Resolving the Security Dilemma in Europe

The German Debate
on Non-Offensive Defence

Also available from Brassey's

BOUTWELL
The German Nuclear Dilemma

CAMPBELL
Germany's Past and Europe's Future

GROVE
Global Security

HIGGINS
Plotting Peace

HOLDEN REID & DEWAR
Military Strategy in a Changing Europe

IISS
Strategic Survey 1990–91

LEECH
Halt! Who Goes Where? The Future of NATO in the New Europe

Resolving the Security Dilemma in Europe

The German Debate
on Non-Offensive Defence

by

BJØRN MØLLER

Foreword by

BARRY BUZAN

BRASSEY'S (UK)
(A Member of the Maxwell Macmillan Group)
LONDON · WASHINGTON · NEW YORK

First English edition 1991

UK editorial offices	Brassey's, 50 Fetter Lane, London EC4A 1AA
Orders	Brassey's, Headington Hill Hall, Oxford OX3 0BW
USA editorial offices	Brassey's, 8000 Westpark Drive, First Floor, McLean, Virginia 22102
Orders	Macmillan Publishing Company, Front and Brown Streets, Riverside, NJ 08075
	Distributed in North America to booksellers and wholesalers by the Macmillan Publishing Company, N.Y., N.Y.

Library of Congress Cataloging in Publication Data
Applied for

British Library Cataloguing in Publication Data
Applied for

ISBN 0 08 041315 3 Hardcover

Typeset by BPCC Techset Ltd, Exeter
Printed in Great Britain by BPCC Wheatons Ltd, Exeter

Dedicated to those I love:

My wife Ulla,
my daughter Ditte,
and my son Hans.

Table of Contents

List of Acronyms

ABC	Atomic, Biological, Chemical
ADE	Armoured Division Equivalent
ADM	Atomic Demolition Munition
AFCENT	Allied Forces Central Europe
ALB	AirLand Battle
APC	Armoured Personnel Carrier
ASW	Anti-Submarine Warfare
ATBM	Anti-Tactical Ballistic Missile
ATGM	Anti-Tank Guided Missile
ATGW	Anti-Tank Guided Weapon
ATM	Anti-Tactical Missile
ATTU	Atlantic-to-the-Urals
BAOR	British Army of the Rhine
C^3I	Command, Control, Communications, Intelligence
CAS	Close Air Support
CBM	Confidence-Building Measure
CDE	Conference on Disarmament in Europe
CDU	*Christlich-Demokratische Union*
CENTAG	Central Army Group
CFE	Conventional Armed Forces in Europe
CMEA	Council of Mutual Economic Assistance
CONUS	Continental United States
CPSU	Communist Party of the Soviet Union
CSBM	Confidence-and-Security-Building Measure
CSCE	Conference on Security and Cooperation in Europe
CSSR	Czechoslovak Socialist Republic
CSU	*Christlich-Soziale Union*
DA	*Demokratische Aktion*
DKP	*Deutsche Kommunistische Partei*
DP	*Deutschlandpolitik*
EC	European Community
ECM	Electronic Counter-Measure
EDC	European Defence Community
EFA	European Fighter Aircraft

EMP	Electro-Magnetic Pulse
ERW	Enhanced Radiation Weapon
FAE	Fuel-Air Explosive
FAR	*Force d'Action Rapide*
FDP	*Freie Demokratische Partei*
FEBA	Forward Edge of Battle Area
FOFA	Follow-On Forces Attack
FOTL	Follow-On to Lance
FRG	Federal Republic of Germany
GDR	German Democratic Republic
GLCM	Ground-Launched Cruise Missile
GNP	Gross National Product
GSFG	Group of Soviet Forces, Germany
IFF	Identification: Friend or Foe
IFSH	*Institut für Friedensforschung und Sicherheitspolitik*
IFV	Infantry Fighting Vehicle
IISS	International Institute for Strategic Studies
INF	Intermediate-Range Nuclear Forces
IOC	Initial Operating Capability
IPW	*Institut für internationale Politik und Wirtschaft*
Km	Kilometre
KT	Kilotons
LDPD	*Liberal-Demokratische Partei Deutschlands*
MAD	Mutual Assured Destruction
MBFR	Mutual and Balanced Force Reductions
MBT	Main Battle Tank
MdB	*Mitglied des Bundestages*
MLF	Multilateral Force
MLRS	Multiple-Launch Rocket System
NCO	Non-Commissioned Officer
NFU	No-First-Use
NN	Neutral and Non-aligned
NOD	Non-Offensive Defence
NORTHAG	Northern Army Group
NSPF	Non-Soviet Pact Forces
NVA	*Nationale Volksarmee*
OCA	Offensive Counter Air
OMG	Operational Manoeuvre Group
OP	*Ostpolitik*
PDS	*Partei des Demokratischen Sozialismus*
PGM	Precision-Guided Munition
POMCUS	Prepositioned Overseas Material Configured Into Unit Sets
PUWP	Polish United Workers' Party
PS	*Parti Socialiste*

RAF	Royal Air Force
RAFG	Royal Air Force, Germany
REFORGER	Return of Forces to Germany
RMA	Restricted Military Area
RPV	Remotely Piloted Vehicle
SACEUR	Supreme Allied Commander Europe
SAM	Surface-to-Air Missile
SAS	*Studiengruppe Alternative Sicherheitspolitik*
SDI	Strategic Defence Initiative
SED	*Sozialistische Einheitspartei Deutschlands*
SLOC	Sea Lines of Communication
SNF	Short-range Nuclear Forces
SPD	*Sozialdemokratische Partei Deutschlands*
START	Strategic Arms Reduction Talks
StruNA	*Strukturelle Nichtangriffsfähigkeit*
StrUnA	*Strukturelle Angriffsunfähigkeit*
TDCW	Totally Destructive Conventional War
TVD	Theatre of Military Operations
UK	United Kingdom
UN	United Nations
USAF	U.S. Air Force
USSR	Union of Soviet Socialist Republics
VTOL	Vertical Take-off Landing
WEU	Western European Union
WHNS	Wartime Host Nation Support
WP	*Westpolitik*
WTO	Warsaw Treaty Organisation
WWI	World War 1
WWII	World War 2

Foreword

For the first time since the beginning of the Cold War more than 40 years ago, the political determinants of military security in Europe are changing much faster than the technological ones. In front of our eyes, and with a rapidity that still seems astonishing, the bipolar political and military order set by the outcome of Second World War is giving way to a new, and as yet unlabelled, historical era.

Among the defining characteristics of this new era is that power is more widely distributed in the system, and that international relations are everywhere shaped and constrained by networks of interdependence. The Soviet Union is the precipitate decline, and even the United States, its victory in the Gulf notwithstanding, is no longer able singlehandedly to bestride the system military and economically as it once did. Though still by considerable measure the dominant military powers in the system, they are becoming simply the best armed among a group of industrial powers.

With the political changes in the Soviet Union since 1985, and in Eastern Europe since 1989, much of the heat and fear has gone out of the superpower rivalry. Both are more concerned with solving pressing domestic problems than with leading ideological crusades. Neither has the appeal of ideological freshness and, with Gorbachev's abandonment of Stalinism, much of the once-strong ideological foundation for the Cold War collapsed.

For Europe, the consequences of these developments are momentous. The Cold War divided not only Germany, but the entire continent. As the most valuable prize on the planet, Europe became the main front line in the superpower rivalry, in the process generating the biggest and most expensive military confrontation in history. But the political, ideological and economic tensions that necessitated such arrangements have now all but vanished, and Western Europe is emerging as a new kind of loosely-structured power centre in its own right. Most of Eastern Europe is trying to reconstruct its political economy along Western lines, in the process drifting into orbit around the new European Community pole. Since 1989, the Eastern Europeans have thrown off the role of front line in an ideological confrontation, and become something more like a permeable buffer between Western Europe and the Soviet Union. Europeans on both sides of a now disintegrated iron curtain are having to find new relationships both with each other, and with their respective superpower allies.

As a consequence of all this, the coming decade will require innovative strategic thinking on that which accompanied the simultaneous onset of the nuclear age and bipolar superpower rivalry after 1945. The political changes now underway are too big to stop, but this does not mean that the transition process will be either quick or easy. A period of political change always contains sufficient uncertainty to justify prudence. But change on this scale, and in so positive a direction, also requires sustained adaptation and a willingness to embrace opportunities to improve mutual security. The military arrangements of the Cold War are no longer suited to Europe, and there is no way of avoiding a period of transition in which new military strategies and deployments are forged to fit a much less confrontational political environment. In part, this is a process of managed change between two historical eras. In part, it is a core element in the development and construction of the new post-Cold War international order.

It should come as no surprise that Germans have been thinking longer and harder about these transformations than others. Their country was divided by the Cold War, and Germans on both sides of the iron curtain lived with the day-to-day pressures of being the front line of the massive East-West military boundary. In addition to the immediate dangers, costs and inconveniences of sharing a small area with large foreign military forces, the Germans have lived with the knowledge that if deterrence failed, many of them, and most of their carefully reconstructed country, would be among the first casualties.

One consequence of this situation was that there developed in West Germany a tradition of thinking about alternative defence arrangements that stretches well back into the 1970s. This tradition was both theoretical and practical, and its central aim was to devise detailed military strategies with a heavily defensive emphasis. The logic of this enterprise was to maintain a credible military defence for West Germany without needing to deploy the massive counter-offensive capabilities that simply justified the threat perceptions of other side. By adopting such a posture, the proponents of non-offensive defence (NOD) hoped that West Germany could begin to break the dynamic of the security dilemma that helped to sustain the East-West confrontation. They also hoped to reduce the intensity of Germany's division, and in so doing to increase the security of all Germans, as well as all Europeans. Although the division of Germany that gave rise to it is now over, the military logic of NOD remains highly relevant to the restructuring of security relations in Europe.

Bjørn Møller's book is an exceptionally timely and useful introduction to this German debate. It is timely because political transformations are making non-offensive defence a much more easily acceptable strategy than it was before. Rather than having to be implemented in the teeth of confrontation, there is now a good prospect that NOD can become the set of principles by which the Europeans, the Russians, and the Americans will unilaterally and multilaterally reconstruct their military relations. It is useful, because by making the German debate available to the English-speaking world Møller does two services. First, he gives insight into German thinking about the difficult central role of Germany in Europe, helpfully setting this into the political and historical context of German policy. Given the importance of Germany for Western security as a whole, and given the novelty and detail of the defence measures proposed, this aspect of the book is essential reading for all those interested in European security. Secondly, and more generally, he opens up what is by far the best developed body of thinking on alternative defence currently available.

All of the major approaches to territorial defence are discussed and criticised in detail, providing almost a textbook for the concept as a whole. This is the only serious work that points towards realistic solutions to the problems of excessive dependence on nuclear weapons and/or self-defeating offensive force structures. On this basis, the German debate is a valuable source of ideas and experience for defence and peace research communities almost everywhere. Although developed in the context of the Cold War, German thinking on NOD contains a wealth of principles and practical ideas applicable to the post-Cold War environment. The literature discussed here is not only of historical interest because of the new importance of Germany, but it is also highly relevant to the current need for new thinking about security generally.

The ideas here are especially important for British and American audiences, because the Anglo-Saxon countries are the most wedded to NATO orthodoxy, and therefore slowest to react to the current wave of change. Britain has been particularly resistant, in part because NATO is the organisation most flattering to British power, and in part because of the peculiar circumstance of the decade-long Thatcher government, with its strong orientation to the NATO role and the American relationship. NATO is in some ways a British creation, and it is significant that Britain is the only country to mirror the full panoply of the American commitment: nuclear forces, supporting naval power, and permanently stationed front-line air and ground forces in Germany. But this situation is unsustainable, both because of the political changes in Europe and, as recurrent crises in defence spending underline, because of inadequate resources. There is no escape from the financial and political logic that is driving the country towards a major rationalisation of its armed forces into a more sustainable, less comprehensive and more specialised, framework.

Despite the success of British arms in the Gulf, change has to come, and there is a pressing need for new ideas to govern how the transition is managed. Debate has so far been restricted by the interlocked combination of an entrenched government and an unelectable opposition. In part, the opposition was unelectable because of the blatant feebleness of its excessively emotional and idealistic thinking about defence. But there are now firm signs that the opposition is recovering its electoral potential, in part by thinking more realistically about defence issues. The Labour party has moved towards NOD thinking, but seems as yet only superficially to understand the issues involved. Exposure to the German debate would strengthen, and set into European context, the intellectual foundations for the development of an alternative vision for British defence policy in the 1990s and beyond. On this basis I cannot recommend this book too highly to all those who have an interest in formulating defence policies appropriate to the quite unprecedented times in which we Europeans now live.

Barry Buzan

Preface

We live in interesting times, indeed. Events in the realm of international relations have been occurring at an infinitely faster pace in 1989 and 1990 than hitherto. What formerly required decades of hard diplomatic bargaining has been accomplished overnight, and established verities about security policy turned out to have been 'writ in water'. One hardly dared watch the evening news for fear that one's entire image of the world would be turned upside down before the set was turned off again. One had to withold one's opinion even on abstract matters until one had heard the very latest news on the radio or television.

European security policies remain in a state of flux, since most of the previous 'pillars of stability' have come tumbling down. The entire post-war construction of the European security system seems on the verge of collapsing, yet without any 'post-post-war' replacement ready at hand. Amongst these uncertainties are the following:

I. Nuclear weapons seem to be on their way out. The overall numbers of strategic as well as 'tactical' nuclear arms are being reduced by the superpowers, both unilaterally and as part of arms control agreements (the INF Treaty, START and the upcoming SNF negotiations). NATO as well as the Soviet Union, along with what is left of the Warsaw Pact, are openly acknowledging the need for a higher nuclear threshold. A panoply of proposals are being made for minimum deterrence, no-first-use, nuclear-weapons-free zones, etc. Finally, and perhaps most decisively, the public seems to have developed a distinct aversion to nuclear weapons, in most countries, and certainly in West Germany with which this book deals.

NATO at its July 1990 summit seems to have finally realised the irreversibility of these trends, and committed itself (apparently upon the insistence of West Germany) to what might be called a 'no-early-first-use' policy for nuclear weapons. Henceforth, nuclear escalation will be a true 'last resort' option, rather than a 'gap-filler' intended to 'mend the holes' in the 'fence' of conventional forces. As a corollary, the genuine battlefield nuclear weapons, i.a. nuclear artillery shells, are scheduled for abolition, once again undoubtedly because the Germans insisted.

On the one hand, most people, including the present author, would tend to regard this partial denuclearization as a fortunate development, since it has the potential of eventually freeing Mankind from the ever-present risk of thermonuclear holocaust. On the other hand, the nuclear deterrence system may have imparted a degree of stability and predictability on international relations that was a partial blessing in disguise. If the nuclear spectre should be effectively removed, may we not be entering an entirely new period, in which war becomes thinkable once again, yet one in which every war might still go nuclear, because the nuclear 'genie' is out of its bottle for good?

II. The alliance system has become 'unhinged' through the dissolution of the WTO, to all practical intents and purposes, although not yet formally. What will replace it does, however, remain to be seen. Will it be a genuine 'peace order', perhaps in the shape of a collective security arrangement? Or might we be unwittingly heading towards a new balance-of-power era, characterised by arms racing, competitive alignment, and perhaps by occasional wars between individual states or *ad hoc* alliances? I shall return in the concluding chapter to the available evidence supporting either hypothesis.

III. The very 'lay-out' of the international game is changing. Until 1989, at least the number of 'players' in the game of international politics was fairly constant. Subsequently, however, some states began to disintegrate, whereas others merged, thus entirely changing the 'format' as well as the rules of the game. In a few years time the familiar pattern of two Germanies versus one Soviet Union will probably have been replaced by the exact opposite: one united Germany and several former constituent parts of the USSR, which have now seceded and become sovereign states. Furthermore, it is quite conceivable that the USA may disengage from Europe, thus ceasing, to all practical intents and purposes, to be a 'European power'.

This raises the fundamental question: Who are going to be the 'players' in the international power game in and around Europe in the 1990s, and what will be the power ratio between them? Will the emerging new configuration be more stable and peaceful than the present one? Or perhaps less so, and more war-prone?

IV. The German question has been one of the most pressing of these questions, since which ever answer was found to it was bound to have repercussions way beyond the boundaries of the two former German states or, indeed, of Central Europe. Will the recently united Germany once again become a source of security concerns on the part of its neighbours? Or might it, on the contrary, develop into a 'greenhouse' for cooperative East-West ventures (to the extent that 'East' and 'West' remain meaningful terms at all)?

It would appear that the former possibility loomed large in the minds of some 'bystanders', particularly the USSR and Poland, for the duration of the unification process. Fortunately, the Germans, along with their Western allies, were attentive to these risks, whence sprang repeated West German as well as East German declarations of a confidence-building content, as well as the decisions taken at the aforementioned NATO summit.

Germany may thus well become the greenhouse in which the seeds of 'cooperative security structures' will be sown, to blossom in the next millennium. On the other hand, the possibility cannot be entirely dismissed that the four powers which in 1990 relinquished their ultimate responsibility for Germany may have given birth to a 'monster' that may upset peace in Europe in the next decade, just as Germany has done on several occasions in the past.

All these and several other elements of uncertainty appear as yet unsettled, in the sense that several different paths into the future remain open. Both worst-case and best-case scenarios (or any combinations thereof) may come true, since it can still go either way. Even though different paths apparently still remain open, the development may, on the other hand, soon reach a point of no return. Whereas decisions may still be taken that could shape the future of Europe well into the next millennium, the time for doing so may soon pass[1].

Most of these decisions will be of a profoundly political nature, dealing with such fundamentals as who are to be regarded as friends and (potential) foes, respectively, and what constitute the 'objective' interests of the various states. To the extent that security policy considerations are going to play a role in shaping these decisions it will undoubtedly be a modified and expanded conception of security wherein non-military threats and opportunities begin to supercede military ones.

Nevertheless, for as long as war remains a possibility (albeit increasingly remote), military considerations will retain some prominence, even if only in the sense that certain military decisions might foreclose perhaps highly promising options of security by political means. With a view to accomplishing the attempted metamorphosis of the two (or one-and-a-half) primarily antagonistic military alliances to political alliances of a cooperative orientation, they will have to pay close attention to their military elements, at least for the transitionary phase. Paraphrasing Clemenceau, it must be acknowledged that military matters are too important to leave to the generals, or other experts for that matter. They are certainly too important to be neglected by politicians.

All the aforementioned uncertainties pose questions of the utmost importance with regard to the physiognomy of the 'post-nuclear, post-bipolar era' in both their military and political dimensions. Militarily, this era will, on the one hand, be one in which nuclear weapons remain, either in the form of a radically reduced residual arsenal, or at the very least as a potentiality.

On the other hand, these will be new circumstances, because the role of nuclear weapons will have been severely curtailed, and they are thus no longer regarded as (deceptive) panaceas for security problems. It is perfectly conceivable (and most would agree: highly desirable) that the role of military force will be reduced in parallel, leaving whatever conflicts might remain between states to be fought out by political means. Still, general and complete disarmament is undoubtedly a prospect for the rather distant future, and conventional forces are therefore bound to continue to play a significant, perhaps even increased, role.

In this context, a debate with important implications for the future security structure of Europe has been conducted for a number of years about the future of conventional defence. One of the most prominent and persistent ideas has been that of building down offensive capabilities and gradually approaching strictly defensive structures. Various terms have been applied for this concept: 'non-offensive defence', 'non-provocative defence', 'non-aggressive defence', 'structural inability to attack', 'defensive defence', 'confidence-building defence', or the catch-all (yet somewhat misleading) 'alternative defence'. In this book I shall prefer the term of 'non-offensive defence' with the convenient acronym 'NOD'.

According to its proponents, including the present author, NOD could provide the solution to the problems of war prevention and disarmament in a 'post-nuclear setting'. Furthermore, NOD would presumably be flexible in the sense of being applicable to both a bloc system, such as the present one, and to a system of more fluctuating nation-states and *ad hoc* alliances. Finally, NOD would presumably be a 'perfect fit' for the united Germany, and was, indeed, contrived partly with this application in mind by its proponents, most of whom 'happened' to be Germans, not entirely by coincidence.

Its novelty notwithstanding, the concept of NOD has experienced an astonishing success (both academically and politically) over the last few years. On the academic level, what started up as a preoccupation of a few isolated peace researchers in the FRG has attracted growing attention from other parts of the academic spectrum as well, both in terms of a disciplinary spread, and in terms of geography. Political scientists and students of international relations are including the topic in their curriculae to an increasing extent. Academics from the 'strategic studies' branch are likewise devoting more attention than previously to conventional forces, and more specifically to ways of strengthening the defence *vis-a-vis* the offence.

This even holds good for the military. Whereas the obvious disarmament perspectives of NOD do not immediately appeal to military men, neither do nuclear weapons or other strictly political tools of military power. A growing number of military officers simply want to do a good job, and have for this purpose 'borrowed' a number of tactical ideas from the NOD schemes, and *vice versa*. A significant number of (usually retired) officers have even developed NOD proposals of their own, as Chapter V below will show.

Furthermore, whereas the ideas are of German origin, NOD has gradually attracted attention in other parts of the world, first of all, as was to be expected, in the FRG's neighbouring countries, e.g. Denmark, the other

Nordic countries, and the Netherlands; and secondly, in the UK, where one might mention the 'Alternative Defence Commission', the 'Just Defence' group and the 'Foundation for International Security', as well as a number of prominent individuals: Frank Barnaby, Hugh Beach, Barry Buzan, Malcolm Chalmers, Gerard Holden, Mary Kaldor, Robert Neild, Gwyn Prins and Adam Roberts, to mention but a few. Furthermore, the growing number of critical analyses by British experts also constitutes evidence of the relevance of the NOD conception. Thirdly, on NATO's southern flank, one might mention individual researchers from Spain as well as a fully fledged research group from Italy. Fourthly, in the USA, where distinguished academics (including Robert Jervis, George Quester, Steven Canby, John Mearsheimer, Michael MccGwire, Stephen van Evera, Jack Snyder, Jonathan Dean, Alvin Saperstein, Paul Walker, Dietrich Fischer, Randall Forsberg, Carl Conetta, Charles Knight, and others) have in one way or the other, perhaps even unwittingly, written about NOD.

On the political level, the general NOD principles have been adopted, either wholesale or selectively, by significant political groupings, most of them in Western Europe, and all of them in opposition, yet with fair chances of gaining government power within the next decade. The Social Democratic Party of Germany (SPD) first included the call for 'structural inability to launch an attack' (i.e. NOD) in its party platform in 1984. Although it is still wrestling with the problem of selecting a specific model from the available panoply of proposals, the party seems firmly committed to the basic idea. The British Labour Party likewise in 1984 adopted a security policy platform which included paragraphs on 'defensive deterrence'. However, its commitment seems much less firm than that of the SPD, probably due to its lack of self-confidence after its conspicuous defeats in the last couple of elections. Finally, the Social Democratic parties of the smaller NATO countries such as Denmark have been following in the footsteps of the SPD, as have the New Democrats in Canada.

Whereas the concept thus appears to appeal above all to the socialist parties, a few parties belonging to the liberal tradition have also embraced the idea, at least partly. This holds true e.g. for a number of 'dissidents' within the West German CDU, for its coalition partner, the FDP (and not least Foreign Minister Hans-Dietrich Genscher), for the Danish Liberal Centre Party and the British Liberal Democratic Party. Even in the USA prominent political figures are beginning to back the idea, or at least elements thereof. The idea of NOD thus no longer bears a leftist 'stigma', if it ever did.

Furthermore, the Social Democratic parties, above all the SPD, have introduced the NOD concept into the East-West dialogue. The SPD for a couple of years pursued a series of 'negotiations' in a party-to-party format with the ruling parties of East European countries, in continuation of their previous *Ostpolitik*. It accomplished agreements on significant draft 'treaties' on e.g. a wide range of CSBMs (Confidence- and Security-Building Measures) for Central Europe, in addition to three overlapping zonal arrangements devised for the same area: a chemical-weapons-free and a nuclear-weapons-free zone, as well as an agreement for a withdrawal of particularly offensive weapons systems from the 'zone of contact' (more on which later).

Whereas NATO initially showed a distinct scepticism towards NOD, this negative attitude seems to be waning: First of all, NATO has acknowledged it to be its goal to reduce above all 'capacities for launching surprise attack and for the initiation of large-scale offensive action'. The historic July 1990 summit, furthermore, promised to review the entire NATO strategy, including the nuclear element as well as 'forward defence'. It seems almost unavoidable that the criterion for this reassessment will become the maintenance of defensive elements simultaneously with an abandonment of offensive options. One reason for this is that an ongoing dialogue on military doctrines and strategies has been initiated, in the context whereof the other side is likely to insists upon it[2].

The USSR (along with, until its collapse, the WTO) has, since 1986-87, adopted the NOD idea as one of the core elements of its 'new thinking' on security policy. Subsequently, nearly all WTO countries have undertaken fairly deep cuts in their military arsenals, and applied the defensive criterion as a guideline, with the result that the remaining forces will not merely be 'leaner', but also somewhat less 'mean'[3].

Furthermore, in March 1989, talks on Conventional Forces in Europe (CFE) were opened in Vienna, and were concluded as early as November 1990: compared with the unsuccessful MBFR (Mutual Balanced Force Reduction) negotiations from 1973 to 1989 a remarkable achievement, indeed. The explicit aim of these talks was identical to NATO's aforementioned objective: to limit capabilities for surprise attack and large-scale offensive operations. Even though the agenda was narrowed down to dealing with major ground force equipment plus aircraft, the eventual results did imply a reduction of offensive capabilities in Europe, in addition to doing away with Soviet conventional superiority.

NOD has thus been firmly placed on the political as well as on the academic agendas. Often, however, the lively interest has been combined with an insufficient awareness of both the research being conducted on this topic around the world, and of the political debate in other countries, undoubtedly partly due to language barriers. This is deplorable, if only because it means that the Anglo-Saxon audience is largely without access to the literature in German, which remains, beyond comparison, the most detailed and profound part of the global body of NOD literature.

The present work is intended as a contribution to filling this gap. Its primary aim is the modest one of providing a historical survey of the NOD debate in the two Germanies, with a distinct emphasis on the FRG. I have acquired a certain background for the task I have taken upon me in three ways. First of all, in my employment since 1985 as a research fellow on a project on 'non-offensive defence in Europe' at the Centre for Peace and Conflict Research at the University of Copenhagen, I have attempted to go through all available German literature dealing directly and indirectly with NOD (as well as a good part of the literature on NOD in English, the Nordic languages, Dutch, French, Spanish and Italian). An educated guess would be that I am familiar with at least ninety percent of all available literature, and that, furthermore, most of the remaining ten percent is of merely secondary importance.

Secondly, I have been able to benefit from my experience as the editor of an international research newsletter on the subject (*NOD: Non-Offensive Defence*). Thirdly, through a rather lively participation in numerous international conferences on the subject, I have been in a position to acquaint myself personally with the majority of the authors dealt with.

A comprehensive and thoroughly documented account has been attempted, taking into account most of the significant contributions to the debate, even such as in my personal opinion are of limited or even negative intrinsic value. A faithful presentation of the most important contributions to the debate has been attempted, although it has been impossible to render full justice to the complexity and sophistication of many arguments.

The work has had a long gestation period. A first version of the manuscript was presented to the publishers in the Summer of 1989, but (as it turned out, by a stroke of luck) the decision to go ahead was postponed until it had become obvious that momentous developments in the field of European security and defence policies were underway, not least pertaining to the two German states. The entire manuscript was subsequently revised in the light of the new developments and finished by Christmas 1990, when it appeared fairly obvious which problems would be solved, and approximately how, even though numerous uncertainties remained.

I wish to thank the Centre for Peace and Conflict Research at the University of Copenhagen for giving me the opportunity of spending so much time on a single work, as well as for providing an inspiring environment in which to do so. I particular, I want to thank my colleagues Prof. Barry Buzan and Prof. Håkan Wiberg for their encouragement and useful comments. Furthermore, Lutz Unterseher of the SAS group (cf. Chapter IV) has been extremely helpful with comments and 'inside information' about the German debate. Needless to say, I alone am to blame for any remaining errors.

Above all, however, thanks are due to my wife and two children for their patience with their husband's and father's preoccupation with these matters, at the inevitable expense of family life.

Bjørn Møller
Copenhagen, Denmark
4 January 1991

CHAPTER I

What NOD is and What it is Not

A survey of the literature on non-offensive defence (NOD) such as the present one is faced with the methodological problem of defining the topic so as to establish criteria for inclusion and exclusion from the relevant body of literature.

Family Resemblances

Not everybody claiming to be an NOD advocate should automatically be accepted as such; and certainly not all opinions expressed by indisputable NOD proponents should be taken as elements in the NOD discourse. Whereas an empirical definition of NOD is thus impossible (and because there exists no definition with any legitimate claim to authority), the only alternative would seem to be an *ad hoc* definition by the present author, who would, of course, enjoy the inalienable privilege of defining the subject *ad libitum*.

I have, however, refrained from trying to establish stringent criteria, taking as an alternative point of departure Ludwig Wittgenstein's notion of 'family resemblances'. This implies assuming that there is no particular characteristic common to all 'family members', but rather 'a complicated network of similarities overlapping and criss-crossing: sometimes overall similarities, sometimes similarities of detail'[1].

Applied to NOD literature, this notion implies that not all 'NOD authors' embody all distinguishing traits, but that all of them incorporate at least one, usually several. It also implies 'grey areas', in which NOD literature shades out into, on the one side, mainstream strategic literature and, on the other side, international relations theory and peace research. What thus emerges as 'NOD literature' is a rather heterogeneous agglomeration of proposals and analyses, which might roughly be lumped into two main categories:

I. Analyses of broader security political problems, the authors of which have recommended a defensive conversion of military structures, without necessarily going into great detail in this respect.
II. Concrete proposals for military restructuring, often intended as contributions to the solution of broader security political problems, yet sometimes motivated primarily by concerns about military efficiency.

These two approaches to NOD interact, in the sense that analysts belonging to the former category tend to integrate proposals from the latter by simply 'reframing' them. On the other hand, analysts who really belong to the second category often attempt to 'sell' their proposals by couching them in terms of broader security political conceptions, thus 'posing' as belonging to the first category. The resultant diversity and heterogeneity of the NOD literature reflects the way that politics and public debate work in practice. The chapters on the political debate will bring out this fact, by showing how political decision-makers have in fact picked and chosen elements from a panoply of different, in fact often logically incompatible, analyses and proposals.

The methodological point of departure for the following survey has thus been what might be called an 'archetypal NOD discourse' that I have attempted to set out in ten concise points, i.e. as a 'Decalogue'. The number of theses is, however, artificial, since one might just as well have spelled out the same discourse in, say, seven or seventeen theses.

Although it is based on a thorough study of most of the literature which informed observers would categorise as NOD literature, it is inevitably somewhat impressionistic. The NOD discourse that constitutes the major part of this chapter presumably possesses a certain inherent logic, although some might dispute the logical stringency at some point. Most NOD authors would tend to follow the same logic most of the way, whilst perhaps departing from it at some point or other, whereas most 'mainstream' strategists would tend to be in only sporadic agreement.

In parallel with the enumeration I have tried to identify some continuities of the 'NOD logic' with, as well a departures from, traditional strategic thinking and international relations theory. Finally, I have tried to eliminate right from the start a few of the most common misunderstandings concerning NOD.

The Decalogue of Non-Offensive Defence

I. Because lasting security is only obtainable in the form of Common Security, states should take the security of their adversaries into due consideration in the design of their armed forces, with a view to making them strictly defensive.

This admonition is based on the theory of the 'security dilemma', according to which dyads of states locked in adversarial relationships tend to interact in such a mode that one state's defensively-motivated steps are misconstrued by the other as potential attack preparations. By taking defensive precautions, a state may thus call forth defensive counter-moves on the part of its adversary which, regardless of the underlying intentions, constitute a threat to the first state. The quest for security may thus become self-defeating, unless the respective adversary's security concerns are taken into due consideration[2].

Unless both sides feel secure, none of them will therefore enjoy any lasting security. 'The security of one nation cannot be bought at the expense of others', as formulated by the Palme Commission whose 1982 report on *Common Security. A Blueprint for Survival* made the notion of Common Security known.

Common Security calls for a configuration of the armed forces (along with a strategy for their employment) which provides an adequate capability for defence, yet none for aggression that might constitute a threat to other nations. Non-offensive defence is thus its military counterpart[3].

II. Scale back the role of nuclear weapons to that of minimum deterrence against enemy nuclear attack or 'blackmail', and adopt, as a corollary, a no-first-use policy based on conventional stability.

Due to the immense destruction that would result from a nuclear war in the era of 'overkill', nuclear war can serve no political purpose whatsoever. Attempts to use nuclear weapons for war-fighting purposes are therefore futile and likely to fuel a nuclear arms race. Even worse, the acquisition by both sides of nuclear weapons suitable for first strikes might result in 'reciprocal fears of surprise attack', as a result of which a war might be launched pre-emptively[4].

The nuclear powers ought therefore to abandon their quest for 'flexible options' and use the possession of nuclear weapons merely to deter nuclear attack, as well as perhaps as a counter to the (probably elusive) prospects of 'nuclear blackmail'[5].

MAD (Mutual Assured Destruction) is with us for good, since defence against nuclear attack is impossible. Strategic defences (such as the SDI programme of the Reagan administration) will therefore be destabilizing, since they might conceivably lead their possessor to hope for a break-out from the MAD stalemate with a view to attaining a war-winning capability. Paradoxically, 'offence is defence; defence is offence; killing people is good; killing weapons is bad'[6]. Any apparent 'family likeness' between NOD and SDI is therefore misleading.

The MAD situation of mutual vulnerability should be maintained, albeit at the lowest possible level of destructive potential, preferably in the form of 'minimum deterrence' arsenals. Consequently, nuclear weapons should be removed entirely from the land-mass of Europe, where they only create ambiguities, and jeopardise strategic stability.

There seems to be no absolute limit to how minuscule the nuclear arsenals may become, due to the 'existential deterrence effect'. The very fact that nuclear weapons have been invented, and cannot be disinvented, means that they will always somehow show up in the calculus of military planners. By implication, any would-be conventional war will henceforth be fought in the nuclear 'shadow', or, as some have called it, in a 'sub-nuclear setting'[7].

A no-first-use (NFU) strategy could safely be adopted as an antidote to counterforce and war-fighting temptations, as a means to improve crisis stability, and as a confidence-building measure[8]. However, the Western alliance has consistently legitimated its first-use strategy with reference to its presumed inability to prevail conventionally against the Warsaw Pact. Regardless of the questionable validity of this view, it will therefore be a political precondition for switching to NFU that conventional defence becomes self-sufficient, both in actual fact, and as mirrored in the perceptions of the states involved.

III. Seek to minimise simultaneously the risks of premeditated war of aggression and inadvertent war through strengthening crisis stability by means of defensive postures.

Any future war might be either premeditated, i.e. initiated by an act of deliberate aggression, or inadvertent, i.e. either of a preventive or a pre-emptive nature[9]. Whereas 1939 (Hitler's attack on Poland) is the paradigm case of the first variety, 1914 (the outbreak of WWI) might serve as the classical example of the second type. 1967 (the June War in the Middle East), in its turn, constitutes an example of the third type[10].

The distinction between the second and third types is primarily one of timing and pace. A preventive war is based on the preference for fighting now rather than later a war which is believed to be inevitable in the long run. Nevertheless, the first blow represents a deliberate political act. A pre-emptive war, on the other hand, is started by one party in the earnest, albeit often erroneous, belief that the other side has already commenced operational preparations for attack, or even launched the initial strike. In such a situation, the military logic may dictate a state to strike first in order to improve its chances.

Under the present circumstances, neither the superpowers nor any of their allies are likely to premeditatedly launch a war, and since 1914 or 1967 scenarios appear less unlikely, the problem of 'crisis stability' deserves serious attention. Whereas the problem of preventing inadvertent nuclear war has hitherto attracted most attention, the most fundamental principles of crisis stability pertaining to the strategic level are, *mutandis mutatis*, applicable to the 'sub-strategic level' as well[11].

Crisis stability is largely about avoiding pre-emption. This, in its turn, requires two sets of precautions, pertaining to intentions and capabilities respectively. On the one hand, either side should refrain from giving its respective opponent any incentive for pre-emption, such as might e.g. arise from fear of an impending attack. On the other hand, either party should deny its respective opponent any such options of pre-emption as might improve the pre-emptor's chances in the ensuing confrontation.

Theoretically, this problem might be handled unilaterally: either a state might successfully avoid any kind of pre-emption vulnerability, e.g. by virtue of possessing an overwhelming military superiority; or it might, conversely, deprive its opponent of any reasons for fear, and *eo ipso* of motives for pre-emption, by way of complete disarmament. Neither of these approaches is, however, entirely satisfactory, i.a. because of the lack of insight into the current, and possible future, intentions of the opponent. Prudence therefore demands a more cautious approach than the latter, whereas the former may safely be dismissed as beyond the means of any state. The appropriate approach is therefore 'dual-tracked', in the sense that a country's defence posture ought to aim at minimizing both options of and motives for pre-emption.

From these considerations flow a number of criteria for crisis stability:

1. **The non-offensive criterion:** States should refrain from the acquisition of capabilities for disarming strikes, which would be destabilizing, since it would merely give the other party an incentive to pre-empt an expected first strike. A secure second strike capability will, on the other hand, be stabilizing, since it will allow its possessor to wait in order to 'ride out' any attack, rather than 'respond' pre-emptively to an anticipated attack, which may never occur. The inversion of this criterion is a deliberate vulnerability towards hypothetical retaliatory strikes on the part of one's opponent. Unfortunately, this criterion at the same time rules out any defence against a first strike.

2. **The no-target criterion:** States should avoid presenting lucrative targets which might lead their opponent to believe himself capable of launching a disarming strike. The more dispersed and/or individually unimportant the military targets, the smaller the incentives for any adversary to attack.

3. **The no-surprise criterion:** Maximizing invulnerability towards disarming strikes also requires minimizing the surprise factor. Only if one party might hope to be able to eliminate the defensive capability of its opponent by means of a bold strike would it make sense to attack in the midst of a crisis. Whereas effective surveillance is important for prolonging the available time for political, rather than military, decisions, the deployment of forces also matters. The shorter the time required to prepare for attack and move forces into position, the greater the potential surprise effect, and the more unstable the situation.

4. **The transparency criterion:** Mutual perceptions are what matter in a crisis, and capabilities as well as incapabilities should therefore be made apparent to the opponent. Such an enhancement of 'transparency' would, furthermore, contribute to mutual confidence-building and thus to a less crisis- and misapprehension-prone climate in the future.

5. **The no self-deterrence criterion:** It is of no avail to be forewarned, unless one is able to respond adequately, whence the importance of escaping what might be called the 'self-deterrence' or 'preparedness-provocation dilemma', of having to choose between two unattractive options: on the one hand, adequate defence precautions which might be construed as preparations for an attack and could thus trigger an otherwise avoidable war; on the other hand, a paralysis of the defence due to self-deterrence, which might allow an adversary to launch a premeditated attack.

IV. Select a military structure that allows for disarmament by promoting 'mutual defensive superiority', and endeavour to establish such a regime by means of a combination of formal arms control negotiations and 'coordinated unilateralism'.

An important factor in the armaments dynamics is the aforementioned security dilemma, manifesting itself in the well-known 'action-reaction phenomenon'. A precondition for 'stepping out of the arms race' and embarking on disarmament is hence to escape the security dilemma, in its turn necessitating an elimination of the inherent ambiguity of military means. Defensive measures and armament programmes should be made clearly recognizable as such, in which case they will call for no 'balancing steps' on the part of the respective adversary[12].

Numerical parity is of little military relevance, since historical evidence does not point to any high degree of correlation between, on the one hand, parity or numerical disparities and, on the other hand, war. Not only is parity thus irrelevant, but the quest for parity may even be harmful. If both sides in an adversarial relationship strive for 'parity', the very elusiveness of the concept is almost bound to lead to arms racing, since both sides are wellnigh predestined to seek what is 'objectively' superiority in order to attain what they subjectively perceive as balance[13].

The only conceivable form of mutual superiority is 'mutual defensive superiority' based on a distinction between offensive and defensive forces, combined with the inherent superiority of the defensive ones. This would allow one side's ability to defend himself to be superior to the other's attack capability[14]. If both sides were aware of this mutual defensive superiority, they would know that they could not hope to win a war by initiating it, but needed not fear defeat if only they remained on the defensive.

As far as the implementation of this sought-for 'mutual defensive superiority regime' is concerned, NOD has often been portrayed by its advocates as a way of making unilateralism a viable option on the part of the West. However viable the unilateral option might be in principle, the West would probably miss a unique opportunity if it did not seek some reciprocity on part of the East, so as to achieve simultaneously a Soviet conversion to a less offensive posture.

Due to their scepticism towards formal negotiations, most NOD proponents would, however, recommend 'coordinated, parallel unilateralism' or 'informal bilateralism', inspired by the strategies of 'gradualism'[15]. In this mode, unilateral restraint might be exercised, and carefully calibrated disarmament and conversion steps taken, in the hope of thereby inducing reciprocation on the part of the adversary.

Under the influence of Soviet 'new thinking', most NOD advocates would appear to be gradually adopting a more positive attitude towards formal negotiations. Indeed, a number of them have gone so far in their 'arms control euphoria' as to almost forget about the unilateral option.

V. Establish criteria for a distinction between offensive and defensive military forces, which should refer to military postures and options rather than to weapons.

The above accomplishments all presupposed the conceptual distinction between 'offence' and 'defence'. These terms might, however, refer both to political ends and to the military means with which to accomplish these ends. 'Means', in its turn, might refer both to particular actions and to the instruments for performing such actions.

It is, first of all, perfectly conceivable that a state might be entirely defensive politically whilst at the same time seeing no other way of defending itself than by means of offensive military operations. This would e.g. seem to be a fairly accurate description of Israeli military doctrine. Furthermore, 'military operations' is, in its turn, also ambiguous, since it may refer to activities on different scales. Whilst intending merely to defend its own territory, a state might, for instance, well envisage doing so by seeking to strike the first blow in every single engagement, thus being strategically defensive, whilst tactically offensive. This has e.g. been the case for guerillas ever since the Peninsular War against Napoleon, as well as in recent Third World wars.

Finally, in the case of alliances, even strategically defensive operations on the part of individual member states might not even suffice for defending the alliance as such, since this would rule out assistance to allies in jeopardy unless the assisting forces were already stationed in peacetime in the country in question.

The physical instruments of defence and offence are in most cases ambivalent, in the sense that the same physical item may be used for offensive and defensive purposes, depending on the circumstances. Attempts at defining 'defensive weapons' have so far been rather unsatisfactory, regardless of whether they have been couched in terms of range and extent of destructive power (Galtung), or in terms of rewarding first- or second-strike approaches (Quester)[16].

Absolute definitions inevitably disregard both historical and geographic factors of considerable importance. Forces which were once offensive (say, the legions of the Roman empire) may no longer be so, and force postures or components which may be used offensively by some countries against certain others, may be useless for the same purposes in wars between other contestants.

Higher levels of analysis than that of individual weapons are therefore needed, but just how high may be a matter of dispute. The division might seem to recommend itself as the appropriate level, constituting the smallest self-contained formation in modern-day armed forces. On the other hand, 'defensive divisions' may merely serve as force multipliers for 'offensive divisions' within the same theatre of war, so that, on closer analysis, an even higher level of aggregation might appear warranted in order to take into due account the synergistic effects of combined-arms operations.

Most NOD advocates have therefore preferred distinctions pertaining to the level of aggregate postures, as in the definition of NOD formulated by Frank Barnaby and Egbert Boeker:

> 'The size, weapons, training, logistics, doctrine, operational manuals, war-games, manoeuvres, text-books used in military academies, etc., of the armed forces are such that they are seen in their totality to be capable of a credible defence without any reliance on the use of nuclear weapons, yet incapable of offence'[17].

Even this very elaborate definition does, however, refer back from structures to their possible use, and it might thus be even better to define NOD functionally, rather than structurally, and by implication speak of options rather than of structures, whilst never forgetting that options are functions of structures. A possible functional definition might be the following:

> 'The state should be capable of a credible defence without any reliance on the use of nuclear weapons, yet incapable of offence'.

This definition also has the advantage of acknowledging the possibility of ensuring non-offensiveness by other means than by a particular configuration of the armed forces themselves, say, by political means. This possibility should certainly not be ruled out, notwithstanding the fact that NOD does focus on the armed forces.

VI. Analyse carefully the relative strength of offence and defence, and capitalise on the intrinsic superiority of the defensive form of combat.

NOD is based on the Clausewitzian assumption of the defence as the intrinsically superior form of combat. This has often been couched in terms of the so-called '3:1 rule', according to which a defender will be able to prevail against an attacker up to three times his own numerical strength. To what extent (or on which level of analysis) this holds true is, however, disputed: Most analysts would agree that it remains valid for tactical engagements in a linear mode, i.e. situations in which two opposing forces meet head-on. Under such conditions, the defender will be able to exploit fully his advantages of prepared combat positions, etc., whilst the attacker will be forced to expose himself.

Occasionally, wars have almost constituted simply such linear engagements 'writ large'. This was i.a. the case for the fighting on the Western front in WWI (World War I), in which the predictions of the Polish banker, Ivan Bloch, were borne out perfectly, whereas the expectations of the military professionals proved entirely false. The war soon assumed the form of an attrition contest, in which the defending side in its barbed-wire protected trenches, armed with machine-guns etc., was able to prevail against the party trying to gain ground through head-on assault[18].

On other occasions, however, in which manoeuvre warfare has dominated, the tactical 3:1 advantage of the defence has been of small avail, since the aggressor has been able to concentrate swiftly, thus achieving overwhelming (i.e. exceeding 3:1) tactical superiority at the decisive points. If skilfully targeted, such tactical scores may even be transformed into strategic victories, such as were the case of Hitler's *blitzkriegs* at the outset of WWII. To which extent either of these two historical lessons apply to today's European scene is disputed, i.a. amongst American analysts, with John J. Mearsheimer standing as the most prominent advocate of what might be called the 'strategic 3:1 rule'[19].

Most European NOD advocates would tend to agree with the assumption that the 3:1 rule is valid on a theatre scale, with the caveat that this might well require deliberate modifications of defensive postures and strategies. Above all, the defender must prevent tactical gains from translating into strategic victory, something which may presumably be accomplished by rules VII-IX below.

VII. Refrain from 'meeting like with like' in favour of an asymmetrical approach that should emphasise elusiveness and avoid presenting lucrative targets to the attacker by means of a dispersed pattern of deployment.

The basic idea of asymmetry has been called, alternatively, 'the indirect approach' (Liddell Hart), 'the indirect strategy' (Andrè Beaufre), or, more recently, 'the paradoxical approach' (Edward Luttwak). To a large extent is goes against the usual military preference for matching (or even better outmatching) an opponent in terms of hardware and numbers. It ought thus to come as no surprise that the principle has appealed above all to irregular military forces. Historically, the asymmetrical approach has primarily been associated with guerilla warfare, the first origins of which may be traced way back into antiquity[20].

The asymmetrical character of guerilla warfare was i.a. captured by Mao Tse-Tung in his famous 'sixteen word formula' according to which 'the enemy advances, we retreat; the enemy camps, we harass; the enemy tires, we attack; the enemy retreats, we pursue'[21]. NOD advocates have applied analogous principles to the Central Front, i.a. by their rejection of the duel-like engagements whereby tanks are used against the tank threat, emphasizing rather such 'asymmetrical' means as anti-tank weapons and ditches, as well as battle avoidance, etc.

The dispersal of forces was what gave guerilla warfare its unique 'elusive' character, but the same principle is also well-known from nuclear strategy, where it has been pointed out that targets should be avoided which might make pre-emptive strikes on the part of the enemy appear worthwhile[22].

Whereas the dispersal principle might seem to violate the renowned 'principles of war' (Jomini) which are held in high esteem by military establishments around the world, the two may in actual fact be reconciled, as demonstrated by Liddell Hart:

> 'The principles of war, not merely one principle, can be condensed into a single word: "concentration". But for truth this needs to be amplified as the "concentration of strength against weakness". And for any real value it needs to be explained that the concentration of strength against weakness depends on the dispersion of your opponent's strength, which in turn is produced by a distribution of your own that gives the appearance, and the partial effect of dispersion. Your dispersion, his dispersion, your concentration—such is the sequence, and each is a sequel. True concentration is the fruit of calculated dispersion'[23].

The dispersal principle also seemingly violates the well-known 'Lanchester laws', particularly the so-called 'square law', according to which an initial force imbalance will be multiplied through successive engagement rounds. NOD proponents have, however, pointed out that Lanchester's observations presupposed particular technological conditions. Hence, due to the increasing accuracies and kill probabilities of modern weapons, the square law no longer applies, and the defender might therefore safely disperse his forces without suffering disproportionate attrition. On the contrary, greater dispersal would reduce the attrition rates of the defender, whilst concentration on the part of the attacker would only make his forces all the more rewarding as targets, and hence exacerbate his attrition[24].

VIII. Structure the defence as a web, thus taking advantage of the prevalent trends in the development of military technology.

In the absence of large-scale mobility, the defender should maintain the cohesion of his forces by means of the 'web principle', so that the aggressor would be unable to close the front around a conquered piece of territory and thus bring resistance to an end.

Any single unit might be assigned to a designated area, and might be (but would not have to be) conscripted locally. The units should be 'reactive' in the sense that they would be unable to go into action until the aggressor had entered their designated area of operations. In this way the defensive nature of the military structure would be underlined, and escalation contained. The individual units might operate under a high degree of autonomy, and the command structure be decentralised to a considerable extent, thereby becoming less vulnerable.

Part of the original impetus towards NOD was the presumed potential of PGMs (Precision-Guided Munitions), which had scored such impressive results i.a. in the Vietnam and Yom Kippur wars. PGMs appeared to have the potential of making the major weapons platforms traditionally associated with offensive warfare 'impotent and obsolete', and thus to benefit the defender. Although some NOD advocates still cling to the belief in small, cheap and effective high technology weapons for anti-tank, air defence and coastal defence purposes[25], most have modified their initial optimism: although PGMs continue to play an important role in most NOD schemes, they no longer tend to be envisaged as panaceas, but merely as one amongst several means to exploit the structural advantages of the defender.

It is more often than not acknowledged that the stipulated aggressor might 'counter-optimise' and adjust his posture to the defender's changing structure, and that counter-measures are likely to be developed against practically any conceivable defence innovation. What still gives grounds for optimism is, first of all, that any adjustment would take time, something which might be exploited by the defending side for the development of counter-counter-measures etc.

Secondly, when seen from the Western side, NOD's emphasis on e.g. PGMs would force the USSR to compete in a field wherein the West has, and is almost sure to maintain, a definite lead, namely the fields of micro-electronics and integrated circuits. A 'PGM-type defence' would hence be 'cost-effective at the margin'.

Thirdly, the decisive and immutable (because structural) advantage of the defender in such a hypothetical measures vs. counter-measures race is his more modest level of ambition: fighting on one's own territory, at close range, and from shielded positions is simply less demanding than invading, and hence less expensive. In spite of this residual optimism, the 'hi-tech euphoria' which characterised the infancy of NOD thinking seems to be over, and increasing emphasis is being given to both ordinary state-of-the-art technology and to distinctly low technology solutions. Ruggedness and cheapness are being acknowledged as important characteristics of the weapons profile of the defender, since it will provide for redundancy, or at the very least for the required area coverage.

IX. Exploit the time factor by avoiding decisive battles in favour of a protracted attrition contest, i.a. by leaving no parts of the territory undefended, whilst insuring an adequate frontier defence.

This principle is based on the simple observation that the defender is in no hurry, and consequently in a position to opt for a strategy of protracted war. The general rule may be deduced from the *prima facie* plausible assumption that an aggressor needs swift and decisive victories. Thwarting his hopes in this respect might hence be expected to exert a considerable dissuasive effect.

Whereas there might, indeed, be exceptions to this rule couched in absolute terms, its validity for Europe under modern conditions appears indisputable. The only war of aggression that might conceivably make sense to the USSR would be a strictly conventional one. However, the attacker might, at most, feel confident in being able to prevent escalation if he were able to finish off the campaign swiftly. Furthermore, even in the case of a strictly conventional protracted war, the USSR would be almost certain of defeat, due to the West's immense mobilizable resources. The USSR would hence need a strictly conventional war, which could swiftly be brought to an irreversible decision[26]. Conversely, thwarting such plans by means of the ability to transform the war into a protracted contest of attrition would have a considerable war-prevention effect.

In order to reap the benefits of the time factor, the defenders should avoid decisive battles; they should defend the entire territory, so as to be able, if need be, to 'trade space for time'. However, to be able to trade space for time does not imply 'inviting the enemy inside', and it has, indeed, been regarded as politically inconceivable to abandon forward defence in a country as densely populated as the FRG (although it does strain the imagination to envisage forward defence maintained subsequent to unification) more about which in due course.

Most NOD proposals amount rather to a forward defence plus a fall-back option of in-depth defence, with the latter presumably recommending itself as more attractive than the nuclear escalation envisaged as the only fall-back option in present NATO strategy. Although in-depth defence of the FRG would beyond doubt cause immense destruction, the devastation would hopefully be less irreversibly catastrophic than that caused by (even 'tactical') nuclear war.

Recently, however, a number of NOD advocates have come to regard the prospects of conventional war as nearly as scaring as those of nuclear warfare. They have been persuaded by what might be called the 'TDCW (Totally Destructive Conventional War) Hypothesis', according to which even conventional war is suicidal. This seems to be a logical trap, since the inescapable conclusion would be a choice between nuclear deterrence and defeatism.

On the one hand, even though nuclear deterrence might well break down, thus causing immense destruction (but, according to the TDCW, not significantly greater than that resulting from conventional war), it might just as well hold, thus reducing destruction to zero—whence might be derived a rationale for nuclear deterrence as the lesser evil. On the other hand, the safest choice might be a set of priorities calling for complete, unilateral disarmament according to the 'better red than dead' logic.

Neither nuclear deterrence for other than 'nuclear purposes', nor an abandonment of defence altogether, are, however, compatible with the foundations of NOD strategy. NOD and the TDCW are thus logically incompatible, but only few of the German NOD proponents seem aware of this[27].

X. Assign a high priority to damage limitation, i.a. by scrupulously respecting the laws of war, and by declaring cities open.

Damage limitation is not 'only' important as a means to ease the suffering of the population during war, and to make post-war recovery possible; it is also important for the sake of war prevention. Without adequate provisions for damage limitation, the state might find itself entrapped in a severe 'defence dilemma'[28], since the damage resulting from defence and war would dwarf that involved with surrender. If the choice were to be between red or dead, most would prudently opt for the former, since it would never be completely irreversible. Damage limitation provisions are therefore a precondition for eliminating (or at the very least limiting) 'self-deterrence'.

Needless to say, damage limitation will be extremely difficult in societies as vulnerable as those in Europe, with high population densities and a high level of urbanization, saturated with possible sources of contamination such as nuclear and chemical plants, etc.[29]. Nevertheless, some degree of damage limitation is not necessarily impossible to achieve, i.a. because the defender may influence the actual course of the war.

The defender is in a position to select the place of battle, since he is the one whom the aggressor has to defeat in order to bring war to an end. To fight in the 'concrete jungles' might, from a narrow military point of view, appear sensible, due to the abundance of shelter provided by urban structures. Nevertheless, with a few isolated exceptions, all NOD advocates have recommended refraining from fighting in densely populated areas, in order to protect civilians from the enemy's fire. Most advise against any form of military defence of cities, whilst some recommend supplementing the military defence of the countryside with non-military forms of resistance on the part of the urban population, so as to prevent the aggressor from seeking shelter in the cities.

The laws of war are acknowledged by most authors as having some effect on keeping escalation within bounds, not so much because treaties *per se* prevent violation, but rather because they constitute 'thresholds'. In the 'nuclear shadow' only wars which remain limited make sense. It is hence in the self-interest of both sides to prevent escalation *in extremis*, something which might be ensured by observing thresholds, such as those represented by the laws of war, whence the recommendation on the part of most NOD proponents to declare the (in a military sense) undefended urban areas 'open towns', in accordance with the laws of war[30].

Hence, likewise, the critical attitude of most NOD advocates towards e.g. Johan Galtung's ill-advised recommendation to introduce an intermediary category of 'para-military forces' between the non-violent fighters (who are by definition civilians) and the regular soldiers. On the contrary, the goal would have to be a maintainance of the distinction between combatants and non-combatants, with a view to providing both sides with all the protection of the Geneva Conventions, etc. Because of their falling beyond the 'jurisdiction' of these Conventions, and because of the risk of blurring the distinctions between the former categories[31], genuine guerillas ought therefore to have no role in the defence model, although regular infantry may well fight according to guerilla-like tactical principles.

Summary

Let me conclude this chapter by briefly recapitulating how the reader might recognise an NOD proposal if he should stumble across one (in analogy with elephants, which may be hard to define, but are easily recognizable on sight). A NOD proposal would include a number of, but not necessarily all of, the following recommendations.

—Build down offensive capabilities to a minimum, whilst maintaining, and preferably enhancing, defensive capabilities.

—Reduce the reliance on nuclear deterrence to, at most, minimum deterrence, combined with a no-first-use strategy.

—Avoid lucrative targets such as fixed sites and force concentrations.

—Reduce offensive-capable as well as particularly vulnerable components in the military posture.

—Refrain from seeking decisive battles, in favour of the ability of conducting protracted resistance.

—Defend the entire territory, whilst providing for at least some forward defence.

—Emphasise various forms of damage limitation.

CHAPTER II

A Country in the Heart of Europe

One of the most obvious distinguishing features of the NOD debate has so far been its being German, both in the sense that a disproportionate number of participants have been German, and in the sense of dealing with problems which are either particular for Germany, or which at least acquire a specific German 'flavour' when applied to this area. The use of the term 'German' rather than 'West German' in this context is deliberate. Although the subsequent account deals almost exclusively with West German problems and suggested solutions, in a certain sense 'West Germany' can only be understood as part of a larger entity, namely the 'Germany' which would be, should be (or perhaps should not, but might be), and which in 1990 became a reality.

That the debate on NOD started in the FRG, and has remained most topical here, is no coincidence. Germany is, indeed, special in a number of respects, as this chapter aims to show. That a German focus does not amount to parochialism (as would a focus on, say, the present author's home country, Denmark) is due to the fact that Germany in more than one sense constituted a microcosmic version of the macrocosmic East-West conflict. Most lessons valid for Germany would hence (*mutatis mutandis*) have at least some validity for the global conflict as well.

—The division of Germany in general, and that of Berlin in particular, symbolised the very division of the European continent into opposing blocs. A valid answer to the 'German question' would thus *eo ipso* point towards a solution to the bloc division as such.

—Although their policies towards Germany constituted a divisive issue in the relations between the major powers, certain 'regimes' nevertheless developed, tending to give all parties involved certain vested interests in their survival. This may have been the case i.a. for the four-power regime pertaining to Berlin. Eventually, such regimes might develop into 'security regimes' based on reciprocal restraint[1]. Indeed, the 'Two-plus-Four' in 1990 could be seen as a logical 'extrapolation' from this regime.

—The military posture of the FRG materialised more than anything else the very multinationality of the NATO alliance by virtue of the deployment

15

side-by-side of force contingents from several allies. Any change of i.a. the FRG's military strategy would therefore have necessitated a change of strategy on the part of all (or at least most) other NATO states, albeit not necessarily in the form of emulation.

—Germany has been a focus of security concerns on the part of friends as well as foes, due to its very size and power, as well as to its recent past. If ways might be devised to solve the security dilemma with regard to Germany, they would probably provide the key to a global escape from this ominous dilemma.

—There is thus a very real way in which the future of Europe, indeed perhaps the entire international system, has hinged on the future of Germany.

The European Security Complex

The present chapter by no means pretends to constitute a treatise on 'the German security problem', but sets itself the much humbler task of placing into context the subsequent account of one particular element in the security political debate, namely NOD. The concept of 'security complex', developed by *Barry Buzan*, seems appropriate for describing the 'setting' of West German security policy, i.e. Europe. In this terminology, a 'security complex' constitutes

> 'a local set of states whose major security perceptions and concerns link together sufficiently closely that their national security problems cannot realistically be considered apart from one another'[2].

The FRG is linked with shared perceptions of external threats to the other West European countries, including previous arch-enemies such as France, and its security problems are only comprehensible within this context. Such a regional security complex constitutes a durable, albeit not permanent, structural feature of the international system, comprising two sets of relationships, both of which may be subject to change: on the one hand, the patterns of amity and enmity between states, and, on the other hand, the relative power distribution within the system.

These relationships are determined by many sets of factors, amongst which geopolitics is merely one. Germany's location does, however, go a long way towards explaining its historical ambitions as well as the shifting patterns of amity and enmity with neighbouring states. First of all, Germany is obviously a country in Central Europe, the connotations of which are better conveyed by the term *Mitteleuropa*, which has a certain romantic and imprecise ring to it; the *Mitteleuropa* to which 'Germany' (whatever the precise meanings thereof have been through the ages) is not so much a political entity, and certainly no formal arrangement between states. It is rather a cultural community, as well as a group of nations (rather than states) sharing in some sense a common destiny.

Furthermore, from a German point of view *Mitteleuropa* has always been 'the new frontier', i.e. an area for expansion: not necessarily in the military sense of the word, but in any case understood culturally and economically. The fact that the region is approached in a similar manner by other states, not least Russia, has, however, constituted a perennial source of conflict, as may be gathered from the repeated struggle over, and occasional partition of, Poland by the rival great powers.

Germany's geopolitical situation is further complicated by the fact that it constitutes the Western part of *Mitteleuropa*, or the Eastern part of Western Europe, depending on the perspective; hence the (not always unproblematic) balancing act between *Ostpolitik* and *Westpolitik*, to which I shall return shortly[3].

Besides geopolitical determinants, a regional security complex is influenced by external actors who may modify both of the above sets of relationships, i.a. by 'overlay' through which their own bipolar relationship is superimposed on the local sets of inter-state relations. This was precisely what happened to Europe in the course of the post-war period, where (due undoubtedly to a great extent, although not exclusively, to the overlay) a 'pluralistic security community' developed between the West European states, so that war between, say, the FRG and France came to be no longer regarded as an option by either side[4].

Whereas the 'security dilemma'[5] was thus rendered largely irrelevant for inter-state relations within Western Europe, it remained relevant for Europe as a whole, at least until the Autumn of 1989 (cf. Chapter XI). Between the two halves of the continent, war certainly remained conceivable, regardless of the overlay; indeed, it might even have become more likely because of it. Hence the security dilemma which faced (and perhaps still faces) Western Europe and *a fortiori* the FRG.

The greater the effort the NATO countries put into their own defence against the (presumed) Soviet threat, the greater this threat tended to become, since the USSR was inclined to reciprocate in a similar manner to what it perceived as a growing Western threat; hence a spiralling armaments dynamic, as well as mutually reinforcing urges towards preventive or pre-emptive war. If, on the other hand, the West had chosen not to put up a viable counter to the looming Soviet menace, then this might, indeed, have materialised into a genuine threat.

A certain variety of the security dilemma was, furthermore, at work in intra-alliance relations, namely the 'alliance security dilemma', a particular instance of which was the 'abandonment versus entrapment dilemma'. If smaller states aligned themselves closely with great powers, *in casu* one of the two superpowers, they might feel reasonably confident of the support of the latter in case of jeopardy. However, they at the same time risked being entrapped in the maelstrom of inter-superpower rivalry, thus ending up parties to conflicts beyond their control. If, alternatively, they should try to loosen the bonds so as to mitigate this risk, they would merely run the risk of being abandoned by their superpower ally, and hence of ending up at the mercy of its rival[6].

As a 'net consumer of security', the FRG has, throughout most of its existence, found itself unable to escape this dilemma, which might help to explain its apparent oscillation between two poles: at the one pole, a loyal 'cold-war attitude' towards the USSR, implying i.a. support for the INF deployment; at the other, a desire for promoting *détente* through accommodation, whence the opposition, in the first instance, to INF deployment (as far as the SPD was concerned) and subsequently to the contemplated FOTL (Follow-On-to-Lance), a negative attitude that came to be shared by the government parties[7].

Another perennial dilemma in West German security political considerations has been the so-called 'defence dilemma', stemming from the fact that even 'successful' defence might be fatal because unable to protect what ought to be defended. Whereas statehood might be successfully preserved by nuclear means, this might only be at the expense of sacrificing the population, as well as the societal structure, of the country in question, the 'statehood' of which would thus become an empty shell[8].

The defence dilemma was, furthermore, not 'only' a wartime phenomenon, but made itself felt, albeit in a different shape, even in peacetime, when the burdens of defence expenditures might reach such heights as to put the survival of the welfare state in question. Both varieties of the defence dilemma were making themselves felt with an increasing intensity in both parts of Germany, as will emerge from the concluding section of this chapter, as well as, hopefully, from the rest of this book.

The Symphonic Structure of German Politics

Having thus constructed a conceptual skeleton, I shall proceed to add some flesh and blood through a (very rough and superficial) description of the actual place and role of (West) Germany within this European security complex. I shall round off this account with a brief presentation of 'the German Question', to the recent development of which I shall return at some length in the Chapter XI. Subsequently, I shall elaborate a little on the security and defence dilemmas as seen from the angle of the FRG. Before that, however, a few words on the dominant themes of West German foreign policy seem in order.

Historically, the foreign policy of the FRG consisted of three basic ingredients, each of which constituted a 'bundle' of policies *vis-à-vis* individual other states:

—*Westpolitik* (WP), i.e. policies towards the Western powers.
—*Ostpolitik* (OP), i.e. policies towards the Eastern bloc.
—*Deutschlandpolitik* (DP), i.e. policies (or a politically motivated lack of policies) towards the other Germany, the GDR.

The most suitable terminology for describing the complicated combination of these policy dimensions might, strange though it may sound, be that of music, rather than that of international relations treatises. One might e.g. conceive of West German foreign policy since WW2 as an elaborate (Bach-style) fugue, wherein two main motifs (WP and OP) have combined and interacted in a polyphonic, indeed contrapuntal fashion, with the DP serving as *basso continuo*. Alternatively, one might depict it as a Beethoven-style symphony, wherein the WP theme dominated in the first part (constituting itself a sonata movement, with all three themes present), followed by a second part wherein the OP theme took the lead, with the DP theme continuously present, albeit periodically almost inaudible, and being rounded off with a grand finale (1989-1990) wherein all three *motifs* interacted in a powerful *crescendo*. Finally, one might liken German politics to a Wagnerian opera, with different *leitmotifs* (e.g. the DP theme of reunification) recurring from time to time in the midst of the epic evolution.

It would, however, require a more profound understanding of musical theory, as well as of German foreign policy, than that possessed by the present author to pursue this terminological path, wherefore I shall revert to the well-known terms of international relations theory.

The three themes have tended to be interlinked in an often seemingly paradoxical manner, reminiscent of the 'indirect strategies' described in the previous chapter, or of the original conception of 'containment' as a basically asymmetrical response to a Soviet political threat, as envisioned by George Kennan. WP has thus been pursued as an approach to OP or DP, rather than for the attainment of WP ends for their own sake; OP has served as an instrument in the WP endeavour; whilst the pursuit of DP goals has only been possible in a roundabout fashion through a mixture of WP and OP, etc. The persistent West German quest throughout 1990 for enlisting the support of its Western allies for assistance to Eastern Europe in general and the USSR in particular, with a view to gaining the approval of the latter for German unification-cum-NATO membership, constituted an eminent example of this complicated pursuit of DP by means of WP directed towards OP[9].

Conversely, the three themes have also constituted 'strings' upon which external powers have been able to play in order to influence West German policy. For it to be effective, however, such influence has also usually had to be exerted indirectly, in a roundabout fashion, whereas brute attemps at direct influence have more often than not proved futile and occasionally counter-productive. James McAdams aptly drew the lesson hereof for the 1989-1990 all-European discussions on the German question:

> 'To a great extent, we may get the Germany that we deserve. (. . .) Rather than imposing demands, it makes more sense to concentrate on deliberately cultivating an environment in which the leaders of a new Germany could agree to such limitations of their own volition and at their own pace'[10].

The constituent elements of all three pervasive themes (i.a. policy dimensions) in German foreign policy have been policies towards other states, i.e. towards other members of the security complex. I shall therefore commence with a brief account of some of the more durable features in the relationship of the FRG with the most important states, highlighting particular 'bonds of amity and enmity' and power relations, as well as shifts therein.

Bonds of Amity and Enmity

Throughout the ages, Germany's neighbours have tended to perceive her as at least a latent threat, and 'enemy images' have flourished which have reached excesses well beyond those pertaining to the Soviet Union during the Cold War. The following statement by Rudyard Kipling was probably merely an extreme expression of a rather widespread 'Germanophobia':

> 'There are only two dimensions in the world today: human beings and Germans. (. . .) Human beings (. . .) desire nothing more greatly than that this unclean thing should be thrust out from the membership and the memory of nations'[11].

What the Germans themselves conceived of as 'the German question' (i.e. how to bring Germany back together), has therefore more often than not, and obligatory lip-service to German demands for unity notwithstanding, received a twist in the minds of Germany's neighbours, thus becoming 'the German problem', the gist of which has been how to keep the Germans apart. In this sense, the post-war division of Germany was so desirable for everybody but the Germans as to be almost inevitable. The German defeat in WWII thus merely provided a convenient opportunity for doing what the other European states had long wanted to do anyway[12].

Even though to admit so would be unthinkable, the truth is that the neighbouring states were probably quite content with the existence of the Berlin Wall. Its ugliness notwithstanding, the Wall constituted a pillar of stability in East-West relations. Even the friends and allies of the FRG were therefore somewhat in disarray when the Wall finally came tumbling down, and the topic of German unification elbowed its way on to the immediate agenda of European affairs[13]. I shall return at some length to this topic in Chapter XI.

Needless to say, the Germans have been far from innocent victims of 'slander', nor can they be absolved from the main responsibility for their present debacle. Germany was either the sole, or at least one of the, instigator(s) of several of the more recent wars in European history, including the two world wars. The blame for WWI may have been somewhat more evenly distributed between the belligerents than subsequently assumed by the victors, and layed down in the controversial Art. 231 of the Versailles Treaty. Be that as it may, the Wilhemine *Kaiserreich* was certainly far from innocent in this respect[14].

Even more clearly, Germany bore the undivided blame for unleashing WWII, in the course of which they committed what were probably the most outrageous atrocities in the entire history of Mankind: 'the most diabolical thing Man has ever done to Man'[15].

The FRG remained burdened with this heritage of the Third *Reich*, not merely in the form of the division of Germany, or of its somewhat circumscribed sovereignty. Above all, none of the FRG's neigbours have yet forgotten about the two world wars emanating from Germany, whence their lack of enthusiasm for German unification, or any strengthening of the FRG's relative power position in Europe.

In the following passage I shall venture a rough, and inevitably superficial, account of (West) German relations with some other European powers (in the 'CSCE sense', i.e. including both superpowers). This is, however, a highly complex matter, i.a. because all of these are more or less interdependent: Franco-German relations are, for instance, entirely incomprehensible without reference to the relationship of both states with Russia/the USSR, in their turn dependent upon the state of US-Soviet relations, as well as on the US-German relationship, etc. Ideally, a multi-dimensional account would thus be appropriate, whereas any attempt at drawing two-dimensional sketches necessitates (over-)simplifications. Since only two dimensions are available, however, I shall sketch a few 'clusters' of West German foreign policies in so far as they are relevant for the subsequent account of the NOD debate.

The USSR has the typical perspective on international relations of a land power in Mackinder's sense, which is practically only vulnerable (on the conventional level) to land attack. Throughout history there has almost only been one source of such threats to Russian/Soviet security (and regional supremacy), namely Germany. German unification and/or the lifting of some of the constraints on West German armaments might therefore raise, in Soviet eyes, the spectre of a revitalised German threat.

Whence, first of all, recurrent campaigns against West German 'revanchism', etc. Secondly, the great significance attributed by the USSR to the Helsinki accords with their codification of 'the Yalta map of Europe'. Thirdly, an understandable Soviet interest in driving a wedge between the FRG and the Western superpower, neither of which would constitute a serious threat on their own, whereas in collaboration they certainly might. Whence, finally, the Soviet recalcitrance in the question of the continued/future membership of the united Germany in NATO, to which I shall return in Chapter XI[16].

Whereas Russia/the USSR has thus often feared Germany, the opposite has been equally true, particularly in the post-war period when the power ratios of previous centuries were inverted, as a result of Soviet expansion and arms build-up occurring simultaneously with German dismemberment and 'emasculation'.

Fears have thus been mutual and reciprocal. However, periods of enmity have alternated with almost as frequent periods of amity, or at least of *ad hoc* and pragmatically motivated collaboration. This was i.a. the case in the 1920s, when the two 'outcasts' from the international system (i.e. the League of Nations) collaborated fairly closely, also in military matters, in circumvention of the prohibitions imposed on the German military by the Versailles Treaty. This collaboration was partly codified in the Rapallo Treaty of 1922, and included the clandestine training of German officers in Soviet Russia as well as a certain cooperation with regard to military production[17].

Even though the rise to power of Hitler's Nazi party was initially a cause of serious concern in the Politbureau of Stalin's CPSU (the Soviet leader had read *Mein Kampf*), the hostile attitude was eventually replaced by almost an *entente cordiale* between the two dictators, subsequent to the Molotov-Rippentrop Treaty of 23 August 1939. Neither of these (diametrically opposed) attitudes towards Germany thus amounted to an unprecedented anomaly, but both were, in a certain sense, 'business as usual'.

Even in the 1980s, Soviet-German relations had a very high prominence for both sides, both of which, furthermore, possessed a considerable leverage *vis-à-vis* the other. The USSR held the key to any solution to 'the German question' in the sense that unification presupposed Soviet consent, both *de jure* and *de facto*. The FRG, in its turn, constituted for the USSR the most accessible source of Western technology, so urgently required for any expansion of Soviet power along the non-military dimensions. Since the USSR has been quite aware of the basically fragile nature of its 'one-dimensional' power, this West German role as high technology supplier has provided her with considerable leverage[18]. By the Winter of 1990-91, the USSR had become even more dependent on German collaboration, i.a. with a view to feeding the Soviet population, threatened by widespread deprivation and downright starvation.

Furthermore, the FRG has been viewed by the USSR as a potential go-between and moderator *vis-à-vis* the rival superpower, since Soviet leaders have realistically counted on a more profound German understanding of their own concerns, as well as on an earnest willingness to accommodate these concerns, at least up to a point. Notwithstanding the persistent Soviet calls for a neutralization of a united Germany, it is therefore open to serious doubt to what extent they have been serious, since German neutralization would deprive the USSR of a conditional, but nevertheless valuable, ally in the Western camp[19]. I shall return at some length in Chapter XI to the most recent developments in this matter.

Since relations between Germany and the Soviet Union have thus always been close, albeit alternating between hostility and *entente*, the prospects of a renewed 'special relationship' were not all that remote, even prior to 1989. In 1990 it soon became clear that something monumental was 'in the offing' pertaining to German-Soviet relations, though the implications were unclear. As a partial *quid pro quo* for Soviet acquiescence with all-German NATO membership, Chancellor Kohl had promised to follow up his immediate financial support for the USSR with a later 'comprehensive agreement', the precise contents of which remained to be settled. Furthermore, in September 1990, a 'Treaty of Good Neighbourly Relations, Partnership and Cooperation' was signed. This was tantamount to a non-aggression treaty, combined with an unspecified obligation to co-operation in various fields. I shall return to this treaty in Chapter XI below[20].

To the 'bystanders', these prospects of an *entente cordiale* between the USSR and Germany have been a matter of great importance, and not merely in the positive sense. One of the most concerned spectators has been France.

France, in its turn, is the FRG's only other potential contender as the mightiest power on the European land-mass, whence a centuries-old relentless struggle for predominance[21]. Franco-German rivalry has historically taken the forms of occasional wars as well as perpetual arms racing and competitive alliance formation. Based on this experience, France came to regard Germany as fundamentally bellicose and aggressive. Although the timing was admittedly the worst possible for Franco-German *entente*, General De Gaulle thus in 1944 expressed what was probably a widespread French opinion about their eastern neighbours:

'A grand people, but one that perpetually tends towards war (. . .) such is the German people'[22].

With such attitudes as their point of departure, it should come as no surprise that France rejoiced in the post-war dismemberment of Germany. Although France did not participate in the Potsdam conference, it was asked to sign the agreement *ex post facto*, and willingly did so, thus assuming its part of the responsibility for the division of Germany. Francois Mauriac is famous for his ironic, yet probably accurate, explanation of this French attitude: 'I am so fond of Germany that I am pleased that there are now two of them'[23].

As West Germany's ally in NATO, France has of course been obliged to pay lip-service to the policy of reunification, in its turn a West German *sine qua non* of NATO membership. French support has, however, been less than enthusiastic and always somewhat conditional. France has tended to see the solution to the German question/problem in a transcendence of it, implying that it be embedded in pan-European, or at least multinational, 'grand schemes'[24].

The original French plans for the European Defence Community, EDC, (which eventually failed, ironically because of lacking French support), were thus put forward in response to Western plans for German rearmament, with the prospects whereof the French felt uncomfortable. Surprising though it may sound, there was also a certain French interest during the 1960s in embedding the German question in a Central European Union, as was the gist of a semi-official proposal. This notion did, however, fly in the face of the traditional French unease with any German talk about *Mitteleuropa*, which has usually been interpreted as a re-emerging *Drang nach Osten*. In the latter vein, the German relations with Poland have always been applied by France as a yardstick for evaluating the orientation and intentions of Germany: if the Germans behaved peacefully towards their eastern neighbour, then contentment was presumed to prevail with the territorial *status quo*, whereas indications of German hostility towards Poland were seen as signs that 'they were at it again', i.e. that the expansionist trend had resurfaced[25].

Furthermore, France has been somewhat ambivalent with regard to the European solution to the German question/problem. On the one hand, France has been opposed to 'West European' solutions, i.a. because these have tended to include the USA, and *eo ipso* to reduce French leverage *vis-à-vis* the FRG. On the other hand, France has tended to see the best prospects for maintaining an approximate balance with West Germany within a clearly West European framework, because pan-European schemes would tend to 'tip the scales' against France, as a consequence of Germany's cultural ties with, and economic access to, Eastern Europe. Caught between the horns of this insoluble dilemma, France has tended to support the preservation of the *status quo* in an almost 'don't rock the boat' fashion[26].

Franco-German rivalry and *rapprochement* have thus partly been of a geopolitical nature, and have usually taken the form of a balance-of-power contest. The traditional ally of France in this respect has been Russia, a policy orientation to which De Gaulle in 1953 gave blunt expression with his utterance: 'France is always an ally of Russia in case of a German threat'. Conversely, France has tended to fear that a German nation-state might follow the traditional Prussian policy of alignment with Russia, in which case France would have no alternative to alignment with an external power strong enough to out-balance Russia, the only viable candidate for which role has traditionally been Britain. *Entente* and collaboration with the UK has, however, been no easy choice for France, locked for centuries in a global contest with this state for colonies and global influence. If Germany were to align itself with the USSR today, the only available alternative to Britain would be the USA, which, however, tends to be too strong for a France that is all but happy with subordination under a hegemonial ally. Whence an uncomfortable choice between subordination under American hegemony and acquiescence with a *pax sovietica*[27].

In the post-war period, the rivalry has undergone a metamorphosis as compared with previous centuries. On the one hand, France's traditional (and indeed geopolitically 'natural') ally, Russia, has been ruled out because of the bipolar 'overlay'. Indeed, in the era of *Ostpolitik* and *détente*, the traditional nightmare of France was almost superceded by its exact opposite. Rather than being frightened about a too strong and bellicose Germany, the French have come to worry more about the spectre of German neutralization and accommodation towards the Soviet Union, i.e. what they regard as weakness. 'For the first time in history, France does not fear the strength but the weakness of Germany', as Raymond Aron aptly described it[28].

On the other hand, German power has been so curtailed through the various post-war arrangements (dismemberment, NATO and WEU membership, etc.) as to no longer constitute any immediate military threat to France, for its part robed in the garments of nuclear power. Nevertheless, the prospects for France seemed increasingly uncertain in the light of unification, and widespread concerns remain about the power and strength of Germany.

Regardless of the remaining ambivalence, the foundations for a more lasting cooperative relationship did emerge. Franco-German *entente* was first codified in the Elysée Treaty of 1963, and has since then developed into what has been called a 'Paris-Bonn axis', in which the emphasis has been placed on security policy in the narrow sense. It has resulted in the establishment of i.a. a joint defence council, in the conduct of joint manoeuvres, etc.[29]. Both sides do, however, remain somewhat ambivalent with regard to the cooperation.

On the one hand, the FRG has needed France's assistance in the quest for emancipation from American hegemony, since she could not risk such a venture on her own, lest this be perceived as a 'break-out' from the Yalta constraints, something which would immediately have revitalised the security dilemma dynamics. On the other hand, the FRG certainly did not want to replace American with French tutelage, but was only prepared to settle for a relationship on equitable terms.

As far as France has been concerned, she has needed the FRG for several purposes: first of all, as a military *glacis* shielding her eastern flank, whence the fear of a new 'Rapallo relationship', which might develop if the FRG should drift too far in the direction of the USSR. Secondly, France has needed the FRG's support in its quest for European integration, preferably on terms which would ensure France a leading role[30].

On the other hand, France is certainly not prepared to give up the vestiges of a major power only in order to accomodate the FRG's anti-nuclear concerns, whence the insistence on maintaining the nuclear *Force de Frappe* as a French force, about the future employment of which France might well agree to consult the FRG, but the actual use of which would have to remain a French prerogative. France also remained unwilling to embrace whole-heartedly the principle of forward defence, although the development of the FAR (*Force d'Action Rapide*) has provided her with some of the wherewithal for fighting a forward battle in Germany. The latter issue may, however, have become irrelevant in the light of German unification and the reassessment of NATO strategy which is in process.

If the above account of Franco-German relations seems confusing, it has in a certain sense accomplished its purpose: to convey an impression of extreme complexity and ambivalence, which is, moreover, likely to increase in the years immediately ahead, when decisions of extreme importance are impending as a consequence of German unification, for instance about the future of the Western alliance, about relations with the USSR and the newly-emancipated East European countries, about the EC, etc.[31].

The traditional attitude of Great Britain towards Europe has been that of an insular counterweight and balancer, seeking to preserve a rough balance of power on the continent, so as to prevent the emergence of a preponderant power, which might constitute a genuine threat. Since WW2, however, the UK has lost some of the wherewithal for orchestrating this balance of power, due once again to the overlay, which i.a. prevented 'playing the Russian card' against Germany.

Furthermore, Britain has relinquished some of her insular 'privileges' and agreed to more permanent stakes in the development on the continent, materialised in the stationing in the FRG of the BAOR (British Army of the Rhine) and the RAFG (Royal Air Force, Germany) wings, along with their integral nuclear arms. Indeed, this commitment has even been increasing relative to the total British defence budget, due to its being defined in absolute terms in an era of increasing scarcity. Britain's main role may thus have shifted from that of a balancer to that of 'the guardian of the overlay', whose main concern was to prevent the FRG from 'leaning' too much towards the East, and who was eager to maintain the U.S. presence on the European continent[32].

The USA has since WWII played the role as the 'resident alien' power, the national interests of which have only partly overlapped with those of the Europeans. American security has always been based, above all, on its 'ultra-insular' location and has never been 'naturally' linked to that of Europe. Whereas the previously mentioned states have thus *nolens volens* been parties to the European security complex, the USA has always had a choice between involvement and disengagement. What determined this choice in the past was probably a mixture of traditional power politics and ideological concerns of an almost 'crusading' nature.

The United States has undoubtedly viewed itself as an unselfish benefactor of Europe, and not least of Germany, which certainly had not 'deserved' Marshall aid. The USA thus tended to understand the 'Truman Doctrine' and the very NATO treaty as benevolent concessions to friends in dire straits, rather than as measures based on shared interests, and by implication beneficial to both sides. Hence the American conviction that the USA had a legitimate claim to hegemony. Whereas some West Germans continue to support such claims, the resurgent FRG (and still less the united Germany) is most unlikely in the long run to acquiesce to such an American predominance.

Relations with the FRG since the end of WW2 have shifted from enmity to amity, due above all to the perceived need for a counterweight to the USSR, in its turn a precondition for successful containment. This continues to play a role for the USA, who tended to view West German rapprochement with the Soviet Union with some concern[33].

The two states would thus seem to be on a clear collision course in the decades ahead, when open clashes may only be averted in the unlikely case of American acquiescence to a more egalitarian relationship. Nevertheless, although the two states are thus drifting apart, this is bound to be a rather slow process of emancipation.

Due to its indisputable contribution to deterring the (presumably inherently aggressive) Soviet Union, the USA may remain an appreciated ally. To the extent that the Soviet threat fades away, however, (as it has already to a large extent) the overlay may be lifted and the unequal relationship come to be felt as increasingly insupportable[34].

In addition to the great powers in focus so far, two minor neighbouring states had high stakes in West German security policy: the GDR and Poland.

East Germany (the GDR) had always had a very ambiguous relationship with the FRG, due above all to its own lack of intrinsic legitimacy. The very existence of the FRG *eo ipso* constituted a security risk for the GDR, because the vast majority of the latter's citizens, if given the choice, would undoubtedly have preferred FRG citizenship—preferences which in 1990 resulted in the GDR being 'swallowed' by the FRG, with the explicit, indeed enthusiastic, consent of its citizens. I shall return to this unique chain of events at some length in Chapters X and XI.

The FRG, in its turn, historically based its very *raison d'être* on being the legitimate offspring of Germany, whence the obstinate denial until the late 1960s of the very existence of the other German state, and the extremely strained and mutually hostile relations (indeed, for a long period of time, non-relations) between the FRG and the GDR.

Subsequent to the break-through for *Ostpolitik* under the Brandt-Scheel government, however, a much more benign 'special relationship' developed, entailing i.a. improvements in living conditions and human rights in the East, as well as a certain 'normalisation' of the status of Berlin. The GDR, in its turn, was only too happy to reap the fruits of *détente* and to exploit fully the benefits of the special inter-German relationship, giving it i.a. almost unlimited access to the EC[35].

Poland has been the country in Europe, whose destiny has been linked most inextricably with the Yalta and Potsdam agreements, and hence the country with most to lose if Germany were 'set free' without constraints and without the debilitating frontier through the middle.

What the Poles feared more than anything else was probably an inherent German expansionism. There were, indeed, a panoply of historical precedents in German history for regarding its eastern border as 'open', as well as for eastward colonization for expansionist purposes. Indeed, the very existence of Poland as an independent state had frequently been questioned by Germany, e.g. by the Chief of the German Army, General von Seeckt, who in 1922 said *expressis verbis* that 'Poland's existence is intolerable, incompatible with Germany's'[36].

The Hitler-Stalin Pact of 23 August 1939, leading to yet another partition of Poland, did not spring out of of the blue, but was in a certain sense in direct continuity with previous German-Russian relations. Having thus on several occasions been dismembered by Germany and Russia, Poland was understandably quite content with the division of Germany and seriously concerned about the talk of (re)unification, especially when such claims were not qualified with explicit support for the Oder-Neisse frontier.

The 'open-endedness' of the border issue persisted throughout the postwar period, because the legal status of the Oder-Neisse border was deliberately kept ambiguous. Some progress was, however, made, i.a. by the signing of the Warsaw Treaty in 1970, 'normalizing' relations between the two countries. Nevertheless, the 1972 *Bundestag* debate on the treaty's ratification merely reopened the issue with the declaration that 'the treaty does not create any legal foundations for the present borders'[37].

Although Germany had, beyond comparison, inflicted far graver suffering on Poland than *vice versa*, Poland had on certain occasions also behaved vindictively, indeed even expansionistically, towards Germany, such as (at least as the Germans understood it) in the early inter-war years, when Germany was victim of the Versailles Treaty constraints. Although clearly dwarfed by the genocide committed by Germans against Poles, the latters' behaviour has also been occasionally rather less than creditable, e.g. in being, until recently, rather ambiguous about the very existence of the (in actual fact quite sizable) German minority in Poland[38].

Subsequent to the 1989 revolutions, the Polish attitude towards Germany remained somewhat ambivalent. On the one hand, the FRG was regarded by the new Polish government as a model for emulation in many respects, particularly economically, whence the keen interest in friendly neighbourly relations with the FRG, as well as with the united Germany in the making. On the other hand, the Poles were uncomfortable with the prospect of unification, particularly because the matter of the Oder-Neisse border was not yet settled[39]. I shall return to this matter in Chapter XI.

The Polish ambivalence towards Germany was intertwined with equally ambivalent Soviet-Polish relations. On the one hand, the Poles had always resented the Soviet presence, legitimated above all by the need for communications with the GSFG (Group of Soviet Forces, Germany) in East Germany. On the other hand, the Soviet presence both in the GDR and in Poland did constitute a guarantee against any resurgent German 'revanchism', whereas Poland might become isolated in the case of a Soviet withdrawal, especially if this were to take place (as is actually happening) simultaneously with German unification.

The FRG thus had fairly complicated relations with a number of her neighbours and allies. In her dealings with one, she constantly had to keep in mind the implications for relations with the rest, i.a. with regard to the combination of the three dimensions (WP, OP and DP) of her foreign policy.

The German Question

No account of West German security policy is conceivable without at least a few words on 'the German question'. This question has almost always been part of the discourse on the *Ostpolitical* or *Westpolitical* aspects of security policy. Often the references to the German question have been almost inaudible, and perhaps not really meant to be taken seriously, but serving rather to legitimise endeavours in other directions. By explicitly 'keeping the question open', political parties may have gained some leeway for the pursuit of other goals, some of which may in actual fact have contributed to 'closing' the question. In the minds of many, the question was thus conceived of as a perennial question, never meant to be answered[40]. It did, however, imbue German politics with an 'open-endedness', appreciated by many a politician.

The division of 'Germany' came to be regarded as an anomaly and has, paradoxically, been seen in this light for centuries, the historical fact notwithstanding that 'Germany' has been a highly elusive term.

First of all, there has only been very little continuity about the 'German nation', politically, territorially or spiritually. Neither has it been tied to any particular political regime or any well-defined stretch of territory; nor is it at all easy to identify what 'German culture' is supposed to mean. Secondly, the German nation (whatever precisely this may mean) has throughout most of its history been divided up into even smaller political pieces than today. As a matter of historical fact, 'Germany' conceived of as a unified nation-state is of a fairly recent vintage[41].

There are, however, strong historical precedents for the present quest for national unification, going back at least to the national liberation movement against Napoleon in the early 19th century. In 1848, when a wave of democratic revolutions swept across Europe, the 'national question' loomed at least as large in the German movement as did the democratic question.

However, although the revolutionaries were united in their calls for ending the undignified *Kleinstaaterei*, they subscribed to quite irreconcilable visions of 'Germany'. Indeed, the 'Germany' they had in mind was not so much a political notion as a romantic *Sturm und Drang* spiritual construction, the translation of which into political terms brought serious inconsistencies to light[42].

The Paul's Church in Frankfurt became the venue of the first Constituent Assembly, the mandate of which was to create a unified German state. Already then, however, divergent sets of priorities were at work, with the party of the *Grossdeutschen* clinging to a vision of a 'Great Germany', including Austria, which would, however, have been a far cry from a democratic nation-state, since 'Austria' in the final analysis encompassed the entire Habsburg Empire (and was quite reactionary, too). The party of the *Kleindeutschen*, on the other hand, pursued the objective of a 'Small Germany', excluding Austria but, as a concequence thereof, certain of being dominated by the far from democratic Prussia[43].

Due to these conflicting sets of priorities, genuine unification was not accomplished until the time of Bismarck, and in the more 'worldly' sense of a political entity, quite unrelated to previous romantic conceptions of 'Germany'. It was also set apart from the visions of 1848 by being far from a creation of the mind but, on the contrary, created through the victorious Franco-German war of 1870-71. In a certain sense, 'Germany' was thus born in war, although Prince Bismarck, subsequent to the creation of the Empire, shifted to a policy of *status quo*, implying a rejection of both expansionist and preventive war[44].

Even after this accomplishment of a fairly rounded nation-state, the 'German question' continued to play a role, partly because Germany did not rest content with the modest objectives, but embarked on a quest for a colonial empire, whence ensued WWI.

The German defeat and the Versailles Treaty, in their turn, led to the emergence of a new 'German question', since the principle of national self-determination was (at least as the Germans saw it) applied by the victors in a somewhat less than equitable manner: wherever it implied cessation from Germany, or the annexation by other states of formerly German territory, it was applied, whereas it was deemed inapplicable wherever it would have benefited the vanquished Germany. Deeply felt German resentments resulted, upon which the Nazi party was able to play, with appeals for bringing the Germans 'back into the *Reich*'. Although Hitler's plans were thus couched in terms of solving the German question, this was in actual fact merely a propagandistic ploy, intended to legitimise much more overtly expansionist designs[45].

Even to the present day, the notion of the German nation has persisted, albeit partly 'rationalised' as a purely political notion. Furthermore, the Germans have made strenuous efforts not to be perceived as nationalistic;

hence the perceived need of embedding proposals for German solutions in broader schemes[46].

The FRG nevertheless understood itself, and codified this understanding in the Basic Law (*Grundgesetz*), as merely a part of a whole, which was defined, according to most interpretations until 1990, as Germany within the borders of 1937. In reality, however, the identification of most West Germans was exclusively with the FRG as a political entity, as such enjoying very widespread, indeed almost total, loyalty from its citizens. That most of the inhabitants of the FRG thus tended to almost forget about the larger 'Germany' of which they were supposedly merely a part might be related to the unpleasant memories connected with this entity, and especially its most recent past[47].

Until recently, few Germans seemed to take the (re)unification option seriously for the near or medium-term future. Although there remained, throughout the last thirty years, a majority of more than eighty percent in favour of unity, opinion polls also revealed a significant decline in belief in the feasibility of unification, reaching an all-time low of three percent in 1987[48]. Until the momentous years 1989-90, the question thus tended to be seen as a task for 'the next government', but almost never for the present one.

A few political groupings deliberately sought to 'close' the question, yet only with a view to approaching it in a more round-about fashion: either by way of 'change through *rapprochement*' (*Wandel durch Annäherung*) such as envisioned by the SPD; or by way of pan-European schemes, such as implied by the 'Green' visions (cf. below, Chapters VIII and XI)[49].

Both WP and OP had obvious implications for DP, i.e. for the German question. Certain options might be foreclosed by an overt Western orientation, likely to alienate the USSR and thus deter it from accommodating the West Germans. Even though the FRG thus succeeded in enlisting the political support of its NATO allies for (re)unification, this in no way helped persuade the USSR to accede to unification. The understanding therefore gradually grew that there was no solution to the German national question on the national level, but that it had to be sought on the level of an East-West European 'settlement', such as the much debated 'European Peace Order'[50].

Defence policy obviously entered into DP considerations as well, and *vice versa*. Just as military force has been *expressis verbis* acknowledged as inapplicable to the German question, it has also usually been acknowledged that an unrestrained military build-up (especially if combined with a distinct Western 'bias') might damage chances of peaceful unification. This seeming incompatibility between rearmament and reunification did, indeed, constitute a prominent theme in the security political debate of the 1950s, as the subsequent Chapter will show. From this derived (and still derive) numerous schemes for some kind of neutralization of Germany as a *quid pro quo* for unification[51]. Such schemes seem in line with public preferences, since as late as 1986, when asked explicitly whether they would prefer unification-cum-neutralization to NATO membership-cum-division, as many as 41 percent declared themselves in favour of the former 'package'[52].

The Security Dilemma

Due to the aforementioned concerns on the part of the FRG's neighbours, West German foreign policy makers have continually faced a security dilemma. First of all, they have had to acknowledge that there were limits to the FRG's attainable power increases, beyond which they would become self-defeating; secondly, that there were limits to emancipation as a way of avoiding 'entrapment', beyond which 'abandonment' might become a serious danger. However, these dilemmas have only been acute during times of increased international tension, whereas under more relaxed conditions it has been easier to 'muddle through', whilst achieving significant results in the process.

The FRG has thus been vitally dependent on the international 'climate' and had a high stake in *détente*. Logical though it may seem, this has not always been so, however. During the Adenauer and Erhardt administrations the very *raison d'être* of the FRG hinged on the maintenance of a degree of East-West tension, giving the Western powers a stake in the survival of 'their' Germany; hence the predominance of the 'abandonment side' of the above dilemma. Since the *Ostpolitical* breakthrough around 1970, however, the stakes in *détente* have grown considerably, both as far as *détente* in general is concerned (i.a. as a precondition for proceeding along the *Ostpolitical* dimension of the *Deutschlandpolitik*), and, in particular, with regard to expanding East-West trade.

In the latter field, *détente*, OP and WP proved difficult to reconcile, because of the incompatibility between the American and the West German approaches to trade relations with the East: Whereas the FRG (as most European states) saw trade as a mutually beneficial relationship, the USA tended to visualise it in terms of assistance to the systemic foe, and thus as a unilateral concession which called for a Soviet *quid pro quo*. A number of conflicts ensued, pertaining i.a. to the appropriate criteria for 'militarily relevant technologies' (the COCOM lists), in which connection the USA has favoured broad and hence restrictive interpretations, while the Europeans, and above all the West Germans, wanted narrower, and thus more permissive, interpretations.

Secondly, conflicts have centred around the extent to which economic sanctions should be applied against breaches of the unwritten 'code' of '*détente* behaviour', most conspiciously in the debate over the gas pipeline deal between the FRG and the USSR[53].

The Defence Dilemma

In the case of the FRG, the 'defence dilemma' has constituted perhaps an even more serious concern for policy-makers than the security dilemma. This has been due, above all, to its extremely central geopolitical location. Ironically, the FRG was large enough to worry its neighbours, but small enough to worry herself.

It also seemed to be in the wrong spot. On the one hand, the FRG was located almost in the exact centre of Europe, and thus in a favorable position to interact with almost all of Europe, in terms of military conquest, trade relations, cultural ties and influence, or political relations. On the other hand, the location of the FRG constituted a handicap in other respects. The most obvious disadvantage was, of course, the extremely awkward location of Berlin, which remained, until unification in 1990, in a potential hostage position *vis-à-vis* the USSR and her (until 1989, faithful and loyal) ally, the GDR.

Furthermore, the FRG had only limited access to the sea and thus slim chances of competing successfully with 'natural' naval powers such as Britain, the USA and Japan. Although this had not prevented occasional quests for a naval great power status, these attempts had invariably failed[54].

The paramount problem was, however, that the FRG, in addition to being an important part of the spoils of any future European war (thanks to her wealth and prosperity), also constituted an obvious battleground by virtue of her very central location. The FRG was both an attractive stationing area and a transit area, almost impossible for any neighbouring states at war with each other to bypass.

These factors might explain why, until 1990, the FRG was, by most accounts the most heavily militarised country in the world (except perhaps for Israel). Vast stocks of conventional, chemical and nuclear weapons were stored on her territory, with very frequent and large-scale military exercises and other peacetime activities taking place. Partly as a cause, and partly as a result thereof, the FRG was almost certain to become the main battlefield in any future East-West war: a war which would have extremely disastrous consequences, even if fought on a strictly conventional level.

I shall refrain from challenging the competing 'beans-counting' with any detailed break-down of force levels or ratios, and limit myself to providing a rough sketch of the types and approximate numbers of forces to be found on West German soil[55]. In recognition that this posture is about to change radically, the past tense seemed most appropriate for this account, notwithstanding the fact that most figures still held at the time of writing.

The grand total of approximately 495,000 West Germans under arms had, until 1990, almost been regarded as a 'magical number', *below* which the FRG could not go. In actual fact, however, it stemmed from the ceiling of

500,000 troops stipulated by the WEU Treaty as a maximum *beyond* which the FRG was not allowed to go[56].

Until 1990, the *Bundeswehr* constituted NATO's second-largest conventional force. The land forces comprised, first of all, a Field Army of 275,000 troops, organised in twelve divisions: six tank, four mechanised infantry, one mountain and one air-landing division; secondly, a Territorial Army with a peacetime strength of 42,000 cadres, capable of 'inflation' upon mobilization to approximately the same strength as the Field Army. The equipment included almost 5,000 MBTs (Main Battle Tanks); more than 6,000 Tank Destroyers, IFVs (Infantry Fighting Vehicles), APCs (Armoured Personnel Carriers), etc.; around 1,500 artillery pieces, including MLRS systems (Multiple-Launch Rocket Systems); 26 *Lance* short-range missiles; 750 helicopters of various types; as well as several thousands of ATGWs (Anti-tank Guided Weapons), SAMs (Surface-to-Air Missiles) and assorted guns and mortars. An impressive force, indeed.

In accordance with the terms of accession to the WEU and NATO, the Field Army as well as the air force and the navy were to remain under NATO command in peacetime, whereas the Territorial Army was placed under West German command. The *Bundeswehr* was also prevented from operating as an independent military force through another organizational feature, namely the 'layer-cake' configuration of allied forces along the inner-German border. The West German forces were thus not merely assigned to two different NATO commands (CENTAG and NORTHAG), but also separated geographically by allied corps strips. This militarily extremely awkward arrangement was probably devised with a view to constraining the FRG, to at least the same extent as it was intended as a 'coupling mechanism' that should ensure the semi-automatic participation of allied forces in forward defence from the very outset of a war.

The FRG's air force had 108,000 troops at its disposal, manning a total of four wings, half of which designed for offensive, and the other half for defensive, purposes. The aircraft inventory (excluding the naval air arm) included the following combat aircraft: 222 F-4, 210 Tornado, 171 Alpha-Jets, plus 115 helicopters of assorted types.

The Federal Navy, in its turn, enlisted a total of 36,000 troops, assigned to the surface and sub-surface fleets, as well as to the naval air arm with a total of 98 Tornados, plus an assortment of planes and helicopters for reconnaissance and similar purposes. The surface navy included seven destroyers, nine frigates, five corvettes, 40 missile craft and 57 mine warfare vessels. The submarine fleet, in its turn, comprised a total of 24 vessels. Whereas the Federal Navy had historically emphasised Baltic and North Sea missions, its operating area had gradually been expanded to encompass also the Norwegian Sea[57]. It thus certainly had significant 'blue-water' ambitions as well as potentials.

In addition to the indigenous forces, a number of allies stationed substantial contingents of forces in West Germany. The US presence consisted, first of all, of the Seventh US Army, comprising more than 200,000 troops, divided into two armoured and two mechanised infantry divisions, plus a great number of smaller formations, and secondly, the 17th U.S. Air Force, comprising around 40,000 troops, assigned to a total of six air wings.

The U.K. stationed in the FRG, first of all, the BAOR, comprising more than 50,000 troops, divided into i.a. three armoured divisions. Secondly, the RAFG, comprising over 10,000 troops, assigned to twelve air squadrons. The last of the three 'occupation powers', France, stationed around 50,000 troops in the FRG, in fairly rearward positions compared to the others. Furthermore, both The Netherlands and Belgium deployed minor contingents of ground troops (5,000 and 26,000, respectively) in the NORTHAG sector, as well as a number of SAM batteries. Finally, Canada deployed a small number of troops (around 7,000) in the FRG as a token of her commitment to NATO's integrated defence.

The foreign military forces stationed in the FRG in peacetime thus amounted to around 400,000 active soldiers. If their relatives, as well as the civilian military employees, were added to this number, the grand total would amount to around 900,000 resident foreigners associated with NATO's integrated defence. In addition to the inconvenience thereof, the foreign military presence also came at a considerable financial cost, because the FRG was obliged to pay part of the upkeep of stationed forces[58].

Furthermore, in addition to the forces actually stationed in the FRG, a great number of other forces were earmarked for reinforcement of West Germany in a case of emergency. First of all, six CONUS (Continental USA) -based US divisions had part of their equipment in storage in the FRG under the POMCUS (Prepositioned Overseas Material Configured Into Unit Sets) and WHNS (Wartime Host Nation Support) arrangements. The return of these forces was rehearsed annually in the framework of huge REFORGER (Return of Forces to Germany) manoeuvres, instituted in 1968 when the USA needed part of the forces stationed in the FRG for its war effort in Vietnam. Secondly, a number of other allies had similar, albeit smaller-scale, arrangements for fighting in the FRG in case of war. This held true even for a country with minuscule armed forces such as Denmark, the bulk of whose ground forces were envisaged as fighting in the northern-most part of the FRG, rather than back home[59].

In addition to the forces themselves came their weaponry, in particular the nuclear and chemical weapons. Ever since the mid-1950s, the USA (and later the UK) had deployed battlefield and short-range nuclear weapons with their forces in the FRG. In addition to these, NATO in the late fifties contemplated the deployment of intermediate-range nuclear missiles in West Germany, capable of hitting targets in the Soviet Union. Eventually, this rather provocative deployment option was abandoned, only to be revitalised in the late 1970s, however, with NATO's 'dual-track decision' and the subsequent deployment of Pershing-2s and Tomahawk GLCMs (Ground-Launched Cruise Missiles) in the FRG.

Many of the nuclear systems were operated under 'dual-key arrangements', and thus not unambiguously foreign, but partly indigenous, at least in some respects. Since the late 1950s the FRG (as most other allies) had, as a matter of deliberate choice, fielded a panoply of dual-capable means of delivery (aircraft, artillery pieces and the like) which were capable of firing nuclear warheads. The latter, however, remained in American custody in peacetime, but could be released to subordinate commanders (including German generals) in case of emergency—slight approximation to the 'German finger on the button', so dreaded by most other countries[60].

A number of the nuclear systems, furthermore, had the (from a German point of view) problematic feature of almost entirely affecting Germany. The short-range and battle-field nuclear weapons were most likely to hit only (West as well as East) German targets, and hence had severe 'defence dilemma implications'. Just how severe, was highlighted in 1955 when the results of the map exercise *Carte Blanche* became known. In the span of a mere 48 hours, NATO's air forces dropped a total of 335 nuclear bombs, including 268 charges on German soil. The casualties were calculated at 1.5-1.7 million dead and five million wounded[61]. Of course, this was merely an exercise, and no 'real-life' test has ever occurred. Still, if these were the realistic costs of defence, then decision-makers were indeed facing a serious dilemma! Might not surrender to an invader be preferable to even a successful defence at such horrendeous costs?

Gradually, some of the most uncomfortable nuclear weapons were withdrawn, such as the ADMs (Atomic Demolition Munitions) which were obviously only suitable for striking at targets in the FRG itself. Some had, however, been replaced with more modern substitutes, so that the total number remained impressive. At least 3-4,000 nuclear weapons remained in Europe till the end of the 1980s, most of them deployed in the FRG[62]. That NATO subsequently (undoubtedly upon West German insistence) decided to withdraw nuclear artillery shells was regarded by most East and West Germans as a step in the right direction, particularly if the Soviets, as stipulated by NATO, were to reciprocate as promised.

In addition to the nuclear weapons, the FRG constituted the only overseas storage site for American chemical munitions. According to some estimates, these comprised 700-1,100 tons of chemical substance, amounting to 6-10,000 tons (or 100-300,000 pieces) of chemical munition, most of which were obsolete and beginning to leak, thus constituting a severe peacetime hazard. In connection with enlisting NATO's support for the production of new binary munitions (a precondition for Congressional funding of production), the USA did, however, commit herself to withdrawing existing stocks from the FRG, whilst preserving the option of a crisis deployment of the new munitions[63]. This withdrawal was originally scheduled to be completed by 1992, but subsequently accelerated considerably to be completed in 1990.

As illustrated by the chemical example, West German worries have not merely pertained to what might happen in case of war, but also to what was happening on a day-by-day basis in peacetime. There were noisy overflights by supersonic aircraft (with occasional crashes); the allocation of large strips of ground to military (including foreign) purposes; great financial expenses; the immeasurable social cost of compulsory enlistment of a large part of the male youth for military service, etc. All of this certainly added up to more than a minor nuisance[64]. Still, the prospects of war loomed even larger amongst the German concerns.

As a mirror-image of the NATO posture, the FRG has always ranked high on the Soviet 'target list', with a good number of divisions poised to invade and a whole panoply of nuclear and chemical weapons targeted against the FRG. Directly across the border stood until recently (and to some extent still stand) more than 400,000 Soviet élite troops belonging to the GSFG (Group of Soviet Forces Germany), the immidiate target for which could hardly be any other country than the FRG[65]. They were, however, under partial withdrawal as a corollary of the unilateral Soviet reductions announced in December 1988, and the Two-Plus-Four agreement stipulated their gradual but complete withdrawal. I shall return to this issue in Chapter XI.

In operational terms, the USSR until recently included the FRG's territory in the Western TVD (Theatre of Military Operations), and apparently planned for deep and swift combined-arms operations across West Germany. The aim would be to create a *fait accompli*, which would render NATO's first-use option unattractive and hence void, as well as prevent the USA from establishing a bridgehead on the European continent. An alternative interpretation has envisaged 'limited' Soviet attacks with only limited goals[66]. In both cases, however, war would primarily be fought on German soil, and with disastrous consequences.

There have, indeed, been many reasons for the prospects of war to appear even more ominous to West Germans than to most others. First of all, the FRG had no hopes whatsoever of standing aloof from a European war, which was bound to be fought (primarily or at least partly) on German soil. Secondly, if the war were to escalate to a tactical and/or theatre nuclear war, the resultant devastation would most likely eradicate the FRG as a functioning industrialised society. Thirdly, even if nuclear escalation should not occur, the FRG would be extremely vulnerable to large-scale and intense conventional war, because of its high population density, the high degree of urbanization, and the presence of large numbers of nuclear reactors and chemical plants, which might lethally contaminate vast areas of the country[67].

Due to these vulnerabilities, the military problem has been of more than academic interest for most German citizens; the defence dilemma has loomed large, and the attraction of 'rather red than dead' appeals has therefore been considerable. Furthermore, the number of conscientious objectors has been steadily rising to an all-time high of 77,432 in 1989, i.e. 22.1 percent, as compared with around 12 percent in the beginning of the 1980s. The very legitimacy of the military defence might thus be at stake, as also indicated by several opinion polls[68].

To find a solution to this defence dilemma, i.e. a non-suicidal form of defence, has therefore been a consistent preoccupation of the majority of the West German proponents of NOD, to whom the following chapters are devoted.

CHAPTER III

The Predecessors

The present chapter is by no means intended as an exhaustive history of the defence debate in the FRG. It merely aims to place the ongoing debate into perspective by showing, first of all, that there are many elements of continuity and, secondly, how the debate on defence alternatives has been interwoven with the three themes of German foreign policy: *Westpolitik*, *Ostpolitik* and *Deutschlandpolitik*. I have taken the 1950s as the main focus, since this decade saw a series of important junctures which were in many respects similar to the ones which the FRG and NATO were facing in 1989-90. Before proceeding with the account of the fifties, I shall, however, insert a brief section on the more distant forefathers, as well as on the offensive tradition which the defence proponents of the 1950s were up against.

The Ancestors

Paradoxical though it may seem, one might trace the roots of NOD back to two German sources: Clausewitz and Kant. From Clausewitz, present-day NOD proponents have, or at least might have, derived the principle of the supremacy of the defensive, as well as a number of tactical and operational principles. A careful reading of the writings of Kant, would, in its turn, reveal the embryo of a philosophy of Common Security, just as it would show the great German philosopher as a kindred spirit by virtue of his calls for disarmament. Since it would far exceed the scope of the present work to elaborate on either of the two philosophies, I shall limit the account to an identification of some points of convergence with NOD theory.

Carl von Clausewitz is above all known for his theories of wars of annihilation and of escalation *in extremis* which are to be found in his *On War*, whence his reputation as an apostle of absolute and offensive warfare. However, he was quite aware of the strength of the defensive which he regarded as *per se* the stronger form of combat[1].

According to Clausewitz, the main reason why actual wars did not escalate beyond bounds was the supremacy of the defensive, enabling the defence to enforce pauses in fighting. Since war constituted merely a means to a political end, the very fact that war became protracted through these pauses might suffice to allow the political end (which might be fairly modest) to take precedence over the military objective, always entailing a subjugation of the enemy.

From this might be derived a rationale for 'pure resistance', perfectly adequate for 'negative objectives', such as maintenance or restoration of the *status quo*, no matter how inadequate for the achievement of 'positive objectives' such as territorial conquest[2]. When applied to the East-West conflict, in which both sides acknowledge the inadmissibility of 'positive objectives' of war, Clausewitz's analysis would be tantamount to a recommendation of pure resistance, i.e. NOD. Thus conceived, it should emphasise protracted fighting with a view to allowing political considerations to predominate in the mind of the aggressor.

One of the reasons why the defence was regarded as superior was that it had the advantages of the terrain or, as Clausewitz expressed it, 'the assistance of the theatre of war'. Furthermore, the defender would benefit from the assistance of the people, which might sometimes be decisive, as Clausewitz acknowledged in the chapter on 'people's war', i.e. guerilla warfare. He acknowledged the invalidity of the 'concentration principle' for this kind of warfare, which required, on the contrary, a large surface on which to operate. He furthermore comprehended one of the unique strengths of guerilla warfare to be its elusiveness, implying that 'the principle of resistance exists everywhere, but is nowhere tangible'[3].

There were thus several elements in Clausewitzian strategy which might point towards NOD. A more immediately congenial theoretical ancestor of NOD was, however, Immanuel Kant. Two centuries ago he formulated the core of the ethical principles which were in 1982 advanced by the 'Palme Commission' under the heading 'Common Security'. In his *Critique of Practical Reason*, Kant called this the 'categorical imperative':

'Act only on that maxim through which you can at the same time will that it should become a universal law.'[4]

Kant also preceded 20th Century peace researchers with his conception, to be found in the pamphlet *On Perpetual Peace* from 1795, of standing armies as a cause of war, and his demand for their eventual disbandment; hence might be derived an advocacy of a militia form of enlistment, such as often recommended by modern NOD advocates[5].

The Offensive Heritage

Neither the above-mentioned 'benign side of Clausewitz' nor the anti-militarism of Kant were, alas, allowed to dominate the development of German military thought. On the contrary, the armed forces of the German *Kaiserreich* inherited from their Prussian ancestors a clear offensive bias and a structure suitable for offensive utilization. The reorganization of the armed forces (based on a principle of general conscription), combined with the general staff system, and the scientific study of strategy conducted under its auspices, provided the Prussian rulers with powerful instruments of war, by means of which they scored impressive victories during the 19th century[6].

Especially the victory over the French at Sedan in 1870 acquired a tremendous symbolic importance for the 'apostles of the offensive', who came to dominate the German general staffs until the First World War: Schlieffen, the younger Moltke and others yearned for 'a second Sedan' and attempted such a feat by means of the 'Schlieffen Plan'. This highly offensive strategy was matched by the equally offensive French 'Plan XVII', inspired by the *offensive a l'outrance* school (Foch, Joffre and others). As a result, by the spring of 1914 two highly offensive-capable armies were poised against each other, encouraged by their belief in the feasibility of swift offensive victories, subsequent to which the soldiers would be 'home before the leaves fall'. This was indeed a recipe for disaster, such as actually ensued[7].

Bellicosity was not a prerogative for the military, however, but was widespread also in the academic community in 19th and early 20th Century Germany. One of the most bellicose thinkers was the political scientist Heinrich von Treitschke, in whose *Politics* one may find the following eulogy of war:

> 'The grandeur of war lies in the utter annihilation of puny man in the great conception of the state, and it brings out the full magnificence of the sacrifice of fellow-countrymen for one another. In war the chaff is winnowed from the wheat.'[8]

Although there were thus quite a few bellicose civilians, the ascendency of the offensive was nevertheless facilitated by the incursion of the military into the political domain. The German military in the 19th Century in fact developed their military thinking into the diametrical opposite of Clausewitz. Whereas the latter had urged the subordination of warfare to political control, his successors ended up by advocating a subordination of politics to military imperatives.

In the war of 1870-71, Chancellor Bismarck e.g. had to write a 'blank cheque' to the General Staff, confirming their complete independence of politics. This development was, in fact, initiated by Helmuth von Moltke with his emphasis on professionalism, in its turn seen as requiring complete autonomy and freedom from interference by 'amateurs', such as politicians[9].

The 'philosophical' foundation for the military predominance could be found in bellicose writings with reminiscences of German romanticism. An example thereof was Friedrich von Bernardi, who in his *On the War of the Future* (1920) delivered the theoretical justification for the complete inversion of Clausewitz, that actually occurred with his radical demand that 'statecraft must restrict itself to paving the way for military success or to utilizing it according to the instructions that are to be issued by the military'[10].

The ordeal of the trench warfare of WWI, along with the fact that Germany lost this war, led to a certain reassessment of war in general, and offensive warfare in particular. Furthermore, it spurred attempts, e.g. on part of the Social Democratic Party of Germany (SPD), at strengthening political control over the military. Some of the controls actually imposed on the German military, however, were compromised by their being part and parcel of the 'Versailles system', which was perceived (not without some justification) as unjust by most Germans, and certainly by the German armed forces. Calls for autonomy for the armed forces, voiced i.a. by General Ludendorff, hence became associated with demands for freedom for Germany, as well as for revenge[11].

For quite some time, however, alternative views thrived, also in the ranks the officers' corps, where almost 'NOD-like' ideas received a certain attention.

The German military was forced to make the best of the situation created by the Versailles Treaty of a clear German inferiority compared with her former, and most likely future, enemies. In the years 1924-25 a group of high-ranking officers in the General Staff around the Chief of the Department of the Army, von Stülpnagel, developed plans which envisaged a defensive strategy as the solution to this problem. Rather than aiming for an unattainable 'decisive victory', Germany should seek merely to prevent (or at least hamper) the occupation of Germany. According to these officers, a future war should thus be fought in two stages, the first of which should be strategically defensive and, above all, seek to gain time; subsequently however, an offensive should be attempted. For the (by 1924) foreseeable future, however, this second stage was regarded as a Utopia, and the emphasis hence placed on the strategic defensive.

The tactical and operational principles were, in many respects, similar to the those advocated by modern NOD proponents: the defender, according to von Stülpnagel, should concentrate on attrition, and combine a forward defence with a protracted in-depth defence on his own territory[12].

In the same vein, the General Staff undertook a reassesment of strategic thinking, in the course of which they rediscovered the old concept of 'people's war', which was, however, abandoned because of unfortunate connotations. Its two constituent elements, border defence and *Kleinkrieg* (i.e. guerilla warfare), were, however, elevated to the mainstays of German strategy[13]. Furthermore, the 'no target-principle' that has become so central for modern NOD was also to be found in these vintage 1924-25 documents, wherein it was emphasised that

'the heavy enemy masses must find no target, such as a fortified line or a concentrated group of artillery, but must encounter individual assault groups, machine gun nests, artillery squads and positions of mixed formations across the terrain, the targeting of which is hardly possible, and not cost-effective at all, and which force the enemy to slowly "eat his way" through the entire German territory, thus weakening him morally as well as materially.'[14]

These were merely plans, however, and the strict controls imposed on Germany through the Versailles system hampered their actual implementation. Moreover, the emphasis on the defensive was merely one of two competing trends, and, at the end of the day, its diametrical opposite emerged victorious.

During the inter-war years, offensive strategies reminiscent of the 'Schlieffen Plan' were developed, this time devised with a view to exploiting the mobility provided by the tank. The German officers' corps (of whom Guderian was merely the best known) developed elaborate and sophisticated strategies of offensive manoeuvre warfare, to some extent in collaboration with likeminded Soviet officers such as Tuchachevsky, under the auspices of the 'Rapallo Treaty'. Whether the German officers actually invented the offensive *Blitzkrieg*, or whether they were, in their turn, inspired by British strategists such as Fuller or Liddell Hart, need not concern us here. Suffice it to say that the new offensive emphasis proved a perfect fit for the German military mind in the late inter-war period, and that it was subsequently put to a real-life test in the form of WW2[15].

The eventual unconditional capitulation of the Third *Reich* thus put an end to yet another era of offensive excesses, and hence motivated a reappraisal of military doctrine amongst the Western powers, albeit not in the USSR. Before bothering about military 'details' (such as doctrine, strategic conceptions, and armaments), the Allies did, however, take a more radical approach to harnessing the military threats emanating from Germany. In addition to the occupation (and actual division) of the country, this included a complete demilitarization, including a disbandment of the entire German officers' corps. On the other hand, this could obviously only be a temporary solution which left the question of a future military settlement open.

The 1950s: The International Framework

During the 1950s, a number of proposals for less offensive military structures were made by both Germans and foreigners, for various reasons:

1. Deployment of tactical nuclear weapons was commencing in Europe, and above all in the FRG, combined with an emerging (and all too apparent) American interest in 'limited nuclear war'[16]. Regardless of how limited such a nuclear war might appear to the USA, it promised to be total to all practical intents and purposes, as viewed from a German angle.

By the early 1960s, the scale of nuclearization even worried avowed 'nuke-lovers' such as West German Minister of Defence, Franz-Josef Strauss, who acquired insight into the nuclear targeting of NATO through 'back channels'. His informant, General Albert Schez, himself expressed profoundly consternation:

'Not merely the number of targets, but also the repetition of attacks against these targets: it's horrible! Nothing of Germany will remain. It is impossible to assume responsibility for.'

Subsequently, Strauss managed to persuade SACEUR, General Norstad, to 'clean up' the target list somewhat, above all by omitting repetitious targeting[17].

2. There was a growing fear (particularly, but not merely, on the Soviet side) that the expected proliferation of nuclear weapons might result in a 'German finger on the nuclear trigger'. Strauss, with his all too obvious longing for a German nuclear potential, did little to allay such fears.

3. The death of Stalin in 1953 gave some hope for *détente*, or at the least for a certain 'thaw' in the Cold War.

4. German rearmament was underway, but was seen as entailing risks of exacerbating political tension in Europe, thus missing the presumed opportunities flowing from the Soviet leadership shift, and jeopardizing German reunification.

The USA from a very early date favoured (West) German rearmament, as may be gathered i.a. from the (top secret) Joint Chiefs of Staff document *JCS* 1769/1, dated 29 April 1947, wherein it was stated:

'Potentially, the strongest military power in this area is Germany. Without German aid the remaining countries of Western Europe could scarcely be expected to withstand the armies of our ideological opponents until the United States could mobilise and place in the field sufficient armed forces to achieve their defeat. With a revived Germany fighting on the side of the Western allies this would be a possibility.'[18]

The USA found herself, in her role as the 'patron' of Europe, facing the dilemma of having to opt for either German or Soviet domination in Europe. The only escape from this dilemma would, according to i.a. George Kennan's analysis (1948), be a federal structure for Western Europe, into which the renascent Germany might be interwoven[19]. This converged with what France had in mind.

France was probably the Western country least eager to see a re-emergence of a mighty, independent German army. As an alternative, the French government launched the 'Pleven Plan' for a European Defence Community (EDC), envisaged as leading to the creation of joint European armed forces, into which the West German army would be so closely integrated as to constitute no threat to her neighbours. Furthermore, the EDC was envisioned as an element in a more elaborate, and primarily economic and political, integrative scheme, whence ensued, in due course, the Coal and Steel Community and the EEC[20].

The EDC itself, however, eventually failed on grounds of lacking support from almost all its envisaged founders, including Britain and the FRG. Neither did France herself, at the end of the day, come out in favour of the EDC, because of a change of government implying a sea-change in the attitude to defence cooperation. The FRG's negative attitude was, of course, due to the second-rate status envisioned for the German forces in the EDC, which were to be assigned *in toto* to the unified command, and integrated into the European army on the level of small (sub-divisional) formations. Upon British initiative the West European Union (WEU) was subsequently founded as an alternative[21], only to descend into oblivion for three decades, until its unexpected 'resurrection' in 1984.

One reason for the failure of the grand cooperative scheme was that, although all three Western powers did agree on the need for German rearmament, their motives for this differed considerably, whence their divergent preferences with regard to the appropriate institutional framework. Klaus von Schubert summed up their lists of priorities thus[22]:

	USA	UK	FRANCE
1.	Military strength	Burden-sharing	Control
2.	Burden-sharing	Military strength	Burden-sharing
3.	Control	Control	Military strength

It proved impossible to 'square the circle' of reconciling incompatible preferences, especially those of a strong West German army which, at the same time, should be under reliable control.

As we shall see below, initiatives for German rearmament met with a positive West German response. At the same time, however, they raised concerns both in the FRG and abroad, whence the wave of disengagement proposals, intended to mitigate the negative repercussions of rearmament. Most of the proposals envisioned either a neutralization of (a reunited) Germany, or a disengagement of forces from Central Europe, including the two German states. Most of the disengagement debate in the West, however, occurred in response to a steady flow of proposals from the East.

In two subsequent notes addressed to the three Western occupation powers, Moscow in 1952 proposed negotiations with a view to signing a peace treaty with Germany, timed so as to pre-empt West German rearmament and NATO membership. Although its sincerity remains disputed, the proposal did include some openings: Germany would be allowed national armed forces; it would be reunited; free elections would be held prior to unification, supervised by the four powers; and the emerging unified Germany would be accorded full sovereignty. The only apparent major concession to Soviet preferences would be a commitment to neutrality on the part of the new German state, along with some constraints on the size and composition of the German armed forces, which were, in retrospect, rather permissive[23].

Regardless of its possible merits, the proposal was turned down by the Federal Government as well as by the three Western powers (to whom it was, for reasons of international law, addressed), albeit not without some public debate and dissent within their own ranks, as well as in those of the SPD[24].

After having thus failed in pre-empting West German rearmament, the Soviet Union embarked on what might be called a 'damage limitation' venture, through which she sought to ameliorate what she must have seen as a sequence of set-backs: NATO's expansion (to which it responded by founding the Warsaw Pact); West German rearmament; and the deployment of tactical nuclar weapons in Europe. This venture took the form of i.a. a series of disengagement proposals, launched both by the Soviet Union and by its allies. A balanced evaluation of these proposals is difficult, because they were, on the one hand, made more credible when Stalin was succeeded by Khruschev, who i.a. initiated a substantial reduction of Soviet conventional forces; on the other hand, the proposals also have to be seen against the background of the major Soviet nuclear build-up in progress[25].

In 1957 the USSR proposed a 'zone of limited armaments' combined with a prohibition of nuclear weapons in Europe, and acompanied by a series of non-aggression treaties. Under the impact of the rapidly deteriorating economic and political situation in the GDR, the USSR in 1959 even tried to re-open the German question with a proposal for a peace treaty with Germany.

Against the background of the 1958-1959 Berlin Crisis, however, it can hardly have come as a surprise to the Soviet leaders that the proposal failed to attract the FRG. In addition to suggesting a confederate structure as a step towards reunifiction, it featured well-known (and already rejected) demands, i.a. for neutralization and for a withdrawal of foreign troops. As far as the national armed forces of a future unified Germany were concerned, the proposal repeated the previous conditions with the specification that weapons of mass destruction, rockets, guided missiles and launchers, bombers or submarines should not be permitted; nor should foreign troops be allowed on West German territory[26].

The Soviet allies were somewhat more successful in convincing the West of their sincerity. The most prominent East European initiative was the Polish 'Rapacki Plan' advanced in four slightly different versions:

1. The first proposal (1957) envisioned 'merely' the creation of a nuclear-weapons-free zone in Central Europe, comprising the two German states, Poland and the Czechoslovakia.

2. The second version (1958) expanded on this by envisaging what has subsequently come to be called 'negative security guarantees' on the part of

the nuclear powers, who should commit themselves *expressis verbis* to refrain from nuclear strikes against the zone.

3. The third version (1958) envisaged a two-stage implementation, commencing with a regional nuclear non-proliferation arrangement, and proceeding with a simultaneous build-down of nuclear and conventional weapons within the zone.

4. The fourth version (1962) differed from its predecessors merely with regard to details of the subsequent phases[27].

Even though it was impossible for the West to agree to, the plan was widely understood to reflect sincere, and perfectly understandable, Polish security concerns. Indeed, its essentials have consistently constituted a central element in Polish foreign policy ever since, from the Gomulka Plan (1963), which envisaged a freeze on nuclear armaments in Central Europe, to the Jaruszelski Plan of the 1980s.

Nevertheless, regardless of the extremely 'delicate' nature of German-Polish relations (stemming from the immense German burden of guilt *vis-à-vis* the tormented Polish people), the Adenauer government refused to negotiate the Polish proposals. However, both the SPD and other political forces felt that the plan deserved a response, and it thus spurred a number of similar disengagement proposals[28].

A number of independent Western observers had been equally concerned about the military build-up in the heart of Europe, and there were a number of disengagement proposals that were only partly a response to the aforementioned Eastern initiatives. I shall refrain from attempting a complete survey and mention only a few of the most prominent proposals.

Whereas the first 'Eden Plan' (named after the British foreign secretary) had launched the WEU, the 'second Eden Plan' from 1955 was of a much more 'benign' nature. It was couched in terms of finding a way to make sure 'that the reunification of Germany, and its right to join with other countries at its own choice, did not entail dangers for anybody else'. It therefore suggested negotiations concerning the level of armed forces in Germany and in the neighbouring countries, and even opened up the possibility of creating a demilitarised zone between East and West[29].

In 1957, the distinguished US ambassador George Kennan, speaking on the BBC, proposed a disengagement of forces in Europe by a withdrawal of superpower forces, combined with the restructuring of continental-European forces into 'para-military ones, of a territorial-militia type, somewhat on the Swiss example'. Furthermore, their main purpose should not be frontier defence, but rather 'defence at every village crossroad'. The possession of what we would today call an NOD-type defence, with a strong civilian-based defence component, would presumably suffice for dissuading any would-be aggressor[30].

In Britain, Denis Healey of the Labour Party in 1958 issued a plan for military disengagement, envisaging a neutralization of the two Germanies, along with Poland, Czechoslovakia and Hungary, perhaps even extended to Romania and Denmark. In the area thus defined, no nuclear weapons were to be deployed, and the level of conventional forces should be severely limited. The armed forces should merely suffice for defence against minor incursions, whereas the appropriate 'defence' against major assault would be security guarantees on the part of the major external powers, guarantees which, as an *ultima ratio*, were to be implemented by means of limited nuclear war (sic!)[31].

Shortly afterwards the chairman of the Labour Party, Hugh Gaitskell, launched a proposal on his party's behalf, deliberately couched in terms of a Western response to the Rapacki Plan. It envisaged a piecemeal withdrawal of foreign troops as well as nuclear weapons from the two Germanies, Poland, Hungary and Czechoslovakia, combined with German reunification, and a series of criss-crossing non-aggression treaties[32].

The 'Gaitskell-Healey plan' received qualified approval from the renowned British military analyst, Michael Howard, according to whom 'on purely military grounds there was much to be said in its favour', even though he predicted problems with regard to its political implementation. He concluded that 'they would have to be carefully balanced against the disadvantages of the existing situation before the West could put it forward as a bona fide proposal for a settlement'[33].

The attentive reader will notice the term 'settlement' which was still prominent, although subsequently wellnigh forgotten. There did, indeed, remain some hope in most minds of 'turning the tide', breaking down the 'iron curtain' and achieving i.a. German reunification; a hope which did, of course, turn out to be vain, at least far as the following decades were concerned.

A settlement was, however, reached in 1955 with regard to the former German ally, Austria, terminating the allied occupation and giving full sovereignty to Austria. *Qua* four-power settlement, this might indicate what sort of arrangements pertaining to other states the Soviet Union might accept (even though Germany was clearly in a different 'league').

In accordance with the 'Moscow Memorandum' of 15 April 1955, Austria accepted a commitment to permanent neutrality. Furthermore, in the 'State Treaty' of 15 May 1955, the Austrian state committed itself to acquiring none of the following military items: nuclear weapons, 'self-propelled or guided munitions'; torpedoes or 'devices which serve for the launch and control thereof'; sea mines; manned torpedoes; submarines; motor torpedo boats; specialised attack vehicles; artillery pieces with ranges exceeding thirty kilometres; and certain specified chemical substances. The former occupation powers also reserved for themselves the right to add further (unspecified) prohibitions.

These prohibitions were, in fact, almost carbon copies of the peace treaties with i.a. Finland, Italy, Bulgaria, Romania and Hungary. In fact, they originally reflected British, rather than Soviet wishes, which may explain the thirty kilometres criterion and the ban on rockets and guided missiles. The UK was simply determined to prevent any repetition of the V-1 and V-2 attacks on the British Isles, but would be out of harm's way if its adversaries were to possess merely weapons with ranges below the width of the Channel[34].

The German Response

The main goal of the FRG under the Chancellorship of Konrad Adenauer was to regain sovereignty, including the entitlement to national armed forces. This required acceptance on the part of the Western occupation powers, whence the emphasis during the first post-war decade on *Westpolitik, in casu* a quest for integration into the Western state system in all its ramifications: the OEEC (later OECD), NATO, the WEU, the Coal and Steel Community and the EEC.

This also explained the rather lukewarm response to the French plans for the EDC, which would only have allowed the FRG 'semi-national' armed forces—a German contingent within a joint West European army, subdivided into small formations under national command, but under multinational command above this level. Whereas Adenauer and his associates did lend this 'Pleven Plan' their support as long as it was believed to be the only framework for rearmament within reach, they clearly preferred the NATO framework, since this implied a higher status for German forces. Nevertheless, the EDC debate did indicate that West Germany was not opposed to the notion of multi-nationality *per se*, but merely resented discrimination and 'singularization' of the FRG[35].

The Adenauer government was quite prepared to sacrifice reunification on the altar of integration with the West. Indeed, there are indications that Adenauer actually preferred a continued division for fear of the fate of a united Germany. According to Sir Ivone Kirkpatrick (British permanent under-secretary in the Foreign Office), Adenauer had in 1955 approached the British ambassador with a plea not to sign any reunification accord with the USSR, because 'he was terrified that when he disappeared from the scene, a future German government might do a deal with Russia at the German expense. Consequently he felt that the integration of Western Germany with the West was more important than the unification of Germany'[36].

It was therefore only logical for the CDU government to fundamentally oppose any *rapprochement* with the East, as well as any accommodation of Soviet demands, lest this might loosen the bonds to the West. The few initiatives that were actually taken in the direction of *Ostpolitik* were thus intended almost entirely as propaganda ventures, tailormade to elicit negative Soviet responses.

Initially, Adenauer sought to exploit the precedent of the Austrian settlement with a proposal (1958) to the USSR of an 'Austrian solution', yet exclusively for 'the middle part of Germany', i.e. the GDR. Whereas this was clearly (and probably purposefully) unacceptable to the USSR of the late 1950s, the proposal was, ironically, quite similar to the 'Genscher Plan' of 1990 and to the actual outcome of the 'Two-Plus-Four' talks (cf. below, Chapter XI).

Subsequently, the government put forward the 'Globke Plan' (1959), envisioning reunification after a five-year transition period, in the course of which the two German states should formally acknowledge each other's diplomatic status, etc. The final step towards reunification would be a referendum on unification, subsequent whereto Germany was to decide between the options of NATO or Warsaw Pact membership, or neutrality[37]. Regardless of their possible intrinsic merits, none of these proposals stood any real chance of Soviet approval, due above all to the obvious attractiveness of the West as compared with the East. The last thing the Soviets would do, therefore, was to give 'their' Germans a free choice of social system.

In addition to opting for integration with the West, the Federal Government as early as 1950 initiated planning for West German armed forces[38]. Adenauer's Counsellor, Count Schwerin, in September 1950 summoned the government's most prominent military advisors to a clandestine (indeed illegal) conference in the Himmerod monastery, on which occasion the famous *Himmeroder Memorandum* on possible German military contributions to the Western alliance was drafted, which has since been called 'the *Magna Carta* of German rearmament'. Its point of departure was the call for equality and non-discrimination for German armed forces, with regard to both command structures and to equipment. It, furthermore, described as imperative that the defence should commence as far East as possible, and dismissed as unacceptable the notion of treating West Germany east of the Rhine as a *glacis*.

What was envisioned, however, was far from a defensive forward defence, but mobile and quite offensive manoeuvre warfare, whence the recommendation for assigning first priority to mechanised, armoured forces, and treating infantry and artillery as ancillary arms. Even though it suggested a postponement of 'large-scale attacks against Russia' until 'the Russian forward march on the ground had been brought to a halt', it prescribed the following strategic principle for the German armed forces:

'The defence must, wherever possible, be conducted offensively. This means that attacks must be launched everywhere, and from the very beginning, wherever it is feasible. (. . .) It must be attempted by all means to carry the fighting on to East German territory'[39].

Furthermore, the Memorandum raised the demand for an effective air defence of the German population as well as for an adequate coastal defence, thus demanding nothing less than full-fledged, three-branched armed forces, with far from negligible offensive potentials.

As was to be expected, these plans, as well as the general policy of Western integration, called forth a broad wave of protest, both from the opposition, from within Adenauer's own party, and from the ranks of the nascent armed forces themselves.

The SPD until 1959 remained highly critical towards the plans for rearmament. The party was concerned that too close bonds with the West might have negative repercussions on the prospects of reunification, as well as being uneasy about the military strategy of the Americans and, by implication, of NATO. By planning for the decisive defensive battle on the Rhine, the envisaged defence would provide no protection at all for vast areas of West Germany, which were thus predestined to become an exposed battleground. On such terms, why take part in Western defence at all?

Such considerations, indeed, induced the SPD to recommend an even more offensive strategic orientation, seeking to carry the fighting into the aggressor's home territory, and establishing the Western defence perimeter along the Vistula, rather than the Rhine[40]. As a precondition for rearmament, the SPD's leader, Kurt Schumacher, therefore demanded that the West 'should defend Germany (and, moreover, all of Germany) offensively with an eastward direction in order to spare itself the gravest devastation of a new war'[41].

Dissenting voices also made themselves heard from within Adenauer's own CDU, the most prominent being that of former Minister of the Interior, Gustav Heineman, who went so far as to resign in protest against the Chancellor's defence policy. As an alternative to the barren and dysfunctional Western orientation, the new German state ought, in his opinion, to seek accomodation with both sides alike. Furthermore, Heineman expected German rearmamant to defer German reunification even further, and was persuaded by the aforementioned Soviet proposals of 1952 that the path of negotiations were to be pursued: 'If Russia is prepared to sacrifice the Communist system in Germany and to let an all-German government emerge from free elections, the West should be prepared to pay the price of renouncing West German rearmament'[42].

The small FDP, likewise, tabled its disapproval of Adenauer's resistance to accomodation with the East. Its plan had been developed by MdB (*Mitglied des Bundestages*, i.e. MP) Georg Pfleiderer and was presented in 1952. It acknowledged the ambiguities of German policy, which was based on the politically offensive goal of reunification whilst arming itself, albeit for strictly defensive purposes. Soviet fears were thus at least understandable, since 'it has always been difficult to demonstrate defensive intentions'. Because, according to Pfleiderer, the Germans did, indeed, yearn for reunification, yet only by peaceful means, they ought to take Soviet concerns into due account. The proposed solution to the dilemma was to maintain the Soviet and Polish occupation of the areas east of the Oder-Neisse border, and a Western 'mirror occupation' of some of the western-most areas. The reunited 'Germany', in the middle, should build up its indigenous forces to an agreed limit, whilst prohibiting the stationing of foreign troops[43].

From within the ranks of the armed forces, Colonel Bogislav von Bonin presented the best known, yet also most controversial, alternative proposal, which made him a direct ancestor of the present NOD proponents. What drove a loyal officer such as Bonin, a high-rank employee of the *Amt Blank* (the predecessor of the Ministry of Defence) to 'step out of line' were, first of all, the recognition that an implementation of Western strategy would lay Germany in ruins. The actual defensive battle would be fought on the banks of the Rhine, and Germany would be treated as a mere *glacis* for France. His second concern was that the deployment of battlefield nuclear weapons would be catastrophic in the densely populated Germany. Bonin's final concern, shared by the SPD, was that rearmament and integration into NATO would render all hopes of German reunification vain[44].

Bonin's proposed remedy was a genuine forward defence, based on anti-tank units. As early as 1952, he urged his superiors to designate the first cadre army formations as barrier units, which should emphasise anti-tank defence. In 1954 he was asked to prepare a study of how to halt a Soviet attack against a Germany in the process of raising armed forces. In this study (classified until 1984) he proposed the creation of a 50 kms. deep barrier zone, featuring anti-tank units. In order to minimise the provocative effects, their armaments should be unmistakably defensive, consisting above all of anti-tank weapons. As Bonin later revealed, he had in mind primarily jeep-mounted 105mm. recoilless rifles, the cheapness of which would allow the purchase of 10,000, along with further expenses on mines, etc. The required force would be in the order of 120-150,000 troops, preferably volunteers, as compared with the twelve mobile divisions, consisting predominantly of conscripts, which were envisioned by the political leadership, as well as by the *Amt Blank*[45].

Bonin was not the only one to have such ideas. For instance, one of his former colleagues, the retired General, Smilo Freiherr von Lüttwitz presented similar proposals, calling for the creation of twelve barrier formations of 10,000 men each. Nevertheless, Bonin's study was in due course assessed by the *Amt Blank*, and its proposals rejected, not so much because of military deficiencies as on the grounds of anticipated political obstacles.

What was problematic, according to Bonin's superiors, Generals Heusinger, de Maizière and Kielmansegg, was, first of all, the fact that because the envisaged anti-tank barrier would not be impenetrable, penetrations could only be met by allied, rather than German, mobile forces.

So much for equality! Secondly, the creation of fortifications and the like in the border zones might presumably cause unrest with the population. Thirdly, and perhaps decisively, the envisaged solution would be a national one, difficult to fit into the ongoing negotiations for an integrated NATO defence, i.a. because the proposal allowed for no stationing of allied forces in the immediate border zones[46].

At the end of 1954, Bonin followed up his classified study with a memorandum, wherein he proposed a defence scheme along the lines of his own proposal as a *sine qua non* of rearmament. Without a genuine forward defence, 'we ought prudently keep our fingers out of rearmament and let ourselves be flooded by the red deluge, in order to save at least a minimum of basis for existence'. On the other hand, Bonin's own proposal would presumably ensure immediate readiness, cost less and, not least 'constitute an assurance to the French and the Russians that such a West German army cannot be aggressive'. Bonin was thus from the outset firmly committed to the non-provocative (i.e. NOD) idea[47].

At a series of high-level meetings in the spring of 1955, Bonin's proposals were discussed by a number of Generals (as well as one Field Marshal), the majority of whom came out against his ideas. He was not isolated, however, enjoying the unreserved support of Generals Lüttwitz, Wenck and Hossbach, as well as a certain, albeit more reserved and conditional, support from Generals Reinhardt, Eberbach, Kunzen, Busse and von Wietersheim, as well as from Field Marshal von Manstein[48].

Out of these meetings and coalitions sprang an appeal to the public, which Bonin first presented to the above-mentioned generals, but which was later published by *Der Spiegel* under the title *Reunification and Rearmament: No Contradiction*. On this occasion, Bonin was joined by Wietersheim and Lüttwitz as co-authors. To go public with such proposals was, however, regarded as inadmissible, and led to the dismissal of Bonin from the *Amt Blank*. The dismissal became the subject of some controversy, i.a. in the security committee of the *Bundestag*, but nobody dared speak out openly in favour of Bonin[49].

The controversial article proposed, in line with the previous classified study, to 'defend the homeland immediately at the border and to protect it, to the greatest possible extent, from the horrors of land warfare', and to do so by means of 'several state-of-the-art barrier formations', albeit with the maintenance of 'a few tank divisions'. The barrier formations should be equipped with anti-tank pieces and automatic weapons, assisted by strong engineer forces, and backed up with a reserve tank battalion for counter-attacks. They should be highly cross-country mobile, deployed along a wide front and yet in great depth (around 50 km.). Notwithstanding the fact that the anti-tank forces should be supported, if need be, by allied nuclear artillery, the authors nevertheless described the suggested posture as 'an outwardly clearly recognizable defensive instrument'. By virtue of their defensive orientation, such armed forces would presumably not block the way for German reunification, since neither the USSR nor France were likely to oppose them[50].

The attentive reader may, however, be slightly puzzled by the fact that the original 'Bonin Plan' envisaged the employment of nuclear artillery. The author did, however, soon abandon this ill-conceived notion, and by the year 1959 we find Bonin's signature under a memorandum demanding a nuclear-weapons-free zone encompassing Germany, Poland and Czechoslovakia. Moreover, as early as 1955, he had distanced himself clearly from the prevalent views on nuclear warfighting, advocating instead a neutral re-unified Germany, devoid of nuclear weapons, foreign troops and foreign airfields, which should have at its disposal strictly defensive armed forces, pending a 'ban on war and a general disarmament'.[51]

Bonin was highly critical towards Adenauer's 'policy of strength' associated with *Westpolitik,* which he regarded as an unsuitable tool for both *Ostpolitik* and *Deutschlandpolitik,* because 'a policy of *détente* can only succeed by way of honest compromise, only according to the *do ut des* principle'.[52] Since the actual balance of power had to be taken into account, Bonin did not regard German reunification as realistic unless it could be accomplished without tipping this balance, in its turn only conceivable if combined with neutralization.

Although he received no substantial direct support, Bonin was not entirely 'a voice who cryeth in the wilderness'. The military expert of the renowned daily *Frankfurter Allgemeine Zeitung,* Adalbert Weinstein, e.g. openly supported Bonin's views, and elaborated on his critique of official security policy. According to Weinstein, the envisaged initial deployment of twelve divisions (which were to be gradually expanded to 24), combined with the Adenauer government's diplomatic approach of 'reunification through strength' was bound to appear highly provocative. The USSR was hence likely to conclude that the FRG had allowed itself to become a stationing area for highly offensive-capable armed forces, and that it had boosted this threat by deploying, in addition, strong West German shock forces.

If the FRG, however, were to limit itself to a very small, yet effective, defensive force, then this would *eo ipso* constitute an appeal to the USSR to reciprocate, something it might do i.a. by limiting the number of Soviet forces in Germany, and by placing limits on the East German militia forces, the *Volkspolizei.* Furthermore, in order to underline the defensive intentions, whatever foreign troops were to remain in the FRG should be stationed behind the Rhine. Thus, a bilateral process towards military balance between the two sides of the 'Iron Curtain' might be launched, something which, in its turn, would open the way for German reunification. In order to meet legitimate Soviet, as well as French, concerns, however, the armed strength of the reunified Germany should not, according to Weinstein, exceed twelve divisions. By implication, neither side ought to field more than half this number prior to reunification[53].

In addition to scattered individual voices such as von Bonin's and Weinstein's, political parties in the FRG thought roughly along the same lines as the above-mentioned foreign advocates of disengagement, at least for a while.

The persistent themes of the SPD's security political views were, first of all, the demand that the reunification option should not be closed through Western integration; secondly, the call for a pan-European security system; and thirdly, the concern with damage limitation, requiring both limits to the nuclearization of the continent, and a strategy of forward (*Vorne*), perhaps even forward-moving (*Vorwärts*), defence, which would salvage the FRG from the ill fate of serving as a battleground.

A first version of these themes was put forward in 1957 when the SPD presented the so-called *Ollenhauer Plan*, envisioning the integration of a reunited Germany into a comprehensive all-European security system, which would, in its turn, be based on political obligations to refrain from aggression, as well as on more tangible arms control measures[54].

The apogee of the SPD's disengagement efforts was reached with the presentation of its *Germany Plan* in March 1959, wherein it called for the establishment of a '*détente* zone' comprising the two Germanies, Poland, Czechoslovakia and Hungary. Within this zone, indigenous troops would be subjected to limitations, and foreign troops scaled down, pending their complete withdrawal. The acquisition of nuclear weapons by indigenous forces should be prohibited (something which was by that time by no means self-evident), and the nuclear armaments of the remaining stationed troops were to be frozen. In due course, a nuclear-weapons-free zone should thus be created, which should be underwritten by a collective security pact. By virtue of such a benign military framework, reunification of the two Germanies would presumably become possible[55].

The 'Germany Plan' stood in direct continuity with the party's previous opposition to rearmament and integration into the West at the expence of reunification, which had i.a. been reflected in its temporary participation in the peace movements (i.a. in *Kampf dem Atomtod* and the *Paulskirche* Movement). However, the plan was only given a very short lease of life: at the SPD convention in Godesberg at the end of 1959 a new programme was adopted which constituted an embrace *in toto* of both rearmament and Western integration. As a consequence, the 'Germany Plan' was explicitly declared obsolete and no longer valid[56].

The FDP presented its own *Germany Plan*, almost simultaneously with the SPD (20 March 1959), and was likewise inspired i.a. by the Polish Rapacki Plan(s). The FDP envisioned a nuclar-weapons-free zone, combined with a withdrawal of foreign troops. Furthermore, the reunited Germany should commit itself to abstain from joining any alliance, whilst, on the other hand, being prepared to participate (on a non-discriminatory basis) in a future all-European security system, in which both superpowers should participate[57].

Even more surprisingly, Defence Minister and leader of the CSU, Franz-Joseph Strauss by March 1958 felt compelled to respond to the Rapacki Plan(s). Whereas he did not out of hand dismiss the concept of nuclear-weapons-free zones as such, he emphasised the need of a wider scope, including the Soviet satellite states. As a corollary, the conventional forces within the zone would have to be built down step-by-step to the level of the strength of the stationed forces in the FRG. Whereas such a scheme would appear to amount to disengagement, on other occasions Strauss explicitly described 'disengagement' as dangerous. To the extent that one should take his original scheme seriously, an explanation might be found in the basic incompatibility between nationalism (deeply entrenched in the CSU) and Western integration, an inconsistency which the party did, however, gradually learn to live with[58].

The outcome of the above debate was the German accession to NATO via the WEU in 1955, under the terms of a compromise formula. On the one hand, the Western powers affirmed the West German *Alleinvertretungsrecht* (i.e. Bonn's right to speak for all of Germany), and pledged themselves to support German reunification. On the other hand, the FRG signed a commitment neither to acquire nuclear, chemical or biological weapons, nor to use force 'to seek reunification of Germany or the modification of the present boundaries of the Federal Republic'.

Since German rearmament was henceforth restrained only by the above 'conventional only' provisions, it was possible to proceed with the build-up of indigenous West German armed forces along the lines sketched in the 'Himmerod Memorandum', with a distinct emphasis on mechanised, ar-moured forces possessing considerable offensive capabilities. Indeed, in the latter half of the 1950s, the FRG (and particularly Defence Minister Strauss) took a number of initiatives with a view to acquiring nuclear capabilities, thus providing the East with one of the motives for the 'disengagement offensive' described above[59].

Via Consensus to Dissent

The SPD's Godesberg convention in 1959 marked a juncture in that it established a basic consensus around the foundations of the FRG's security and defence policy. Henceforth, and until the beginning of the 1980s, the security political debate was therefore essentially limited to two fields; on the one hand, a dispute on the 'details' of armaments and arms control and, on the other hand, a dispute on the appropriate foreign policy towards the East (*Ostpolitik*), which did, however, almost entirely neglect the military impli-cations. Since both issue-areas are somewhat peripheral to our main concern, I shall only deal with this period very superficially, highlighting a few of the most conspicuous themes and events, to the extent that they had implications for the NOD debate of the 1980s.

As already described in the previous chapter, *Ostpolitik* has always constituted a recurrent theme in the 'symphonic structure' of German international relations. Whereas the competing theme of *Westpolitik* had been dominant in the first part, i.e. the period from 1945 to 1960, in the second part the *Ostpolitical* theme came to dominate. Furthermore, whereas the CDU/CSU had played the leading theme in the first part, this was now taken over by the SPD in a somewhat fragile coalition with the FDP. Finally, the *Deutschlandpolitical* theme in the *basso continuo* gradually became more audible, since an important motive spurring the SPD's drive for accommodation with the East was the desire for 'reopening the German question', not in the monotonous, almost *praeterea censeo* fashion of the previous CDU governments (which had always maintained that the question remained open, whilst in actual fact closing it), but in a more constructive, and less dogmatic way.

Most observers seem to agree that the original impetus to reorientation was, paradoxically, the construction of the Berlin Wall in 1961. This demonstrated irrefutably that the Communist regime in East Berlin (and the USSR behind it) intended to remain in power at almost any cost, and that they had the means to ensure this, not least by the existence of several million potential German hostages, namely the populations of the GDR and of West Berlin. If the fate of these Germans was to be ameliorated, agreements with the East German regime were required, whence the need for an, at least *de facto*, recognition of the GDR as a state.[60]

This new theme was first struck by Egon Bahr who in 1963 launched the notion of of 'change through *rapprochement*' (*'Wandel durch Annäherung'*)[61]. The SPD's accession to power was followed by a series of cautious overtures to the East, above all to the USSR, but indirectly also to Poland and the GDR. Not all overtures were cautious, however: Chancellor Willy Brandt e.g. made a highly symbolic gesture during a visit to Warsaw when he knelt in veneration for the Polish victims of German aggression.

The culmination of this period came with the signature of the *Ostverträge* with all three Eastern powers, implying a recognition of the GDR, an acceptance of the Oder-Neisse border, and (in an agreement with all four occupation powers) a more satisfactory status for West Berlin. The FRG thereby renounced its 'revisionist' ambitions, and became a *status quo* power with no claims beyond that of security, thus also laying the political foundations for a defensive military strategy[62].

This also led to a sea-change in the West German attitude towards *détente*. Previously, a certain degree of tension between the blocs had constituted the *conditio sine qua non* of Bonn's foreign policy, including the 'Hallstein Doctrine' of non-recognition of the GDR and the accompanying

Alleinvertretungsanspruch[63]. Now, however, *détente* came to be seen as the precondition for *Ostpolitik* and by implication for successful *Deutschlandspolitik*. Furthermore, whereas the relationship (or non-relationship) between the two German states had previously been a constant source of tension, it now gradually developed into almost 'a bed-rock of *détente*', a much more solid and robust relationship than e.g. that between the superpowers[64]. Ever since, the FRG has been a staunch supporter of East-West *rapprochement* and supported quests for accommodation in non-military issues (i.a. through the CSCE process), as well as attempts to lower the risks of armed conflict, i.a. by way of arms control.

Finally, this sowed the seeds for transatlantic conflict, stemming from a growing divergence between European and American approaches to *détente*, with the West Germans standing for the 'European approach' *par excellence*. For the last couple of decades, the West European countries have, as a general rule, tended towards a *realpolitical* approach to the USSR as well as to the 'Yalta map of Europe', and have willingly accommodated the former by codifying the latter, i.a. in the CSCE documents. The USA, on the other hand, only reluctantly acquiesced, and was all but happy with the eventual outcome[65].

This European attitude, in its turn, paved the way for a businesslike approach to the systemic conflict, wherein fields of common concern (such as e.g. environmental protection) as well as expanding and mutually beneficial trade relations received growing attention. The West Germans in particular expanded their trade with the East considerably, whence emerged powerful vested interests in a maintenance of *détente*. Whereas the Europeans thus became increasingly determined to stabilise the situation on the continent in order to reap the fruits of *détente*, the USA stuck to a more ideological type of adversity and sought to prevent this *détente* process from 'getting out of hand'.[66]

An analogous divergence of interests could be seen through the 1960s and 1970s in the military field, although any dissent from American views tended to be expressed *sotto voce* until the 1980s. I shall limit this account to a few highlights with more far-reaching implications.[67]

During the 1960s and 1970s, the military debate tended to focus on issues pertaining to nuclear weapons, and caused by the inherent fragility of the American commitment to the defence of Europe in an age of mutual assured destruction. It was soon realised on both sides of the Atlantic that to execute the threats of 'massive retaliation' implied by Eisenhower's 'new look' strategy would amount to deliberate US suicide in the defence of Europe, whence the quest for more credible options than that of all-out nuclear war. This led, in due course, to NATO's adoption of the Flexible Response strategy in 1967, which did, however, remain open to several incompatible interpretations, as described in the previous chapter[68].

The Americans tended to visualise the flexible options in a warfighting perspective, whilst caring only little about 'coupling', whence their plans in the mid-1970s for the production (with a view to deployment in the FRG) of Enhanced Radiation Weapons (ERW), the so-called 'neutron bombs'. Whereas such weapons (intended primarily for anti-tank purposes) did fit well into warfighting schemes by virtue of their reduced residual radiation, which would facilitate manoeuvre on the nuclear battlefield, they were utterly unacceptable to the Germans. On the one hand, their deployment might lower the nuclear threshold and thus make nuclear war, including the use of 'ordinary' nuclear weapons, more likely. On the other hand, the prospects for limiting damage were unsatisfactory, since the ERW promised to 'kill the inhabitants, whilst sparing the buildings', as it was put by the peace movements which were called into being by the plans[69].

A similar disagreement lurked beneath the surface of formal consensus regarding NATO's 1979 dual-track decision. Helmuth Schmidt, in his 1977 IISS speech, had expressed concern about the viability of American extended nuclear deterrence in the face of new developments: first of all, strategic parity as codified in the SALT agreement, and secondly a regional Soviet preponderance, created not merely by the deployment of SS-20s, but to at least an equal extent by the Soviet build-up of conventional forces. He had therefore called for NATO measures to safeguard 'coupling' by means of regional balance, but had not been particularly concerned about the exact military implementation thereof. The USA, on the other hand, appears to have wanted weapons incorporating actual warfighting capabilities, whilst caring less about the coupling implication. Hence the compromise implied by the dual-track approach, which envisaged both negotiations with a view to attaining regional balance, and a deployment of the Pershing-2s and Tomahawk GLCMs in Europe, above all in the FRG[70].

This decision raised both Soviet concerns about a new 'strategic' (from their point of view, albeit not in the SALT vocabulary) threat from German soil, and concerns among the West German population about becoming, to an even greater extent than before, a high-priority target for Soviet nuclear strikes. The dual-track decision thus inadvertently placed the entire nuclear question on the agenda, not merely in Europe, but also in the USA. A debate on no-first-use of nuclear weapons (NFU) ensued, in the course of which the FRG was unable to reach a consensus stand. Whereas NATO traditionalists such as the West German 'Gang of Four' opposed NFU out of fear of 'de-coupling', others favoured the proposal because of its potential for limiting damage and, to some extent also, because it improved crisis stability.[71]

Closely related to this controversy was another on the creation of a nuclear-weapons-free corridor in Central Europe, such as proposed by the 'Palme Commission' in 1982. Here, once again, the consensus split, with the SPD eventually coming out in favour of the proposal, just as they did in favour of NFU and against the INF deployment. The FRG had thus acquired a politically significant (albeit still minority) anti-nuclear community on an obvious collision course with the USA[72].

A side issue of the nuclear deterrence debate pertained to nuclear proliferation. This was, likewise, originally caused by scepticism concerning the credibility of American strategic guarantees, whence sprang a growing interest in the acquisition of national nuclear weapons in both France (which eventually succeeded) and the FRG (which did not). This, in turn, raised the spectre of uncontrollable nuclear proliferation, a development which would benefit neither world peace and stability, nor American superpower interests. The USA therefore launched a proposal for a joint US-European nuclear force, the MLF (Multilateral Force). Although the British as well as the FRG supported the initiative, it eventually failed due i.a. to its uncertain operational implications, as well as to the fear of raising Soviet concerns about 'a German finger on the button'[73].

The nuclear controversy reached new peaks with the launching of the SDI programme by President Reagan in March 1983, by which the USA committed itself to the goal of 'making nuclear weapons impotent and obsolete', thus raising the spectre of de-nuclearization. This policy reorientation seemed to be confirmed at the superpower summit in Reykjavik, when Reagan allegedly almost reached agreement with Gorbachev on an elimination of nuclear missiles.

Seen from this angle, the SDI might have appeared as a consolation to the growing anti-nuclear constituency in the FRG, including the SPD. However, the plans for an 'astrodome defence' seemed to fit in too neatly with two other trends. First of all, the trend away from 'pure deterrence' towards war-fighting, which was absolute anathema to the anti-nuclear public and the SPD; and secondly, the trend towards neo-isolationism which might eventually imply American disengagement from Europe, and consequently a decoupling of European (and not least West German) security from that of the USA. If the USA could be protected against Soviet nuclear missiles, whilst Western Europe remained defenceless, the very foundations of NATO would be in jeopardy, whence the concerns raised by the SDI in the minds of the West German 'establishment', and the subsequent plans for a European counterpart to the SDI, in the shape of an ATBM (Anti-Tactical Ballistic Missiles) defence.

Whereas the SDI might thus *prima facie* have been expected to appeal to both the 'peace community' and the 'establishment', by virtue of its timing and layout it in actual fact alienated both. The establishment was furthermore, somewhat concerned about the prospects of being left behind in a momentuous drive towards high technology defence, with presumed 'spillover' effects into the civilian sectors of the economy. There was, therefore, a certain urge to 'jump the SDI bandwagon', as the FRG did by signing a (secret) cooperation agreement with the USA[74].

The entire nuclear controversy was closely linked with the conventional field. First of all, West German observers were understandably concerned about the massive Soviet conventional build-up, which occurred after the ousting of Khruschev in 1964. Secondly, they were concerned about the prospects of American withdrawal from Europe, as implied by the 'Mansfield Amendments'. Hence the great importance attributed to the MBFR negotiations, intended not merely (although probably primarily) as a *quid pro quo* for the CSCE, but also as a means of actually improving the conventional balance, hopefully thereby achieving a certain cut-back (or at least a freeze) on the Soviet forces but, more realistically, preventing a unilateral American troop withdrawal, which raised the spectre of decoupling. I shall not venture into an account of the MBFR experience, but merely record the actual accomplishment. Whereas the result in terms of force reductions was nil, the Americans did stay on in Europe, and not until 1989 was a withdrawal again taken into serious consideration by an American administration, now, however, under much more benign conditions[75].

One reason why the prospects of a (partial) American withdrawal were taken more lightly than before may have been the fact that the development through the 1980s of American conventional strategy had also raised some concerns in the FRG. The 1982 'Air-Land Battle' doctrine (ALB) of the US Army had raised the spectre of conventional manoeuvre warfare on (East as well as West) German territory. This, in turn, would either cause widespread devastation (if conducted on NATO, i.e. West German, territory), or it would implicate the FRG in offensive schemes that would be incompatible with the constitution, if successful in carrying the war to the enemy.

Furthermore, the long-term plans of the US Army and Air Force ('ALB 2000', 'Army 21', etc.) pointed towards even more offensive and manoeuvre-oriented types of warfare. Although the *Bundeswehr* tried to accommodate the new American strategic trends, i.a. by signing the so-called *Glanz-Meyer Paper*, amounting to a joint ALB-2000 plan, in actual fact neither the political leadership nor the military staffs were probably entirely happy with these new trends[76].

In addition to pursuing the arms control track, the FRG has also pursued the armaments track with a steady improvement of the *Bundeswehr*, making it, in due course, into NATO's second mightiest conventional land force. This has proven to be one of the most problematic features, which has, in its turn, spurred the NOD debate, since it brought to mind historical precedents: that of the numerically inferior, but qualitatively superior *Wehrmacht* embarking on imperialist conquest[77].

We have thus seen through the 1960s and 1970s the emergence of a number of military as well as non-military problems facing West German security political decision-makers:

—A growing militarization of both the FRG and its immediate surroundings.

—A growing split between the USA and its European allies, with the FRG in the forefront amongst the 'dissenting' states.

—A break-down of the fundamental consensus on security politics.

Perhaps of greater importance than anything else, the 'glue' which had hitherto prevented a break-down of the security political system, i.e. the perception of a genuine Soviet threat, seems to have undergone radical change during the reign of Gorbachev. Previously, disagreements on military strategy and other matters tended to be silenced by reference to the need for not alienating the Americans, lest the Soviet Union would take advantage of the split. However, as Gorbachev's official visit to the FRG in June 1989 demonstrated, the popularity of this leader of the previous 'arch-enemy' country was enormous. Regardless of how genuine the Soviet threat might thus be in reality, in the eyes of the West Germans is had almost completely vanished; whence a perceived need for reassessing a wide range of hitherto unasked questions.

In the light of the problems and emerging opportunities described in this and the previous chapter, it should come as no surprise that there has arisen a debate on the fundamentals of military strategy pertaining to the FRG. One of the most prominent conceptions in this new debate has been that of 'structural inability to attack', i.e. what I have chosen to call NOD (Non-Offensive Defence).

In the following pages, I shall give a comprehensive account of this debate. I have sought to record the most significant contributions to the debate, although a few may well have escaped my notice. For the sake of simplicity and clarity, I have categorised the various contributions by high-lighting in each case one particular feature. Such a categorization does not, however, render full justice to the authors concerned, who have almost without exception embedded their proposals in elaborate security political analyses. To some extent I have tried to present the gist of these arguments, whilst focusing on the concrete defence alternative proposals. Hence the 'vertical slicing' of the debate (according to authors) rather than a 'horizontal slicing' according to the concrete nature of the defence proposal.

CHAPTER IV

Models of Non-Offensive Defence

In this lengthy chapter, I shall provide an overview of the various NOD proposals ('models') that have been put forward, particularly by members of the West German academic community, through the last decade or so.

The distinction between the authors dealt with in this and the subsequent chapter on 'military defectors' is, admittedly, somewhat arbitrary, i.a. because some of the model designers in the present chapter are not academics, but retired officers, whereas some of the employees of the armed forces do hold academic degrees. Furthermore, there is some overlap with the chapters on the political debate, in particular with that on the SPD.

Territorial Defence

Territorial defence is in many respects the obvious answer to the question addressed by NOD advocates of how to devise a military structure lacking offensive capabilities, yet with the ability to defend territory and *ipso facto* population. A territorial defence specialises in defending the homeland, whilst envisaging no operations beyond its borders. It is thus largely stationary in the sense of possessing no 'strategic' (long-range) mobility, whilst often emphasizing 'tactical' mobility along 'internal lines'.

There have been a number of proponents of such a defence in other countries, i.a. the UK, and it has appealed to neutral and non-aligned states such as Sweden, Finland, Switzerland, Austria and Yugoslavia, the defence postures of which tend to be approximations to the pure territorial defence type[1]. In West Germany, the most prominent advocate of such a defence has been Horst Afheldt, who might be regarded as the 'grand old man' of German NOD thinking. First of all, although the core NOD ideas might be traced back to the 1950s (see Chapter III), Afheldt was the instigator of the new wave of NOD debate in the 1970s and 1980s. Secondly, he laid the theoretical foundations for NOD thinking by formulating most of the basic principles, the validity of which have since been acknowledged by most NOD advocates. Unfortunately, since Afheldt has only rarely written in English and has very seldom been translated, he has not received the attention in the Anglo-Saxon countries which he deserves. In fact, others better versed in the English language (such as Albrecht von Müller, to whom I shall return in due course) have been able to gain a reputation for themselves with ideas 'borrowed' from him.

Afheldt's NOD theory evolved gradually, beginning in the early 1970s, when the problems inherent in the prevailing security arrangements first became apparent to him. In 1976, he presented the broad outlines of his 'defensive defence' model, which has subsequently been modified and elaborated upon, particularly in a work published in 1983. Until his retirement in 1989, Afheldt was 'still going strong', even though his particular model had now been 'demoted' to merely one amongst a host of different proposals. Immediately prior to his retirement, he took stock of the accomplishments in the NOD field with an *opus ultima* which also allowed him to take the prospects of German unification into account[2].

The point of departure for Afheldt, as for most of his successors, was the danger of nuclear war. He had participated in a research team, which in 1970 published a path-breaking report on *War Consequences and War Prevention*. The detailed studies herein on the economic, biological and environmental effects of a 'tactical' nuclear war fought on German soil led him to conclude that a nuclear defence of the FRG would result in its complete devastation as an independent, industrialised society[3]. As the only viable escape from the dilemmas posed by the available 'mainstream' defence options, Afheldt pointed to 'political solutions' in a very broad sense. These would require a rather fundamental change of attitude, since states should not merely renounce war as an instrument of politics, but would also have to eschew arms racing as a medium of their struggle for power[4].

In his 1976 work on *Defence and Peace*, Afheldt likewise took as his point of departure an examination of the dangers emanating from the nuclear arsenals. The arrival of MAD (Mutual Assured Destruction), for one thing, made it imperative to acknowledge that 'the Clausewitzian decisive war between the superpowers no longer represents a viable means of politics'[5].

To avert nuclear war, as well as to achieve at least a modicum of damage limitation, have ever since remained paramount goals for Afheldt. However, limiting damage was not 'merely' argued on humanitarian grounds, but was also viewed as a precondition for a credible deterrent which presupposed that its actual implementation might be a rational option from the point of view of the defender[6].

Strategic stability was acknowledged as being of paramount importance for the sake of averting war. In order to be satisfactory in this respect, however, it had to be sought in two different varieties:

—Crisis stability, i.e. the prevention of inadvertent war.
—Stability during war, i.e. the avoidance of unintentional and irrational escalation.

Both objectives, in their turn, demanded that the employment of nuclear weapons be kept under strict political control and utilized exclusively for political purposes. Military logic should therefore be prevented from influencing nuclear decision-making on either side.

First of all, military logic might induce the opponent to use nuclear weapons against the FRG. In order to avert this danger, the FRG should avoid presenting any targets which might make Soviet nuclear utilisation appear cost-effective. This principle formed the analytical point of departure into the realm of defensive conventional defence, since it appeared to rule out the creation of fronts, and thus made forward defence look questionable[7].

Secondly, whereas NATO would need nuclear weapons, along with an option of nuclear first-use, as the ultimate means of restoring the *status quo ante bellum*, the USA should rise above military logic and wield this threat as a strictly political tool, by means of which a 'politically determined, mutually adjusted employment of nuclear weapons' might be utilised for 'inflicting unacceptable damage on the opponent'[8]. The targets should be carefully selected for their political leverage, since the deciding factor would be the will of the opponent, as prescribed by Clausewitz[9]. The most efficient leverage would presumably result from threatening the very survival of the Soviet empire through nuclear strikes against Eastern Europe.

However, since the ethical problems entailed hereby were obvious, Afheldt subsequently (i.a. in his work from 1983 on *Defensive Defence*) shifted towards an NFU advocacy with regard to nuclear weapons, also because he shared the widespread sense of alarm over the direction in which the nuclear arms race seemed to be heading in the early 1980s, i.a. with NATO's 1979 dual-track decision[10].

In a work published in 1984 on *Nuclear War. The Curse of Politics by Military Means*, he delivered a scathing criticism of traditional thinking on nuclear matters with its misplaced emphasis on 'balance', as had been apparent i.a. in the INF issue. The only 'balance', which he was willing to acknowledge as serving peace, was a negative one between two parties, both of which were incapable of employing their military means for political purposes, a 'balance of incapabilities', so to speak[11].

Furthermore, regardless of its superficial attraction, Afheldt also regarded 'conventional balance' as a very misleading goal indeed. Since the armies of both NATO and the Warsaw Pact were true descendents of the tank armies of World War II, they promised success to the side possessing the initiative, i.e. the attacker. Under these conditions, the side determined not to attack, not even at the last minute, was at a severe disadvantage, and particularly under conditions of parity[12].

On the basis of his critical analysis of 'stable deterrence', Afheldt developed what he called 'the general structure of a peace policy by military means'. The 'normative principles' herein have subsequently constituted the theoretical foundations for the entire NOD discourse[13]. These principles i.a. included the following:

Short-term objectives should be prevented from jeopardizing longer-term goals; military means should not be self-perpetuating, but preferably lend themselves to a gradual replacement with political means of war prevention; the military means should allow none of the parties to a conflict to defeat the other side decisively; they should allow neither side to benefit significantly from starting a war in times of crisis ('no premiums on prevention or pre-emption'); they should allow for unilateral arms reductions without damage to one's own position; they should provide the opponent with no meaningful, and certainly no decisive, options of military utilisation of nuclear weapons; in order for threats to be credible deterrents, they should lend themselves to implementation in a rational manner; only such options should hence be sought as might be controllable, even in the gravest of crises.

The basic rationale for these norms was summed up thus:

'Any military option should be able to stand the test of whether or not it could be imitated. If it is likely that a military option would be imitated, this option is only compatible with a peace policy if its imitation by others, with a likelihood close to certainty, would not harm, but rather promote, world peace.'

In a later work, Afheldt reiterated this demand, couching it in terms borrowed from Kant as 'the categorical imperative of the nuclear age: merely to undertake military measures which, if undertaken by the opponent, would be acceptable, because they would not increase the military threat'.[14]

Proceeding from this analysis, the aim was identified as the abolition of the military functions of nuclear weapons by means of a credible conventional defence. Conventional defence thus had a rather modest level of ambition, since it was by no means conceived of as a defence that should stand alone, but would merely be called upon to prevent a *fait accompli*. Thus 'buying time' would presumably ensure the FRG of American assistance, including nuclear first-use, and the impossibility of achieving a *fait accompli* would hence deter the USSR from embarking on aggression in the first place[15].

The conventional defence should thus be able to slow down and hamper, but would not have to suffice for preventing altogether (except through deterrence) a Soviet conventional attack. Nor would it need the ability to force the enemy out of the country. This would be a task for politics, underpinned by strategic nuclear weapons.

The above norms i.a. called for military postures that were immune to arms-racing, in contrast to the existing armed forces which had an unfortunate tendency of interacting and mutually legitimising each other, due to the entrapment of states in the 'security dilemma'. To escape this dilemma was the rationale for the recommended shift to defensive forces, since Afheldt had to acknowledge (as did the American political scientist Robert Jervis at about the same time) that the defensive character of a state's military forces was the decisive factor in halting the arms race[16]. Only through eliminating an element in the armaments dynamics, *in casu* the action-reaction phenomenon[17], might arms control and disarmament become realistic objectives to strive for.

With regard to the mode of transition to defensive forces, Afheldt, on the one hand, advocated 'cooperative arms control', whilst, on the other hand, maintained the viability of unilateral implementation, for instance in a step-by-step manner. Such a process might commence with the creation of defensive 'islands' in the offensive 'sea', combined with invitations to (rather than demands for) reciprocation on the part of the adversary[18].

The other analytical path leading towards the same emphasis on defensivity was the call for a mutual incapability of defeating the respective opponent for the sake of war prevention, i.e. the aforementioned 'balance of incapabilities'. This recommendation followed from an analysis of possible paths towards war, according to which inadvertent wars of the '1914 type' were more likely than the '1939 type'[19].

Since the aggregate probability would equal the sum of the probabilities of aggressive war and the various types of inadvertent war, a prudent defence planner ought to seek to minimise all probabilities simultaneously, rather than concentrating on one side of the problem and compounding the other. Whereas neither 'flexible response' nor 'deep strikes' were deemed viable answers, since they would create incentives to pre-empt[20], an effective, yet strictly defensive, defence was believed to be precisely what was required.

On the conventional, just as on the strategic level, damage limitation would be of paramount importance, according to Afheldt, since even a traditional conventional war would cause horrendous devastation, in addition to possibly inducing the respective opponent to cross the nuclear threshold. First of all, therefore, HA underlined that his defence scheme should not be assessed as a war-fighting strategy, but rather as a war-prevention strategy in its own right[21]. The frequent allegations against NOD for causing excessive damage have, indeed, tended to be based on flawed comparisons between war damage under NOD conditions and the near-zero damage resulting from successful nuclear deterrence, whereas the only meaningful comparison would be between the war damage resulting from a break-down of either forms of dissuasion.

Secondly, the damage limitation principle led Afheldt inescapably to a recommendation for leaving cities undefended, i.e. 'open towns' in the sense of the Geneva convention[22]. In order to prevent the invader from using cities as strongholds, he advocated the employment of non-military forms of resistance in urban areas, a point on which he, however, did not elaborate in any detail. To explore this option, Afheldt's research team collaborated with the 'grand old man' of German non-violence, Theodor Ebert, whose assessment of the viability of such a scheme was not, however, altogether favourable[23]. Since then, however, other proponents of civilian-based defence have arrived at more positive conclusions (cf. below).

Thirdly, in order to accomplish a satisfactory damage limitation, it became important to find a defence structure that would present as few lucrative military targets as possible, particularly for the adversary's nuclear weapons. The defence ought thus to be dispersed to the greatest possible extent, a requirement which ruled out forward defence because of its concentrated front line that would inevitably constitute a lucrative target[24]. Forward defence would, furthermore, make break-through assaults all the more tempting for the aggressor, because of the prospects of reaching undefended territory behind the forward line. In order to prevent this, the defence would have to be territorial, i.e. cover the entire territory, so that there would simply be no undefended rear into which anybody could hope to penetrate. Afheldt therefore recommended an abandonment of the renowned principle of forward defence, i.e. a departure from one of the most central principles of West German security policy.

Although forward defence has usually been presented as the damage limitation measure *par excellence*, Afheldt did not agree with this assessment. Besides violating the no-target criterion, forward defence was, according to him, simply an elaborate bluff, since the Alliance could neither be expected to, nor really believed in its ability to, halt a WTO attack. After the break-through which had to be anticipated, the only recourse would hence be escalation, an option for which the label 'deliberate' would be inappropriate. Rather, the outcome would amount to 'desperate escalation', reducing the opportunities of damage limitation to zero[25].

Furthermore, forward defence might actually exacerbate civilian destruction, since it would require long logistic chains, which would inevitably run through densely populated areas, and which would attract enemy fire. Furthermore, if the defence of a line were attempted, this effort would have to imply the defence of any part of the line, including major cities such as Hamburg or Lübeck which happened to be inconveniently located on the very forward line. Fighting would thus inevitably take place in the midst of the civilian population. A 'retreating defence' would, however, be no better in this respect, since this would likewise lead to intense fighting in the midst of the population[26]. The only solution was thus believed to be a renunciation of mobility in favour of a largely stationary territorial defence.

In order to achieve an effective defensive capability, the defender should renounce symmetry and opt instead for asymmetrical ('indirect' or 'paradoxical') responses to the moves of the adversary[27]. He should, above all, capitalise on the advantages inherent in the defensive role, the tasks of which were intrinsically less demanding in terms of structure, since the defender would be in a position to renounce wide-ranging attacks (whence less demanding logistic requirements), as well as the ability of movement under fire (whence no need for armour protection of vehicles and weapons systems)[28].

These were, briefly stated, the strategic principles which formed the point of departure for Afheldt's 'techno-commando' model. As far as its concretization in operational and tactical terms was concerned, he was inspired by other authors, not least by Guy Brossolet and Emilio Spannochi, whose works were published in German simultaneously with his own[29]. These two authors had (with a view to application in France and Austria, respectively) developed a number of operational and tactical principles, including the prudence of eschewing operational and strategic mobility, whilst emphasizing tactical mobility; the potentials of light and man-portable ATGMs (anti-tank guided missiles) and other PGMs (precision-guided munitions); the strength of small-unit combat techniques applied in a guerilla-style 'strategy of non-battles'; the logic of a deliberate quest for 'buying time'; the advantages of a modular configuration of the defence; the relative invulnerability of the network structure, etc.

Horst Afheldt transposed elements of these conceptions to the German theatre, molding them into a model of 'defensive defence'. Although it has undergone some modification between the 1976 and the 1983 version, its basic structure has remained largely unchanged:

The basic elements were so-called 'techno-commandos' or *Jäger* squads, consisting of light infantry troops, with which Afheldt recommended saturating the entire territory, thus departing from Brossollet who had envisioned merely a wide defence zone. By dispersing the 'commandos' almost evenly and randomly over the entire territory, they would neither present lucrative targets for the enemy's means of mass destruction, nor would there be any, narrow or broad, line of defence against which an attack might concentrate[30]. Since the model was exactly this, rather than a concrete proposal, he was satisfied with operating in statistical terms, rather than with concrete geography. However, he did explicitly state that the coverage should, naturally, adapt to terrain features, and the units hence not be distributed completely at random.

He, furthermore, modified the proposals of his predecessors by envisioning a complete abolition of heavy armoured forces, on the grounds that they would, likewise, represent fairly lucrative targets[31]. For the same reason, he recommended abolishing aircraft altogether (sic!), primarily in order to avoid fixed, and thus highly vulnerable, airfields.

The *Jäger* squads should be completely stationary in order to capitalise on the defender's inalienable advantage of being able to prepare defensive positions. However, every platoon should have several alternative fighting positions in order to make them more difficult to locate. The stationary deployment was regarded as being in conformity with the demands of modern weapons technology, particularly PGMs, the enhanced accuracy of which would presumably allow the destruction of any target within sight. The only way to survive on the modern battlefield would thus be to remain concealed, by renouncing movement. The attacker, on the other hand, would, for obvious reasons, have to move about, thus exposing himself to the precision fire of the defenders.

The *Jägers* were to be assigned to the prime task of anti-tank defence, but their targets should not merely be the tanks themselves, but, to at least an equal extent, their long and vulnerable logistic 'tail'. For these purposes the techno-commandos should be armed with anti-tank PGMs such as the 'Milan'[32], as well as with more sophisticated PGMs, etc. Furthermore, each individual commandos should be accorded pre-defined tasks, a precaution which would relieve the burdens placed on the command structure, just as would the elimination of the risk of enemy break-throughs[33].

A defence of this type would supposedly have a de-escalating effect because it could only be used reactively, since each individual commando would be unable to go into action before the enemy had reached its area of responsibility. The defence would hence not reward, but rather penalise, pre-emption on the tactical level[34].

Horst Afheldt's cousin, Brigadier General (ret.) Eckardt Afheldt provided some further detailed suggestions for the *Jäger* network, albeit within the context of an interim model which still envisaged the maintenance of a considerable number of mechanised forces[35]:

—A *Jäger* platoon would consist of 25 troops, defend an area of 10-15 sq. kilometres and be armed with 'PARS' and 'Milan' anti-tank PGMs, *Fliegerfäuste*, grenade launchers, machine guns, rifles etc.

—A *Jäger* company would consist of four platoons, a medical unit, a command unit, a few 'TOW', mortar and pioneer squads, in total approx. 130 troops, defending a territory of 50-80 sq. kilometres.

—A *Jäger* battalion would consist of four *Jäger* companies plus command, communications and medical staff, a reserve *Jäger* platoon and further reserve troops; a total of 600 troops, defending approx. 250-350 sq. kilometres.

—A *Jäger* brigade would consist of four battalions plus command staff, logistical units and a *Jäger* platoon for self-defence—total of 2,600 troops, with responsibility for an area of approx. 1200-1500 sq. kilometres.

In addition to the stationary units, Horst Afheldt in 1976 recommended mobile air defence squads, integrated within the *Jäger* network[36]. They were to be armed with SAMs as well as various man-portable air defence weapons, and their main role would be to prevent enemy airborne landings. In addition, they were to be equipped with anti-personnel weaponry for use against paratroopers or other forces which might have succeeded in disembarking. Furthermore, recognizing the need for preparing the terrain in terms of obstacle-building, emplacement of sensor arrays, etc., Afheldt in 1983 proposed to supplement the regular light infantry with pioneer troops. Since the aggressor would have the advantage of being able to select points of concentration, the defender would be faced with the dual task of being present everywhere, whilst at the same time able to concentrate his defence effort where needed. Whereas area coverage was deemed attainable without mobility by way of the 'network principle', the need for concentration was seen to require supplementing the *Jäger* network with additional means, *in casu* a network of missile commandos.

In 1976, Afheldt put his faith in emerging technologies such as TGSMs (terminally guided sub-munitions) armed with armour-piercing warheads. As potential launchers for these, 'Lance' missiles and conventional cruise missiles were mentioned, preferably in miniaturised versions and with ranges from 25 to over 100 kms. By such means, it would presumably be possible to concentrate fire against the decisive points without having to physically move the launchers, something which would inevitably have exposed them to enemy fire[37]. The (in fact enormous) problem of target acquisition would allegedly be reduced through the elimination of the well-known IFF (Identification Friend Foe) problem: since the defenders would remain stationary, every moving unit would by implication be a legitimate, i.e. 'foe', target.

For the 1983 version the proposed armaments profile had been modified slightly, if only because cruise missiles were now considered too problematic, due to the ambiguity created by the impending INF deployment. The no-target philosophy still exerted a predominant influence on Afheldt's thinking, and seemed to rule out tube artillery altogether, whilst pointing towards 'fire-and-forget' systems as the ideal type of weaponry, in their turn calling for miniaturisation and cheapness. The concrete implications of these requirements were elaborated primarily by Lt-Col. Acker, who participated in Afheldt's research team in Starnberg[38]. The resultant proposal envisaged both small, relatively short-range missiles assigned directly to the *Jägers*, and heavier, longer-range missiles, which were to be assigned to special battalions of rocket artillery.

The rockets should be almost exclusively single-shot systems, against which an attacker would be most welcome to direct his counter-battery fire. Fortunately, he would only be able to do so when he had located the launchers, which would presumably only become possible when they exposed themselves by firing, subsequent to which they would be empty. In order to make the enemy target the missile batteries, and thus expend his ammunition, Afheldt eventually came to regard it as advisable to maintain some reload systems, whilst keeping the adversary guessing as to which were reload and which were single-shot systems[39].

The dense *Jäger* web and the coarser missile web should, of course, be interconnected by a C³I (Command, Control, Communications, Intelligence) network, which would emphasise redundancy, e.g. by integrating the civilian communication arrays with military planning[40]. The overall defence posture would thus comprise three overlapping networks:

—A network of *Jäger* commandoes
—A network of rocket artillery
—An information network

The total personnel requirements were in 1976 assessed to be in the range of 390,000 men, to which should be added a mobilizable home-guard, for defence against i.a. airborne landings. The cadres of these would amount to a peacetime force of about 50,000, which would bring the total peacetime requirements to around 450,000 men.

In 1983, the balance sheet was somewhat less optimistic: on average, a total of three infantry troopers (*Jägers* as well as pioneers) plus one artillery trooper per sq. kilometre, adding up to a total of 940,000 troops. This high number was nevertheless assessed as realistic, also because a considerable percentage would be reserves, particularly in the Western parts of the country[41].

One still had to search in vain for any role for the air force in Afheldt's model(s), since he (surprising though it may seem) envisaged aircraft being phased out entirely. This appeared as the only way of meeting the no-target requirement, since fixed airfields would inevitably represent worth-while targets. As a consolation, he pointed out that the very structure of the defensive land force posture would tend to minimise the effects of enemy air power, since there would e.g. be no lucrative targets for enemy figter-bombers or CAS (Close Air Support) aircraft. As far as the (genuine) threat from helicopters was concerned, man-portable systems belonging to the *Jäger* commandoes were assessed as the appropriate counter.

A defence posture such as this would presumably be able to meet the primary threat, namely that of a massive armoured Soviet attack with the mission of swiftly establishing control of the entire West German territory. Afheldt was, however, well aware of some of the conceivable weaknesses of his model: would it be able to resist an enemy who reorganised his forces by placing a greater emphasis on infantry, i.e. 'an infantry steam-roller'? Would it be able to evict an invader from German territory, its deliberate incapability of even counter-attack notwithstanding?

Alas, he was unable to give any final answer to these questions, and merely pointed out that the current defence structure suffered from analogous deficiencies. Therefore, a viable solution would have to be sought on the political level[42].

As far as the implementation of his proposal was concerned, Afheldt envisaged a step-by-step approach. Furthermore, he subsequently collaborated in framing the interim proposals of Eckardt Afheldt and Albrecht von

Müller to be outlined below. This may appear somewhat surprising, since von Müller's model is regarded by most analysts as only seemingly non-offensive, whilst in actual fact pointing towards a more offensive posture, due to its combination of a defensive 'shield' with offensive-capable 'swords' (cf. below). In general terms, however, Afheldt remained alert to the risk that some schemes, by improving defensive capabilities whilst retaining significant offensive capabilities, might indeed enhance overall offensive capability. Depite his collaboration with von Müller's team (until finally firing the latter), Afheldt therefore remained sceptical towards his associate's concept of 'conditional counter-offensive capability'. If this were envisaged as a permanent feature, it would negate the chances for arms control provided by a genuine defensive defence. Furthermore, according to Afheldt, NATO did not really need any war-winning capability for effective deterrence, since the ability to conduct a protracted war of resistance would suffice for this purpose[43].

As regards the scope of implementation, Afheldt in the final analysis had all of Europe in mind. Nevertheless, one of the advantages he saw in his 'defensive defence' was that it would not necessarily require reciprocity, but might be implemented unilaterally. He therefore urged NATO to commence the restructuring of its forces unilaterally, whilst inviting, rather than demanding, WTO reciprocation. Not even a complete NATO consensus was deemed a *conditio sine qua non* for commencing restructuring, since individual countries might in fact, via their national policies, impose an overall non-offensive structure on the rest. Even if e.g. the USA did not concur, the US Army would not possess any genuine offensive capability in Europe if it were to be deprived of the support of its allies for offensive operations.

The FRG, in its turn, would have a special interest in changing present strategy, to which should be added a special responsibility. Since the FRG would inevitably have to bear the main burden of any conventional arms build-up, it had the potential of becoming the strongest conventional army in Europe. Because of the German historical heritage, however, such a power position would only be acceptable to Germany's neighbours if the option of its offensive use was credibly excluded[44].

Without abandoning unilateralism, Afheldt had by 1988 (under the spell of Gorbachev) begun to take the prospects of a bilateral implementation of defensive defence more seriously. Under these circumstances, he recommended commencing with a build-down of tanks as well as self-propelled artillery. However, if a 'mere' reduction of the number of tanks on both sides were to be accomplished, this might even compound instabilities, since the remaining tanks on either side would not suffice for defending the entire front, due to 'force-to-space constraints', whereas they might suffice for break-through assaults along narrow axes. A second element of the defence reform would thus have to be the creation of a 'defensive rim', consisting of barriers, infantry, artillery and missiles, intended to bring any attacking tank formations to a standstill[45].

Afheldt's proposals have served almost as a lightning rod for criticism from different quarters. This is partly because they have been (correctly) regarded as the 'archetypal' model of NOD, and partly because they have in some respects been easier targets than some of the more 'mature' proposals, which have been able to respond to the initial critique voiced against him. The criticism may be lumped into three categories.

First of all, the 'left' has argued that the proposals were either not radical enough, since they would leave the NATO structure intact and thus not really matter; or that they were unrealistic, precisely because they did necessitate fundamental changes. Furthermore, it has been alleged that a unilateral West German defence conversion might simply result in a division of labour within the Alliance, by which the FRG would take over the defensive tasks, whilst the allies would be in a position to perform their offensive missions even more effectively, shielded by the defensive *Bundeswehr*[46].

Secondly, criticism has been raised against the theoretical basis of the proposal, as well as against some of the underlying assumptions. Some critics have claimed that NATO did not possess any genuine offensive capability anyway, and that nothing therefore had to change. The same critics have claimed that nothing needs to be done on the conventional level, since the WTO's superiority was anyway largely fictitious. NATO might thus simply adopt a NFU strategy, without any resultant need for conventional improvement, according to the 'If it ain't broke, don't fix it!' logic[47].

Thirdly, there has been criticism (primarily from military circles) of the efficiency of the model. The main instances hereof have been the observations that the model did not allow for force concentration; that the FRG was in no position to trade space for time (such as envisaged by Afheldt), because of its insufficient depth and too high population density; that many techno-commandos would remain inactive, because they were beyond range of the combat zone; that a stationary deployment would necessitate a substitution of redundancy for mobility and therefore would be unaffordably expensive; that the attacker might change his posture in the direction of infantry-heavy formations; that the aggressor in fact need not defeat the armed forces of the defender, since he might target the decision-making bodies and the social infrastructure instead; that the deterrent value was insufficient, because the aggressor's own territory would be spared, whereas all combat would take place with the defender; that the technological prognoses were too optimistic, since small and cheap weapons with sufficient ranges and accuracies would not become available as soon as expected; that the possibilities of counter-measures had not been taken sufficiently into account; and finally that the envisioned form of combat (autonomous fighting, even behind enemy lines and in complete isolation) did not suit the frame of mind of modern man in industrialised societies[48].

In 1989, Afheldt published his *opus ultima* entitled *The Consensus* with the subtitle 'Arguments for the Policy of Reunification of Europe'. Even though it predated the momentous events in the autumn of that year, the author nevertheless did deal *expressis verbis* with the implications of the multipolar Europe that was presumably in the making.

His point of departure was that German unification, even economically, would create a power that could not be outbalanced by the other European states[49]. Indeed, the relative power of Germany would tend to grow in parallel with a shift of emphasis from military to other means of power, creating an uncomfortable dilemma:

'The more cooperation comes to replace confrontation in Europe, the smaller becomes the importance of military means of power, and the greater that of economic power. To put it clearly: German power grows, whilst the English and French, but also the Russian and American, power in Europe declines'[50].

These problems notwithstanding, Afheldt did regard it as a relevant aim-point to overcome the division of Europe, in its turn presupposing that the security interests of both Eastern and Western Europe be safeguarded[51].

As far as the military element in the emerging multipolar structure was concerned, which Afheldt regarded as *per se* more stable, he recommended what he now preferred to call a 'reciprocal structural defensive superiority'. On closer analysis, this concept did, however, reveal itself as largely synonymous with a situation in which 'defensive defence' had been implemented by all sides[52].

True to his long-standing critique of the arms control approach, he, furthermore, urged all states to convert to such structures unilaterally whilst consulting, rather than negotiating, with each other in the process of doing so. It would, in fact, be unilaterally advantageous to convert to defensive defence, i.a. because attack capability (according to the stipulated new Soviet thinking) had ceased to be a trump-card and had become a burden[53].

In order for Europe to play the truly independent role, which it was called upon to play in the emerging multipolar 'concert', it presumably needed a leading power, the only feasible candidate for which role would, according to Afheldt, be France[54].

In spite of the many truly weak points in his thinking (amongst which perhaps the proposal just mentioned), Horst Afheldt deserves credit as the 'founding father' of a new discipline, which has since then produced so many fruitful ideas, as will hopefully emerge from the following survey of his successors.

The High-Tech Defence Wall

Horst Afheldt was not the only one to recognise the potentials of new military technology, as they had been demonstrated e.g. in the Yom Kippur War, the Israeli invasion of Lebanon or the Falklands/Malvinas war. However, whereas Afheldt saw the perspectives in dispersal, decentralization and area coverage, others were more interested in the potential for a highly centralised, forward defence.

The diametrical opposite of the Afheldt model was developed by a former staff officer of the *Bundeswehr*, Lt-Colonel Norbert Hannig, now working as a consultant for the aircraft industry. He had for some time criticised NATO's prevalent defence conceptions, and in 1984 he presented a full-fledged NOD proposal[55].

Whereas Afheldt had emphasised the need for defending the entire territory and, as a corollary, abandoning forward defence, the core element of Hannig's defence scheme was a 'linear border defence by means of fire barriers'[56]. As merely a special type of forward defence, it was in this respect considerably less radical than Afheldt's territorial defence scheme. On the other hand, it was no less radical in its proposal to abandon mobile, armoured formations entirely, with a view to ruling out even small-scale manoeuvre warfare.

Linear defence and the reliance on fixed barriers and fortification has acquired a bad reputation since the blatant fiasco of the French Maginot Line in 1940[57]. Hannig therefore went out of his way to emphasise the difference between his proposal and any 'Maginot-line strategy'. Whereas the latter relied on fixed barriers and fortifications, he placed his faith in the decisive component, namely fire-power. The impenetrable barrier which he proposed to establish along the border would thus be no physical structure at all, but rather a potential barrier of fire, i.e. a form of 'killing zone'.

The fire, by means of which the enemy's movement was to be impeded, should preferably come in the form of passive munitions, as an example of which Hannig pointed particularly to anti-tank mines (AT-2) with sophisticated fuzes. According to his calculations, a saturation of e.g. 0.4 mines per sq. metre would put thirty percent of the attacking vehicles out of action. If the saturation were to be increased to 0.8 mines per sq. metre, any attack would presumably be brought to a stand-still. To complete the picture, these mine-fields with their area-covering effects should be combined with precision strikes against point targets, delivered from infantry units, operating in a combined arms mode[58].

The ideal launchers would be rockets and missiles, which Hannig regarded as more cost-effective than the obvious alternative, namely manned aircraft. He pointed i.a. to the potentials of 'modular' missiles, which should serve primarily as submunition dispensers, in which role they would represent all-round platforms for both anti-tank, air defence and anti-personnel purposes, that might meet the requirements for a wide panoply of missile systems of different ranges and sizes[59]. He mentioned especially the 'Milan 1/2' combined anti-tank and air defence system (with a range of approximately two kms.) and 'HOT' anti-tank missiles. For the latter, he did, however, recommend elevatable platforms as an alternative to helicopter deployment.

The predominant means for establishing the fire barrier would, however, be mobile multiple rocket launchers, assigned to the artillery. Of these systems, both light and heavy versions would be required along with the medium-sized MLRS currently under deployment. The ranges should likewise vary from 20 up to 200 kms. For the even longer ranges, i.a. for offensive counter air (OCA) missions, Hannig went so far as to recommend the employment of a conventional version of the 'Pershing-2' as a munitions dispenser, armed e.g. with Fuel Air Explosives (FAE) for shelter attack, and/or with runway cratering munitions[60]. These ideas resembled those associated with NATO's FOFA (Follow-On Forces Attack) doctrine and related 'deep strike' proposals, schemes which Hannig nevertheless criticised emphatically for providing genuine offensive options[61].

His claim to genuine non-offensiveness thus rested on a quite permissive criterion of defensivity and a correspondingly narrow definition of 'offence'. According to him, genuine offence logically implied occupation. In the absence of invasion and occupation capabilities, a state could constitute no genuine threat to any opponent, regardless of whether its military potential might contain weaponry capable of inflicting severe damage on the territory and society of its adversaries.

The various types of launchers should be deployed at different depths well behind the FEBA (Forward Edge of Battle Area), where they would be relatively well protected against enemy counter-battery fire[62]. As a rule of thumb, their stationing should match their range in such a way that they would only be able to reach the border, but not enemy territory. From their rear launching stations, these missiles and rockets would be capable of saturating the designated forward zone with mines in a 'killing zone' mode at the very outbreak of an attack, so as to create a veritable fire barrier. Hannig envisaged a zone with a depth of around four kms., which assessed as sufficient to bring any forward march of the enemy to a halt.

Whereas the potentials of rockets and missiles should primarily be exploited for land warfare purposes, he also paid some attention to their suitability for the aerial and sea environments. The air force should be relieved altogether of the task of ground attack, including tactical air support, and its mission structure would thus be largely reduced to surveillance and air defence. The latter was, furthermore, merely envisioned as a temporary expedient, pending the development of a full-fledged air defence system relying entirely on SAMs[63]. In due course, aircraft should thus be decommissioned entirely for combat roles and henceforth mainly serve as aerial surveillance platforms.

As far as coastal defence was concerned, Hannig anticipated it to gradually become possible to rely entirely on land-based missile systems, as a substitute for surface ships. By means of mobile multiple rocket launchers with ranges of around fifty kms., and deployed up to forty kms inland, highly efficient counters to invasion fleets and similar threats would be available. In the longer run, anti-ship missiles with ranges up to 200 kms. should enable the German defenders to cover the coastal areas in both the Baltic and the North Sea with the same set of missile launchers, deployed in the rear of Schleswig-Holstein.

These prospects ought to be welcomed, since major surface combatants were anyhow facing obsolescence due to their low cost-efficiency, even though Hannig did envisage a residual role for them for ASW (anti-submarine warfare) missions. Whereas land-based missiles were thus deemed sufficient for coastal defence purposes, the question of 'blue water missions' did, however, remain open. Apparently, Hannig simply wanted to abandon as unrealistic any protection of the transatlantic SLOCs (Sea Lines of Communication), the vital importance of which he flatly denied[64].

By employing the same missile modules for land, air and coastal defence, he hoped to pave the way for an integrated command system, which would do away with the obsolete and dysfunctional division of the armed forces into separate service arms. As an alternative, a genuinely hierarchical system with a high degree of centralization ought to be sought[65].

The proposed defence scheme was supposed to be very capital-intensive, and i.a. to have only modest manpower requirements. The number of troops required would be in the range of 500,000 men upon full mobilization[66], a very realistic figure even under the most pessimistic demographic assumptions.

The model was presumably ripe for implementation and would, according to Hannig, require no reciprocity on part of the WTO. Preferably, it should be initiated as a common NATO endeavour. If need be, however, the FRG might take the lead in the reform, or even, if consensus should prove unachievable, implement it unilaterally on a national scale.

This unilateralist conviction notwithstanding, Hannig did nevertheless embrace the possibility that had become apparent since 1986-87 of a simultaneous and coordinated conversion in both blocs. This, in its turn, might presumably take the form of a 'disarmament spiral', in which gradual nuclear disarmament was to be combined with conventional conversion and arms build-down[67].

Hannig's original 'vintage 1984' model has since then been developed further, partly in collaboration with Johannes Gerber, a professional soldier with the rank of General (ret.), who had developed an similar barrier model as an alternative to NATO's present posture[68]. The rationale for the two proposals differed somewhat, however, with Gerber being motivated primarily by considerations of cost-effectiveness.

He did not regard current defence planning as compatible with the budgetary and demographic 'squeezes' facing the *Bundeswehr*, and recommended, as a remedy, to switch to a more capital-intensive form of defence[69]. For this purpose, he envisaged an integrated terrestrial, aerial and maritime 'fire belt' to be 'deployed' all along the border by the defenders with the help of sensor arrays. These should provide target coordinates for a system of missile launchers with different ranges and stationed at variable distances from the intended belt along the border.

Gerber did, however, envisage the maintenance of a number of armoured regiments and anti-tank helicopters, at least for the interim period, intended to serve as 'hammers' against any enemy columns which might succeed in penetrating the fire barrier, conceived of as an 'anvil'. This conception, of course, stood in sharp contrast to the principled stance of Hannig, who had expressly mentioned the need for a complete abolition of such systems. Indeed, Hannig had warned against the risks involved in not phasing out such offensive-capable systems simultaneously with the establishment of the defensive posture lest an even more offensive-capable structure might result[70].

These differences of opinion notwithstanding, a 'model merger' was accomplished, the offspring of which was the so-called 'DEWA (Defence Wall) Concept'[71]. The core concept remained that of a fire barrier, consisting of passive munitions, fired into a pre-defined killing zone along the border. This would allegedly create a 'defence wall' which would be capable of destroying intruding tanks etc. The mines envisaged for this purpose would presumably be even better capable of destroying state-of-the-art tanks (outfitted with composite armour etc.) than the ones of the original model, thanks to their ability to hit the targets from below, where their armour is thin.

The DEWA concept was envisaged as an almost completely stationary defence, which would rely almost entirely on fire-power. It should capitalise on dispersal and concealment of the launchers (mostly rocket artillery), as well as on a far-reaching centralization of C³I structures. For the sake of protection, however, the rocket launchers were to be mobile, something which might obviously provide them with a certain offensive capability, unless checked. In order to minimise this potential, the two authors recommended the application of only light armour to the launching vehicles with a view to deliberately rendering them immobile under enemy fire. As a result, they would be mobile whilst inactive, but stationary whilst involved in combat.

Although the rocket artillery was envisaged to bear the brunt of the defence effort, the infantry would play an important (albeit mainly auxiliary) role as well, primarily as far as anti-tank and air defence were concerned. For this component of the defence, a novel feature in the DEWA version (as compared with Hannig's original proposal) was introduced, namely an extensive employment of rather unconventional infantry fighting vehicles, which should be capable both of digging themselves in and of creating additional obstacles.

Taking advantage of this feature, the two authors recommended a more extensive use of shelters for various force components, including the command staffs of the smaller units. This, in its turn, might allow for a somewhat greater decentralization, so that the DEWA model could meet the no-target criterion more satisfactorily than had been the case for the original, highly centralized, model[72]. In the latter, the hierarchical structure represented an obvious point of vulnerability, since the enemy might simply target the command posts, thus perhaps paralyzing the entire defence system.

Since the resultant 'defence wall' would allegedly represent an impenetrable barrier, any need for counter-offensive capabilities would *eo ipso* be eliminated. Even if certain minor penetrations should occur, the fire from the launchers deployed in depth would presumably be capable of covering the entire area of the FRG.

The assumptions with regard to the proposal's manpower and financial implications remained highly optimistic: According to the authors, the envisioned defence posture would allow for reduced manpower levels. By way of i.a. arms control agreements, these might be brought down to a total of 800,000 troops for all of NATO in Central Europe (land forces: 760,000, air forces: 21,000 and maritime forces: 18,000). An implementation of the proposed reform would thus allow for considerable savings, on the precondition that it would take place gradually, say, over a fifteen year span.

Disengagement Models

As we have seen in the chapter on the historical background, disengagement is quite an old idea. Particularly during the 1950s, proposals for disengagement abounded, both in Germany itself and abroad. However, even in the latter case, the authors had above all Germany in mind for the application of their proposals.

Disengagement has been conceived of in both political and military terms. The target of political disengagement has been the alliance structure *per se*, and proposals to this effect have been motivated by the desire to loosen the bonds between allies so as to avoid mutual 'entrapment'. This approach has primarily been taken by smaller states with a view to preventing their being inadvertently drawn into a conflict by their great-power allies[73]. Thus severing some of the integrative bonds and (as the opposite side of the same coin) extending the scope for autonomous action on the national scale has been the goal of political disengagement, occasionally referred to as 'decoupling', 'dealignment' or 'neutralization'[74].

Disengagement proposals have sometimes been motivated by nationalism, and particularly so in the case of Germany. Since it has been a consistent Soviet demand ever since 1945 that German unification should not lead to any strengthening of NATO, neutralism in various specific shapes has been regarded as a possible way of meeting these Soviet concerns, thus paving the way for unification. This line of reasoning, in its turn, has appeared in two varieties, which might be called 'rightist' and 'leftist' disengagement, respectively. Whereas the former variety has tended to regard the concessions to Soviet security concerns as enforced and deplorable, albeit realistically necessary, the latter has often embedded disengagement schemes in a 'Common Security' conceptual framework. Whereas the former variety, furthermore, has tended to be 'minimalist' with regard to disengagement (no more 'concessions' than one is forced to), the latter has tended towards 'maximalism': as many insurances for the opponent as would be compatible with one's own security.

A good example of 'right-wing' and 'minimalist' disengagement is General Günter Kiessling, to whom we shall return in the next chapter. The 'left-wing' and 'maximalist' disengagement advocates in the FRG have tended to cluster around the Green Party (cf. below, Chapter VIII). Furthermore, numerous authors belonging to the academic community have advocated left-wing disengagement, with Professor Ulrich Albrecht of the Free University, West Berlin, standing out as a prominent example.

Disengagement as envisioned by Albrecht would amount to the creation of a 'non-nuclear neutral security zone' in Central Europe, the military element of which would not merely be a removal of nuclear weapons from the heart of Europe, but also a withdrawal of offensive-capable weapons systems such as heavily armoured shock divisions[75].

The political element would be a deliberate decoupling, in its turn manifesting itself in a 'neutralist option', the objective whereof would, however, be a transformation of the alliances, rather than 'old-fashioned' absolute neutrality. It would presumably allow individual states to assert their sovereignty *vis-à-vis* their superpower hegemon, and thus to opt out of the East-West confrontation.

The 'Scandinavian model' might, in Albrecht's opinion, be adapted to Central Europe, implying a 'Swedenization' of the FRG, and a 'Finlandization' of the GDR, as well as a scaling down of the alliance commitments of the Benelux countries to the same level as those of Norway and Denmark[76]. Such a differentiated 'security zone' or region would presumably constitute a valuable *glacis* for both East and West, and might thus serve as a buffer zone.

Since the FRG would constitute the nucleus of such a security arrange ment, its national defence posture would be of vital importance for the stability of the whole:

'West Germany would have to be militarily strong enough to ensure that its territory could not be used for aggressive purposes by either side in the event of a European war, but not so strong as to pose a threat to its neighbours. German defences would have to be organised in a benign, non-provocative manner, more in keeping with the strictures of Germany's postwar constitution. The more offensive NATO concept of a forward-based defence would thus have to be rejected.'[77]

In the light of the reemerging German question, Albrecht pointed out that (re)unification of Germany did constitute a security risk. Most European states, and not merely the Soviet Union, would prefer a divided Germany, whence the imperative of finding less threatening forms of German unity. In continuity with his previous writings, he pointed to the Nordic community as a viable model for the rest of Europe, including the two Germanies. His recommendations thus continued to amount to a Central European non-nuclear, neutralised zone[78].

Another example of politically motivated disengagement-cum-NOD has been the Bremen Professor Dieter Senghaas who was one of the 'founding fathers' of German peace research[79].

Writing in 1986, he envisaged for the short term a continuance of the political *status quo* in Europe, including the continent's division into two opposing alliance systems. Under these framework conditions, he advocated disengagement, as well as a piecemeal creation of defensive military structures, as ways of promoting mutual confidence and co-existence, and thus of opening up the perspectives of an all-European common identity. He emphasised that the starting point for disengagement would have to conventional forces. In particular, a gradual disentanglement of heavy equipment and large man-power concentrations would be important, since this would relieve worries about conventional aggression, and thus deprive nuclear weapons of their predominant rationale. As a result, an NFU strategy as well as considerable reductions in the nuclear inventories would become realistic[80].

Disengagement should, furthermore, be attempted within the framework of the alliances. Indeed, the very multi-nationality of the military posture on the Western side was assessed as a political guarantee against attack[81]. For the same reason, multi-nationality ought to be maintained, even under the reduced force levels.

Subsequently, Senghaas went somewhat more into detail with the military aspects of his proposal[82], and i.a. specified the width of the envisaged disengagement zone to 50 kms. on the Western and 100 kms. on the Eastern side of the dividing line, the difference supposed to reflect geographical asymmetries. Furthermore, he specified which types of weapons systems to withdraw, namely tanks, combat helicopters and other heavy, mobile systems, along with bridging equipment. At the same time, both sides should remain at liberty to construct tank barriers of various kinds in their respective zones. The withdrawal of tanks etc. should be combined with a considerable reduction in their numbers, e.g. implemented through a transformation of heavy formations into mechanised or light infantry formations[83].

As far as longer-term perspectives were concerned, Senghaas saw a disengagement scheme such as the one described as merely a first step towards the establishment of an all-European system of collective security. This, in its turn, should be conceived merely as a preparatory phase, pending a conversion to what he called 'cooperative security'. I shall return to these visions for the future in Chapter XI below[84].

As the examples of Albrecht and Senghaas illustrate, proposals for political disengagement require a military component. Others have, however, approached the topic of military disengagement more directly, and one might, in fact, single out a category of NOD proposals for their emphasis on this type of measures.

The distingushing feature of military disengagement as compared with other NOD models, has been that they have not so much envisaged a change in the composition of existing forces as modifications of their deployment patterns. The underlying idea has been that certain types of weaponry were *per se* undesirable from an NOD point of view. Nevertheless, they have been regarded as impossible to eliminate, either because they were deemed militarily imperative, at least for a transitional phase, or for other (e.g. political) reasons.

Such weapons would, however, presumably be less offensive and provocative the further back they were to be deployed. This description holds true both for proposals for 'offensive-weapons-free zones' (e.g. tank-free zones) and for the more traditional varieties, pertaining to weapons of mass destruction. In actual fact, most proposals combine the two.

The redeployment of offensive-capable forces implied by disengagement would almost inevitably require changes in the residual arsenals, and hence be bound to affect strategy as well. In this manner, disengagement proponents have been forced to think through the implications and have, more often than not, ended up with concrete proposals for NOD defence schemes.

Just as disengagement proponents have been directed towards NOD, NOD theorists have also been led towards disengagement concepts, both along the path mentioned above, and in a search for temporary expedients. By realistically envisaging a piecemeal implementation of their NOD scheme, the obvious starting point has been identified as the immediate zones of contact (i.e. the border regions) with the longer-term perspective of a gradual expansion of the 'NOD zones'. This was also the case for Afheldt's *prima facie* very radical model, which should be seen in connection with the following.

Brigadier General (ret.) Eckardt Afheldt is a cousin and close collaborator of Horst Afheldt. In 1983 he presented his contribution to the joint results of the research team headed by the latter, in the form of a very detailed interim model called *Defence Without Self-Destruction. Proposal for the Deployment of Light Infantry.* The gist of his proposal was to substitute to a considerable extent infantry for armoured forces, especially in the forward areas. The proposal would allegedly lend itself to implementation in a step-by-step manner, just as it, in its turn, would merely constitute a step towards the all-encompassing territorial defence scheme.

As an alternative to the current posture, Eckhardt Afheldt proposed the creation of a 70-100 kms. wide forward zone, defended by means of a web of light infantry ('*Jägers*'), a proposal occasionally couched in terms of a 'tank-free zone' of the same width. The creation of such a '*Jäger* zone' would presumably make two to three tank divisions redundant, the savings from which would suffice for financing the force of 100,000 *Jägers*, who were to operate in the forward zone, from which the armoured forces would be banned[85].

The *Jägers* were to be deployed in-depth and widely dispersed, with an average of two *Jägers* per sq. kilometre. Even though no 'standard equipment' was envisaged, since the appropriate equipment would have to depend on tasks and location, Eckhardt Afheldt nevertheless mentioned as typical equipment i.a. ordinary light infantry weapons, obstacle construction gear, anti-tank missiles and artillery rockets, the latter primarily for the emplacement of land-mines. Elsewhere, he dealt with the possibility of a focused development of weaponry for such an infantry web, for which purpose the emphasis should be placed on rocket launchers for close combat (with maximum ranges of two kms.), multiple rocket launchers (with ranges up to eight kms.) in both stationary and mobile versions, precision-guided ballistic missiles, and the like. As a long-term perspective he even envisioned the employment of e.g. laser weapons and other beam weapons, as well as a wide spectrum of electronic warfare devices[86].

Eckhardt Afheldt's model was far less radical and consequential than that of his cousin Horst. He wanted, for instance, to maintain armoured forces, albeit in a more rearward deployment, from where they would be able to exploit the time gained by the *Jäger* network. Furthermore, in addition to the mechanised divisions, he proposed to employ other force components which have usually been considered suitable elements of an offensive posture, such as high-precision ballistic missiles with ranges up to 60-80 kms.[87].

Nevertheless, he proposed to employ the same tactical principles as proposed by his cousin: disperse forces, so as to present no lucrative targets, with a view to preventing escalation to a nuclear or chemical level; to deploy the forces in a stationary mode, so as to be able to exploit terrain advantages; to fight only from full cover (for which purpose he advocated the development of remotely launched and directed weapons systems); to preserve the defenders' own combat strength by eschewing battles on unfavourable terms[88], etc.

Even less radical than these proposals were those of the serving *Bundeswehr* officer Manfred Bertele, who intended 'merely' to achieve conventional stability without in any fundamental manner altering nuclear posture or strategy. His analytical point of departure was the mis-match between NATO strategy and posture. Because of the shortage of available forces, these would simply be incapable of performing their stipulated tasks, i.a. because of the immutable force-to-space requirements so often referred to by military authors[89].

As a remedy, Bertele advocated a model of stability to be implemented bilaterally, e.g. in the framework of an MBFR settlement, such as was by that time conceivable, however unlikely. For this purpose, he proposed a division of Europe into three wide zones on either side:

I. A zone of 250 kms. along both East and West borders, in which the parties should be allowed to deploy a maximum of 35 divisions each. These divisions should, furthermore, be predominantly of a new type: thirty infantry divisions with no 'shock power', albeit including one armoured regiment each. To these should be added a mere ten traditional armoured brigades, serving as an operational reserve, capable of counter-attack.

II. Two parallel zones of 750 kms. on either side behind the inner zones, wherein no standing armoured forces should be deployed at all.

III. A rear area, for which there would be no limitations.
The lack of offensive capability should be ensured through the lack of shock power in the forward line (zone I), combined with the impossibility of a surge deployment from zone III, above all because of the prohibitive distance. The intermediary zone would thus primarily serve a buffer function.

The divisions permitted in zone I should emphasise the infantry element, and be heavily armed with anti-tank missiles and guns, artillery and air defence systems, as well as equipped with a small number of tanks and armoured personnel carriers. The two latter offensive-capable categories were to be cut by three-fourths, whereas anti-tank weaponry should be multiplied by a factor of 2.5, and the infantry component doubled. Each of the new divisions would thus contain the following numbers, as compared with their predecessors[90]:

	New	Old
Infantry troops	4,320	1,800
Anti-tank missiles	585	180
Artillery systems	168	150
Air defence systems	72	36
Battle tanks	41	260
IFVs	41	270
Combat battalions	18	10–16
Regiments (combat troops)	5	3–4

Sword and Shield

What one might call 'sword and shield' conceptions are in some respects very similar to the disengagement proposals described in the previous section. Both envisage a withdrawal of offensive-capable forces and the deployment of strictly defensive forces up front. The difference is rather one of emphasis and rationale.

Whereas most disengagement proposals have maintained offensive forces merely as a temporary measure out of political pragmatism, 'sword and shield' models have tended to invest the residual 'sword forces' with a positive value and emphasised the military synergy between the two elements. They have hence maintained offensive capabilities as a matter of deliberate choice, and merely added defensive elements to the total posture, thus shifting the emphasis, but neither intending nor effecting any strategic sea-change. In this respect they resemble the 'integrated forward defence' to which the subsequent section is devoted.

The fact that 'sword and shield models' might be compatible with even fairly offensive orientations may explain why these models have attracted considerably less criticism from the strategic 'establishment' than the more radical proposals.

Brigadier General (ret.) Jochen Löser had participated in Horst Afheldt's research team at Starnberg. His other main source of inspiration was military history in general, and the writings of the 'great captains' in particular. He acknowledged a special debt to proponents of the 'indirect approach', such as Mao Tse-Tung and André Beaufre[91]. He did, however, depart from this tradition by regarding their prescriptions for annihilation of the enemy as invalid under present circumstances, since striving for this might well lead to the destruction of what ought, above all, to be protected, namely the population[92].

In 1982 Löser, in collaboration with a number of retired as well as a few active officers, pulished his best known work with the title *Neither Red Nor Dead. To Survive Without Nuclear War. An Alternative*, wherein he upheld the main ideas of Afheldt, in principle at least: not to possess any significant offensive capabilities; to avoid presenting any targets which might lead to escalation; to shun decisive battles, etc. Where he departed from his mentor was in the question of forward defence, for which Horst Afheldt (deliberately) lacked any capability, but which Löser regarded as a political imperative. However, he did not deem forward defence a realistic option under the prevailing circumstances, because of Soviet conventional superiority in combination with a poorly adapted NATO strategy[93]. To establish a credible and effective forward defence henceforth remained one of Löser's main concerns.

His threat perceptions were very sombre, indeed. The Soviet aim was believed to be an expansion of world communism by means of threats to use military force. Inspired by his collaboration in General Hackett's best-seller *The Third World War*, Löser developed a detailed scenario, stipulating a Soviet *blitzkrieg* attack in the 1980s, in the course of which the aggressor would use chemical weapons etc., and which would rapidly escalate to the nuclear level. This presented the Western states with an uncomfortable 'choice between red or dead'[94].

To escape this dilemma was his paramount goal, and appeared to necessitate an elimination of nuclear arms from NATO's military arsenal. Conventionalization would presumably be a precondition for reassembling the scattered popular consensus around NATO, since it offered the possibility of a modicum of damage limitation, whereas people could not be expected to support a strategy envisaging, for whatever purpose, their own annihilation. Furthermore, denuclearization would bring NATO strategy into compliance with international law, prohibiting, in Löser's interpretation, indiscriminate attacks against population centres. *A fortiori*, it would bring military planning on the part of and pertaining to the FRG into compliance with the Constitution prohibiting 'aggressive war'[95].

NATO strategy presumably failed because of its inability to protect the population, an imperative which Löser proposed to meet by means of a 'total defence', wherein civil defence should be accorded the same priority as military defence. It should encompass an elaborate programme for shelter construction, ensure the provision of vital necessities, etc. Furthermore, as a way of minimizing civilian casualties, population centres ought to be kept outside the zones of combat by being declared 'open towns' and, as a corollary thereof, be left militarily undefended[96].

In the absence of such damage limitation, the actual implementation of no strategy would be rational. It would therefore not be credible, and hence possess dubious deterrent value. The latter could, in the final analysis, only spring from defensive capability, which would depend to a great extent on 'intangibles' such as the 'will to defend', which, in turn, presupposed a solution to the problem of 'alienation' of the armed forces from society[97].

These criteria led Löser to recommend what he called an 'area covering defence' (*Raumdeckende Verteidigung*), occupying a half-way position between Afheldt's territorial defence (*Raumverteidigung*), possessing no forward defence capability at all, and the current strategy of forward defence with no fall-back provisions for in-depth defence. Löser's scheme thus comprised three zones:

I. A frontier area defence (*Grenzraumverteidigung*).
II. An area-covering defence web (*Raumverteidigungsnetz*).
III. A rear area.

The state of readiness in the three zones would differ, since a mobilization period of merely twelve hours would have to be the planning guideline in zone I, whereas as much as 24 hours might be available for zone III[98].

The area-covering defence web in zone II was roughly similar to Afheldt's. It should consist of *Jäger* brigades of 3000 troops each, responsible for the defence of an area of 600-800 sq. kilometres, and including both light and heavy *Jäger* units, as well as special forces. All *Jäger* squads should be armed with light anti-tank and air defence weapons (*Panzerfäuste* and *Fliegerfäuste*, respectively) as well as with mines and grenade launchers, in addition to which the heavier squads should be equipped with light multiple rocket launchers or mortars with ranges of approximately eight kms. On higher levels of command, the *Jäger* web should include missiles with ranges from ten to forty kms, as well as light armoured vehicles and anti-tank helicopters[99].

Furthermore, the web should include special air defence units, equipped with (preferably man-portable) low-level air defence systems such as 'Mistral'. For target acquisition, they should have access to an air-space surveillance array, i.a. mounted on television masts. This air defence network would shoulder the main burden of air defence, a task that would be facilitated by the fact that the elimination of aircraft for CAS and air defence missions would largely solve the IFF (Identification: Friend or Foe) problem. Henceforth almost everything in the air would be a legitimate target[100].

The tactical principles envisaged for the *Jägers* owed a great deal to Afheldt, Brosollet and others. They were to be deployed in-depth with five to seven brigades stationed behind each other, in order to confront attacking Soviet tank columns with a continuous resistance. Whereas Löser agreed with Horst Afheldt on the importance of restricting mobility in order to remain unambiguously defensive, he nevertheless envisaged a greater, albeit still merely tactical, mobility, and was e.g. unwilling to eschew the capability of movement under fire. The availability of several prepared positions per squad and an optimal utilization of the familiar terrain would presumably facilitate mobility. Man-made changes notwithstanding, the physical environment was still believed to provide good cover for the defenders, if only they adapted to its novel features, for instance by the employment of elevated weapons platforms, etc.[101].

The defenders should take advantage of their ability to position sensor arrays etc. in order to attain a superiority with regard to battlefield surveillance, also by means of jamming communication between the aggressor's units. The defenders were likely to prevail in the ensuing 'electronic battle', since they would be relatively immune to ECMs (Electronic Counter-Measures) by virtue of their greater independence of C³I structures. In order to magnify this independence, Löser recommended the employment whenever possible, of *Auftragstaktik*, i.e. what has also been called 'directive control'. Not everything, however, should be left to improvisation, but quite a lot planned in advance in terms of fire and obstacle-laying plans, so as to provide field commanders with a panoply of options from which to choose[102].

As additional means of gaining the initiative, Löser envisaged supplementing the 'shield forces' described so far with 'sword forces', which should be capable of counter-offensives, and which would therefore have to comprise armoured vehicles. In the short term these should consist of ordinary tanks, whereas a replacement with lighter armoured vehicles was envisioned as a longer-term perspective. The sword forces should be employed i.a. for the final annihilation (on the tactical scale) of enemy units that had already been brought to a halt and had been attrited by the shield forces. For the sake of minimizing genuine offensive capability, however, they should operate primarily in the rear zone, a conception which revealed the semblance between Löser's model and the disengagement models.

These 'sword' formations should consist of both allied and West German armoured forces. Whereas this multinationality might go some way towards minimizing offensive potentials, the defensive character should be further underlined by reducing their state of readiness, i.e. by 'skeletonizing' or cadering the formations. In general, the defence should to a considerable extent be made up of reserves: at the border, up to one third of the personnel should be reserves, whereas the percentage might reach two thirds in the rear areas. On other occasions, Löser even mentioned a three-thirds (sic.) cadering of units, presumably amounting to a mere storage of equipment[103].

An additional potentially offensive element in Löser's model was the maintenance of the air force. Due to the air defence capability integrated in the *Jäger* formations, the air defence tasks would be minimised, and an increased number of aircraft thus made available for other missions. In his opinion, these were to be assigned, first of all, to the ground forces (including the sword forces), albeit no longer for ordinary close air support. Secondly, they were to operate independently with e.g. deep interdiction missions against targets in the enemy's hinterland, a mission that most other NOD proponents have recommended to be abolished as too offensive[104].

The final component of the military defence would be the rear or home guard, consisting of volunteers (including women), and tasked with the defence of the least exposed areas, i.a. against air landings and enemy formations which might have accomplished penetrations. Furthermore, the home guard should collaborate with the police and the regular military forces in the struggle against covert operations and subversive activities on the part of the enemy, in Löser's opinion an underestimated threat which merited much more serious attention[105].

One advantage of Löser's defence scheme, according to its author, was that it would lend itself to a step-by-step implementation. It might e.g. be implanted in an arms control strategy in accordance with which NATO should challenge the USSR to emulate a sequence of steps undertaken by the Western Alliance, in a manner resembling that envisioned by the 'gradualists'[106].

The result would be a disengagement process through which both sides would gradually withdraw their offensive-capable forces from the frontier, resulting in a zonal arrangement:

—In a 150 kms.-deep zone along the border only infantry forces should be deployed, whereas combat aircraft, armoured vehicles and tactical nuclear forces would be prohibited.

—In the adjacent 400 kms.-deep zones armoured units might be stationed, whereas INF systems should be banned[107].

Along with INFs, tactical nuclear weapons might be abolished as henceforth entirely superfluous. Indeed, the main purpose of the proposal was precisely to make an NFU policy viable, faithful to which goal Löser, incidentally, participated in the research team appointed by the American 'Union of Concerned Scientists', that in 1983 issued one of the best known NFU defensorates[108].

Since the publication of his original model, Löser has added little to its military essentials, whilst elaborating on its ramifications, occasionally with rather odd results. In a book written in collaboration with Harald Anderson on *The Answer to Geneva. Security in East and West*, Löser *mirabile dictu* attempted a merger of his own concept with the US Army's ALB (AirLand Battle) doctrine which has been regarded by many observers as a modern *offensive a l'outrance*. He interpreted the notorious 1982 edition of the *Field Manual* 100-5 in which the new doctrine was most authoritatively expressed as a sign that 'strategy was moving exactly towards the point of view expressed in *Neither Red nor Dead'*. He even reframed his own area-covering defence as a contribution to making ALB applicable to Europe, even though this had been explicitly ruled out by SACEUR (Supreme Allied Commander, Europe) Bernard Rogers[109].

Furthermore, Löser expressed satisfaction with the 'Rogers Plan' (subsequently known as FOFA: Follow-On Forces Attack) because of its emphasis on the interdiction of the WTO's second echelon forces[110]. As a final tribute to the offensive renaissance in progress, he acknowledged *ex post facto* the wisdom of NATO's dual track decision, thus *expressis verbis* contradicting his own previous critique[111].

Already in the original model, the role of the defensive shield forces had been somewhat ambiguous, since the 'shield' might, indeed, simply serve as a force multiplier for the offensive-capable sword formations. This ambiguity about what was actually meant by 'defensive' was subsequently compounded by Löser's favourable interpretation of the SDI (Strategic Defence Initiative) launched by the Reagan administration. He saw this as a confirmation *ex cathedra* of the need for defensive forces as an alternative to offensive deterrence. In all fairness it must, however, be added that he did recommend substantial reductions of strategic nuclear forces for the duration of the transition period pending full-scale deployment of SDI[112]. Nevertheless, this SDI advocacy set Löser apart from the entire NOD, indeed from the entire centre-left, political community in the FRG. Perhaps in order to avoid such a rightist 'stigma', he seems to have had second thoughts on the matter, and subsequently denounced SDI *expressis verbis* as fuelling the arms race and 'perverting' the defensive idea[113].

Simultaneously with such ill-advised attempts at 'mergers' with various emerging trends in 'mainstream' military doctrine, Löser has also sought to subsume more 'dovish' ideas within (or as a framework for) his own proposal, as, for example, with the concept of 'Common Security'[114].

He has furthermore slackened his allegiance to NATO as such, coming forward with proposals for gradual disengagement and loosening of the bloc structures. He was particularly outspoken to this effect in a work published in 1984 in collaboration with Ulrike Schilling on *Neutrality for Central Europe*, wherein he advocated a gradual neutralization of Central Europe, implying i.a. a withdrawal of the US Seventh Army.

As a means towards the end of a more independent Europe, he urged the European NATO members to gradually adopt a non-provocative defence posture, and both superpowers to disengage from Europe. In the first phase, they should withdraw most of their armed forces as well as nuclear and chemical weapons from the two Germanies, to the area behind the Weser-Lech line and the Oder/Sudenten-Gebirge/Hohe-Tatra line, respectively. In a second phase, all forces and nuclear weapons were to be completely withdrawn, whilst leaving behind depots etc. for the US Air Force. In the third phase, these should, finally, be withdrawn as well[115].

Such a military disengagement, in its turn, would allow the two Germanies to adopt a neutral stand, 'along the Austrian example'. Indeed the two authors paid tribute to this country with an entire chapter in their book entitled *Tu felix Austria* . Eventually, the whole of Central Europe was to become a 'zone of peace', joined together by a confederation encompassing the two Germanies, the Benelux countries, Czechoslovakia, Poland, Hungary, Austria, Romania and Yugoslavia. In due course, this zone might constitute the embryo of the 'Common European House' advocated by the USSR[116].

In the same category of NOD advocates as Löser, one might count Former Minister of Research and Technology and *Staatssekretär* in the Ministry of Defence, Andreas von Bülow. He has, however, earned himself a reputation as one of the leading German advocates of defence reform primarily in his capacity as a prominent member of (and MdB for) the SPD, and I shall therefore relegate him to the chapter on this party.

Conditional Counter-Invasion

Most of the ideas outlined in the previous chapters may be traced back to Horst Afheldt. The same goes for the model to which this section is devoted, although its author might be said to have strayed so far from the original idea as perhaps not to deserve the label 'non-offensive' at all. This is all the more surprising because of Afheldt's personal involvement in this project.

In 1984, a research team at the Max Planck Institute in Starnberg, near Munich, launched a project on 'Stability-oriented Security Policies', under the joint directorship of Afheldt, the renowned physicist Hans Peter Dürr and the young philosopher Albrecht A.C. von Müller. The latter served as administrative leader, after the post had first been offered to Lutz Unterseher of the SAS group (cf. below). The aim was to transform Afheldt's basic ideas into a zonal model, which should be ripe for implementation and emphasise, above all, crisis stability. In addition to Afheldt's, particularly the ideas of von Müller came to play the decisive role[117].

Von Müller's theoretical foundations were very elaborate, and the format of the research project was correspondingly ambitious. However, no major publications ever flowed from the ambitious project, even though preliminary results were made available in the form of a number of articles and manuscripts, written primarily by von Müller (or at least presented in his name), and most of them 're-cycled' in numerous, almost identical, versions.

With the retirement of Afheldt in 1989, the project was terminated, although he and von Müller had earlier parted company, apparently 'more in anger than in sorrow'. Subsequently, the latter had established himself at a new 'institute' called EUCIS: 'European Centre for International Security'. Its impressive name and list of supporters (including e.g. Robert McNamara) notwithstanding, it was little more than a 'one-man show', collaborating with a similar institution in Copenhagen until the death of the latter's director, Anders Boserup, in May 1990.

The 'power basis' of both branches of EUCIS was the Pugwash Movement, under the auspices of which a sub-group on 'Conventional Forces in Europe' had been working since 1984, convened jointly by Boserup and von Müller[118]. Taking advantage of the emerging Soviet interest in NOD, the two convenors had facilitated the introduction of West German NOD conceptions into the Soviet debate, albeit more often than not depicting themselves as their true inventors.

Because of their questionable relevance for the genuine NOD debate, the ideas of von Müller will only be treated very cursorily, and their elaborate philosophical underpinnings (set out in a book from 1984 on *The Art of Peace*[119]) not at all. Suffice it to say about the latter that the degree of complexity in the presentation was not always matched by the originality or relevance of the substance.

Metaphysics aside, two separate political paths seem to have led von Müller towards NOD: on the one hand, the quest for 'security partnership' as an element of a stable international order, and, on the other, the search for an escape from the otherwise insoluble contradiction between defence and security, i.e. the socalled defence dilemma.

Besides philosophical reasoning, the methodology employed in the project has featured in the notion of 'Force Ratio Development Functions' (FDFs), by means of which the comparative attrition of defending and attacking forces were to be measured; a methodology resembling (and probably 'borrowed' from) the more sophisticated American force comparison models, such as Joshua Epstein's 'dynamic analysis' and Barry Posen's 'Attrition-FEBA Expansion Model'[120]. The preliminary conclusion from applying this method was that a stable situation required the aggressor to suffer the severest attrition, until his attack would eventually falter. To bring this about was presumably one of the main objectives of NOD.

Presently, neither of the alliances was assessed as satisfying the stability criterion, even though, in von Müller's assessment, NATO was currently incapable of large-scale offensives. It was, however, 'structurally capable' and the deficiency consisted simply in a quantitative shortage of military means. On these preconditions, the WTO might conceivably construct worst-case scenarios of NATO interventions in Pact-internal crises, etc., fears which could only be effectively removed by way of structural change. The WTO, on the other hand, was assessed as being both structurally and in actual fact capable of large-scale offensives, with the resultant well-known fears on the part of NATO as a consequence[121].

For the concept of NOD, von Müller framed the cumbersome and grammatically perplexing term 'structural non-attack capability' (*strukturelle Nichtangriffsfähigkeit* with the acronym *StruNA*), sometimes rendered (more understandably, but less literally) as 'structural inability to attack'. This term was, according to the author himself, first used in *Frankfurter Rundschau*[122], and it has since then (alas!) become prominent in the German debate.

The 'integrated forward defence' which formed the core of the 'StruNA' proposal was an eclectic model, combining ideas borrowed from the two Afheldts, Hannig, Löser, von Bülow and, not least, the SAS (cf. below). True to his usual style, however, von Müller simply subsumed these proposals into his own, without acknowledging his sources of inspiration.

The concrete proposal essentially consisted of a zonal model[123] combining three zones with a rear area:

I. A five kms.-wide fire-belt, almost devoid of troops, but saturated with fire delivered by means of MLRS systems, attack drones etc., preferably in the form of 'smart' passive munitions, such as sophisticated mines. This zone closely resembled Hannig's proposals. It furthermore envisaged combining this fire-barrier on the FRG's own territory with 'close interdiction' on to enemy territory to a depth of 40-60 kms.

II. A 75 kms.-wide 'network zone' behind this, defended by infantry, armed with PGMs and fighting in a guerilla mode. Here, the inspiration from the two Afheldts was unmistakable.

III. An appr. 60 kms.-wide 'manoeuvre zone' with traditional armoured units. These should, however, be deployed in greater dispersal than presently, and serve primarily as an 'internal rapid deployment force', such as envisaged by the SAS. In contrast to the latter, however, the armoured and mechanised forces should, as a matter of deliberate choice, entail substantial (counter-) offensive capabilities (cf. below).

Behind these zones, the rear area should be subjected to no restrictions. All the same, it should form a defence web, containing both stationary and mobile units, and have the primary task of deterring and defending against air landings.

The scheme allegedly met Afheldt's no-target criterion, since the two forward zones would contain no lucrative targets for massive attacks, and even the armoured formations stationed further back would do so to a lesser extent than presently, due to their more dispersed deployment. Furthermore, the system was allegedly structurally defensive, although, as we have seen, the fire-belt would be capable of extension into the territory of the attacker in times of war. This 'close interdiction' should be conducted by means of e.g. drones and missiles etc. to a depth of approximately fifty kms.[124].

Since the presentation of the original proposals, only marginal alterations have been made. In the 1988 version, the two forward zones had been merged into a 25 kms. deep 'web zone' of light infantry and obstacle-building units. In spite of its rather low density (40,000 troops in peacetime rising to 120,000 upon mobilization), it would allegedly be capable of considerably delaying and attriting the intruding formations, by capitalizing on a systematic development of close interdiction capabilities. For this purpose, a total of 2,000 sq. kilometre of sensor arrays were envisaged to be emplaced in the border region in order to provide guidance for combat drones. However, the central components would remain various types of mines along with mine-launchers[125].

Emerging technology played a central role in the approach of the Starnberg team, for which purpose they even aligned themselves with the near-by arms producing firm Messerschmidt-Bölkow-Blohm. The proposal envisioned an exploitation of trends in modern technology, which presumably, according to the authors, tended to benefit the defender[126].

The munitions to employ for the fire-belt should above all be so-called 'stochastic mines', moving about in a random pattern, and thus making evasive manoeuvering by the target, in casu the enemy tank, impossible. The particular type of mines envisaged would be able to hit the tanks from the sides and bottom, i.e. where they were rather 'soft-skinned'. The mines would allegedly be cheap (an estimated US$ 3,000 per mine), so that substantial numbers might be procured in order to ensure sufficient coverage.

For 'close interdiction', a combination of attack drones and missiles were to be employed, which would compound the threats to the enemy's tanks by being able to hit them from above, so that the armour requirements for complete protection would henceforth become prohibitive. The missiles and drones would rely on real-time information provided by reconnaissance drones, connected by means of fibre-glass cables to ground data processors. The reconnaissance drones were estimated to cost around US$25,000 each.

A central element in the defence would be the sensor array, which would presumably provide the defenders with redundant means of near real-time surveillance of the battlefield. In order to be survivable, the sensors were to be dug in to a depth where they would be out of reach of enemy artillery. Since the weight of an advancing tank would be its most difficult feature to obscure by means of various sorts of decoys, the sensors should primarily be of the seismic type. The sensors should be interconnected by means of fibreglass cables, which would be both comparatively cheap and resistent to both EMP (Electro-Magnetic Pulse) and ECMs.

The original cost estimate for the envisioned scheme amounted to the following, with the subsequently revised figures[127] in brackets:

PROCUREMENT	MILL.	$
2,000 km sensor net	200	(400)
3,000 simple combat drones	75	(150)
Intelligent passive munitions	125	(250)
Mobile mines and launchers	165	(339)
Total investment costs	565	(1,130)

In both the original and the modified version, von Müller envisaged as the outcome a situation of 'conditional offensive superiority', which he *mirabile dictu* saw as merely a special case of 'mutual defensive superiority'. The latter was the stabilizing ratio between offensive and defensive capabilities discovered by the Frenchman André Glucksman on the basis of Clausewitz, and since then popularised by von Müller's collaborator, the late Anders Boserup[128]. However, von Müller went a bit further than these by explicitly demanding an inversion of the offence-defence ratio.

When the attacking forces had penetrated the two forward zones, they would presumably, due to the heavy attrition suffered so far, find themselves outnumbered to such an extent that the defenders would have an offensive counter-attack option, allowing them even to invade the home territory of the attacker[129]. This was conceived of as a solution to a problem with the original Afheldt model, which was presumed to be (though not by Afheldt himself) severe, namely that it had no satisfactory answer to the question of how to evict the aggressor and thus restore the *status quo ante bellum*.

However, von Müller's idea also resembled the controversial proposal by Samuel Huntington for 'conventional retaliation', which envisaged offensive manoeuvre warfare on enemy territory, albeit merely for deterrence purposes. The latter proposal has attracted considerable criticism, both on pragmatic grounds as being well beyond NATO's abilities, and on more principled grounds, as having offensive implications, incompatible with the defensive nature of the Western alliance[130].

Whereas von Müller believed that 'StruNA' might lend itself to unilateral implementation, he nevertheless emphasised that reciprocity would speed up the process, and that some kind of arms control settlements ought hence to be sought[131]. In actual fact, he seems to have drifted rapidly from the unilateralist towards a more traditional arms control position.

In early 1988 he put forward a set of proposals, worked out jointly with a prominent East European researcher, Andrzej Karkoszka of the Polish Institute for International Affairs. Herein the two authors proposed ceilings for various weapons categories at roughly fifty percent of the present force level of the inferior, i.e. in most cases NATO. Whilst building down in the especially offensive-prone categories, both sides should be at liberty to 'maintain or even acquire as much passive munitions and barrier technology, anti-tank and anti-air weapons and "close interdiction" systems (with ranges shorter than 50 kms) as they deem necessary against the remaining threat'.

Under the precondition of such a successful conventional disarmament, it was envisaged that the nuclear arsenals in Europe would be able to stand some deep cuts. However, it appeared sensible to the two authors to leave behind a residual force of perhaps 500 warheads for land and air-based systems, of which, moreover, only 100 would be allowed to be on rockets[132]. This represented a departure from von Müller's previous advocacy of a residual force of a mere 200 warheads assigned to Europe, deployed exclusively at sea and with yields ranging from ten to 250 KTs (kilotons)[133]. This more forthcoming attitude towards NATO's pro-nuclear wing may have been motivated by a 'eagerness to please', but did, however, seem misplaced at a time when land-based 'nukes' were being questioned from all sides in the FRG.

Only a few months later, von Müller presented yet a new joint proposal, this time compiled in collaboration with a retired four-star General, Gerd Schmückle. As far as nuclear weapons were concerned, it was envisioned that the warheads assigned to the defence of Europe should be built down to 'a few hundred', a figure that was elsewhere specified to a maximum of 400 single-warhead missiles without terminal guidance and with ranges below 500 kms. Furthermore, von Müller explicitly proclaimed himself in favour of maintaining nuclear weapons in Europe 'for the foreseeable future', depicting them as a factor of stability and as contributing to war prevention. Nuclear artillery ought, however, to be phased out entirely, and all nuclear weapons were henceforth to be assigned to a special corps under the command of SACEUR. In order to allow for a European say pertaining to nuclear employment, a special 'crisis cabinet' should be formed around the US President, consisting of experienced European politicians[134].

Spider and Web

The model developed by the 'Study Group Alternative Security Policy' (SAS) might be described as a 'mature' model. It 'stands on the shoulders of' its predecessors; it has been elaborated in great detail; and it encompasses proposals for the two environments that are all too often neglected, particularly by German NOD proponents—the air and the sea.

The SAS is a multinational group which includes researchers from the FRG (amongst whom Lutz Unterseher, Wolfgang Vogt, Hans Günter Brauch, Hartmut Bebermeyer and Bernd Grass), the former GDR (Wolfgang Schwarz and Manfred Müller, with the previous Minister of Finance Walter Romberg closely affiliated), the Netherlands (Sjef Orbons and John Grin), the U.K. (David Stevenson and Malcolm Chalmers), Denmark (the present author), and the USA (Carl Connetta and Charles Knight). In addition to the academics, the members include officers of the *Bundeswehr* (Franz Borkenhagen and others) as well as leading SPD members (MdB Hermann Scheer and Senator Volker Kröning). Furthermore, the social science research firm SALSS is collaborating closely with the SAS, since its co-director happens to be the SAS chairman and *primus motor*, Lutz Unterseher. Finally, the SAS has wide-ranging ramifications and contacts abroad, thanks primarily to Unterseher, who has been a fellow at the Royal Staff College, Camberley, a consultant to the Austrian Ministry of Defence, as well as a frequent lecturer in the USA and elsewhere.

The SAS has in many respects been more directly political than most of the authors dealt with so far. First of all, it has constantly tried (with considerable success) to enlist political support for its proposals and analyses, primarily within the SPD. In this respect, Unterseher's affiliation with the party's *Bundestag* caucus in his capacity as advisor to Hermann Scheer (the party spokesman on arms control and disarmament) has been of special importance. The SAS has, however, also been consulted by parliamentarians from the Green Party, although the latter have subsequently been reprimanded by 'fundamentalists' in their party. Advice has nevertheless been provided, albeit clandestinely. Of even greater importance was that the short-lived Ministry of Defence in the post-revolutionary GDR took a great interest in alternative defence plans, including those of the SAS.

Secondly, the SAS has consistently dealt directly with ongoing defence planning, issuing concrete evaluations, as well as recommendations for reforms, of *Bundeswehr* planning. In 1985 it issued a critique of the FRG's defence planning, formulated jointly by a professor at the Bundeswehr Academy in Hamburg, a minister of economics in Saarland, a senator from Bremen, and two members of the SPD executive[135].

In the following account I shall limit myself to research carried out under the auspices of the SAS and SALSS, as well as individually by West German members, whilst largely omitting the research activities of the non-German SAS members (such as the present author himself). The East German members are dealt with in Chapters X and XI below.

One of the points of departure for the SAS has been threat analysis. In general, the SAS has assessed the Soviet threat as somewhat less ominous than assumed by NATO and *Bundeswehr* authorities. In 1984 SALSS e.g. analyzed the Central European balance of conventional ground forces. As a preliminary, they reminded the audience that such an exclusive focus on land forces was somewhat unfair, since this was the one area in which the WTO was superior, whereas NATO superiority in the air and at sea was just as glaring[136]. Secondly, they found that any possible WTO ground force advantage was bound to be short-lived, due to NATO's superiority in terms of mobilization potential.

In terms of divisional comparisons, the WTO was, indeed, assessed as being superior, a fact which, however, primarily reflected organizational differences rather than any disparity of actual strength. If merely WTO divisions in a high state of readiness were counted, the advantage would shrink considerably. In other word, the superiority would only emerge in case of a 'standing start' attack, subsequent to which it would soon wither away. Furthermore, even as far as present forces were concerned, the WTO could only be reckoned as superior if the NSPFs (Non-Soviet Pact Forces) were counted as well, in spite of their highly dubious reliability[137]. In terms of major weapons systems, the numerical advantages of the WTO should to a considerable extent be seen as reflecting qualitative inferiority. If compared by the yardstick of ADEs (Armoured Division Equivalents) the WTO would have merely a marginal superiority in the magnitude of 1.2:1, a ratio which might improve to 2:1 for a short interval, if NATO was slow to mobilise.

This was, on balance, a rather optimistic assessment, since it has generally been deemed necessary for an attacker to attain a superiority exceeding 3:1 on the tactical scale in order to prevail. Indeed, Soviet planners appear even more 'conservative' and would hardly be comfortable with ratios below 4:1 or 5:1[138]. None of the scenarios taken into consideration thus appeared to provide any worthwhile options for a WTO attack.

In 1987, Unterseher undertook a more detailed investigation of the 'tank threat' in collaboration with Malcolm Chalmers of the Bradford School of Peace Studies. In this study the two authors took into account qualitative factors in their force comparison, with the result that the weighted numerical superiority of the WTO tank fleet shrank to very manageable proportions indeed (between 1.3:1 and 1.6:1). In spite of this optimistic threat assessment, however, the authors did not regard the situation as stable, but called for a defensive restructuring as the only remedy[139].

Just as it has been critical of official threat assessment, the SAS has on many occasions criticised *Bundeswehr* planning, i.a. for not taking into due consideration the pending manpower shortage, due to the *Pillenknick* (i.e. the declining birth-rates since the end of the 1960s, commonly associated with 'the pill') and the resultant unfavourable age pyramid. In a few years time there would simply not be enough young male citizens around to continue manning a *Bundeswehr* of the present size[140]. Neither were the ideas emanating from the defence ministry (for an extension of the conscription period, for female conscription, for a greater contingent of professional soldiers and the like) regarded as acceptable. Even though this problem has now largely disappeared thanks to unification (implying a larger pool of eligible young males) and the scaling down of the *Bundeswehr* to 370,000 troops, it was certainly a severe problem until then.

Furthermore, the maintenance of the *Bundeswehr* was criticised for placing far too heavy a burden on the shoulders of the taxpayers, and hence of undermining the economic fabric of the society which was supposed to be defended: the peace-time variety of the 'defence dilemma'[141]. In a democratic society such as the FRG, defence planning had to comform with the priorities of the electorate, who tended to prefer maintaining the welfare state to spending unwarrantedly great (and increasing) percentages of the GNP for defence. If the government did not modify its policies in accordance with this popular mood, the public legitimacy of any defence (and indeed of the entire security political system) might vanish[142].

The SAS was also highly sceptical towards the 'Rogers Plan' and similar deep strike concepts (FOFA, 'Counter Air 90', etc.), partly because of their unwarranted faith in the potentials of emerging technologies, partly on grounds of a presumed obsolescence. According to the analysis of the SAS, the WTO was about to switch over to structures that would deprive any would-be NATO deep strike planners of worthwhile targets. In these assessments, the group was undoubtedly somewhat inspired by the American defence analyst Steven Canby[143], who had to a certain extent collaborated with Unterseher. Furthermore, deep strikes were rejected for creating pre-emptive urges and for placing a premium on striking first, thus severely damaging crisis stability[144].

The somewhat related conceptions of a switch on the part of NATO towards deep manoeuvre warfare (such as implied by the ALB doctrine and the Huntington proposals for 'conventional retaliation') were likewise dismissed as inevitably entailing vast numbers of civilian casualties. If the battlefield was allowed to become 'fluid' as a result of manoeuvre warfare on both sides, fighting could not possibly be banned from populated areas[145].

As far as nuclear weapons were concerned, the SAS proposal emphasised the imperative of presenting no targets for enemy nuclear strikes, whence its criticism of the INF deployment and other nuclear 'modernisation' pro-grammes. Nevertheless, the SAS did considered the maintenance of a limited nuclear arsenal for 'minimum deterrence' as warranted, at least temporarily. The group did, however, regard no-first-use on the part of NATO as envisaged by the 'Gang of Four' and others as a perfectly realistic strategic option[146].

This advocacy of minimum deterrence-cum-NFU notwithstanding, the real problem was not deterrence, since a replay of a '1939' scenario was regarded as very unlikely, whereas a path towards war resembling the events in 1914 was deemed much more conceivable. Crisis stability thus assumed paramount importance, and the strictly defensive nature of the military means was considered to be the best way of preventing such inadvertent wars[147].

The SAS member Hans Günter Brauch has delivered a substantial input to this criticism of traditional and 'alternative' NATO planning. He has been a very prolific writer, and has published extensive critical accounts on a number of aspects of present NATO strategy and posture.

With the aforementioned objective of enhanced crisis stability in mind, Brauch approached the topic of alternative defence from the angle of confidence-building measures (CBMs). Confidence, in its turn, was not merely regarded as a precondition for handling crises, but also for successful arms control and disarmament in general. Compared with these far-reaching goals, Brauch saw the previous accomplishments in the CSCE in general, and the CDE (Conference on Disarmament) in particular, as valuable, albeit all too cautious, steps in a promising novel arms control and disarmament process.

What made these negotiation fora particularly promising was primarily their sensible goal of reducing, above all, the risks of surprise attacks. This presumably constituted a first step in a new direction which might eventually lead out of the *cul de sac* in which arms control had hitherto almost invariably ended. In such an endeavour, alternative defence concepts could obviously play an important role. More specifically, certain proposals for CSBMs (Confidence- and Security-Building Measures) actually tabled at the CDE Conference were given a very favourable assessment. One of these was the 1983 Yugoslav proposal for restrictions on manoeuvres in border areas, and reductions of foreign-based troops. The Western approach to CBMs, on the other hand, was criticised for focusing excessively on enhancing transparency, whilst ignoring the realities, such as offensive and possibly provocative military concepts[148].

In spite of the high priority assigned by the SAS to crisis stability, the SAS Chairman Unterseher did not accept the well-known arguments for disengagement as a stability-enhancing measure, and went out of his way to set the SAS model apart from disengagement proposals. According to his assessment, spatial disengagement might be even less stable than the present postures, since both sides would have an obvious incentive to break the disengagement rules at an early stage of a crisis, something which might lend itself easily to misinterpretation. A forward movement to combat positions up front was the last thing one would want to have to undertake in a crisis[149].

The group saw its own approach as somewhat eclectic, and has in fact incorporated a number of elements from other models, along with ideas of an Anglo-Saxon origin, such as those developed by i.a. Steven Canby and Richard Simpkin. On numerous occasions, group members have also surveyed and criticised other proposals for alternative defence[150]. As a matter of fact, the present work could be seen as the hitherto most elaborate contribution to this endeavour.

The group acknowledged its indebtedness to Horst Afheldt whose ideas were considered a 'structural confidence-building measure'. Nevertheless, a number of deficiencies in this 'pure' form of NOD were identified.

—It relied on a specific type of anti-tank weapons, a fact which would enable the opponent to optimise counter-measures.

—It was characterised by 'mono-culture' on the tactical as well as on the technical level, something which would enable the aggressor to counter-optimise, e.g. by means of highly mobile infantry troops.

—The missiles to be deployed in the rear would be vulnerable to sabotage.

The SAS therefore envisaged supplementing the Afheldt-like units in its defence scheme with mobile combat reinforcements. These were to be stationed within the web, albeit concentrated along the border. Lighter forces should be stationed closer to the front than the heavier ones, which were to be deployed approximately eighty kms. behind the border[151].

Despite some superficial similarities between the SAS model and Löser's 'sword and shield' model, the latter was criticised for his notion of making the defence web itself mobile. Mobility was only deemed possible under armour, and the 'combat reinforcements' would therefore have to be armoured. To provide the lighter forces with armour would, however, prove unaffordable. Furthermore, the envisaged combination of 'shields' with 'swords' was regarded as potentially destabilizing, since the defensive 'shield' might simply serve as a force multiplier for the offensive sword. Hence the even more critical evaluation of the von Müller and von Bülow proposals, in which particularly the option of 'conditional offensives' was considered highly problematic[152].

Hannig's proposal was appreciated for its non-provocative character, but its dependency on unbroken communication chains to the missiles tasked with establishing the fire-belt was identified as a point of vulnerability. Presumably, however, this problem might be solved by means of a redundant fibre-optical network[153].

The actual alternative model of the SAS was distinguished by a number of unique features:

1. By its employment of almost entirely available and tested technology rather than emerging technologies of dubious reliability.
2. By its requiring substantially lower troop numbers than the present structure without at the same time necessitating unaffordable investment costs.
3. By its providing for a genuine forward defence, combined with an in-depth territorial defence.
4. By its possessing substantial tactical mobility whilst renouncing any strategic mobility that might amount to an offensive capability.

The latter arrangement was what gave the model its name, since the mobile forces were likened by Egbert Boeker and Unterseher to a 'spider in its web'. Within its web, a spider was highly mobile, but beyond it, it was severely handicapped[154].

The SAS model has been worked out in great detail, the full complexity of which is impossible to convey in a short presentation such as the present one. In the SAS's *Concept of Land Forces for the* 1990s, the recommended defence posture included three components[155]:

I. The Containment Force was to consist partly of present, and partly of cadred forces. The present forces were to be deployed in an approximately 32 kms.-wide zone, commencing at the border. They would be stationary and interlinked in a network structure, in such a manner that any single unit might be assisted by the neighbouring units. They would fight from prepared positions, but each squad would have four to five interchangable positions at its disposal. The basic unit would be a 28-man platoon (or 'module') with the responsibility for defending approximately 16 sq. kilometres.

Their equipment would consist of automatic rifles, light grenade launchers, sniper's rifles, flame throwers, *Panzerfäuste* with ranges around 500 meters, anti-tank missiles and volley launchers with ranges around 2.5 kilometers, in addition to a variety of mines. For transportation, each module should be equipped with two ordinary trucks.

The higher echelons would include the company level (four modules plus support elements, i.e. a total of 142 men), and the battalion level (four companies plus support elements, i.e. a total of 690 troops). The latter level should provide the lower echelons with air defence by means of *Fliegerfäuste*, anti-tank missiles on elevatable platforms, mine-laying vehicles and mortars with ranges of 10 kms. Above battalion level, no further force components, but merely sanitation and C³I service functions, would be added.

Altogether, the standing element of the containment force would comprise about 1,664 modules with a total of 80,000 troops. It should, however, be supported by the cadred element of the containment force, deployed behind the present units in a 48 kms.-wide zone. It would consist of 5,000 modules with a total of approximately 224,000 men, out of which only 50,000 should be enlisted men (volunteers or conscripts). They would be mobilizable within no more than 18 hours, thanks to their regional organization. Their organization and form of combat would be the same as for the present forces. On the other hand, their equipment should generally be less up-to-date, and each module would be expected to defend only half the area defended by an analogous present module.

The logistics for the stationary modules would be almost non-existent: when a module had run out of ammunition, it should simply be allowed to fall back or be evacuated. However, small numbers of light infantry weapons (of older vintage) should be stored in dispersed depots within the containment web for replenishment[156].

II. The Rapid Commitment Force (also called the 'fire brigade') was envisaged as the mobile element of the defence posture, intended i.a. for reinforcement of exposed stationary units. It was to be deployed in the same areas as covered by the containment force, and would consist of three different types of forces:

II.1. *Jäger* Battalions, each consisting of three infantry companies mounted on APCs, one tank company with a total of ten light tank destroyers, and a mortar company, as well as various support elements, i.a. for air defence and communication. The total strength would be 775 men. These battalions were intended for combat in covered terrain, and were supposed to fight dismounted on most occasions.

II.2. Cavalry Regiments, each consisting of two companies with ten tank destroyers each, two companies with ten IFV, and one mortar company, as well as support elements, e.g. for communication and air defence: a total of 640 men. They were intended to serve as an avant garde collaborating with the heavier units. Their high mobility should make them suitable for the task of serving as connection links between, and crisis support for, stationary modules. In addition, they might also take part in the evacuation of these troops.

II.3. Shock Units each consisting of three battle tank companies with a total of 30 tanks and one mechanised infantry company with 11 IFVs, a mortar company and support units: a total of 550 men. These were the heaviest units, capable of fighting in open terrain and of mobility under enemy artillery fire. They should be capable of reconquering lost terrain, e.g. by launching flanking attacks on the approaching enemy.

Whereas the brigade level would be eliminated, certain support elements for both the containment force and the rapid commitment force were to be found at the divisional level: an ABC (Atomic, Biological, Chemical) protection unit, C³I elements such as e.g. RPVs (Remotely Piloted Vehicles), helicopters and scout vehicles, 14 anti-tank helicopters, 18 mobile SAMs, 24 light multiple rocket lauchers (with ranges up to 25 kms.), in addition to a variety of engineer troops i.a. for bridge-laying.

The corps level should comprise five divisions plus support elements, such as a heavy combat helicopter unit (28 helicopters), an air defence unit (18 systems), an MLRS unit (24 systems with ranges up to 40 kms.), and a reserve of cavalry regiments.

The total man-power requirements for the 'rapid commitment force' would be only 76,000 men. These should be almost completely standing forces, and consist of around half professionals and half conscripts. They would be assigned to a total of 36 heavy shock units, 17 *Jäger* batallions and 17 cavalry regiments. Of these, the cavalry should be deployed furthest forward, the others more to the rear, albeit still within the fighting area of the stationary network. The logistics for the 'fire brigade' would consist of numerous small depots distributed in an almost random pattern across the defended terrain[157]. In this way, a considerable independence could be achieved for the mobile elements, by relieving them of the need for a cumbersome logistical 'tail'.

Even more important, by virtue of this arrangement, strategic mobility would be effectively ruled out, and the non-offensive character of the defence posture thus ensured. Mobility would, furthermore, be hampered beyond the confines of the web, because most of the communication facilities would consist of stationary, robust and EMP (Electro-Magnetic Pulse)-proof fibre-optical networks[158]. Beyond the web, the mobile units would thus not merely be deprived of support, but also effectively blind.

III. The Rear Protection Force might be likened to a home guard. It should be divided into two elements: a stationary element, intended for protection of key objects, and a mobile element intended for supplementary territorial defence, e.g. against air landings. Both would consist of infantry troops, albeit of an inferior quality as compared with the 'containment force'. Their equipment would consist of older weapons and ninety percent of the personnel should be reserves. Upon mobilization the total force would comprise 120,000 troops, four fifths of whom would be assigned to object protection.

The land force concept has since then been modified somewhat, e.g. by the addition of a 14 kms.-deep 'fire zone', reminiscent of Hannig's fire barrier. It would be 'located' in the very forward line, i.e. in front of the web, and physically consist of mines and sensor arrays. This fire zone would emphasise mine-fields (e.g. scatterable minelets) which should be combined with natural barriers such as canals, rivers, forests etc.[159].

The equipment and tactics of the ground forces was outlined in great detail. A more recent study has dealt with a 'standard battalion of line infantry', and thus not directly with the SAS concept[160]. Nevertheless, the new features were eventually incorporated in the SAS model. In addition to the ones already recorded, Unterseher e.g. mentioned the following weapons systems as particularly relevant:

—Heavy (115-155 mm.) recoilless rifles with ranges up to 500 metres.
—Remotely-controlled recoilless rifles with laser range finders and 'HEAT' warheads.
—Second-rate recoilless rifles with triggering devices to be used as 'directional mines'.
—Mortars.
—Mines, including so-called 'stochastic mines'.
—Fibre-optically guided combat drones (with ranges up to ten kms.), capable of hitting tanks from above, where their armour is relatively thin.

In the recent book published by the SAS, Unterseher provided the 'final' version of the SAS land forces, wherein the role of the containment forces was further clarified. Due to their relative 'lightness' they were not supposed to engage the armoured forces of the invader directly, but rather to 'divide and channel' these forces, whereas the heavier 'spider forces' were to be assigned to the role of delivering the final blow of annihilation. In addition, the containment web was supposed to decimate any intruding airborne units or reconnaissance teams as well as clear the way for the friendly 'spider' forces. Furthermore, they were to support the latter in terms of logistics and surveillance. In this way, the containment web would serve not merely as a 'space multiplier' but also as a 'time multiplier', and thus as a true 'force multiplier'[161].

As far as the weapons mix was concerned, the SAS further de-emphasised those fairly long-range indirect fire systems, that have been preferred by most alternative models, in favour of distinctly short-range systems. The group had likewise abandoned its own previous illusions about the bright future of third generation 'fire and forget' ATGMs, and of the persistent minefields. As far as the latter were concerned, their being indiscriminate would raise problems in terms of the laws of war (which would have to be scrupulously respected); or they would be too easily cleared by the invader. On the other hand, it was acknowledged that the tube artillery (so resented by most NOD advocates on the grounds of its representing lucrative targets) would have important roles, i.a. for the delivery of cheap 'dumb' munitions[162]. By thus modifying its concept, the group frankly admitted to being engaged in a continuous learning process, rather than having found the ultimate panacea with validity for an indefinite future.

In general, the trend in the model's development could be seen as moving away from relatively few, highly sophisticated, but fairly expensive systems towards a greater number of simpler, yet more robust and affordable, weapons. What mattered most for the efficiency of the defence scheme would not be particular magnificent technologies, but rather a set of appropriate tactical principles which would allow the defender to capitalise on the synergies of a diversified defence system.

A distinguishing feature of the SAS model has been its inclusion of fairly concrete and detailed proposals for the aerial and maritime environments. As far as the tactical air forces were concerned, the SAS identified, as its point of departure, a clear Western superiority. Whereas the WTO had a very marginal numerical preponderance (1.04:1), NATO was qualitatively far ahead. This overall disparity in the West's favour was further compounded by an offensive bias, reflected i.a. in the high ratio of offensive-capable fighter-bombers to predominantly defensive fighters (1.7:1), whereas the ratio was inversed in the East (1:1.76). A predeliction for the offensive on the part of the West might also be identified in the realm of doctrine, where OCA (Offensice Counter Air) played an important role. This, in its turn, boded ill for crisis stability[163].

In order to avert such an inadvertent war reminiscent (in terms of operations) of the June War in the Middle East[164], both unilateral conversion and arms control endeavours would be called for. In both cases, the guideline should be to build down offensive capabilities as well as to remove lucrative targets, so as to simultaneously minimise incentives for, and options of, pre-emption.

A further problem with present air force postures were the sky-rocketing procurement costs, which had been experienced already with the 'Tornado' project in the 1970s. The *Bundeswehr*'s participation in the joint European EFA (European Fighter Aircraft) project therefore appeared ill-advised: not only would the resultant aircraft be too offensive-capable, but the cost overruns were also likely to be so substantial that the total number of planes would be too small to overcome the pending fighter shortage[165].

When outlining their alternative to the present aerial postures, the SAS maintained a rather low level of ambition, deliberately ruling out a number of the most 'sexy' aerial missions. The defender should resist the temptation of deep interdiction missions, as well as of OCA, both because of the destabilizing effects thereof, and because of their low cost-effectiveness. Air defence was to be acknowledged as the central task, even though CAS above the defender's own territory would remain a legitimate objective. The latter should therefore be maintained in the panoply of missions, if only a cost-effective method could be devised that would also solve the runway vulnerability problem[166].

As far as the air defence mission was concerned, the SAS scheme envisaged it as a joint task for the ground-based air defence and the residual number of fighter-interceptors, which might e.g. result from a conversion of the 'Tornado' fleet. The main burden of air defence would, however, fall on the mobile SAMs which had the advantage of not being dependent on airfields and thus of conforming to the 'no targets' criterion. For target acquisition, the SAMs should be able to rely on redundant, but partly mobile, sensor networks. Whereas the SAS did, on the one hand, envisage modernizing the present combined IHAWK/Patriot belt so as to keep it up-to-date, on the other hand they warned against providing the latter with an ATM (Anti-Tactical Missiles) capability (such as envisioned by the USA), lest this be seen as the first step in the creation of the 'European Defence Initiative', supplementing the SDI[167].

The CAS mission might best be performed by VTOL (Vertical Take-off Landing) aircraft such as the British Harrier, by virtue of being able to utilise a number of small-scale airstrips, such aircraft would (in conformity with the SAS philosophy) represent a great number of individually rather unimportant targets, rather than a small number of lucrative targets[168].

As far as the arms control path to enhanced aerial stability was concerned, the SAS proposed, as a preliminary, to include aircraft in the CFE talks, by then in progress, but not yet dealing with aircraft. However, due to the intrinsic strategic mobility of even tactical aircraft, regional reductions would not make much sense in isolation, hence the need for an area of application exceeding even the ATTU format.

The overall offensive air forces of both alliances ought to be reduced, by the year 1995, to 1,000 aircraft each. Paradoxically, although this would imply asymmetrical Western cuts (due to the initial Western preponderance in this category of aircraft), the West would nevertheless end up with a superiority (due to qualitative factors), which the East would be obliged to accept. As a *quid pro quo*, the East should be allowed to 'balance' the Western lead with a surplus of air defence forces. As a result of such an arms control process, a total of around 5,000 aircraft would have been taken out of service, and the residual air forces would have been converted to more defensive structures[169].

As far as the naval (or, better, maritime) component of the SAS model was concerned, Hartmut Bebermeyer and Unterseher took as their point of departure a critical analysis of current trends. First of all, offensive high sea ambitions ('the lure of the blue waters') seemed to be re-surfacing within the German Navy. Similar ambitions during the imperial era, associated with the name of Admiral Tirpitz[170], had reflected 'a chauvinist policy in sharp contradiction with all political, geographical and military realities, which had ended in the First World War'. A replay of this chain of events had to be prevented.

Secondly, the new (Forward) Maritime Strategy of the US Navy was criticised for being excessively offensive and oriented towards war-winning[171].

These two negative trends were, on the other hand, not entirely mutually supportive, since the Maritime Strategy would provide the allied navies with merely marginal roles. Still, according to current planning guidelines, the German navy would be assigned to the role of securing access for NATO naval forces into the Baltic Sea (rather than of preventing the Soviet Baltic Fleet from exiting). In this way it would contribute to NATO's offensive threat against the USSR. The Soviet Navy, which was regarded as, on balance, defensively oriented, would thus have as its main task to prevent NATO intrusions into the Baltic Sea[172].

The SAS alternative to these trends in naval strategy was to limit the missions of the German Navy to those of defending the Baltic Sea (in collaboration with the Danish navy), as well as the southern parts of the North Sea: hence '*Hochsee Adee!*' ('Farewell, Blue Waters!'). With such limited ambitions, German naval planners should come to realise that destroyers and frigates as well as major submarines were henceforth superfluous, since their tasks in the North Sea might be performed by corvettes and mine warfare ships.

The prime task would be the defence of the Baltic Approaches. The main threat to this area, however, was assessed as consisting in Soviet air landings and amphibious assaults against Jutland, against which threat offensive naval forces would obviously be of no avail. Rather, the need was for emphasizing land defence. The naval element of the defence was hence in the original version envisaged as consisting entirely of 'an evidently defensively oriented coastal defence with ships, combat helicopters and good blocking equipment'. To these elements, the 1989 version of the proposal added land-based anti-ship missiles, inspired perhaps by the Danish debate on naval defence[173].

As a result of these analyses, the two authors made a number of concrete proposals for the Federal Navy's development in the years to come[174]:

—The present 110 'Tornado' aircraft with anti-ship missiles should be maintained until the beginning of the 1990s. However, they should henceforth be employed as a 'coastal fire-brigade' operating along the coast, rather than as means for striking from the coast deep into enemy waters and territory. In order to limit their vulnerability, rear operating bases would have to be established. In due course, they would be modified to air defence missions, and after serving their time no replacement appeared warranted.

—The present nineteen anti-submarine and patrol aircraft should be maintained, yet gradually replaced with a new maritime patrol aircraft. The current number of combat helicopters should be increased from 22 to 40, if possible by a redeployment of the 'Sea Lynx' from the frigates to shore.

—The destroyers and frigates should be retained until obsolescence, but be employed merely for sea control purposes in the southern North Sea, for which mission they were advised to cooperate closely with the Dutch Navy. They should only be very moderately modernised and not replaced after their end of service.

—Six corvettes should be built with envisaged IOC (Initial Operational Capability) for the latter half of the 1990s, and be assigned to the mission of controlling the southern North Sea and the Skagerak, as well as of providing escorts for individual ships and convoys approaching the North Sea harbours.

—The submarines should continue to serve in the Baltic Sea until their withdrawal from service.

—The present fleet of forty fast patrol craft should be maintained, and later be replaced with (Danish-designed) 'Stanflex' boats.

—The 50-60 mine warfare vessels should be maintained and modernised, and the overall mine-laying capacity further expanded with guided mines and torpedo batteries, integrated in a multi-sensor web.

—The landing craft should be employed for the reinforcement of exposed points ashore, but be reduced considerably.

—On-board air defence should be improved, e.g. by means of a 'navalization' of the army's *Fliegerfäuste* (short-range, man-portable air defence missiles).

—Anti-ship missiles should be procured (or developed) with ranges of 20-25 and 50-70 kms., respectively. They should be deployed on helicopters, patrol craft and corvettes, as well as on mobile coastal defence batteries ashore.

—An 'old-fashioned' coastal artillery (employing remotely-activated automatic guns) should be deployed at particularly exposed coastal stretches.

With this plan, the SAS delivered the first concrete proposal for a defensive maritime defence of the FRG. Unfortunately, however, the German SAS authors did not deal in any detail with 'blue-water' naval missions, including that of SLOC (Sea Lines of Communication) protection, a task which the present author has, however, taken upon himself on several occasions, to some extent on behalf of the SAS[175].

One presumed advantage of the SAS model is that it would be realistic, i.a. by virtue of its being entirely NATO-compatible. It was thus envisaged that allied forces would be assigned a role in the defence of the FRG, even among its most forward elements. Indeed, a maintenance of the present 'layer-cake' structure along the Central Front was recommended, i.a. as a way of minimizing offensive capabilities on the part of individual states.

Nevertheless, a certain role specialization was recommended: Allied troops should gradually assume greater responsibility for air defence and naval matters pertaining to Central Europe, whereas the indigenous forces should mainly be responsible for land defence. However, as a longer-term perspective, a certain American disengagement from Europe was envisioned, which would leave the USA primarily with the role of nuclear deterrence of nuclear threats[176].

In a collaborative effort with American researchers (Charles Knight and Carl Conetta), concrete suggestions for a restructuring of the US Seventh Army in the FRG have been made. According to these proposals, part of the US troops might be withdrawn from Europe, i.a. because their tasks would henceforth be performed by the 'containment web'. Some of the remaining US divisions should, however, serve as 'rapid commitment' forces, i.e. 'spiders'[177].

The SAS model would presumably lend itself to a piecemeal implementation. According to Unterseher it would not, however, make any sense to let the successive steps be made conditional on the other side's reciprocation, as envisaged in the gradualist approach. The realization of the concept should therefore not be embedded in any arms control framework, be it explicit and oriented towards negotiations, or more informal. It would have to be predominantly a unilateral endeavour on the part of the countries involved. On the other hand, great care should be taken to 'send the right signals', i.a. because phasing in defensive elements simultaneously with phasing out offensive ones might be perceived by the other side as just another arms build-up. An intensified dialogue on 'NOD topics' with the 'enemy' was therefore recommended[178].

The SAS did try to keep pace with events in the years 1989-90. Lutz Unterseher thus (in a lecture to East German officers, 5 July 1990) outlined how the future military posture of the present GDR might be configured within a modified 'Genscher Plan' framework. The length of military service should be shortened to twelve months, and the total size of the NVA (*Nationale Volksarmee*) thus amount to 75,000 troops. These might be divided into five 'territorial commands' with 'web character' and assigned to each of the five *Länder* governments. These five commands would be equivalent to a total of 25 regiments, the major part of which should be twenty infantry regiments with strong pioneer and anti-tank components as well as with some artillery.

In addition to these, there should be a minimum of 'spider forces', namely four tank regiments with main battle tanks (T-72s) and other armoured vehicles, as well as one helicopter regiment. In conformity with the SAS philosophy, the 'spiders' should be manned to ninety percent (because their mobilization might be ambiguous), whereas the 'web' should be cadred down to 45 percent (because they might be brought up to full combat readiness without undesirable repercussions). In addition to these land forces, the posture should include a (somewhat reduced) surface-to-air component as well as a total of two fighter wings, based on the present 'MIG-23s' and 'MIG-29s'. The command of Mecklenburg (the only *Land* with a coastline) should, in addition to the above elements, have at its disposal the present mine warfare units (only slightly reduced) as well as a few minor surface combatants.

Thanks to the great opportunities it would provide for an alliance-wide division of labour, the SAS model would also seem suitable for the united Germany within NATO, under which conditions the remaining allied forces in Germany could well be, say, aerial forces or (small-scale) 'spiders'. Finally, the very small overall size of the SAS posture would seem highly compatible with the future total size of the all-German ground forces, i.e. could easily be made compatible with the agreed-upon 370,000 man limit.

In the most recent version of the SAS model[179], it was thus envisaged shrinking the overall strength considerably. The total strength of the *Bundeswehr* might immediately be reduced to 350,000, and that of the allied forces in West Germany to 150,000. Within the next eight to ten years, the armed forces of the united Germany might be brought down to 250,000 troops along with a reduction of the allied element to 100,000. If these figures appear rather conservative compared with, say, the figure of 105,000 suggested by Dieter Lutz (cf. below), the reason is that the SAS did acknowledge the need for, first of all, maintaining an effective defence capability, and secondly, of ensuring an ordered process of disarmament, in the course of which due account should be taken of the problems of re-employment of military personnel and the like.

Some members of the SAS (i.a. Brauch, Chalmers and the present author) have also, in the light of the new circumstances of 1989-1990, begun to analyse the opportunities for creating genuine collective security structures to include NOD. I shall return to these analyses in Chapter XI below.

The 'Missing Link' Approach

Combat under modern conditions is a complicated affair, and offensive operations are in many respects even more complicated than defensive ones. They require the coordination of many types of forces, only the combination of which might thus merit the label 'offensive', regardless of any inclusion of defensive elements. This very complexity has provided the point of departure for a particular variety of NOD which might be called the 'missing link approach', since it attempts effectively to deprive force postures of their offensive potentials by means of the smallest possible alterations, *in casu* by removing one central component.

Whereas this approach has exerted some attraction on i.a. American arms control thinkers, only one author in the FRG has consistently pursued this path: Erwin Müller of the Institute of Peace Research and Security Policy at the University of Hamburg (IFSH).

Müller had for some time been studying i.a. CBMs, in the course of which research he had concluded that NOD would be a viable approach to confidence-building, indeed the CBM *par exellence*[180]. In 1984 he, furthermore, put forward a set of proposals which might be considered a model. Its point of departure was the recognition that the parties to a conflict had neither reliable knowledge about their respective opponents' intentions, nor any way of proving that their own intentions were strictly defensive except by transforming their capabilities to make them unsuitable for offensive utilization.

This requirement for unambiguously defensive military means had different implications for the conventional and nuclear spheres. In the nuclear realm, the defensive criterion called for a strict 'deterrence by punishment' strategy, in its turn requiring an arsenal that was 'first-strike resistant, yet first-strike incapable', for which combination he coined the term 'defensive in the second grade'. Even though its main purpose would be to deter nuclear attack, the very possession of it would inevitably exert a certain deterrent effect on the conventional level as well. A *prima facie* conventional conflict would thus take place in the 'shadow' of nuclear weapons and not be truly conventional in the classic sense[181].

In the conventional sphere, the armed forces would have to be restructured as a 'defensive potential of the first grade', capable only of 'deterrence by denial', and incapable of offensive operations. A defence potential of this sort would presumably have a considerable dissuasive effect, since it would not merely deter, but 'de-motivate' any Soviet attack[182].

As far as the actual design of such a defensive posture was concerned, Müller rejected 'easy' solutions and e.g. pointed out that 'offensive capability' was a relative concept, which only made sense when 'measured' with the yardstick of the opponent's capabilities. In this sense, the conventional defences would also be 'of the second grade', albeit having a different connotation from when applied to nuclear forces[183].

He also differed from most NOD proponents in his greater confidence in the rationality of the present structure, of which he would prefer to maintain as much as possible, though without its offensive capabilities. He did i.a. consider some mobility to be imperative for concentration purposes, since the only alternative would be weapons systems with undesirably long ranges. Furthermore, he recommended maintaining the principle of forward defence with a view to protecting the inhabitants of the FRG from the horrors of a war in their midst. Finally, he regarded a certain deep interdiction capability as indispensible e.g. for the destruction of bridges and airfields in Eastern Europe[184].

These offensive elements notwithstanding, a strictly non-offensive defence would presumably be achievable by simply renouncing at least one of the following components, which were necessary for strategic offensives, thus deliberately creating a 'missing link':

1. Air defence capability beyond one's own airspace.

2. Anti-tank capability on enemy soil, which would be absent if anti-tank weapons were to be located in stationary positions on one's own territory.

3. River-crossing capability. Regardless of the availability of amphibious vehicles etc., this would require bridge-building equipment: without this, logistical problems would pile up and combat support would be unobtainable during an intrusion into enemy territory.

From this vantage point, Müller was able to sketch seven possible defensive postures, each of which lacked some combination of the above offensive components. As the most effective alternative, he pointed to a posture maintaining both 1 and 2, and merely lacking 3.

An obvious problem with this proposal was, of course, that the missing component might be pre-stocked elsewhere, *in casu* in the USA, only to be deployed to Europe in an emergency. As a way of maintaining defensive credibility in the face of this potentiality, Müller suggested giving the WTO a right to on-site inspection[185].

With regard to the specific weapons systems, he was likewise more in line with military tradition than most other alternative defence proponents. He thus suggested arming the defence forces with quite long-range missiles (e.g. Patriot and Lance derivatives), cruise missiles and MLRS systems armed with highly lethal 'Skeet' submunitions. Even though the envisaged arsenal would thus contain both dual-capable and deep-strike systems, this presence of *per se* offensive-capable weapons would allegedly not constitute a genuine problem in the absence of any capability of ground force offensives, whence the recommendation to abstain from the fielding of MBTs and aircraft. In these respects, he came quite close to the scheme of Hannig described above[186].

Müller contributed further to NOD theory with an analysis of 'conventional stability', a concept which has become prominent in the NOD discourse, as well as across the entire political spectrum, under the influence of the CFE. In line with the above analysis, he rejected the prevalent definition of offensiveness that referred to the very capability of undertaking offensive operations, and advocated a narrower identification of offensiveness with the ability to prevail under such conditions. Only a state which could win a war of aggression would thus be truly offensive[187].

A stable situation would be one in which neither side had this ability, and should preferably be brought about through a shared weakness in the offensive, rather than by any strengthening of defensive capabilities. Nevertheless, the resultant 'structural non-attack capability' (StruNA) would be a relative term, denoting a ratio between one party's weakness in the offensive and the respective adversary's strength in the defensive. To bring about true stability would therefore presuppose that the military power of either side could be amplified substantially when applied on its respective own territory, as compared with its strength when used on the opponent's territory.

In practical terms, however, a state attempting unilaterally to create such a situation would inevitably end up in an optimization dilemma, having to choose between emphasizing defensive strength, or the incapability of attack. Müller saw the only escape from this dilemma in a mutual and coordinated implementation, either in the form of a withdrawal of offensive-capable weapons systems, or by way of the above 'missing link approach'. However, when trying to translate the latter notion into operational terms, one would encounter logical problems: an abstention from anti-tank or air-defence capability on foreign territory would be nonsensical, e.g. if the other party possessed neither tanks nor aircraft.

As an alternative, Müller pointed to 'asymmetrical missing links': One party might e.g. abstain from anti-tank capability, whilst maintaining his aircraft, while the other might eliminate his mobile air defence capability, whilst maintaining his tanks, etc. As the ideal model, he pointed to a bilateral agreement on a 'dual missing link': no long-range weapons systems, and no cover (i.e. armour) on foreign territory. On friendly territory, however, the defenders should be able to capitalise on heavy (but stationary) weapons systems, cover etc.[188].

The Common Security Approach

The survey of Erwin Müller's contribution to the NOD debate takes us immediately to his host institute, the Institute for Peace Research and Security Policy at the University of Hamburg (IFSH). Besides the work of Müller, the IFSH's main contribution to the NOD theoretical endeavour has been the analysis of Common Security (CS), to the 'basics' of which I refer to Chapter 1 above.

Since the theory of CS is relatively new and has hitherto enjoyed little theoretical, as opposed to political, attention[189], by no means all the potential ramifications of the concept have been worked out. The endeavour to fill this gap has for several years constituted the major part of the research at the ISFH, under the guidance of its director, Egon Bahr of the SPD.

In this connection, the IFSH team has also investigated the inter-relationship between CS and NOD, which most NOD proponents have taken for granted, but few have actually analyzed in any depth[190]. The outcome of this research has been analyses of the relationship between various alternative security concepts, including NOD, and CS. Furthermore, the institute has taken upon itself the task of bringing together the 'NOD community' at a series of hearings, with a view to facilitating a comparison of their recommendations[191].

The survey of Egon Bahr's outstanding contributions to CS and NOD theory is covered in the chapters on the SPD below, but noteworthy research in the same fields has also been carried out by Bahr's deputy, Dieter S. Lutz and his collaborators. Through their industrious and systematic efforts, they have established the IFSH as a centre of CS research in the FRG, although their contribution to NOD theory in a narrower sense has been somewhat less significant (with the exception of aformentioned Erwin Müller).

Lutz has been a very prolific writer, but has only recently taken up the issue of NOD after having for a number of years focused on the broader political aspects of security as well as on the flaws in deterrence logic[192], etc.

The latter analysis led him to recommend CBMs as means to enhance crisis stability, particularly CBMs of the 'restrictive' kind, i.e. what are often referred to as CSBMs.

As relevant CSBMs, he pointed i.a. to the establishment of buffer zones, a withdrawal of logistics and armaments so as to create 'infrastructural barriers', as well as a renunciation of the development and deployment of such weapons technologies as would tend to accelerate a conflict by providing only short warning. Of even greater relevance from our current point of view, he recommended 'agreements on doctrines, including the assimilation of military behaviour, and the development of defensive strategies'[193].

CSBMs of whatever variety would, however, only marginally modify the military postures at the root of the problems facing Europe, whence the need for more far-reaching alternatives. As candidates for this role, Lutz analyzed a wide range of security political conceptions, before focusing specifically on defence structures. These conceptions included neutrality, a 'European Peace Order', a 'System of Collective Security', and CS.

As will hopefully have become apparent by now, neutrality has always had a certain attraction for the Germans. It, therefore, made sense for Lutz to subject the concept to a closer analytical scrutiny. On the one hand, he found significant evidence of neutrality's positive effects, both theoretically and in the actual practices of the European neutrals which might serve as models for emulation. These countries tended to be, and be perceived as, non-threatening, partly by virtue of their benign strategies of dissuasion, by means of which they merely sought to exact a high entrance and staying price from any would-be aggressor, rather than to wield any threats of retribution. The territorial defence postures of the European neutrals and non-aligned countries (Sweden, Finland, Switzerland, Austria and Yugoslavia) were strictly defensive and could not possibly be construed as threats to any other state, but might be regarded as confidence-building structures.

On the other hand, Lutz was unwilling to acknowledge such defence postures as prerogatives of neutrals, but found that they might lend themselves to implementation also by alliance members, such as the FRG. The case for neutrality was hence found to be inconclusive[194].

Another concept which has always appeared attractive to Germans (and not least to Social Democrats) has been that of a 'European Peace Order', perhaps because of its resemblance to the notion of a 'settlement'. Attempting to bring some clarity to this hitherto (perhaps deliberately) somewhat blurred notion, Lutz expanded its scope considerably. In his conception, a 'New European Peace Order' (NEPO) would imply internal democratization, the creation of a Collective Security System (SCS), the weaving of a web of interdependencies and mutual obligations across Europe and a global accomodation of interests between North and South. I shall return to these visions in Chapter XI below[195].

For the last couple of years, Lutz has focused more specifically on the CS approach, whereas the more abstract theorizing on the concept itself has been the task of other members of the IFSH research staff, particularly Reinhard Mutz. Lutz, for his part, surveyed its history and political status in great detail as well as analysed its security political implications at considerable length[196]. Whereas, according to him, CS was in principle incompatible with military alliances such as NATO and the WTO, both of these presumably differed from previous alliances by virtue of their pro-claimed defensive goals, so that a certain continuity might be counted on when approaching CS[197].

One of the most disputed issues in the CS literature has been the relationship between deterrence and CS. 'Minimalist' CS proponents (in-cluding the present author) have regarded CS as a reflection of the shared vulnerability resulting from mutual deterrence, and therefore found an 'abolition of deterrence' to be both impossible to achieve and undesirable (whilst acknowledging the need for mitigating the malign side-effects of deterrence strategies)[198]. 'Maximalists' amongst CS advocates, including Lutz and the rest of the IFSH staff, have, on the other hand, declared CS incompatible with the 'deterrence system', because of the latter's ominous implications in terms of nuclear retaliation against populations. They have found the only legitimate form of dissuasion to be that deriving from the ability to exact a high admission and staying price from any aggressor, whilst posing no threat to him, i.e. a 'structural inability to launch an attack' (StruNA, i.e. NOD)[199].

Embarking from this vantage point on the analysis of NOD, Lutz expressed dissatisfaction with the previous usage of the term, proposing a distinction between a wider and a narrower sense of StruNA: whereas StruNA/NOD narrowly conceived would refer to changes in the structure and armaments of military forces, the wider sense would signify a society's inability to carry out aggression. Thus conceived changes in the internal structure of society (restraining the military industrial complex, building down enemy images, promoting research on disarmament and conversion options, etc.) would presumably constitute contributions to StruNA in this wider sense[200].

Although he thus urged against narrowing the focus down to mili-tary issues, Lutz did not disregard these entirely, although he did not elaborate on the military 'details' of StruNA. As far as the implementation of the shift to StruNA was concerned, he acknowledged that traditional arms control might play a certain role, albeit only as means to the more general end of CS. For this auxiliary role arms control ought to focus on measures such as nuclear-weapons-free zones, limitations of particularly threatening conventional weapons systems, range limitations for aircraft and missiles, moratoria on research and development, and the like[201].

Lutz managed to integrate a number of the security political conceptions mentioned above in his grandiose design of CS-cum-NOD. Neutrality might constitute an element therein, gradualism a method of implementing it, collective security a step towards it, etc. This 'conceptual integration' has in fact been the main analytical accomplishment of the IFSH's research, in addition to which the Institute staff has attempted to 'map out' the implications of CS for the issue-areas of various disciplines, such as psychology, economics, international law, etc.[202]. In the course of these exploratory studies, additional theoretical paths towards NOD have emerged:

The legal implications of CS proved to be yet another reason for a conversion to StruNA (i.e. NOD). Already, the FRG's constitution contained a number of paragraphs which e.g. prohibited FRG from waging wars of aggression as well as doing anything intended to, or merely likely to, disturb peaceful co-existence. Considerable scope for diverging interpretations of the text, however, remained, in respect of which Lutz (a lawyer by training) advocated a more restrictive interpretation than hitherto adhered to by the shifting governments of the FRG.

He argued i.a. that it was incompatible with the constitution to prepare for 'disproportionate' nuclear retaliation, such as entailed in 'flexible response'. Nor would it, according to this reading, be permissible to plan for absorbing nuclear strikes on German soil, regardless of whether these were launched by enemies or allies, both of which were in actual fact targeting the FRG with their short-range and battlefield nuclear weapons. Whereas the present structure was thus allegedly revealed as unconstitutional, StruNA would be perfectly compatible with even the most restrictive interpretation[203].

As mentioned above, Lutz consistently advocated NOD or StruNA as the military component of the CS strategy, but not before 1987 did he venture into any more thorough analysis of the concept. When finally doing so, his first theoretical contribution was yet another term for the same concept. The implications of such terminological modifications are extremely difficult to convey satisfactorily in English, but at the very least the patient reader may grasp the specific German 'flavour' of the argument.

First of all, Lutz proposed to improve on the language by replacing the linguistic nonsense (invented by Albrecht von Müller) '*Strukturelle Nichtangriffsfähigkeit*' ('Structural Non-Attack Capability') with '*Strukturelle Angriffsunfähigkeit*' ('Structural Inability to Attack'). Secondly, he suggested a refinement of acronyms, substituting his own (rather perplexing) 'StrUnA' for the previous 'StruNA' (notice the change in capital letters), and to employ the English acronym 'SIA'. Thirdly, he recapitulated his distinction, mentioned above, between the narrow and the wide sense of 'StrUnA' or 'SIA', thus ending up with the rather cumbersome acronym '*StrUnA (i.e.S.)*' for the narrow version, i.e. for what we have called 'NOD'[204].

Lutz thus saw NOD as the military strategy corresponding to Common Security, which, in its turn, was seen as a theory on how to realise 'Common Peace', attainable by way of the new peace order, in which the collective security would form an element. NOD's role was thus primarily to constitute the conventional military component of a broader war prevention strategy. This, in its turn, should represent an alternative to deterrence, by providing a form of 'inoffensive deterrence' or better, 'defensive dissuasion' (*'defensive Abhaltung'*)[205].

As far as the more operational aspects of NOD were concerned, Lutz rejected the permissive definitions of offensiveness, which have narrowed it down to invasion capabilities (Hannig, Erwin Müller et al.). Rather, he maintained the demand for a complete 'prohibition of cross-border capabilities for launching an attack', implying e.g. an unconditional abstention from aerial or missile strikes against enemy territory. He thus ended up with a quite restrictive definition of NOD, which would prohibit capabilities for both occupation and invasion, for any offensives and counter-offensives, for (complete and partial) disarming strikes, as well as for retaliation.

Even under these 'anti-efficiency criteria', the relevant aim for StrUnA would have to be 'defensive superiority', rather than parity, dismissed as, at best, fictitious, ephemeral and irrelevant. If both parties were to become superior in the defensive roles, to their respective opponent assuming an offensive stance, then a considerable degree of conventional stability would presumably be accomplished, both in the sense of arms race stability, crisis stability and 'escalation stability'. Strategically, StrUnA should strive to make aggression appear not worthwhile by virtue of its ability to exact a prohibitive admission and staying price. Should dissuasion nevertheless fail, the defence should emphasise damage limitation and the preservation of the values to be protected[206].

This damage limitation, however, would primarily be attainable through mutual 'transarmament' (i.e. a conversion from offensive to defensive capabilities), requiring the adversary to likewise destroy his weapons of mass destruction. This objective of mutuality notwithstanding, StrUnA might presumably be unilaterally implementable as well. In order for, say, a German conversion not to remain an isolated step, a gradualist strategy would presumably recommend itself, envisaging a series of small, unilateral steps being reciprocated by the adversary, etc.

That such reciprocation might be a realistic prospect was confirmed by other studies from the IFSH. These pointed to a growing diversity in military as well as political matters within the WTO, and hence to rather favourable prospects of achieving reciprocation, both on the part of the USSR and of the smaller WTO states, most interestingly the GDR[207].

In the years 1989-90 Lutz resurfaced his previous proposals for collective security, as usual in a number of almost identical articles. I shall relegate the account thereof to the concluding chapter, and limit myself to mentioning the concrete implications which the new situation, according to Lutz, had for concrete defence requirements.

Whereas he envisioned supranational to supplant national armed forces, Lutz foresaw a mixture of the two during the transition period. For this mix to be acceptable, however, the national armed forces would have to be deprived of all their offensive potential. The need would presumably be for a grand total of around 700,000 troops for all of Europe, a number which would warrant the fielding of no more than 105,000 German troops. These would have to be unmistakably defensive and, in particular, configured and of a size so as to be clearly inferior to Poland's armed forces (sic.)[208].

The 'magic number' of 105,000 troops was (perhaps by coincidence) only 5,000 in excess of the so much resented maximum imposed on Germany by the victorious Entente in the framework of the Versailles Treaty[209]. Despite this unfortunate resemblance, the number recurred in a proposal published by the IFSH in April 1990 for a *European Security Concept*. It envisaged a build-down of the armed forces of the united Germany to the said 105,000 soldiers, structured strictly for defensive purposes, in the context of a Europe where the level of armed forces should be built down from the present 2.5 million to half a million troops, supplemented by an embryo of multilateral forces, amounting to a sort of 'European police force'[210].

In addition to thus devoting itself to the conceptual clarification of NOD and to security political grand designs, the IFSH has given some attention to the more humble job of investigating the implications of CS and NOD for naval forces and strategies. The one volume hitherto published contained, first of all, fairly elaborate and highly critical analyses of the naval strategies of the two superpowers, criticizing above all the US 'Maritime Strategy'. Secondly, it included an analysis of NATO's reliance upon the sea for reinforcements etc., which left no doubts about the necessity of somehow elaborating naval strategic conceptions that were compatible with the aims of common security and StruNA[211]. The latter task was effectively left to Erwin Müller and Andreas Pott, respectively.

Müller analyzed the previous experience with naval arms control, in the course of which he found the Washington naval treaty of 1922 confirmed the assumption that 'cooperative arms control' was, indeed, possible[212]. Pott dealt more specifically with this option of cooperative naval arms control, which could, hopefully, avoid the pitfalls of previous negotiations: those of ignoring the underlying political conflicts, of focusing on numbers rather than qualitative factors, etc. According to Pott, in order to stand a better chance of success, the aim should be more stable, i.e. more defensive, naval postures. States ought thus to renounce wide-range mobility and concentrate on the defence of their own shores, for which purpose small vessels would presumably suffice[213].

However, he had previously acknowledged the incompatibility of such naval postures with collective security[214], i.a. because it would be impossible for the USA to come to the aid of its allies in times of war, unless NATO were able to protect its transatlantic SLOCs. Furthermore, a defence of only coastal regions might result in Europe abandoning the idea of the seas as 'the common heritage of mankind', if other nations were unwilling to show similar restraint. The problems involved with these incompatibilities were, however, left unresolved.

Almost simultaneously with NATO's move towards arms control in the air at the May 1989 summit, Lutz published a preliminary study on this subject. It was, however, even more sketchy than the above naval analysis, and only seems worth mentioning because of an absence of substantial analyses on non-offensive air strategies, almost as glaring as the lacuna on naval matters: a few ideas by Hannig and the SAS group (including the present author)[215], but nothing like an exhaustive study of the subject.

Lutz's point of departure was the aforementioned restrictive definition of NOD, ruling out, besides invasion capabilities, also those of pre-emptive strikes and 'counter-value' attacks against the adversary's rear. Due to the inherent flexibility of airpower, it was not, however, possible to distinguish between permissible and undesirable aircraft merely on the basis of range, but relevant criteria would have to include functions and missions.

As relevant arms control aims, Lutz recommended reductions of strategic bombers (in the framework of the START negotiations) as well as the elimination of INF bombers and a piecemeal scrapping of all fighter-bombers in the entire ATTU area; and reduction to as small residual air fleets as possible (e.g. twenty percent of current NATO holdings). Further-more, in the Central Region of ATTU no tactical aircraft were to be allowed for air-to-ground combat: a most perplexing recommendation that was, unfortunately, not elaborated upon. Moreover, a rearward re-location of the remaining aircraft should be embarked upon, i.a. with a view to creating a 100 kms.-wide corridor, in which no aircraft might be stationed. Finally, he recommended a reduction in the number of airfields, runways, hangars and other infrastructure (a reform that would, incidentally, seem to violate the 'no-target principle' so central for NOD, since it would imply a concen-tration, rather than a dispersal, of aircraft).

The envisioned agreement would be accompanied by adequate verification procedures, i.a. encompassing on-site inspections, as well as by stringent non-circumvention clauses that would prohibit e.g. the acquisition of combat drones or cruise missiles as aircraft substitutes. This was also rather perplexing, because no range specifications were given, so that it was unclear whether the author really intended to prohibit drones with ranges of, say, forty kilometers. As a substitute for all these prohibited and/or limited items, air defence would be strengthened by means of surface-to-air means, especially SAMs[216].

Due to the fact that the IFSH has been promoted by the SPD, and that its director, Egon Bahr, has been a figure of such high standing within the party, it should come as no surprise that the political aspirations of the Institute have been more pronounced than has been the case for most other peace research institutes.

First of all, Deputy Director Lutz has been a consultant member of the commission responsible for the defence policy of the SPD (cf. below, Chapter XII). In addition, he has published a number of articles directly intended as inputs into the political deliberations in the party as well as into the debate with other parties, as e.g. the 'Greens'. Secondly, the IFSH has published a number of papers representing concrete recommendations intended for 'political consumption', e.g. a critique of the NATO's deep strike concepts[217], as well as a proposal for the establishment of 'defensive zones'.

The latter took a bit further the ideas of Egon Bahr (recorded below, chapter VII) for a 'zone without weapons for attack', but was also reminicent of the zonal concepts described above, not least the proposals from the Starnberg group around von Müller. Not surprisingly, the IFSH recommended the establishment on a bloc-to-bloc basis of two pairs of zones:

1. 'Defensive zones', from which all nuclear weapons, tanks, artillery, fighter-bombers and heavy combat helicopters should be withdrawn, along with other equipment necessary for wide-range offensives, primarily bridge-building equipment. The zone should be defended by means of infantry armed with anti-tank weapons and obstacle-construction equipment.

2. 'Reduction zones', in which all military forces, but particularly those best suitable for offensive operations, should be built down[218].

Social Defence

Some authors have attempted to combine proposals such as those above with another variety of alternative defence, namely strictly non-military, civilian-based or 'social' defence (SD). Although it is to some extent peripheral to the main topic of this book, I shall therefore give a brief account of the strategy of social defence.

Even though it has certainly not been its exclusive purpose, SD has occasionally challenged military strategy on its own terms, by claiming to be a viable substitute for military defence. Presumably, it would be capable of meeting the same threats, either by virtue of its deterrent (or 'dissuasive') potential, or by actually conducting a successful struggle in case of a failure of deterrence.

Indeed, SD has occasionally been depicted as a particularly skilful application of the Clausewitzian principles of strategy. Since the objective in a war, once started, has been presumed to replace the original purpose, the strategy of an attacker would inevitably have to strive for victory, necessitating a breaking of the will of the defenders. The latter would thus be in a position to define the centre of gravity of the struggle, and by implication, at liberty to leave some 'areas' undefended, without this necessarily detracting from the effectiveness of their defence. The defenders might thus e.g. charge the opponent's will directly, rather than indirectly through attacking the adversary's military wherewithal[219].

This strategy has often been based on the realization that 'the opponent' constitutes an abstraction, beneath which inevitably lies a complex political structure, consisting of rulers, opposition, public opinion, etc. By demonstrating the futility of aggression to parts of the opponent's system other than the immediate instigators of the aggression, the non-violent defenders might hope to induce the former to exert pressure on the decision-makers, in order to make them give up the aggression, or, in the last resort, to bring about a political change in the opponent's political system[220]. Such prospects have received growing attention in recent years, due to the rapidly increasing 'transparency' of all societies, which allows almost unimpeded access to the opponent's political system. Taking advantage of this opportunity would obviously call for spectacular actions, aiming at demonstrating how the aggressor's cause was either unjust or futile, or indeed both.

Furthermore, the rulers of the aggressor country would have to rely on aids for their conquest and occupation. First of all, they would rely on individual soldiers, the sheer number of whom would imply that they would inevitably represent a fair sample of the opponent's population. Even though soldiers had been 'socialised' by the military system to perform 'roles' according to this system, 'beneath' these roles they were bound to remain ordinary human beings, susceptible to the same influences as everybody else. SD accordingly recommended a differentiated approach to the occupation forces, shunning all contact and collaboration with them as soldiers, whilst fraternizing with them as people. In this way, the hope was to undermine the 'morale' of the enemy, in perfect conformity with the well-known dictum of military strategy that the morale factor is decisive in combat[221].

Apart from seeking to break the will of the enemy, SD has furthermore emphasised the need for making the defenders' own will unbreakable. The immediate way of doing so would be the conduct of SD exercises etc., but more fundamentally it was seen as imperative to avoid deep cleavages in society, and to achieve a basic consensus[222].

In addition to their military personnel, the occupants would rely on administrative staff, for which the same strategy would apply: personal relations should be promoted, whereas collaboration should be denied to the foreigners in their role as administrators of the conquered society[223]. This might appear to entail a dilemma, since the defenders of a modern society, dependent to an increasing extent on the administrative apparatus for its smooth functioning, would risk jeopardizing popular morale if they were to impede the vital functions of society—yet another version of the 'defence dilemma' mentioned in chapters I and II above.

SD proponents have sought an escape from this dilemma in the catch-phrase 'continued work without collaboration', implying a continuance of society's vital functions for the benefit of the inhabitants, combined with a prevention of the utilization of these administrative functions by the occupants, at the very least for repressive purposes[224].

With the dual aim of safeguarding morale and of depriving the enemy of blackmail options, some SD advocates have, furthermore, recommended enhancing society's invulnerability, i.a. by decentralization, economic self-sufficiency, etc., whereas others have maintained that any such strategy of seeking to exploit vulnerability for coercive purposes would anyhow be futile, and hence warned against making profound changes in society a precondition for SD[225]. SD proponents have, however, tended to agree on the need for careful advance preparation, including that of the administrative structure, so as to be able to provide the population with at least the essentials for survival[226].

SD might also be depicted as an application of 'the indirect approach' or 'the indirect strategy', which are associated with Liddell Hart and André Beaufre, respectively. SD has thus been appropriately likened to 'political ju-jitsu' by Gene Sharp[227]. The plans of the enemy were to be countered asymmetrically, i.e. in a different 'coinage'. The tanks of the enemy were to be opposed with neither tanks nor anti-tank weapons, but rather with an absence of lucrative targets for tank fire, combined with the obvious unattractiveness of firing into crowds of unarmed civilians. The enemy's nuclear weapons were to be met with a stubborn unwillingness to surrender to coercion, rather than with threats of retaliation, or with strategic defences[228], etc.

The indirect approach of SD has also been couched in 'contest of will' terms. Since SD rejected embodying the entire 'will' of society in its military forces, this will would become harder to break, at least by means of military forces, suited only for defeating opposing military forces, but not for exerting influence on the minds of the opponents. Since SD did not embody its will in the integrity of the national territory either, even successful occupation would not necessarily spell the end of resistance or any collapse of the defenders' will. SD's indirect approach has even occasionally been couched in terms of manoeuvre warfare, depicting SD as an 'encirclement of the invaders by the entire population'.

In any case, the time factor should be deliberately played upon in the ensuing contest, redefined as a contest of wills and endurance. The aggressor would inevitably have to aim for a quick victory, so that time would work to the advantage of the defender, who should hence seek to slow down combat intensity. In this way, SD revealed its affinity to guerilla strategy[229].

In some, theoretically somewhat less sophisticated, versions SD has been identified as a form of 'deterrence by denial'. In order to demonstrate the effectiveness of SD in this respect, specific goals on the part of the aggressor have been stipulated, and the impossibility of attaining these goals when confronted with non-violent resistance demonstrated. If the aggressor were to aim for ordinary 'imperialist' goals, such as access to material resources, then he would obviously require the collaboration of the population. In order to deny him these gains, the defenders might, besides general non-collaboration, employ such means as sabotage of production facilities or lines of transportation[230].

The obvious problem with the above arguments is, of course, that other scenarios are conceivable (indeed probably more likely) than that forming the basis for the SD strategy, which has been based on the precedent of Nazi Germany. A number of SD advocates have acknowledged this deficiency, but often countered it with the allegation that *per se* conceivable alternative scenarios would be rendered irrelevant by a conversion to SD.

First of all, a country defended by non-violent means would pose no offensive military threat, the neutralization of which might appear to warrant a preventive or pre-emptive attack; hence only premeditated aggression would be relevant. Secondly, territory would possess no intrinsic value, but only matter as a means to a different end, be this exploitation of natural resources or military conquest by means of 'bridgeheads'. The latter case was, however, not considered relevant, since it would merely amount to a circular explanation of an urge for minor military conquest by reference to an urge for major military conquest. The fundamental motives for aggression could presumably only be exploitation or ideological victory. As far as the latter was concerned, SD would obviously be superior to military strategy as an ideological struggle *par excellence*[231].

This line of argument implicitly assumed a global implementation, since military threats posed by some countries to others might under certain circumstances warrant attack on third parties, in order to prevent these from being used as bridgeheads. 'A' might thus feel inclined to attack 'B' in order to stand a better chance in an expected war with 'C', a war which might, in its turn, very well be preventive or pre-emptive. History, in actual fact, abounds with attacks based on such considerations, and it is by no means clear how a social defence would oppose an invasion force which intended merely to establish a military bridgehead.

A few SD advocates have acknowledged this as a problem, without, however being able to provide any wholly satisfactory answer, apart from (not really convincing) recommendations to blockade runways etc. in a non-violent fashion[232].

SD has sometimes been criticised by adherents of traditional and nuclear strategy on the grounds that its implementation would inflict severe suffering on the population, carrying out the struggle with the enemy in their midst.

Partly as an answer to this criticism, SD advocates would appear to have placed an increasing stress on the dissuasive effects of SD, as compared with its 'war-fighting' potentials. SD has thus been proclaimed to possess a considerable dissuasive effect, due to its ability to exact a high staying price from the aggressor. At the same time it has also been acknowledged that these capabilities would have to be made apparent to the would-be aggressors in order to achieve the intended effect, for which purpose 'SD exercises' have been recommended.

Occasionally, the very concepts of 'defence' and 'security' have been broadened by SD authors, who have pointed out the significant dissuasive effects of e.g. 'good services': The more useful a country were to be in peace, the more any aggressors would have to lose by upsetting this peace, a factor which the stipulated would-be aggressors would have to take into account in his cost-benefit calculations with regard to the contemplated attack[233].

However, SD has also claimed a better damage-limiting capability than present strategy in the hypothetical 'if deterrence fails' situation, first of all, because SD would not envisage nuclear strikes, and hence would not invite pre-emptive nuclear attack; secondly, because SD would make the opponent's use of weapons of mass destruction pointless[234]; thirdly, because it might presumably be able to decrease the general level of violence in any ensuing combat, by avoiding any escalatory moves.

Although many SD advocates have argued their case in rather absolute terms, most have acknowledged the extreme improbability of SD simply supplanting military defence at one stroke. Inevitably, a transition period would thus have to be anticipated, in the course of which military forces would be built down and non-military means of defence gradually introduced. Indeed, Gene Sharp even warned against the dangers of a too rapid introduction, since this might invite 'defence disasters'[235]. The total defence posture would thus at any given time consist of a mixture of military and social means, or at least options.

There have been different answers to the question of how to mix, with some advocating a geographical and others a temporary division of labour[236]. Still others have warned against any mix, on the grounds that the two types of defence would obstruct each other, because of their logical incompatibility[237].

Amongst the proponents of mixes, some have argued for confining military defence to the countryside, leaving the densely populated areas demilitarised and 'open' in the sense of the Geneva Convention. In order to prevent the aggressor from simply taking cover in the cities, these should be defended by the methods of social defence[238].

Others have recommended utilizing SD, at least during the transition period, as a 'fall-back defence line'[239], implying that the military defence should take the first blow and attempt to stop the enemy at the border. After a certain period, however, the armed forces should lay down their arms, to let protracted civilian-based defence take over. Moreover, the would-be aggressor should be made aware of this fall-back option, so as to enhance dissuasion by presenting the prospects of protracted struggle. Others have, however, regarded the availability of any such fall-back options as dysfunctional, since it would detract from the credibility of the first line[240].

Still others have advised against any rigid divisions of labour, and simply pointed out that SD would be a useful option for certain, unspecified contingencies[241]. The latter may, in fact, be the most precise and all-embracing definition possible.

In recent years, SD proponents have tended to become more favourably inclined towards combinations of SD and military defence, whilst underlining the need for limiting military means to strictly defensive ones, i.e. to NOD[242]. I shall return to this option at greater length below.

Having thus presented the case for and partly against social defence, a comparison of it with NOD becomes possible. First of all, a number of similarities between SD and NOD are fairly obvious:

—Both are inherently non-offensive, although some authors have emphasised the offensive capabilities of SD, e.g. by infiltration etc.[243].
—Both reject the use of nuclear weapons for military purposes.
—Both constitute asymmetrical approaches to strategy.
—Both attach major importance to the time factor, and to the capability for protracted struggle.
—Both seek to deprive the opponent of worthwhile targets.

Secondly, however, there are also a number of important differences:

—They take different scenarios as their point of departure, and thus emphasise different types of capabilities: SD's paradigm case is a '1939-type' invasion, and SD proponents thus emphasise deterrence by denial. NOD's paradigm case is an inadvertent '1914-type' war, and NOD advocates thus tend to emphasise crisis stability.
—SD is considered a long-term perspective, whereas NOD is intended for almost immediate implementation.
—The techniques are, of course, entirely different, SD rejecting the use of weapons, and NOD basing itself on military means.

As mentioned above, some authors have deliberately tried to combine social defence with military NOD. One plausible rationale for this might be to achieve a better *tout azimut* coverage, taking also into account other types of threats besides the strictly military ones. Another rationale for combination might be a desire to gradually supplant military with non-military forms of defence, as a contribution to a piecemeal de-militarization of society.

A number of the above models (e.g. Afheldt's and Löser's) have, indeed, envisaged a certain role for social defence, although they have not elaborated on this theme in any detail. Likewise, some of the proponents of social defence (i.a. Theodor Ebert) have taken a stand on the military NOD proposals, and often appreciated them, at least as 'lesser evils' or as potential steps towards the implementation of social defence. However, whereas in other countries there have been a number of attempts to deliberately integrate the two forms of defence, in the FRG only the two Nolte brothers appear to have taken up this challenge.

Wilhelm Nolte is a serving *Bundeswehr* officer with the rank of Lt-Colonel, presently working as a 'documentalist' at the military academy in Hamburg. Despite his professional affiliations, he has been extremely critical towards the prevailing trends in both nuclear and conventional strategy[244]. He has thus remained a strict nuclear abolitionist, and his alternative proposals have thus aimed primarily at 'making nuclear weapons impotent and obsolete'. He developed his concrete model in collaboration with his brother, Hans-Heinrich, a historian with some expertice in the field of civilian defence. The two brothers called their model 'autonomous dissuasion', the aim of which would be to 'combine elements of civilian resistance with elements of military defence in such a way that one can renounce nuclear weapons entirely'[245].

Their goal was thus the complete abolition of nuclear weapons, rather than any 'mere' reduction of nuclear deterrence to political functions, to which goal most other NOD proposals have modestly limited themselves. The strategy for accomplishing this ambitious goal was a 'holistic' defence concept. It should be strictly defensive, and emphasise 'holding capability' (*'Behauptungsfähigkeit'*), which was allegedly the prime distinctive feature of a 'structural incapability of attack'[246]. Such a defence should be capable of replacing the current 'total defence' conceptions of some NATO member countries, which include nuclear deterrence. Autonomous dissuasion would consist (as do already the more traditional 'total defence' concepts of countries such as Denmark) of three elements: military defence, civil defence and civilian resistance. However, as compared with 'established' total defence, the one envisioned by the Noltes would downgrade military defence relatively. Furthermore, it would take a much broader view on 'civilian resistance', by making it a task for the entire population, rather than just for the administrative personnel. However, the defence structures of certain neutral countries such as Switzerland and Austria appeared much more in line with the Nolte proposals[247].

The division of tasks between the different elements of the defence was to be primarily spatial. Military defence should only take place in (primarily rural) areas of low population density, whereas civilian resistance should take over in population centres. In this way, cities would become 'refugee fortifications' into which the population from the rural districts could be evacuated, just as they were in the Middle Ages. The suburban areas, in their turn, were envisioned as a connective link between the two defence zones, and the authors accordingly considered these as 'the real gravitation points of the defence'.

The civilian-based defence of cities should i.a. serve the strategic task of preventing an aggressor from exploiting cities as 'bases' in his forward-moving conquest of the country. In addition, this precaution would force the aggressor to disperse his forces, particularly in a 'structural' sense: by having to bring along forces for administrative tasks etc., since he would no longer be able to 'live off the country'[248].

Unfortunately, the military aspects of the defence model were not developed in any detail, and neither weapons systems nor tactical principles were specified. However, the authors proposed to exploit terrain advantages by the creation of barriers, as well as to emphasise the depth of the defence deployment, so as to be in a position to launch attacks against the flanks of the approaching aggressor's forces, apparently in some kind of guerilla-like tactic. In the original presentation, the authors referred to the proposals of Afheldt, Bülow, Löser and the SAS, without, however, making any definite choice between these. Since then, however, Wilhelm Nolte has explicitly opted for the SAS proposal, although remaining somewhat critical towards its nuclear component[249].

The humanitarian norms of warfare were accorded considerable weight. Combined with the intended lack of incentives for an aggressor to cross the nuclear threshold, or to escalate beyond bounds in general, these norms would presumably make civil defence a viable option. The civil defence component should attempt to create real chances of survival for the population, e.g. by taking care of supplies for the civilians who had been evacuated into the cities. The prospects of considerable damage limitation would be further improved by the intended limitation of escalation. Millions of lives (and, indeed, the survival of mankind as such) might thus be saved, according to the authors' assessment, although their worst-case prognosis still anticipated a war causing millions of casualties. The maintenance of cities as 'open' should serve the same purpose by keeping actual fighting 'at arms length'. Still, for further protection of the evacuees, civil defence measures would be required as protection against the hazards of conventional warfare. Against nuclear attack, on the other hand, any civil defence (as e.g. blast shelters) was deemed futile[250].

Whereas the military defence was to be conducted by regular troops, the resistance forces should (despite the embryo of a command structure) be civilians and hence 'non-combatants', enjoying all the legal protection accorded to these[251]. For the same reason, the authors were sceptical of proposals (such as Johan Galtung's) for the interposition of an intermediary category of paramilitary forces. Despite the similarity between the tactics etc. of their military component and those of guerillas, the Noltes hence advised strongly against all forms of genuine guerilla warfare[252].

The authors emphasised the compatibility of their defence proposal with the existing social structure. Despite the mobilization of greater parts of the populace for the defence effort, this would by no means result in any 'militarization of society', but rather in a 'civilization of the military'. Taking the 'citizen in uniform' tradition of e.g. von Baudissin as his point of departure, Wilhelm Nolte repeatedly appealed to the military profession's sense of duty, not as a way of boosting their fighting spirit, however, but rather as a recommendation of more independent thinking[253].

Conscripts would form a part of the civilian resistance, and their particular form of combat should be rehearsed in peacetime. It might take the form of i.a. acts of strikes, sabotage, demonstrations, maintenance of a communications system, appeals to the international community, etc. In addition, by means of civilian defence, an appeal should be made to the 'false morality' of the occupation forces.

Which type of service to opt for should be voluntary, something which would give conscientious objectors a useful and 'legitimate' task. Indeed, even women should be allowed to participate in the defence effort. The Noltes furthermore emphasised their proposal's potential for gathering a consensus, embracing also the 'alternative movements' (as e.g. the Greens) which were currently 'alienated' from the defence endeavours of society. Such groups, indeed, would most likely become the central 'bearers' of social defence in case of an invasion[254].

The authors, likewise, maintained the compatibility with NATO membership, although they have acknowledged that difficulties might arise in connection with the provision of mutual support in a Collective Security system, if e.g. the FRG were to convert to a more civilian-based form of defence. In order to be compatible with a system of Collective Security, an introduction of a full-fledged non-violent defence would hence have to be undertaken collectively. However, within the NATO framework, the FRG might initiate the process of conversion to civilian-based defence, taking advantage of the greater scope for autonomy allegedly afforded by the proposed defence scheme[255].

This, in its turn, might be further expanded by promoting role specialization within the Alliance. If the FRG were to have the main responsibility for land defence, whereas the allies would shoulder the main burden of air defence, then the FRG would be more at liberty to initiate incremental changes in the direction of 'autonomous dissuasion'. The first steps would have to include the withdrawal of nuclear weapons from German soil, as well as a formal declaration to the effect that the FRG renounced any nuclear 'guarantee', combined with an invitation to the WTO, to emulate this step.

As a precondition for initiating such a gradualistic process of 'transarmament', the Noltes were prepared to accommodate American interests to a large extent, e.g. by excluding certain parts of the FRG from their defence scheme. In this gradualistic endeavour, the 'transposition suitability' of the defensive military schemes (i.e. the viability of gradually replacing them by non-military means) was assessed as a great advantage, compared with traditional military postures[256].

Recapitulation and Evaluation

I shall round off this lengthy survey of the West German NOD 'designers' and theorists with a brief recapitulation as well as evaluation of the various approaches and proposals.

As will have become apparent, one might distinguish between three 'pure versions' of NOD, flanked by various combinations as well as half-way approximations. The pure versions are, first of all, the stationary territorial defence, such as envisioned by Horst Afheldt; secondly, the presumably impenetrable forward defence such as proposed by Norbert Hannig; and thirdly, the exclusively non-military or social defence. None of these would possess any border-crossing offensive capabilities whatsoever, the first because of its lack of mobility as well as long-range strike capabilities; the second because of its lack of mobile land forces, capable of taking and holding ground; and the third because of the complete absence of armed forces.

These three forms of defence have been combined with each other in various ways, such as e.g. attempted by Albrecht von Müller and the SAS group. They have also, usually with a view to devising immediately implementable defence alternatives, been combined with the present postures, such as was the case with the various disengagement and 'sword and shield' models.

None of the NOD proposals developed so far is flawless, but then again, neither is NATO's present strategy. Whereas one might criticise each and every one of the proposals for some deficiency, this does not necessarily mean that some are not better than others. I shall conclude with enumerating some of the obvious weak points in the most prominent proposals, as well as with trying to weigh the pros and cons.

The argumentation for non-violent Social Defence has not really appeared persuasive to anybody taking the risks of aggressive war of conquest seriously. The evidence supporting its efficiency is, to put it mildly, inconclusive, and it appears to focus on rather irrelevant scenarios. To the questions raised by more plausible scenarios, furthermore, SD simply has no answer, and the conclusion thus seems inescapable that SD simply will not be adequate against aggressors with only limited territorial conquest in mind, and caring little about controlling society.

This negative assessment should not be taken to imply a complete dismissal. One could conceive of circumstances in which SD means of resistance might become relevant, both for certain regular defence purposes, for the struggle against subversive activities on behalf of foreign states, and for defence against purely internal enemies. Although the relevant circumstances may be hard to define, a state may indeed find the availability of such options useful in a case of emergency.

Even more so would it be useful to be able to combine the regular (i.e. armed struggle) with civilian-based defence in urban areas, such as envisaged by the Noltes. A war initiated in the erroneous belief that it would be swift and successful may in actual fact become protracted. Indeed, this is exactly what most NOD proposals aim at. If so, the aggressor might fall back on the cities, hoping in this way to be able to outlast the resistance. For such circumstances, non-violent means for urban resistance might indeed come in most handy.

Its theoretical merits notwithstanding, the military critics were right that Horst Afheldt's scheme did constitute something of a monoculture. It did not take into sufficient account the wide range of counter-measures available to a would-be aggressor. It was, furthermore, probably based on unwarranted optimism with regard to the potential of missiles for firepower allocation; and the intended area coverage by means of fire alone might hence well prove, by an order of magnitude, more expensive than anticipated.

Any assessment of these proposals as 'mere' strategy or operational art would, however, be misleading, since Afheldt's goal was not to enable states to wage wars effectively, but to prevent war by ruling out certain military options which might be attractive for a would-be aggressor, particularly the quick *fait accompli* on the conventional level. Even though an aggressor might succeed with other strategic options on an operational scale, but these would not necessarily make much sense for a political leadership contemplating whether or not to launch a war.

A more fair criticism might be that Afheldt (along with most other Western observers) erroneously believed in Soviet 'petrification' and grossly underestimated the potential for change. When he emphasised the unilateral option, and focused his attention on changes in NATO strategy, it was hence not necessarily out of undue self-criticism (and certainly not out of sympathy for the USSR), but rather because this focus appeared as the only realistic way of getting a process started.

One of the weak points in Norbert Hannig's proposal for 'impenetrable fire barriers' was probably its 'all-eggs-in-one-basket' character. If the centralized command system were to be incapacitated by means of e.g. 'surgical' attacks, then the entire defence structure might end up in total disarray. Furthermore, if the forward barrier should, against all expectations, nevertheless be penetrated, the defender would have no means of forcing the intruders out. If the attackers were to disperse after their penetration, they would be extremely difficult to target by means of exclusively indirect fire, especially if they were to enjoy the support of ground-attack aircraft, long-range artillery or similar means, suitable for counter-battery fire. The model would also appear to put quite unwarranted faith in the promises of emerging technologies, and to neglect the wide range of counter-measures available.

Hannig's technological optimism also appeared excessive with regard to his proposals for relying almost entirely on land-based anti-ship missiles for coastal defence, and on SAMs for air defence. Whereas the potential of these means has been acknowledged by the majority of NOD advocates, most have recommended some back-up in the form of small vessels and fighters.

A final problematic aspect of Hannig's concept would seem to be its rather permissive use of long-range firepower. Although the argument that genuine offensive capability presupposes mobile (i.e. mechanized and armoured) land forces does have a certain logic, it may put too great a strain on objectivity, and neglect perceptions. Capabilities for offensive counter-air and (retalia-tory) counter-value attacks may not imply offensive capability, if seen in isolation, but they are certainly far from confidence-building. Furthermore, if some (not necessarily all that numerous) mobile land forces were to be added, the resultant mix might well have a significant offensive capability.

A final 'deficiency', for which Hannig should not be blamed, is that the notion of forward defence has apparently been rendered obsolete in the light of the German unification. It is now far from obvious where to locate the envisaged fire barrier.

Just as disengagement is both a political and a military concept, it may be criticised from both angles. Politically, some of the disengagement schemes may be criticised for going too far in the direction of neutrality and a complete dismantling of the present alliance structure. Whereas a certain neutralisation and softening of the alliance structure would seem likely to promote *détente*, it is by no means self-evident that German neutrality would do the same. As described in the Chapter II, the country is simply too large, located too strategically and haunted by too horrendous a past to be left unchecked without hereby invoking mistrust on the part of its neighbours.

Militarily, disengagement of offensive-capable forces seems, on balance, capable of improving stability, since it will eliminate any options of attack 'from a standing start'. The implied need for mobilisation and/or forward movement of formations will provide the defender with valuable additional warning time. By so doing, it may allow him to build down the state of readiness, e.g. by relying to a greater extent on reserve forces. This very fact will extend the warning time available to the opponent, and hence allow him to reciprocate with a lower state a readiness. By thus at any conceivable moment pushing the risk of war days or weeks into the future, disengage-ment may well promote mutual trust and thus serve as an important confidence-building measure.

On the other hand, if the withdrawal of forces is implemented without any simultaneous structural changes, the benign peacetime effects may have to be weighed against potentially malign effects in times of crisis. In a 'moment of truth', when the threshold is crossed beyond which a war suddenly comes to appear possible, both parties may come to fear an attack from the other. There may therefore emerge certain incentives to violate the disengagement rules by moving forces up front so as to meet the potential attack as close to the border as possible. Such a movement of mobile and structurally offensive-capable forces may, however, be highly ambiguous when seen from the other side, which is hence likely to fear an impending attack, if only for the motives described by Thomas Schelling: 'He thinks we think he'll attack; so he thinks we shall; so he will; so we must'.

This caveat does not imply that disengagement of offensive-capable forces is a bad idea, only that it should not be allowed to stand alone, but be combined with a considerable reduction of such forces, and with the creation of efficient non-offensive means of forward defence.

A more principled criticism might be raised against the 'sword and shield' models of Jochen Löser, Andreas von Bülow and others. It is by no means self-evident that overall offensive capability will automatically be reduced by substituting 'shields' for 'swords', since all combat requires both. Taking the terms literally, it is e.g. perfectly conceivable that a Roman legionnaire with both a sword and a shield would be able to defeat a samurai (or whatever) with two swords, and that an army equipped in this manner with both offensive and defensive means would hence possess a considerable, indeed enhanced, offensive capability.

Under certain circumstances, 'pure' offensive capability is merely 'pseudo-offensive', whereas a genuine offensive capability would have to amount to offensive plus defensive forces. Some ratios of substitution of defensive for offensive forces may thus yield undesirable results, whereas there may, of course, well be other ratios of substitution which would actually diminish genuine offensive capability.

Under modern conditions, genuine offensive potential will often be dependent on the availability of e.g. a 'defensive' air cover, and on the 'tactically defensive' capability of holding conquered terrain against the counter-attacks of the 'true' defenders, etc. On the one hand, replacing tanks with anti-tank weapons, mine-clearing with mine-laying equipment, aircraft with SAMs, etc. may well lead in the right direction (and may, furthermore, be the only realistic way to implement a NOD reform). On the other hand, if extreme care is not taken, then in the course of the transition period certain offence-defence mixes may emerge which are all but defensive.

Finally, it appears questionable whether crisis stability will automatically be improved because of a cadering of offensive capable forces, or by their rearward deployment. A mobilization race and/or a forward deployment race might ensue, which might well reach a point when the temptation to pre-empt might be almost irresistible, also because the risks associated with 'standing down' without absolute certainty that the opponent did likewise might turn out to be considerable.

The 'conditional offensive capability' envisioned by Albrecht von Müller further amplified the above problem of the appropriate combination of 'swords' with 'shields'. Because he made the offensive wielding of the 'swords' a matter of deliberate political choice, rather than a deplorable side-effect, he might rightly be considered 'a wolf in sheep's clothing', for whom the label 'non-offensive' would be entirely unwarranted. Indeed, implementing the envisioned 'conditional offensive' would be incompatible with NATO's defensive political and strategic orientation, and would constitute a clear violation of the FRG's Constitution.

Furthermore, the envisaged form of forward defence seems to have been rendered obsolete by German unification: Should the Oder-Neisse frontier be saturated with sensor arrays and the like? And would the (by now democratic) Poland really deserve to be made the target of (not so close) aerial interdiction, to say nothing of counter-invasions against the USSR that would inevitably have to transit through Poland?

Whereas all of the above proposals have revealed serious flaws, that of the SAS seems far more ripe for implementation. It would be militarily efficient, by virtue of its reliance on well-tested weapons technologies and 'robust' tactical principles. It would, furthermore, be unmistakably defensive and thus confidence-building by virtue of the deliberate incapability of border-crossing military operations. The 'spiders' would be inextricably tied to the 'web' of stationary forces on friendly territory. The SAS scheme would thus combine the advantages of forward defence with those of in-depth territorial defence, and would appear immediately applicable to the united Germany.

CHAPTER V

Military Defectors

The military services constitute powerful institutions in almost every society. These 'men on horseback' (Samuel Finer) always exert some political influence, as do all institutions. The armies, navies and air forces tend to collaborate in their joint competition with the civilian sectors for a greater share of the societal 'cake', but tend to struggle amongst themselves for the distribution of this military slice of the cake. However, in spite of the widespread inter-service rivalries e.g. over weapons procurement programmes, an important factor in the bargaining power of the military v. their civilian competitors has historically been the high degree of internal cohesion and the unswerving loyalty to the common cause of raising military budgets. Defection has therefore usually been regarded as a very serious matter, indeed[1].

Another factor in the military bargaining power has traditionally been the promise of disproportionately high pay-offs to military investments. This discourse has often been linked with assumptions of the primacy of the offensive. On the one hand, military budget claims have been argued with reference the easy gains to be reaped through offensive wars of conquest, such as seems to have abounded prior to WWI, not least in Germany. On the other hand, the military has sometimes argued in favour of increased military outlays for strictly defensive purposes, which were presumably required for the dissuasion of adversaries from an (allegedly cheap and swift) war of aggression[2].

The Defection Phenomenon

Since the bargaining power of the military thus tends to depend both on internal cohesion, and on the claim of the supremacy of the offensive, it is a very serious matter indeed for an officer to 'step out of line' and voice dissenting views on the primacy of the defensive, since this may jeopardise his career prospects, etc. The phenomenon of military 'defectors', in the sense of active or retired officers joining the peace and anti-nuclear movement, has nevertheless been well-known around the world.

In the USA, for instance, quite a few admirals and generals have raised their voices against nuclear policy, interventionism, exorbitant military expenditure, etc. A number of their colleagues have even formed an international association of 'Generals for Peace'[3].

The phenomenon of dissent has, unfortunately, been most widespread amongst retired officers (in German with the suffix 'AD' for '*Ausser Dienst*'), whereas there have only been rather few supporters amongst their colleagues within the ranks. The reason for this significant difference may, of course, be a genuine aversion in the military mind to the defensive. However, an alternative explanation might be that a latent favourable attitude has simply been muted by the constraints of career considerations and obedience, only to come out into the open after retirement.

The Prussian heritage notwithstanding, the 'defection phenomenon' has been fairly widespread in the FRG, where would-be dissenting officers have been emboldened by the anti-militarist attitude of the majority of politicians as well as the public, eager to maintain political and societal control over the services, so as to avoid any repetition on the 1914-18 and 1939-45 disasters. The image of the armed forces as 'citizens in uniform' has thus been deliberately promoted as an alternative to the 'state within the state' allegory[4].

The following is a list of present or former officers from the FRG, who have openly supported at least the main tenets of the 'NOD philosophy'[5]:

I. Active Officers

Alexander Acker, Colonel
Franz H.U. Borkenhagen, Major
Wilhelm Nolte, Lt-Colonel
Elmar Schmähling, Rear Admiral (subsequently dismissed)
Franz Uhle-Wettler, General.

II. Retired Officers

Eckardt Afheldt, Brigadier General
Gert Bastian, Brigadier General
Ludger Dünne, Captain
Helmut Funk, Colonel
Georg Füreder, Colonel
Helmut W. Ganser, Major
Johannes Gerber, Brigadier General
Ingo Günther, Brigadier General
Norbert Hannig, Colonel
Hermann Hagena, Brigadier General
Günter Kiessling, General
Jochen Löser, Brigadier General
Alfred Mechtersheimer, Colonel
Gerd Schmückle, General

Martin Tetzlaff, Captain
Günther Vollmer, Brigadier General.

I have already dealt with a number of the above under other headings, and I shall return to some of the others in the following chapters. This chapter is thus devoted to the residual category of NOD advocates belonging somehow to the armed forces, but falling outside the scope of the other categories.

Light Infantry Advocates

The idea of giving infantry, and especially light infantry, a more prominent role in the overall defence posture has consistently had its proponents 'within the ranks'. The motives for such recommendations have varied, however. Whereas some have argued the case for the infantry on grounds of its military efficiency, pointing out e.g. its virtues under particular terrain conditions, others have stressed the non-provocative character of infantry. Some infantry advocates, such as Liddell Hart and Ferdinand Otto Miksche, have even pleaded its case as a potential (complete or partial) substitute for nuclear weapons.

The same fascination with light troops may be found in the 'light infantry renaissance' within the US Army, spokesmen for which have recommended 'light forces' on the grounds of their flexibility and hence suitability for 'low intensity conflict' in the Third World; for their potential role as force multipliers for the offensive-capable land forces; and for their eminent 'fit' for rugged terrain[6].

Whereas such proposals have not previously been particularly defensive, they have now assumed a new significance, because of the option of integrating them into NOD schemes. A distinctly 'mainstream' military trend has thus tended to merge with more alternative tendencies, regardless of whether the individual infantry advocates have so intended or not.

One of the most prominent 'infantry advocates' within the German military has been General Franz Uhle-Wettler, who later left his post in the *Bundeswehr* for an assignment at the NATO Academy in Rome. In spite of his career in the armoured forces, Uhle-Wettler had for quite some time been a proponent of a greater emphasis on infantry. He had published a work in 1966 suggesting a greater role for it in the defence of Central Europe, to the detriment of armoured forces[7]. In 1980, he took up the idea again in a book on *The Battleground Central Europe*.

Uhle-Wettler saw the main threat to NATO's defence posture in the trend towards 'over-technification' of the armed forces: the number of fighters (the 'teeth') had, as a consequence hereof, been steadily declining in comparison with the 'tail', so that the current 'teeth-to-tail ratio' was allegedly around 10:90. This conflicted with the very *raison d'etre* of military forces:

'The purpose (*Zweck*) of our army is manifested in the tank, in the rifleman and in the ordnance, not in the staffs, command and logistics troops or in the ministry, despite the importance of these. The entire rear apparatus, the shaft of the spear, for which we assign our best conscripts, loses its purpose and *raison d'être* if the edge of the spear is blunt.'[8].

The disproportionate increase in logistics tended to hamper mobility and to increase vulnerability, since even a slow cumulative attrition would soon effectively incapacitate formations. If a division were to lose merely fifty percent of its manpower, it would no longer be fit for combat. The major part of the logistic chains would inevitably consist of 'soft-skinned', and hence vulnerable, trucks and the like, the break-down of which could cause the entire defence effort to falter. The logistic system therefore required protection by means of fighting units, whence a further decline in the number of these available for fighting the actual battle. Furthermore, the rear services had an unfortunate tendency to recruit the best qualified personnel with a resultant deterioration in the quality of the actual fighters, both 'objectively' and through a decline in the morale of the infantry[9].

An associated problem was the lack of adaptation on the part of the defence structure to the specific German geography. The FRG did not have forces at its disposal specifically designed for combat in industrial areas, forests or mountanous regions, despite the prominence of such terrain. Thirty percent of the area was covered by forests, and, on average, there was a village of 230 inhabitants for every square kilometre. Any war waged on German soil would thus be a fight over villages or woods, and often enough a fight in the mountains, for which purposes neither armoured battalions or even mechanised infantry companies, nor the artillery would be suitable. Hence the recommendation for mechanised forces to be de-emphasised, since their long range was anyhow only usable in open spaces, which formed merely a small part of the FRG's territory.

However, Uhle-Wettler rejected the common notion that 'confined spaces' as e.g. urban and suburban areas would automatically represent difficult terrain for mechanised invaders. On the contrary, if such areas were left undefended, the aggressor might simply seek shelter there, particularly in the context of a manoeuvre-oriented type of warfare. An appropriate defence for such terrain was thus deemed imperative, and only attainable by means of light infantry[10].

Over-technification was problematic i.a. because of the rapidly increasing costs of major weapons systems, whence the emphasis on quality rather than quantity. As an alternative hereto, Uhle-Wettler pointed to the potential of anti-tank missiles, which might allegedly be made extremely cheaply[11]. The fact that this option had not been adequately exploited, and the resultant over-mechanisation of the *Bundeswehr*, he explained with reference to the 'legacy of Guderian', which had, ever since the 'Himmeroder Memorandum' of 1950 (cf. above, Chapter III) led to an unwarranted predilection for the offensive. One consequence thereof had been the complete mechanization of the army, intended to provide the armed forces with 'capability of wide-range offensives and large-scale manoeuvre warfare'. According to Uhle-Wettler, however, 'only an attacker today has to mechanise his fighting forces entirely'[12].

The defender's alternative option was to adapt to the particular terrain features, such as forested areas, industrial and population centres, i.e. 'ecological niches' that were eminently suitable for a defence with simpler, and hence cheaper, weapons, particularly missiles. Furthermore, by means of missile strikes, the invader could be driven away from the open and tank-friendly terrain into confined spaces, where the defence could take up combat by means of specialised weapons.

According to Uhle-Wettler, the defence thus needed two types of divisions: mechanised divisions for combat in open territory, and light infantry divisions for fighting in closed terrain. The latter should compensate for their lack of mobility by way of dispersal, a measure which would, in addition, provide some protection against heavy artillery barrages as well as nuclear strikes. To a considerable extent the defender would be at liberty to choose the terrain, although he would have to satisfy the requirements of forward defence simultaneously with providing for complete fire coverage of the defended area.

At liberty to choose, the light infantry ought, of course, to opt for 'infantry terrain' such as villages and suburban areas, industrial areas, woods, marshes and sub-alpine mountaneous regions. In such terrain, the aggressor would be at a disadvantage and unable to play his 'trump-cards'. The defenders should, furthermore, seek to force the aggressor to dismount in order to slow down his advance, gain time to deploy their own reserves and, finally, engage the opponent under conditions where his 'trumps' (long-range fire and mechanised mobility) would be to no avail. Against such a defence, it would only be possible for an aggressor to establish control over the target country by means of infantry, something which would considerably slow down the forward momentum of his attack and, by so doing, fulfil one of the goals of the defender[13].

The tactics advocated by Uhle-Wettler resembled and were partly inspired by partisan warfare. The infantry should yield to a superior opponent and allow him to penetrate deeper, only to strike at his logistical columns. In this way, the defenders would i.a. force the aggressor to protect his rear by means of fighting units, thus depleting his front-line strength. Thus the defenders would 'buy time with space', in analogy with Afheldt's recommendations.

In order to improve mobility and agility, the weaponry of the infantry should be as light as possible, and the troops were primarily envisaged as moving about on foot, although light (and cheap) transport vehicles, as well as helicopters would also be called for. The latter would allow the infantry to serve as a kind of airborne 'fleet in being', reminiscent of naval strategy, which in collaboration with the stationary light infantry should tie up the opposing forces[14].

Uhle-Wettler envisaged taking the decentralization of forces very far indeed. The basic unit would be the 1/12-man squad (one NCO and 12 privates), itself operating in three sub-teams. The platoon would integrate three squads plus a platoon unit for radio communication etc. and a platoon leader. At the company level, three platoons would be mated with various heavier weapons. These would be assigned to a special platoon, consisting of two squads armed with four light mortars as well as *Panzerfäuste* or ATGMs. The logistical requirements would likewise be handled at the company level. The higher levels as e.g. battalion, would exercise only an absolute minimum of command functions, giving platoon and company leaders as long a leash as possible[15].

This would be a rather manpower-intensive form of warfare, requiring, furthermore, a great percentage of active troops. The form of combat of the infantry would be very demanding, and it would accordingly have to consist of active soldiers with long training. The overall number of troops might hence have to be increased, according to Uhle-Wettler's assessment. However, the fact that these forces would be very weak in the offensive should make this acceptable without causing insurmountable security political problems[16].

As a way of implementing his proposed scheme, Uhle-Wettler did not merely envisage unilateral conversion, but also recommended refocusing the MBFR talks (still in progress in 1980 when his work was written), implying a shift of emphasis from manpower levels to armoured forces. In this manner, mutually satisfactory agreements would appear to be within reach.

Three-Dimensional NOD

The most recent substantial military proposal in the realm of NOD has been presented by Captain Ludger Dünne, writing under the auspices of the Institute of Peace Research and Security Policy at the University of Hamburg, IFSH (cf. above, Chapter IV).

As his point of departure, Dünne took a rather permissive definition of 'structural inability to attack' (i.e. NOD), implying an incapability of border-crossing operations with political or military significance[17]. Neither should small-scale incursions without political consequences be regarded as violations of this principle, nor would even rather large-scale 'stand-off' attacks fall outside the bounds of the permissible, since they would lack political significance unless accompanied by ground force incursion.

The focus was thus on options, rather than on postures as such, and the author explicitly stated that the defender required an 'option of victory', albeit only the defensive one of restoring the *status quo ante bellum*. He rejected not merely Afheldt's radical ideas, but also other more moderate proposals for a stationary defence, on the grounds of their inability to reconquer lost terrain, or to provide a sufficient area coverage without becoming prohibitively costly. However, the current (alleged) forward defence was not deemed credible either, since the attacker might simply mass forces for breakthroughs, and thus force NATO to apply its only fall-back option, namely nuclear escalation with the resultant destruction of the FRG[18].

Dünne's own alternative was a skilful adaptation to the terrain combined with well-known military technologies. Far from recommending emerging technology as a panacea (such as many other NOD proponents), he proposed the exact opposite: as a general rule, well-known and tested, rather cheap and robust technologies should receive the main emphasis[19].

The organizational structure was to be simplified by abolishing the divisional level entirely, making the brigade the basic formation, responsible for defending a pre-defined stretch of front. Above the brigade level would be the corps level, with a total of 8-10 corps sectors in the FRG, each encompassing 4-6 brigade sectors. The brigades should be partly skeletonised, with a permanently-ready 'brigade formation' responsible for the integration of reservists into the fighting brigades upon mobilization, a process to be repeatedly rehearsed in peacetime[20].

The weapons systems should belong either to the brigade or to the corps level. To the level of the corps would be assigned:

—Armoured air defence vehicles mounted with both guns and missiles.
—Helicopters, primarily for combat, but also for anti-tank purposes.
—MLRS systems for use against enemy airborne landings.
—Air-mobile armoured vehicles, i.e. infantry fighting vehicles and small tanks, primarily as reserves.

To the basic level of the brigades would be assigned the same types of systems, all highly mobile and suitable for use under even the most demanding terrain conditions. The main weapons system would be the above-mentioned airborne armoured vehicle, but the MLRS would also be extremely important, i.a. for remote mine-laying in the enemy's midst, in its turn presumably constituting a most effective counter-mobility device. As a means of further impeding the enemy's freedom of manoeuvre, Dünne pointed to landscaping: the transformation of tank-friendly into tank-hostile terrain by the plantation of woods, the digging of canals, etc.—a most effective, albeit for obvious reasons long-term, means of defence[21].

The 'third dimension' was to be exploited to a great extent, both as a medium for transport (by means of helicopters), for anti-tank operations, and for similar operations against intruding ground forces. Since helicopters were envisaged as the main vehicle for these aerial military activities, the proposal thus implied taking the fullest advantage of what others have called 'the rotary-wing revolution'[22]. In order to deny this advantageous use of the aerial dimension to the enemy, however, all units would have to be equipped with a full range of air defence guns and missiles.

The posture resulting from the recommended reforms would be a genuine combined arms posture, yet without offensive capabilities. This was due to one important deficiency, namely that of ordinary tanks, without which no major border-crossing operations were conceivable. Whereas the posture would contain air-mobile armoured vehicles, these would, on the one hand, be hopelessly inferior in direct combat with the enemy's tanks on his territory; on the other hand, their reliance on rotary-wing aerial transport would limit their long-range mobility, thus making them suitable only for tactical mobility[23].

Dünne's proposal thus incorporated a number of ideas from its predecessors in the NOD literature surveyed in the previous chapter, including Hannig's concept of the complete abolition of armoured formations, paving the way for a rather permissive approach to aerial systems, and the SAS concept of mobile 'spiders', which were to be effectively immobilised beyond a state's own territory, etc. One of the most obvious deficiencies of Dünne's scheme was, however, the insufficient attention given to implementation, making the envisioned posture stand out against the present as perhaps more radical than intended.

A Controversial Admiral

Rear Admiral Elmar Schmähling has been one of the highest-ranking active officers ever to promote the NOD cause. This had earned him a reputation as a 'lone ranger' in the *Bundeswehr*, as well as a few official reprimands i.a. for his public denouncement of the flexible response strategy in the spring of 1989. He had i.a. participated actively in the Pugwash Study Group on 'Conventional Forces in Europe' mentioned in the previous chapter. In this context, he had taken advantage of his naval background to contribute to filling the 'maritime gap' in German NOD literature.

His general attitude to naval matters differed radically from what one might expect from an Admiral. He e.g. explicitly predicted that the pride and glory of the navy, the major surface ships, were facing obsolescence. As the fate of the HMS *Sheffield* in the Falklands/Malvinas War demonstrated, they would henceforth be unable to prevail in the contest with the much cheaper anti-ship munitions, which might even be launched from land-based weapons platforms. This was due primarily to the increased precision of missiles, which allowed powers to control vast sea areas without surface combatants. In war, duels would thus no longer be fought between opposing ships, but rather between one party's ships and the other's missiles, launched from ashore. Alternatively, the surface warships would be engaged by submerged submarines, which were most likely to prevail in the ensuing duels[24].

Whereas navies, under the spell of the aforementioned objective trends, have often tried to legitimise the maintenance of a surface fleet with reference to military tasks short of war, Schmähling was prepared to acknowledge surface ships as neither a *sine qua non* of successful crisis management, nor really suitable for this task, above all because of their unfortunate tendency to end up in 'high noon situations'[25].

He did not even accept the validity of the often-heard argument that NATO, as a transatlantic alliance, was vitally dependent on SLOCs. Whereas this might hold true for the present, in the years to come the European need for overseas reinforcements could easily be reduced substantially. In actual fact, Western Europe should be perfectly able to 'make ends meet' without any such reinforcements. The present author has even (at a conference in Amsterdam in November 1988) had the curious experience of trying in vain to persuade the Admiral of the continuing validity of this traditional naval point of view[26].

The Admiral thus recommended a shift of emphasis in naval postures from surface ships towards 'many small, possibly camouflaged and/or mobile weapons carriers at the coast or offshore'. The submarine, on the other hand, was forecast a much longer lease of life, by virtue of its ability to remain concealed, out of reach of an opponent's sensor systems.

Schmähling has dealt with the land forces as well. Here too, he has criticised the obstinate adherence amongst his colleagues to obsolete military postures. On the one hand, the present land defence was, according to him, fraught with a number of deficiencies and inconsistencies:

—It was limited to the defence of a narrow strip of land, but possessed neither any modern state-of-the-art barrier concept, nor light troops optimised for such a task.

—It was trapped in a process of 'structural disarmament' due to the rapidly rising unit costs for military equipment.

—It emphasised types of weaponry which entailed first shot premiums (cf. the 'high noon' analogy above), whilst being constrained by a doctrine of allowing the opponent the first strike.

—The forces were stationed too far away from their planned war-time stations, with a resultant need for early mobilization and demanding redeployments, which might be destabilizing in a crisis situation.

—The integration of nuclear arms in the conventional structure held back means that were needed for immediate defence[27].

On the other hand, NATO's approach to squaring these deficiencies was assessed as counter-productive. With its focus on long-range deep interdiction, NATO would miss the opportunities provided by the so-called 'window of efficiency'. Schmähling's argument resembled the well-known admonition by commanders: 'Don't shoot until you can see the whites of their eyes!' Under modern conditions, weapons systems such as tanks were particularly vulnerable at a certain distance, within range of the counter-weapons, yet beyond their own weapons' range. The most cost-effective moment at which to neutralise a tank would therefore be when it was within this 'window', rather than far beyond it, as envisioned in FOFA planning[28].

He thus assessed the basic ideas of the alternative models as more in line with objective trends in military technology, by virtue of their recommendations for substituting long-range, accurate, and thus highly effective, fire for the movement of the weapons systems on the battle-field. The defence should take advantage of the friendly terrain, and not succumb to the deceptive lure of cost-ineffective all-purpose forces. The friendly terrain was to be prepared in several ways: by laying optical fibre networks; by emplacing seismic sensors below ground in the border areas and plugged into the optical fibre network; by mounting sensor systems on high-rise buildings; by integrating civilian radio transmitters and cable networks into the war-time communication network; by constructing underground command posts; by storing mines, munitions, bridge-building equipment and the like in the areas where they would be needed, etc. In this manner a centralised, real-time combat management would become possible, and present plans for sub-delegation of command might thus be revised.

The main components of the envisaged defence posture would be state-of-the-art obstacle-creating systems such as dynamic mines, belonging to the third generation of mines, featuring multi-sensored, 'smart' and mobile mines, capable of saturating a considerable area. Furthermore, various types of explosives might be used for creating artificial tank barriers, which would, in their turn, bring the enemy's tank columns to a stand-still and expose them to the fire from friendly artillery. These artillery systems should be stationary and fire from sheltered positions, albeit from alternating stands as a way of hampering localization and resultant counter-battery fire.

As far as the manning of such weapons systems was concerned, Schmähling recommended an organisation along militia lines, implying that the soldiers would fight on home ground, and that any plans for crisis-destabilizing redeployments might be abandoned[29].

The goal would be a territorially fixed (*Raumgebunden*) defence structure, incapable of major offensive operations: a criterion that NATO's present structure did not satisfy, according to the Admiral, who with this statement contradicted the almost unanimous assessment of his colleagues. Since the recommended defence scheme would *per se* improve NATO's defensive capabilities, it would make no sense to make mutuality a precondition for the reform, even though a WTO reciprocation would, of course, be most welcome. A situation of 'mutual defensive superiority' would thus come within reach, something which would amount to the 'conventional stability' so often mentioned as the goal. As a corollary hereto, nuclear weapons ought to be built down radically, perhaps by way of establishing nuclear-weapons-free zones, but in any case by depriving them of their war-fighting roles, leaving only a residual role of deterring the enemy from nuclear attack[30]. On the basis of such considerations Schmähling was not in the least disturbed by the INF settlement, but publicly recommended proceeding along the same path, including a 'third zero' solution. On other occasions, he recommended a denuclearization of the fleets, something which was, on the one hand, fairly unproblematic from the point of view of the (anyhow conventional) German navy, but which, on the other hand, could be interpreted as disloyal to the US Navy[31].

As mentioned above, his overt dissent from the official policy of the FRG motivated his employers in the Ministry of Defence to give him a severe reprimand, implying a temporary stop to further promotions.

In the beginning of 1990, the controversial Admiral published a fully-fledged book in which his dissent from the official security policy of the FRG was elaborated, entitled *The Impossible War*—soon to become a best-seller. It was a very polemical work which respected no 'taboos'. It criticised in harsh words the very foundations of the Atlantic Alliance, and the entire strategy of NATO and the *Bundeswehr*, as well as the practices of security political decision-making in the FRG that left much to be desired from a democratic point of view.

The notion of the USA as the unselfish benefactor from overseas was questioned by pointing to the actual 'privileges' of the USA with regard to vulnerability and risk. From the American point of view, NATO constituted, according to Schmähling, above all an instrument for US national power politics. Seen in this light, the hegemonic status enjoyed by the USA within NATO appeared as a privilege, indeed unfair as compared with the much more exposed European members of the alliance. Particularly the FRG was at an unjustified disadvantage in this respect, with the role of constituting the future battle-ground, yet enjoying only a restricted sovereignty in alliance matters, i.a. with regard to whether, how and where a future war were to be fought.

Burdens and influence thus needed redistribution, which ought to entail a greater West German influence on matters of strategy pertaining to its own soil, in accordance with the 'most affected' principle. Furthermore, full and equal sovereignity for the FRG should be demanded. Finally, in the European cooperation on defence affairs 'German and European interests should be in the forefront. Western Europe cannot forever subordinate its policy to the security political objectives of the USA'[32].

NATO's strategy of flexible response was severely criticised for being both logically flawed, based on false or questionable premises, and as most likely to have disastrous consequences if it were ever to be put to a real-life test. The claims of NATO that the absence of war in Europe was a result of nuclear deterrence was likened to the effect of salt on elephants: one might just as well claim that salt kept elephants away because very few people had ever had elephants in their kitchen![33]

Conventional forces and strategy did not fare much better in Schmähling's evaluation. As a result of its complete mechanization and emphasis on armour, the *Bundeswehr* allegedly possessed an offensive potential that was quite unwarranted in view of its officially envisaged combat tasks. Whereas it was meant to fight only on West German soil, it did have substantial capabilities for border-crossing operations. In this connection, he pointed to a few offensive elements hitherto ignored by other NOD proponents. In addition to air landing capabilities and mobile bridge-crossing capabilities (the possession of neither of which was warranted), there were, likewise, no defensive requirements for military priests, courts, medical services or the like, since all of these services would be available from the civilian sector in a war fought on the FRG's own soil[34].

With regard to his alternative to present strategy, Schmähling merely elaborated on his previous ideas: the defence should be strictly conventional, and nuclear weapons should serve the sole purpose of deterring nuclear attack or 'blackmail', something which would, however, be difficult to ensure in an 'extended deterrence mode'. The FRG should not allow other nations to decide about the launch of nuclear weapons from West German soil, but should only accept a 'nuclear guarantee' which allowed it a decisive say. If such a guarantee should prove unobtainable, the Admiral advised the FRG to reconsider the matter of an indigenous nuclear potential (sic.)[35]. This last recommendation seemed very ill-advised indeed, but may have been simply a 'slip of the tongue' (or meant ironically), since it was nowhere elaborated upon.

Furthermore, the FRG ought to exploit what was actually a unique opportunity for creating a genuine national, territorial defence (*Landes-verteidigung*), by virtue of its legal obligation to defend only its own territory. The best way of doing so would be by means of a territorial militia, the size of which needed not exceed 300-350,000 men. The 'magic figure' of 495,000 for the *Bundeswehr* was, he claimed, by no means founded on military considerations, but merely intended to exploit to the limit the maximum of 500,000 allowed by the WEU[36].

The militia forces were to receive only a short initial training, but, as a compensation, be called up for frequent refresher training, as a way of facilitating which they were to be locally based. They should be equipped with modern weaponry, including ATGMs, mines, SAMs and the like, designed according to the 'small, plenty, cheap' principle. The terrain should be prepared for combat to the greatest possible extent compatible with civilian needs, e.g. by constructing bunkers, communication posts and the like as an integral part of civilian urban society. The maritime defence forces should be structured in conformity with the principles set out above, i.e. concentrate on land-based anti-ship missiles, sea mines and submarines[37].

The conventional military defence was to be supplemented with a civil defence, enjoying a considerably higher priority with regard to budgets and resources than was presently the case. The aim would be a genuine 'total defence' adequate for the needs of the immensely vulnerable post-industrial society. Whereas this might be understood as amounting to a militarization of society (also because the Admiral apparently envisaged extending military service to women), this trend might be contravened by furthering democratization of the armed forces[38].

The latter recommendation proved to be highly relevant for Schmähling's own case. The outspoken criticism outlined above apparently became 'the last straw', which brought the career of Admiral Schmähling to an abrupt end. In the beginning of 1990, at the age of 52, i.e. more than seven years before his retirement age, he was placed into early retirement, i.e. sacked, without any elaborate attempts by his employers to conceal the reasons, namely his open dissent from the official line of the government.

Whereas such an official reaction may perhaps seem understandable to observers accustomed to a greater degree of service 'loyalty', it actually went against West German practice, i.e. the 'citizen in uniform' tradition. Two years before the 'Schmähling case', the Constitutional Court had ruled *expressis verbis* that soldiers (regardless of their rank) had an inalienable right to 'deal critically with defence political issues, and in this connection, also to contradict the opinion of comrades and superiors'. The opposition parties, the Greens and the SPD, criticized the decision by Defence Minister Stoltenberg, and defended the courage and loyalty of the retired Admiral, without, however, being able to reverse the decision[39].

Since his retirement, the now '*AD*' Admiral made a great effort to support the peace movement and like-minded political forces in both Germanies, e.g. as a main speaker at the 'Easter March', convened by the peace movements in 1990, for the first time ever in both halves of Berlin. On this occasion, he proposed a dissolution of both alliances, in view i.a. of the development in the German question[40].

A Neutralist General

An colleague of Schmähling's of even greater prominence has recently joined the alternative defence 'crowd': General (ret.) Günter Kiessling with the prestigious title of Former Deputy SACEUR. In a work entitled *Neutrality is No Treason. Sketch of a European Peace Order*, published in the spring of 1989, Kiessling went so far as to advocate neutrality for a future united Germany. The rationale for this was very reminiscent of the debate in the 1950s, not least of Colonel Bogislaw von Bonin (cf. chapter III above), whom Kiessling also specifically mentioned as 'a man of character'. Just as it had been for Bonin, German unification was the paramount goal for him, whereas 'ties with the West cannot be the goal, but merely a detour on the way towards the goal'[41].

Consequently, if alliance obligations should stand in the way of unification, they would have to yield. This was believed to be exactly the situation facing West Germany as of 1989, just as it, in retrospect, had been in 1952 when the Soviets made their offer of unification-cum-neutralization in the famous 'Stalin Note'. Acording to Kiessling, the Soviet offer had been meant seriously, motivated by an earnest concern about the implications for Soviet security of German rearmament in the context of NATO. West Germany had therefore probably missed an almost unique opportunity[42].

Today, just as in the 1950s, German unification, according to Kiessling, presupposed the acquiescence of both East and West, and hence demanded that the position of neither would deteriorate as a result of unification. Viewed in this light, the present situation might present a 'window of opportunity', because both blocs (and especially both superpowers) were eager to maintain balance at as low a level of armaments and military expenditure as possible. If only the unavailability of the all-German military potential for both East and West could be ensured, then neither bloc was likely to oppose unification and the ensuing loss of the military potential of 'their Germany'. That the Soviets would accept a unilateral withdrawal from 'their Germany' was (in retrospect, erroneously) dismissed as wild fantasy[43].

The four former wartime allies would thus have to guarantee the status of a united Germany, which should be permitted to enter no alliance directed against any one of the signatories. Whereas the NATO allies of Germany were not, in Kiessling's assessment, likely to oppose German withdrawal from the alliance, Europeanization as pursued by certain political groups in the FRG might well damage the prospects of unification. The rejuvenation of the WEU, as well as any possible future modicum of military cooperation within the EC, ought thus to be rejected[44].

In his view, the great powers were likely to prefer an armed Germany to a military vacuum in the centre of Europe. As a minimum, the united Germany would therefore have to possess armed forces capable of an effective border defence, but preferably also possessing some endurance so as to escape the need for early employment of nuclear weapons[45].

It was, however, just as imperative that the united Germany should not be perceived as a military threat by its neighbours, whence the need for refraining (in a binding treaty with adequate verification) from the acquistition of or access to nuclear weapons. With regard to the conventional forces, Kiessling suggested a force of 300,000 troops, distributed as follows:

Central staff	10,000
Navy	20,000
Air force (including air defence)	70,000
Army	200,000.

The emphasis should be placed on the land forces, whereas the navy would comprise little more than a number of small coastal protection assets, and the air force, in its turn, little more than air defence means. The army should consist of forty brigades: twenty for border defence and twenty 'intervention' brigades. While the former should be composed of militia type troops, the latter should comprise ten armoured brigades and ten air cavalry brigades of regular forces. In order to meet any concerns on the part of other states, the conventional forces should be subjected to certain constraints, i.a. a prohibition on long-range rockets and a ceiling of 2,000 on the number of tanks[46].

Kiessling had no objections to the notion of the four powers deciding upon the military status of Germany, as would be the case with the envisioned peace treaty, since this would only limit sovereignty towards the outside, leaving the Germans at liberty internally. Furthermore, he envisaged the suggested solution to the German problem as a step in the direction of an all-European peace order, although the configuration of this was left blurred. It would, however, imply a wide-ranging disengagement of the blocs, i.e. what he called 'horizontal disarmament'. Whereas the first step in the disengagement process would consist in the neutralization of Germany, other countries could join in the next step. As likely candidates for arrangements similar to those of Germany, the General mentioned Poland, Czechoslovakia, Austria and Hungary from the eastern side, and the Benelux countries as well as Denmark from the western, something which would presumably amount to a 'Central European peace order'[47].

Whereas it was, indeed, unusual for such a high-ranking officer to advocate such a radical break with the official security policy of his country, Kiessling was by no means alone in this respect. His neutralist example has e.g. been followed by his colleague, General (ret.) Gerd Schmückle (also a one-time Deputy SACEUR) who prophesised the inevitable dissolution of NATO, along with the disappearing threat it had been formed to meet. According to him, however, the western alliance, along with its eastern counterpart, might be replaced by a new Euro-Atlantic system, which should include the USSR[48].

The Curse of Low-Level Flying

Whereas Kiessling had devoted his attention to broader security political conceptions, the alternative thinking of Brigadier General Hermann Hagena has had a somewhat narrower scope, focusing on a critique of NATO's aerial strategy with its emphasis on the offensive.

Deep aerial operations were not 'only' problematic because of their crisis stability implications, but also because of the peacetime costs. Low-altitude flying with its diabolical noise placed a severe burden on the civilian population of West Germany, particularly on the inhabitants of areas close to USAF and RAFG air bases. Furthermore, it entailed risks of severe accidents, as had been illustrated in Ramstein and Remscheid in 1988[49].

The military rationale for low-level flying, however, was that it was presumably the only way of penetrating the dense air defence array of the WTO. Whilst acknowledging this, Hagena nevertheless expressed doubts whether low-level flying was really worth the cost, and regarded it as 'imperative only according to the conceptual calculus, according to which offensive combat is an appropriate means for the weaker to defeat the stronger'. However, he regarded 'an unprejudiced reassessment of the strengths of the defensive' as long overdue[50].

In the spring of 1990, Hagena elaborated on his scepticism in a book on *Low-Altitude Flying in Central Europe*, featuring i.a. a detailed historical analysis of low-level flying in actual wars. The experience gathered from the Vietnam War, the June and Yom Kippur Wars in the Middle East, the Falkland/Malvinas War and in Afghanistan was found to neither corroborate the assumption of the effectiveness of low-level flying, nor to present any convincing case for offensive aerial operations in general[51]. On the basis of a technological analysis, he furthermore found state-of-the-art SAMs (especially man-portable ones such as 'Stinger') to pose a serious, and highly cost-effective, threat to even the most sophisticated aeroplanes in the most demanding flight patterns, a trend that was more likely to continue than to be reversed by any decisive break-through in aeronautics.

There were also security political considerations militating against offensive aerial operations such as OCA, above all that they tended to depend for their effectiveness on the surprise factor. In this respect, however, NATO was at a severe disadvantage, since the WTO (as the stipulated attacker) would be at liberty to select the time and place of the initial strike. If low-level flying for penetration purposes was at all warranted, it would therefore be for the WTO, but not for NATO[52].

NATO's previous rejection of Soviet proposals for an inclusion of air forces in the CFE talks had broken down with the acceptance, at the June summit of 1989, of equal ceilings for combat aircraft in the ATTU region. This was, understandably, assessed positively by Hagena, who recommended focusing on a build-down of offensive aerial potentials. The conceptual guideline for this endeavour should be a shift of emphasis from OCA and deep interdiction towards 'defensive counter-air', battle-field interdiction and close air support (coincidentally almost exactly the same set of priorities as recommended by the present author at about the same time). On such a conceptual basis, NATO would, according to Hagena, be in a position to achieve a positive response from the WTO by building down its offensive capability without in any way impairing its defensive capabilities[53].

Military Research

As a general rule, military research institutions have not dealt with NOD. An exception, however, has been the University (formerly: Academy) of the *Bundeswehr* in Munich. A couple of researchers from the Institute for Applied Systems and Operations Research (IASFOR) at this institution, headed by Professor Reinar K. Huber, have for a number of years dealt extensively with the problems of conventional stability, including the potential contribution of NOD. In this connection, Huber has i.a. participated in the Pugwash Study Group, as well as collaborated with the Starnberg research team mentioned in Chapter IV. Most of his contributions to the debate have, as was to be expected, been very technical and couched in mathematical formulae, qualities to which the present author is, alas, unable to render full justice in the following account.

As was perhaps to be expected from a civilian and academic 'man on horseback', Huber consistently stressed the importance of military efficiency, not however as an end in itself, but rather as a *sine qua non* of higher-ranking goals such as stability. However, the various forms of stability were not, unfortunately, always mutually supportive. Whereas post-WWII Europe was assessed as having enjoyed quite a high degree of crisis stability, this appeared to have been bought at the expence of a correspondingly high degree of 'arms race instability' which the public could not be expected to accept indefinitely.

In his view, the presence of nuclear weapons might go a long way towards explaining the high level of crisis stability in Europe, in which case NATO might be facing serious problems due to the present trend towards denuclearisation, which obliged the Western alliance to seek alternative means of stabilising the conventional level[54].

Unfortunately, however, coventional crisis stability would be hard to attain with two antagonists equipped with general-purpose forces, designed to operate in all, including offensive, combat modes. Huber defined this crisis stability as a situation where 'in a given crisis neither side perceives an advantage in attacking first', 'advantage' simply meaning that the relative force ratios would improve as the conflict progressed. A thorough mathematical analysis confirmed that 'a high level of security may only be attained through superiority', amounting to a severe security dilemma[55].

Both alliances in Europe were assessed as being presently structurally capable of offensive operations, with the inescapable conclusion that the situation was inherently rather crisis-unstable. *A fortiori*, the programmes currently underway in NATO (FOFA, etc.) were deemed dysfunctional because they would add new vulnerable high-priority targets to NATO's current target profile, a particularly severe problem if the implementation of the programmes would weaken forward defence against the WTO's first echelon forces[56].

Whereas there were thus similarities between NATO and the WTO in their common offensive-capable structure, a basic difference between the security conceptions of the two alliances could be identified. While NATO had generally striven for security by way of uncertainties, the USSR had sought security based on the certainty of being able to repel any aggressor by virtue of superiority. Furthermore, 'the more the credibility of nuclear deterrence diminishes for whatever reason, the higher will be the likelihood that a Soviet-type stability attitude will be adopted by both antagonists', in which case the only way of achieving satisfactory crisis stability would be to ensure a significant defence advantage[57].

Arms control endeavours aiming merely at reducing force levels would represent no solution, but might in actual fact contribute to a deterioration. Although the IASFOR had collaborated to a certain extent with the Starnberg Group, they criticised some of Albrecht von Müller's arms control proposals rather harshly. In a rebuttal of his proposals for numerical reductions, they proclaimed that what really mattered was to test scientifically the validity of the 'defence efficiency hypothesis' (derived from Clausewitz), according to which the defence was per se the stronger form of combat[58].

The defence efficiency hypothesis was thus revealed as the sine qua non of stability. In order to either validate or falsify it, the IASFOR research team had already developed a sophisticated computer simulation model by means of which they have attempted to test the various proposals[59]. I shall not go into any detail with this simulation model, but merely alert the reader to some of its limitations (openly acknowledged by its designers), as well as recapitulate some of the principal findings:

—The simulation scenarios all belonged to the tactical (i.e. regiment and battalion) level, whereas neither the operational nor the strategic levels were taken directly into account.

—The team had merely tested components of various models, rather than aggregate postures, with the result that potential synergies, stemming from the collaboration of various components, were not automatically given due credit.

—The components were tested for their effectiveness as supplements to traditional armoured forces, rather than as substitutes for these.

—The tests evaluated the effectiveness of the proposals for a forward defence. Even a territorial defence of Afheldt's type was therefore merely tested for its ability to halt an attack, not to prevent it by other means.

—The simulations operated on the assumption of a constant threat, and hence took into account neither the effects of e.g. the elimination of incentives for pre-emptive attacks, nor the effects of the lack of worthwhile targets.

—A number of immeasurable factors, as e.g. the surprise factor and the morale of the troops, were disregarded.

Such limitations were, of course, unavoidable, and their being openly acknowledged by the authors merely testified to their scientific rigour. However, they should be kept in mind as a hedge against jumping to unwarrented conclusions.

The simulation model tested the following active (i.e. traditional) force structures:

A: A normal, reinforced, armoured infantry (*Panzergrenadier*) battalion.

B: A mixed reinforced, armoured infantry battalion.

C: A mixed, reinforced tank battalion.

D: A reinforced 'Armoured Infantry Battalion 90' as envisaged in current *Bundeswehr* planning.

For the sake of comparison, the following reactive (ie. defensive) model components were tested:

E: Afheldt's techno-commandos.

F: The infantry forces of the Swiss territorial defence.

G: The infantry forces of the (vintage 1984) SAS model.

H: The infantry forces of the Austrian territorial defence.

I: The 'shield forces' of Löser's area-covering defence.

K: The 'cavalry battalions' of the SAS model.

L: The anti-tank groups of Füreder's 'cellular defence'.

M: Gerber's anti-tank and SAM belt.

N: Hannig's fire belt.

O: The proposal of the authors themselves—a light infantry battalion as a component of a barrier brigade with the mission of creating a selective fire belt.

All the defence structures tested were armed with up to three of the following five types of weaponry: machine guns, automatic guns, guns, guided missiles and 'fire-and-forget' missiles, in addition to artillery pieces and rocket launchers. It was stipulated that the defence forces were to defend a front sector of five kilometres, that they had prepared the terrain in advance, and that time had allowed them to assume combat position. The attacking force was stipulated as a motorised rifle regiment or a tank regiment, in either case consisting of three battalions, supported by artillery and helicopter forces.

The results of the approximately 500 simulation runs were relatively predictable: the modernised traditional forces were reasonably effective, as compared with the currently deployed ones, which performed poorly. The static territorial defence concepts proved themselves incapable of creating points of main effort, and only F was assessed as possessing an adequate effectiveness, although G also fared rather well. Afheldt's units proved incapable of preventing break-throughs (something which they, incidentally, were never intended to do). The dynamic territorial defence concepts (I-L) generally performed poorly, as did the integrated fire belt concepts (M-N).

The selective fire barrier concept (O) performed best, a fact which might arouse a certain scepticism, since this concept represented the choice of the authors and designers of the simulation model. It was, of course, not a question of the authors 'fiddling the figures', but of their having been able to optimise their own proposal to the demands implied by the simulation set-up.

On the basis of these tests, the authors recommended options F and O for further study, which should include simulations at higher levels as e.g. division and corps units. The authors have since worked on creating a model which could take the higher levels into due account, but the results are not yet available[60].

Evaluation

With the civilian, pro-disarmament researchers at the Munich Military Academy we have come a very long way indeed from the image of the militaristic 'men on horseback'. Undoubtedly, the promotion of the alternative vision of 'citizens in uniform' has accomplished significant results in erasing the image of the Prussian, offensive-minded officer corps.

There certainly remains a predominant scepticism on the part of the officers of the *Bundeswehr* towards the new NOD ideas. Nevertheless, the many officers recorded in this, as well as other, chapters of this book as supporting (either unreservedly or at least partly and conditionally) the NOD ideas have shown that the negative stand was by no means so unanimous as to confirm the allegations often made by sceptics and critics that 'these may be nice ideas, but military expertise rejects them'.

This, in itself, may have been a significant accomplishment, since the resultant 'neutralization' of military 'authority' provided greater scope for arguments of substance. Although the NOD discourse has (partly) been about military affairs, there has never been any compelling reason why it should be acknowledged as a prerogative of the military services.

Furthermore, even within the top-brass, 'main-stream' military establishment, there seems to be a growing acceptance of the NOD ideas, perhaps thanks to the fact that the strictly unilateral option of Western NOD conversion had been rendered obsolete by the Eastern openings in this direction.

General Wolfgang Altenburg (until October 1989 Chairman of NATO's Military Committee) was a good example of the gradual acceptance of at least some of the NOD conceptions that is slowly emerging even in main-stream military circles, and at the very highest level. In his contribution to an anthology published for Horst Afheldt's 60th birthday, he wrote i.a.

'First of all, future military structures and conceptions may well be influenced by elements associated with the names of numerous authors of the present volume: a higher share of infantry and a lesser of armour, a higher degree of stationary deployment (*Bodenständigkeit*) in the defence posture, combined with mobile elements, further development and utilization of new technologies of an explicitly defensive character, such as intelligent mines; a higher degree of cadering and dependence on mobilization. (. . .) It will become apparent that many an idea has sprung from the 'alternative strategies' that has subsequently proven itself fruitful, when its time has come, and when it is being adopted by both sides'[61].

CHAPTER VI

The Political Scene Before 1989

Having now analysed a wide range of independent proposals for defence reform, stemming either from the academic community or from (mostly retired) officers, I shall devote the following chapters to a survey of the political NOD debate in the FRG.

Needless to say, the distinction between 'academic', 'military' and 'political' proposals is somewhat artificial. On the one hand, academics in general, and peace researchers in particular, have always taken a vivid interest in politics, as have most officers. On the other hand, some politicians (in the FRG actually quite a few) hold academic degrees. What sets politicians apart from the others is, however, their immediate influence on authoritative decision-making. Whereas the other two groups must thus seek to persuade politicians in order to realise their plans, the latter simply have to make up their minds and bargain amongst themselves.

Before proceeding with the attitudes of the political parties towards NOD, a brief description of the role of the parties within the political system seems appropriate for context-setting. However, since this work is not intended as a treatise on comparative politics, the following account is very superficial.

Political parties form the core of the political system of the FRG, as it has developed since 1945. Indeed, in contrast to most democracies of an older vintage, the parties are explicitly mentioned in the Constitution (or, to be more precise, in the 'Basic Law') of the FRG as 'constitutional' institutions. Furthermore, the FRG is a parliamentary system, based on proportional representation, which provides better opportunities for 'third parties' than, say, the American or British electoral systems, and which contributes to a somewhat more even distribution of power across the system, i.e. a certain decentralisation[1].

Another aspect of the decentralisation of power has to do with the federal status of the FRG, in which the constituent 'states' (*Länder*) are relatively autonomous in a wide range of issues, albeit not in terms of security or defence policy. Neither the head of state, i.e. the Federal President (a predominantly representative post), nor the leader of government, the Federal Chancellor, are vested with powers comparable with those of, say, the American or French presidents. Still, the Federal Chancellor wields considerable power, i.a. by virtue of his being empowered to appoint the government[2].

The various branches of the executive, i.e. the Federal Government (*Bundesregierung*), likewise, have considerable influence on policy-making, above all through their power of the initiative (and hence 'agenda-setting') and their near-monopoly on information. In the fields of security politics, the two most important actors are the Defence Ministry and the Foreign Office which dominate the key areas of defence policy and arms control, respectively. Both these actors do, however, make a significant input to policy-making within the primary domain of the other, and their areas of responsibility overlap and intersect to a considerable extent, both of them e.g. having 'NATO desks'. 'Bureacratic politics' may thus go quite a long way towards explaining West German politics, as e.g. the MBFR experience showed[3].

The FRG is a highly stable political system. This may be partly due to two factors: One, the threshold for admission to parliament of five percent of the votes (*Sperrklausel*) has prevented an 'atomisation' of the party spectrum in the *Bundestag*, such as has been seen in e.g. the Italian or (to a lesser extent) the Danish parliaments; and two, the requirements for 'constructive votes of non-confidence' have prevented frequent premature elections or government crises. A government simply cannot be deposed before a workable alternative is available.

The FRG has a multiparty system. Until recently, the *Bundestag* in effect comprised merely three (or four, dependening on how one counts the CDU/CSU) parties, which thus formed the core of the political system. Only they are really relevant for the political process, either as government candidates in their own right, or as potential coalition partners for the others. From right to left, they are: the CDU (*Christlich Demokratische Union*) and its sister party, the CSU (*Christlich Soziale Union*), the FDP (*Freie Demokratische Partei*) and the SPD (*Sozialdemokratische Partei Deutschlands*).

To these should be added occasional 'third (i.e. fourth or fifth) parties' with a distinctly marginal status, such as e.g. previously the neo-nazi NPD party and its successor, the present Republicans. Recently, one such formerly marginal party has gained what should probably be regarded as a permanent presence: the Greens (*Die Grünen*). They have, on the one hand, established their presence in the *Bundestag*, whilst, on the other hand, remaining to some extent marginalised in the sense of not being regarded as potential allies by either side. The latter characteristic may, however, be a thing of the past, as the temporary collaboration of the SPD with the Greens in the city council of Berlin (West) indicated[4].

Parties in a system such as this constitute 'institutional interest groups' with the function of 'articulating and aggregating demands' from the population into the political system with a view to effecting an 'authoritative allocation of values for society', most effectively by gaining positions of power. However, contrary to i.a. the American party system, West German political parties are not mere mechanisms for the aggregation of public demands, nor mere instruments for gaining power, but have a distinct ideological basis.

Parties thus channel demands into the political system, wherein included demands pertaining to alternative defence. But parties also mould public opinion as well as modify such demands, both in accordance with their ideological and other dispositions, and for reasons of political tactics. The demands included in the party platforms therefore serve several, both open and hidden, functions. Some of these may represent demands coming from the public, and thus serve to legitimise the party *vis-à-vis* its voters, especially the 'marginal voters'. However, they are not necessarily demands for which the party is willing to invest any major effort. Other demands may reflect ideology, and as such constitute concessions to the 'core voters', but may, once again, not be points for which the party is willing to expend a major effort.

In both cases, the demands in the party platforms thus serve 'hidden functions' (in the sense that they are intended for other than their implied purposes) in addition to their obvious ones. A demand for a change in security policy may thus not primarily be intended to actually transform security policy. The real motive for making such a demand may be the desire to attract marginal votes simultaneously with maintaining the hold on the core votes, with a view to attaining a position of power for the party. Other demands may, of course, represent 'actual policy', for which the party does seriously strive. Even in the latter case, however, the demands are meant as objects for bargaining, and are therefore more often than not deliberately vague, so that the manifest functions may be served only indirectly and partly.

When the parties either adopt or reject demands such as that for alternative defence, it is thus significant. But it ought to come as no surprise if the parties should prefer to remain vague and be reluctant to commit themselves to any concrete proposal.

The realm of security policy is in some respects special, since it has been dominated by a persistent quest for consensus, at least in the sense that governments have been striving for broad majorities, encompassing all the parties constituting the 'body politic'. This makes radical departures from established security policy viewpoints even more significant than changes in other fields.

In the following chapters, I shall concentrate on the SPD, which has been the party having the most intense debate on NOD. The other parties might in fact be interpreted as primarily responding to SPD challenges in this field, rather than as taking independent initiatives. However, as far as the SPD is concerned, it, too, might be understood as responding to changes in its environment, above all to changing perceptions of the 'public mood'.

In general, the political debate in the 1980s took place against the background of a somewhat higher salience of security policy issues in the general public debate, as well as of changing attitudes amongst the population. The belief in an overwhelming WTO superiority was waning, as was the general feeling of being threatened. The opinion was rather widespread that survival (in terms of war avoidance) was more imperative than the defence of freedom, and the willingness to spend more on defence was limited.

Nevertheless, it would be a gross overstatement to say that these public moods were the decisive factor in the re-orientation occurring in the political parties, since defence and security issues remained only one 'cluster' amongst a number of clusters of factors influencing voting patterns. Be this as it may, public opinion thus represented a framework to which the political parties somehow had to adapt[5].

One might also argue that no dramatic shifts occurred in the West German public's attitude to security policy questions throughout the 1980s. There remained in the public at large a nearly undamaged support for NATO as well as for the dual-track approach of defence-cum-*détente*, and the same held true for the 'elite' in national security policy. There thus seemed to be a very broad consensus on the 'Harmel policy'. Even the 'peace through strength' group (around the 'Steel Helmet' faction in the CDU/CSU) remained 'to the left' of their apparent counterparts in the USA, since they did not question *détente* as such, only favouring a 'realistic *détente*'[6].

The autumn of 1989, and particularly the fall of the Berlin Wall in November, in many respects constituted a decisive juncture for West German politics, when the 'rules of the game' were changed radically almost overnight. Whatever the parties might have to say on matters of security policy suddenly had to be assessed in a different light, namely in the light of a future unification of the two Germanies. The 'shadow of the future', in which day-to-day politics is always conducted, suddenly changed shape.

It therefore seemed appropriate to divide the subsequent account of West German political attitudes towards NOD into two parts: before and after 1989, which divide fairly clearly on most issues. Whereas discontinuity thus prevails, there remain elements of continuity, i.e. political developments not directly linked to the p ospects of unification. Whereas, as a general rule, the account of most matters in the subsequent three chapters is therefore discontinued in November 1989 only to be continued in Chapter XI, there are occasional exceptions. Furthermore, it seemed appropriate to intersect a chapter on the other Germany, i.e. the GDR, which subsequently became part of the new, united Germany.

CHAPTER VII

The SPD Before 1989

As will have become apparent from Chapter III above, there were numerous precedents for the views that became prominent in the SPD in the last half of the 1980s. The 'new' ideas of the party might thus be merely interpreted as the 'pendulum' taking another swing, once again landing the party in positions held in the past.

An ideologically-founded anti-militarism had deep roots in the party, going back to the proclamation by Karl Marx and Friedrich Engels that 'the proletariat has no fatherland', based on their theory of the state as an instrument of oppression in the hands of the ruling capitalist class. Although the latter part of the statement was challenged by the other main theorist, Ferdinand Lasalle, the conclusion remained that of anti-militarism.

The demands for an abolition of standing armies in favour of general conscription, as well as for a democratisation of decision-making over peace and war were to be found in the party platforms adopted in Eisenach (1869), Gotha (1875) and Erfurt (1891), to which has since 1891 been added the demand for international arbitration and conciliation, i.a. through the League of Nations. The anti-militarist attitude prevailed, both within the SPD and in the entire Second International, at least until 1914, when the SPD for the first time cast its vote in favour of military spending, as did its sister parties around the world[1].

Immediately after the Second World War, the party remained neutralist and 'flirted' with disengagement for about a decade, until the end of the 1950s. This orientation may be seen both as a return to anti-militarism, and as a reflection of the party's concerns about the future of Germany. The SPD, indeed, consistently opposed the division of the country, and even warned against the prospects thereof in their 1934 programme, with the main purpose of alerting the democratic nations to the barbarism and risks of war implied by the Nazi dictatorship[2].

In spite of this neutralist and nationalist background, the SPD had since 1959 endorsed the FRG's official security policy, including NATO membership, the stationing of nuclear weapons on German soil and a strong *Bundeswehr*. Even before that, however, the SPD under Kurt Schumacher had, in general terms, supported the political commitment of the FRG to a 'roll-back' strategy *vis-à-vis* the East, as well as the prevalent plans for border-crossing counter-offensives[3].

Second Thoughts on the Deterrence System

Part of the reorientation of the SPD's security policy in the 1980s had occurred in collaboration and consultation with other Social Democratic parties, especially within the framework of the so-called 'Scandilux group'. This consisted of a core of Scandinavian and Benelux parties, with the SPD, the British Labour Party and the French PS (*Parti Socialiste*) attending as observers. The SPD representative, Egon Bahr, played a prominent role in the deliberations of this group, and ideas traceable back to him might in actual fact be seen as gradually permeating the sister parties. It is possible to identify three new 'common perspectives' in the security policy reorientation of the Scandilux parties, including the SPD[4]:

I. The concept of Common Security.
II. The desire for greater (West) European independence.
III. The alternative defence strategies.

I shall, very briefly, sketch the developments in the first two fields before concentrating on the SPD debate on the third issue:

Although the neutron bomb had also been a contested issue, it was primarily the INF issue which spurred the debate on security policy (including the defence debate) within the SPD. From a position as supporters of the dual-track decision, the SPD gradually swung around to a rejection of INF deployment, with a dramatic peak of the debate occurring at the extraordinary party Convention in November 1983. The shift was controversial and, amongst others, former Federal Chancellor Helmut Schmidt vehemently opposed the new policy[5]. The INF issue directed public focus on nuclear weapons as such, with the NFU debate standing out as a central issue. By implication, the very core of 'deterrence thinking' was placed on the agenda[6].

It was as an alternative to the nuclear orientation in security policy that the concept of Common Security gradually gained ground. The decisive impetus was provided by the publication of the Palme Commission's report in 1982, amongst the authors of which was Egon Bahr[7]. He was presumably the one to invent the very term of Common Security, the rationale and core idea of which he formulated thus:

'For the first time in history, we have developed the means to destroy ourselves (. . .). The hope for victory is no longer valid, and we must instead strive for common security, i.e. security *together with*, and not *against*, a potential enemy.'[8]

For Bahr the avoidance of nuclear war remained the paramount objective, and other goals by implication had to recede into the backgound, a fact which he stated more unreservedly than most other politicians would have dared[9].

He was aware of the ambiguities surrounding the relationship between CS and deterrence, which he attempted to solve by distinguishing between 'deterrence as a fact' and 'deterrence as a doctrine'. The fact consisted primarily in the mutual interdependence between the nuclear contestants, which, however regrettable, was bound to remain. The doctrine, however, was depicted as a futile and dysfunctional quest for preventing wars by means of war-fighting capabilities, with arms racing etc. as the inevitable consequence[10]. Bahr's proposal to organise security in collaboration with the adversary ('security partnership') was thus envisioned as an alternative to this deterrence doctrine, but would not, on the other hand, contest the very fact of deterrence.

Realistically, however, he was only able to envisage the shift from deterrence doctrine to common security as a piecemeal process, in which arms control measures would have to play a prominent, albeit in principle only ancillary, role. As a first step Bahr proposed a withdrawal of nuclear weapons from the countries not themselves possessing them, an idea about which he felt so strongly that he had his minority position to this effect recorded *expressis verbis* in the Commission's report[11].

As a precondition for gradually making nuclear deterrence superfluous (and hence for implementing CS), Bahr consistently emphasised the need for conventional stability. In 1983, he e.g. demanded a rough conventional balance in Europe as a pre-condition for an NFU policy on the part of NATO, but did not conceive of this balance in terms of parity. Rather, it would amount to a situation in which none of the parties would possess a superiority which might be used militarily for an attack[12], a formulation which came quite close to explictly defining a 'NOD criterion'. Although the introduction of NOD ideas into the SPD's security-policy thinking has often been attributed to Andreas von Bülow, Bahr thus actually preceded him in this respect.

There has been a certain ambiguity in the SPD's conception of CS pertaining to the question of whether to conceive of CS as an alternative to the blocs, or as a new strategy to be implemented within the framework of the alliance structure. In the report of the working group on 'New Strategies' (established by the party executive in 1983 and chaired by Bahr), it was explicitly stated that CS was to be implemented within the alliances. Nevertheless, the possibility has consistently remained that 'bloc-transcending structures' might eventually make the alliances redundant. Furthermore, minority factions within the party have expressly favoured a dissolution of the blocs, and some have even gone so far as to advocate a unilateral neutralisation of the FRG[13].

This problem has been intertwined with the debate on 'Europeanisation'. The underlying desire for a greater independence *vis-à-vis* the USA stemmed primarily from a growing unease with the novel American tendencies during the first term of the Reagan administration, most emphatically formulated in Oskar Lafontaine's *Fear of One's Friends*. The quest for greater independence and autonomy has, however, always been coupled with a fear of isolation. This led the SPD to emphasise the role of the 'European pillar'. In the resolution of the party convention in 1986 Western Europe was thus urged to assume a more independent role in the future'[14].

The quest for autonomy spurred a search for potential allies, amongst whom France was apparently at the top of the list. Mitterrand's party, the *Parti Socialiste* (PS), has shared the SPD's desire for a European pillar in general terms, and the two parties for a couple of years conducted regular consultations on security policy matters, as did, of course, the two governments[15].

Helmut Schmidt was among the most prominent advocates of a such an intensified Franco-German collaboration, and i.a. suggested a burden-sharing formula: that the FRG should assume primary responsibility for conventional defence to which she should contribute eighteen divisions, whereas France, as a *quid pro quo*, should devote its nuclear potential to the common defence but be obliged to field only twelve conventional divisions[16].

In general, the SPD has supported the steps taken towards improved Franco-German cooperation, such as the joint manoeuvres, the common Defence Council, etc. The issue has remained somewhat controversial, however, since not everybody in the SPD has rejoiced in the prospect of replacing an American with a French extended nuclear deterrence 'umbrella'. The main point of controversy within the SPD (as in the bilateral relations between the two states) has therefore been the nuclear accent in French strategy. Associated with this, a bone of contention has been the French rejection of the very principle of forward defence[17].

Whereas 'Europeanisation' in this 'Western' sense has thus been somewhat controversial, there has been an almost universal consensus within the SPD on the need for improving relations with the East. This, in its turn, has often been legitimised with explicit references to the 'pan-European' perspective. An erosion or loosening of the bloc structures in Europe was thus a consistent SPD endeavour for decades, leading it to emphasise *détente* as well as a certain accommodation with the East, not least with the smaller East European countries.

This objective in the 1970s found its manifestation in the *Ostpolitik*, whereas in the 1980s it was attempted by way of a bilateral diplomacy undertaken from the opposition benches[18]. The latter endeavour did accomplish some spectacular results in the form of draft agreements on various arms control issues: with the then ruling party of the GDR, the Socialist

Unity Party, SED, draft treaties were negotiated for a chemical-weapons-free zone as well as for a nuclear-weapons-free zone for Central Europe.

Even more conspicuously, perhaps, the SPD and the SED in August 1987 signed a joint document on *The Ideological Struggle and Common Security*, wherein both parties acknowledged the other's ability, in principle, to maintain a lasting peace, as well as the need for conducting a 'controversial dialogue'. The latter, on the one hand, should not be allowed to jeopardise peaceful coexistence. On the other hand, neither should it be obliged to observe any 'taboos', as e.g. on human rights issues. In addition, defensive military doctrines and the lack of capabilities for attack were mentioned as valuable contributions to bringing about a CS regime[19].

As we shall see in the subsequent chapters, these rather close (albeit, as a matter of principle, explicitly not friendly) relations with the party of Honecker became a liability in the wake of the autumn 1989 revolution in the GDR and compromised the SPD in the eyes of many onlookers.

Almost the same held true for the relations of the SPD with other subsequently overthrown Communist parties in Eastern Europe. In 1985 an agreement was e.g. reached with the Polish United Worker's Party (PUWP), on CBMs, as a follow-up to which the two parties in 1988 presented a new common document on *Criteria and Measures for Confidence-building Security Structures in Europe*, containing principled recommendations for NOD. Subsequently, the SPD and the PUWP issued a joint proposal on *Confidence—and Security-Building Measures and Arms Control in the Baltic Sea*, featuring concrete suggestions for less offensive postures on the Baltic Sea[20].

The Defence Debate

The defence debate in the SPD has been no less lively than that on broader security policy, but partly conducted behind closed doors. As a very large party with a clear ideological orientation, the SPD included within its ranks a number of highly competent experts and theorists, a surprisingly large number of whom had, furthermore, found the time to elaborate on their views in books and lengthy articles. Although these party leaders by no means constituted a representative sample of the party's rank-and-file, they were nevertheless those whose views would to a large extent decide the party's position.

I shall therefore briefly outline the views of some of the most prominent participants in the debate, before tracing the evolution of the commitment to NOD within the party apparatus[21].

The aforementioned Egon Bahr served as the first chairman of the party's working group on 'New Strategies', appointed by the executive in 1983 to the recommendations of which I shall return in due course. Ever since, Bahr consistently supported the NOD idea, both within the party and *vis-à-vis* external critics, whilst neither taking a stand on neither of the competing factions, nor comitting himself to any specific model. In general terms, he advocated the establishment of a non-offensive zone along the border, subsequently refined somewhat in the form of a joint set of recommendations issued by the staff of the Hamburg peace research institute (cf. chapter IV), whose director he was[22].

In 1988, Bahr formulated his ideas at greater length in a book on *European Peace. A Response to Gorbachev*. As indicated by the title, it was written in a radically improved international climate, in which the problem was no longer Soviet recalcitrance, but the exact opposite. Subjected to the bombardment of Soviet initiatives in the realms of arms control, disarmament and confidence-building, the West seemed in complete disarray. On the other hand, this Soviet sea-change opened up unique opportunities for improvements in the situation in Europe, not least as far as the FRG was concerned.

Bahr was genuinely surprised by the congeniality of the new Soviet leader, who had apparently wholeheartedly embraced the concept of Common Security. He also assessed favourably the Soviet conception of the 'Common European House', requiring in turn an improved 'culture of struggle': on the one hand, fundamental disagreements were bound to persist, but, on the other hand, they ought to be allowed to jeopardise neither *détente* nor peace. The peace process already set in motion should be pursued to a 'point of no return', which might not have been reached yet, but which was well within sight. This would be tantamount to 'the elimination of the Soviet threat plain and simple'[23].

The Soviet leader's panoply of initiatives furthermore created unique opportunities for attaining genuine conventional stability in Europe. No longer would it be necessary for Western peace researchers and others to approach the problem in a roundabout fashion (such as the gradualist approaches favoured by many German left-wingers), since 'the direct road to common security in Europe is open'. In concrete terms this would imply, according to Bahr, first of all a scaling down of the wherewithal of nuclear deterrence and, secondly, a 'common security regime' in Europe requiring a conventional stability based on a situation in which neither side could hope for gains by launching an attack, regardless of whether it would be undertaken from a standing start, after a short warning period, or after complete mobilisation[24].

As a point of departure for any East-West negotiations, agreement should be sought on a definition along these lines. The next step would be to agree upon the principle of parity with regard to the most important systems particularly suitable for attack, i.e. MBTs, IFVs, artillery, combat helicopters and bridge-building equipment. All-European ceilings should be combined with regional sub-ceilings, most importantly for Central Europe (in the broad sense, i.e. including Denmark, Poland and Hungary), where e.g. neither side should be allowed to station more than 4,000 tanks. Even better, the parties might seek agreement to withdraw the offensive-capable systems entirely from this 'zone of contact'.

The resultant 'non-offensive corridor' would contribute immensely to stability, especially if appropriate safeguards against reintroduction of the prohibited items into the zone could be agreed upon. It would constitute the nucleus of a bilateral 'structural inability to attack' regime and *eo ipso* of conventional stability. For the sake of defence efficiency, however, various types of weaponry of strictly defensive utility should be deployed in the restriction zone so as to further hamper any transgressions[25].

This situation of robust conventional stability would presumably render nuclear weapons on European soil entirely superfluous, not only objectively, but also in the eyes of the European populations. The required scope would thus be created for agreeing on a 'third zero' solution, which would rid Europe of short-range nuclear weapons, and hence relieve the Germans of their present worries that 'the shorter the range, the deader the Germans'. Even under the assumption of a complete withdrawal of nuclear weapons from Europe, the continent would, however, not be denuclearised in any meaningful sense of the word. There would remain i.a. 200 nuclear reactors, which no potential aggressor could be sure not to hit inadvertently. The result would be a tremendous radioactive pollution which would not spare the aggressor's own home-land[26].

One of the very first in the SPD to take 'defensive defence' seriously was member of the party presidium Erhard Eppler. In his 1981 book *Ways Out of Peril*, he took as his point of departure the INF debate as a manifestation of a seemingly perpetual arms race. As an alternative for the FRG, he recommended, first of all, 'defensive defence' (i.e. a reform along the lines of Horst Afheldt's proposals) as a way out of the *circulus vitiosus* of the arms race; secondly, he urged the FRG to support a more independent Europe, implying that 'the European shirt must be closer to her body than the Atlantic coat'[27].

Whereas Eppler may have been the first within the party to under-stand the substance of NOD, the first to use the unfortunate term 'structural non-attack capability' (*Strukturelle Nichtangriffsfähigkeit*) invented by Albrecht von Müller (cf. chapter IV above) was apparently the editor of the party's theoretical journal *The New Society* (*Die Neue Gesellschaft*), Peter Glotz. He supported the idea, both as an alternative to the trends towards 'deep strike', and as a *détente* measure. Furthermore, he presented it as the military component of a 'second *Ostpolitik*', which, in its turn, should pave the way for a 'system of collective security'[28].

The person to make the SPD's attitude towards NOD known to a broader public was, however, the controversial Andreas von Bülow. He had for quite some time been pleading for a more realistic threat assessment, but his own essay on the matter attracted just as widespread criticism for what was regarded as a fatal underestimation of the Soviet threat, along with numerous factual errors[29].

As early as in 1984, von Bülow had begun advocating a new defence strategy with clearly discernible non-offensive elements[30], the purpose of which would be to place NATO in a position to abandon early first-use of nuclear weapons. In September 1985, he set out his proposals in somewhat greater detail, by drafting a plan which was intended merely as an internal working paper for the party leadership. It leaked to the press, however, quickly became known as the 'Bülow paper', and became the focus of a rather heated debate.

In addition to its critical analyses, the paper outlined a proposal for an alternative defence of the FRG. The defence concept therein was very akin to the 'integrated forward defence' proposals of the Starnberg team, although likewise inspired by Löser model, the 'sword and shield' terminology which von Bülow frequently employed[31].

Although it focused on the FRG, the proposal was not intended for unilateral implementation, but rather as a plan for a bloc-to-bloc settlement. Indeed, one of the main objectives of any NATO defence reform would be to induce the USSR to renounce its 'forward-moving' ('*Vorwärts-*') strategy. As a *quid pro quo*, NATO was urged to abandon its strategy of early employment of nuclear weapons, and move in the direction of a minimum deterrence strategy. In the conventional sphere, von Bülow recommended both parties to emphasise the build-down of capabilities for surprise attack and deep operations into the rear of the opponent, whereas he left open the option of 'conditional offensive capability'.

On the ground, the requirements for achieving such a stabilising situation would be a defence structure emphasising anti-tank capabilities rather than tanks, even though NATO might still have to retain a fleet of tanks for the reconquest of lost territory. Along the border, a 25-70 kms.-deep belt was envisaged to be defended by means of a dense web of dispersed anti-tank forces, which would not themselves present lucrative targets. This network was to be equipped with third generation mines, drones with optical wire guidance, 'fire-and-forget' anti-tank missiles, elevated weapons platforms, anti-tank helicopters, etc. In the air, the need would be for an effective area-covering air defence system 'of the Swedish type'. The proposals bore witness to a fascination with modern technology, and the vision of a 'brave new world' of high technology weaponry working to the benefit of the defender was subsequently elaborated upon at some length[32].

The proposed defence scheme would be a forward defence, which should not give up space in order to gain time. It would presumably be better capable of absorbing reserve forces than the present structure, by virtue of which it might safely be 'thinned out' considerably, whilst maintaining the capability of rapid local mobilisation that would bring the skeleton-ised formations up to full combat strength. In order to facilitate this mobilisation, the service period for conscripts should be shortened to 7-8 months, supplemented with frequent refresher exercises. As an organisational reflection of this, the distinction between the field and territorial armies was to be abandoned in favour of a 'total defence organisation' structured along territorial lines.

For the sake of NATO compatibility, the defence web should allow for an integration of allied forces in the forward zone. Furthermore, it allegedly entailed brighter prospects for Franco-German collaboration, since the envisaged structure would be a perfect match for the French FAR (*Force d'Action Rapide*). In the course of the next one or two decades, it was envisioned that Western Europe should become self-reliant in the realm of conventional defence. The superpower forces would, accordingly, be gradually withdrawn from both the FRG and the GDR, except for a token force contingent stationed in West Berlin. This disengagement perspective, incidentally, brandished von Bülow in much of the public debate as a neutralist in disguise.

To an increasing extent he came to stress the need for negotiated, rather than unilateral, implementation. In all fairness it must be said, however, that he never made mutuality or bilateralism a *conditio sine qua non* of conversion, but maintained that intermediary steps were perfectly suitable for unilateral implementation[33]. As a way of promoting the bilateral option, he furthermore took part in informal consultations with Soviet authorities, in collaboration with a number of peace researchers from other European countries.

In 1988, von Bülow, jointly with Colonel (ret.) Helmut Funk, presented a concrete proposal for a bilateral scaling down of offensive capabilities in Central Europe, which was subsequently published in numerous versions and with a great amount of detail[34]. The core element of the proposal was to establish parity at lower levels on armoured vehicles within what has come to be known as the ATTU area: 5,000 MBTs, 2,500 IFVs and 2,500 tank destroyers. These ATTU ceilings should, moreover, be combined with geograpical subceilings for three zones, revealing the proposal's similarity to the various disengagement schemes:

I. 60 kms. on both sides of the border (i.e. the parts of the FRG, the GDR and Czechoslovakia): No armoured forces at all.

II. The rest of the FRG plus Denmark and Luxemburg, as well as the rest of the GDR, Czechoslovakia and Hungary: Forty percent of the global ceilings.

III. The Netherlands, Belgium and France, plus Poland and the USSR to the Urals: Sixty percent of the global ceilings.

In 1988, von Bülow published a book jointly with Albrecht von Müller and the above-mentioned Helmut Funk, featuring i.a. a proposal for an alternative structure of the *Bundeswehr*[35]. Herein he maintained his previous proposal for merging the Territorial Army with the Field Army in a unified structure, i.a. in order to meet the impending manpower 'squeeze'. The level of 400,000 standing forces might thus presumably be maintained without extending the term of service for conscripts, such as contemplated by the CDU government.

The Territorial Army was to be distributed in regiments numbering 2,000 man and defending 300 kms sq., which were to be cadered down to ten percent in the forward zones, and eight percent in the rear areas. They should make ample use of the civilian infrastructure, i.a. for means of transportation and telecommunications. In an attempt to meet the criticism for providing cheap 'cannon fodder', von Bülow proposed to let the 'poor bloody infantry' fight exclusively from sheltered positions, and to give them similar opportunities for requisitioning reinforcements as the formations of the Field Army enjoyed.

The resultant expansion of the Territorial Army would allow for a 'thinning out' of armoured formations and thus minimise offensive capabilities. Furthermore, it would presumably be compatible with a mutual build-down of armed forces, without jeopardising the principle of forward defence.

To work out the detailed implications of this posture was left to Helmut Funk, who labelled his model 'the integrated forward defence' (not to be confused with von Müller's proposal bearing the same name). He calculated the required number of territorial 'shield forces' to be 330 regiments of 2,000 troops each, plus an additional ten brigades for the defence of major cities in the border areas (thus departing from the almost universal NOD recommendation not to defend cities militarily). Each regiment should be equipped with 216 machine guns, 224 *Panzerfäuste*, 80 'PARS' (anti-tank missiles), 16 *Fliegerfäuste* and 118 anti-tank drones of the 'Wespe' type. As a way of transforming the high degree of urbanisation in the FRG from a liability into an asset, these regiments should be 'based on' cities in terms of supplies and other support, and fight predominantly in terrain unsuitable for tanks[36].

Having thus exposed himself by adding detail to the Bülow-Funk model, Colonel Funk was fiercely attacked by i.a. representatives of the SAS group (cf. above, Chapter IV). They criticised him i.a. for 'fiddling the figures' in order to conceal two facts: first of all, that the proposal would by no means imply a reduction, but in actual fact rather an expansion, of the armoured forces; and secondly, that the manpower requirements were grossly underestimated, and that the real numbers would be quite unrealistic[37]. It is, however, beyond the scope of the present survey to go into this controversy in any detail. Suffice it to say that the calculations of Funk were, to say the least, questionable.

Whereas von Bülow was rather closely associated with the Starnberg research project around von Müller, another prominent spokesman of the party in security matters, Hermann Scheer, has for a number of years been a member of the SAS Group[38]. These two research teams might thus be said to have been competing for the SPD support through of their respective advocates within the party leadership.

In 1986, Scheer set out his personal ideas on a peace strategy in a book entitled *The Liberation from the Bomb*, wherein he took as his point of departure an elaborate critique of current strategic trends[39]. His main purpose, however, was to outline a comprehensive peace strategy, comprising political as well as military elements.

Politically, the two Germanies were urged not to see the division as a 'wailing wall', but rather as a historic opportunity. Because both states were members of their respective alliances, whilst sharing a deeply entrenched attachment to *détente*, they should collaborate in building down tension and reconciling the bloc division of the continent. Eventually, the three (*sic!*) German states (the FRG, the GDR and Austria) were envisioned as becoming the locus for a peaceful Europe, due to their belonging to the two blocs as well as to the NN 'bloc' of neutral and non-aligned states[40]. He might thus be seen as seeking to combine historical 'Great German' ('*grossdeutsche*') aspirations with a modern pan-European ideology.

According to Scheer, the appropriate strategy for building *détente* would be a step-by-step demilitarisation, underpinned by political and economic integrative tendencies, which should be deliberately promoted, with an all-European Union (including a common security and defence policy) as the ultimate aim. Such a development would gradually expand the scope for internal change in Eastern Europe as well. The culminating point in this long process would be the dissolution of the two blocs.

By means of arms control, the policy of deploying nuclear weapons on the territory of states not disposing of them themselves should be discontinued[41]. This would constitute a partial disengagement, and thus presumably enhance crisis stability. Disengagement should pertain to troops etc. as well, but the withdrawal of nuclear weapons would have to precede measures on the conventional level. As first steps, the Pershing-2s should be withdrawn, and the opportunities of a Euro-strategic balance should be investigated. This would have to take the British and French nuclear forces into due account, restrict the deployment of cruise missiles to the sea, and rule out any further build-up of nuclear weapons, such as Euro-strategic aircraft[42].

Scheer saw no compelling need for accompanying de-nuclearisation with any conventional arms build-up, since 'the conventional inferiority of NATO does not exist any longer', as he bluntly stated. As far as the MBFR negotiations (then still in progress) were concerned, he urged the FRG to do its utmost to achieve a speedy MBFR agreement, and subsequently promote follow-up negotiations which should focus on particularly offensive types of weaponry[43].

Whereas Scheer should probably be placed somewhere slightly left-of-centre within the party, on the far left wing of the SPD the 'Frankfurter Circle' was to be found, under the auspices of which a 'Working Group Peace' was formulating recommendations for the party's security policy. The main speaker for this faction was Konrad Gilges, who in 1985 put forward his views on security affairs in a book with the revealing title *Peace Without NATO*. Explicitly taking Marxism as his theoretical frame of reference, Gilges found it obvious that both the EC and NATO were instruments of capitalism which true socialists could not possibly support[44].

He subjected the resolution passed by the 1984 Party Convention (cf. below) to a very elaborate critique. He was at odds with its call for a 'security partnership' within the framework of the existing military blocs; with its demand for 'minimum deterrence' which he found far too modest; with the long transition period envisaged for the adoption of *StruNA* (i.e. NOD); and, finally, with the narrow military sense in which the term was usually employed. In his *StruNA* should rather be conceived of as a comprehensive strategy for peace and *détente*, which would require changes in national as well as international policies, by virtue of which recommendation Gilges came close to Dieter Lutz's conception of '*StruNA i.w.S.*', i.e. 'Structural Inability to Attack in the Broader Sense' (cf. above, Chapter IV)[45].

Nevertheless, he suppported *StruNA* even in its 'narrow' military sense, whilst emphasising the need for unilateral implementation, in which context *StruNA* ought to be combined with a radical military build-down, reducing the standing forces of the FRG to 100-200,000 troops, combined with a militia-like structure[46].

The deputy chairman of the SPD and the party's unsuccessful 1990 candidate for the chancellorship, Oskar Lafontaine, had for quite some time been highly critical of NATO strategy, as may be gathered from the title of his 1983 bestseller *Fear of One's Friends*, wherein he had sharply criticised above all the nuclear strategy of the Alliance in general, and the USA in particular. In 1988, he analysed the accomplishments of the first *détente* period, identifying the absence of genuine disarmament as one of its main deficiencies. Furthermore, the decision-makers on both sides of the iron curtain had clung to obsolete patterns of thought, whereas the peace movement had been the first to open up new alleys.

One of the main tasks for the coming decades would have to be a more independent European stand, which would necessitate a cooperation on defence policy within the European Communities (EC). This, in turn, would release resources sufficient to allow for an abandonment of US extended nuclear deterrence, since 'a community of 320 million people should be able to defend itself with conventional means against states that are far inferior on industrial and technological terms'.

Whereas, in the short term, the nucleus of the envisaged cooperative scheme would be continuing Franco-German collaboration, the entire integrative endeavour would have to be seen in a long-term pan-European perspective. In order to pave the way for such a development, the West should accept the recent WTO challenges and enter into East-West consultations on military doctrines (as has subsequently happened). Furthermore, NATO ought to embark on a conversion of its armed forces to a non-offensive posture, combined with the establishment of a nuclear-weapons-free corridor in Central Europe[47].

The party's security policy speaker in the *Bundestag*, Karsten Voigt, had largely succeeded in standing aloof from the controversies within the party, whilst lending his unswerving support to the basic notion of NOD.

He has pointed to the goal of 'conventional stability' as the relevant goal for East-West negotiations, and mentioned as the main criterion for such stability a situation in which both parties were structurally incapable of attack. He has pointed, furthermore, to the need for bilateral consultations in order to bring about such a situation: the parties ought to exchange information on what each regarded as especially offensive and threatening on the other side. Although Voigt thus supported some of the WTO's proposals, he also maintained that in whatever negotiations on conventional forces might come about, the resultant reductions would have to be asymmetrical, since the Soviet strategy for wide-ranging offensives still constituted the main source of instability[48].

In 1988 Voigt published a detailed comparison of the various proposals of Afheldt, Hannig, Löser, von Müller, von Bülow and the SAS. Afheldt's model was deemed inadequate on grounds of inefficiency, and that of Hannig because it would present too may lucrative targets, but Voigt also expressed serious doubts about von Müller's and von Bülow's proposals. Not in spite of, but because of, their (alleged) military efficiency, their strictly defensive character was deemed hardly credible. He hence had to dismiss them as less than optimal, on the criterion of 'strategic stability'.

The SAS concept conformed better to this requirement, although it did fail, in Voigt's assessment, on account of its insufficient deterrent effect, due to its (deliberate) inability to pose any threats to the aggressor's homeland. He therefore suggested adding an offensive component to the SAS model, as a precondition for making this 'SAS plus' his preferred alternative[49]. The SAS spokesman, Lutz Unterseher, however, was (prudently) not very forthcoming in this respect, considering offensive capabilities to be superfluous and, indeed, dysfunctional.

At the *Wehrkunde* Conference in February 1990, Voigt commented on the prospects of conventional arms control in the following words, which probably represented what had by now become the 'mainstream' SPD opinion:

'The concept of reciprocal structural inability to attack does, on the one hand, envisage a maintenance of forward defence. On the other hand, it makes an abandonment of both flexible response and the previous form of forward defence imperative. Such an abandonment is urgent, because without it NATO would end up in the political *cul de sac* of a structural inability to disarm'[50].

The SPD has consistently had former officers on the party's pay-roll as consultants. One of these has been Major Franz H.U. Borkenhagen who has served as the SPD's advisor on *Bundeswehr* issues in the *Bundestag*. His attitude towards NOD was quite positive, and he had, indeed, been personally involved in NOD research in two different contexts: as a member of the Afheldt team, and more recently through his affiliation with the SAS. Being very critical of the current trends in NATO planning for conventional defence, he unreservedly supported the NOD idea, whilst criticising the concrete proposals for their lack of precision[51]. In 1985 he presented his personal contribution to such a refinement, albeit couched in terms of a military posture that would presumably be compatible with a 'system of collective security' (SCS)[52].

In order to accomplish both the external and internal defence tasks, the SCS should comprise 'systemic' as well as national armed forces. The first should be recruited from amongst national armed forces, and only come under SCS command in case of an emergency. However, in addition to these forces, the SCS should also have at its disposal armed forces (with associated infrastructure and logistics) which were exclusively under supranational command.

As far as the national armed forces were concerned, Borkenhagen envisioned these as specialising in certain tasks in such as way that no national armed forces would constitute a 'balanced force' in the traditional military sense. In this way, a considerable reduction of national offensive capabilities would be ensured. When he came down to specifics regarding the structure of the national armed forces (or rather service arms), he pointed (as was to be expected) to the defence conceptions of the SAS group[53].

As might be expected for a new concept, the support for NOD within the SPD has not been unanimous. The most eloquent opponent of the concept has been General (ret.) Christian Krause, who after his retirement had joined the research team of the party's 'Friedrich Ebert Foundation'. His criticism notwithstanding, his opposition to NOD was neither 'hawkish', nor was he ever completely alien to the basic ideas underlying NOD. When, in 1984, he e.g. listed the criteria for an alternative military strategy, he did for instance acknowledge that it should be defensive and seek no military victory over the attacker[54].

Nevertheless, Krause has delivered a comprehensive, as well as highly competent, critique of the basic assumptions underlying NOD[55]. The gist of his argument was that 'if it ain't broke, don't fix it'. He simply could not agree with NOD proponents that NATO had a problem, since both alliances were already *de facto* incapable of successful attack. Because the balance of forces was, in actual fact, approximately even, NATO might simply abandon its first-use strategy without further ado[56], a step which he had actively supported, i.a. as a co-signatory to the Union of Concerned Scientists' *No-First-Use* report of 1983.

Furthermore, Krause criticised the NOD models (and particularly that of Afheldt) for relying too much on emerging technologies, as well as for making unwarrantedly optimistic assumptions about the efficiency of their models. He was even more sceptical towards the von Bülow and von Müller proposals, which might, according to this author, inadvertently enhance, rather than minimise, offensive capabilities[57].

Finally, none of the proposals had taken into account what Krause regarded as the only threat worthy of serious concern: that of limited attacks with limited goals. What was really needed for such contingencies was a capability for crisis management, without ensuing risks of inadvertent war, i.e. for CBMs as well as a certain redeployment of forces, but certainly not for any fundamental restructuring of the armed forces[58].

The Decisions

Proposals for NOD combined with other security policy alternatives have thus abounded within the SPD. Some have been couched in fairly general terms, whereas others have been more specific. As far as the latter category is concerned, the proponents have almost formed competing factions, which have occasionally attacked each other ferociously. As the following account will show, by the end of 1990 this competition was far from over, and the party had not yet committed itself to any specific model. On the other hand, the advocacy of NOD had steadily become more explicit and unequivocal.

As already mentioned, the SPD in 1983 appointed a working group under the auspices of the party executive with Egon Bahr as chairman, a post which was later taken over by Andreas von Bülow. The preliminary recommendations of this working group included a number of criteria, to which a new defence strategy should conform, i.a. those of being strictly defensive, of lending itself to disarmament and confidence-building, and of rendering nuclear weapons superfluous for extended deterrence. The party did, however, remain somewhat ambiguous with regard to 'deep strike'. Whereas the need for deep interdiction capabilities was acknowledged in principle, it was emphasised that these would have to be clearly discernible from any capabilities of territory-conquering offensives, as well as distinguishable from nuclear weapons[59].

Since many points remained unsettled, the exploratory work was continued, as a contribution to which the SPD took the initiative to a hearing on 'Alternative Strategies' in the *Bundestag* in 1983-1984[60]. The SPD made sure of inviting researchers such as Horst and Eckardt Afheldt, Dieter Lutz, Lutz

Unterseher and Carl Friedrich von Weizsäcker, thus placing NOD on the parliamentary agenda for the first time ever, without, however, any decisions being taken, or any recommendations made.

At the SPD conference in Essen in 1984, the goal of *StruNA* (i.e. NOD) was for the first time recorded in a binding decision, which stated that 'a new security concept must (...) gradually establish a defensive conventional structure, so that in the long run a structural incapability of attack is achieved ...'[61].

It was envisaged reaching a consensus pertaining to specifics at the 1986 Party Conference in Nurenberg[62], but eventually the party refrained from going into detail. It did, however, unanimously adopt a resolution on *Peace and Security Policy*, constituting the first both elaborate and authoritative SPD statement on NOD. As a preliminary, it was declared that 'we need a NATO strategy that dispenses with the early, or perhaps even first, use of nuclear weapons', as a precondition for which 'the structure and equipment of NATO armed forces must unambiguously serve defence purposes and must not obstruct the achievement of a European peace settlement'. In order to meet this requirement 'the structure and equipment of the armed forces must provide the parties with a credible forward defence capability; i.e. the forces must tax any potential aggressor with an unbearable military risk. They must in no case be operationally suitable for a border-crossing attack with territorial objectives'.

As far as the specific directions for the *Bundeswehr* were concerned, the SPD explicitly pointed to the need for a structural incapability of attack (albeit without using the term): 'A reform of the structure of the armed forces must serve the function of improving the stabilising capability of forward defence, and especially strengthen the functions of anti-tank defence, obstacle-construction and air defence'[63].

Subsequently, the party continued labouring internally to work out the implications of the above recommendations, all the time with outsiders (such as the peace research groups surveyed in this book) trying to 'sell' their specific ideas to the party via supporters within the party executive.

With regard to specifics pertaining to the *Bundeswehr* procurement programmes, the party expressed agreement with programmes such as anti-tank helicopters, submunitions for the MLRS, improvements of the 'Roland'/'Gepard' air defence systems, a new fighter aircraft (but not the planned 'Fighter 90'), medium-range SAMs (yet without ATBM capabilities), and a new frigate, yet procured in limited numbers. At the same time, the party expressed disapproval of weapons acquisition programmes such as new MBTs, and any modernisation of the Pershing-1A or other long-range surface-to-surface missiles[64].

At its 1988 convention in Münster, the SPD adopted a document on *Peace and Disarmament in Europe*, wherein the focus had (in the light of Soviet build-down and impending CFE negotiations) shifted from unilateral conversion towards arms control measures, and more specifically, to the interconnection between nuclear and conventional arms control. The party emphatically rejected any modernisation of the theatre nuclear arsenal, including the Lance missiles, and furthermore proposed a new set of negotiations with the goal of a complete abolition of battle-field and short-range nuclear weapons.

As far as the conventional talks were concerned, the SPD recommended their being focused on 'a reduction of armed forces to such an extent that they remain capable of defence, but become structurally incapable of attack'. For the initial round of negotiations, the SPD recommended an goal of equal ceilings around fifty percent of present NATO holdings of MBTs, heavy artillery systems, combat aircraft and combat helicopters, combined with density limits intended to rule out force concentrations in preparation of attacks. Furthermore, the SPD envisaged (evidently inspired by the SAS) 'a reduction of logistics so as to allow mechanised formations the necesary mobility, whilst making them dependent on support from stationary depots and service facilities every two to three days', along with reductions of mobile bridge-building equipment and forward deployed munition storage to the level required for three days of combat[65].

In July 1989, the SPD executive issued a comprehensive set of proposals for the CFE negotiations by then in progress, authored jointly by Egon Bahr, Andreas von Bülow and Karsten Voigt. Although its title, *European Security 2000*, indicated a forward-looking character, the major part of the document was in fact devoted to proposals for very concrete and short-term arms control measures. These were, however, couched in terms of 'making war in Europe impossible' and of creating 'a state of mutual incapacity to attack'.

The envisaged outcome of the arms control endeavours until the year 2000 was a simultaneous cut-back of WTO and NATO forces to fifty percent of current NATO levels, combined with some restructuring of the remaining forces and the creation of 'restricted military areas' (RMAs) close to the border wherein no potentially offensive forces should be stationed. In the RMA (with a depth of about 100 kms. on each side) both sides should, on the other hand, be free to deploy whatever non-mechanised, less mobile and/or stationary means of defence they might wish, as well as to construct various forms of barriers. However, the RMA should constitute a prohibited area for offensive-capable weapons systems such as battle tanks, armoured personnel carriers and infantry fighting vehicles, artillery, combat helicopters and combat aircraft, ballistic missiles and various forms of equipment suitable for offensive operations (such as bridge-building). The RMA would thus be largely identical to the 'offensive-weapons-free zone' previously proposed by i.a. Egon Bahr[66].

The proposal was not restricted to ground forces, but did take the other environments into account. First of all, the aerial means of combat had to be subjected to restrictions as well. For the same reason, the party's speakers applauded President Bush's new initiatives on air force reductions, launched at the NATO summit May 1989. In the subsequent debate in the *Bundestag*, party Chairman Hans Jochen Vogel welcomed the Bush initiative as 'the first constructive answer from the West to the disarmament initiatives of the Soviet Union' and expressed satisfaction with the inclusion of air forces in the negotiations[67].

In its own proposal, the SPD envisaged some constrainst on both fixed-wing and rotary-wing aircraft within the confines of the RMA. Furthermore, the party proposed an elimination of asymmetries through the establishment of common ceilings (below present NATO holdings) for medium-range and fighter bombers, as well as (unspecified) common ceilings for interceptors. Secondly, the SPD proposal envisioned some restraint on naval forces, i.a. in order to prevent circumvention of the ground force limitations by means of amphibious forces.

Finally, the SPD maintained their demands for removal of nuclear artillery munitions and short-range nuclear systems, and stated explicitly that such a denuclearisation would be made possible through the creation of a situation of inability to attack. In conformity with this view, the party speakers also expressed dissatisfaction with the outcome of the NATO summit in terms of its attitude to nuclear disarmament. As the party's chairman pointed out in the *Bundestag*, the very strategy of deterrence was a relic from the Cold War, which had to be abandoned. Horst Ehmke hence explicitly called for a replacement of NATO's flexible response strategy with a new strategic concept, based on the principles of common security, and Katrin Fuchs pointed out that the discussion on a new strategy was long overdue[68].

The 'European Security 2000' proposal won no consensus in the party on either the party's version of NOD or its arms control policy. One voice of dissent was that of Hermann Scheer, who in collaboration with member of the party presidium Heidemarie Wieczorek-Zeul, published an elaborate critique of the Bahr-Bülow-Voigt proposal. According to the two authors, the proposal would imply a postponement of the withdrawal of tactical nuclear weapons until the accomplishment of conventional incapability of attack; it treated 'minimum deterrence' as a lasting solution; it placed undue emphasis on negotiated conversion to the detriment of unilateral steps; it falsely assumed that parity would create stability (although numerical equality would amount to a Western superiority, because of qualitative differences); and it erroneously treated heavy forces as *per se* 'evil' and destabilising. As an alternative to the ill-advised recommendations of the Bahr/Voigt/Bülow trio, the Scheer/Wieczorek-Zeul duo recommended the SAS proposal for a 'spider-web defence'[69].

By March 1990 (i.e. now in the light of the unification prospects), the SPD put forward a proposal in the *Bundestag*, which dealt i.a. with concrete *Bundeswehr* planning. The guide-line in this respect, according to the party, had to be 'a structure which combined far-reaching disarmament goals with a sufficient defensive capability and a structural incapability of attack'. The goal should be a peace-time strength of 240,000 troops with a commensurate reduction of the mobilisation strength; conscription should be shortened to twelve months; the EFA should not be procured; low-level flying exercises over the FRG should be terminated immediately; arms exports to non-OECD states should be prohibited; and a concept for conversion from military to civilian production should be presented.

With regard to arms control, the party reiterated its previous proposals, including that no nuclear short-range missiles should be deployed, and that battlefield nuclear weapons should be withdrawn. The goal was to be a third zero solution for all nuclear weapons with ranges up to 500 kms. Furthermore, the Federal government should work for a conclusion of the first phase of the CFE by June 1990; preparations for the second phase of the CFE should be taken; and the goal for this 'CFE-bis' should be a fifty percent reduction compared with CFE-I[70].

Evaluation

As will hopefully have emerged from the lengthy account above, the SPD has steadily moved closer to the NOD conceptions recorded in Chapters IV and V. The fact that it has thus adopted positions very akin to those promoted by the peace movements and the peace research community is certainly significant, if only because the SPD remains the best hope for NOD advocates of having their proposals implemented. Because of this unquestionable significance, the change of SPD security policy has given rise to concerns from both the left and the right sides of the political spectrum.

Is the SPD serious in its dissent from traditional NATO views, and if so, to what extent is the shift irreversible? Such questions have been asked by many observers from the left, who have been concerned that the anti-nuclear, pro-disarmament and pro-conversion policies promoted by the SPD over the last five to six years might prove ephemeral. They might, indeed, represent attempts to 'swim with the tide' in the surge of a disarmamental mood among the West German public, so as to hold on to or regain votes. If this should prove to be the case, the SPD, when or if returned to power, might thus revert to its previous positions, fall back into line and join ranks with the 'NATO traditionalists'.

Such scepticism is, of course, impossible to refute beyond any doubt. The 'vote-winning' argument does not, however, appear to be supported by available evidence. Simultaneously with its sea-change on security policy, the SPD in actual fact lost votes, and had to relinquish the reins of government to the CDU/CSU-FDP coalition. If anti-nuclearism was thus contrived as a tactical scheme, it would have to be assessed as an obvious fiasco, and a reversal would probably have occurred. There is hence every reason to believe that the SPD has in fact been sincere in its dissent. However, the pendulum may, of course, swing back again if the party should regain governmental power, either because of a shift in the internal 'balance of power', or under the influence of the mighty NATO apparatus. On the other hand, the SPD would seem to have committed itself so firmly to certain positions that they could not be abandoned without creating severe credibility problems. The party could not easily shift its position from opposition to support for nuclear modernisation, increased military expenditures, more offensive strategies, or the like. Some degree of irreversibility may thus in fact have been accomplished.

This has, of course, been exactly what critics from the right have feared: that the SPD, if returned to power, will exacerbate the problems of NATO, deepen the divide between the two sides of the Atlantic, proceed in a neutralist direction, etc. The only consolation for these critics may be that any changes would inevitably be gradual. Whereas the SPD has, indeed, promoted a more independent European and West German policy within NATO, it has by no means lent support to proposals for neutrality. Although opposed to any net growth in the military budgets, and advocating shifts in the strategic concepts, the SPD had (at least until the spring of 1990, cf. Chapter XII below) by no means abandoned either the basic principles of 'flexible response' or of 'forward defence', but merely proposed alternative ways of implementing these principles. To the extent that the SPD has subsequently come to question even these fundamentals in the light of German unification and the end to the Cold War, it has been joined by almost the entire political spectrum in the FRG and, indeed, in NATO itself.

CHAPTER VIII

The Peace Movement Before 1989

The peace movements in the early 1980s exerted a significant influence on the political parties almost all over the world. They did so, above all, by changing the popular mood, and thus influencing the framework conditions for politics. All political parties were forced to take into account the unpopularity of nuclear weapons and the arms race, either by actually adopting the same viewpoints as the peace movements, or by couching their policies in different and more accommodating terms. Nuclear build-up could henceforth only be advocated as a means to build-down, and even programmes such as the SDI had to be couched in terms of 'making nuclear weapons impotent and obsolete'.

General Description

The peace movement in the FRG was, for obvious reasons, larger than in most other countries. All the Pershing-2s and a good part of the GLCMs (ground-launched cruise missiles) were to be deployed here, and the Germans were understandably concerned about the prospects of housing 'first strike weapons' in their midst, representing obvious targets for Soviet pre-emption. Scientists and others developed scenarios for 'nuclear war in Hessen'[1] and the like, demonstrating the immense devastation to be expected from a nuclear war, not least for the Germans.

Such apocalyptic visions were further dramatised by the theories on 'nuclear winter', according to which not merely those 'responsible' (in the widest possible sense of the word) for a nuclear war, i.e. the peoples in the Northern hemisphere, but also the rest of humanity would suffer from the climatic aftermath of a nuclear war; and how not 'merely' mankind, but in fact most living species might be annihilated through the resultant climatic changes and the changes in the biosphere.

The term 'nuclear war' thus acquired a more profound and ominous meaning, which may have had a particular appeal to exactly those who thenceforth manned the peace movement's 'picket lines': the young generation characterised by a deeper ecological consciousness and a sense of solidarity with the impoverished Third World, combined with fundamentally anti-authoritarian attitudes[2].

The peace movement(s) continued to grow steadily, right up to the 'moment of truth' when INF deployment actually commenced. The size of the demonstrations grew; the support from organisations such as churches and trade unions surged; more and more high-ranking politicians 'jumped the bandwagon' (often out of deep personal conviction) and joined the movement; and more and more new imaginative forms of protest were employed, with a resultant growth in media attention[3].

The movement(s) did, however, remain a rather amorphous lot, comprising devoted Christians, concerned mothers and grandmothers, fanatic communists, eloquent anti-authoritarians, and many others. This proved to be a strength as well as a weakness. On the one hand, it prevented the peace movement from forcefully articulating a comprehensive set of demands, since the political basis for joint activities had to be the highest common denominator, in actual fact amounting to little more than 'No to cruise and Pershings'. On the other hand, the diversity may have given the peace movement a longer lease of life.

Although the size of demonstrations shrank rapidly after the peak in 1983, other activities have continued till the present day, albeit on a much more modest scale, because the ideas had taken root in new groups: amongst women, in the churches, in the trade union movement, etc.[4]. Above all, however, the basic ideas promoted by the peace movement had taken root in the popular mood, in which the fear of war remained significant and nuclear weapons anathema, etc.

Whereas the peace movements were thus tremendously successful in bringing across their negative message, they were considerably less effective in formulating, and still less in promoting, concrete alternatives. Almost everything formulated, except for trivialities, was the work of individuals, to a sample of whom I shall devote the following section. For obvious reasons, I have made this selection only from amongst those who have dealt explicitly with alternative defence.

Although these individuals might be (and probably would not resent being) called 'peace movement ideologues', this should not be understood in any pejorative sense, and certainly not as implying any lack of scholarly rigour, which may well go hand-in-hand with emotional affinity to, and active support for, popular movements such as the peace movement(s).

Peace Movement Ideologues

The Frankfurt professor of international relations, Andreas Buro was one of the founders of the 'Easter March Movement' in the FRG. In his more academic capacity, he was a member of the 'Socialist Bureau' as well as of the 'Committee for Basic Rights and Democracy' (cf. below). In these capacities, he had published a number of studies criticising the security policies of the FRG and the military strategy of NATO[5].

Buro's basic approach to alternative defence strategies was distinctly 'disarmamentalist' and abolitionist, entailing i.a. a rejection of any reliance on nuclear weapons whatsoever. Furthermore, he dismissed the narrow military approach to the matter in favor of a broader view, pointing i.a. to the need for a multi-pronged disarmament strategy: attempts at disarmament by way of defence conversion (i.e. NOD) should thus be combined with efforts to control the internal armaments dynamics (the 'military-industrial complex', etc.). In order to accomplish this, the conversion to defensive forces would need to be embedded in a more comprehensive strategy of democratisation. Furthermore, any disarmament attempts would have to be supplemented with political strategies aimed at limiting the overall conflict potential[6].

In 1987, Buro characterised the present situation in Europe as one of 'organised peacelessness', whilst identifying 'positive peace'[7] as the relevant goal. This, in its turn, was utterly incompatible with mutual threats, whence the requirement for a complete elimination of offensive capabilities. He assessed the military potentials of both blocs as structurally capable of attack. Not only was he thus unwilling to absolve NATO of its part of the blame; he also pointed to a number of negative current trends in Western military thinking, which would make it increasingly threatening, even aggressive.

The Soviet Union and its allies, in their turn, were described as 'bureaucratic class societies', but were nevertheless attributed with a genuine interest in disarmament and positive peace, due to their immense economic and political problems. Under these circumstances, the European NATO countries might play a constructive role in inducing the USSR to adopt a more defensive posture *vis-à-vis* NATO, at least on the regional scale. For the Soviet Union to participate in a European quest for positive peace, she would not necessarily have to relinquish her superpower status, but only to change her military structure and doctrines related to Europe. This would presumably be facilitated if Western Europe were to shift to non-threatening defensive conceptions'[8].

'Transarmament' therefore ought not to be made conditional on mutuality, but should be embedded in a comprehensive process of transformation and confidence-building. The obvious resemblence notwithstanding, Buro was, however, very sceptical towards the gradualistic approach[9], since this could allegedly contribute to cementing 'enemy images'. Rather, unilateral action ought to be combined with multilateral consultations (up to the point of negotiations).

In line with his rejection of the narrow military approach to NOD, Buro repeatedly warned against the risk of a 'de-politicisation' of the debate. If the debate were e.g. to be couched in terms of 'conventional stability' etc.

(as actually seems to have happened), the military criteria of efficiency would tend to overshadow the more important political criteria of relinquising threatening postures[10].

His proposals had distinctly neutralist implications. As a consequence of West European 'transarmament', he envisioned at the very least a withdrawal of US troops from Europe, an outcome which he would by no means deplore. In his view, NATO was no guarantor of peace, and he e.g. flatly dismissed, as simply a shrewd way of avoiding genuine transarmament, the often-encountered NATO argument that the very multinational nature of many of its formations contributed to their lack of offensive capability[11].

Buro and Ulrich Albrecht (cf. Chapter IV above) collaborated under the auspices of the Committee for Basic Rights and Democracy, to which also belonged scholars such as Ekkehart Krippendorf, Eva Senghaas-Knobloch and (explicitly taking only limited responsibility for the group's recommendations) Egbert Jahn. The committee might thus be described as a smaller-scale German predecessor of the 'Alternative Defence Commision' in the UK. In 1981 the group published a comprehensive report on *Peace With Other Weapons. Five Proposals for an Alternative Security Policy*[12]. In this work, a comprehensive and 'citizen-oriented' conception of security was adopted, and the main principles of Common Security were proclaimed, prior, in fact, to the publication of the 'Palme Report': 'Security as well as liberty necessarily includes the security and liberty of the other (. . .) Security is not possible by way of reducing the security of others.'[13].

The deterrence strategy of NATO was criticised at length, both for its consequences 'if deterrence fails', for its provocative side-effects, for its contribution to the arms race, and for its inherent need for enemy images, etc. As an antidote, a sobre analysis of the Soviet threat was attempted, which did nevertheless corroborate the assumption of the WTO as the main threat to the FRG[14].

The work analysed five different options for meeting this threat. Although the authors of the individual options were nowhere revealed, I have indicated my 'educated guess' as to their identity:

1. Disengagement and nuclear-weapons-free zones
2. Neutralism
3. Strictly defensive defence concept
4. Civilian or social defence
5. Unilateral and complete disarmament

Options one and two were treated practically as one, and were both assessed as realistic options, requiring only relatively minor changes. The FRG might e.g. adopt a position akin to that already taken by the Nordic NATO countries: with no nuclear weapons on its soil etc. According to the author (Ulrich Albrecht?) not only nuclear warheads, but, in addition, their means of delivery and related C^3 systems, as well as conventional shock formations with large tank components, would have to be withdrawn from the Central European disengagement zone[15].

Option three implied a shift to NOD, conceived of primarily in political terms and envisioned to transform the 'deterrence system' in the direction of disarmament. Such a major change would presumably require a spectacular alternative, in order to set in motion 'social learning processes'. The recommended 'big step' should consist in abandoning deterrence and defence strategies relying on nuclear or other means of mass destruction. The actual military forces proposed by the Committee (Andreas Buro?) resembled the techno-commandoes of Horst Afheldt, but the author rejected the underpinning by nuclear weapons originally envisaged by him. As a hedge against militarisation, a nationalisation of the arms industry along with a thorough democratisation were strongly recommended. Furthermore, any collaboration with other NATO states pertaining to arms production should be restricted to defensive weapons systems only, and arms exports permitted only to countries with strictly defensive military strategies[16].

I shall not dwell on Option four at any length, but simply refer to the account of of non-military defence in Chapter IV above. Its author (Egbert Jahn) took a rather favourable, albeit pragmatic, stand on the previous option, welcoming any defensive reformation of the armed forces, not least because of its beneficial politico-psychological effects on the troops as well as on the population at large[17].

The fifth option was based on a threat assessment entirely different from the rest, since its author (Ekkehart Krippendorff?) dismissed as fictitious any 'assertive' threats emanating from the USSR and the WTO, considering inadvertent war to be the only serious risk. On this premise, complete disarmament had to appear as the logical choice, since it would eliminate any threats to the other side which might provoke aggression. The (presumed) author has subsequently published an elaborate and profound analysis of the interconnection between militarism and the State, thus adding to his anti-militarist 'ammunition'[18].

The committee as a collective body was predictably unable to choose between these five options, all of which were nevertheless unanimously assessed as possible improvements on the present situation. Indeed, the five options might even be conceived of as a sequel, with disengagement and neutralism recommending themselves as 'starters', which might gradually pave the way for the more ambitious proposals, with complete disarmament as the ultimate goal[19].

To an even greater extent than any of the former authors, Joachim Wernicke and Ingrid Schöll might most appropriately be viewed as 'intellectual peace activists'. Their joint work from 1985 on *Defend Rather than Annihilate. Escapes from the Nuclear Trap* might thus be regarded as a contribution to the internal peace movement debate. Whilst their critical analysis of present NATO strategy was quite in line with 'traditional' peace movement analysis, the authors had felt a need to present a convincing alternative as well, because 'brilliant analyses, loud protests and horror scenarios cannot be all there is to it. Somewhere there must be a way out of our situation, which could convince in a positive manner, for only in this way do ideas get a realistic chance in a democracy'[20].

The two authors criticised NATO strategy along with certain NOD conceptions for being *de facto* area defence concepts, planning for combat in the midst of the densely populated FRG, with utterly unacceptable damage as the inescapable consequence. In their opinion, a genuine defensive defence should amount to an effective frontier defence, wherein the FRG's own armed forces would have to assume the prime responsibility for the most forward elements, whereas foreign troops were be relegated to the rear areas, as well as built down to an absolute minimum.

In such a defensive defence scheme, civil defence might, once again, come to make sense, i.a. because it would no longer lend itself to misinterpretation as an underpinning of a war-fighting strategy. As a civil defence measure, the population might have to be evacuated from the areas closest to the border, where the combat would concentrate[21].

The Green Party

The Green party is not a political party in the traditional sense, but might be more appropriately described as a mixture between a party and a mass movement.

On the one hand, it constitutes an integral part of the peace movement as well as the 'green movement', and shares their anti-authoritarian and, in a certain sense, anti-political sentiments, as well as their 'basic democratic' structure. As part of this movement, the Green Party constitutes an innovation by virtue of its combination of many causes (ecology, peace, international solidarity, etc.) into a more holistic alternative, which presumably transcends traditional left-right or socialist-liberal dichotomies.

On the other hand, the Greens do in fact constitute a party, running for power positions in local constituencies as well as in Parliament and even in supranational bodies such as the European Parliament. As such, the Greens have been obliged to largely play by the 'rules of the game', from which have arisen certain challenges (or temptations) of actually wielding power, e.g. through coalitions with other parties. This has caused a certain split within the party, between the fundamentalists ('*fundos*') and the pragmatists ('*realos*'). The former have preferred to remain 'pure' and 'uncontaminated' by political 'dirty compromises', whereas the latter have preferred a piecemeal implementation of the party's policies to permanent marginalisation[22].

In security policy issues, as well with regard to environmental protection, the Greens have in a certain sense acted more as a catalyst than as a political force in their own right. They may thus, for instance, have pushed the SPD to take up a number of hitherto unnoticed issues i.a. in the realm of security and defence policy. Playing this 'catalytic' role was facilitated by the fact that the Greens shared most of the SPD's critical positions towards NATO strategy, i.a. the opposition to nuclear strategy in general, and the SDI in particular.

Furthermore, the Greens warn against the dangers associated with deep strike strategies, and oppose any conventional arms build-up on principle, even when it was couched in terms of 'conventionalisation'. Finally, whereas they favour Europeanisation in principle, they were extremely critical in practice of the actual European collaborative institutions, such as the WEU, as well as of cooperative ventures, such as the emerging 'Paris-Bonn axis'[23].

Despite these points of partial convergence, the distance between the Greens and the SPD was considerable, and in actual fact prevented any semblance of a coalition for the purpose of parliamentary elections, numerous proposals to this effect notwithstanding. The main divisive points were the radical stands of the Greens on alliance and defence matters as well as their rejection in principle of the very notion of 'Common Security'[24].

In alliance matters, the Greens have always been ideologically committed to neutrality, and have favoured unilateral withdrawal from NATO, even though they have been rather quiet about this goal for the last few years. They have, however, consistently and vehemently opposed any measures that might further integrate the FRG into the Western Alliance, including (perhaps wrongly) the trend towards increasing Franco-German cooperation[25].

In defence matters, the Greens have been committed to the goal of non-military, i.e. social, defence. They thus shared the SPD's criticism of current military trends, yet without being prepared to support what, from their point of view, might have been considered 'the lesser evil', namely a more defensive military posture. However, in spite of (or perhaps even because of) their deeply rooted scepticism towards military thinking, the Greens have followed, and to a certain extent contributed to, the NOD debate. In June 1984 in the *Bundestag* they arranged a major hearing as a follow-up to that of the SPD, for which event they invited renowned peace researchers and 'NOD designers'[26].

Furthermore, the Greens have issued a number of critical analyses of the NOD concept in general, as well as of the 'von Bülow paper' (cf. above, Chapter VI) in particular. The latter was primarily criticised for not taking the NATO context into due consideration. If combined with a maintenance of offensive-capable systems in the rest of NATO, any improvement of the defensive capabilities of the FRG would presumably simply enhance overall offensive power. In addition to this criticism, the Greens have found any maintenance of nuclear weapons, even for 'minimum deterrence' purposes, such as envisaged in most NOD proposals, to be unacceptable[27].

One of the most eloquent members of the Greens has been Dr. Alfred Mechtersheimer, a former Colonel as well as *mirabile dictu* a former member of and *MdB* for the CDU. Under the influence of the peace movement he left this job and was excluded from the CDU, only to join the Green party. He has ever since been a highly controversial public figure, most recently due to his alleged affiliation with Col. Qadafi of Libya who may have contributed to Mechtesheimer's work with considerable sums of money (to which the Latin phrase *non olet* would perhaps not fully apply).

Mechtesheimer founded and became the director of a private peace research institute in Starnberg. His research and publications effort has dealt, first and foremost, with the INF issue, but he has also seen it as his task to deliver other forms of 'ammunition' to the peace movement, such as contributions to a more realistic threat assessment and a 'military atlas' of the FRG[28].

As far as alternatives were concerned, he supported a certain European-isation, as well as a thorough democratisation of the military alliances. His overall goal was the demilitarisation and denuclearisation of Europe, for which purpose he advocated 'transarmament', albeit in a somewhat luke-warm tone. He furthermore alerted the peace movement to some of the inherent dangers in this approach, i.a. the risk of 'falling victim to the tendency of thinking in terms of technocratic panaceas'. Hence, he urged the peace movement not to waste its energy on future defence conceptions, but first pave the way for their political implementation'[29].

This caveat notwithstanding, Mechtesheimer did support a reform of the *Bundeswehr* that should satisfy three criteria:

—Area coverage of the entire FRG.
—Increasing density in the Eastern parts of the FRG.
—Reinforcement along the likely avenues of attack.

As relevant equipment for the armed forces, he recommended light anti-tank and air defence missiles, along with other weapons that were easy to handle, affordable, and difficult for an opponent to neutralise. The defence should be deployed on a local basis to the greatest possible extent. In addition, it should be combined with non-military forms of defence, especially as far as cities were concerned, which should be declared 'open', and hence remain militarily undefended[30].

The Impact Of The 'Peace Forces'

Grass-root movements such as those described in this chapter have become a permanent feature in most Western democracies (as well as, more recently, in the previously totalitarian East). As such, they have constituted an innovation which the political system will have to accommodate, also because they reflect widespread (and sometimes, though not always, predominant) public moods.

This has been the case for the peace movements during the 1980s, when opinion polls have consistently shown public opinion to be more in line with the views of the peace movements and the Greens than with those of the established political parties[31]. What has saved the 'old parties' from ultimate electoral catastrophe has probably been the relatively low prominence of peace issues as compared with e.g. economic issues. Due to this, the established political forces have enjoyed a considerable leeway for adopting policies diverging from the views of their electorates. Nevertheless, as a long-term factor, the change in public attitudes is almost bound to effect party policies, as may be gathered i.a. from the account of the CDU-CSU in the subsequent chapter.

As might be expected, the policies advocated by the peace movements and the Green party have not been entirely consistent: It is e.g. by no means self-evident that neutrality might be combined with disarmament, such as implied by the Greens. Such a combination would militate against traditional interpretations of The Hague conventions and other relevant pieces of international law, as well as against historical evidence, *in casu* the actual defence policies of European neutrals[32].

The very fact that the popular movements have ventured into a field as inherently complicated and technical as that of conventional strategies deserves credit. Whereas the peace movements were previously mostly protest movements, with few and rather trivial positive demands, a quest for viable alternatives to the 'deterrence system' is now discernible everywhere. Due to the novelty and intrinsically complicated nature of the subject, however, it should come as no surprise that the peace movements have not yet come up with alternative ideas that would stand any chance when confronted with actual expertise.

Despite these deficiencies, and by virtue of their devotion to disarmament and an anti-militarist attitude, authors such as those referred to above may prove a valuable addition to the ongoing defence debate, preventing it from forgetting the fundamental truths that prevention of war is above all a task for politics, and that disarmament in general as well as nuclear disarmament in particular should remain the goal.

CHAPTER IX

The Government Parties Before 1989

The government in Bonn has since 1982 been a coalition between the CDU-CSU (between the two components of which the distinction has henceforth been omitted for the sake of simplicity) headed by Federal Chancellor Helmut Kohl, and the small FDP, headed by Minister of Foreign Affairs, Hans Dietrich Genscher.

Despite this temporary coalition, there have always been significant differences between the two parties, as becomes apparent from the fact that the FDP has joined ranks with the SPD for a number of years (1969-1982), whereas the CDU-CSU has only been willing to do so for a very brief interlude (1966-1969). Although the fact of the present coalition has by no means eliminated these disagreements, it has restrained both parties from expressing openly their diverging opinions. The actual distinctions are hence more difficult to identify, since politicians tend to mix up their roles as ministers and as party representatives. Nevertheless, I shall attempt a separate treatment of the two parties.

The Christian Democrats

The CDU-CSU has all along belonged to the 'traditionalist camp', as recorded in Chapter III above. Indeed, from its very infancy, the party, under the leadership of Federal Chancellor Konrad Adenauer accorded first priority to integration with the Western system (NATO, WEU, EC, etc.), even at the expense of reunification. Ever since, acceptability *vis-à-vis* the other NATO partners, and above all the USA, has been a decisive criterion for CDU-CSU security policy. Only very recently have the actual disagreements come out into the open, with the debate on short-range nuclear modernisation[1].

As might be expected, the CDU-CSU has therefore been extremely critical of all the alternative concepts described in the previous chapters. The only exception has been the issue of 'Europeanisation', wherein they have consistently lent their support to a strengthening of the European 'pillar', and actively promoted Franco-German collaboration, without, however, being prepared to sever the transatlantic bonds as a consequence thereof[2]. The basic attitude towards *détente* as such has undergone significant shifts. During the first decade of the FRG's existence, *détente* was perceived as a menace, since it might undermine support for the 'Hallstein Doctrine', and perhaps even lead to reunification on less than satisfactory terms, e.g. with an SPD-led all-German government. Since then, the CDU-CSU has, however, been somewhat more accommodating towards the East, particularly during periods of US-Soviet 'thaw'. Whereas the party had previously attacked the *Ostpolitik* of the SPD-FDP government, it gradually came to embrace the concepts almost wholeheartedly, and to emphasise the 'special relationship' between the two Germanies as a 'bedrock of *détente*' in the maelstrom of the 'second cold war'.

The CDU-CSU was somewhat ambiguous, albeit predominantly negative, towards the novel concepts of the 1980s, such as Common Security and NOD. However, whilst remaining critical of the (social democratic) CS approach[3], the then defence minister Rupert Scholz launched the phrase of 'reciprocal security' (*gegenseitige Sicherheit*), which constituted an alternative more in terms than in substance:

'We lend our support to a concept of reciprocal security. It requires from neither side more than the renunciation of absolute military security, i.e. it requires the willingness on the part of both parties to allow each other the same measure of security. It requires the abstention from trying to solve political problems by military means. The concept of reciprocal security rests on the balance of mutually secured defence capability, on a system of reciprocal confidence-building measures, as well as on *détente* and disarmament'[4].

Furthermore, after some hesitation the CDU-CSU came to support the INF agreement and vehemently opposed, even at the cost of open disagreement with the USA and the UK, the plans to 'fill the gaps' with short-range nuclear systems such as the 'follow-on to Lance'[5]. However, far from shifting to an anti-nuclear attitude, the party has supported maintaining the deterrence system, preferably indefinitely.

Part of this theoretical endeavour has been undertaken at the party's research institution, the 'Konrad Adenauer Foundation'. Researchers belonging to this institution have i.a. been seeking a blueprint for post-START and post-INF nuclear arsenals, which might maintain deterrence whilst meeting the German concerns. As it has repeatedly been stated by prominent CDU-CSU spokesmen, this was incompatible with any expansion of short-range nuclear forces, which should preferably be reduced substantially[6]. In their attempt to salvage a modicum of nuclear deterrence, certain CDU-affiliated researchers have even come to embrace the notion of NOD, albeit only conditionally[7].

As a general rule, however, the CDU-CSU has been reluctant to become involved in the actual NOD debate, and when it nevertheless has, its attitude has been highly sceptical. For instance, the 1985 *White Book* of Manfred Wörner's Ministry of Defence included an official critique of NOD, undoubtedly reflecting CDU viewpoints. On the other hand, 'forward-moving' (*Vorwärts-*) defence was just as unequivocally ruled out, since 'neither pre-emptive war nor offensive and preventive operations on to the territory of the opponent (. . .) are politically conceivable or militarily feasible options for NATO'[8].

Regardless of this critical attitude, the leader of the right-wing *Stahlhelm Fraktion* ('Steel Helmet Faction') within the party, Alfred Dregger, recently introduced parts of the NOD vocabulary into the debate, albeit with a distinctly 'hawkish' bias. In a 1988 article he e.g. stated his recommendations for NATO's post-INF strategy. They amounted to 'bringing about a mutual non-aggression capability', even though he was unwilling to acknowledge that this might necessitate changes on the NATO side as well[9].

A similar bias may be found in the party's decisions of its 36th Federal Convention in 1988, bearing the title *Our Responsibility in the World*, wherein it was stated that 'the CDU demands additional steps towards balanced and verifiable disarmament at all levels'. The envisioned steps included the elimination of the WTO's conventional superiority in general,. and the Soviet invasion capability in particular, for the purpose of which a preparedness to enter into discussions on military doctrine and strategy was expressed. The aim should be to attain 'a situation in which also the armed forces of the Warsaw Pact are only capable of defence'.[10]

In principle at least, the CDU-CSU thus seemed to have no problems with either the central NOD notion of restricting armed forces to the purpose of defence, or the notion of self-restraint as such. Minister of Defence, Gerhard Stoltenberg confirmed this impression with his statement at the *Wehrkunde* Conference in February 1990 that: 'International politics is today faced with the imperative of self-restraint, of the moderation of political goals. (. . .) The political purpose of armed forces can and must in our time be nothing but defensive'.[11]

In addition to such conditional, and partly somewhat ill-conceived, recommendations of NOD, a small group of (mostly local) CDU-CSU leaders have been genuinely influenced by the peace movement activities as well as by their Christian beliefs. They hence felt a need to distance themselves from the security policies of their party. In 1986 this group of Christian Democrats in Favour of Steps Towards Disarmament (CDSA) published a collection of articles, many of which advocated concepts such as CS and NOD[12].

The well-known TV personality Franz Alt had already made a public stand on his religiously-founded opposition to the dual-track decision, and he now, once again, pointed out the incompatibility of the Christian faith with arms build-up and deterrence[13]. Whereas he thus emphasised the 'C', i.e. the Christian basis of the CDU, others emphasised the 'D', i.e. the democratic principles. Kurt Biedenkopf (Chairman of the party organisation on North-Rhine-Westphalia) was especially concerned with the lack of public consensus behind nuclear deterrence[14]. Other members of the group emphasised the need for understanding the perceived security requirements of the USSR, including the historical Soviet fear of the Germans, whence the logical conclusion was drawn to support the principles of Common Security[15].

Albert Deittert and Heinrich Niesporek pursued this line of reasoning by *expressis verbis* advocating a conversion to NOD, i.e. a defence which would serve only to dissuade aggression by exacting a high admission and staying price, and which would be entirely non-threatening. As steps towards the political implementation of such an alternative defence, Wolfgang Pfeiler proposed consultations between the two alliances on military doctrines, and Diethelm Gohl advocated a gradualist approach towards a withdrawal of particularly offensive-capable weapons systems from the border areas, along with the creation of nuclear and chemical-weapons-free zones[16].

The CDSA, of course, constituted only a minuscule minority within the CDU-CSU. Furthermore, at least one of the dissidents, Franz Alt, subsequently left the party for good[17]. The very existence of the group did, however, testify to emerging cracks in the 'traditionalist' front. Furthermore, it served to remove the 'leftist stigma' on the ideas of CS and NOD by showing how these might actually appeal even to people of more conservative leanings.

More recently, the renowned research institution close to the CDU, the 'Foundation Science and Politics' in Ebenhausen, has also taken up NOD for serious consideration. Hans-Dieter Lemke (a serving army officer) in a research paper identified the elimination of offensive capabilities as the paramount objective of arms control. The goal should be a situation wherein both sides possessed armed forces of an exclusively defensive nature, so that even numerical disparities would become rather irrelevant. More specifically such a situation would be characterised by the following combination, reminiscent of the SAS proposal (cf. Chapter IV above):

'The distinguishing features of defensive superiority and strategical attack incapability would thus be a combination of strong main forces, which are only capable of defence, and weaker (. . .) formations, which are also capable of operational and tactical counter-offensives within the boundaries of the defence'[18].

There have thus been a number of indications that the CDU might be slowly approaching an adoption of at least some of the central NOD conceptions.

As a further indication of how far the NOD ideas had permeated into CDU thinking one might mention repeated statements by the holder of the highest office in the FRG, Federal President Richard von Weizsäcker. Although he was by virtue of his office elevated above the party-political level, he nevertheless remained a former CDU parliamentarian, and might thus be expected to express views at least compatible with those of his party.

By virtue of his having consistently sought the position of the presumed 'moral high ground', whilst taking the Christian ideals more seriously than most of the CDU, von Weizsäcker had for a number of years represented what might be called the more 'serious' conservative position. He had been deeply concerned about the division of Germany and the unsettled status of Berlin, as well as about the perpetual arms race.

On more than one occasion, he made statements very positive towards NOD, perhaps to some extent inspired by his brother Carl Friedrich, who, in addition to being a most renowned scientist in his own right, has been a close collaborator and 'mentor' of Horst Afheldt[19]. During his visit to Moscow in 1987, the Federal President gave a speech, in which he said *expressis verbis* that 'a balanced defence without the capability of attack is of importance'.

During the official visit of his then colleague from the GDR, Erich Honecker, in September 1987, the Federal President even went so far as to use the term 'structural inability to attack' (*strukturelle Nicht-Angriffs-fähigkeit*), thus deliberately disregarding the fact that this had been so closely associated with the SPD, and by so doing bridging the gap between government and opposition, as a president is supposed to do[20].

During the Soviet President Mikhail Gorbachev's visit to the FRG in June 1989, the government took yet another step towards supporting the defensive ideas. In the joint communiqué issued after the meeting, the idea of CS was to be found along with a formulation of the NOD principle which was (perhaps deliberately) left open to different interpretations. The FRG might imply nothing more than the allegations found in any NATO communiqué against Soviet offensive superiority, whereas the USSR might understand it more even-handedly, as an admonition to both sides to build down offensive capabilities:

'The Federal Republic of Germany and the Soviet Union declare that one cannot accomplish security for one-self at the expense of the security of others. (. . .) Both sides seek to (. . .) reduce the military potentials to a stable balance at a lower level, which is sufficient for defence, but not for attack'.[21]

As a means to soothe Soviet worries; the CDU-CSU was also forced to take NOD seriously because of the inescapable need for military build-down. In the light of disarmament, receding threat perceptions and an increasing scarcity of resources, the *Bundeswehr* (including its political masters) had to face the problem of how best to distribute cut-backs, rather than merely preparing lists of desirable additional procurements.

The 1990 budget thus fell well short of the three percent real increase envisaged by NATO ever since 1978. In fact, defence spending was now below the level suggested by the Social Democrats in the early 1980s. By December 1989, the West German Cabinet had thus agreed on a reduction of the *Bundeswehr* to a grand total of 470,000 troops, distributed between 420,000 active personnel, 10,000 reservists and another 40,000 in ready reserve status. The planned extension of the conscription period from fifteen to eighteen months had, furthermore, been scrapped.[22]

A reason for this development may be that it had become increasingly difficult for the proponents of the 'business as usual' school (to which the CDU-CSU have tended to belong) to justify their views with reference to external threats. In his speech to the *Wehrkunde* Conference in February 1990, Minister of Defence, Gerhard Stoltenberg thus had to concede that 'Never before since 1945 were the dangers of a great war on our continent so small as in our time'.[23]

The Free Democrats

The CDU-CSU's smaller coalition partner, the FDP, all along had a much more balanced, indeed almost positive, assessment of NOD, thanks both to the party's long experience with constructive *Ostpolitik* and to the party leader, Foreign Minister Hans Dietrich Genscher's profound understanding of the requirements of arms control. As early as in 1986, Genscher had *mirabile dictu* officially proclaimed NOD as the relevant goal for Europe:

'It is necessary to create cooperative security structures in Europe. The existing alliances should continue, but with regard to the weapons systems, the logistics, the force structure, the geographical deployment and the respective doctrines, our armed forces should be shaped in such a way that both sides have only the capabilities for defence, but not for offence and invasion'.[24]

Genscher was, furthermore, expressly positive towards Gorbachev's notion of the 'Common European House' and acknowledged the need for comprehensive disarmament as an element therein[25].

Since 1988-89, the latter topic in general, and the CFE talks in particular have, for obvious reasons, been a special preoccupation of the Foreign Minister. In this connection, he apparently waged an intra-governmental struggle against then Minister of Defence, Manfred Wörner, on the appropriate targets and concrete proposals for the CFE negotiations. The foreign office was thus tasked with elaborating a concept of conventional stability reflecting Genscher's, and presumably his party's, preferences. It was envisaged herein to seek reductions to equal ceilings 'somewhat below the current NATO level', necessitating a build-down on both sides, albeit most drastic as far as the WTO was concerned. This accomplishment should be followed by a phase which would focus on restructuring forces by emphasising defensive capabilities at the expense of attack capabilities[26].

Genscher largely prevailed in this intra-governmental struggle, as became apparent from the West German government's concrete recommendations for the CFE negotiations, which implied a preference for 'agreements on equal ceilings at lower levels for such weapons systems as are of special importance for the ability to carry out territory-conquering offensives', as examples of which were mentioned MBTs, tank destroyers and artillery[27].

Subsequently, Genscher elaborated in considerable detail his views on conventional arms control, hereby revealing an unmistakable inspiration from the NOD debate, most conspicuously from the SAS. He e.g. pointed to the need for modifications of C^3 structures, logistics, engineer support and the like so as to 'tie' the mobile, and *per se* offensive-capable, formations to their home territory[28].

Evaluation

As will have become apparent from the above account, the demand for NOD is no longer a prerogative of Social Democrats or other 'leftists'. Even 'centrists' and right-wingers frequently employ the term, and concur with the identification of offensive capabilities as the fundamental problem. There remains, however, an important distinction between the basic lines of argumentation of the SPD and the CDU.

Whereas the SPD has tended to conceive of conversion to NOD as a joint endeavour, requiring changes in both alliance systems (albeit more profound ones in the East), the CDU has tended to cling to the present NATO structure, whilst being increasingly eager to build down Soviet offensive capabilities via arms control. From discussions with younger colleagues associated with the CDU, the present author has got the impression that the problem has gradually come to be couched in rather surprising terms: not of how to achieve mutual force reductions, but of how to convince the German public of the need for maintaining the present level of forces in the face of an obvious unilateral Soviet build-down.

This attitude has tended to be based on the opinion that only the Eastern side possessed any margin for reductions, whereas NATO was already 'stretched too thin', whence the shift of the argument away from the emphasis on uneven 'force-to-force ratios' towards that of fixed 'force-to-space ratios'. Regardless of how much the other side might be willing to build down, there would allegedly be absolute limits to how small the defending forces (i.e. NATO's) might be—as a matter of coincidence, almost identical to the current force level.

Such an argument was, however, bound to run into problems. First of all, the public was unlikely to buy it, but might be expected to take the government up on its previous argument: 'If the huge Soviet preponderance was the reason why we needed an arms build-up in the past, then a Soviet build-down must logically allow us to build down as well'. Second, unless both sides had a margin for negotiated reductions, why negotiate at all? NATO might just as well sit back and wait for the unilateral Soviet build-down, which might indeed be likely to happen anyway.

CHAPTER X

The 'Other Germany' Before 1989

The account has so far concentrated on Western Germany, for obvious reasons. In the other German state, political developments were slow, boring, indeed almost non-existent.

A Solid Monolith?

To all practical intents and purposes, the Socialist Unity Party, the SED, led by Erich Honecker, possessed an unchallenged monopoly of power, although they formally shared this with certain 'interest groups' as well as with a group of 'bloc parties'. None of these were, however, at all comparable to their seeming western counterparts. The 'interest groups' (i.a. trade unions) were led by the SED, and the interests they saw themselves called upon to defend were primarily those of 'society' (i.e. the state, i.e. the SED regime) rather than the 'particular' interests of their members. The independence of the bloc parties was also close to a figment of the imagination, and they had little besides the name in common with their 'sister parties' in the FRG[1].

This near-monolithic power structure seemed astonishingly solid, and no major instances of civil unrest had been recorded since the rebellion in 1953 which had been crushed by the SED and their Soviet allies. The prevailing feeling amongst the population was one of apathy and lack of political interest, a fact that did not seem to bother the SED, except for the occasional instances where cheering crowds were of some importance[2]. This apathic calm was based i.a. on two factors:

First of all, on a fairly decent level of economic growth (at least until recently) which meant that the standard of living in the GDR was well above that of all its East European neighbours. This, in its turn, was based i.a. on the near-membership of the EC informally enjoyed by the GDR thanks to its 'special relationship' with the FRG. Secondly, it was based on a system of repression and censorship that managed to 'nip' most dissident currents 'in the bud'[3].

Foreign Policy

The very existence of the GDR was always based on the (above all military) power of the USSR, which regarded the GDR as one of the main pillars in its alliance system. Upon being accorded formal sovereignity in 1949, it was hence a foregone conclusion that the GDR would join the Soviet state system with all its ramifications: the Warsaw Treaty Organisation (WTO), the Council of Mutual Economic Assistance (CMEA, also know as 'Comecon'), etc. Furthermore, the GDR perceived itself (probably correctly) as enjoying a more limited room for political manoeuvre than the other and less important members of the East European 'community'.

The leaders of the SED, i.e. Walter Ulbricht and his successor Erich Honecker, along with their entourage, made a virtue out of this necessity by almost making loyalty towards the USSR their political *raison d'être*[4]. They were thus loyal, almost enthusiastic, participants in the 'Cold War', and e.g. supported, indeed urged, the invasion of Czeckoslovakia in 1968, as well as the imposition of martial law in Poland in 1981.

In a certain sense, the Cold War was (until the 1970s) seen as the *sine qua non* of maintaining the GDR as a separate state, and hence of the continued power of the ruling élite. Were *détente* to proceed beyond a certain point, German unification might become feasible, as a result of which the SED dictatorship was sure to be overthrown. It was thus hardly surprising that Walter Ulbricht in 1950 turned down the Western proposals for free elections in both parts of Germany, as allegedly envisaging 'mumbo-jumbo (*Hottentotten-*) elections' with a view to 'allowing the great land-owners, entrepreneurs and bankers from the West back in Berlin, from whence they had fled'[5].

From being a beneficiary of the Cold War, the GDR did, however, gradually become accustomed to the *détente* of the 1970s, to the point when they verged on refusing to join the USSR in the new Cold War in the early 1980s[6].

The unswerving loyalty to the common cause of socialism was undoubtedly partly motivated by 'existential concerns' on the part of the East German leaders, stemming above all from the fact that the GDR lacked a true national identity. This became obvious when the GDR in 1974 adopted probably the most absurd constitution in the whole of Europe, which omitted any reference to the German nation, whilst explictly mentioning the alliance with the USSR. In contrast to other repressive regimes in Eastern Europe, the GDR did not constitute a nation-state, but was an obvious political artefact, 'an entity without identity'[7]. Until around 1970, the GDR was not even regarded by the international community as a state at all, partly (but not merely) as a result of the West German claim to be the sole legitimate representative of 'Germany' in the international community ('*Alleinvertretungsanspruch*').

The best the GDR could hope for in this respect was to shield itself off from the other Germany, to which the overwhelming majority of the country's population would have preferred to belong. The formula of 'two German states of one German nation' (or 'one German territory') thus became the sacrosanct formula for the SED's policy towards West Germany, indeed in a certain sense for the totality of the country's foreign relations.

Relations With The FRG

Relations with the FRG were thus predestined to be strained, to say the least, and the FRG refused to have diplomatic relations with the GDR until 1972 when the 'Basic Treaty' was signed[8]. Even subsequent to this treaty (in its turn merely one element in a criss-crossing pachwork of treaties between the FRG and the WTO states), the GDR was not regarded by the Federal Government as a 'real state', and citizens of the GDR were hence automatically treated as citizens of the FRG, rather than as foreigners.

The GDR has made frequent allegations against the FRG for sponsoring subversion in the GDR, even officially proclaiming the Berlin Wall to be an 'anti-fascist protection wall', shielding the innocent East German citizens from their dangerous compatriots in the West[9]. Although this allegation was obviously ridiculous, it does seem inherently plausible that the FRG was, in fact, secretly 'pulling some strings' in the GDR.

The GDR, in its turn, was consistently involved in various forms of subversive activities in the FRG. Since the 1989 revolution, it has e.g. been revealed that the GDR's Ministry of Defence had been involved in the paramilitary training of members of the (West) German Communist Party (DKP). Mainly responsible for these activities was, however, the hated *'Stasi'* (*Staatssicherheitsdient*)[10]. Furthermore, the GDR also hosted (presumably wittingly) regular terrorists, such as members of the *'Rote Armee Fraktion'*, i.e. the 'Baader-Meinhof Group', and the infamous 'Carlos'[11].

In practical terms, however, relations were normalised and the GDR increasingly opened itself up to the West. Old-age pensioners were allowed to emigrate, other citizens were given better (than the previously almost non-existent) opportunities for travelling to the FRG, jamming of West German television broadcasts ceased, etc. In return, the GDR established highly lucrative trade relations with the FRG and by implication indirectly with the entire EC, which allowed for a rising standard of living, comparing favourably with the rest of Eastern Europe. The only standard of comparison according to which the GDR failed miserably was, indeed, that of the FRG. However, the latter was, alas, the only obvious yardstick in the minds of the East Germans, who were able to watch, and envy, their fellow-countrymen in the West every night on television.

The SED leadership attempted, albeit largely in vain, to imbue their subjects with an artificial sense of national identity, whilst erasing the 'old' one, i.e. the reminiscences of the united Germany. In the beginning, they sought to amplify the (in truth not negligible) accomplishments of socialism in the GDR whilst simultaneously belittling the (actually much more impressive) accomplishments of the capitalist FRG. They actually portrayed the GDR as 'the first truly democratic state in German history', whence the name 'German Democratic Republic'. The utter absurdity of this endeavour did, however, gradually become apparent, i.a. because of the intensified contacts, which decreased the prospects of lying almost to nil[12].

Subsequently, the SED leadership shifted to another strategy, namely that of portraying the GDR as the (or at least a) legitimate heir to the German traditions, in terms of culture and the like. National historical figures such as Martin Luther, Frederick the Great and others henceforth enjoyed a new attention (especially so, if they happened to have been born, or have spent some time in, what was now the GDR), and 'progressive' elements in their thinking were amplified, occasionally beyond recognition[13].

Neither of these quests for 'national identity' were, however, at all succesful, and the population of the GDR continued to regard themselves as 'Germans', who had the bad luck of living in the wrong part of the divided country, rather than as East Germans in their own right.

Gradually, the relationship between the two Germanies intensified both in economic terms and with regard to personal contacts between the leaders as well as populations of the two Germanies, to the point when it had become almost cordial. Part of the explanation for this was the shared interest of both German states in the maintenance of peace, based on their shared understanding of being singled out as a future battleground for a potential war beyond their own control. Any major conventional war in Europe, as well as most conceivable varieties of 'tactical' and theatre-scale nuclear war, would be completely devastating to both Germanies, perhaps even more so for the East than for the West[14].

Defence Policy

The uncomfortable front-line status of the GDR has obviously reflected, above all, Soviet military priorities. It is, however, beyond the scope of the present work to undertake a in-depth analysis of Soviet military strategy[15]. Suffice it therefore to recapitulate the two (or two-and-a-half) alternative explanations for the Soviet military presence in the GDR, which might be called the 'defensive' and the 'offensive' interpretation, respectively.

1. According to the defensive interpretation, the Soviet Union did in all honesty, albeit erroneously, fear an attack from the West, and was eager to prevent a repetition of Napoleon's or Hitler's invasions. Hence the perceived need for a 'buffer zone' to protect the Soviet heartland from the most likely

enemies. Prominent amongst these were the USA and Germany (now in the shape of the FRG), two states that would individually constitute serious threats, but who now collaborated according to some diabolical scheme directed against the USSR. One element in this collaboration was the stationing of powerful US forces and a whole panoply of nuclear weapons on the territory of the FRG, poised against the Soviet Union. The only appropriate answer to this threat was to be found in a counter-positioning of Soviet forces on the territory of the GDR, intended as a first defence line.

1a. Whereas the above explanation might be convincing with regard to the very presence, as well as perhaps the size, of the Group of Soviet Forces Germany (GSFG), it falls short of explaining their highly offensive configuration. As an additional explanation thereof, a Soviet predeliction for preventive or pre-emptive, yet basically still defensively motivated, warfare has been provided. According to what might be called the 'defensive-through-offensive' interpretation, the Soviets had contingency plans for a preventive high-speed invasion of Western Europe, which might be effected once a war was believed to be inevitable. Such an invasion would, for obvious reasons, have to pass through the FRG, and the ideal location for the forces assigned to this task (requiring a high offensive potential) would be the GDR[16].

2. According to the offensive interpretation, the Soviet Union had always been inherently expansionist, and hence obviously needed, for implementing these objectives, forces with as high a shock power as possible, and stationed as far forward as possible with a view to capitalising on the surprise factor.

Although the present author subscribes to some variety of the (1a) 'defensive-through-offensive' explanation, there is no conclusive evidence in favour of either hypothesis. Be that as it may, the fact remained that the Soviet Union had, ever since the war, stationed very powerful forces (around twenty divisions) on the territory of the GDR, with a panoply of highly offensive-capable weapons systems at their disposal: MBTs, heavy, self-propelled artillery, IFVs, frontal aviation and 'tactical' missiles, as well as nuclear and chemical munitions[17].

The GDR, in its turn, had since 1955 been 'allowed' to field indigenous military forces, which were assigned, even in peacetime, to the WTO (in analogy with the West German forces, assigned to NATO). They had been subordinated entirely to WTO (i.e. to all practical intents and purposes: Soviet) command, and should probably be understood to be, above all, a far-flung support structure for the GSFG. Their capabilities for independent operations, say of a territorial defence character, had to be assessed as very circumscribed, and they had no indigenous military doctrine which might have prescribed such operations[18].

Just as was the case for the other NSPFs (Non-Soviet Pact Forces), however, the reliability of the East German forces had always been somewhat questionable. On the one hand, the 'National People's Army'

(NVA), undoubtedly possessed high professional skills, and an high discipline, and would thus most likely have been loyal in most contingencies. On the other hand, the rank-and-file NVA soldiers would most likely have been unreliable when confronting their fellow countrymen, i.e. in the only really realistic contingency[19].

The total strength of the NVA had grown from 85,000 in 1962 to 179,000 by 1988, including i.a. four motorised and two tank divisions, an airborne battalion, 337 fixed-wing combat aircraft and 150 helicopters. In addition to these regular forces were the border guards and internal security forces, numbering an impressive 77,500 troops, bringing the grand total to 239,000, among a total population of only 16 million inhabitants. By any comparison, the GDR was thus at least as militarised as the FRG, probably more so[20].

A distinctly military spirit was deliberately cultivated by the authorities, both by means of 'Prussian-style' military parades and marches, and through 'pre-military' education in the schools. Furthermore, in line with the cultivation of the historical traditions, the NVA came to be portrayed as the heir to the best of the German/Prussian military tradition[21].

Ideology and the Academic Community

The official state ideology of Soviet-style Marxism-Leninism was given a high priority by the authorities, not least as a would-be substitute for a sense of national identity. In this respect orthodoxy was more complete in the GDR than in most other East European countries. This orthodoxy, as well as the loyalty to the Soviet Union, was manifested i.a. in a relentless stream of German translations of Soviet theoretical works on Marxism-Leninism (undoubtedly with a very limited readership). In addition to such expressions of 'proletarian internationalism', the GDR was also a mass producer of indigenous propaganda material and pseudo-analyses i.a. in the realms of political science and international relations.

Regardless of the manpower resources spent on these ideological efforts, the genuine intellectual output until the revolution remained far from impressive, indeed almost pathetic. A steady flow of publications, completely devoid of innovative or critical thinking, but as a meagre substitute abounding with quotations from Erich Honecker and the Marxist classics, poured out from the 'paper-mills' of the various 'think-tanks' servicing the SED, such as the huge IPW (Institute for International Politics and Economy) in East Berlin. Due to censorship as well as an actual unavailability (i.a. for currency reasons) of Western literature, the GDR publications showed an almost complete ignorance of the new thinking flourishing not least in West Germany.

The NOD debate described in the previous chapters was thus just one example of innovative Western thinking that was hardly noticed in the GDR. Nevertheless, the total lack of openness with regard to military

matters, be they Soviet or East German, made the deficiency even more
glaring in this field than in so many others. It should thus come as no
surprise that the NOD debate emerged from the rich and pluralistic
intellectual environment of the FRG, rather than from the barren and
monotonous one of the GDR.

It has since the revolution been openly acknowledged, even by former
'accomplices', that political science in the GDR was in a sorry state and
in acute need of renovation[22]. Even prior to the revolution, some of
the ground-work had nevertheless been done for the wave of new thinking
that sprang out into the open after the fall of Honecker and the Wall.
A number of the elements of new thinking (including 'Common Security'
and NOD) were, at least latently, to be found in pre-revolutionary
writings, especially in the years since 1985, and undoubtedly inspired by
the 'Gorbachev phenomenon'. I shall return to these elements shortly.

Although the above attitudes were, until the revolution, the predominant
ones in the GDR, they were not all-pervasive. There had consistently been
dissenting and critical voices, albeit often muted by the censorship and the
Stasi regime. Some of these persons and groupings were subsequently to be
found in the forefront of the political èlite of the post-revolutionary GDR.
Whereas a good deal, indeed most, of the criticism has been raised against
the internal policies of the SED regime, I shall disregard these, and
mention but a few of the dissenting opinions with regard to foreign, and
especially military, policies.

Although the distinction is, admittedly, somewhat artificial, and even
though the border between the two is blurred, it nevertheless seems sensible
to distinguish between 'dissidents' and 'critics'. Whereas the former contested the very legality of the by then prevailing regime and, as a consequence, made a point of dissenting, the latter category tended to voice their
dissenting views on specific points, and to do so 'more in sorrow than in
anger' and *sotto voce*. Needless to say, neither of these categories *per se*
have held 'the moral high ground'.

Contrary to the situation in the West, the peace movement was
not always to be found amongst the critics. As a matter of fact, the
'Peace Council' of the GDR remained a loyal supporter of the SED
regime, and it was hence more a matter of coincidence when it was to be
found on the same side as the Western peace movements, e.g. in the INF
debate[23].

Amongst the dissidents were to be found i.a. conscientious objectors
(including, ironically, the later defence minister, Reinar Eppelmann) and
other genuine peace groups (i.e. such as criticised both blocs equally),
'greens' and other ecological groups. Amongst the critics were to be found,
first of all, the Federation of Protestant ('evangelical') Churches, collaborating with the state apparatus whilst nevertheless preserving their independence, including the right to criticise official policies[24].

The most prominent amongst the 'defence intellectuals' of the churches was the professor of mathematics at the Academy of Sciences, Walter Romberg, whom we shall encounter in the subsequent chapter as Minister of Finance (for the East German SPD) in post-revolutionary GDR. As early as 1986, he published a major study on *Crisis-stable Military Security in Central Europe*, which constituted, to the knowledge of the present author, the first substantial work on NOD by any East German (or by any East European, for that matter). It was cautiously marked 'Only for use within the churches'.

Romberg's point of departure was a series of positive authoritative statements (from as early as 1982) by the protestant churches about common security and the need for 'typically defensive conceptions of defence'. His theoretical point of departure was, however, rather the Western discussion of crisis stability, in which problem he saw the most serious challenge to peace in Europe. Whereas the existing military structures in Europe entailed incentives for both preemption and escalation, an alternative structure was conceivable which would minimise these incentives, thus improving stability. It should combine a structural incapability of 'strategic offensives' (understood as major operations on the territory of the respective opponent) with ensured defensive capabilities, understood as the ability to exact a high entrance as well as staying price.

Neither alliance, according to Romberg, complied with these criteria, i.a. because the socialist states adhered to 'an offensive strategy for military defence'. The various NOD models were, likewise, compared by the author according to the same criteria, and those were criticised which included significant strategically offensive elements (such as Jochen Löser's), whereas other 'mix models' (i.a. that of the SAS) were assessed as more positive contributions to stability[25].

The political point of departure for Romberg's own concrete proposal was the 'Palme Zone', and the proposal itself thus amounted to a disengagement proposal reminiscent of the ones described in Chapter IV above. It envisioned a three-stage disengagement process:

1. In the first stage, all battlefield nuclear weapons were to be withdrawn from a narrow zone (50-100 kms. on either side), along with all heavy, mechanised forces: vehicles weighing more than 20 tonnes, weapons with calibres exceeding 100 mms (for tube artillery) or 140 mms (for rocket artillery), respectively. In the thus depleted zone, light infantry and stationary territorial militia formations should be deployed, and various forms of barriers and fortifications constructed.

2. In the second stage, the same weapons systems should be withdrawn a further appr. 50 kms. with the exception of rocket artillery and missile launchers, which should be allowed a slightly larger calibre of 240 mms (in order to allow for i.a. deployment of the US-West German MLRS and the corresponding Soviet systems).

3. In the third and final stage, the remaining parts of the territories of the FRG and the GDR should be rid entirely of nuclear weapons, and the numbers of offensive-capable major weapons systems should be reduced substantially[26].

Since then, Romberg has been a frequent participant in the international debate on NOD, and had i.a. maintained close links with the SAS, mentioned in chapter IV above. His concrete proposal subsequently remained largely unchanged, but the author has embedded it more explicitly in a gradualistic framework[27].

In this connection Romberg assessed very favourably the series of unilateral steps on the part of the WTO since 1988, including the pre-revolutionary unilateral arms reductions announced (albeit for lack of time not actually implemented) by the Honecker regime, to which I shall return below. Romberg advocated proceeding along the same path, i.a. by gradually extending the 'agenda' of gradualistic unilateralism to include constraints on naval forces and a modicum of 'preventive arms control' in the form of restrictions with regard to military research and development[28].

Since he was not overtly oppositional, his activities were tolerated by the SED authorities. After the revolution, he was nevertheless regarded as an obvious candidate for one of the ministries related to security policy (foreign or defence minister), but it just so happened that he had to assume responsibility for the finances of the rapidly collapsing GDR. His post-revolutionary contributions to the NOD debate have therefore been fairly limited, albeit far from negligible. I shall return to these in the next chapter.

The Gorbachev Factor

Under the impact of the generational change in the Soviet Union, the personality of Mikhail Gorbachev, and the new political approaches of *glasnost* and *perestroika*, things were set in motion in the GDR as well as in the Soviet Union itself. As the new 'climate' spread gradually to the entire Soviet sphere of influence, the SED leadership began to sense increasing pressure, even prior to the autumn revolutions of 1989.

They were, indeed, in an unenviable position, having all along based their claim to power on Soviet support and now felt the rug being pulled away underneath their feet. Ideological dogmas upon which the SED had based its presumed legitimacy were undergoing reassessment, and history was being scrutinised, threatening to reach the 'blind spots' in East German history which the SED preferred to forget about. The very societal structure in the other countries of the socialist community was undergoing a slow, but apparently unstoppable, transformation[29].

Under the influence of the new Soviet thinking, a number of new themes appeared in East German security political literature, which have subsequently blended in with the Common Security and NOD discourse:

—The notion of 'peaceful coexistence' as a semi-permanent stage in international relations, based in its turn, on a reassessment of the orthodox thesis that capitalism tends towards war[30].

—A positive assessment of interdependence as a contribution to peace as well as development[31].

—The conception of the 'Common European House'[32]

—The acknowledgement of 'global problems' transcending the systemic divide, i.e. of problems under which capitalism and socialism suffer alike, for which neither is exclusively to blame, and the solution of which must hence be a joint responsibility[33].

—The notion that modern industrial (or 'post-industrial') societies were unfit for any type of war, whether nuclear or conventional. According to this 'TDCW (Totally Destructive Conventional War) hypothesis', as I have called it elsewhere, even victorious conventional warfare would prove suicidal, due to the tremendous vulnerability of urbanised and industrialised societies, such as the GDR. Consequently, Clausewitz's dictum on 'war as a continuation of politics' presumably no longer applied. Although the present author happens to disagree with this hypothesis, it served to emphasise the primacy of war prevention, and hence *prima facie* strengthened the case for disarmament. As a matter of fact, however, the TDCW is logically incompatible with NOD, since it implies also that defensive war makes no sense. None of the authors in the GDR (or in the FRG) who have simultaneously advocated NOD and the TDCW have, however, seemed to be aware of this logical inconsistency[34].

—The notion of Common Security, which had previously been rejected for its implications that even inherently peaceful socialist states might constitute security risks for their neighbours[35].

—Since around 1987, NOD was also being explicitly promoted by East German researchers, albeit most often with the curious twist that only NATO was portrayed as being currently offensive[36]. The focus was placed on certain new NATO conceptions, such as the FOFA doctrine, an emphasis which was perfectly understandable in view of the fact that the GDR was located within the firing range of most of the envisaged FOFA systems.

To the extent that security policy analysts in the GDR did at all take the WTO's military posture into account, they tended to promote conversion and NOD as a bilateral endeavour, preferably to be implemented via CSBMs and/or some type of disengagement, i.e. 'offensive-weapons-free zones'[37]. Analysts from the GDR have, however, just as their colleagues from the other Eastern countries, tended to be sceptical towards more high technology NOD schemes, regarding these as simply initiating a new round in the arms race, and, moreover, a round which the technologically backward WTO was almost certain to lose.

Many of these new ideological themes were given expression in the 1987 semi-official joint paper by the SPD of the FRG and the SED of the GDR on *The Struggle of Ideologies*[38], wherein both sides acknowledged each other's ability, in principle, to maintain peaceful relations, and wherein a wide range of common interests were enumerated, including a conversion to NOD.

As a general rule, academic 'new thinking' did not precede that of the political rulers, at least as far as the published views were concerned. It is, of course, conceivable that these academics, many of whom had unofficial positions as advisors, may have 'whispered into the ears of the rulers' some of the ideas, which the latter subsequently made official policy, and which were eventually also expressed openly, and elaborated upon by the academics. To verify this assumption is, however, impossible, and it must hence remain merely an 'educated guess'.

Researchers from i.a. the IPW or the diplomatic academy had previously been closely associated with the SED government (e.g. as speech-writers for Honecker). They had often made it their business to contribute to the 'paper-mills' of official propaganda, and had thus sacrificed (at least some of) their scholarly integrity.

Subsequent to the revolution, several of these academics had begun to appraise the past critically. This phenomenon is open to several different interpretations, in analogy with the phenomenon dealt with in Chapter V of the retired officer turned anti-militarist: either the apparent change of mind was due to opportunism of the 'bandwagoning' kind ('since the old regime has gone, let's make friends with the new one'); or it might reflect personal intellectual tragedies. These political scientists and academics from other disciplines (many of whom were highly gifted in their respective fields) might have held dissenting opinions all along, but might have felt compelled to keep them to themselves, for fear of losing their jobs.

The present author's personal impression is that there were examples of both, and that the difference was partly generational. Particularly younger academics seemed positively delighted to finally be able to voice what they had thought all along, whereas some of their elder colleages and often superiors appeared opportunistic and only engaged in (probably futile) attempts at salvaging their positions, with the infamous Max Schmidt of the IPW, who has now been sacked along with many of his closest collaborators, as the most pathetic example.

Manfred Müller of the diplomatic academy in Potsdam was another example. After having followed the SED line unswervingly (indeed, being a member of the Central Committee), he realised the need for 'new thinking' too late. By 1988 and 1989, he had reached the stage of acknowledging NOD as a valid objective in principle, without, however, being prepared to go into the implications for the military structure of the WTO or the NVA in any kind of detail. By 1990, however, he had come a long way, indeed, and now published a proposal (in West Germany) for the role of the united Germany in the European security system. Herein he envisioned e.g. the total merger of the two alliances, i.e. the accession of all present WTO member states to NATO, as well as a number of constraints imposed upon German military structure; and a reduction of the *Bundeswehr* to 200,000 men, and the NVA to 50,000. In addition to this, until 1999 both superpowers were to maintain their military presence in both Germanies[39].

Gerhard Basler of the IPW was probably a good example of the former category. At the beginning of 1990, he delivered a scathing criticism of the former foreign policy of the GDR in the West German foreign policy journal *Europa-Archiv*, accusing the SED i.a. of not comprehending the dialectical relationship between external and internal factors, from whence had ensued isolationism[40].

The same held true for Wolfgang Schwarz, who was probably the first East European to earn a Ph.D. degree for a dissertation on NOD, with the title *Structural Inability to Attack in Europe*. Apart from the above-mentioned work of Romberg, this constituted the only major contribution of GDR scholars to the theory of NOD which deserves to be mentioned alongside the substantial West German works.

Predictably, Schwarz criticised NATO's offensive military plans (FOFA, ATBM and the like) as not 'merely' destabilising, but also incompatible with the alleged 'inability of modern societies to wage war'. Even a conventional war such as envisaged by NATO (to say nothing about nuclear war) would completely devastate the countries upon the soil of which it were to be waged, due to the abundance of nuclear reactors, chemical plants and similar highly lethal facilities, which were allegedly almost certain to be hit, be it advertently or as collateral damage. Furthermore, the entire infrastructrure of such industrialised urban societies was so vulnerable that it would surely break down under the impact of fighting, with a paralysing effect on society, as well as on the armed forces themselves[41].

Although the implied TDCW (cf. above) seemed rather detached from strategic considerations, such an image of a future war did become prevalent in the GDR, as well as in certain circles in the FRG. Indeed, the present author had the curious experience of trying in vain to convince not only said Schwarz but also professional officers from the GDR (i.a. teachers at the Military Academy in Dresden) that defence by military means might still make sense under certain circumstances. Although no agreement was reached on this point, the authors from the GDR, and especially Schwarz, agreed that the major risk was entailed by the offensive military potential, whereas defensive forces did constitute a lesser risk. In a war waged between military alliances such as NATO and the WTO with offensive military configurations, the concept of a 'rear area' would lose all meaning, and the entire territory become the battleground for high-intensity warfare. in all likelihood with highly disastrous consequences for the civilian population. Even operational-scale counter-attacks thus constituted strategic challenges to a country of the size and location of the GDR[42]

Since war prevention would thus be the foremost imperative, the appropriate yardstick for the military forces of both sides would be 'sufficiency', conceived of as a combination of an adequate ability to defend with an inability to attack. Whereas this has been the distinguishing common feature of all West German NOD proponents, these were nevertheless criticised by Schwarz for supporting the official NATO view that war prevention might be possible through the ability of waging war. Furthermore, NOD proponents were, according to Schwarz, too uncritical with regard to the NATO threat images of the aggressive Warsaw Pact[43].

As his alternative, he suggested a very comprehensive conception of NOD, including not merely the land forces, but also naval and aerial forces. Furthermore, he regarded NOD as unobtainable through unilateralism, but as requiring a concerted effort by both sides. Furthermore, Schwarz emphasised that this bilateral conversion endeavour should aim at reduced numbers of forces, whilst requiring only very marginal additional investments. He was therefore highly sceptical towards the more demanding and high technology-dependent NOD schemes, above all because they would place unacceptable economic burdens on society[44].

Whereas the analysis of Wolfgang Schwarz did not add many new elements to the transnational body of NOD theory, it did provide a solid basis for the debate on NOD in the GDR, which subsequently accelerated, i.a. with said Schwarz as a central participant, in his post-revolutionary capacity as government advisor.

Reform Before the Revolution

Even prior to the revolution, the SED leadership had taken up a number of the themes prevalent in the West German security debate, namely those that were compatible with a 'stabilisation' of the East-West conflict, including their own remaining in power and the continued division of Germany. The themes emphasised by the SED included denuclearisation, couched above all in terms of a nuclear-weapons-free corridor in Central Europe, as well as chemical disarmament, likewise envisaged, in the first stage, through the creation of a chemical-weapons-free zone.

With regard to both issues, the SED negotiated 'draft treaties' with the SPD of West Germany, as mentioned in Chapter VII above. Furthermore, they undertook a major propaganda effort, including (some financial, but above all political) support for parts of the peace movement in West Germany.

This behaviour placed a number of political groupings in the West in a dilemma. They could hardly refuse some political collaboration with the SED (or at least with its 'front organisations' such as the 'Peace Council') on matters where there was no political disagreement. Both sides were in agreement on the need for halting the INF deployment and supported the creation of zones free of nuclear and chemical weapons, etc.: demands which were of an indigenous Western origin, conceived of as gradualistic and incremental ways of halting the arms race, and demands which, according to most peace activists and peace researchers remained sensible, no matter who supported them. On the other hand, the support by the SED (as well as the USSR) did contribute to 'fouling the waters'. The peace movement became somewhat vulnerable to charges of falling victim to Soviet 'disinformation campaigns', etc. The dilemma was not really soluble, and only demonstrated the wisdom embedded in the old proverb: 'God protect me from my friends. My enemies I can take care of myself!'.

The same was true for the NOD issue, which likewise (after initial indifference and dismissal) gained the approval of the GDR leadership, subsequent to the Soviet adoption of the objective. This led to the publication of a number of analyses of offensive elements in Western military strategy and posture (i.a. from the aforementioned 'paper-mills'), as well as to authoritative political statements to the same effect. The SED also began to take an interest in the western NOD debate, above all for its inherent criticism of Western military structure.

The trouble was that the SED was less forthcoming with regard to self-criticism, i.e. in the form of the identification of offensive elements in WTO military strategy and posture. In addition to these propagandistic and partly diplomatic endeavours, however, the GDR had for some time been following the lead of its Warsaw Pact allies and had embarked upon reductions and a certain restructuring of its armed forces.

At the beginning of 1989, Erich Honecker thus announced reductions in the size of the armed forces by 10,000 men (i.e. six percent) as well as a ten percent cut in the defence budget. A total of six tank regiments were to be dismantled by 1990; some tanks were to be transferred to training units or converted to other uses; most were to be scrapped. There was also a certain discussion in the highest circles on the need for restructuring forces to a more defensive configuration. Motor rifle units, for example, were to be stripped of their tank units and some assault engineer units replaced with more anti-tank and obstacle-building elements[45].

Subsequent to the first stage of the revolution, i.e. the replacement of first Honecker with Egon Krenz, subsequently the latter with Hans Modrow, the defence reform continued. The newly-appointed Defence Minister, Vice Admiral Theodor Hoffmann, outlined substantial military reforms which were to include a reduction in service length for naval conscripts from two years to 18 months, bringing the navy in line with the ground forces. He indicated, furthermore, that East Germany would also follow the Soviet Union's lead in publicly adopting a 'defensively oriented' military doctrine. The changes were to be implemented for the most part by the end of 1990, according to Hoffmann[46].

It does not appear sensible to conclude this chapter with an evaluation since, with the democratic revolution of 1989/90, life itself provided an 'evaluation' of the SED regime as well as, indeed, of the GDR as a sovereign state. In both cases, the findings of the evaluation were negative, as will become apparent from the subsequent chapter.

CHAPTER XI

The Year of Upheaval

The twelve months following the summer of 1989 became the most momentuous period in the entire post-war history of both German states. During this short period, developments occurred at a breath-taking pace, and of such tremendous impact on the future as nobody had believed possible. Subsequent to what could only be called a revolution, albeit an entirely peaceful one, in East Germany, the two Germanies embarked upon a process of unification, the pace of which took everybody by surprise. Even the most daring and radical schemes of unification[1] were rendered hopelessly conservative and obsolete by the actual course of events. Furthermore, Germany once again became the focus for high-level East-West negotiations, this time, however, conducted in an infinitely more constructive and almost cordial atmosphere than had been the case in the 1950s.

It might almost seem as if Germany, the former bone of contention, had now become a unifying factor, indeed perhaps the groundstone for a far-reaching restructuring of international relations. A 'security regime' may be in the making, which may, in due course, manifest itself in, say, a genuine system of collective security, i.e. a new structure worthy of the name 'peace order'. I shall, however, postpone these more visionary considerations (with important implications for the very NOD idea) to the concluding chapter and devote the present one to a more sober account of what actually happened during the 'year of upheaval'. In this account, I shall give a special emphasis to how NOD ideas entered into the deliberations in the two Germanies, as well as elsewhere, but with regard to Germany.

Since an exhaustive account of these developments is beyond the scope of the present work, what follows is inevitably selective and fragmentary. I shall commence with a brief sketch of the autumn revolution in the GDR. Subsequently, I shall identify the main steps in the unification process, followed by an account of the reactions to this process from abroad. These all constitute the framework conditions, under which the security and defence debates in both German states were conducted, to which I have devoted the concluding parts of this chapter. Needless to say, such a division is very artificial, since what actually occurred was an interaction, or perhaps even 'an interaction between interactive processes'. Nevertheless, I have found this ordering of the subject more satisfactory that the purely chronological account.

A Peaceful Revolution

The momentuous events in the autumn of 1989 were, in a certain sense, initiated from abroad, albeit not from the FRG, as it was claimed by the, by then almost desperate, SED Politbureau in a statement dated 11 October 1989. In this declaration, they claimed that the steady flow of refugees were 'victims of a grand-scale provocation', and charged the FRG with 'interfering in the internal affairs of the GDR, in violation of the laws of nations'[2].

What really set the process in motion was, first of all, the fact that the Soviet leadership had since Gorbachev's accession to power in 1985 steadily loosened its grip on Eastern Europe, as well as provided an example for emulation in terms of openness (*glasnost*) and restructuring (*perestroika*). It thus became clear to the East German population that the SED was on its own, and that any opposition would merely have to defeat the indigenous holders of the reins of power, rather than (as happened in 1953) the Soviet occupation forces.

The USSR may have been reconsidering its attitude towards the German question for some time before 1989, just as it appears to have had second thoughts on the very value of Soviet dominion in Eastern Europe. The former attitude had emphasised the military factors, and as a consequence found comfort in the maintenance of a 'buffer zone' shielding the USSR from the presumably aggressive West. The Soviet Union had, furthermore, remained eager to check the military power of (West) Germany, i.a. through the division of the country.

Both policies had required a military presence abroad, intended both as a means of maintaining Soviet dominance, and as actual fighting forces. In the latter role, Soviet forces had been intended to conduct swift offensives into Western Europe, most likely as a means for 'offensive defence', yet conceivably for the purpose of aggression, should the opportunity arise.

These policies did, however, come at a price which gradually came to be seen as exceeding any accruing benefits, namely the price of continued 'cold war' with all its implications in terms of poor international relations, unaffordable defence expenditures, etc. With the advent to power of the new generation of communist (or perhaps not so communist?) leaders around Gorbachev, the time had come for a thorough re-evaluation of previous policies[3].

One of the most productive elements in 'new thinking' pertaining to German unity was the notion of a 'Common European House', which was obviously incompatible with arrangements under which 'tenants' were kept apart by force, or some apartments were occupied by other tenants. If the

Soviet leadership wanted the West to take the notion seriously, they had to put their own part of the 'house' in order[4].

Secondly, democratisation in Hungary (which had long been underway, but which was also helped along by the favourable Soviet attitude) implied e.g. an opening of the border to Austria in September 1989. Thus emerged an obvious escape route for dissatisfied East Germans wanting to emigrate to the FRG who were now able to do so via Hungary and Austria. The steady and increasing flow of migrants soon acquired the proportions of a surge exodus, above all of the productive age-groups. The consequences were grave both in material terms (an increasing shortage of labour) and for the GDR's international image, which was severely damaged by the televised reports of streams of refugees as well as of East German tourists seeking refuge in foreign embassies and consulates across Europe. The situation became obviously untenable[5].

The Fortieth Anniversary of the GDR in October 1989 thus became a rather absurd spectacle: celebrating the accomplishments of socialism at a juncture when it was obvious to everybody (including the invited foreign guests) that most people only remained in the GDR because forced to. The most prominent of these foreign guests, Soviet President Gorbachev used the occasion to signal to the world, as well as to the Honecker entourage in the SED, that he regarded reform as long overdue (thus 'pulling the rug away' from under the SED's feet). In his official speech, he said i.a.:

'History has its own laws, its own pace and rhythm, which is determined by the maturation of objective and subjective factors of development. To disregard this would mean creating new problems'[6].

On a less ceremonial occasion, he expressed the same in less veiled terms: 'Who is too late will be punished by life'[7].

The stream of refugees continued, in due course also causing economic and social problems in the West. The hands of the West Germans were, however, tied when dealing with these problems, since it was inconceivable to treat their Eastern compatriots as foreigners[8].

Some, i.a. in the SPD, tried to belittle the problem, such as Egon Bahr who was cited for the rather unfortunate, and blatantly false assessment that '99.5 percent of the people will stay in the GDR'. Only the prime minister of Saarland, the party's vice chairman and designated candidate for the post as chancellor, Oskar Lafontaine dared to propose controls on immigration to the SPD convention in December[9].

Meanwhile, demonstrations became the order of the day in the East, and their numbers swelled until a decision had to be made by the SED leadership—either resign, or crush by force what had by now assumed the proportions of a rebellion. It would go beyond the scope of the present volume to track in detail the subsequent chain of events, the cumulative effect of which was nothing less than a revolution[10].

First, Honecker was ousted at a Politbureau meeting, apparently after having failed to push through an order for suppression by force (and according to some accounts, after having received clear signs from Moscow that the Soviet forces, i.e. the GSFG, would not side with him, but perhaps even support the opposition). Honecker's successor became Egon Krenz, who sought to meet the opposition half-way, but obviously did 'too little too late'[11]. The borders to the West were opened, most symbolically by tearing down (parts of) the Berlin Wall on the night 8-9 November; civil rights were expanded, etc.

Without the artificial protection of the Wall, however, the economic problems of the GDR simply increased due to the inefficiency of the command economy in combination with the considerable 'magnetism' of the FRG. Whatever was economically viable (including skilled labour) was 'sucked out' of the economy, thus creating a situation which soon became obviously untenable. Unification hence soon became an inescapable necessity, i.e. the only way of preventing a total collapse of the GDR[12].

Not only was the economy revealed as inefficient. The belated *glasnost* also uncovered numerous other hitherto ignored problems. One of the most serious was the pollution of the environment which had assumed such proportions that it constituted acute health hazards, as did the nuclear power plants which were in a dreadful state. A number of ecological grass-roots movements appeared, some of which had formerly been administratively repressed by the authorities. Furthermore, the former pride of the SED regime, the health services, were now revealed as grossly inadequate, in certain instances almost entailing a violation of the human rights of the patients. As a result, citizens of the West simply had a longer life expectancy than their fellow country-men in the East[13].

The economic and social crises were compounded by an even graver political crisis, spurred in the first place by the obvious moral collapse of the SED. Reports of large-scale corruption swelled the by now uncensored newspapers, and still uncompromised SED members fled the party in a mass exodus. The new leadership under Krenz convened an extraordinary party convention, 8-9 and 15-16 December 1989, on which occasion a dissolution of the party was seriously contemplated.

It did not come to that, however, but a complete break with the past was attempted. The leadership was replaced almost entirely, and the party tried to provide itself with a new 'profile'. First of all, it changed its name, first to 'SED-PDS' (i.e. 'Socialist Unity Party-Party of Democratic Socialism'), and subsequently simply to 'PDS'. Secondly, it sought to make the break with the past apparent by replacing 'the old gang' almost entirely. An uncompromised figure with considerable public relations skills, Gregor Gysi, who had i.a. defended dissidents in court, was chosen as party leader. Other former local SED leaders and public officials (such as the mayor of Dresden, Berghofer) were co-opted into the party leadership. Although these personalities undoubtedly made an honest effort to turn the party around completely, they soon came to realise the futility thereof and by January 1990 had resigned from the party[14].

The post as prime minister was taken over by the (likewise uncompromised) Hans Modrow, who made a serious effort to rally the support of the opposition for rather fundamental reforms of the entire political system. The opposition was given a formal political role (almost comparable to that of 'Her Majesty's Opposition' in Britain) by being seated at the 'Round Table' and consulted by the SED government on all matters of importance. Furthermore, it was announced that free elections would be held in May 1990.

When even these measures turned out to be insufficient, the opposition seated at the 'Round Table' was invited to join the cabinet, an invitation they accepted. A result hereof was i.a. that the first East German (indeed, probably the first person in the entire Eastern bloc) ever to take NOD seriously, the mathematician Walter Romberg (cf. Chapter X above) was appointed Minister, representing the newly founded GDR-SPD. In addition to these measures, Modrow further announced the holding of parliamentary elections earlier than originally planned, i.e. on 18 March, 1990[15].

By now, time was running very short, indeed. Notwithstanding the abundance of West German plans for economic and political renovation of the GDR[16], it soon became apparent that there was no alternative to unification. Gradually, the public mood in the GDR became almost frantic, as all political groupings hurried to prepare for the election.

The former 'bloc parties' in the GDR sought to disengage themselves from their past as collaborators of the SED, as subsequent events showed, successfully. Most of the parties effectively became 'clones' of their sister parties in the FRG, which had all along maintained a modicum of relations with various parties in the GDR, albeit in different forms[17].

The CDU maintained relations with its East German 'sister party', in actual fact conceived of by the SED as a counterpart to the West German CDU. Likewise, the FDP had had close ties with the East German LDPD (*Liberaldemokratische Partei Deutschlands*). The SPD was in a different situation, due to its previous existence in the Soviet Occupation Zone, before this became the GDR. It had, however, effectively been 'swallowed' by the Communist Party after the war, thus becoming part of the 'Socialist Unity Party', SED. Thus deprived of any approximate counterpart, the SPD had maintained relations (albeit explicitly not friendly ones) with the SED. The SPD was thus forced to undo the involuntary forty-years-old merger, distance itself clearly from the SED, and constitute itself as an independent party. It was founded as such in October 1989, only to embark almost immediately on the first steps in an election campaign[18].

Other party groupings were formed by the popular movements that had brought the revolution to victory. Beyond the range of the democratic parties, finally, the political scene also witnessed the less pleasant spectacle of right-wing extremists of an almost neo-nazi persuasion: the 'skinheads' and the so-called *'faschos'*. Some of these went to extremes in terms of racism, particularly anti-semitism, and chauvinism, which were unanimously condemned by all the democratic parties[19].

Democracy was, however, too young in the GDR and rested on too fragile organisational foundations for it to escape domination by the strong, well-staffed and experienced political parties of the other Germany. Undoubtedly reflecting this influence, the results of the elections in March 1990 came as a surprise to most observers: an overwhelming victory for the CDU and its allies (the CSU and DA) with a total of 48 percent of the votes, whereas the SPD merely gained 22 percent. Surprisingly, the PDS got as many as 16 percent, whereas the popular movements (*Neues Forum* and others) received a mere three percent of the votes[20]. Since a two-thirds majority in parliament was, however, a precondition for passing the amendments to the constitution, which were required for the unification process, a coalition government had to be formed which included the SPD and the FDP. The SPD thus gained the important ministries of Foreign Affairs (Markus Meckel) and of Finance (Walter Romberg), until they were dismissed in August 1990[21].

By this time, however, it had become abundantly clear that the GDR was in an *interregnum* situation, because unification was the order of the day. Before proceeding with the political developments in the GDR, including the defence policies pursued by the shifting governments, a brief account of the unification process does, however, seem appropriate.

The Process of Unification

Soon after the dethronement of Honecker and his entourage, it became obvious that the 'German question' had forced its way on to the agenda, and that it would only be a matter of time before unification was accomplished. In the East, Prime Minister Hans Modrow took cautious step towards *rapprochement* with the West (along with a promise of more to come) in his speech to the *Volkskammer* (Parliament) on 17 November 1989 wherein he introduced the notion 'contractual community' (*Vertragsgemeinschaft*)[22].

In the West, Helmut Kohl gained the initiative with his *Ten Point Programme for Overcoming the Division of Germany and of Europe*, presented to the *Bundestag* on 28 November, 1989. The Federal Chancellor sought to strike a delicate balance between raising hopes for the Germans (whilst simultaneously perhaps slowing down, rather than accelerating, unification[23]), and allaying concerns abroad by explicitly embedding his proposed solution to the German question in a European framework. He even, probably intentionally, alluded to the Soviet 'common house' vision with his expression that 'we are now all called upon to shape a new architecture for the European House'.

In addition to immediate relief measures, the gist of the ten points was to pursue practical cooperation with the GDR in a number of fields, whilst making an expansion thereof conditional upon a decision in the GDR to embark on 'a fundamental and irreversible transformation of the political and economic system of the GDR'. As a slightly longer-term prospect, Kohl envisioned the contractual community, yet with the perspective of building 'confederative structures between the two states in Germany, the goal being to create a federation'.

Before concluding with a reminder that 'reunification, i.e. the complete re-attainment of the political unity of Germany remains the political goal of the Federal Government', the Chancellor made sure to embed this goal in an all-European framework with the expression that 'the future architecture of Germany must be enclosed in the future architecture of all of Europe'. As far as the practical implications thereof were concerned, Kohl pointed to an openness on the part of the EC towards the states of Central, East and Southern Europe, as well as to the CSCE process as 'the core of the all-European architecture'. He also emphasised that unification and the accompanying end to the bloc division in Europe presupposed 'far-reaching and relevant steps in disarmament and arms control'[24].

These ten points raised a number of concerns amongst the FRG's allies as well as traditional adversaries. I shall return to this external dimension of the unification process in due course. Suffice it at this stage to remind the reader that West German politicians were performing a demanding balancing act. On the one hand, they had to be seen as courageous and forward-looking by the public back home, i.e. by their electorate. On the other hand, they also had to appear cautious and 'sensible' to the international community, so as allay fears caused by the rapid unification process.

Not all West German politicians succeeded in this balancing act, but everybody tried, with two possible exceptions. First of all, the extreme right-wing party, the Republicans, led by former SS officer Schönhuber placed an increasing emphasis on nationalism. It demanded i.a. the 'recreation of Germany as a nation' and an 'internal rejuvenation of the German people', whilst making it unmistakably clear that the 'Germany' they had in mind would have the 1939 borders (i.e. including Austria), rather than 'merely' those of 1937[25].

Secondly, the left wing criticised what they regarded as a new wave of nationalism, and declared the nation-state to be obsolete. Paradoxically, this rejection of nationalism was also the ideological basis for those few who fought for the maintenance of two German states. The only ones to oppose unification *expressis verbis* were thus small groups of Greens along with members of the Communist Party, DKP. The latter was deeply compromised by the revelations about their collaborators in the East, the SED, as well as in dire straits because of a drying up of funds. Previously, these had flowed magnanimously, but they now ceased, leaving the party with no alternative to putting the majority of its former staff on the dole. That the DKP followed the example of their allies in the GDR and changed its name into 'PDS' hardly helped at all to remove the 'stigma' of complicity with the East German debacle. The opponents of unification were thus no serious political force in the FRG[26].

The SPD had at first welcomed Kohl's Ten Point Programme, and even claimed credit for being its true inventor[27]. Subsequently, however, at the urging of Oskar Lafontaine and Horst Ehmke, the SPD attached a number of conditions to its approval, i.a. a recognition of the German-Polish border, a decision by the *Bundestag* against nuclear modernisation, and immediate relief for Berlin[28]. Regardless of such reservations, unification was henceforth a subject to be taken seriously as a matter of day-to-day policy-making, even as far as the SPD was concerned. At its conference in Berlin in December 1989, the SPD hence adopted a platform on *The Germans in Europe*, wherein the point of departure was unreserved support for unification.

In December 1989, the heads of governments of the two German states, Helmut Kohl and Hans Modrow met in Dresden (GDR). In the joint statement issued after the talks, the idea of a 'contractual community' reappeared, signifying at the very least a common understanding that a quantum leap in the relations between the two states was required. Understandably, however, the GDR was not yet prepared to sign what may have been regarded (in retrospect, correctly) as its own death sentence, namely a commitment to actual unification, a position legitimised with references to the European considerations[29].

Nevertheless, under the influence of the continuing flow of refugees and the mounting economic problems, the GDR finally had to acquiesce to the inevitable, and by 1 February 1990, Hans Modrow presented his *Plan For a United Germany*. It had many reminiscences of the Ten Point Plan, which by that time was, however, regarded in the West as overtaken by events. Amongst the points of agreement were the commitment to, first, an economic, and monetary union, and secondly, a confederation. Gradually, he envisioned a transfer of sovereign rights to 'organs of power of the confederation or a German federation'. As a precondition for this development, however, Modrow mentioned military neutrality for both the GDR and the FRG[30].

Part of the background for this shift of attitude may also have been the agreement reached with Soviet President Gorbachev by both Modrow himself and his West German colleague, on the need for unification (cf. below). Henceforth, both sides were in agreement that unification was the order of the day, and that further discussions would thus merely be concerned with the pace and the modalities of this unification.

Increasingly, the Germans came to regard this as their exclusive prerogative, becoming more and more self-confident and self-assertive. Chancellor Kohl thus undoubtedly expressed the prevalent mood with his declaration in Paris on 17 January 1990 that 'nobody should seek to combine this development with conditions, which in the final analysis would amount to rendering the right of self-determination of the Germans void.'[31].

Political realities thus soon dictated that everybody with a claim to being taken seriously must commit himself to unification. The SPD undertook a rapid change of course. Formerly it had advocated the cautious strategy of 'change through *rapprochement*', implying i.a. a stabilisation of the GDR as an independent state, and envisaging a very protracted process of unification. Now the SPD had to shift its perspective entirely. Stabilisation of the other Germany seemed out of the question, and unification was obviously proceeding at a breath-taking pace:

Egon Bahr was a good example of this intellectual and political development. He had urged his fellow countrymen to 'see the historical opportunities in the division', and *expressis verbis* declared the German question to be 'open' no longer, at least for as long as NATO and the WTO were to exist. Indeed, he had even suggested what might have been tantamount to closing the question for good by signing two separate peace treaties with the two German states, a proposal which had aroused fierce criticism as not merely unwise, but unconstitutional[32]. Now Bahr, too, had to 'swim with the tide' of the unification process.

Amongst those in favour of unification, an intense debate raged as to both the pace and the terms. Events soon overtook Kohl's (in retrospect, cautious) November plan, and even Foreign Minster Genscher soon advised against any further use of the term 'contractual relationship', since it might be seen as cementing the two-state status[33].

In legal terms, two different modes of unification recommended themselves: either an accession of the GDR to the Federal Republic according to Article 23 in the FRG's constitution, which would require merely a re-creation of the five former constituent states (*Länder*) in the East; or the formal creation of a new state, encompassing the population and territory of the two German states, an eventuality provided for in the constitution's Article 146[34]. As it happened, the former option turned out to be the most convenient.

As a first step towards unity, as well as a much called-for attempt at salvaging the GDR's economy, Chancellor Kohl in February 1990 offered the establishment of a economic and monetary union. Whereas no direct conditions were attached to this offer, it was explicitly stated that 'a monetary union only makes sense if the GDR immediately initiates comprehensive reforms in the direction of a market economy'. No matter how uneasy the prospects might be for the East Germans, this constituted 'an offer they could not refuse', unless they were willing to face the prospects of total economic collapse of their country[35].

On the other hand, much also pointed towards immense economic problems ahead for the GDR as a consequence of the monetary union, whence the widespread criticism, above all from the West German left who expected it to benefit capital to the detriment of the workers, and who were sceptical about the prospects for modernisation of the East German economy[36].

At least parts of the SPD were equally critical, the main opponent amongst whom was Oskar Lafontaine, who refused to assume responsibility for an arrangement he expected to cause mass unemployment and social problems in the GDR. Lafontaine, Horst Ehmke and others thus for quite a while blocked the SPD's approval of the economic and monetary union. This opposition was all the more serious, first of all, because Lafontaine enjoyed considerable leverage within the party, thanks to his designation as SPD candidate for the chancellorship; and secondly, because the SPD, after the *Länder* elections in May 1990, occupied a majority of the seats in the Federal Council, thus possessing an actual power of veto. It took quite a lot of 'arm-twisting' to persuade Lafontaine to accept economic realities, thus leaving the road open for the introduction of the *Deutschmark* in the GDR by 1 July 1990 ('D-Day'). The law on the union (the *Staatsvertrag*) was passed by the Bundestag with only a few SPD members (i.a. Peter Glotz) voting against it[37].

Subsequently, the pace accelerated further, and soon everybody was counting on the first all-German parliamentary election before the end of 1990. The urgency was partly caused by the above factors, partly by a constitutional coincidence: *Bundestag* elections were due for December 1990, and there were no legal provisions whatsoever for a postponement, something the ruling Chancellor and his party were hardly eager for anyhow, hoping. on the contrary, to be able to benefit from the apparent CDU-CSU majority in the GDR. Finally, the urgency also stemmed from the danger that the GDR might 'short-circuit' the process in an unpredictable manner, say, if a motion for immediate accession to the FRG were to be tabled in the *Volkskammer*, a proposal which all parties would be very hesitant to (be seen to) oppose[38].

On 23 August 1990, the *Volkskammer* of the GDR decided to dissolve the GDR as an independent state by 3 October. Unification subsequently proceeded according to schedule. The unification treaty was signed on 31 August, and the 3 October went down into history as 'the day of German unification'. In a message to all governments around the world, Chancellor Kohl made the following solemn promises:

'Our country will with its regained unity serve the interests of peace in the world, and the unification of Europe. (...) Only peace will in the future emanate from German soil. We are fully aware that the inviolability of borders and the respect for territorial integrity and sovereignity of all states in Europe is a fundamental precondition for peace. Therefore we have confirmed the final character of the borders of the united Germany, herein included the border with the Republic of Poland'[39].

A precondition for this development was, however, that the occupying powers acceded hereto.

The External Dimension of Unification

Whereas unification has so far been described as an internal process (which it was, of course, to a large extent), it is impossible to understand the dynamics of unification without taking the external participants in the process into account. It was these foreign powers who, to a very large extent, determined the security policy and defence-related aspects of the various unification schemes, devised i.a. with a view to accommodating (or at least not alienating unnecessarily) these powers. In the following account I shall briefly survey the development of the attitudes of the most relevant external powers, referring the reader back to Chapter II for some of the background for the present and future attitudes.

As soon as Kohl presented his Ten Point Programme, the first expressions of concern were heard, from both Francois Mitterrand, Margaret Thatcher, James Baker, and Eduard Shevardnadze, who were unanimous in cautioning the Germans to be patient[40]. This initial unanimity notwithstanding, it was on all accounts the USSR which constituted the greatest obstacle to the unification process. I shall now briefly analyse the development of the attitudes of the main actors towards Germany.

THE USSR: Signs of a more positive and constructive Soviet attitude towards the Germans had long been visible. Indeed, during Kohl's official visit to Moscow in October 1988, relations had been cordial, and the Soviets had seemingly forgotten the Chancellor's unfortunate comparison of Gorbachev with Goebbels. Relations became even friendlier during Gorbachev's return visit to the FRG in June 1989, when he was practically feted by the West German public[41].

The Soviet Union began to 'hint' at German unity by late 1989, when the demise of the GDR had become obvious, and when calls for unification were beginning to make themselves heard. An opening was i.a. offered when Soviet Foreign Minister Shevardnadze in December 1989 declared that 'each German state retains its right of self-determination', albeit with the caveat that 'this right must only be exercised in the context of other standards and principles of international law'. He recalled the previous Soviet preference for 'a united democratic and demilitarised Germany', adding that 'this idea may now deserve more attention'[42].

It did, however, take until the beginning of 1990 before the USSR was prepared to give the final 'go-ahead' for German unification. This happened during East German Prime Minister Hans Modrow's visit to Moscow in January 1990, when President Gorbachev accepted that 'the unification of Germany has never been questioned in principle by anybody', whilst adding that the two Germanies, the four powers and the European process had to be coordinated[43].

The Soviet President went even further than this on the occasion of Chancellor Kohl's visit in February 1990. The communiqué of the meeting included what almost amounted to a Soviet 'blank check' for unification:

'Gorbachev stated, and the Chancellor agreed, that there were, for the time being, no differences of opinion between the USSR, the FRG and the GDR concerning the matter that the Germans should solve the problem of the unity of the German nation on their own, and themselves decide in which political form, at what time, at which pace, and on what conditions they would implement this unity'[44].

Now one particular question became the focus, namely the status of Germany in relation to the alliances. The Soviet position initially focused on the alleged unacceptability of a unified Germany's membership of NATO, whilst hinting at the possibility of dual membership, i.e. simultaneous membership of both NATO and the WTO. According to Foreign Minister Shevardnadze, this dual membership would 'bring us all closer to the establishment of European security structures. It would turn Germany into a testing-ground for constructive interaction of both blocs'. This vision was subsequently elaborated upon by Soviet academics, some of whom proposed, as a corollary of dual membership, the establishment of joint military formations consisting of troops from both WTO and NATO, under supranational command, to be stationed in Germany[45].

The ensuing debate did, however, largely disregard such more visionary notions, and concentrated on the Soviet demand for neutrality, in sharp contrast to the firm and unanimous refusal by the West to even contemplate this option. Gradually, the notion of neutrality did, however, become implanted in visions of 'all-European security structures' to such an extent that it came as no surprise when the USSR eventually dropped the demand for neutrality. What we were witnessing in the Spring of 1990 was thus probably a diplomatic bargaining process, in the course of which the Soviet Union chose to advance 'maximalist' proposals so as to have all the more to bargain with. The USSR continued to stick to their position until they finally 'folded' in mid-July 1990, not surprisingly, yet somewhat earlier than most had expected. What remained of the former positions was, however, first of all, a Soviet emphasis on preventing a simple expansion of NATO territory, and, secondly, the Soviet advocacy of 'all-European security structures'[46].

President Gorbachev used the highly symbolic occasion of the anniversary of the Soviet victory over Germany in the 'Great Patriotic War' to propose a peace treaty with Germany. Such a peace treaty would, however, presuppose that 'only peace must emanate from German soil', in its turn requiring the creation of all-European security structures, as well as an acceptance of the post-war borders.

This notion of 'security structures' was subsequently elaborated upon by the Foreign Minister, who mentioned as elements therein such arrangements as: regular summits and even more frequent meetings between foreign and defence ministers as well as Chiefs of Staff of NATO and WTO member states; joint NATO and WTO institutions and joint manoeuvres; and, finally, militarily-depleted zones intended to shield both sides against surprise attacks (i.e. a modified 'NOD regime'). This would presumably transform the present alliances from military blocs into primarily political organisations, as well as deprive them of their adversarial nature in favour of a more cooperative orientation[47].

Subsequent to the agreement on German unification that was accomplished in the 'Two-Plus-Four' negotiations (cf. below), the FRG and the Soviet Union signed what might almost seem tantamount to a new 'Rapallo Treaty', had it not been for the fact that it was not directed against any other states—the *Treaty of Good Neighbourly Relations, Partnership and Co-operation*. Besides a general commitment to cooperation in various fields, the treaty provided directions for the narrow security policy relations between the two states. The treaty was tantamount to a mutual non-aggression treaty, but its scope extended to all of Europe, since both states solemnly commited themselves to respect the territorial integrity of all European states. Furthermore, the treaty contained what might be called 'a NOD clause':

> 'The Federal Republic of Germany and the Union of Socialist Soviet Republics will work for a substantial reduction of armed forces and armaments through binding and effectively verifiable agreements, along with unilateral measures, with a view to creating a stable balance on a lower level, particularly in Europe, which will suffice for defence, but not for attack'[48].

POLAND was probably the country in Europe that was most concerned, but at the same time ambivalent, with regard to the prospects of German unification.

One of the most problematic ingredients in the debate on the 'German question' had always been the 'Polish question' beneath it, i.e. the fact that Poland's present borders had been established at Germany's 'expense', by moving them westwards, accompanied by a deluge of German refugees.

Behind this lay, however, a bloody history of German aggressions and atrocities against Poland, most recently in WWII.

Fortunately, most Germans were aware of their tremendous burden of collective guilt towards their Polish neighbours, and thus realised the urgent need for confidence-building *vis-à-vis* the Poles. This endeavour was not facilitated by the equivocation involved with Chancellor Kohl's aforementioned 'Ten Point Programme', which contained no reference to the German-Polish border. Furthermore, its author was most reluctant to add any such a reference, even when *expressis verbis* asked to do so. Rather, the routine reply became a reference back to various former treaties and agreements still in force, such as the German-Polish Treaty of 7 December 1970, in its turn including an almost (but not quite) clear acknowledgement of the Oder-Neisse border, the continued validity of which had last been confirmed in the joint statement issued by Kohl and Tadeusz Mazowiecki on 14 November 1989[49].

Whereas the CDU might thus no longer question the Oder-Neisse frontier, the party did, on the other hand, seem to find it extremely difficult to say so *expressis verbis*, thus consistently sending rather unfortunate diplomatic signals.

From these concerns about the Oder-Neisse sprang also a terminological dispute, which may, seen from the outside, have a somewhat 'scholastic' appearance, but which had serious implications for those concerned: was German unity a matter of unification or of *re*unification? Whereas the first term seemed to imply nothing more than a 'merger' of the two existing German states, the second was much more ambiguous and open-ended, whence e.g. East German premier Hans Modrow's blunt 'no reunification'[50].

Diplomacy did not fare much better, when the Chancellor during his visit to Poland in 1989 made the somewhat less than fortunate statements that 'Germans and Poles (...) have mutually inflicted deep wounds on each other, especially in recent times', wherein the term 'mutually' might all too easily be taken as an insult. Kohl's subsequent linkage of the matter of borders with the questions of minority rights for Germans in Poland, as well as with reparations, assuaged concerns neither in Poland nor abroad.

The first condition was unfortunate, because it could be seen as implying Polish ill-treatment of ethnic Germans, by coincidence the same charge Hitler had used as part of his excuse for attacking Poland in 1939. The second seemed absurd, because Poland had explicitly renounced its claims to reparations as early as 1953. The clumsy Federal Chancellor struck no luckier chord in his speech in Paris, 17 January 1990, wherein he sought to allay Polish fears only through recalling the ill fate of the German *Heimatvertriebenen*, for which the Poles could not reasonably be blamed[51].

Polish Prime Minister Tadeuz Mazowiecki i.a. expressed the Polish worries in a speech before the *Sejm*, 18 January 1989, wherein he declared that 'to commence the process in the course of which the German people regains its political unity is only possible when both German states respect, and do not question, the present borders with their neighbours', explicitly adding that this was not merely a principled matter of national self-determination, but concerned the neighbours of the German state as well[52]. Eventually, Poland did, however, decide to settle for an official interpretation of the equivocations as a commitment to the existing borders [53].

Poland was far from isolated in these respects, but received support from all over Europe, i.a. from its traditional ally, France. French Foreign Minister Roland Dumas thus made his country's position abundantly clear with the statement: 'The final, i.e. untouchable, character of the Western border of Poland must be acknowledged without reservations'[54].

What the Poles wanted from the Germans was, however, not entirely clear. On the one hand, they seemed to prefer a Germany 'tied down' by its NATO membership to a neutral Germany which might be more volatile and unpredictable. On the other hand, they seemed eager to preserve a modicum of alliance with the USSR, i.a. as a counter-weight to Germany, whence their need for not alienating the Soviets by opposing them too openly. However, Poland did not want to alienate Germany either, i.a. because of their need for some financial assistance (or, as a minimum, good economic relations). Poland thus had a challenging balancing act to perform, and generally sought to accomplish this by transcending the German question and embedding it in an all-European framework, which would, hopefully, be able to satisfy both sides.

When the Polish Foreign Minister, Krzystof Skubiszewski, visited NATO, 21 March 1990, he therefore stressed the 'necessity of building a new security system in Europe', whilst specifying that 'NATO and the American military presence in Europe have a stabilising effect'. Even more at odds with official Soviet positions, he declared that 'Germany should not be neutral: it must therefore belong to an alliance'. Furthermore, he expressed sympathy with the 'Genscher Plan', which would allay Polish concerns by not allowing NATO armed forces to advance beyond the current line of separation between the two Germanies[55].

When addressing the WEU Assembly the following day, Skubiszewski elaborated on the latter notion by advancing the idea of substituting mixed (e.g. Polish-German, Czech-German or Franco-German) brigades for the Soviet troops presently stationed on the territory of the GDR. Furthermore, whilst not ruling out the stationing of purely German units in the GDR either, he specified that these would have to be entirely without offensive capabilities (i.e. be structured according to NOD principles)[56].

With regard to the need for counter-balancing the united Germany, whilst embedding it in larger cooperative frameworks, there have, furthermore, been some Polish thoughts on establishing a confederation of Poland, Czechoslovakia and Hungary, which should be associated with the EC, as well as a member of the Council of Europe. The Poles have thus been particularly eager to pursue the pan-European path in a 'Europe of the regions' form[57].

The Polish desire for grand pan-European schemes combined with an emphasis on *Mitteleuropa* regionalism seems to be matched by the newly democratised Czechoslovakia, likewise a country with historically somewhat mixed experiences with Germany. The President of Czechoslovakia, Václav Havel, has therefore been a staunch supporter of regionalism as a way of safely embedding German unification in a larger framework, as well as of facilitating his country's reintegration with Europe as a whole[58].

The attitude of the Western powers has been somewhat ambivalent. On the one hand, they were, in principle, committed to the general notion of national self-determination, as well as, more specifically to their West German ally's demands for a unification of Germany. On the other hand, they were concerned about the implications for *détente* and stability in Europe, as well as, perhaps, for the growing power of the future united Germany.

FRANCE: For the reasons mentioned in Chapter II above, the French attitude towards Germany, and *a fortiori* towards German unity, has been almost as ambivalent as the Polish one. President Francois Mitterrand expressed this ambivalence at the press conference during his official visit to the GDR (22 December 1989), on which occasion he said:

'I have by no means the intention of dictating to Germany what its future status should be. (...) But as soon as it concerns the status of Europe, then it is our business, and we must take care that no disparity arises, which could eventually lead to a re-creation of the Europe of the wars.'[59]

The French may, in the final analysis, only have regarded unification as desirable for as long as it was deemed impossible. Once unification did prove to be possible, however, France could not go back on its word and openly oppose it. Furthermore, according to recent opinion polls, as much as sixty percent of the general French public did support unification, whereas the *classe politique* tended to remain somewhat sceptical. The main interest of the latter may have been to slow down the process of unification, i.a. until the EC had passed the various 'hurdles' on its way towards '1992'[60].

The French government may have felt they scored a major success when they joined the (now united) Germany in a ('French style') major initiative, according to which the WEU and the EC were to 'establish a clear organic relationship', subsequent to the latter's transformation into a genuine political union. Whether anything would come out of this grandiose scheme remained to be seen by the time these lines were written, but considerable scepticism did appear warranted in the light of the fate of similar schemes in the past[61].

The American and British publics, likewise, tended to support unification, although the British press tended to be somewhat concerned[62].

THE USA: The American administration may have been somewhat worried about the prospects of a Soviet-German *rapprochement*, whence an eagerness to prevent a 'new Rapallo'. The equivocation stemming from this eagerness became apparent in President Bush's address to the NATO Summit in December 1989, in which he stated four basic principles pertaining to Germany:

1. Self-determination.
2. Continued commitment towards NATO and the EC.
3. A peaceful and gradual process.
4. Support for the Helsinki principles.

That points 1 and 2 might be incompatible (if, say, the Germans were to opt for neutrality) was, however, hardly noticed[63].

The FRG and the USA maintained continuous consultation through the entire process of unification, i.a. because the last thing the West Germans wanted was to alienate the USA. An agreement seems to have been reached during the visit of Kohl and Genscher to the USA in February 1990. Even though their host, President Bush, declared that 'we believe a unified Germany should remain a full member of the North Atlantic organisation, including its participation in the military structure', he did not rule out the possibility that, after unification, the territory of the former GDR might receive a 'special military status', in respect for the security interests of the USSR[64]. The support of the US President for at least the rough contours of the 'Genscher Plan' had thus been enlisted.

NATO: Just as (some variety of) the 'Genscher Plan' was thus endorsed by President Bush and Secretary of State James Baker, NATO also gave its approval at its February meeting in Ottawa[65].

Furthermore, the Genscher Plan also enjoyed the support of its author's former rival in Bonn, Secretary General Manfred Wörner, now speaking *ex cathedra* on behalf of NATO, rather than as a CDU politician. He explicitly mentioned the possibility of a 'special military status' for the GDR within NATO, as well as the option of not including the GDR in the military integration of NATO at all. Whilst calling for full membership of the united Germany in the Atlantic Alliance, including a maintenance of NATO's integrated military structure on the territory of the FRG, Wörner explicitly promised military self-restraint on the part of NATO, in the sense of refraining from the stationing of troops beyond West German territory. When regular consultations on German unification were started on the Alliance level, the Secretary General, furthermore, stressed that the allies were unanimous about Germany's full membership in the Alliance, but that, on the other hand, NATO had no intention of upsetting the balance in Europe to the detriment of the USSR[66].

Some concrete thoughts may also have been given by parts of the NATO apparatus to the modalities of such a grand compromise, i.e. on how to remove the impression of increasing NATO's offensive potential *vis-à-vis* the Soviet Union. In this connection, Staff officer at the AFCENT NATO Headquarters, Colonel David Miller put forward some interesting ideas on a division of labour as a contribution to non-offensiveness (albeit not in so many words):

'NATO is under firm democratic, political control, making it impossible for one state to attain a position of absolute power. That being so, it is to the Soviet Union's advantage for Germany to be a NATO member, where restraints (should they prove necessary) can be exercised by its allies within the structure of the alliance. Two further safeguards are possible within such an alliance. One is to designate national specialisations such that no nation has an independent offensive capability but can only form a balanced force in combination with other nations. This might, for example, lead to different nations providing particular types of equipment, undertaking particular roles, or operating in specific geographical areas. Another approach is to create multinational formations, made up of national units commanded by a multinational headquarters (horizontal integration) or by forming multinational units (vertical integration). By forming a number of such multinational formations, integrated horizontally, or preferably vertically, the power of any one nation is limited yet further'[67].

These were, however, unofficial viewpoints, whereas NATO as such remained unwilling to reconsider its strategy until the July summit of 1990, notwithstanding the fact that, according to SACEUR, John Galvin, the traditional NATO scenario of a Soviet surprise attack through the so-called 'Fulda Gap' in southern West Germany had been made redundant by the imminent unification of Germany[68]. At the aforementioned July summit, however, NATO did acknowledge the need for a reappraisal of strategy, including a shift towards a 'no-early-first-use' policy for nuclear weapons.

What the concrete findings of this reappraisal may, in due course, turn out to be was impossible to predict by the time these lines were written. Furthermore, history testifies to the extreme difficulty in finding a new compromise formula to replace the present flexible response-cum-forward defence, due to the divergent national interests involved. An educated guess might be that the Alliance will, in due course, settle for yet another way of 'papering over' its internal disagreements, perhaps in the form of a less offensive-capable posture, relying more on mobilisation, and with a lesser emphasis on nuclear escalation, yet without any radical breaks with the past.

THE WEU: The West European Union has for historical reasons been vested with a special responsibilty for Germany, since it was through this organisation that Germany entered NATO in 1955, and only on certain preconditions which were left to the WEU to monitor. The WEU therefore had to form an opinion on German unification.

Judging on the basis of statements by the WEU Secretary General, Willem van Eekelen, the organisation seems to have been pursuing the same logic as the aforementioned Col. Miller. Mr. Eekelen e.g. lent his support to the notion of establishing multinational European forces as the appropriate military corollary of German unification, on the assumption that such multinational forces would be more acceptable to Moscow than the stationing of national forces on the territory of the former GDR. In order not to discriminate against, i.e. 'singularise', Germany, however, similar force contingents would also have to be accepted by other countries, above all France and the Benelux countries[69].

THE EC: The European Community has also had a certain say on the matter of German unification, above all because of the need for (the former) East Germany to join. The EC President, Jacques Delors, did, fortunately, at an early stage make clear that the GDR would be acceptable to the EC. This forthcoming attitude may have been motivated by a fear that 'the FRG, inspired by the prospects of reunification and by the role it might come to play in some kind of large Central Europe, might lose its interest in the Community'. As a result of the replacement of the previous informal and indirect membership of the GDR in the EC with a formal membership, the need had, furthermore, to be acknowledged for the EC to engage in some form of *Ostpolitik*[70].

The contours of a 'grand settlement' were thus visible with the acceptance of all involved states and international organisations of German unification, as well as with a rough agreement on the approximate modalities thereof. There remained, however, the matter of 'detail', including the legal procedures for unification.

TWO PLUS FOUR: Agreement on the 'Two-Plus-Four' format for negotiations was reached during informal talks on the fringes of the Ottawa meeting on 'Open Skies'. Partly by virtue of its historical foundations, this format proved appropriate for handling an issue of such complexity, and involving so many nations and transnational organisations, as German unification. The four occupying states (the USA, the UK, France and the USSR) thus enjoyed a formal veto, but the two German states had the initiative, as symbolised by placing the 'two' before the 'four'[71].

A timetable for the talks was agreed upon at the first meeting (5 May 1990): in the first stage (June), the politico-military matters were to be discussed, whereas the second stage (July) should deal with the issue of frontiers, with the participation of the Polish foreign minister. Subsequently, ministers were to meet in Moscow with a view to, hopefully, sealing the agreement, so that it could be ready for the CSCE summit in the autumn of 1990.

The foreign ministers of all six states agreed on the need for linking the process intimately to the all-European one. Furthermore, a certain *rapprochement* occurred with regard to timing, when the Polish participant accepted that a German-Polish border agreement would be signed subsequent to formal unification, rather than (such as previously insisted upon) as a precondition thereof. The said agreement was eventually signed on 14 November 1990, wherein Germany and Poland solemnly declared that 'the border between them is inviolable now and in the future'[72].

Chancellor Kohl did, however, responded negatively to the Soviet proposal, made during the first round of talks, to separate the issues of unification and the future military and security policy status of Germany. This would presumably infringe the sovereignty of Germany, according to Kohl, who insisted on settling the two matters in parallel, and eventually prevailed[73].

During the meeting of the 'two plus four' in mid-July 1990, agreement was finally reached on the permissibility of all-German NATO membership, as well as on the termination of the rights of the four powers in Germany by the end of 1990, a concession that was apparently 'bought' i.a. with a West German obligation to settle the border issue with Poland in a binding way[74].

The final agreement was signed on 12 September, 1990, stipulating i.a. the following:

1. The Oder-Neisse border was made final and inalterable, and Germany renounced, once and for all, all outstanding territorial claims (§1.1).

2. Germany reiterated its commitment to abstain from anything that might jeopardize peace, and particularly the preparation of aggressive war (§2).

3. Germany renounced its right to produce or dispose of ABC weapons (§3.1).

4. The armed forces of the united Germany would not exceed 370,000 troops, to be formalised in the CFE treaty, the signing of which was planned for 19 November 1990, immediately before the CSCE summit in Paris (§3.2).

5. The Soviet forces in the former GDR were to be withdrawn by 1994, and the FRG should resume all responsibilities for their upkeep from the former GDR. For as long as the Soviet forces were to remain in Germany, the other three former occupying powers would maintain a contingent of forces in Berlin (§4.1, §5.2).

6. Until 1994, neither such German forces as were integrated in NATO structures of command, nor other NATO forces would be stationed in the former GDR (§5.1).

7. After 1994, Germany would be free to station NATO-integrated German forces in the former GDR, yet without nuclear weapons or means of delivery. Allied forces would, however remain prohibited (§5.3)[75].

In connection with the signature of the CFE Treaty, the Federal

Government solemnly confirmed its commitment to the 370,000 troop limitation, to commence upon the entry into force of the CFE agreement[76].

This final settlement probably constituted one of the most important decisions in the entire post-war era. It reflected the end to the Cold War and the emergence of a much more constructive and cooperative relationship between the major powers in Europe. Furthermore, the agreement pointed towards the future, in the first instance towards the CSCE summit in November to which I shall return in the concluding chapter.

All the above international interests in the German question *eo ipso* constituted strings on which the FRG could play, and the fact that they were both partly coinciding and partly incompatible allowed the FRG to, at least up to a point, play one against the other.

This seemed to be precisely what the FRG sought to do at the EC summit meeting in Dublin, on which occasion it attempted to enlist the EC in an elaborate 'linkage' scheme. According to this scheme, the EC should promise economic assistance to the Soviet reform process (in support of Gorbachev and *perestroika*), but only do so on condition that the USSR dropped its objections to the NATO membership of the united Germany. On this occasion, however, Germany's allies refused to go along, and made the promised assistance conditional only upon economic reforms in the Soviet Union. Subsequently, however, the FRG has taken the lead in providing financial and other support for its former arch enemy, the Soviet Union, i.a. in the form of immediate relief for the Soviet population with whom the average German citizen felt a deep sympathy, even if they did not wish to receive a mass immigration[77].

Security Policy in a New Light

The security policy debate in both Germanies during 1989-1990 was different from what it had been, first of all, by being very intense. Secondly, it covered a much wider range of issues than previously, for the obvious reason that things had to change radically, in whatever direction, and that previous 'taboos' were therefore lifted. Thirdly, its complexity increased, due to the delicate balancing act described above, the necessity of which was understood by most political groupings in the FRG. I shall commence the account of this debate with the government parties, followed by the SPD.

THE FDP: What united the government parties was not least their unanimous rejection of the neutralist option. As far as the FRG was concerned, this attitude was motivated by the fear that 'a neutralisation of Germany would lead to the Germans breaking loose from the European context' and thus 'create undesirable insecurity and volatility in Central Europe'.[78]

What did, however, set the FDP apart from its coalition partners was its greater willingness to meet Soviet concerns, whence the 'Genscher Plan', envisioning a 'special status' for the territory of the GDR. According to same logic, numerical reductions of the forces about to 'change sides' might presumably mollify Soviet objections to a unified Germany remaining in NATO. The Foreign Ministry staff hence developed proposals for scaling down the all-German forces to a level below what had hitherto been envisioned for the *Bundeswehr* alone, according to Genscher not much more than 300,000 troops. Furthermore, along the former demarcation line only German units were to be deployed, whereas allied forces should be withdrawn 'as far as possible' to the West. Finally, it was envisaged that the two German states should make a solemn joint declaration confirming their renunciation of the production and possession of atomic, chemical and biological weapons[79].

Such conceptions obviously also required NATO to change its strategy somewhat, part of which had, however, already been rendered obsolete, according to Genscher. Hinting at the (by then not yet shelved) plans for short-range nuclear weapon modernisation, he asked: 'Does one really want to acquire new nuclear rockets which can just reach the Poland of Lech Walesa and of democratic development, or the Hungary of humanity and democratisation?'[80]. As an appropriate medium for this transformation, Genscher pointed towards the Vienna CFE negotiations, whilst stressing the need of beginning to prepare for the subsequent 'CFE-II' negotiations, which should include the stationing of foreign troops, nuclear artillery and short-range nuclear weapons.

Whereas Genscher and his party viewed the alliances as useful for the transition period, as a longer-term perspective the FDP envisioned their restructuring and eventual replacement with a collective security system. The central catch-phrase became one borrowed from NOD and Common Security literature, namely 'cooperative security structures'. The West in general, and the FRG in particular, should declare their preparedness to collaborate in creating such structures, above all because 'we want to convince the Soviet Union that the united Germany constitutes a contribution to European stability, and thus also an advantage for the Soviet Union'[81].

One element in this process would be 'transforming the Alliance from the previously antagonistic military one to a security-promoting political one' based on the principles of 'security not against, but with each other', i.e. what Genscher called 'cooperative stability'.[82]

Through pursuing this logic, the FDP also found a new rationale for its longstanding advocacy of European federalism as the most suitable framework for accomplishing what everybody acknowledged as imperative, namely embedding German unification in a broader context. What the FDP had in mind was a grand European federation that would include, amongst other states, a federation of all Germans[83].

THE CDU-CSU were in principle in agreement with their coalition partner on the need for a European framework for unification. Even prior to launching his confederation scheme, Chancellor Kohl thus made sure to combine his calls for national self-determination with calls for a 'European Peace Order', 'shaped by the peoples of Europe in free self-determination' (November 1989). Once the process was underway (December), he even sought to please the Soviet Union by alluding to their vision of the 'Common European House', by stressing that 'the German House, our common house, must be built under a European roof', an image he stuck to when expressing his gratitude towards the USSR for their acceptance of unification. On this occasion, the chancellor solemnly declared that 'the unification of Germany must be embedded in the all-European architecture'[84].

Neither such solemn declarations nor terminological pleasantries, however, sufficed to solve the problem that the Soviets were less than comfortable with seeing a former high-priority ally simply shifting sides. The Soviet concerns in this respect were hardly allayed by declarations by West German Defence Minister Stoltenberg (16 February) to the effect that the entire united Germany had to become NATO territory. Even Stoltenberg did, however, take Soviet security concerns into some account by envisaging no forward deployment of regular NATO troops on to the territory of the GDR, but merely German troops falling outside the integrated NATO command, i.e. the Territorial Army. The number and configuration of these troops was, furthermore, to be determined under the auspices of the CFE. Stoltenberg's proposal was, however, publicly rejected by his colleague in the Foreign Ministry, on the grounds that it would, in the final analysis, indirectly displace NATO's border to the Polish border[85].

In addition to officially declaring (15 February 1990) that 'no units or facilities of the Western alliance will be re-located forward into the present territory of the GDR', Kohl proclaimed himself prepared for additional confidence-building measures. He i.a. declared it to be his firm intention to maintain the self-imposed abstention from the acquisition of ABC weapons, to adhere to the NPT (Non-Proliferation Treaty), as well as to allow all sorts of on-site inspections with a view to monitoring these matters[86].

With the same goal of allaying eastern (this time above all Polish) fears, the *Bundestag* (including the CDU-CSU) in the beginning of March decided to propose to the Parliament soon to be elected in the GDR a solution, according to which both parliaments were to solemnly declare their intention not to raise the border issue in the future, to be followed, subsequent to unification, by the all-German government's signing a formal agreement to that effect with the Polish government[87].

Furthermore, Kohl expressed understanding of the need for intermediary solutions, i.a. with regard to the Soviet presence in the GDR. During his visit to the USA in February 1990, Kohl e.g. promised that half the 380,000 Soviet troops stationed in the GDR might be allowed to stay in the country until further negotiations had determined their future. However, he also declared that a unified Germany 'could not belong to two different security systems', thus seemingly revealing the former as a very temporary expedient, indeed[88].

Be that as it may, some of Kohl's fellow partisans did in fact accept this notion of a continued Soviet presence in the GDR, i.a. with a view to not letting it block the road towards a speedy unification. CDU Prime Minister Lothar Späth e.g. declared himself prepared to accept a Soviet presence in the GDR for a certain time, and to let the Federal Republic take over the financial responsibilities for their upkeep (around 3.5 billion DMs)[89].

Some thought has subsequently been given to the matter of Soviet withdrawal, which according to the Two-Plus-Four agreement is to be completed by 1994. The actual implementation thereof is, however, bound to be quite demanding, i.a. because to bring back 375,000 Soviet troops along with their weaponry will require a total of 70,000 railway waggons, to which should be added a further 50,000 waggons for the transportation of the families, furniture, etc. of the Soviet officers stationed in the GDR. Finally, the munition of the GSFG has been assessed to weigh somewhere between three and four million tonnes, the transportation of which would also be a demanding logistical task, if only because of the required security precautions[90].

Whereas all of the above could be seen as diplomatic manoeuvering with a view to allaying fears in the East, the West German government also had some confidence-building to do vis-à-vis the West, i.a. so as not to be seen as being too preoccupied with the German question, at the expense of the European integrative process. The day after the elections in the GDR, Kohl thus mentioned that 'we want to build a united Germany with Europe and in Europe, and not against Europe', to which he added (in a speech to the CSCE follow-up conference on economic cooperation, 18 March, 1990) that 'nowhere are the hopes for a peaceful Europe stronger than in Germany'[91].

To satisfy the demands of friends as well as (former) foes, however, was far from an easy matter, i.e. because of the different velocities and the resultant difficulties with synchronisation, as explained by Federal President Richard von Weizsäcker (13 December 1989):

'We have, if I may say so, three different velocities: there is a German dynamic, then there is a dynamic in Europe. How can cooperation be established here, economically, scientifically, culturally? And, thirdly and finally, how will the two pacts, the two alliance systems, provide for an umbrella of security, that we continue to need, and underneath which we can pursue the dynamics with regard to Europe and Germany in a peaceful manner. It is important that these three velocities remain within reach of each other'[92].

On the unofficial level could be seen a more principled dispute between the three competing groupings within the CDU-CSU, which might be called the 'Atlanticists', the 'Europeans' and the 'Nationalists', respectively. One of the questions at issue was whether to commence reconsidering NATO strategy in the light of unification, thus running the risk of being perceived as disloyal; or whether to risk unification for the sake of remaining an unswervingly loyal NATO partner[93].

An example of the Atlanticist group might be Minister of Defence, Gerhard Stoltenberg, who during his visit to Washington in the beginning of May warned against the 'strategic misunderstanding' that NATO might be rendered obsolete by the disintegration of the Warsaw Pact, and who argued against a total withdrawal of American forces, as well as against making Europe nuclear-free. To the Europeanist grouping belonged i.a. the security policy expert Karl Lamers, who proposed the near replacement of NATO by a genuine European Defence Union[94].

The nationalist grouping was i.a. represented by Former Defence Minister Rupert Scholz who went so far as to explicitly advocate a 'review' of the forward defence conception. Whereas this notion, as well as his advocacy of an abolition of short-range and battlefield nuclear weapons, nearly made him an SPD fellow-traveller, Scholz remained at odds with the SPD with regard to the appropriate replacement for forward defence. Far from envisaging any form of in-depth and non-offensive defence, he urged NATO to shift to a strategy of 'mobile defence', that might well entail offensive capabilities. Moreover, to refrain from stationing NATO forces in the present GDR could, according to Scholz, only be a temporary solution, since 'a reunited Germany with two different, or even opposing, security zones is inconceivable'. As a temporary expedient, he proposed to merge the East German NVA with the West German Territorial Army[95].

Its previous criticism notwithstanding, the CDU in the course of its principled deliberations, *mirabile dictu* came close to an advocacy of NOD, as might emerge from the following expressions by the leader of the CDU parliamentary caucus, Alfred Dregger:

'We Germans are in any case prepared to make military concessions to our eastern neighbours and the Soviet Union, as far as possible. (. . .) What will be of importance in the years to come, not only in a security policy sense, is disarmament to a minimum of conventional and nuclear weapons, as well as a transformation of the structures of armaments, implying a strengthening of the defender and a weakening of the potential aggressor, depriving either side of any invasionary potential *vis-à-vis* the respective other side.'[96].

Dregger, furthermore, proposed a replacement of forward defence with an alternative defence posture, to be embedded in a structure of 'mutual defensive sufficiency' with some reminiscences of the various disengagement proposals recorded in Chapter IV. The forward area (i.e. the territory of the previous GDR) was to be defended by 'territorial forces, not under NATO command, whereas allied forces were to be organised in multinational mobile formations, stationed in the rear 'not merely on German territory'[97].

The General Secretary of the CDU, Volker Rühe, likewise, advocated a reassessment (indeed, a 'rapid replacement') of NATO's concept of forward defence, based on the conviction that the present posture could not possibly be maintained in what would soon become the midst of Germany. Furthermore, because it would be imperative to allow the USSR to withdraw its troops from its western *glacis* without thereby exposing itself, the West ought to be forthcoming, i.a. by acknowledging that NATO no longer felt a need for any successor to Lance[98].

Both the government parties were thus quite forthcoming towards Soviet interests, and might almost be seen as taking over the SPD's policies, including the advocacy of NOD, in their attempts to allay Soviet concerns.

THE SPD was somewhat in disarray as a result of the impending collapse of the GDR, because they had consistently cautioned against hoping for speedy unification and had sought to stabilise (or at least not to destabilise) the GDR, i.e. they had been engaged in what was now believed to have been all along a futile endeavour. Furthermore, the SPD had been in a direct *tête-à-tête* with some of the leaders of the SED who had by now been unmasked as incompetent and corrupt. The SPD nevertheless made an effort to attain both 'the moral high ground' and the political initiative, also with a view to the parliamentary elections by the end of 1990.

At its conference in Berlin in December 1989, the SPD adopted a party platform on *The Germans in Europe*, wherein it sought to combine its awareness of the NOD ideas with its new (or rejuvenated) quest for German unification. As a preliminary, the party declared that 'we can now begin to realise what for a long time appeared as a utopia: to complete the unity and freedom of Germany'. It did, however, make sure to emphasise that 'the unification of Europe and the uniting of the Germans are closely inter-related. One cannot be obtained at the expense of the other'. Furthermore, it strongly condemned 'whoever speaks about the restoration of the *Reich* within the borders of 1937' and demanded 'an unconditional acknowledgement of the Polish western border'.

Furthermore, the SPD urged both German states to take initiatives to accelerate disarmament, for which purpose it recommended a follow-up to the CFE negotiations 'with the goal of structural incapability to attack' (i.e. NOD). Immediately after the first CFE agreement, new negotiations were to commence 'with a view to attaining a reduction of armed forces by at least fifty percent and an adequately verifiable incapability to attack'. The party, furthermore, envisioned a withdrawal of all nuclear weapons from German territory, attaching a particular urgency to the removal of short-range and battlefield weapons.

With regard to the more distant future, the SPD envisioned that 'the existing alliances could then be replaced by an all-European security system. Our goal is to replace the military alliances with a European peace order'.

In the subsequent security policy debate within the SPD, the views of one particular politician were of special importance, namely those of the Prime Minister of Saarland, Vice Chairman of the party, Oskar Lafontaine. His appointment in the Spring of 1990 as the SPD's candidate for chancellorship for the upcoming elections gave him a very central position in the party, with considerable leverage, since the last thing the SPD would want was to change 'front figure' in the midst of an election campaign.

Lafontaine sought to exploit this leverage (e.g. by means of threats of resignation) to force the SPD to turn down the economic and monetary union with the GDR, as described above. Eventually, he did, however, bend to the party's arm-twisting, perhaps having then succeeded in what he actually wanted, namely refusing to take responsibility for the problems caused by the arrangement, without having to later face, as Chancellor, the problems ensuing from not having it. Furthermore, he seemed certain of becoming leader of the united SPD, once the merger with the GDR-SPD had been accomplished.

According to opinion polls and popularity indexes, Lafontaine was tremendously popular, both within the party and beyond, and his popularity did not exactly suffer either when he became the victim of a clumsy assassination attempt in the first days of May 1990[99].

Lafontaine was aware that the SPD apparently had some explaining to do so as to prevent misunderstandings. First of all, whereas the previous SPD approach of 'change through *rapprochement*' was outdated (something nobody would question any longer), it had previously been the only appropriate approach, because 'the key which will open the gates to freedom in Eastern Europe is kept in Moscow'[100].

Furthermore, the SPD might appear compromised by having taken Marxism-Leninism (in the particular SED variety) far too seriously, i.a. by pursuing the ideological dialogue with the SED, in the course of which the two parties had uncovered quite a lot of 'common ground'. The last thing the SPD wanted in the present situation was, however, to be seen as merely being a more benign species of the same genus as Honecker and entourage (the impression which the CDU sought to convey, i.a. during the election campaign in the GDR). According to Lafontaine, however the controversial 1987 document on '*The Struggle of Ideologies*' had been 'nothing less than a further step intended to promote the free societal dialogue in the GDR on the basis of the CSCE principles on human rights'. He even claimed that 'the oppositional groupings could henceforth take this paper as their point of departure'[101].

Personally, Lafontaine might also have felt that he had some explaining to do. He had previously (i.a. with his book *Afraid of One's Friends*, cf.

above, Chapter VII) appeared to come very close, indeed, to a genuinely neutralist position. By 1989-90, however, he made an effort to remove this impression, i.a. by coming out explicitly against neutrality for the new Germany. According to him, neutrality might mean that Germany would be positioned as a kind of *cordon sanitaire* between NATO and the Warsaw Pact. However, 'the loss of the functions of NATO and the Warsaw Pact should not lead to a return to the security structures of the 19th century,' as he told the Socialist group in the European Parliament. Rather, the need was for pursuing the integration path, even to the point of transcending the East-West division, with the longer-term perspective of a future European security system encompassing the Soviet Union and continuing cooperation with America and Canada. He even envisaged East European countries joining NATO, and would not even rule out an audacious application from Gorbachev for Warsaw Pact membership in NATO[102].

On other occasions, however, Lafontaine appeared to be arguing against NATO membership for the united Germany. As his preferred alternative, he advocated a European Defence Community, i.e. a collective security system, encompassing all European states, and collaborating with the USA, Canada and the USSR. By March 1990 (in an address to the French Socialist Party), he came out, once again, aginst German neutrality, whilst at the same time ruling out any stationing of NATO troops on territory formerly belonging to the Warsaw Pact. As an alternative, he pronounced himself in favour of 'the United States of Europe', in the context of which he even envisioned a Polish-German brigade modelled on the Franco-German brigade (as envisioned by Polish Foreign Minister Skubiszewski)[103].

He sought to distance himself from the government parties by an emphasis on the inviolability of borders. He emphatically stressed that 'for us Social Democrats, Germany will be complete when the Federal Republic and the GDR are united'[104].

One of the SPD's leaders to come out most unequivocally against Germany's remaining in NATO (as presently configured) was the Chairman of the 'Working Group on Disarmament and Arms Control' in the SPD's parliamentary caucus, Hermann Scheer. In collaboration with Heidemarie Wieczorek-Zeul (member of the Presidium) he in March 1990 issued a memorandum on *Germany and NATO*. Whilst arguing against membership of the united Germany in NATO in its present form, the two authors did not regard neutrality as any constructive contribution to the new European perspective either. As an alternative they recommended NATO to abandon the integration of the armed forces of member countries, including the joint supreme commands, along with the entire strategy of flexible response.

With regard to Germany they advocated a partial demilitarisation, i.e. a build-down of German armed forces to a very low level, combined with a restriction to merely defensive equipment, i.e. NOD. As a confidence-building measure, Germany should submit its armed forces to international control, to be conducted by an Arms Control Agency, with its headquarters in Berlin. In parallel with this conversion on the part of Germany, the troops of the four powers in Germany should be drastically reduced and eventually withdrawn, subsequent to the entry into force of a 'European Peace and Security Arrangement'[105].

The SPD was, generally speaking, keenly aware of the need for confidence-building and for embedding unification in broader integrative schemes. The honorary chairman of the party, former Chancellor Willy Brandt was therefore open towards conceptions such as the 'Genscher Plan', but went a step further, almost to the point of endorsing the plan connected with his successor as Mayor of Berlin, Walter Momper. The latter has suggested that, for an intermediary period, the powers enjoyed by the four powers in Berlin might be extended to the GDR. Willy Brandt, in an interview with *Spiegel* took up this idea:

> 'Try to envision that, in principle, the military status of Berlin might be extended to the part of Germany which is added. In Berlin, there are, as a matter of principle, no German troops, regardless of the fact that the NVA was allowed to violate this status. That there may be some special status for an otherwise united German territory is thus nothing new.'[106]

The 'European connection' has consistently been given high priority by SPD spokesmen, albeit in different versions. One of the party's most influential spokesmen, Karsten Voigt, thus propounded several different, perhaps not entirely compatible, versions of this 'Europeanization'. He e.g. emphasised the need for strengthening the WEU, whilst at the same time stressing the need for supplementing, and in due course supplanting, the confrontational function of the blocs with cooperative functions. For the latter purpose, he recommended placing greater emphasis on the other 'leg' in (West) European integration, the EC, which presumably had the potential of overcoming the division of Europe, i.a. by opening up towards Eastern Europe.

Finally, in a speech to the SPD's (left wing) 'Frankfurter Circle' (16 March 1990), he proposed the establishment of a 'European Security Treaty', the parties to which should be all states presently participating in the CSCE. The treaty was envisaged to oblige all signatories to maintain peaceful relations, both without and within. Furthermore, it should prohibit regional sub-alliances, and place constraints on the armed forces of the member countries, both quantitatively and in qualitative terms, e.g. by restructuring them into strictly defensive forces.

As far as the intermediary steps were concerned, Voigt proposed a maintenance of US troops on the soil of the former West Germany, and Soviet forces in the former East Germany, not merely in order to please the Soviets, but also as a sort of security guarantee for Poland. On the present territory of the GDR, formations of the *Bundeswehr* should neither be stationed nor allowed to operate. Rather, the 'GDR' should be defended by means of either a defensive German territorial defence or an 'emergency police force'. The *Bundeswehr*, in its turn, was to remain integrated in the multilateral structures of NATO. Finally, on other occasions, Voigt emphasised the need for ensuring that NATO's infrastructure would not be extended to the territory of the present GDR, as well as for preventing the Soviet security guarantees to the former GDR from being applied 'by default' to the FRG[107].

Others have taken an even more 'pan-European' attitude. This holds true i.a. for Peter Glotz, the editor of the SPD's journal *Die Neue Gesellschaft*, who proposed to seek an answer to the so-called stability-instability dilemma in pan-European federalism:

'A European federalism of the peoples with extensive rights for minorities and ethnic groups, and above that supranational, supra-territorial structures and ties, which allow Europe to continue playing a role in the political and economic power game of world politics'[108].

The first West German 'ambassador' to the GDR (1974-1981), Günter Gaus suggested what might be regarded as a temporary approximation to this goal in the form of a Central European Confederation, consisting of both German states, Poland, Czechoslovakia, Hungary and Austria, with a 'capital' in the latter. According to the author, this would both ensure Poland's borders, and (i.a. by so doing) facilitate German unification. Whether this would actually prove to be as confidence-building as undoubtedly intended seems debatable, however, i.a. because of the resemblance to the *Mitteleuropa* schemes of the past which have often been regarded as protected German 'spheres of influence'. Other (and more prominent) SPD representatives have accordingly expressed grave scepticism with regard to such schemes[109].

The inclusion of NOD conceptions in a number of the above security policy proposals will be apparent. Indeed, even the SPD's 'resident disbeliever', General (ret.) Christian Krause 'mellowed' considerably with regard to NOD. In a couple of short studies published in the spring of 1990, he tried to come to grips with the 'new architecture' of Europe, which, according to the author, was bound to become truly pluralistic. Indeed, neutrality would cease to be an anomaly or an exception, and become wellnigh the rule, with the number of neutral and non-aligned countries likely to increase to seventeen, whereas the number of aligned states would most likely decline to fifteen.

In this pluralistic European landscape, there would remain the need for an all-European factor of order, whilst no longer any need for deterrence. However, no military weak spots should be permitted which might invite transgressions, whence Krause derived the need for defensive structures: 'In this sense, the principle of inability to attack will remain useful in the future'.

He had thus come to regard NOD as a recommendable goal, even though he pointed to a presumable contradiction involved with the notion of bilateral conversion to defensive structures:

> 'When there are no longer any armed forces capable of attack, there will also no longer be any need for defence. In the final analysis the implications of this conception were to make the armed forces redundant'[110].

Few NOD proponents, and certainly not the present author, would argue with that, but rather see it as one of the main advantages of NOD: that it might eventually make armed forces, and by implication itself, superfluous.

East German Security Policy Debate

Although the shifting governments in East Germany were, of course, disengaging themselves increasingly from their former Soviet allies, simultaneously with approaching NATO (*in casu* the FRG), they made a great effort to do so in a manner that would meet, as far as possible, the Soviet concerns. They primarily sought to accomplish this in the same manner as their colleagues in the West, namely through developing security policy conceptions, according to which a state's 'shifting side' was not all that important.

In their joint statement in December 1989 (i.e. when the talks were still about the 'contractual community', rather than on genuine unification) Chancellor Kohl and Premier Modrow expressed their agreement 'that good neighbourly relationship, based on a common responsibility for peace and a contractual community between the two states is of great importance for stability in Europe and constitutes a contribution to a new European architecture.'[111].

The IPW research institute, which had all along been close to the SED government (cf. Chapter X above) was subsequently given the task of elaborating on the plan for 'contractual community'. By December 1989, the IPW came out with i.a. the following recommendations, wherein a clear link was established to NOD thinking:

> 'The contractual community should assign first priority, and regard it as its paramount obligation, to allow both German states to make a responsible contribution to *détente* and disarmament in the spirit of the CSCE process. This would imply substantial contributions on the part of the GDR and the FRG to the piecemeal creation of mutual incapability of attack.'[112].

When unification had paved its way irreversibly on to the agenda, the question of NATO membership for the GDR naturally became the most controversial issue. As his alternative thereto, Premier Modrow came out in favour of a demilitarisation of his country 'in parallel with a piecemeal demilitarisation of Europe.'[113]. Proceeding from the same premises, aforementioned Walter Romberg (cf. Chapters IV and X), conducted discussions in Moscow (now as a member of government for the SPD) with Marshal Achromeyev and others i.a. on the military aspects of unification. According to Romberg, the two were in agreement that the membership of a united Germany in NATO was unacceptable[114].

Subsequent to the March 1990 elections, the new parliament in a unanimous declaration, passed 12 April 1990, made a sincere effort at confidence-building, i.a. by acknowledging their share of the responsibility for the horrors of WWII ('We feel sorrow and shame and acknowledge this burden of German history'), a legacy which had been repressed by the former government with its postulation that the GDR (in contrast to the FRG) represented a complete departure from the German past. Furthermore, the parliamentarians solemnly acknowledged their respect for the results of WWII, including the German borders[115].

In his first speech as the new leader of government, Lothar De Maizière (CDU) attempted to steer carefully between the 'Scylla' of neutralism, and the 'Charybdis' of contributing to threat perceptions on the part of Germany's neighbours. He did so by emphasising that 'the road must pass through European disarmament', rather than through neutrality. The new government, furthermore, committed itself to what it called an 'ecologically-oriented, social market economy', and paid tribute, as far as its foreign policy was concerned, to the confidence-building imperative, to a much greater extent than, say, the CDU in the other part of Germany:

'Germany lies in the middle of Europe, but is must not, once again, seek to grow into the power centre of Europe. (...) The unification of Germany must contribute to a stabilisation of Europe, and promote the creation of an all-European order of peace, democracy and cooperation. (...) It is the task of the government of the GDR to pursue a policy of promoting the replacement of the military blocs with alliance-transcending structures, in their turn constituting the beginning of an all-European security system'[116].

The government declaration even included what was probably the first commitment to NOD on the part of a near-Western (or 'soon-to-be-Western') government:

'For a transitionary period, there will, in addition to the Soviet armed forces, be a radically reduced and strictly defensive NVA, with the task of defending this territory. Our loyalty towards the Warsaw Pact will i.a. find its expression in our constant taking into consideration the security interests of the Soviet Union and the other Warsaw Pact states. The government of the GDR seeks a drastic reduction of all

German armed forces. We will initiate a restructuring of the People's Army and a piecemeal build-down of the military obligations of the GDR. The political cooperation in the framework of the Warsaw Pact should, on the other hand, be intensified'[117].

In the course of the foreign policy endeavours that were to follow, the GDR continued its difficult balancing act between West German and Soviet preferences and concerns. During a visit to the Kremlin on 20 april, de Maizière thus defended the idea of a united Germany belonging to NATO, whilst specifying (in reply to Gorbachev's description of the notion as 'unacceptable') that the GDR could not conceive of such a membership unless the Atlantic Alliance were to reform its strategy and structure[118].

During their first meeting, on 27 April, the defence ministers of the two Germanies (Stoltenberg and Eppelmann) declared their aim to be the membership of a united Germany in the Atlantic Alliance, however without NATO's military structures or installations being extended to the territory of the GDR: i.e. a commitment to the 'Genscher Plan'[119].

Intersecting Defence Debates

Simultaneously with this broader security policy debate at least three defence debates were conducted, albeit closely interconnected:

—The debate in the GDR on the structure of the NVA
—The debate in the FRG on the structure and size of the *Bundeswehr*
—The all-pervasive debate on the future of the armed forces of the united Germany, which tended to transform the two former debates into make-believe debates: 'Let's pretend that we will survive, and discuss the terms afterwards'.

In the GDR, the debate was very intense, indeed, with certain almost absurd features. For instance, official and semi-official representatives of the former ruling party (now the PDS) who had previously uncritically defended any arms build-up on the part of the USSR and the GDR, were now to be found amongst the most radical proponents of disarmament. This was i.a. the case for the infamous Max Schmidt of the IPW (and former advisor as well as speech-writer to Honecker), who now declared that the NVA had lost all purpose, since 'no enemy to deter exists any longer'[120].

As early 17 November 1989, newly-appointed Prime Minister Hans Modrow committed himself to adhering to the NOD commitment of the previous government, whilst now actually implementing the necessary reforms, rather than merely talking about them:

'Supported by its traditions of peace, the GDR intends to work in a novel way for the objective of reducing the capabilities of reciprocal attack and destruction of the Warsaw Pact and NATO states to such an extent that no existential challenges remain. In conformity herewith we must redefine our military doctrine'[121].

The chairman of the SED-PDS, Gregor Gysi followed his lead by proposing in January 1990 a *German-German Security Model* 2000, conceived of as an element in a 'contractual community', into which NOD entered as an important element. The concrete proposals of Mr. Gysi included cutting the armed forces of both German states in half; halting all modernisation; prohibiting any stationing of formations above company level within 50-80 kms. from the border; prohibiting submarines and amphibious landing craft by either state in the Baltic Sea; appealing to both alliances to withdraw their forces completely by 1999, starting with the border areas; and, finally, demanding a complete withdrawal of nuclear and chemical weapons, to be completed by the year 1991[122].

A further curious spectacle was that of (even top-brass) military officials questioning the utility of military power for whatever purpose. This was i.a. the case for a number of officers and teachers at the 'Friedrich Engels Military Academy' in Dresden, who as early as the autumn of 1989 were demanding very radical reforms indeed, as the present author experienced personally during a visit to the Academy in December 1989. Furthermore, the journal of the armed forces 'Military Affairs' (*Militärwesen*) rose to the status of the military journal with the most extensive debate on NOD[123] in the world.

Seen from the 'professional angle', the debate was carried out under the worst possible circumstances, since the NVA was visibly disintegrating. First of all, the rank-and-file of the NVA on more than one occasion mutinied, i.a. when on 6 February 1990 the 'Eighth Reconnaissance Battalion' in Schwerin was able to enforce, amongst other demands, the dismissal of five officers, including the commander of the battalion. There were repeated mutinies over working conditions, which i.a. forced newly-appointed Defence Minister Theodor Hoffmann to negotiate with the mutineers, and in the last resort accede to the improvements called for[124].

There were repeated proposals for a shortening of service from eighteen to twelve months, and there was a continual defection of officers. By early 1990, more than 2000 officers were thus reported to have approached the *Bundeswehr* with applications for jobs, but their chances were regarded as slim, i.a. because they had, almost without exception, been members of the SED. The NVA was thus visibly shrinking, and its reliability approached zero, to the extent that the WTO supreme command had to make the decision no longer to make any use of the NVA, i.a. after the refusal of an infantry regiment to conduct joint manoeuvres with the Soviet forces. Although Hoffmann told commanders that the NVA would continue to participate in WP exercises as long as these treaty obligations existed, such assurances turned out to be 'writ in water'[125].

Defence Minister Hoffmann was thus in an unenviable position, whence probably his apparent vacillation. On 23 February 1990, he issued a proposal for a joint German army of 300,000 men. After correction by the WTO supreme commander, however, he changed his view and proposed the formation of a professional army of 70,000, without, however, gaining the approval of the (by then very powerful) citizens movements of the 'Round Table'. By February, Hoffmann had modified his proposal for the future of the country's armed forces, and now recommended a joint army of the united Germany numbering around 300,000 men. The new force should number around 300,000 men (i.e. be reduced by fifty percent), be called the *Bundesheer* (Federal Army), be strictly defensive, and comprise mobile border militia and army units. Initially, the two Germanies should, however, remain members of their respective alliances[126].

By now, however, the monolithic intellectual climate in the GDR had changed radically, and a pluralistic environment had emerged, the liveliness of which surpassed that in the FRG. One participant in the debate on defence matters was the 'Study Group for the Demilitarization of Security' (SES), founded in January 1990. Its members included aforementioned (Chapter X) Wolfgang Schwarz (of the IPW), André Brie (of the Diplomatic Academy in Potsdam) and Siegfried Fischer (of the aforementioned Military Academy, with the rank of naval Captain). The SES took it upon itself to analyse very radical options, indeed, for the military future of the GDR. In a commentary to the CSCE Seminar on Military Doctrines in January 1990, the SES e.g. stated that 'the discussion now in progress on military doctrines should not take the defensive nature of these doctrines as its yardstick for comparison, but rather their conformity with the tendency towards demilitarisation'.

Siegfried Fischer, furthermore, publically advocated neutrality-cum-demilitarisation for the GDR, to be implementied through a ten-year plan for the disbandment of the armed forces of the GDR. Furthermore, he rejected the notion of NOD on the grounds that it was not radical enough, since 'even the preference for the defence eliminates neither offensive capabilities, nor the threat emanating herefrom'.

As the present author was able to personally ascertain during a lunch in Copenhagen, Fischer was, furthermore, a firm believer in the futility and utter destructiveness of any type of war on the European continent, even a strictly conventional one, i.e. he subscribed to what I have called the 'TDCW hypothesis' (cf. Chapter X). What the GDR really needed was therefore not a new military doctrine, say, a strictly defensive one, but a programme for complete demilitarisation[127].

The same attitude was taken by Professor at the Military-Political Academy in East Berlin, Colonel of the NVA Wilfried Schreiber, who in his presentation to a colloquium in Brussels by the end of February said that 'for the states along the line of contact, the question of the offensive or defensive character of the military strategy in question becomes secondary'. Whilst acknowledging NOD as a lesser evil than offensive strategies, he nevertheless maintained that 'any defence by the Warsaw Pact states on the soil of the GDR is completely unacceptable. In this sense, not only offensive but also defensive military strategies are incompatible with the security interests of the peoples and states of Europe'[128].

A further participant in the intense defence debate was the aforementioned Walter Romberg, who was not, unfortunately, in a position to devote his undivided attention to defence matters, having assumed responsibility for the catastrophic finances of the GDR. Nevertheless, in March 1990 he published a fairly detailed proposal for the military future of Germany, according to which the four allied powers should maintain 30,000 troops in Germany, whereas the German armed forces should consist of 100,000 on the territory of the FRG, and 30,000 in the present GDR[129].

A final peculiarity of the defence debate in the GDR was that the peace movement was now in a position to talk *ex cathedra*, by virtue of the fact that Rainer Eppelmann became the new Defence Minister of the GDR. A Protestant priest, convinced pacifist and former conscientious objector, he once spent eight months in prison for refusing to take the oath of allegiance, and who subsequently became a leader in the peace and human rights movement in the early 1980s. In conformity with this persuasion, Eppelmann made it a precondition for his assumption of the post that the ministry was renamed 'Ministry of Disarmament and Defence', as a matter of deliberate choice, in that order[130].

Under the auspices of the new ministry, a regular journal was launched with the telling title 'Military Reform in the GDR' (*Militärreform in der DDR*), as an indication that the government in general, and Eppelmann in particular, were serious about the desirability of public debate on defence matters.

In an almost programmatical speech to the officers of the NVA, 2 May 1990, the new Defence Minister outlined his, and the new government's, goals with respect to disarmament and conversion, the latter in the dual sense of 'conversion from offensive to defensive structures' and 'conversion from military to civilian purposes'. After a pacifist admonition ('A border-transcending policy is more humane than border-crossing military operations'), the Defence Minister continued:

'Nevertheless, the GDR intends, for as long it it continues to exist as an independent state, to maintain its people's army of an appropriate size and strictly defensively structured, in the interest of its external security. Also subsequent to unification, there will be a second German army on the territory of the GDR, which will perform its own territorial defence functions, integrated in no military alliance, and structured, equipped and trained in accordance herewith. (...) There will, however, be no

NATO troops on the territory of the present GDR. (. . .) On the territory of the present GDR, there must be no military vacuum. Hence a demilitarisation in the sense of a rapid disbandment of the NVA is unacceptable to us.'[131].

Paradoxically, Eppelmann now spoke out against an abolition of conscription in the GDR, which he explicitly declared to be 'a piece of democracy'. On the other hand, the leader of the PDS (former SED, i.e. the party that had previously imprisoned Eppelmann for his refusal to do military service), Gregor Gysi, by now advocated an abolition of armed service[132].

Subsequent to assuming his new position, Eppelmann announced that the NVA was to be extensively restructured with a view to reflecting the new role it would play within the Warsaw Pact in the light of impending German unification. Referring to the CFE negotiations, he outlined the main weapons systems he wanted to maintain in the NVA's arsenal:

—The air force should retain 225 combat aircraft and 44 combat helicopters.

—The ground forces would operate 1,060 MBTs, 2,352 other AFVs and 735 artillery systems of 100 mm calibre and above.

—The NVA's official peacetime strength of 168,000 was to be reduced to 100,000 by 1992-93.

—Territorial troop strength would be in the order of 5,200-6,000 troops. The territorial commands would equate to the *Länder* structure that was due to be established in East Germany.

—The field troops were to include 39,000 troops in two army corps, with eleven or twelve brigades and support units. There should be no purely armoured formations; instead all brigades should be uniformly structured and include motor-rifle as well as armoured elements.

—The air defence forces should have a strength of 22,000 troops, organised in two air defence and one air defence support divisions. They would most likely field a total of four air defence wings, three SAM brigades, and six signals battalions, with separate units for transport and helicopters.

—The navy would comprise 12,000 men, and consist of one flotilla each of missile craft and coastal protection craft. There would be two coastal defence brigades (one of which was to be a mobilisation brigade) and separate naval aviation and helicopter units[133].

In both Germanies 'citizens initiatives' transcending the border between the two German states had by now also emerged, and began to demand a say in the future of the German armed forces. A call for a referendum to abolish the army and demilitarise both East and West Germany was issued in the GDR by various peace groups. In the proposal it was stated that 'this demilitarisation will be an exemplary step in the direction of a demilitarised Europe'.

In the FRG, the 'Federation for Social Defence' (*Bund für Soziale Verteidigung*) launched a similar campaign for 'The FRG Without an Army'. In the proclamation of the campaign it was stated that 'even without weapons we are not defenceless', since 'by means of the methods of non-violent resistance (also in the form of civilian insubordination) we can implement our goal of an abolition of armaments and military'.

From a joint demilitarisation conference held by the Greens (FRG) and the new Green Party (GDR) in Magdeburg, on 14 March 1990, an appeal was issued which, in a similarly radical vein, stated that

'demilitarisation, i.e. the piecemeal disbandment of military formations, is the political alternative to the restructuring of the *Bundeswehr* and the NVA which is now being promoted, be it in the direction of "defensive armaments" or in that of a professional army. Both are unacceptable to us'[134].

The two governments have also consulted with each other. The two Ministers of Defence Stoltenberg and Eppelmann by the end of April held the first set of negotiations, and at a subsequent meeting it was agreed to develop a 'comprehensive cooperation' between the two armies: contacts would be intensified, both at the political and expert level, but also at the professional military, level. It was stressed that the shared objective was to reduce the personnel of both armies, even though the outcome of the CFE and 'Two-Plus-Four' talks would have to be awaited[135].

The debate in the FRG in the Spring of 1990 was much less intense and innovative than its counterpart in the East. It might almost seem as if the West German parties were competing as to who dared propose the lowest figures for the future united German armed forces, without caring all that much about their configuration. The distinctions have conformed fairly accurately to the traditional left-right dimension: the further to the right, the higher numbers, and *vice versa*.

—According to Volker Rühe (CDU), the peacetime level of the all-German forces could be 'below 400,000', provided the disarmament talks succeeded. This would allow for a reduction of service to twelve months.

—The FDP called for a reduction of the *Bundeswehr* to 350,000 troops, combined with a reduction of the length of service from fifteen to twelve months.

—In a document dated 23 March, Egon Bahr and Katrin Fuchs of the SPD argued in favour of a fifty percent cut in *Bundeswehr* personnel, to 240,000 in peacetime and 600,000 in a crisis (instead of 1.3 million). In addition, they called for a reduction in main battle tanks from around 5,000 to 1,000 and the withdrawal from service of *Luftwaffe* fighter-bombers, as well as giving up the Tornado aircraft[136]. The last item on the list was the only one in which some attention was apparently given to the structure, rather than merely the numerical size, of the armed forces.

As mentioned above, the Greens launched a campaign in collaboration with what was left of the peace movement(s) for the total abolition of German armed forces, whilst criticising NOD conceptions as reflecting the last desperate attempts on the part of the armed forces to prevent the only sensible solution: a complete demilitarisation of Germany. The Greens even went to such lengths as to call upon conscripts to desert, in case they were to be sent to the Persian Gulf[137].

The Defence Ministry eventually also deciphered the 'writing on the wall', and embarked on an examination of the future size of the armed forces subsequent to unification. The outcome of these deliberations was only revealed subsequent to the authoritative decision to build down the *Bundeswehr* to a mere 370,000 men.

Defence Minister Gerhard Stoltenberg on 12 November 1990 presented his plans for the restructured *Bundeswehr*, according to which the army was to be reduced to a ceiling of 260,000 men (as compared with the former 302,000 in West Germany and 57,300 in East Germany); the air force to 83,800 (as compared with 98,000 and 22,700, respectively); and the navy (hitherto numbering 36,200 and 8,700, respectively) to 32,200, pending a further reduction to 26,200 by the year 2000. The number of army divisions was be reduced from twelve to eight and brigades from 48 to 30, whereas the navy should halve the number of its vessels from the present 180 to 90 by the year 2005[138].

There remained the somewhat delicate matter of how to deal with the former East German forces, weapons systems and military installations. It was decided to build down immediately the NVA from 90-100,000 troop strength to 50,000 upon unification, and to finish the integration by 1994, at the latest. Some opportunities for professional retraining were to be offered to those leaving the NVA. Among the units to be disbanded immediately and in their entirety were notably the border guards (numbering 19,000 troops), the last task for whom would, ironically, be clearing the mine-fields along the former border and dismantling what was still left of the Berlin Wall.

A West German officer, Lieutenant-General Jörg Schönbohm was appointed to head the *Bundeswehr*'s newly-established Eastern Command (covering the former GDR), to be assisted by 240 *Bundeswehr* officers and 360 former NVA officers and NCOs. The new command was to administer two military district commands (Leipzig and Neubrandenburg), and super-vise the transformation of the former NVA divisions to six home defence brigades, in addition to which there were to be four home defence regiments, various command, combat support logistics and medical troops, as well as 15 military region commands, including Berlin.

As far as equipment was concerned the naval staff of the former GDR had wanted more than 50 of its ships to be incorporated into the Federal Navy, but West German naval planning left no room for these. By the end of the day, the only equipment taken over (for a transitional period) by the united German armed forces were the MIG-29 *Fulcrum* fighters, which the Defence Minister decided, against the advice of his planning staff, to continue operating, tasked with patrolling East German airspace[139].

Not only were the German forces thus scheduled for a major cut-back. The latter half of 1990 also saw what looked like the preparations for a major exodus of allied forces from Germany[140]. In the light of impending unification, several allies unilaterally announced their intentions of partial or complete withdrawal from the FRG. By September, the Western Allies had reached agreement for an orderly withdrawal, according to which the former 410,000 Western troops stationed in the FRG will be reduced to around 150,000 by the end of the 1990s. This build-down e.g. entailed a US withdrawal of 60,000 troops by 1997; a British halving of the BAOR over the same period; a French pull-out of 20,000 troops (out of 50,000) troops over two years; and a partial withdrawal of the 8,000 Dutch and the 25,000 Belgian troops[141]. Few Germans appeared to be worried about these prospects, which would previously undoubtedly have triggered the 'abandonment' element of the 'abandonment-entrapment dilemma' mentioned in Chapter II above.

As an immediate 'relief measure' for the German population, an agreement was, furthermore, reached on a discontinuation of low-altitude flying by USAF aircraft. Whereas they had previously flown at altitudes as low as 75 metres, they were now expressly prohibited to go below 300 metres, thus mitigating somewhat the 'peace-time defence dilemma' (cf. Chapter II) hitherto experienced by the involuntary neighbours to USAF bases[142].

All of the above debate took place in the light of the first all-German elections in December 1990, and the parties to a certain extent used security policy and defence issues as means of improving their credibility, i.a. by modifying or even erasing their former public images. The PDS desperately sought to disengage itself from the SED and DKP images, yet with only limited success, whereas the SPD largely succeeded in making the electorate forget about their former relations with the SED, whilst playing upon the theme of social security. The government parties did, however, score the largest successes of all, perhaps due more than anything else to their good fortune in having been in power at the time of the revolution in the GDR. The results of the elections were as follows[143]:

Party	Percentage of votes	Seats in the *Bundestag*
CDU	36.7	268
CSU	7.1	51
FDP	11.0	79
SPD	33.5	239
Greens	3.9	0
PDS	2.4	17
Others	1.2	8

Subsequent to this electoral defeat, the SPD rapidly changed their leader, with Oskar Lafontaine withdrawing to his post as Premier in Saarland, and his colleague from Schleswig-Holstein, Björn Engholm taking over the post as candidate for chancellor[144].

Collective Security and Out-of-Area Challenges

In the light of the positive developments with regard to East-West relations during 1989-1990, a number of the *dramatis personae* of the previous chapters had begun to take the conception of 'collective security' seriously. A few had done so all along, amongst whom Egon Bahr's deputy as director of the IFSH in Hamburg, Dieter S. Lutz.

His conception of what he called a 'System of Collective Security' (SCS) had, however, been rather ahistorical, 'idealistic' and legalistic, and had therefore been regarded as rather untimely. He had e.g. conceived of SCS as an integral part of the so-called 'NEPO' (New European Peace Order), and thus as a follow-on to a 'common security (CS) regime'. The level of ambition, and by implication the envisaged timeframe, of SCS had been a half-way station between a CS regime and NEPO. On the one hand, SCS would expand on CS by also entailing provisions for collaboration in times of war, i.a. in the form of collective sanctions. On the other hand, SCS would limit itself to promoting 'negative peace', in Johan Galtung's sense of a 'mere' absence of war, whereas NEPO also promoted 'positive peace', in the sense of building down 'structural violence'. The main target of SCS, according to Lutz, should thus have been war prevention, for which purpose supranational armed forces would be the ideal solution. However, national forces ought not to be excluded, so long as their role was restricted to that of territorial defence, along with an obligation to unconditional and immediate assistance to other SCS members subjected to aggression from external or internal enemies[145].

In the years 1989-90 Lutz resurfaced his previous proposals for collective security, as usual in a number of almost identical articles. Although the concrete proposal was very similar to its predecessors, it was now put forward under infinitely more benign conditions which made it much more timely.

As far as the institutional format of SCS was concerned, DSL envisaged a combination of the following:

—A European security council
—A permanent secretariat
—A General Assembly
—Various institutions for peaceful conflict resolution
—A multitude of mechanisms for mutual consultation.

Whereas supranational armed forces at the disposal of the SCS should eventually replace national armed forces, for the transition period Lutz assessed it as most realistic to aim for a mixture of national armed forces (without any offensive potential) and supranational armed forces. As mentioned in Chapter IV, he suggested a grand total of 700,000 troops for all of Europe, including 105,000 unmistakably defensive German troops[146].

In 1990, Lutz's institute, the IFSH, put forward a joint set of recommendations (authored primarily by Egon Bahr and Reinhard Mutz) in the light of the 'Two-Plus-Four' talks by then in progress. The authors envisioned a regional (or perhaps rather subregional) collective security system, comprising the united Germany, the Benelux states, Denmark, Poland, Czechoslovakia and Hungary, i.e. an enlarged Central Europe.

The main purpose of the arrangement should be war prevention through prophylactic conflict resolution, combined with the dissuasive effect of an automatic obligation to mutual assistance in case of attack. The authors were aware of the conflicting requirements flowing from such an arrangement: on the one hand, the armed forces should suffice merely for defensive purposes (i.e. of NOD type), but on the other hand, they should also possess a considerable long-range mobility that might be almost tantamount to offensive capability.

The presumed solution to this dilemma was 'a bifurcation (*zweiteilung*) of the armed forces', implying that 'the bulk of the national armies would be defensively structured and equipped and tasked with the traditional defence. A smaller contingent of more mobile forces could perform the function of an "intervention force" or a "Euro-police force", and would be available for assistance in case of attack'. Ideally, however, the latter element should be completely detached from the national structure, and placed under multinational command.

The proposal attracted some criticism, i.a. from Martin Müller of the nearby *Bundeswehr* academy in Hamburg. His main objection was that even though 'this security community would surely threaten nobody, neither would it be taken seriously by anybody, because it would be unable to provide for the security of its members in terms of dissuasion or defence'. Furthermore, as a way of embedding German armed forces in a multinational framework, the 'small European' format envisaged by the IFSH would be inadequate, because German power would be preponderant. Others have, however, seen the implied Central European focus as geopolitically 'natural' for Germany, i.e. as a form of benign revival of the centuries-old infatuation with *Mitteleuropa*[147].

Egon Bahr of the same instutute, as well as of the SPD, likewise proposed the creation of a genuine European Security Community, including a decision-making body that should not be 'handicapped' by veto powers as well as armed forces to carry out its decisions. Whereas the ideal solution, according to Bahr, would be a Soviet NATO membership, he had to acknowledge this to be a very long-term prospect, indeed, whilst still envisaging some sort of association agreements between NATO and the WTO. His fellow partisan, Karsten Voigt thought along the same lines, and e.g. proposed the creation of 'CSCE peace forces'[148].

With the exception of Bahr and his institute, however, NOD theorising had formerly (occasional 'ceremonial' lip-service to the desirability, in principle, of CS notwithstanding) tended to be couched in 'realist' terms, i.e. it had taken as its level of analysis the state, conceived of as a unitary actor pursuing 'national interest', and assumed an 'anarchic setting' for international politics along with a lasting potential for conflict. In the light of the developments in 1989-1990, however, at least some NOD theorists tended to acknowledge the emergence of a new paradigm for international relations and, as a corollary thereof, to envisage the creation of collective security structures.

Amongst these 'converts' to the idea of collective security (to which category the present author belongs himself), was also to be found Dieter Senghaas (cf. Chapter IV above), who by 1990 had come to regard the entire East-West conflict as a thing of the past, whence presumably sprang unique opportunities for creating a 'structure of lasting peace' in Europe within the span of a decade. These prospects also forced him to acknowledge his previous advocacy of 'a civilisation of the East-West conflict' as obsolete. The massive Soviet attack which had hitherto constituted the point of departure for military planning had now ceased being merely unlikely and become totally inconceivable; hence the opportunities for far more drastic disarmament than had so far been negotiated in Vienna[149].

According to Senghaas, the main pillars in the lasting European peace structure that had now become a realistic goal should be the CSCE and the EC. The absence of military elements in the EC was regarded as a strength, rather than a weakness, i.a. because EC integration would, by virtue of this 'deficiency', constitute an appropriate framework for a German confederation. As far as the narrow security policy terms of unification were concerned, he did, however, envision, for a transitionary period, a German dual membership of both military alliances. In the long run, however, the time for the alliances had passed, and they should be replaced by a genuine peace order.

The collective security system intended to embody this should be based on a radical disarmament through a sequel of 'CFE' negotiations. As far as the united Germany was concerned, he suggested a build-down to one fifth of the present strength, i.e. no more than 100,000 troops. In addition to being structurally incapable of major offensives, the German armed forces should be 'balanced' by approximately 175,000 troops in the neighbouring countries, as well as by the maintenance of 65,000 foreign troops stationed in Germany.

On the supranational level, a European Security Council should be established, having at its disposal a standing peace-keeping force of 'Blue Helmets'. Although these should have the capabilities for military intervention (i.e. be *per se* 'offensive'), the emphasis should be placed on 'therapeutic conflict intervention'[150].

Members of the SAS (cf. above, Chapter IV) have also begun exploring the opportunities for collective security structures. Malcolm Chalmers and Hans Günter Brauch both advocated a gradual institutionalization of the CSCE, along with a shift of emphasis from NATO towards the EC, as a more appropriate framework for the search for cooperative forms of security, to eventually supercede the present confrontational forms. Both, furthermore, acknowledged the need for gradually demilitarizing intra-European relations, whilst taking the military problems during the transitional phase seriously, above all by seeking an all-European conversion to NOD postures and strategies. The present author (likewise an SAS member) published largely similar proposals which will be outlined in the concluding chapter[151].

By the end of 1990, there were quite a few encouraging signs that the available opportunities might, indeed, be taken up. At its aforementioned July summit, NATO did acknowledge its willingness to start constructing all-European cooperative institutions, i.a. by providing the CSCE with a modicum of institutional permanency: a secretariat, etc. Furthermore, regular consultations between the two alliances (or, perhaps more realistically, between NATO and the USSR) were envisioned, as was an invitation to the newly-emancipated and democratised East European countries to join the European Council in Strasbourg. Since these proposals matched the previous Soviet ones well, the stage was set for substantial progress in the field of pan-European security structures.

The CFE treaty was signed in Paris on 19 November, on the fringes of the CSCE summit meeting. Whereas the talks had started out as 'the 23-Nation Talks', the number of signatories was by now down to 22 as a result of the unification of the two German states. The treaty was intended to, and probably did, remove any capabilities for surprise attack on the part of the two alliances through a build-down to lower ceilings for each alliance pertaining to five categories of major weapons systems: heavy tanks (20,000), armoured vehicles (30,000), artillery pieces (20,000), combat aircraft (6,800), and combat helicopters (2,000).

The united Germany was 'hit' particularly hard by the various ceilings, sub-ceilings and 'Two-plus-Four limitations', and was i.a. obliged to destroy 3,000 tanks (as compared with the previously envisaged 600 for West Germany alone); 2,500 artillery pieces (previously 150); and 500 combat aircraft (previously 110). The prevailing sentiment in Germany was, however, that of contentment and understanding for the fact that unification did, indeed, have its 'costs'. There did, however, remain a daunting task of physically converting or destroying the tanks and other weapons systems to be withdrawn, a task which seemed to appeal to German ingenuity and entrepreneurship[152].

The CFE treaty was accompanied by the aforementioned German declaration and declarations pertaining to land-based naval aviation and military personnel, as well as by a solemn joint declaration, wherein all 22 states proclaimed no longer to be adversaries, but willing to extend their hands to each other in friendship. In this context they also committed themselves formally to what might best be described as 'a NOD obligation':

> 'They commit themselves only to maintain such military potentials as are necessary for war prevention and an effective defence. They intend to remain alert to the relationship between military potentials and doctrines'.[153].

Furthermore, two days later the *Paris Charter for a New Europe* was signed by all 34 CSCE member states, wherein it was solemnly declared that 'a new era of democracy, freedom and unity' was commencing in Europe. The signatories further decided to launch a certain institutionalisation of the CSCE process, i.a. through the establishment of the following:

—A council of Foreign Ministers that was to meet at least annually.
—A committee of high-ranking civil servants in permanent session.
—A Secretariat, to be housed in Prague.
—A Centre for Conflict Prevention, to be housed in Vienna.
—A Bureau for Free Election in Warsaw.
—A parliamentary assembly.

Whereas the concrete implications of these principled decisions remained to be worked out, by the time these lines were written, the decisions of the Paris Summit certainly seemed to be wellnigh tantamount to 'a happy ending' to the East-West conflict[154]. Certain 'loose ends' nevertheless remained, to which I shall return in the concluding chapter.

The general picture was, however, made more complicated by the fact that the debate(s) on European security and the contribution of the two (and subsequently one) Germany hereto, from the autumn of 1990 became intertwined with a debate on the 'out-of-area' question.

The Iraqi invasion of Kuwait highlighted several facts hitherto ignored by most security political decision-makers. First of all, it reminded everybody of the vital necessity for Germany (as a highly industrialized country with a high degree of dependence on raw material imports) of keeping the international flow of commodities in working order[155].

Secondly, it reminded everybody that there was a world beyond the the Bosphorus or the Urals, indeed even south of the Tropic of Cancer, where NATO's area of responsibility ended. It, furthermore, did so at a point in time when Germany (for the good reasons described in the previous sections) had issued a host of assurances and accepted a number of commitments and obligations, i.a. to the principles of collective security. These commitments were now open to interpretation as blank cheques which might eventually be 'cashed in'.

Many observers felt that the moment had arrived, and that the FRG should participate fully in the UN-imposed blockade of Iraq, as well as, if need be, in a war against this country. Others, however, fought for a maintenance of the restrictive interpretation of the *Grundgesetz*, according to which the FRG was not permitted military operations outside the NATO area. Whence ensued a principled debate which remained unresolved by the time these lines were written.

Whereas the *Bundesmarine* had already taken some part in the WEU's operations in the Gulf, e.g. by sending minesweepers on patrol in the eastern part of the Mediterranean in support of the allied forces operating beyond Suez, it was quite a different matter to take part in what might well develop into a shooting war outside NATO's area of responsibility[156].

According to *Bundeswehr* Chief of Staff Admiral Dieter Wellershoff, Germany should be able to deploy troops outside the NATO area and independent of a UN mandate, as he argued in November, whilst making sure to emphasize that such a change to Germany's constitution could only be made by politicians and not the military. The FDP, however, criticised the Admiral for having 'stepped outside his brief', not because it was against a change in the Constitution, but merely on the grounds that any involvement of German troops beyond the NATO area should take place under UN auspices. Others have suggested that out-of-area operations should be initiated gradually and cautiously, say, with peacetime naval operations.

Defence Minister Gerhard Stoltenberg (CDU) supported his Chief of Staff in the latter's call for a change in the *Grundgesetz* with a view to allowing Germany to participate in out-of-area operations under UN auspices, and unexpectedly even the Federal President Richard von Weizsäcker came out in support of this constitutional change. Nevertheless, the party was in disagreement in this matter, with i.a. the Chairman of the CDU's defence committee, Fritz Wittman speaking out against Stoltenberg, perhaps out of fear that the SPD would try to include a ban on arms exports in the contemplated revision of the *Grundgesetz*.

SPD leader Hans Jochen Vogel had e.g. suggested that it would be unacceptable to have German forces fighting (even under UN auspices) against adversaries armed with German weapons, and honorary party Chairman Willy Brandt emphasised the advantages of German non-involvement in the Gulf because of the opportunities this provided of playing a diplomatic role in resolving the conflict.

Aforementioned (Chapter VII) MdBs for the SPD Hermann Scheer and Heidemarie Wiezoreck-Zeul took an even firmer stand against involvement in a war in the Gulf. They recommended a continuation of the blockade, yet excluding food and medical supplies; the establishment of a true UN peace-keeping force, and the withdrawal of all non-Arab, non-UN forces from the area; an immediate cessation of all arms exports to the former adversaries of Iraq (i.e. Iran); and the summoning of a peace conference for the region, which should also include the Palestinian issue in its deliberations[157].

As already mentioned, the peace movement(s), along with the Greens, took an even stronger stance against any German involvement in the Gulf, as well as against any military intervention in general, even under UN auspices. Regardless of the questionable morality behind this attitude, it appeared to be in conformity with public opinion. According to opinion polls conducted in the autumn of 1990, there was a majority of around 53 percent against the deployment of the *Bundeswehr* beyond NATO territory, whereas a mere 32 supported the suggested changes[158].

Evaluation

The year 1989-90 was, indeed, one of frantic activity with regard to, and heated debate on, defence as well as broader security political matters. Furthermore, it was beyond a shadow of a doubt a year when decisions were taken that could shape the future well into the next millennium, not only as far as Germany was concerned, but with regard to the whole of Europe.

Some lessons seemed to have been learned, either from the futile efforts at combining rearmament and reunification in the 1950s, or from the new security policy 'philosophy' of the late 1980s, particularly the elements thereof connected with 'Common Security' and NOD.

—The security concerns of Germany's foes as well as friends were taken seriously, even if it has not always been considered feasible to meet them entirely. The 'common security' approach has thus taken roots in Germany, across the entire political spectrum.

—It was attempted to downgrade the military element with a view to building German security on a different basis, either that of 'cooperative structures' or some similar term. The perspective became that of removing the spectre of war from Europe so as to make military contingency planning and force structures largely irrelevant.

—Nevertheless, it was realised that military structures (as well as the size of the armed forces) did matter, at least for the transitional period. If care were not taken to make these less threatening, the military logic might block whatever progress might otherwise be accomplished in the non-military field.

These lessons were understood and internalised to different degrees by the various political forces in West Germany (but, *mirabile dictu*, apparently by nearly everybody in the new GDR): most profoundly by the SPD, followed closely by the FDP (at least as far as the immediate entourage of Foreign Minister Genscher was concerned), with the CDU-CSU 'lagging behind' a bit in terms of understanding, but basically speaking the same language and reasoning according to the same logic.

CHAPTER XII

Summary and Conclusions

As has hopefully become apparent from the previous chapters, some 'conceptual bridges' seem to have been constructed, and something approximating a consensus has emerged on certain fundamental verities on security and defence policy. This may prove extremely valuable in the years immediately ahead when the security structure of Europe is going to be built to replace that of the Cold War. A few suggestions to this effect will be ventured as the conclusion to this chapter, after a brief recapitulation of the findings of the investigation so far.

The NOD Debate in Germany

The account provided on the pages above has attempted to show how a rich variety of different proposals for NOD have flourished in the FRG for the last decade or so, the origins of which were to be found in the academic community as well as in political and military circles. Many of these proposals were quite incommensurate, since some dealt primarily with political issues, whereas others focused on military 'detail', and still others struck a balance between the two.

I shall not, therefore, pretend to be able to draw any conclusions in a stringent scientific sense, but limit myself to recapitulating what seems to be common ground, as far as most proposals are concerned. The following theses would appear to roughly capture the essence of the NOD discourse in the FRG, at least as it was conducted until the momentuous period of 1989-1990.

—It is imperative to devise a form of defence the implementation of which will not be tantamount to national suicide.

—It is therefore important to build down the nuclear arsenals, at the very least to a minimum deterrence level, as a corollary whereof a no-first-use strategy should be adopted.

—As a matter of particular urgency, battle-field and short-range nuclear weapons should be withdrawn from Germany.

—Nuclear build-down, in its turn, requires a stabilisation of the conventional level, i.e. a situation where neither side has anything to gain from war.

—Conventionalisation should imply neither any major build-up of conventional forces, nor any substantial increase of defence expenditures.

—Stabilisation is only possible by way of building down offensive capabilities, whilst retaining, or preferably improving, defensive capabilities.

—The most likely cause of war is not a premeditated attack in the '1939 style', but rather a crisis somehow 'sliding off the tracks' as in 1914, whence the paramount importance of crisis stability for peace and stability.

—It is important to avoid giving the opponent any incentives for pre-emptive attack, above all by not posing any threat to him which he might feel inclined to neutralise.

—It is particularly urgent to eliminate the risk of short-warning conventional attacks, by prolonging warning time and removing lucrative targets for enemy strikes, thus depriving any would-be aggressor of options for pre-emption.

—It is therefore particularly important to build down conventional weapons categories such as main battle tanks, self-propelled heavy artillery, fighter bombers, long-range missiles, and major surface ships.

—Pending a complete elimination of such weapons, crisis stability might be improved by withdrawing these to rearward positions.

—The above categories of weapons should be replaced with others, characterised by shorter ranges, limited (i.e. only tactical) mobility, pin-point accuracy and modest requirements with regard to platforms.

—By means of such weaponry and through a skilful adaptation to the terrain, a high defence efficiency may be attainable *vis-à-vis* the major weapons platforms and formations of the attacker.

—Military steps towards improved conventional stability should be combined with political steps towards confidence-building, *détente* and mutual trust and cooperation.

There was approximate unanimity between NOD advocates on the above points, whereas there was considerable disagreement on whether to aim for unilateral or negotiated implementation. Furthermore, NOD proponents tended to disagree on whether to view NOD as a contribution to reforming NATO strategy whilst maintaining the alliance as such, or to use it as a stepping stone on the way towards a dissolution of the blocs, Europeanisation or even German unification-cum-neutralisation. Finally, of course, there was significant disagreement between the various proposers on the preferred configuration of defence forces.

It would be quite unrealistic to expect any of the concrete proposals to be implemented wholesale, since any proposal would have to pass through the 'grinding mill' of political bargaining within and between the parties before being singled out for implementation. Secondly, the task of implementation will in any case remain a prerogative of the armed services, which are unlikely to relinquish this privilege to 'amateurs', and certainly not to civilians. At most, a NOD advocate might thus hope for a political commitment to certain basic principles, along with some involvement in the implementation thereof.

An indication that this might actually happen is the fact that the basic ideas of NOD seem to have gradually permeated into the minds of both politicians and military men, not only in the FRG, and (for as long as it lasted) in the post-revolutionary GDR, but also in other European countries. Come what may, these ideas are thus bound to contribute to the European security policy and defence debate in the coming years.

In a certain sense, however, the NOD idea was a creature of the Cold War and the accompanying bipolarity, as well as of a certain Eurocentrism. The years 1989-1990 uncovered problems hitherto almost unnoticed by NOD proponents (and most others, for that matter), to which existing NOD theory had no solutions ready to hand, and posing questions which remain unanswered, such as:

—Might not a substantial build-down of the level of forces (such as accomplished through CFE) suffice for removing any serious risks of war, particularly when accompanied by a general improvement of the international climate? Might NOD not have become 'a solution in search of a problem'?

—Has not the Soviet threat which NOD was designed to meet disappeared for good, with the *de facto* dissolution of the WTO as well as the systemic change apparently underway in, and the gradual disintegration of, the USSR itself?

—What about the world outside Europe, particularly south of the Tropic of Cancer, where the responsibility of NATO ends? Would the general NOD principles be applicable here, or is their validity limited to Europe?

—What is the appropriate response to outright aggression such as that of Iraq against Kuwait? Would strictly defensive forces have sufficed for dissuading such an attack? And even more problematic, how might an unsuccessfully dissuaded aggressor be evicted from conquered territory by means of defensive forces, deprived of strategic mobility?

I shall not pretend to have the answer to these extremely tricky questions, but merely advance some thoughts on the potential relevance of NOD for the decades ahead.

Towards the Next Millennium

Everybody seems to realise that decisions of tremendous importance are being taken, which will determine the European, and to some extent global, security political 'landscape' well beyond the year 2000[1]:

—Through the arms control and disarmament negotiations now in progress (START, CFE, and others), military structures in Europe are undergoing a fundamental transformation.

—Through the CSCE process, including the November 1990 summit, the broader security political structures of Europe are being remodelled.

—Both parties to the former East-West conflict acknowledge it as having passed away, and the foundations for a more cooperative relationship between the European states and nations appear to have been layed.

—Through the German unification process, the borders of one part of Europe have been revised, thereby perhaps opening a Pandora's box of outstanding border issues.

This impressive agenda entails both opportunities and risks. Although the former presently seem to outweigh the latter, things may go wrong, as 'Murphy' warned us: 'If anything can go wrong, it will, and at the worst possible moment'. Even though this saying is probably far too pessimistic, it does contain more than just a grain of truth, and ought at the very least to serve as a reminder and as a spur to carefully thinking through the implications of decisions now on the agenda.

I shall therefore conclude with a preliminary analysis of some of the ensuing risks as well as accruing opportunities, taking as my point of departure the German question which has been the focus all through this work. Needless to say, such an analysis can only scratch the surface and will have to leave most 'stones' unturned. Which stones have actually been turned has, above all, been determined by whether NOD was deemed to have any impact on the problems to be uncovered.

One of the most basic problems pertaining to Germany, and one of which Germans and foreigners alike are keenly aware, is that Germany may develop into an economic and political 'regional superpower' with the inalienable potential of becoming a military superpower as well. Following unification, Germany has become a power of such an economical and political standing, that it will *volens nolens* constitute a latent military power of impressive proportions. It will therefore be extremely important to prevent Germany from being perceived as a military threat, since this would only induce its neighbours (and through chain reactions perhaps most of Europe) to build up their defences.

Through the dynamics of the 'security dilemma' and the associated competitive armaments dynamics, such behaviour would, moreover, most likely be countered by Germany, whence a spiralling arms build-up might well ensue. This would not 'only' divert resources from more pressing civilian purposes (such as environmental protection), but might also, in a longer-term perspective, entail risks of war.

The only solution to this problem seems to be to circumvent the inherent dynamism in the armaments competition: to devise ways of making Germany's neighbours more secure without thereby jeopardising Germany's own security, and *vice versa*; and to provide Germany with an adequate defensive capability, even for the worst imaginable contingency, whilst ensuring that this does not provide her with the ability to attack others.

This would, indeed, be tantamount to creating a regime of 'mutual defensive superiority' as described in previous chapters, i.e. a situation in which the relative strength of two contestants would be directly dependent upon who were the attacker and the defender, respectively. Whoever attacked should *ipso facto* be weakened, and whoever merely defended himself strengthened relative to the attacker, so that both sides might simultaneously be 'superior' and *eo ipso* secure.

A fortiori, this would constitute an example of a 'common security regime', i.e. a situation where all states behaved according to the fundamental tenet of the common security philosophy: that genuine security is unobtainable at the expense of other states, but can only be achieved as a 'common good'.

The creation of such a 'mutual defensive superiority regime' would not merely call for reductions in the armed forces, but also for a restructuring and reconfiguration of these forces. They should be designed with a view to specialising in defensive operations on the territory of the state fielding them, i.e. according to NOD criteria. Although most NOD schemes pretend to possess these features, not all of them have struck an appropriate balance between the twin requirements of adequate military efficiency (i.e. defensive capability) and defensiveness, i.e. the absence of offensive potential.

Whilst still standing in need of continuous modification, the 'Spider-in-its-Web' conception of the 'Study Group Alternative Security Policy' (SAS), described in Chapter IV, seems most suitable for meeting these requirements, particularly as far as Germany is concerned. An 'SAS defence posture' would, first of all, possess no capabilities for border-crossing military operations, thus being quite unsuitable for offensive purposes. By virtue thereof, it would deserve its name of 'confidence-building defence'. Secondly, it would allow for an adequate defensive capability, thus also allowing for a defensive self-confidence which could make nuclear deterrence utterly superfluous.

The Spider-and-Web conception might also go a long way towards solving a second problem looming on the horizon: that 'forward defence' might be abandoned by NATO as its guideline, only to be replaced with offensive manoeuvre warfare.

It does, indeed, strain the imagination to envisage a maintenance of a forward defence strategy, for two reasons. First of all, the notion of 'forward' has become exceedingly ambiguous in the light of German unification, since the previous forward line is now located in the middle of Germany, and thus hardly forward in any meaningful sense. However, a forward relocation to the new eastern border of Germany would both be very costly, and undoubtedly quite unacceptable to both Poland and the

USSR. The 'Genscher Plan', on the other hand, effectively implies an abandonment of forward defence in favour of a modified in-depth defence, even though the details of its implementation remain to be worked out. The above is not merely a German problem. If 'forward defence' will be, or has already *de facto* been, abandoned as far as Germany is concerned, i.a. along the previous 'Central Front', it strains the imagination to envisage it maintained elsewhere, since it has always been a particularly German imperative.

Secondly, provisions for genuinely deep cuts in the conventional forces in Europe have already been made under the auspices of the CFE Treaty, and it seems likely that 'CFE-II' (etc.) will cut back the armed forces even further. At some point in this process, however, there simply may not be enough remaining divisions to go round, due to force-to-space constraints. Regardless of improving force-to-force ratios, you can only stretch a traditional division's area of responsibility to a certain limit, beyond which it ceases to defend 'a little less' and ends up not defending at all.

The obvious solution to this problem may come to be seen in some kind of offensive manoeuvre warfare, based on rather small, yet highly mobile and lethal units, in the style of the 'OMG' (Operational Manoeuvre Group) or 'AirLand Battle 2000'. By means of such forces, a modicum of 'conventional retaliation' might come to replace forward defence, as suggested by Samuel Huntington, and (implicitly) by the proverbial 'wolf in sheep's clothing' amongst German NOD proponents, Albrecht von Müller.

There are several indications that NATO is in fact moving in this direction. NATO Secretary General Manfred Wörner has e.g. written that forward defence henceforth will require no stationing of NATO forces along borders in concentrated formations. Rather, the Alliance should investigate the advantages of smaller, more mobile and flexible units. With a view to stressing not only NATO solidarity, but also the strictly defensive intentions of the Alliance, he did, however, envision these formations as multinational forces, and furthermore pointed to a reduced readiness of NATO active units, i.e. a greater reliance on mobilisation.

As SACEUR, John Galvin followed up these ideas by i.a. mentioned cutting the eight corps currently stationed in Germany in half, and transforming them into smaller multinational forces over the next two years. The envisioned multinationality was to be achieved at corps level, with the various corps consisting mainly of forces of one nationality, but including divisions of one or several other nationalities. Finally, the defence ministers of NATO gave their formal approval to proceeding along these lines in the communiquè from the Defence Planning Committee meeting in December 1990, wherein it was stated:

'Our future force posture will be based on smaller, more mobile and flexible active forces, able to respond to aggression from any quarter.

A considerable portion of our forces will be held at lower levels of readiness and availability, but able to be built up and reinforced if the need arises. We will increasingly rely on multinational formations, which will enhance cooperation between Allies and underline the collective nature of our defence arrangements'.

As what might become the first step in this direction, the Franco-German brigade was officially activated by on 17 October 1990. In his speech on this occasion, West German Minister of Defence Gerhard Stoltenberg explicitly mentioned this brigade as a possible model for other multinational forces[2].

Whereas the envisioned multinationality would go a long way towards depriving these forces of their inherent offensive capabilities, some concern may nevertheless be warranted. One might e.g. fear a future situation in which comparatively small-scale, but highly mobile, forces come to be poised against each other. Either of these forces might hope to accomplish a swift and decisive victory through bold strikes in the style of the 'Schlieffen Plan' by means of, say, missiles, aircraft and heliborne forces, seeking to take advantage of the fact that the defending forces are both stretched too thin and not really geared for defensive combat. Under such conditions, 'reciprocal fears of surprise attack' might conceivably arise, and a pre-emptive conventional war just might erupt as a result.

The best way of solving this problem would, once again, seem to be to adopt a genuine non-offensive defence structure, such as e.g. advocated by the SAS. This would place the main emphasis on territorial in-depth defence, whilst still maintaining a modicum of 'forward defence', based primarily on static means, and entailing no offensive capabilities whatsoever. Even a relocation of such frontier defences to the actual border would thus constitute no threat to any neighbouring country. Furthermore, it would enable states to circumvent or transcend the postulated (and partly genuine) force-to-space constraints which only hold true for a mobile defence. The border might thus be defended by means of much smaller numbers of armed forces[3].

One of the advantages of the Cold War was its predictability, implying i.a. that it was fairly clear who would be at war with whom, if at all. This comfortable, and analytically convenient, predictability may already have become a thing of the past. The risk implied by the end of the Cold War and the resulting bipolarity is that Europe may revert to the balance-of-power and war system of previous centuries. This might, conceivably come about as a result of three political processes combined with one military trend.

First of all, the USSR may (indeed, seems predestined to) disintegrate into its constituent parts, roughly contiguous with the present union republics, which may henceforth become sovereign states. Under the influence of a veritable avalanche of nationalism, the Russians may soon come to find the 'burdens of empire' outweighing any accruing benefits, and may hence willingly bid the other non-Russian republics farewell.

Secondly, the USA may 'contract', i.a. by disengaging almost entirely from Europe. Historically, all major empires have evolved through cycles of expansion and contraction, the latter most often preceded by a (sometimes protracted) period of increasingly costly and counterproductive over-extension, during which the discrepancy continues to grow between the marginal costs of, and the marginal gains accruing from, foreign presence[4]. The USA may well be in the middle of this intermediary stage and hence on the verge of contraction. A partial or complete withdrawal and disengagement from Europe would seem to be the obvious response.

Thirdly, as already mentioned, Germany has the potential to become a very powerful state, indeed, both economically and politically, as well as in terms of 'latent military power', regardless of whether this potential is exploited or not.

As a result of these shifts in the correlation of forces, we may end up with a truly multipolar system, in which power differentials matter a great deal more than at present. For the very same reason, realignment may have an impact exceeding what it has at present, when it is the superpowers that, in the final analysis, count.

Whereas these three interrelated trends point towards some form of re-emergent balance-of-power system, it takes a further trend to set the stage for a regression to the 'war system' that traditionally went hand-in-hand with the balance-of-power system: a system in which wars are regarded as viable means for attaining political ends (such as shifting the balance-of-power to one's own advantage). The precondition for this is that wars must, once again, come to be seen as less than suicidal, i.e. 'limited'.

This final ingredient may, at least according to worst-case analysis, be about to make its appearance. As a result i.a. of arms control accomplishments (INF, START and the negotiations of a 'third zero' likely to soon be embarked upon), nuclear weapons may be built down to very low numbers indeed, as compared with present arsenals. The 'nuclear spectre' might thus conceivably be effectively removed, making war appear, once again, a viable political option for the external relations of states. Europe may become 'safe for conventional war'.

Although its validity is impossible to verify empirically, the assumption that nuclear weapons have hitherto deterred war does possess a certain inherent plausibility. The fact that nuclear weapons of immense destructive power are available and usable implies that the prospects of war become highly unattractive, since the immense (indeed, most likely infinite) costs of nuclear war would invariably outweigh any prospective gains. As a consequence thereof, wars that might otherwise have been fought may have been avoided.

Were nuclear first-use, however, to become entirely incredible, nuclear weapons would no longer deter anything but direct nuclear attack on the state in their possession. 'Extended deterrence' would thus have to be abandoned, both geographically and functionally. States would no longer be capable of extending any nuclear 'umbrellas' over other states; nor would they henceforth be able to deter conventional and 'sub-conventional' aggression by means of nuclear deterrence. The result might be a re-emergence of the option of 'Clausewitzian war', i.e. wars waged for positive purposes such as territorial conquest.

There are, however, certain mitigating factors. First of all, even though they can be removed and abolished, nuclear weapons cannot be 'disinvented'. Even after their hypothetical complete abolition, their 'shadow' will inevitably remain. No party to a conflict will ever be in a position to feel entirely sure that his respective adversary may not have concealed some warheads, or may not clandestinely build some. In this sense, 'existential deterrence' is bound to be an enduring feature of the post-1945 world, which can never entirely vanish[5].

Secondly, the USSR and its (former) allies, along with a growing number of Western analysts (including numerous of the *dramatis personae* of the present work), have come to believe that conventional war would inevitably be nearly as totally destructive as nuclear war, due to the extreme vulnerability of post-industrial societies. Even though from a strictly scholarly viewpoint the premises for, as well as with the logic of, this hypothesis seem untenable and flawed, the very belief in this 'TDCW hypothesis' (cf. Chapter X) is bound to militate against any reemerging bellicosity, and thus undermines the thesis of the 'safe conventional war'[6].

There is no obvious panacea for solving the above bundle of inter-related problems all at once, but their solution necessitates a concerted effort along many parallel paths, and by many states acting in unison.

Germany's Responsibility

Germany might take the lead in some of these respects. It might, first of all, take advantage of its former status as the 'bone of contention', according to the persuasive logic: 'If this works here, it is bound to do so elsewhere as well'. Secondly, it might exploit the uniqiue opportunities stemming from 'starting from scratch'. This, in its turn, raises the question of what Germany might do in order to play this role?

First of all, Germany might show conspicuous disregard for traditional balance-of-power considerations, just as she has already done to a considerable extent. Even though East Germany's departure from the Soviet bloc constituted an obvious case of realignment, the Germans remained insistent that this had no negative effects on the party thus deprived of a former ally, *in casu* the USSR. From this endeavour, and the lessons it has *eo ipso* constituted, some important facts may have been grasped by other actors in the international system as well.

Secondly, Germany might embark on what might be called 'prophylactic confidence-building', i.e. relieving fears before they arise, as she has, in fact, done to a large extent already. Some of the required steps would be of a clearly non-military nature, such as promises of economic assistance to the East, of continued commitment to the EC (and NATO for that matter), etc. Others would have to deal more directly with relieving fears on the part of neighbouring states that the wherewithal of a regional military superpower might be exploited for aggressive purposes, bearing in mind that the German past has been anything but confidence-inspiring.

The fact that Germany renounced the acquisition of nuclear weapons was an important element in this confidence-building. Even though there have been isolated voices in favour of a 'controlled nuclear proliferation' in general, and a German rise to nuclear status in particular (John J. Mearsheimer[7]), most of Germany's neighbours would feel very unconfortable, indeed, with German nuclear weapons.

The build-down of the *Bundeswehr* to the 370,000 men agreed upon in the 'Two-Plus-Four' negotiations, likewise, went some way towards military confidence-building, but one has to keep in mind the German reputation for efficiency. Even a force this size consisting of Germans might be quite awe—and perhaps fear-inspiring in the eyes of less potent foreigners.

There thus remains a need for qualitative measures alongside the quantitative restrictions. One again, changing to an NOD structure would appear to be the obvious solution, and might imply various restrictions and/or self-imposed constraints with regard to equipment, deployment patterns, etc.

This, however, is not an entirely unproblematic objective to pursue. Bearing in mind the ill fate of the Versailles Treaty which imposed constraints on Germany's military potential, it remains imperative to avoid any semblance of German 'singularization'. Germany should not be allowed to feel that any military precautions with regard to her military might were discriminatory. They hence have to be embedded in broader schemes of restructuring the armed forces of other states as well as of remodelling the entire international system.

The appropriate conception for this purpose may be that of Collective Security, combined with some notion of a European 'settlement', i.e. a genuine European 'Peace Order'. Such ideas have until very recently appeared as too 'idealist', and indeed far-fetched, to most analysts of a more 'realist' persuasion (including the present author). The time may, however, have come to reconsider the matter.

Collective Security in Europe and Beyond

The reason why collective security was (correctly) regarded as unrealistic in the past was that it did not take into account the East-West conflict, which was considered (also correctly) to be a genuine conflict of interest, rather than merely a figment of the imagination or, indeed, a propaganda ploy contrived by militarists.

Although this premise used to be true, it is becoming less and less so. The Soviet Union has adopted the defensive principles, is in the process of withdrawing from Eastern Europe, and has embarked upon a programme of internal reform which will most likely bring it very close, indeed, to a 'Western' type of society, with multiple political parties competing for power, a free public debate without censorship, and with at least a modicum of a market economy. The entire East-West conflict thus seems about to vanish into thin air. A number of Western authors have taken this *ad notam* and have, as a corollary, begun to seriously contemplate collective security regimes[8].

Because the East-West conflict must be acknowledged as being a thing of the past, and because there may no longer be any compelling need for a military defence of the West against the East (or *vice versa*), the time may have come to embark upon a truly radical transformation of the military relationship, a change that would require a genuine 'paradigm shift' in all security policy thinking.

Collective security may, indeed, be the appropriate conception in this respect. It might provide the only acceptable form of external intervention into the internal affairs of European countries, such as might e.g. have been called for, had the *Securitate* prevailed in the internecine struggle in Romania in December 1989. It might, likewise, be the most realistic framework for peace-keeping, and perhaps peace-restoring, operations with regard to intra-European conflicts in the future, say, between Greece and Turkey, Romania and Hungary, or whatever.

A collective security arrangement might, furthermore, be a pre-condition for all individual countries scaling down their defence postures to strictly defensive, territorial defence systems, which entail no options of military operations beyond their own borders. Combined with a build-down of alliance commitments, such a restructuring might place small, remote, or otherwise particularly vulnerable, countries (such as Norway, Iceland, Luxemburg or Albania) at the mercy of their great-power neighbours, such as the USSR or Russia, the USA, the UK, Germany or Yugoslavia. Since such countries would remain in need of external aid for certain contingencies, and since such aid would no longer be available from allied countries (whether on a national scale, or as alliances), a collective security arrangement might be the only realistic fall-back option.

A Collective Security regime would be tantmount to such an enormous transformation of military and security policy affairs that it could not possibly be implemented over night. Furthermore, the modalities would need to be thought through carefully. The following are a few (highly tentative) suggestions herefore, which place a special emphasis on the all-too-often neglected military element.

—The 'European Collective Security Organisation' (ECSO) should comprise all European states, including the USSR, the USA and, if it so desires, Canada.

—ECSO should be registered as a regional UN organisation, and non-European states should be represented as observers (perhaps most realistically on a rotational basis) in its bodies, as well as have the right to be consulted.

—The highest authority in ECSO should be a General Assembly, subordinate to which should be an executive power, comprising a Security Council as well as a permanent Secretariat.

—The voting rules in the General Assembly should be a combination of the 'one state, one vote' and 'one man, one vote' principles, best attainable through a two-chamber arrangement. In the 'Chamber of States', the former principle should prevail, and all states, from the USSR to Liechtenstein, should thus be treated as equals. In the 'Chamber of Peoples', however, the larger states should have a proportionally greater say.

—In the Security Council, decisions should, in most matters, be reached by consensus, but in matters of extreme urgency and/or severity a majority of, say, two-thirds or four-fifths in both chambers of the General Assembly might overrule this veto.

—Subordinated to the Security Council should be a military organisation (ECSOM).

—ECSOM should have at its disposal assigned forces from the member states (with shares proportional to a weighted means of GNP and population) as well as major weapons systems in secure storage during peacetime (e.g. in an arrangement implying that British troops would serve as 'custodians' for German weapons stored on Soviet territory, and *vice versa*).

—The military means at ECSOM's disposal should include weapons systems with a clear offensive potential, such as MBTs, major surface combatants, fighter-bombers, etc. Some of the assigned forces should be heliborne troops and amphibious forces.

—ECSOM should conduct frequent staff exercises as well as regular small-scale field exercises, say, with the participation of 1,000-10,000 troops. The responsibility for providing the participating troops as well as for hosting the exercises should be distributed on a rotational basis.

—No indivudual state should be allowed to field military forces in excess of one-third of the total number in Europe.

—National armed forces should be strictly non-offensive, i.e. no state party to ECSO should be allowed to field military forces with any offensive potential, the criteria for which should be worked out by ECSOM and decided by the ECSO General Assembly.

—All states should have the right to conduct challenge on-site inspections on the territory of any other member state in order to verify that this rule is abided by. Suspected violations could be brought before the Security Council and the General Assembly, subsequent to consultations by the ECSOM staff.

Such a collective security regime might constitute one of the foundations for the construction of a genuine 'common security regime' (on a regional level), which might, in its turn, amount to what is often called the 'Common European House'. In such a house, all the 'tenants' would have basically common interests in the wellbeing of their common house. Each European state should thus assume a share of the responsibility, both for preventing war and for violent internecine struggle, as well as for promoting prosperity and wellbeing elsewhere in Europe. They should all join ranks in the fight against the common problems they are all facing: pollution, wasteful consumption of natural resources in short supply, human rights violations, etc.

There remains, however, the perennial 'out-of-area problem', the severity of which the world was reminded by Iraq's attack on Kuwait. This event was quite unexpected (except perhaps by area specialists), and raised new problems not foreseen by the 'NOD community'. The available NOD literature, likewise, gave no answers to the question of how to handle such an instance of outright aggression in violation of all the principles of international law.

An apparent answer, which is not really satisfactory, might be that if only Kuwait had adopted an NOD defence posture, and perhaps joined forces with likeminded states in the region in a strictly defensive alliance, the Iraqi invasion could never have happened.

Seductive though such an argument might appear, the forces of Saddam Hussein did in fact invade and successfully so, at least from a narrow military viewpoint. Furthermore, they henceforth enjoyed the advantages of the defender which have so persistently been pointed out by NOD advocates. The situation of the 'attacker-turned-defender' is militarily quite advantageous, if only because it forces the victim of aggression to operate under the disadvantageous role of 'defender-turned-attacker': Whereas the original invader is able to 'dig in' and defend his conquest from prepared positions, the actual defender is forced to expose himself on open ground, and to operate on exterior lines; he is dependent on better than 3:1 ratios on the tactical level, etc. Finally, the aggressor could employ a nearly risk-free 'scorched earth' strategy, since the country subjected to devastation is not his own.

This is neither tantamount to saying that the situation of the defender-turned-attacker (i.e. Kuwait and its allies) is hopeless, nor that the invader can enjoy the fruits of his victory unchallenged. It does, however, point to the existential risks still facing small states with stronger and unscrupulous neighbours, even in the 'post-Cold War era'.

These problems also constitute a challenge to NOD thinking, lest it be relegated to the status of a policy and/or strategy of merely historical relevance for a particular region in an era which already belongs to the past. The problem does, furthermore, appear to be two-pronged.

First of all: how is the present situation to be resolved, i.e. Iraq made to return to the *status quo ante bellum* with a minimum of bloodshed and suffering on both sides? Secondly: how is a repetition of such aggression to be prevented in the future, not merely as far as the Gulf region is concerned, but everywhere.

The blockade was an *ad hoc* response to an unexpected challenge, and as such pretty much the best that could be hoped for under the circumstances. It would, however, have been better if the UN had been invested beforehand with the formal power and the material wherewithal to impose and enforce the blockade, i.e. if a genuine and working collective security system had been in existence.

This might also be the appropriate answer to the second question of how to prevent similar contingencies from ever arising again. A combination of regional-scale conversion to NOD with regional and global collective security arrangements might preserve peace in the future, in the Third World as well as in the Europe of tomorrow where the 'ties of amity and enmity' are less durable and dependable than today.

The conversion of national armed forces to strictly NOD-type forces could go a long way towards averting aggression, by strengthening defensive capabilities whilst diminishing any pre-emptive urges. The collective security arrangement would serve as a 'safety net' under (particularly smaller) states which might nevertheless be attacked, since it would ensure them of assistance in times of peril.

However, in order for such a collective security system to perform its role (and, by so doing, make individual states comfortable with strictly defensive postures) it would need at its disposal military means which would have been rightly called 'offensive' if fielded by individual states: forces with long-range ('strategic') mobility, with the ability to move forward under fire, to break through prepared defence lines, etc.

Whereas such capabilities are correctly rejected as destabilising in a national context, they would be far from threatening if fielded by a global organisation. It may thus be time to work out schemes for a combination of the new conception of NOD with the old (but wellnigh forgotten) notion of collective security.

Notes

(See Bibliography for publishing details of works quoted)

Preface

1. Cf. Buzan & al. 1990, 165-185; Wagner, Richard L. 1990; Møller 1990.
2. Cf. Hamm & Pohlmann 1990; 1990a.
3. Garthoff 1988; Holden 1989; 1991; MccGwire 1987; 1988; 1988a; 1988b; Krause 1988; Snyder 1987; 1988; Holloway 1989.

Chapter I: What NOD is and What it is Not

1. Wittgenstein 1953, 32.
2. Herz 1950; Jervis 1976, 58-93; 1978; Buzan 1983, 171-213.
3. Independent Commission 1982; Bahr & Lutz, eds. 1986; cf. Møller 1988a; 1989b; 1990a.
4. Schelling 1960, 227-229.
5. Cf. Betts 1987.
6. Newhouse 1973, 176.
7. Bundy 1986; Beaufre 1960, 73-75; 1965, 107-123; Boserup 1989; Neild 1990, 46-73.
8. Bundy & al. 1982; Union of Concerned Scientists 1983; Steinbruner & Sigal, eds. 1983; Blackaby & al., eds. 1984; Møller 1988.
9. Schelling & Halperin 1961, 9-17; Frei 1983.
10. Tuchman 1962; Miller, ed. 1985; O'Ballance 1972.
11. Cf. Wohlstetter 1958; Brodie 1959; Schelling 1960; McNamara 1968, 51-67; cf. Freedman 1983, 121-257; Ball & al. 1987; Møller 1989d.
12. Jervis 1978, 187; cf. Rathjens 1973.
13. Cf. Møller 1987a; 1990d; idem & Wiberg 1989; Neild 1989.
14. Glucksmann 1967, 42-43; Weizsäcker 1976, 116, 150, 165-166; Boserup 1985; 1990a; Møller 1987a.
15. Osgood 1962; Etzioni 1962; cf. George 1988.
16. Galtung 1984, 172-176; Quester 1986, 23; cf. 1977, 83.
17. Barnaby & Boeker 1988, 137.
18. Bloch 1898, esp. vol. 6.
19. Mearsheimer 1982; 1988; 1989; cf. Boserup 1990b.
20. Hart 1967; Beaufre 1963; 1972; 1974; Luttwak 1987.
21. Mao 1936, 213.
22. Wohlstetter 1958; cf. Kaplan 1983, 85-110.
23. Hart 1967, 334; cf. Jomini 1811, vol. 4, 275-286.
24. Neild 1986; cf. Lanchester 1916; Lepingwell 1987.
25. Digby 1975; Kaldor 1981; Hannig 1984; Barnaby 1986; idem & Boeker 1982.
26. Vigor 1983.
27. Cf. Møller 1989e; 1989f.
28. Buzan 1983, 156-172.
29. Smit 1989; cf. Schwarz 1989, 15-21.

30. Best 1983, 315-330; De Lupis 1987, 233-235...
31. Galtung 1984, 180-184; cf. Walzer 1977, 176-196.

Chapter II: A Country in the Heart of Europe

1. Jervis 1982; George & al. 1988; Dean 1988a.
2. Buzan 1986, 8; 1983, 105-115; 1986; idem & al. 1990, 31-44; cf. Møller 1989c.
3. Mead 1990; Papcke & Weidenfeld, eds. 1988; Schlögel 1989: Voigt 1988a; Weidenfeld 1988.
4. Deutsch & al. 1957; Schlotter 1982.
5. Herz 1950; Jervis 1976, 58-93; 1978; Buzan 1983, 173-213.
6. Snyder, G. 1984; Sharp 1987.
7. Krell 1990, 7; Binnendijk 1989; Ramsbotham 1989, 72-74; Szabo 1990, 5.
8. Buzan 1983, 156-172.
9. Cf. Hart 1967; Beaufre 1963; Luttwak 1987; Gaddis 1982; Kennan 1987; Buzan & al., 117.
10. McAdams 1990, 371, 373.
11. Kipling, quoted in Uhle-Wettler 1989, 117.
12. Burley 1989, 65; Krell 1989, 4; cf. Loth 1989, 18; Buzan & al. 1990, 108-109.
13. McAdams 1990, 358-361.
14. Michalka & Niedhart, eds. 1980, 123-140; Mann 1968, 14-16; cf. for the opposite opinion, Geiss 1985; 1985a; 1990.
15. Mann 1968, 225.
16. Mattes 1985; Dibb 1988, 42-44; Smith, R. 1985, 8-11.
17. Michalka & Niedhart, eds. 1980, 141-142; Hecker 1989, 15-27; Mann 1968, 33; Gorlov, ed. 1990.
18. Haberl 1989, 231-237; cf. Dibb 1988.
19. Loth 1989, 121-128.
20. Der Spiegel, 1990:29, 16-18; Frankfurter Allgemeine Zeitung, 16.09.1990.
21. Brigot 1989.
22. Quoted in Weisenfeld 1989, 22-23.
23. Weisenfeld 1989, 16-27, 59-60.
24. Loth 1989, 56-64; Weisenfeld 1989, 84, 95, 110-111.
25. Loth 1989, 61-63; Weisenfeld 1989, 175, 207; Schilling 1989.
26. Bauer 1989; Manfrass-Sirjacques 1990.
27. Weisenfeld 1989, 15, 33, 66, 125.
28. Aron, quoted in Weisenfeld 1989, 164.
29. Kaiser & Lellouche, eds. 1987, 308-313; cf. Herbst 1989, 193-206; Gnesotto 1987; Ruehl 1986a; Renouard 1986; Fritsch-Bournazel 1987; Ehrhart 1987; Pleiner 1987.
30. Buzan & al. 1990, 151.
31. Moisi 1990.
32. Bluth 1988; Freedman 1988; Bertram 1988; Alford 1988.
33. Baring 1988; Hanrieder 1990.
34. Smyser 1989.
35. Bredow 1989; cf. Hassner 1983.
36. Michalka & Niedhart, eds. 1980, 144, 367-368; Müller, R.-D. 1990.
37. Bingen 1989, 161-166; Posser 1990; Bundesregierung 1977, 32-35.
38. Mann 1968, 67-68; cf. Michalka & Niedhart 1980, 208; Miksche 1990, 60-69; Hartmann 1990.
39. Erb 1989.
40. Stürmer 1989, 722.
41. Weidenfeld 1983, 24-25;'Ai/Sa' 1990.
42. Bussmann 1983, 65; Rovan 1983; Schulze 1987; Rudolf Augstein in Der Spiegel, 1990:27, 30-39.
43. Vossler 1974, 87-99; Stadelmann 1970, 119-141; Jessen, ed. 1973, 131-194, 289-351; Bussmann 1983; Brandt, H-H. 1987.
44. Bussmann 1983, 78-81; Stürmer 1983; Hamerow 1973, 87-144, 266-267.
45. Mann 1968, 11-12, 147; Geiss 1985; 1985a; Stürmer 1983, 97.
46. Seiffert 1986, 57-68.

47. Weidenfeld 1983, 38; Krockow 1983, 166-167; Hättich 1983, 278-279; Rausch 1983, 120-122, 130-145; Seiffert 1986, 269; Mommsen 1983, 171-174.
48. Jansen 1989.
49. Hacker 1989; Schweisfurth 1989; Bahr 1985b; Bark & Gress 1989:1, 510-513.
50. Seiffert 1986, 8-9, 15-16, 144-161.
51. Seiffert 1986, 144-161; Kiessling 1989; Loth 1989, 65-88; Jesse 1989.
52. Jansen 1989.
53. Becker 1986; Jacobsen 1986; Ritter 1985; Stent 1987; Lucas 1990, 115-176; Garthoff 1985, 45-46; 1029-1038; Wörmann 1987.
54. Kennedy 1978, 227-358; Wolter & Meuner 1970, 234-283; Wagner 1988; 1990.
55. Based on Mechtersheimer & Barth 1986; IISS 1988; Arkin & Fieldhouse 1984; Duke 1989, 56-148.
56. Cf. Schmähling 1990, 177.
57. Wagner 1988; 1990.
58. Mechtersheimer & Barth 1986, 25-54; Duke 1989, 66-68.
59. Duke 1989, 63, 83.
60. Stromseth 1988, 23-25; Kelleher 1987.
61. Stromseth 1988, 18, 23; Mechtesheimer & Barth 1986, 111.
62. Arkin & Fieldhouse 1984, 102; Arkin 1986.
63. Mechtersheimer & Barth 1986, 134; cf. Robinson 1986, 38-43, 69-70.
64. Hagena 1990; Bebermeyer 1984; 1989; 1990; idem & Grass 1984; Grass 1984; 1990; Schmidt, H.F. 1988; Bernhardt 1988; Thimann 1989a.
65. Lippert 1987.
66. MccGwire 1986, 117-139; Farwick 1985.
67. Weizsäcker, ed. 1971; Smit 1989; Vogt 1989a.
68. *Frankfurter Rundschau*, 27.01.1990; Wiesendahl 1989; Vogt 1989; 1990.

Chapter III: The Predecessors

1. Clausewitz 1832, 20-21, 360-66 (Book I.1 and VI.1-2, respectively); cf. Wallach 1967, 13-51, 103-118; 1986; Aron 1983, 144-171; Gat 1988.
2. Clausewitz 1832, 29-30, 34 (I.1), 43, 49-50 (I.2), 193-197 (III.16); cf. Boserup 1990.
3. Clausewitz 1832, 369 (VI.3), 521-528 (VI.26); cf. Hahlweg 1986.
4. Kant 1788, 53; cf. Piepmeier 1987; Independent Commission 1982.
5. Kant 1795, 17-18; cf. Bald, ed. 1987; idem & Klein, eds. 1988.
6. Ropp 1962, 152-160; Holborn 1986; Howard 1976, 86-87, 100-101; McNeil 1983, 242-256; Jones, A. 1988, 392-408; Gat 1989, 156-198.
7. Tuchman 1962, 33-161. On Germany, see: Holborn 1941; Wallach 1967, 52-181; 1972, 89-135; Howard 1985; Evera 1985; Snyder, J. 1984, 107-156; Rothenberg 1986; Geiss 1985a, 42-57. On France, see: Snyder, J. 1984, 57-106; Wallach 1972, 137-164; Possony & Mantoux 1941.
8. Treitschke, quoted in Hamerow 1973, 307-308.
9. Holborn 1986; Bald 1990, 2-7.
10. Bernardi, quoted in Bald 1990, 6.
11. Wieland 1990; cf. Bald 1990, 5.
12. Bald 1987, 20-26; cf. Stülpnagel (1924), ibid., 68.
13. Bald 1987, 26-30.
14. Stülpnagel in Bald 1987, 29-30; cf. Afheldt, H. 1983.
15. Perret 1985; Posen 1984, 179-219; Geyer 1986, 54-57; Griffith 1978, 9-11; cf. Scott & Scott, eds. 1982, 27-65; Hart 1951; Mearsheimer 1988a; Gorlov, ed. 1990.
16. Cf. Kaplan 1983, 185-201; Freedman 1983, 91-120.
17. Strauss in *Der Spiegel*, 1989:39, 123-126.
18. Etzold & Gaddis 1978, 73.
19. 'PPS 23' (24.02.1948), in Etzold & Gaddis 1978, 118.
20. Wettig 1967, 363-375, 450-487, 523-589; Mayne 1970, 196-197, 204-205; Schubert 1970, 26-31, 98-121; Herbst 1989, 87-104; Fritsch-Bournazel 1987, 65-69; Gnesotto 1986, 6-7.
21. Mayne 1970, 216; Bluth 1988, 3-7.
22. Schubert 1970, 34.

278   NOTES

23. Griffith 1978, 55-56; Foschepoth 1988a, 45-50; Schubert 1970, 165; cf. Daniil Melnikow in *Der Spiegel*, 1990:49, 185-190.
24. Schubert 1970, 165-175; Herbst 1989, 117-126.
25. Freedman 1983, 139-154; Holloway 1984, 15-55.
26. Schramm & al. 1972, 388, 402-407; Blechman & Kaplan 1978, 356-385; Adomeit 1982, 183-311.
27. Schramm & al. 1972, 388-390, 392-394, 401-402, 410-413; cf. Stefanic 1988; Dobrosielski 1990.
28. Schramm & al. 1972, 413-414; Griffith 1978, 81-83; Stehle 1989.
29. Schramm & al. 1972, 5-6; Albrecht, ed. 1986, 68; cf. Howard 1958.
30. Kennan 1958, 66; cf. 1972, 249; Brinkley 1987.
31. Albrecht, ed. 1986, 81-88.
32. Schramm & al. 1972, 13-17; Albrecht, ed. 1986, 71-76.
33. Howard 1958, 81.
34. Ropper 1964; Vetschera 1985; 1985a; idem & Rocca 1985; Aichinger & Maiwald 1989.
35. Foschepoth 1988; 1988a; Herbst 1989; Schubert 1970, 104-121; Sommer 1988; Schröder 1988, 130-132.
36. Quoted in Foschepoth, ed. 1988, 289-290.
37. Griffith 1978, 85-87; Foschepoth 1988a, 65-65.
38. Schubert 1970; Wettig 1967; Bark & Gress 1989:1, 272-291; 366-372; Brill 1987.
39. Schneider 1984, 64; Fischer 1975, 32-34; Schubert 1970, 65-66; Brill 1987, 90-93; cf. for the quotation: Rautenberg & Wiggershaus 1977, 40.
40. Schubert 1970, 42-48; Brill 1987, 82, 190-192.
41. Quoted in Afheldt 1989a, 15.
42. Schubert 1970, 45-46, 164-165.
43. Albrecht, ed. 1986, 60-65.
44. Brill 1987, 81-82.
45. Bonin 1954; Brill 1987, 93-94, 150.
46. Brill 1987, 120-129.
47. Brill 1987, 130-131.
48. Brill 1987, 138-150.
49. Brill 1987, 150-165.
50. Bonin & al. 1955, 24.
51. Albrecht, ed. 1986, 133-135; Bonin 1955.
52. Bonin 1955a, 50; cf. Griffith 1978, 59-80; Foschepoth 1988a; Klessman 1988.
53. Brill 1987, 176-189.
54. Schramm & al. 1972, 9-11; cf. Hacker 1989, 48-49.
55. Albrecht, ed., 17-18.
56. Rosolowsky 1987, 13-30; Hacker 1989, 51-53.
57. Schramm & al. 1972, 18-19.
58. Schramm & al. 1972, 11-13, 19-20.
59. Griffith 1978, 69; Brandstetter 1987; Bark & Gress 1989:1, 499-509.
60. Griffith 1978, 102; Bender 1986a, 77.
61. Barke & Gress 1989:1, 510-513.
62. Longerich, ed. 1990, 230-233; Griffith 1978, 115-120, 131-225; Rosolowsky 1987, 43-44; Bender 1986a, 115-151; Schramm & al. 1972, 150-154, 166-168, 217-227; Joffe 1984, 175-177; Bark & Gress 1989:2, 90-112, 166-223, 321-331.
63. Foschepoth 1988a, 33-34.
64. Dean 1985a; McAdams 1986.
65. Garthoff 1985, 473-479.
66. Kaser 1987; Schmitt 1988, 16-26; Wörmann 1986; Jacobsen 1986; Ritter 1985.
67. Cf. Risse-Kappen 1988.
68. Stromseth 1988.
69. Scoville 1982; Newhouse 1989, 309-311; Borkenhagen 1984b; Szabo 1990, 22-27.
70. Cf. Haftendorn 1986, 11-31; Lodgaard 1982; 1983; Brauch 1983a; 1983b; Joffe 1987, 60-90; Szabo 1990, 27-30.
71. Bundy & al. 1982; Kaiser & al. 1982; Krell & al. 1983; Krause 1986; Lübkemeier 1988.
72. Independent Commission 1982, 147-149.

73. Freedman 1983, 313-330; Bowie 1963; Buchan 1964; Stromseth 1988, 75-88.
74. Yost 1984; Deschamps 1987, 31-42; Lucas 1986; Bluth 1986. On the EDI, see, Wörner 1986; Rühl 1986; Enders 1986; cf. Brauch 1989. On SDI cooperation, see Engels & Scheffran 1987.
75. Rühl 1982; Dean 1987a, 153-184; Müller, M. 1988a.
76. FM 100-5, 1982; Kipp 1987; Grünen im Bundestag 1984, D35.
77. Hennes 1985; Huffschmid & al. 1986.

Chapter IV: Models of Non-Offensive Defence

1. Cf. Roberts 1976; Agrell 1979; Ries 1988; Lukic 1984; Bundeskanzleramt 1985.
2. Afheldt 1971a; 1976; cf. Trempnau 1983; Afheldt 1983; cf. 1985a; Weizsäcker, ed. 1984; Carton 1984; Afheldt 1989.
3. Weizsäcker, ed. 1971; particularly Afheldt 1971a, 50.
4. Afheldt 1971b, 438.
5. Afheldt 1976, 53.
6. Afheldt 1977, 447.
7. Afheldt 1976, 220.
8. Afheldt 1976, 86.
9. Afheldt 1976, 230; cf. Clausewitz 1832, 17 (Book 1.1.2).
10. Afheldt 1976, 269, 289, 297-298; 1983; 1984a.
11. Afheldt 1987c, 67.
12. Afheldt 1989a, 36-37.
13. Afheldt 1976, 324-325 et passim; cf. 1978b, 263-279; cf. Reich 1990.
14. Afheldt 1984a, 61; cf. Kant 1788, 53.
15. Afheldt 1976, 231.
16. Afheldt 1978a, 640; cf. Jervis 1978. On the security dilemma, see e.g. Herz 1951; Jervis 1976, 58-93; Buzan 1983, 171-213; Møller 1992.
17. Rathjens 1973.
18. Afheldt 1984c, 19; 1983, 44, 59-60.
19. Afheldt 1976, 147; 1983, 149, 151; cf. 1987c, 34-41.
20. Afheldt 1983, 81; cf. 1987c, 220-229.
21. Afheldt 1984c, 19.
22. Cf. Best 1983, 315-330; De Lupis 1987, 233-235.
23. Afheldt 1983, 133-143; Ebert 1984.
24. Afheldt 1976, 218.
25. Afheldt 1987c, 292.
26. Afheldt 1988, 404-405; cf. 1989a, 102, 153.
27. Cf. Hart 1967; Beaufre 1963; Luttwak 1987.
28. Afheldt 1983, 47-49.
29. Brossolet 1976; Spannochi 1976.
30. Afheldt 1976, 247.
31. Afheldt 1976, 249.
32. Afheldt 1976, 263; cf. Afheldt, E. 1984, 77,88.
33. Afheldt, H. 1983, 126.
34. Afheldt 1976, 270.
35. Afheldt, E. 1984, 53-63.
36. Afheldt, H. 1976, 255-258.
37. Afheldt 1976, 261-262.
38. Afheldt 1983, 57-58, 89-91; cf. Acker 1984.
39. Afheldt 1989a, 117.
40. Freundl 1984.
41. Afheldt 1976, 263; cf. 1983, 128.
42. Afheldt 1983, 83, 131.
43. Afheldt 1987a, 9; 1987c, 302-303.
44. Afheldt 1987b, 165.
45. Afheldt 1988, 406-407.
46. Mechtersheimer 1987, 149-150; Schulze-Marmeling 1987, 222-223.

47. Krause 1987a, 49.
48. Hinrichs 1977; Loquai 1982; Steinsäcker 1982; Willmann in Afheldt, E. & al. 1985, 116-117; Lather 1982; Informationsdienst Sicherheitspolitik 1984, 5; Bergstein 1985; Schulte 1985, 476; Krause 1987b.
49. Afheldt 1989a, 20.
50. Afheldt 1989a, 22.
51. Afheldt 1989a, 29-30.
52. Afheldt 1989a, 92-97, 162-163.
53. Afheldt 1989a, 170-176, 204.
54. Afheldt 1989a, 208, 214.
55. Hannig 1984; cf. 1986a; 1979; 1981.
56. Hannig 1984, 34-51.
57. Cf. Gibson 1941; Posen 1984, 105-140.
58. Hannig 1984, 60-62, 47.
59. Hannig 1984, 66-69, 82-89.
60. Hannig 1984, 95-103, 114, 129.
61. Hannig 1986b; cf. e.g. ESECS 1983.
62. Hannig 1984, 130-131.
63. Hannig 1984, 110-111.
64. Hannig 1984, 116-120.
65. Hannig 1984, 134-139.
66. Hannig 1984, 152-154.
67. Hannig 1988, 449-450.
68. Gerber 1985; 1987.
69. Gerber 1984; 1988.
70. Hannig 1987, 31.
71. Hannig 1986c; 1990.
72. Hannig 1986c, 20.
73. Snyder, G. 1984.
74. Alternative Defence Commission 1987; Ørvik 1986.
75. Albrecht 1982a, 148; 1985, 155.
76. Albrecht 1985, 156-165; cf. Møller 1989c; 1989d; 1990a; 1990b; Bomsdorf 1989.
77. Albrecht 1985, 159-160.
78. Albrecht 1990, 124-130.
79. Senghaas 1986; 1987; 1988; 1989.
80. Senghaas 1986, 103-107; 1988, 78-81.
81. Senghaas 1986, 106.
82. Senghaas 1987; 1988, 81-87.
83. Senghaas 1988, 82.
84. Senghaas 1986, 114-116.
85. Afheldt, E. 1984; cf. 1984a, 115-116; idem & al. 1985, 117.
86. Afheldt, E. 1984, 51-53, 63-67.
87. Afheldt, E. 1984, 51, 64.
88. Afheldt, E. 1984, 56-70.
89. Bertele 1982, 381.
90. Bertele 1982, 392, 394.
91. Löser 1982a, 19-70, 207-218; cf. Mao 1936; Beaufre 1963; 1965; 1972; 1974.
92. Löser 1982a, 73.
93. Löser 1982, 51, 130-133.
94. Löser 1982, 9, 22-45; cf. Hackett & al. 1979.
95. Löser 1982, 15, 54-55, 62-65, 77-79; cf. Lutz 1989c.
96. Löser 1982, 89-95, 195-201, 133, 179; cf. Best 1983, 315-330; De Lupis 1987, 233-235.
97. Löser 1982, 81, 83.
98. Löser 1982, 184, 187.
99. Löser 1982, 259-266.
100. Löser 1982, 129-30.
101. Löser 1982, 115, 118-119, 131, 185-189, 264-266.
102. Löser 1982, 132, 265; cf. Simpkin 1986, 227-240; Creveld 1985, 270-271.

103. Löser 1982, 259-266; cf.1985a, 530.
104. Löser 1982, 265; cf. Møller 1989a.
105. Löser 1982, 266, 184, 96-105.
106. Löser 1982, 192-194, 177, 208; cf. Osgood 1962; Etzioni 1962; cf. George 1988.
107. Löser 1982, 209-10.
108. Löser 1982, 176; UCS 1983; cf. Löser & Anderson 1984, 80-81.
109. Löser & Anderson 1984, 69-70, 75-76, 143-144, 151; FM 100-5; cf. Møller 1987a; Kipp 1987; Rogers 1985.
110. Löser & Anderson 1984, 45, 55; Löser 1985a, 525-26, 531; cf. on FOFA: Rogers 1983; 1985; Wijk 1986; Sutton & al. 1984; Farndale 1988; OTA 1987.
111. Löser & Anderson 1984, 53, 57-62.
112. Löser 1985a, 525-526; 1986a, 530.
113. Löser 1987a, 59.
114. Löser & Anderson 1984, 121; Löser 1985b, 295; 1990, 135-137.
115. Löser & Schilling 1984, 145-166; Löser 1985b.
116. Löser & Schilling 1984, 24-37; 142; cf. Löser 1985b, 301-02; 1987b; 1990, 142.
117. Dürr, Afheldt & Müller 1984.
118. Cf. Boserup & Neild, eds. 1990.
119. Müller, A. 1984a; cf. 1988b.
120. Müller 1987b, 9-10; 1989, 122-125; cf. Epstein 1985; 1988; 1990; Posen 1984; 1988; Biddle 1988.
121. Müller 1987a, 60.
122. *Frankfurter Rundschau*, 1. 06. 1983; cf. Müller 1987a, 60.
123. Müller, A. 1986a, 248-49; 1986b, 216-220; 1989, 129-130.
124. Müller, A. 1989, 128-129.
125. Müller, A. 1988c.
126. Müller, A. 1985, 276-279; 1986b, 205-208; 1987b, Annex; 1989, 127-129.
127. Müller, A. 1988c, 91.
128. Glucksman 1967, 42-43; cf. Clausewitz 1832, 360-363 (Book 6.1); Boserup 1985.
129. Müller, A. 1986a, 253-254; 1987c, 519; 1988c, 92-93.
130. Huntington 1983; Papp 1984; Dunn & Staudenmeier 1985.
131. Müller, A. 1987a, 61.
132. Müller & Karkoszka 1988; cf. Müller, A. 1988.
133. Müller, A. 1987a, 62.
134. Schmückle & Müller 1988; cf. Müller, A. 1989a, 340-341.
135. Haeberlin & al. 1985.
136. SALSS 1984a; Unterseher 1987a, 78; 1990a.
137. Cf. Johnson & al. 1980; Herspring & Volgyes 1980; Volgyes 1982; McCausland 1986; MacGregor 1986.
138. Mearsheimer 1982; 1988; 1989; cf. for critique: Epstein 1989; Luttwak 1987, 118-120. On Soviet standards, see Hines 1982; Erickson & al. 1986, 161-163.
139. Chalmers & Unterseher 1987, 57-58.
140. Grass 1984; 1990; Hartwig 1989; Thimann 1989.
141. Bebermeyer 1984; 1989; 1990; idem & Grass 1984; cf. Buzan 1983, 156-172.
142. Cf. Vogt 1989; 1990.
143. Canby 1985; 1985a.
144. SALSS 1984a, 33-34; cf. Møller 1987a.
145. Unterseher 1987b; 1989h, 299-308; 1989, 149-151; 1989e; cf. FM 100-5, 1982; Huntington 1983.
146. Unterseher 1984b, 111-115; SAS 1984b, 156; Møller 1988; cf. Bundy & al. 1982; Steinbruner & Sigal, eds. 1983; Blackaby & al., eds. 1984.
147. Unterseher 1987a, 77, 80; Møller 1989d; cf. Tuchmann 1962; Miller, ed. 1985.
148. Brauch 1987a, 26-31, 39-41, 52.
149. Unterseher 1984b, 126.
150. SALSS 1984b; Unterseher 1984c, 214-222; 1987, 286-288; Boeker 1986, 55-69; idem & Unterseher 1986, 89-109; Brauch 1984; 1988; idem & Unterseher 1984; 1988; Orbons 1988; 1989; cf. Canby 1983; Simpkin 1986.
151. Unterseher 1984b, 123-126.

282 NOTES

152. Unterseher 1984a, 99; 1987a, 79; 1987c; SAS 1984b, 157.
153. Boeker & Unterseher 1986, 99-100.
154. Boeker 1986, 62-65; Unterseher 1989h, 317-318.
155. SAS 1984b; Unterseher 1989h, 318-327.
156. Dick & Unterseher 1986, 242.
157. Borkenhagen 1984.
158. Unterseher 1989h, 320.
159. Dick & Unterseher 1986, 240.
160. Unterseher 1987c.
161. Unterseher 1989, 154-155; 1989a.
162. Unterseher 1989d; Cf. De Lupis 1987, 183-188.
163. Unterseher 1988b, 3.
164. Cf. O'Ballance 1972, 49-84.
165. Unterseher 1989b, 192-193; cf. White 1974, 42-60; Smith 1977; Saw 1987.
166. SAS 1984a; Unterseher 1989b; cf. Møller 1989a.
167. Cf. Smit 1986.
168. Unterseher 1989b, 201; 1989h, 327; cf. on VTOL: Stanley 1986; Brown 1986, 184-186, 259-263.
169. Unterseher 1988b.
170. Cf. Wolter & Meurer 1970, 265-283; Ropp 1962, 211-214.
171. Bebermeyer & Unterseher 1986; 1989, 170-173. On the Maritime Strategy, see e.g. Watkins 1986; Brooks 1986; Friedman 1988; cf. for critical views: Mearsheimer 1986; Møller 1987.
172. Bebermeyer & Unterseher 1986, 10, 29; 1989, 173-175; cf. on German naval plans: Wagner, Jay 1988; 1990; and on the Baltic: Møller 1990b; Boserup 1990c.
173. Bebermeyer & Unterseher 1986, 31, 33; 1989, 181; cf. FRAG 1986; Møller 1987; 1989.
174. Bebermeyer & Unterseher 1986, 37-41; 1989, 182-185.
175. Møller 1987; 1989.
176. Unterseher 1990b, 113; 1984b, 127; 1987a, 81; SAS 1984b, 173.
177. Knight 1988; Conetta & idem 1989; 1990.
178. Unterseher 1987a, 80.
179. Unterseher 1990c.
180. Müller, E. 1982, 105-115; cf. Møller & Wiberg 1990.
181. Müller, E. 1984, 82-92, 133-137; cf. Bundy 1986; Beaufre 1963, 73-75; 1965, 107-123; Boserup 1989; Neild 1990, 46-73.
182. Müller, E. 1984, 130.
183. Müller, E. 1984, 105.
184. Müller, E. 1984, 142-144.
185. Müller, E. 1984, 151-154.
186. Müller, E. 1984, 144, 155-159.
187. Müller, E. 1987, 50.
188. Müller, E. 1988, 51-61.
189. Cf. Väyrynen, ed. 1985; Bahr & Lutz, eds. 1986; 1987; Møller 1988a; 1989b; 1990a.
190. One of the few examples of such an analysis is the present author's Ph.D. dissertation, a revised version of which will be published in 1992.
191. Böge & Wilke 1984, 91-137; Theilmann 1986; Lutz, ed. 1987; Bahr & Lutz, eds. 1988.
192. Lutz 1981; 1982a, 38-45.
193. Lutz 1982a, 48.
194. Lutz 1982b, 16-42; cf. Roberts 1976; Fuhrer 1987; Danspeckgruber 1986; Agrell 1979; Ries 1989; Cramer 1984; Däniker 1987; Lukic 1984; Bebler 1987; Wiberg 1987.
195. Lutz 1983; 1985b; 1987f.
196. Lutz 1986d; 1986e; 1986f; 1986g; idem & Theilmann 1986; cf. Mutz 1986.
197. Lutz 1986f, 47.
198. Lübckemeier 1988; Møller 1989b; 1992.
199. Lutz 1986f, 47-52; cf. Mutz 1986, 103-108; Pott 1987.
200. Lutz 1986f, 52-53.
201. Lutz 1986f, 55-57; cf. Rix & Wilke 1986, 210-215.
202. Lutz 1986f, 60-64; cf. Rix & Wilke 1986, 216-219; Bahr & Lutz, eds. 1987.

203. Lutz 1987a; 1986c.
204. Lutz 1984; 1987b; 1987c; 1987d, 26; English version: Lutz 1988.
205. Lutz 1988, 28-33, 45.
206. Lutz 1988, 37, 41-43, 49-60, 63, 80-84.
207. Lutz 1988, 69-74; cf. Osgood 1962; Etzioni 1962; George 1988; cf. Baechler & Rix 1987.
208. Lutz 1990, 42-45, 58-59; cf. 1989d; 1990a; 1990b; 1990c.
209. Michalka & Niedhart, eds. 1980, 137.
210. Tageszeitung, 28. 04. 1990.
211. Pott 1986a; idem & Lutz 1986; Lutz 1986c.
212. Müller, E. 1986b; cf. Bull 1973; Hill 1989; Prawitz 1990.
213. Pott 1986b.
214. Pott 1985, 350.
215. Møller 1989a.
216. Lutz 1989b, 3-6, 17-19; cf. 1989a.
217. Lutz 1985a; 1986a; 1986b; IFSH 1985.
218. Bahr & al. 1987; cf. Lutz 1988c; Bahr 1987.
219. Boserup & Mack 1974, 148-182; Muller 1984, 212-215.
220. Sharp 1973, 665-678; Jahn 1984, 85.
221. King-Hall 1959, 27-30; Galtung 1971, 89; 1965.
222. Mellon & al. 1985, 149-166.
223. Roberts 1967a, 243-245.
224. Sharp 1973, 421-423; Ebert 1968b, 80-82; 1981a, 30-51, 78-119, 141-191.
225. Examples of the former view are: Fischer 1984, 147-151; Galtung 1984, 192-197; Mellon
     & al. 1985, 179-182. An example of the latter is Boserup & Mack 1974, 56.
226. Ebert 1967a.
227. Sharp 1973, 109-113, 495-496; cf. Hart 1967; Beaufre 1967.
228. King-Hall 1959; Nolte & Nolte 1984.
229. Muller 1984, 206; Boserup & Mack 1974, 154; Ebert 1968, 16-17.
230. Ebert 1981a, 141-191; Sharp 1985, 90-100; Muller 1984, 234.
231. Sharp 1985, 85; Muller 1984, 204; Mellon & al. 1985, 126-127; King-Hall 1959, 39-67.
232. Galtung 1968, 384; Roberts 1967a, 226-227; Ebert 1980a, 188-189; Mellon & al. 1985,
     34-35; cf. Boserup & Mack 1974, 41-42, 135.
233. Ebert 1970a, 155-156; 1981a, 90-119, 141-191; 1981b, 73-103; Roberts 1967a, 218-219;
     Muller 1984, 209-212; Mellon & al. 1985; Galtung 1984, 198-204; cf. 1968, 394; Fischer
     1984, 124-125.
234. King-Hall 1959, 75, 100-103, 140-144; Roberts 1967a, 231-235; Ebert 1981a, 9-29; Sharp
     1985, 16-18, 100-106; Boserup & Mack 1974, 130.
235. Sharp 1985, 70.
236. Roberts 1967b.
237. Ebert 1981a, 141-191; 1981b, 73-103; Niezing 1987, 24-36; Muller 1984, 296-297.
238. Nolte & Nolte 1984.
239. Ebert 1969a, 41; Sharp 1985, 61-63.
240. Klumper 1983;; Schmid 1985, 375-382; Alternative Defence Commission 1983, 228-230;
     cf. for the rebuttal: Boserup & Mack 1974, 141.
241. Roberts 1978; cf. Mellon & al. 1985, 184-187; Wiberg 1977, 117-119.
242. Alternative Defence Commission 1983, 227; Nolte & Nolte 1984; Fischer & al. 1987;
     Salmon 1988.
243. Jahn 1972; King-Hall 1959, 111-119.
244. Nolte, W. 1984.
245. Nolte & Nolte 1984, 142.
246. Nolte, W. 1987a, 65.
247. Nolte & Nolte 1984, 143-145.
248. Nolte & Nolte 1984, 236-241.
249. Nolte & Nolte 1984, 159, 221-25; cf. Nolte, W. 1990; 1987c, 221-23; 1987a, 70; 1986b, 186;
     1988a, 465.
250. Nolte & Nolte 1984, 211, 160, 245, 235.
251. Nolte & Nolte 1984, 146-147; cf. Best 1983, 217-285; De Lupis 1987, 241-244, 271-274.
252. Nolte & Nolte 1984, 236; Nolte, W. 1987c, 226; cf. Galtung 1984, 180-184.

253. Nolte & Nolte 1984, 220; Nolte, W. 1987b; cf. Baudissin 1986.
254. Nolte & Nolte 1984, 148, 219, 273-274.
255. Nolte & Nolte 1984, 150, 275; Nolte, W. 1985, 319-320.
256. Nolte, W. 1987a, 67; 1987c, 221; 1990; cf. Nolte & Nolte 1984, 277.
257. Schelling 1960, 207.

Chapter V: Military Defectors

1. Finer 1976; Allison & Morris 1975; Steinbruner & Carter 1975; Enthoven & Smith 1972; McNamara 1968, 87-106; Greenwood 1975; Head 1983.
2. Evera 1984, 206-398; idem 1985; Snyder, J. 1984; 1985; Posen 1984, 179-219.
3. Kade 1981; cf. the many examples in Prins, ed. 1984.
4. Baudissin 1986; cf. for a critique: Bald & al. 1981.
5. Based, with a few additions, on Fischer & al. 1987, 99.
6. Hart 1937; 1939; Miksche 1955, 160-194; 1959, 168-216; Petraeus 1984; Olson, W. 1985; Dupuy 1985; Wickham 1985; Kafkalas 1986; Downing 1986.
7. Uhle-Wettler 1966.
8. Uhle-Wettler 1980, 30.
9. Uhle-Wettler 1980, 19-21, 27-36.
10. Uhle-Wettler 1980, 25; 1984, 22-26, 46-49; idem 1990, 128-129; cf. Bracken 1976.
11. Uhle-Wettler 1980, 59-62, 78, 87.
12. Uhle-Wettler 1980, 74, 76.
13. Uhle-Wettler 1980, 61, 72-73, 93-94, 103, 107; cf. idem 1990, 126-127.
14. Uhle-Wettler 1980, 116-118, 120-123; cf. on the 'fleet in being' conception: Till 1982, 111-113.
15. Uhle-Wettler 1980, 124-139.
16. Uhle-Wettler 1980, 143-146.
17. Dünne 1989, 13-14.
18. Dünne 1989, 22-26, 32-40.
19. Dünne 1989, 82-83.
20. Dünne 1989, 90-94.
21. Dünne 1989, 123-124.
22. Simpkin 1986, 117-132; cf. 1983, 75-78, 112-115, 174-179.
23. Dünne 1989, 128-129.
24. Schmähling 1986a.
25. Schmähling 1986b, 5; cf. Cable 1979.
26. Schmähling 1988a, 62; cf. Møller 1989.
27. Schmähling 1988c, 544; 1988a, 66-68.
28. Schmähling 1988a, 70.
29. Schmähling 1987, 77; 1988a, 71-73.
30. Schmähling 1987, 73-76; 1988b, 472.
31. Schmähling 1988; 1989; 1989a; 1989b.
32. Schmähling 1990, 17-19, 139, 268, 99.
33. Schmähling 1990, 20-29, 37, 55-92.
34. Schmähling 1990, 32-33, 145-148.
35. Schmähling 1990, 91.
36. Schmähling 1990, 142-145, 172-183.
37. Schmähling 1990, 181-183, 237-251, 284-290.
38. Schmähling 1990, 206-229, 294-299; cf. 1989c.
39. *Die Zeit*, 26. 1. 1990; *Atlantic News*, 19. 1. 1990.
40. *Tageszeitung*, 17. 4. 1990.
41. Kiessling 1989a, 42, 165.
42. Kiessling 1989a, 37-42.
43. Kiessling 1989, 384-389; 1989a 90-99, 198-200.
44. Kiessling 1989a, 177-186.
45. Kiessling 1989, 390; 1989a, 160, 228, 264-265.
46. Kiessling 1989a, 213, 264-276.
47. Kiessling 1989, 261; 1990, 143, 154.

48. *Der Spiegel*, 1990:6, 32-34.
49. Cf. Mechtersheimer & Barth 1986, 167-180; Szabo 1990, 56.
50. *Der Spiegel*, 1989:40, 41-43.
51. Hagena 1990, 32-53.
52. Hagena 1990, 82-83.
53. Hagena 1990, 92-97; cf. Møller 1989a.
54. Huber 1988a, 1; 1988b, 1; 1986, 1.
55. Huber 1986, 11.
56. Huber 1988b, 25-28.
57. Huber 1988a, 2, 9, 12.
58. Huber & Hoffmann in *Süddeutsche Zeitung*, 20-21. 02. 1988; Huber 1988b, 12-15; cf. Clausewitz 1832, 361 (Book 6. 1. 2).
59. Huber & Hoffmann 1984a; Hoffmann, Huber & Steiger 1986a; 1986b.
60. Huber 1987, 37.
61. Altenburg 1990, 312.

Chapter VI: The Political Scene Before 1989

1. Grosser 1988, 145-182; Blumenwitz 1989.
2. Niclauss 1988; Grosser 1988, 116-144.
3. Blechman & Fisher 1990, 75-87; cf. on MBFR: Müller, Martin 1988a.
4. Rosolowsky 1987, 77-114.
5. Rattinger 1985, 114-128; Joffe 1987, 93-130; cf. Rochon 1989, 156-178.
6. Krell 1990, 8-20.

Chapter VII: The SPD Before 1989

1. Marx & Engels 1848, 479; Lasalle 1862; Dowe & Klotzbach 1984, 175, 181, 190, 213, 224; cf. Grebing 1970, 50-60, 134-145; Abendroth 1965, 63-86.
2. Rosolowsky 1987, 13-36; Dowe & Klotzbach 1984, 236.
3. Rosolowsky 1987, 37-47; Krell 1989, 4; 1990, 5-6.
4. Petersen 1984.
5. Schmidt 1984; Brauch 1983.
6. Kaiser & al. 1982; Krell & al. 1983; Krause 1986; Joffe 1987, 45-92.
7. Independent Commission 1982; Lutz 1986d; Kelstrup 1987.
8. Bahr 1985a, 31.
9. Bahr 1985a, 32.
10. Bahr 1985a, 33; 1986, 18-19.
11. Independent Commission 1982, 182-183.
12. Bahr 1983, 144-145.
13. Bahr 1984, 278; cf. 1986, 21-22; Gilges 1985.
14. Lafontaine 1983; SPD 1986, 1270; cf. Meyer, B. 1987, 23-36.
15. Huntzinger 1985, 400; Gnesotto 1986.
16. Schmidt 1986, 58-59; 1987.
17. Scheer 1985a, 734; Nehrlich 1986; Berger 1986; Gloannec 1986; Schulze 1986; Renouard 1986, 52-53; Valentin 1986; Ehrhart 1987.
18. Ehmke & al., eds. 1986; Griffith 1978; Krell 1988; Bender 1986.
19. Voigt 1985; 1987a; SPD & SED 1985; 1987a; 1987b; cf. Hahn 1987; Meyer, T. 1987; Birkenbach 1989; Eppler 1988.
20. SPD & PVAP 1985, 1515; 1988; Ehmke 1986.
21. Cf. Borkenhagen 1987; Szabo 1990, 72-78.
22. Bahr 1986; 1987; 1987a; 1987b, 26-28; idem & al. 1987.
23. Bahr 1988, 24, 30-33; 37; cf. Eppler 1988.
24. Bahr 1988, 52, 61.
25. Bahr 1988, 61-68.
26. Bahr 1988, 75-77.
27. Eppler 1981, 82-90, 211, 213-216.

28. Glotz 1985, 113-114; 1987; idem quoted in Lutz 1987d, 14.
29. Bülow 1984a; 1985a; cf. Rühle 1984.
30. Bülow 1984b.
31. Bülow 1985b; cf. idem & Funk 1987, 15.
32. Bülow 1985b; cf. 1986a, 127.
33. Bülow & Funk 1987, 15.
34. Bülow 1989a; idem & Funk 1988; 1988a; Bülow, Funk & Müller 1988.
35. Bülow 1988b.
36. Funk 1988; 1988a.
37. Gupta 1988; Thimann & al. 1988.
38. Cf. Scheer 1986b.
39. Scheer 1986a; cf. 1984; 1985b.
40. Scheer 1986a, 226, 237-238; cf. Bahr 1985b.
41. Scheer 1986a, 233; 229, cf. Bahr in Independent Commission 1982, 182.
42. Scheer 1986a, 231, 252-253, 279-285.
43. Scheer 1986a, 251, 268.
44. Gilges 1985, 22.
45. Gilges 1985, 37, 40, 123.
46. Gilges 1985, 42, 49, 126.
47. Lafontaine 1988, 126-133, 142-147, 151; cf. Hamm & Pohlmann 1990; 1990a.
48. Voigt 1987c, 417.
49. Voigt 1988.
50. Voigt 1990a, 149, 152.
51. Borkenhagen 1984; 1984a; 1985a; 1987.
52. Borkenhagen 1985b; 1987b, 261.
53. Borkenhagen 1987b, 267-271.
54. Krause 1984, 126.
55. Krause 1987a; 1987b; 1987c.
56. Krause 1986; 1987a, 49.
57. Krause 1987; 1987b, 189.
58. Krause 1987a, 48; 1987b.
59. Bahr 1984, 281, 283.
60. Biehle, ed. 1985; Schuster & Wasmuth 1984; Horn & Buch 1984.
61. Antrag 259, Parteivorstand: *Für eine Neue Strategie des Bündnisses*, quoted in Lutz 1987, 15.
62. Schubert 1985, 110-111.
63. SPD 1986.
64. Horn 1988.
65. SPD 1988.
66. Bahr & al. 1989.
67. *Plenarprotokoll des Deutschen Bundestages*, 11/146, 10801-10802.
68. *Plenarprotokoll* 11/146, 10801-10805, 10816, 10818.
69. Wieczorek-Zeul & Scheer 1990.
70. *Frieden und Abrüstung*, 1990:1, 17-20.

Chapter VIII: The Peace Movement Before 1989

1. Albrecht 1982b, 111-125.
2. Wasmuth 1987, 123-128; cf. Galtung 1988; Szabo 1990, 35-39.
3. Bredthauer & Mannhardt 1981, 157-180; Brauch 1983a, 153-185; Wasmuht 1987, 101-172; Mushaben 1986; Rochon 1989.
4. Galtung 1984, 19-32.
5. Buro 1982a; 1982b.
6. Buro 1982a, 85-86; 1983a; 1983b.
7. Cf. Galtung 1969.
8. Buro 1987, 19.
9. Cf. Osgood 1962; Etzioni 1962; George 1988.
10. Buro 1988.

11. Buro 1987, 20-21.
12. Komitee 1981; abbreviated English version: Committee 1983; cf. Alternative Defence Commission 1983; 1987.
13. Komitee 1981, 18.
14. Komitee 1981, 103.
15. Komitee 1981, 124.
16. Komitee 1981, 158-181.
17. Komitee 1981, 203.
18. Komitee 1981, 214; cf. Krippendorf 1984.
19. Komitee 1981, 234-236.
20. Wernicke & Schöll 1985, 12.
21. Wernicke & Schöll 1985, 168, 176.
22. Galtung 1986; Holmes 1984; Rosolowsky 1987, 77-97; Wasmuht 1987, 139-141; Rochon 83-86.
23. Grünen im Bundestag 1984; Grünen, eds. 1985; Rosolowsky 1987, 77-79; Meyer, B. 1987, 47-52.
24. Voigt 1986; Lutz & Theilmann 1986, 229.
25. Rosolowsky 1987, 77-97; Die Grünen im Bundestag 1988; Schierholz 1986; Statz 1988.
26. Grünen 1981; cf.Bruckmann 1984.
27. Schulze-Marmeling, 214-236; Böge & Schulert 1986, 163.
28. Mechtersheimer, ed. 1982; 1984, 95-151; 1985; idem & Barth, eds. 1983; 1986.
29. Mechtersheimer 1984, 201-203.
30. Mechtersheimer 1984, 209, 218.
31. Rattinger 1985; Vogt 1989.
32. Hakovirta 1988, 14-36; De Lupis 1987, 139-142; cf. Isak 1986.

Chapter IX: The Government Parties Before 1989

1. Griffith 1978, 31-106; Herbst 1989.
2. Meyer, B. 1987, 9-22.
3. Lutz & Theilmann 1986, 224-228.
4. *Bulletin der Bundesregierung*, 26.08.1988.
5. Cf. Kamp 1988; Ramsbotham 1989; Binnendijk 1989.
6. Enders 1988; 1988; idem & Siebenmorgen 1988; cf. Dregger 1988, 407-408.
7. Enders 1990a.
8. Bundesministerium der Verteidigung 1985, 30, 80-81; cf. Wörner 1985.
9. Dregger 1988, 411.
10. *CDU-Dokumentation*, 1988:19.
11. Stoltenberg 1990, 142.
12. Gohl & Niesporek, eds. 1986.
13. Alt 1986; cf. 1983.
14. Biedenkopf 1986.
15. Jaeschke 1986, 49; Krüger 1986, 105.
16. Deittert 1986, 121; Niesporek 1986; Pfeiler 1986; Gohl 1986, 159.
17. *Der Spiegel*, 1988:29.
18. Lemke 1989, 15, 19; cf. 1990; 1990a.
19. Weizsäcker, R. 1985; cf. Weizsäcker, C. 1979; 1983; 1990; idem, ed. 1971; 1976; 1984; 1990.
20. Weizsäcker, R. 1987, 627; idem, quoted in Lutz 1987d, 5.
21. *Bulletin*, 61, 15.06.1989, 543.
22. *Jane's Defence Weekly*, 1989:24, 1325.
23. Stoltenberg 1990, 141.
24. Genscher, quoted in *NOD. Non-Offensive Defence. International Research Newsletter* (Copenhagen: Centre for Peace and Conflict Research), 1986:6, 4.
25. Genscher 1987, 443.
26. *Der Spiegel*, 30. 11. 1987.
27. Genscher: Speech to the CSCE follow-up conference 5. 07,1988, *Bulletin*, 1988:92, 858.
28. *Bulletin*, 1988:83, 785; cf. *Frankfurter Rundschau*, 7. 04. 1988.

Chapter X: The 'Other Germany' Before 1989

1. Walter 1989; Lapp 1990.
2. Ash 1989, 13-25.
3. Grunenberg 1983.
4. Cf. Spanger 1989.
5. Ulbricht quoted in Zieger 1988, 21.
6. Spanger 1990.
7. Rudolph 1983; Walter 1990.
8. Bundesregierung 1981, 43-45.
9. Zieger 1988, 90-96.
10. *Süddeutsche Zeitung*, 28. 02. 1990; *Der Spiegel*, 1990:34, 64-68; 1990:35, 64-73.
11. *Der Spiegel*, 1990:25, 22-25, 97-103.
12. Hättich 1983; Weidenfeld 1983, 33-37; Bredow 1983, 109-111; Rudolph 1983; Seiffert 1986, 93-114; Walter 1989, 126-133; Zieger 1988, 67.
13. Thadden 1983, 57-58.
14. MacAdams 1986.
15. See e.g. Vigor 1983; MccGwire 1986.
16. MccGwire 1986, 128-139; cf. Lippert, G. 1987; Erickson & al. 1986.
17. Lippert, G. 1987; Arkin & Fieldhouse 1985, 38, 265-266; Erickson & al. 1986, 38.
18. MacGregor 1989; Jones 1981a; 1984.
19. Johnson & al. 1980, 98-102; MacGregor 1986; McCausland 1986.
20. MacGregor 1989, 131.
21. Doehler & Haufe 1989; Bredow 1983, 111-114.
22. Bleek 1990; cf. *Der Spiegel*, 1990:30, 136-141; 1990:40, 284-288; 1991:1, 24-25.
23. Schlaga 1990.
24. Knabe, ed. 1989; Fritzsche 1989; Walter 1989, 108-109.
25. Romberg 1986, 2, 5-35, 71.
26. Romberg 1986, 53, 56-60; cf. Independent Commission 1982, 146-149.
27. Romberg 1988; 1989; 1989a; cf. Osgood 1962; George 1988.
28. Romberg 1989a, 242.
29. Holden 1989, 101-109, 115-146; 1991; Shenfield 1987; Holloway 1989.
30. Klein, D. 1988; Heininger 1989; Schmidt & Schwarz 1989d.
31. Maier 1988.
32. Schmidt & Schwarz 1988; 1989c; 1989d; cf. Adomeit 1989.
33. Türpe 1989.
34. Møller 1989e; 1989f.
35. Schmidt & Schwarz 1989a; Benjowski & Schwarz 1989.
36. Müller, Manfred 1988; 1989; Peter 1989.
37. Schirmeister 1989; Brie 1989; Schmidt & Schwarz 1989; 1989b; 1990; Schwarz 1988; 1989; 1989a; Scheler & al., 196-201, 218-223.
38. SPD & SED 1987b; cf. Meyer, T. 1987.
39. Müller, Manfred 1990.
40. Basler 1990.
41. Schwarz 1989, 14-21, 39-59.
42. Schwarz 1989, 21-30, 70; cf. Møller 1989e; 1989f.
43. Schwarz 1989, 35, 62, 65.
44. Schwarz 1989, 67-75.
45. *Jane's Defence Weekly*, 2. 09. 1989 and 23. 09. 1989.
46. *Jane's Defence Weekly*, 1989:23, 1275.

Chapter XI: The Year of Upheaval

Because this present chapter deals with such recent events, most of the documentation takes the form of articles in newspapers and journals. The following abbreviations have been used:

AN   *Atlantic News/Nouvelles Atlantiques*
Bulletin   *Bulletin (Presse—und Informationsamt der Bundesregierung)*

Blätter   *Blätter für deutsche und internationale Politik*
DA   *Deutschland-Archiv*
EA   *Europa-Archiv*
F&A   *Frieden und Abrüstung*
FAZ   *Frankfurter Allgemeine Zeitung*
IHT   *International Herald Tribune*
JDW   *Jane's Defence Weekly*
SD   *Süddeutsche Zeitung*
Spiegel   *Der Spiegel*

1. E.g. Seiffert 1986; Venohr 1990b.
2. *EA*, 1989:24, D699.
3. Cf. Wagenlehner 1989; Riese 1990; Wettig 1990.
4. Gorbachev 1988a, 195-196; cf. Adomeit 1989; Wagenlehner 1989, 1008-1009.
5. Baumann et al. 1990, 134-143.
6. *EA*, 1989:20, D586.
7. Baumann et al. 1990, 151.
8. *Spiegel*, 1989, 33, 18-32; 1989:36, 16-24; 1990:4, 28-53; Kohl (8.11.89), *EA*, 1989:24, D708.
9. *Spiegel*, 1989:38, 16; 1989:52, 68.
10. *Spiegel*, 1989:46, 18-30; Baumann & al. 1990, 146-254.
11. Cf. the letters from Krenz and Schabowski, in *Spiegel*, 1990:43, 103-10.
12. Ehrhart 1990; Wagner 1990.
13. *Spiegel*, 1989:46, 48-50; 1990:2, 27-32, 35-46; 1990:23, 37-53, 100-104; 1990:30, 39-46; 1990:38, 138-139; 1990:47, 145-149; 1991:1, 52-59; Baumann et al. 1990, 163.
14. Kuppe 1990; *Spiegel*, 1989:51, 26-29; Spittmann 1990, 190.
15. *DA*, 1990:3, 466-468.
16. *Spiegel*, 1990:12, 33-44.
17. Lapp 1990.
18. Richter 1989; Fink 1990; Leonhard 1990; Ammer 1990. On the merger of the SPD and the KPD into the SED, see *Spiegel*, 1990:39, 116-127; 1990:40, 127-145.
19. Fischer, Benno 1990; *Spiegel*, 1990:2, 19-20.
20. Baumann et al. 1990, 255-259.
21. *DA*, 1990:4, 497-501; Mantzke 1990; *Spiegel*, 1990:34, 16-18.
22. *EA*, 1989:24, D727.
23. Cf. Buzan & al. 1990, 125-126; MacAdams 1990.
24. *EA*, 1989:24, D730-734.
25. Lenk 1990; cf. Szabo 1990, 110-113.
26. Charlier 1990; *Spiegel*, 1990:8, 52-64.
27. Karsten Voigt in the *Bundestag* (28.11.89), *Plenarprotokoll*, 13514; *Spiegel*, 1989:49, 25.
28. *Spiegel*, 1989:49, 29.
29. Hans Modrow (11.1.90), *EA*, 1990:4, D92, D107.
30. *EA*, 1990:4, D119-120.
31. *EA*, 1990:4, D113.
32. Bahr 1985b; 1988a, 95; cf. Lummer 1988.
33. *Spiegel*, 1990:6, 17.
34. *Spiegel*, 1990:12, 48-57; 1990:19, 72-77; 1990:21, 34-45; 1990:23, 32-35; 1990:24, 18-21; Joffe 1990, 132; Frowein 1990.
35. *DA*, 1990:3, 475-477; cf. *Spiegel*, 1990:22, 110-112; 1990:32, 18-28.
36. *Spiegel*, 1990:19, 18-26; 1990:26, 20-29; 1990:36, 134-135; Brückner 1990.
37. *Spiegel*, 1990:21, 28-29, 1990:22, 26-29; *FAZ*, 22.06.1990.
38. *Spiegel*, 1990:24, 18-21; 1990:25, 40-48; 1990:25, 18-20; 1990:26, 16-19.
39. *Spiegel*, 1990:35, 18-23; *EA*, 1990:21, D537-D564; 'Einigungsvertrag', *Bulletin*, 1990:104, 877-890.
40. *Spiegel*, 1989:50, 16-19.
41. Wagenlehner 1989; Riese 1990; Wettig 1990; Hatschikjan & Pfeiler 1989.
42. *AN*, 22. 12. 1989.
43. *DA*, 1990:3, 468-471.
44. *EA*, 1990:8, D192.

45. Shevardnadze, in *TASS*, 7.04.90; *APN* 27.04.1990; cf. Dmitri Dnailow (IMEMO), *Moscow News*, 1990:5.
46. *IHT*, 17.07.1990; *EA*, 1990:18, D480-490; *Spiegel*, 1990:30, 16-27.
47. *Spiegel*, 1990:20, 26; 1990:26, 21-22.
48. *Frankfurter Allgemeine Zeitung*, 16.09.1990 (unofficial translation).
49. *EA*, 1989:23, D672, D679.
50. *Spiegel*, 1989:49, 35.
51. *EA*, 1989:23, D675; 1990:4, D115.
52. *EA*, 1990:7, D179.
53. Teltschik 1990; *Spiegel*, 1990:10, 23-25; Skubiszewski 1990, 195.
54. *Spiegel*, 1989:51, 17.
55. *AN*, 23.03.1990; cf. Skubiszewski 1990:198.
56. *AN*, 24.03.1990.
57. Skubiszewski 1990, 200-201.
58. Interview with Havel, *Spiegel*, 1990:40, 198-211.
59. *EA*, 1990:4, D96-D97.
60. Schütze 1990, 133-134; Moisi 1990, 30; cf. Foreign Minster Roland Dumas, *Spiegel* 1990:23, 165-173.
61. *AN*, 1990:2281 (12.12.1990).
62. Haltzel 1990; Davy 1990; Glaessner 1989.
63. Greiner 1990; Haltzel 1990, 129-130.
64. *Neue Zürcher Zeitung*, 6.02.1990; *AN*, 1990:2197 (28.02.1990).
65. *FAZ*, 13.02.1990.
66. *SD*, 9.02.1990; *AN*, 18.04.1990, 4.05.1990.
67. *JDW*, 1990:18, 838.
68. *JDW*, 1990:11, 486.
69. *AN*, 6.04.1990.
70. Ungerer 1990; Stürmer 1990; Beise 1990; *Spiegel*, 1989:44, 184.
71. Oeser 1990.
72. *Blätter*, December 1990, 1518-1519; *Spiegel*, 1990:38, 18-21; 1990:46, 25.
73. *AN*, 9.05.1990; 11.05.1990.
74. *IHT*, 17-18.06.1990.
75. *EA*, 1990:19, D509-D514.
76. *AN*, 1990:2273.
77. *FAZ*, 25-26.06.1990; *Spiegel*, 1990:27, 18-20; 1990:48, 23; 1990:50, 158-169.
78. Genscher (11.04.1990), *EA*, 1990:9, D222.
79. *AN*, 28.03.1990; *Spiegel*, 1990:8, 17-18; 1990:17, 20.
80. *Spiegel*, 1989:39, 26-27.
81. *AN*, 24.03.1990; *Spiegel*, 1990:10, 26-31; 1990:20, 29.
82. *EA*, 1990:9, D-222.
83. *Spiegel*, 1989:39, 26.
84. *EA*, 1989:24, D705, D707 (8.11.1989); 1990:4, D89 (19.12.1989); 1990:8, D194 (13.02.1990).
85. *AN*, 21.02.1990.
86. *EA*, 1990:8, D201; 1990:9, D215.
87. *EA*, 1990:9, D214.
88. *AN*, 28.02.1990.
89. *Spiegel*, 1990:22, 50.
90. *Spiegel*, 1990:24, 20-21; 1990:29, 26-27.
91. *AN*, 21.03.1990; *EA*, 1990:9, D213, D214.
92. *EA*, 1990:4, D87.
93. Gutjahr 1990; cf. Szabo 1990, 105-106.
94. Stoltenberg in *SD*, 3.05.1990; Lamers in *Tageszeitung*, 5.03.1990.
95. *AN*, 4.04.1990; Scholz 1990, 244-246.
96. *Die Welt*, 31. 01. 1990.
97. *FAZ*, 22.03.1990.
98. *AN*, 4.04.1990.
99. *Spiegel*, 1990:22, 21-25, 34-35; 1990:23, 18-20, 26; 1990:24, 24-27; 1990:25, 18-20; 1990:26, 40-50.

100. *Spiegel*, 1989:39, 20.
101. *Spiegel*, 1989:39, 21; cf. SPD-SED 1987b.
102. *AN*, 30.03.1990.
103. *FAZ*, 5.03.1990; *AN*, 21.03.1990; cf. *Spiegel*, 1989:52, 67.
104. *AN*, 30.03.1990; cf. *Spiegel*, 1989:39, 21.
105. Wieczorek-Zeul & Scheer 1990a.
106. *Spiegel*, 1990:6, 28.
107. Voigt 1989a; 1990; 1990c:566; *F&A*, 1990:1, 2-4.
108. Glotz 1990, 45.
109. Gaus 1990, 317-318; cf. Voigt 1988a.
110. Krause 1990, 10, 13; 1990a, 6, 9.
111. *EA*, 1990:4, D91.
112. *Blätter*, 1990:2, 243.
113. *EA*, 1990:8, D209.
114. *ADN*, 1.03.1990.
115. *EA*, 1990:10, D242-D243.
116. *Spiegel*, 1990:6, 20; *EA*, 1990:10, D249.
117. *EA*, 1990:10, D258-D259.
118. *AN*, 3.05.1990.
119. *AN*, 3.05.1990.
120. *Spiegel*, 1990:17, 20.
121. *EA*, 1989:24, D726.
122. *Blätter*, 1990:2, 237-238.
123. *Spiegel*, 1989:49, 98; Hagena 1990; 1990a; Plügge 1990.
124. *Bild*, 15.02.1990; *Spiegel*, 1990:10, 37.
125. *Spiegel*, 1990:10, 34-48; *JDW*, 1990:21, 1012.
126. *Spiegel*, 1990:10, 48; *AN*, 28.02.1990.
127. *F&A* 1990:1, 23-30; Fischer, S. 1990; cf. for a critique: Møller 1989e; 1989f.
128. *Rheinischer Merkur*, 2.03.1990.
129. Romberg, quoted in Lutz 1990, 45.
130. *Spiegel*, 1990:17, 22-24; 1990:30, 33-37; *JDW*, 1990:16, 736.
131. *Militärreform in der DDR*, 1990:17.
132. *Spiegel*, 1990:24, 29-31; *Neues Deutschland*, 23.04.1990.
133. *AN*, 18 April, 1990; *JDW*, 1990:25, 1276.
134. *F&A*, 1990-1, 52-53; cf. Buro 1990.
135. *Die Welt*, 26.04.1990; *AN*, 3.05.1990.
136. *Express*, 1.04.1990; *FAZ*, 31.03.1990; *AN*, 28 March, 1990.
137. 'Soldaten und Rekruten der Bundeswehr and the NVA!', open letter from the Greens to the soldiers and privates of the *Bundeswehr* and the NVA, issued from the extraordinary party convention, 23 September, 1990, in *Blätter*, December 1990, 1523-1526; Pax Christi: 'Für eine neue Friedenspolitik', *Publik-Forum*, 1990:19 (5.10.1990).
138. *AN*, 1990:2271.
139. Hagena 1990c; Holzweissig 1990; Holtzendorff 1990; Reeb 1990; *AN*, 1990:2253; *JDW*, 1990:8; 1990:15, 254; 1990:13, 567; 1990:14; *Spiegel*, 1990:39, 86-90; 1990:41, 32-37; 1991:1, 22-23.
140. Mager 1990; *JDW* 1990:5, 152; 1990:9, 301.
141. *AN* 1990:2257; Fechner 1990; cf. the break-down of the US withdrawal in *Frankfurter Rundschau*, 20.09.1990.
142. *AN*, 1990:2248; cf. on protests against low-altitude flights: *Spiegel*, 1990:37, 81.
143. On the PDS, see *Spiegel*, 1990:44, 61-65; 1990:45, 21-25. For the results of the elections, see *Bulletin*, 1990:140, 1481; *Spiegel*, 1990:50, 18-29.
144. *Spiegel*, 1990:50, 18-25.
145. Lutz 1985b; cf. Galtung 1969.
146. Lutz 1989d; 1990; 1990a; 1990b; 1990c.
147. IFSH 1990; Kaestner 1990; cf. Müller, Martin 1990; Mutz 1990; Mead 1990, 632.
148. Bahr: 'Sicherheit durch Annäherung', *Die Zeit*, 29.06.1990; Voigt 1990d, 209-210.
149. Senghaas 1990, 7-8, 11-14, 21; 1990a.

150. 1990:23-31, 46, 54-55, 87, 91; cf. 1990b; 1990c; idem: 'Abrüstung und ein fairer Umgang mit der Sowjetunion', *Frankfurter Rundschau*, 22.06.1990.
151. Chalmers 1990; Brauch 1990; Møller 1990; 1990e; 1990f.
152. *JDW*, 1990:19, 936; *Spiegel*, 1990:40, 229-232.
153. *Bulletin*, 1990:138 (28.11.1990), 1425-1472; quotation from 'Gemeinsame Erklärung von zweiundzwanzig Staaten', ibid. 1990:137 (24.11.1990), 1422-1423.
154. *Bulletin*, 1990:137 (24.11.1990), 1409-1421.
155. Cf. Souchon 1990.
156. Eekelen 1990.
157. *Spiegel*, 1990:34, 121-123; Wellershoff in *JDW*, 1990:20; cf. Souchon 1990, 59-60, 180-181; Weizsäcker in *Frankfurter Rundschau*, 13.11.1990; Stoltenberg in *FAZ*, 13.11.1990; Wittman and Vogel quoted in *JDW*, 1990:19, 933; Brandt in *Wochendienst* (SPD *Bundestag* caucus), 15.11.1990; cf. Norbert Gansel: 'Deutsche Truppen unter UNO-Kommando?, *Zeitschrift für sozialistische Politik und Wirtschaft*, 1990:55, 7; Scheer & Wiezoreck-Zeul: 'Für einen politischen Kurswechsel zur Kriegsvermeidung in der Golfregion', undated press announcement (November 1990).
158. For a peace movement view, see Brandt, H-E. 1990. For the poll figures, see *Landesverteidigung*, 1990:77-78, 3-6.

Chapter XII: Summary and Conclusions

1. Cf. Buzan & al. 1990, 165-185; Wagner, Richard L. 1990.
2. Wörner: Foreword to *Jane's NATO Handbook* 1990-91, cited in *Jane's Defence Weekly*, 1990:15; Galvin: Interview with *Times*, cited in *Atlantic News*, 1990:2262; DPC communique quoted from *ibid.*, 1990:2280, annex; cf. *Der Spiegel*, 1990:42, 26-30; Stoltenberg, quoted in *Atlantic News*, 1990:2263; cf. Lowe & Young 1991.
3. Cf. the critical analysis in Epstein 1990.
4. Cf. Kennedy 1988.
5. Bundy 1986.
6. Cf. Møller 1989e; 1989f.
7. Mearsheimer 1990.
8. Schütze 1990; Chalmers 1990; 1990a; Lübkemeier 1990; Senghaas 1990; Møller 1990; 1992; Brauch 1990.

Bibliography

The following list contains all the works quoted in the text, as well as a selection of other works, particularly by the authors dealt with. As a general rule, only the first version of each article has been included.

Note on the ordering:

The German letters with *umlaut* (ä, ö, ü, Ä, Ö and Ü) are treated as individual letters, and placed immediately after the respective letters without *umlaut*. The German letter ß has been replaced throughout with a double s. The Scandinavian letters æ, ø and å (Æ, Ø and Å) are placed last in the alphabet, in that order.

Items by the same author are ordered chronologically, but individually authored items are listed before edited volumes and joint products, The order might thus be Lutz 1989; Lutz, ed. 1987; Lutz & al. 1985; Lutz & al., eds. 1983.

Abbreviations and references:

The following is a list of journals that have either been abbreviated in the list below, or which were presumed to be difficult for Anglo-Saxon readers to 'track down'.

AdP	*Adelphi Papers*
AP	*AFES-Papers* (Mosbach: AFES-PRESS)
APR	*AFES-PRESS Reports* (same publisher)
AR	*AFES-Reports* (same publisher)
AuP	*Aussenpolitik*
AZ	*Aus Politik und Zeitgeschhichte. Beilage zur Wochenzeitung Das Parlament*
BAS	*Bulletin of the Atomic Scientists*
Berichte	*Berichte des Bundesinstituts für ostwissenschaftliche und internationale Studien* (Köln)
Blätter	*Blätter für deutsche und internationale Politik* (Köln: Pahl-Rugenstein Verlag)
BPP	*Bulletin of Peace Proposals* (Oslo, Peace Research Institute, Oslo, PRIO)
BB	*Bremer Beiträge zur Militär- und Sicherheitspolitik* (Bremen: Steintor Verlag)
Bulletin	(Bonn, Presse- und Informationsamt der Bundesregering).
CRPV	*Current Research in Peace and Violence* (Tampere, Finland: Tampere Peace Research Institute, TAPRI)
DA	*Deutschland Archiv. Zeitschrift für Fragen der DDR und der Deutschlandpolitik* (Köln: Verlag Wissenschaft und Politik)
DDA	*Defense and Disarmament Alternatives* (Brookline, Massachusetts: Institute for Defense and Disarmament)
Dialog	*Dialog. Beiträge zur Friedensforschung* (Stadt-schlai-ning: Österreichis-ches Institut für Friedensforschung und Friedenserziehung)
EA	*Europa-Archiv. Zeitschrift für internationale Politik* (Bonn: Deutsche Gesellschaft für auswärtige Politik)
EW	*Europäische Wehrkunde. Wehrwissenschaftliche Rundschau* (Herford: Verlag Europäische Wehrkunde)
F&A	*Frieden und Abrüstung* (Bonn: Initiative für Frieden, inter-nationalen Ausgleich und Sicherheit)

HB	*Hamburger Beiträge zur Friedens- und Konfliktforschung* (Hamburg: Institut für Friedensforscung und Sicherheitspolitik)
HI	*Hamburger Informationen zur Friedensforschung und Sicherheitspolitik* (same publisher)
HSFK-B	*HSFK-Berichte* (Frankfurt a.m.: Hessische Stiftung für Friedens- und Konfliktforschung)
IDR	*International Defense Review*
IPW-B	*IPW-Berichte* (Berlin, GDR: Institut für internationale Politik und Wirtschaft)
IPW-F	*IPW-Forschungshefte* (same publisher)
IPW-P	*IPW-Papers* (same publisher)
IS	*International Security*
IW	*Internationale Wehrrevue*
JPR	*Journal of Peace Research* (same publishers as BPP)
JSS	*The Journal of Strategic Studies*
Kurzp.	*Kurzpapier der Abteilung Aussenpolitik und DDR-Forschung* (Bonn: Friedrich-Ebert-Stiftung)
Mediatus	(Starnberg: Forschungsinstitut für Friedenspolitik)
NG	*Die Neue Gesellschaft. Frankfurter Hefte* (Bonn: Verlag J.H.W. Dietz Nachf./Friedrich-Ebert-Stiftung)
NSN	*NATO's Sixteen Nations*
ÖMZ	*Österreichische Militärische Zeitschrift* (Bundesministerium für Landesverteidigung, Vienna)
PRIF-R	*PRIF-Reports* (Frankfurt: Peace Research Institute Frankfurt
S + F	*S + F. Vierteljahresschrift für Sicherheit und Frieden* (Baden-Baden: Nomos Verlag)
Studie	*Studien der Abteilung Aussenpolitik und DDR-Forschung* (same publisher as Kurzp.)
U.P.	University Press
WP-CPCR	*Working Papers* (Copenhagen: Centre for Peace and Conflict Research at the University of Copenhagen)
WPJ	*World Policy Journal*
WQ	*The Washington Quarterly*

Abendroth, Wolfgang 1965: *Sozialgeschichte der Europäischen Arbeiterbewegung* (Frankfurt: Suhrkamp).

Abenheim, Donald 1990: 'The Citizen in Uniform: Reform and its Critics in the Bundeswehr', in Szabo, ed., 31-51.

Acker, Alexander 1984: 'Einsatz von Raketenartillerie im Verteidigungsnetz', in Weizsäcker, ed., 89-120.

Adomeit, Hannes 1982: *Soviet Risk-Taking and Crisis Behaviour. A Theoretical and Empirical Analysis* (London: George Allen & Unwin).

1988, 'Gorbatschows aussen—und sicherheitspolitische Initiativen: Chancen für Westeuropa?', *S + F*, 2, 65-69.

1989: 'The "Common House"': Gorbachev's Policies Towards Western Europe', in Clesse & Schelling, eds., 212-224.

1990: 'Gorbachev and German Unification: Revision of Thinking, Realignment of Power', *Problems of Communism*, 39:4, 1-23.

Adrets, André 1986: 'Franco-German Relations and the Nuclear Factor in a Divided Europe', in Laird, Robin F., ed.: *French Security Policy. From Independence to Interdependence* (Boulder, Col.: Westview), 105-120.

Afheldt, Eckhardt 1984: 'Verteidigung ohne Selbstmord. Vorschlag für den Einsatz einer leichten Infanterie', in Weizsäcker, ed., 41-88.

1984a, 'Verteidigen, ohne Selbstmord zu Begehen', in Schröder, ed., 115-132.

—, **Horst Afheldt,** Andreas von **Bülow,** Walter **Kons** & Helmut **Willmann** 1985: 'Streitgespräch, Alternative Strategien', *NG*, 2, 112-121.

Afheldt, Horst 1971a: 'Analyse der Sicherheitspolitik durch Untersuchung der kritischen Parameter', in Weizsäcker, ed., 23-74.

1971b: 'Entwicklungstendenzen der Sicherheitspolitik in Europa und umfassendere Ansätze zur Friedenssicherung', in Weizsäcker, ed., 417-456.

1976: *Verteidigung und Frieden: Politik mit militärischen Mitteln* (München: Carl Hanser).

1977: 'Das Problem der Sicherheitspolitik für die Bundesrepublik heute: Rationale Einsatzoptionen für den Ernstfall?', in Schwartz, Klaus-Dieter, ed.: *Sicherheitspolitik. Analysen zur politischen und militärischen Sicherheit*, second edition (München: Osang), 443-458.

1978a: 'Friedenspolitik mit militärischen Mitteln in den neunziger Jahren', in Schwartz, Klaus-Dieter, ed.: *Sicherheitspolitik. Analysen zur politischen und militärischen Sicherheit*, third edition (München: Osang), 639-656.

1978b: 'Tactical Nuclear Weapons and European Security', in SIPRI, eds.: *Tactical Nuclear Weapons: European Perspectives* (London: Taylor & Francis), 262-295

1983: *Defensive Verteidigung* (Reinbek: Rowohlt).

1984a: 'The Necessity, Preconditions and Consequences of a No-First-Use Policy, in Blackaby & al., eds., 57-66.

1984b: 'Neue Ansätze in der Sicherheitpolitik: Isolierte oder umfassende Problemlösungen', in SAS, eds., 87-102.

1984c: 'Defensive Verteidigung-Warum?', in Weizsäcker, ed., 13-28.

1985a: *Pour une défense non suicidaire en Europe*, Preface by Jean Klein. Postface by Georges Buis (Paris: Decouverte).

1985b: 'Abrüstung der Staaten und die kollektive Organisation des Weltfriedens?', in Lutz, ed., 64-81.

1985c: 'Frieden durch Überlegenheit oder Frieden durch Stabilität. Vorstufen zur kollektiven Sicherheit?', in Lutz, ed., 245-259.

1987a: 'Was heisst strukturelle Nichtangriffsfähigkeit?', *S + F*, 1, 5-9.

1987b: 'Defensive Verteidigung als politisch-strategische Konzeption', in Bühl, ed., 155-172.

1987c: *Atomkrieg. Das Verhängnis einer Politik mit militärischen Mitteln*, second edition (München: dtv).

1987d: 'Überlegungen zu einer defensiven Verteidigung in Theorie und Praxis', in Heisenberg & Lutz, eds., 291-305.

1988: 'Konventionelle Stabilität, Zivilschutz, Defensivüberlegenheit. Redebeiträge', in Bahr & Lutz, eds., 402-408.

1988a: 'New Policies, Old Fears', *BAS*, 44:7, 24-27.

1989: 'Alternative Defence Postures for NATO and the WTO', in Tromp, ed., 187-198.

1989a: *Der Konsens. Argumente für die Politik der Wiedervereinigung Europas* (Baden-Baden: Nomos).

1990: 'European Security and German Unity', in Brauch, ed., 9-20.

— & Hellmuth **Roth** 1971: 'Verteidigung und Abschreckung in Europa', in Weizsäcker, ed., 285-302.

— & Phillip **Sonntag** 1971: 'Stabilität und Abschreckung durch strategische Kernwaffen, eine Systemanalyse', in Weizsäcker, ed., 303-416.

Agrell, Wilhelm 1979: *Om kriget inte kommer. En debattbok om Sveriges framtida försvars— och säkerhetspolitik* (Stockholm: Liber).

Aichinger, Wilfried & Arthur Friedrich **Maiwald** 1989: 'Die Grossmächte und die europäischen Neutralen', *ÖMZ*, 2, 105-115.

"Ai/Sa", 1990: 'Deutschland im Wandel der Zeit', *ÖMZ*, 2, 109-114.

Albrecht, Ulrich 1982a: 'Western European Neutralism', in Mary Kaldor & Dan Smith, eds.: *Disarming Europe* (London: Merlin), 143-161.

1982b: *Kündigt den Nachrüstungsbeschluss* (Frankfurt: Fischer).

1983a: 'The Political Background of the Rapacki Plan of 1957 and Its Current Significance', in Steinke & Vale, eds., 117-135.

1983b: 'Neutralismus und Disengagement. Eine Alternative für die Bundesrepublik', in Deutsche Geselschaft für Friedens- und Konfliktforschung, eds.: *DFGK Jahrbuch 1982/83. Zur Lage Europas im globalen Spannungsfeld* (Baden-Baden: Nomos), 479-504.

1985: 'Alternative Designs of European Security, the Palme Commission Report and the Conventionalization of Forces', in Paul, ed., 141-183.

1987, 'Rüstungsdynamik und technologische Entwicklung', in Heisenberg & Lutz, eds., 386-395.

1988: 'The Role of Neutral and Non-Aligned Countries in a World of Global Powers', *CRPV*, 11:3, 130-135.

1989: 'The Role of Military R&D in Arms Build-Ups', in Gleditsch & Njølstad, eds., 87-104.

1990: 'The Role of Germany in Perspective', in Randle & Rogers, eds., 121-140.

—, ed. 1986: *Europa Atomwaffenfrei. Vorschläge, Plane, Perspektiven. Mit einem Essay von Berthold Meyer* (Köln: Pahl-Rugenstein).

Alford, Jonathan 1988: 'British Defence Choices in the 1990s and the Implications for Germany', in Kaiser & Roper, eds., 137-145.

Allison, Graham T. & Frederic A. **Morris** 1975: 'Armaments and Arms Control, Exploring the Determinants of Military Weapons', *Daedalus*, Summer, 99-129.

Alt, Franz 1983: *Frieden ist möglich* (München: Piper).

1986: 'Die geistige Atombombe: Vertrauen', in Gohl & Niesporek, eds., 21-28.

Altenburg, Wolfgang 1990: 'Die Zukunft der NATO', in Weizsäcker, ed., 303-316.

Alternative Defence Commission, 1983: *Defence Without the Bomb* (New York: Taylor & Francis).

1987, *The Politics of Alternative Defence. A Role for a Non-Nuclear Britain* (London: Paladin).

Altmann, Jürgen, Benoit **Morel,** Theodore **Postol** & Thomas **Risse-Kappen** 1987: 'Anti-Tactical Missile Defences and West European Security', *PRIF-R*, 3.

— & Joseph **Rotblat,** eds. 1989: *Verification of Arms Reductions. Nuclear, Conventional and Chemical* (Berlin: Springer).

Ammer, Thomas 1990: 'The Emerging Democratic Party System in the GDR', *AuP*, 4, 377-387.

Ammon, Herbert 1990: 'The Uncertainties of *Détente* and the Necessity of a Political Alternative to Bloc Confrontation in Europe', in Randle & Rogers, eds., 109-120.

— & Peter **Brandt,** eds. 1981: *Die Linke und die nationale Frage* (Reinbek: Rowohlt).

Anon., ed. 1969: *Civilian Defence: Gewaltloser Widerstand als Form der Verteidigungspolitik* (*Tagungsbericht*) (Biehlefeld: Bertelsmann).

Arkin, William M. 1986: 'Fewer Warheads in Europe', *BAS*, 8, 4-5.

— & Richard **Fieldhouse** 1985: *Nuclear Battlefields. Global Links in the Arms Race* (Cambridge, Mass.: Ballinger).

Aron, Raymond 1983: *Clausewitz. Philosopher of War* (London: Routledge).

Ash, Timothy Garton 1989: *The Uses of Adversity. Essays on the Fate of Central Europe* (Cambridge: Granta).

Augstein, Rudolf 1990: 'Die deutsche als eine europäische Nation', in Weizsäcker, ed., 343-346.

Baechler, Günther & Christiane **Rix** 1987: 'Sicherheitspolitische Differenzierungsprozesse, Wandel der Rolle des Militärischen in den "Ost-Ost-Beziehungen"', *HB*, 21.

Bahr, Egon 1983: 'Peace: A State of Emergency', in Steinke & Vale, eds., 141-154.

1984: 'Bericht der Arbeitsgruppe "Neue Strategien" beim SPD-Parteivorstand vom Juli 1983', in Brauch, ed., 275-290.

1985a: 'Observations on the Principle of Common Security', in Väyrynen, ed., 31-36.

1985b: 'Die Chancen der Geschichte in der Teilung suchen', *S + F*, 2, 70-72.

1985c: 'Gemeinsame Sicherheit, Voraussetzung für Kollektive Sicherheit', in Lutz, ed., 98-106.

1986: 'Gemeinsame Sicherheit: Einführende Überlegungen', in Bahr & Lutz, eds., 15-27.

1986a: 'Von der Strategie der Abschreckung zur gemeinsamen Sicherheit', in Ehmke & al., eds., 95-102.

1987: 'Korridor ohne Waffen für den Angriff', *EW*, 3, 140-143.

1987a: 'Strukturelle Nichtangriffsfähigkeit: Aktuelle Anmerkungen', *S + F*, 1, 3-5.

1987b: 'Gemeinsame Sicherheit. Ein Weg aus der Sackgasse', in Bahr & Lutz, eds., 19-28.

1988: 'Militärische Konfrontation. Konventionelle Stabilität. Strukturelle Nichtangriffs-fähigkeit', in Bahr & Lutz, eds., 13-24.

1988a: *Zum Europäischen Frieden. Eine Antwort auf Gorbatschow* (Berlin: Siedler).

1989: 'Das Bündnis und deutsche Interessen', Manuscript for a speech to the III International Wehrkundetagung 1989 in Munich, *F&A*, 29 (1/89), 29-36.

1991: *Sicherheit für und vor Deutschland*, (München: Hanser).

—, Andreas von **Bülow** & Karsten **Voigt** 1989: *European Security 2000: A Comprehensive Concept for European Security From a Social-Democratic Point of View* (Bonn: Presseservice der SPD). (In German: 'Europäische Sicherheit 2000. Überlegungen zu einem Gesamtkonzept für die Sicherheit Europas aus Sozialdemokratischer Sicht', *F&A*, 30 (2/89).

—, Dieter S. **Lutz**, Erwin **Müller** & Reinhard **Mutz** 1987: 'Defensive Zonen. Stellungnahme der IFSH zur Strukturellen Nichtangriffsfähigkeit und Konventionellen Stabilität in Europa', *HI*, 3.

— & Dieter S. **Lutz**, eds. 1986: *Gemeinsame Sicherheit. Idee und Konzept. Bd. 1: Zu den Ausgangsüberlegungen, Grundlagen und Strukturmerkmalen Gemeinsamer Sicherheit* (Baden-Baden: Nomos).

— & —, eds. 1987: *Gemeinsame Sicherheit. Dimensionen und Disziplinen. Bd. 2: Zu rechtlichen, ökonomischen, psychologischen und militärischen Aspekten Gemeinsamer Sicherheit* (Baden-Baden: Nomos).

— & —, eds. 1988: *Gemeinsame Sicherheit. Konventionelle Stabilität, Bd. 3: Zu den militärischen Aspekten Struktureller Nichtangriffsfähigkeit im Rahmen Gemeinsamer Sicherheit* (Baden-Baden: Nomos).

Bahr, Hans Eckehard 1990: 'Von der Armee zur europäischen Friedenstruppe', in idem, ed., 9-48.

—, ed. 1990: *Von der Armee zur europäischen Friedenstruppe* (München: Knaur).

Bajusz, William D. & Lisa D. **Shaw** 1990: 'The Forthcoming "SNF Negotiations"', *Survival*, 32:4, 333-347.

Bald, Detlev 1987: 'Die Lage Deutschlands und der Krieg der Zukunft. Sicherheitspolitische und militärische Planungen des deutschen Generalstabs in den Jahren 1954/25', in —, ed., 15-70.

1987a: 'Erfahrungen des Weltkrieges und Ansätze zu einem alternativen Verteidigungskonzept in den fünfziger Jahren, die Miliz', in —, ed., 71-82.

1989: 'Traditions in Military-Strategic Thought in Germany and the Problem of Deterrence', Paper presented to the 30th ISA Convention.

1990: 'Zum aussen—und sicherheitspolitischen Grundgesetz der deutschen Staaten. Der völkerrechtliche Rahmen der 2 plus 4 Verhandlungen', *S + F*, 8,2, 59-65.

—, ed. 1987: *Militz als Vorbild? Zum Reservistenkonzept der Bundeswehr* (Baden-Baden: Nomos).

— & Paul **Klein**, eds. 1988: *Wehrstruktur der neunziger Jahre. Reservistenarmee, Miliz oder ...?* (Baden-Baden: Nomos).

—, Thomas **Krämer-Badoni** & Roland **Wakenhut** 1981: 'Innere Führung und Sozialisation. Ein Beitrag zur Sozio-Psychologie des Militärs', in Steinweg, Reiner, ed. 1986: *Unsere Bundeswehr? Zum 25-jährigen Bestehen einer umstrittenen Institution* (Frankfurt: Suhrkamp), 134-166.

Ball, Desmond & al. 1987: *Crisis Stability and Nuclear War*, (Ithaca: AAAS).

Baring, Arnulf 1988: *Unser neuer Grössenwahn. Deutschland zwischen Ost und West* (Stuttgart: Deutsche Verlags-Anstalt).

Bark, Dennis L. & David R. **Gress** 1989: *A History of West Germany*, 1: *From Shadow to Substance* 1945-1963, 2: *Democracy and its Discontents* 1963-1988 (Oxford: Basil Blackwell).

Barnaby, Frank 1986: *The Automated Battlefield*, (New York: Free Press).

— & Egbert **Boeker** 1982: 'Defence Without Offence. Non-nuclear Defence for Europe', *Peace Studies Papers*, 8, (Bradford: School of Peace Studies).

— & Marlies ter **Borg**, eds. 1986: *Emerging Technologies and Military Doctrine. A Political Assessment* (London: Macmillan).

Bartke, Matthias & Margret **Johannsen**, eds. 1990: 'Zur Zukunft Deutschlands. Reden vom 2. internationalen Ost-West-Workshop über Gemeinsame Sicherheit', *HB*, 44.

Basler, Gerhard 1990, 'Die "Herbstrevolution" und die Ost-West-Beziehungen der DDR', *EA*, 1, 13-18.

Batscheider, Tordis & Peter **Schlotter** 1989, 'Angst vor den Deutschen? Über Sicherheitsdenken und Sicherheitspolitik in Frankreich', in Vogt, ed., 99-108.

Baudisch, Kurt, ed. 1988: *European Security and Non-Offensive Defence* (Berlin: WFSW).

Baudissin, Wolf Graf von 1986: 'Dreissig Jahre Bundeswehr. Licht und Schatten', in Borkenhagen, ed., 15-32.

Bauer, Harald 1989, 'Frankreich und die Zukunft Europas. Jalta überwinden oder sich am status quo festklammern?', in Ehrhart, H.-G., & A.P. Teicht, 'Sicherheitspartner im Werden? Frankreich und die europäische Sicherheit', *HB*, 39, 34-64.

Baumann, Eleonore & al. 1990: *Der Fischer Weltalmanach*. *Sonderband DDR* (Frankfurt: Fischer).

Baumann, Wolf-Rüdiger 1989: 'Die deutsche Frage aus der Sicht der CDU', in Blumenwitz & Zieger, eds., 99-108.

Beaufre, Andrè 1963, *Introduction a la Strategie* (Paris: Armand Collin).

1965: *Deterrence and Strategy* (London: Faber and Faber)

1972: *La guerre revolutionnaire. Les nouvelles formes de la guerre* (Paris: Fayard).

1974: *Strategy for Tomorrow* (London: Macdonald and Jane's).

Bebermeyer, Hartmut 1984: 'Verteidigungsökonomie am Scheideweg', in SAS, eds., 9-34.

1989, 'Die Sicherheit und ihre Kosten', in SAS, eds., 118-136.

1990, 'The Fiscal Crisis of the Bundeswehr', in Brauch & Kennedy, eds., 128-147.

— & Bernd **Grass** 1984, 'Unsere Streitkräfte auf dem Weg in die Ressourcenkrise', in Brauch, ed., 176-189.

— & Lutz **Unterseher** 1986: *Eine künftige Bundesmarine im Rahmen einer defensiven Verteidigungskonzeption* (Bonn: SAS).

1989: 'Wider die Grossmannssucht zur See, Das Profil einer defensiven Marine', in SAS, eds., 165-187.

Bebler, Anton 1987: 'Jugoslawiens nationale Verteidigung. Parts 1-2', *ÖMZ*, 4-5, 301-310, 414-422.

Becker, Kurt 1986: 'Möglichkeiten der bilateralen Zusammenarbeit', in Kaiser & Lellouche, eds., 194-200.

Behrmann, Günter C. 1988: 'Volk, Verfassung, Staat, Kultur, Geschichte und Nation. Das nationalpolitische Orientierungsfeld der Deutschen im Wandel', in Jeismann, Karl-Ernst, ed.: *Einheit-Freiheit-Selbstbestimmung. Die Deutsche Frage im historisch-politischen Bewusstsein* (Frankfurt: Campus), 81-103.

Beise, Marc 1990: 'Die DDR und die Europäische Gemeinschaft. Vertiefte EG-Beziehungen als Vorstufe zur deutschen Einheit?', *EA*, 4, 149-158.

Bender, Peter 1986: 'Sicherheitspartnerschaft und friedliche Koexistenz. Zum Dialog zwischen SPD und SED', *NG*, 4, 342-348.

1986a: *Neue Ostpolitik. Vom Mauerbau bis zum Moskauer Vertrag* (München: dtv).

1988: 'Die Notgemeinschaft der Teilungsopfer', in Papcke & Weidenfeld, eds., 76-86.

Benjowski, Klaus & Wolfgang **Schwarz** 1989: 'Militärische Aspekte der Sicherheit-gemeinsame Sicherheit statt Abschreckung', in Schmidt & al., 106-122.

Berger, Markus 1986: 'Vom Nutzen der französischen Nuklearmacht', in Kaiser & Lellouche, eds., 187-193.

Bergstein, Svend 1985: 'Kritik af tekno-forsvaret', *Forsvaret Idag*, 5, 8-9.

Bernhardt, Georg 1988: 'Wehrpflicht und Wehrdienst in den 90er Jahren. Probleme für Führung, Ausbildung und Motivation, in Bald & Klein, eds., 41-56.

Bertele, Manfred 1982: 'Struktur und Dislozierung von Landstreitkräften in Europa. Mögliche Funktionen vereinbarter Beschränkungen bei der Schaffung militärischen Gleichgewichts', in Nehrlich, Uwe, ed.: *Die Einhegung sowjettischer Macht. Kontrolliertes militärisches Gleichgewicht als Bedingung europäischer Sicherheit* (Baden-Baden: Nomos), 375-420.

Bertram, Christoph 1988: 'Britain's Nuclear Weapons and West German Security', in Kaiser & Roper, eds., 201-209.

Best, George 1983: *Humanity in Warfare. The Modern History of the International Law of Armed Conflict* (London: Methuen).

Betts, Richard K. 1987, *Nuclear Blackmail and Nuclear Balance* (Washington: Brookings).

Biddle, Stephen D. 1988: 'The European Conventional Balance: A Reinterpretation of the Debate', *Survival*, 30:2, 99-121.

Biedenkopf, Kurt H. 1986: 'Die Akzeptanz einer Friedenssicherung mit Waffen', in Gohl & Niesporek, eds., 28-44.

1989: *Zeitsignale. Parteienlandschaft im Umbruch* (München: Bertelsmann).

Biehle, Alfred, ed. 1985: *Alternative Strategien. Das Hearing im Verteidigungsausschuss des Deutschen Bundestages, Die schriftlichen Gutachten und Stellungnahmen* (Koblenz: Bernard & Graefe).

Bingen, Dieter 1989: 'Westverschiebung Polens und Revisionsanspruch der Bundesrepublik Deutschland. Die polnische Westgrenze als Stein des Anstosses in den polnisch-deutschen Beziehungen', in Haberl & Hecker, eds., 155-176.

Binnendijk, Hans 1989: 'NATO's Nuclear Modernization Dilemma', *Survival*, 31:2, 137-155.

Birkenbach, Hanne-Margret 1989: 'Die SPD-SED-Vereinbarungen über den "Streit der Ideologien und die gemeinsame Sicherheit". Eine Fallstudie zu den Chancen und Schwierigkeiten kommunikativer Friedensstrategien', *HB*, 37.

Bischof, Henrik 1989: 'Die Krise der SED-Ideologie im Lichte der Reformprozesse im Realsozialismus', *Kurzp.*, 5.

Blackaby, Frank, Josef **Goldblatt** & Sverre **Lodgaard**, eds. 1984: *No-First-Use* (London: Taylor & Francis).

Blechman, Barry & Cathleen **Fisher** 1990: 'West German Arms Control Policy', in Laird, Robbin, ed.: *West European Arms Control Policy*, (Durham: Duke U.P.), 71-122.

Bleek, Wilhelm 1990: 'Der Aufbau der Politikwissenschaft in der ehemaligen DDR', *DA*, 21:11, 1678-1688.

— & Johannes L. **Kuppe** 1990: 'Deutschlands-Perspektiven', in Baumann & al., 45-96.

Bloch, Jean de 1898: *La Guerre* (Traduction de l'ouvrage russe La Guerre Future), vols. 1-6 (Paris: Paul Dupont).

Bluhm, Georg 1990: 'Deutschland: Entspannung und der Frieden in Europa', in Weizsäcker, ed., 54-76.

Blumenwitz, Dieter 1989: 'Die deutsche Frage im Spiegel der Parteien. Ein Schlusswort zu den verfassungsrechtlichen Grenzen der Deutschlandpolitik der Parteien', in Blumenwitz & Zieger, eds., 173-178.

— & Gottfried **Zieger**, eds. 1989: *Die deutsche Frage im Spiegel der Parteien* (Bonn: Wissenschaft und Politik).

Bluth, Christoph 1986: 'SDI: the Challenge to West Germany', *International Affairs*, 2, 247-264.

1988: 'British-German Defence Relations, 1955-80. A Survey', in Kaiser & Roper, eds., 1-40.

1990: *New Thinking in Soviet Military Policy* (London: Pinter).

Boeker, Egbert & Lutz **Unterseher** 1986: 'Emphasizing Defence', in Barnaby & Borg, eds., 89-109.

Bomsdorf, Falk 1989: *Sicherheit im Norden Europas. Die Sicherheitspolitik der fünf nordischen Staaten und die Nordeuropapolitik der Sowjetunion* (Baden-Baden: Nomos)

Bonin, Bogislaw von 1954: 'Juli-Studie', in Brill, ed. 1989, 69-101 (with appendices).

1955: 'Die militärische Bedeutung atomarer Waffen', in 1976, 32-52.

1955a: 'Das Gleichgewicht der Kräfte', in 1976, 49-52.

1955b: 'Angst vor Neutralität?', in 1976, 53-57.

1955c: 'Wiederbewaffnung und gleichzeitig Sicherheit. Ein Lösungsvorschlag für Regierung und Opposition', in Brill, ed. 1989, 132-141.

1956: 'Januar-Denkschrift', in Brill, ed. 1989, 255-266.

1958: 'Unfähigkeit oder böser Wille? Eine kritische Betrachtung der Militärpolitik der Bundesregierung', in 1976, 58-70.

1958a: 'Befehl im Widerstreit?', in 1976, 71-84.

1966: 'Die Schlacht von Kursk. Ein Modell für die Verteidigung der Bundesrepublik', in 1976, 94-105.

1976: *Opposition gegen Adenauers Sicherheitspolitik. Eine Dokumentation zusammengestellt von Heinz Brill* (Hamburg: Neue Politik).

— & Arthur **Stegner** 1955: 'Stegner-Bonin-Plan', in Brill, ed. 1989, 248-253.

—, Wend von **Wietersheim** & Smilo Freiherr von **Lüttwitz** 1955: 'Wiedervereinigung und Wiederbewafnung—kein Gegensatz', in Bonin 1976, 21-26.

Booth, Ken 1990: 'Steps Towards Stable Peace in Europe: A Theory and Practice of Coexistence', *International Affairs*, 66:1, 17-45.

Borg, Marlies ter & Wim **Smit**, eds. 1989: *Non-provocative Defence as a Principle of Arms Control and Its Implictions for Assessing Defence Tecnologies* (Amsterdam: Free U.P.).

Borkenhagen, Franz H.U. 1984: 'Anmerkungen eines Logistikers', in SAS, eds., 174-175.

1984a: 'Grundzüge einer effizienten Logistik in einem militärischen Defensivkonzept', in Weizsäcker, ed., 29-40.

300   BIBLIOGRAPHY

1984b, 'Die Neutronenwaffe, Militärische und sicherheitspolitische Perspektiven', in SAS, eds., 79-86.

1985a, 'Gefahren für eine defensive Vorneverteidigung', ÖMZ, 1, 47-52.

1985b: 'Militärische Defensivkonzepte in einem System der Kollektiven Sicherheit, in Lutz, ed., 260-274.

1987a: 'Aspekte der sicherheitspolitischen Diskussion in der Bundesrepublik Deutschland. Aus dem Blickpunkt der SPD.', ÖMZ, 2, 138-145.

1987b: 'Strukturwandel im Einklang mit dem Bundnis. Mögliche Rahmenbedingungen für eine Strukturelle Nichtangriffsfähigkeit', NG, 5, 448-451.

1988a: Anhörung "Konventionelle Stabilität', in Bahr & Lutz, eds., 412-418.

1988b: 'Der europäische Pfeiler der westlichen Allianz, AZ, B 18/88 (29 April), 35-45.

1989: 'Soldat neben der Gesellschaft?', in SAS, eds., 102-107.

—, ed. 1986: Bundeswehrdemokratie in Oliv. Streiträfte im Wandel (Berlin: Dietz).

Boserup, Anders 1985, 'Non-offensive Defence in Europe', in Paul, ed., 194-209.

1990, 'Krieg, Staat und Frieden. Eine Weiterführung der Gedanken von Clausewitz', in Weizsäcker, ed., 244-263.

— & Andrew Mack 1974: War Without Weapons. Non-Violence in National Defence (London: Pinter).

— & Robert Neild, eds. 1990: The Foundations of Defensive Defence (London: Macmillan).

Boutwell, Jeffrey 1990: 'Party Politics and Security Policies in the FRG', in Szabo, ed., 123-148.

Böge, Volker 1986: 'Grüne und sozialdemokratische Friedenspolitik im Vergleich', S + F, 4, 199-202.

1987: 'Rüstungssteuerung am Ende. Mit einseitig-unabhängiger Abrüstung einen neuen Anfang machen!', in Heisenberg & Lutz, eds., 737-750.

1988: 'Common Security—An Alternative?', Green Peace Policy, 13, 11-12.

— & Irene Schulert 1986: 'Abrüstung und Umrüstung bei Andreas von Bülow. Zur Kritik des "Bülow-Papiers" aus Grüner Sicht', S + F, 3, 162-164.

— & Peter Wilke 1984: Sicherheitspolitische Alternativen. Bestandaufnahme und Vorschläge zur Diskussion (Baden-Baden: Nomos).

Bölkow, Ludwig 1990: 'Ist Verteidigungsdominanz technisch möglich?', in Weizsäcker, ed., 113-122.

Bracken, Paul 1976: 'Urban Sprawl and NATO Defence', Survival, 18:6, 254-260.

Brandstetter, Karl J. 1987: 'Der Griff nach der Bombe. Die Auseinandersetzung zwischen den Regierungen Eisenhower und Adenauer um die Atombewaffnung der Bundeswehr', Blätter, 7, 892-909.

Brandt, Harm-Hinrich 1987: 'The Revolution of 1848 and the Problem of Central European Nationalities', in Schulze, ed., 107-136.

Brandt, Willy 1988, 'The SIPRI 1987 Olof Palme Memorial Lecture, "Security and Disarmament, Change and Vision" ', in SIPRI Yearbook 1988. World Armaments and Disarmament (Oxford: Oxford U.P.), 539-547.

Brauch, Hans Günter 1983a: Die Raketen kommen. Vom NATO-Dobbelbeschluss bis zur Stationierung (Köln: Bund).

1983b: 'INF and the Current NATO Discussion on Alliance Strategy: A German Perspective', in Holm, Hans Henrik & Nikolai Petersen, eds.: The European Missile Crisis: Nuclear Weapons and Security Policy (London: Pinter), 156-202.

1983c, Perspektiven einer europäischen Friedensordnung. Kann das Europäische Parlament eine Rolle beim Zustandekommen einer Europäischen Friedensordnung spielen? (Berlin: Militärpolitik und Rüstungsbegrenzung, 3).

1984: 'Sicherheitspolitik im Umbruch. Aussenpolitische Rahmenbedingungen und Entwicklungschancen sicherheitspolitischer Alternativen', in Vogt, ed., 145-159.

1984a: Der Angriff aus dem All. Rüstungswettlauf im Weltraum (Bonn: Dietz).

1985: 'Perspektiven einer europäischen Sicherheitspolitik', in Strübel, Manfred, ed.: Friedens—und Sicherheitspolitische Alternativen. Konzepte: Kontroversen, Perspektiven (Giessen: Schmitz), 27-46.

1987a: 'Vertrauensbildende Massnahmen (VBM) und Konferenz über Vertrauens—und Sicherheitsbildende Massnahmen und Abrüstung in Europa (KVAE): Eine Einführung', in —, ed., 21-64.

1987b: 'Vertrauensbildung und Vertrauens—und Sicherheitsbildende Massnahmen zwischen Rüstungsdynamik und Rüstungskontrolle, Überlegungen zur Weiterentwicklung des V(S)BM-Konzepts', in idem, ed., 401-421.

1988: 'The Federal Republic of Germany, Searching for Alternatives', in Rudney, Robert & Luc Reuchler, eds.: *European Security Beyond the Year 2000* (New York: Praeger), 79-102.

1988a: 'West German Alternatives for Reducing Reliance on Nuclear Weapons', in Hopmann & Barnaby, eds., 146-182.

1989, 'Europäische Raketenabwehr, Eine trügerische Defensive', in SAS, eds., 34-47.

1989a: 'Nuclear Weapons in Europe after the INF Agreement', in Harle & Sivonen, eds., 155-178.

1990: 'German Unity, Conventional Disarmament, Confidence Building Defence and a New European Order of Peace and Security', in idem, ed., 21-74.

1990a: 'Europa—Haus des Friedens. Ein Fundament, drei Pfeiler und ein Baustein für eine europäische Friedensordnung', in Vogt, ed., 52-70.

—, ed. 1984: *Sicherheitspolitik am Ende. Eine Bestandsaufnahme, Perspektiven und neue Ansätze* (Gerlingen: Bleicher).

—, ed. 1987: *Vertrauensbildende Massnahmen und Europäische Abrüstungskonferenz. Analysen, Dokumente und Vorschlage* (Gerlingen: Bleicher).

—, ed. 1990: 'German Unity and the Future European Order of Peace and Security', *APR*, 38.

— & Rip **Bulkeley** 1988: 'The Anti-Ballistic Missile Treaty and World Security', *AR*, 14.

— & Lutz **Unterseher** 1984: 'Getting Rid of Nuclear Weapons', *JPR*, 21:2, 193-200.

1990: 'A Survey of the German Debate on Conventional Alternatives for the Defense of Central Europe', in Brauch, Hans Günter & Robert Kennedy, eds. 1990: *Alternative Conventional Defense Postures in the European Theatre. Vol. 2* (New York, Taylor & Francis, forthcoming).

— & Robert **Kennedy**, eds. 1989: *Alternative Conventional Defense Postures for the European Theatre. Vol.1: The Military Balance and Domestic Constraint*. (New York: Taylor & Francis).

Bredow, Wilfried von 1983: 'Geschichte als Element der deutschen Identität?', in Weidenfeld, ed., 102-118.

1989: 'Die deutsch-deutschen Beziehungen, ein Sonderfall', in Haberl & Hecker, eds., 207-225.

Bredthauer, Karl D. & Klaus **Mannhardt**, eds. 1981: *Es geht ums Überleben. Warum wir die Atomraketen ablehnen* (Köln: Pahl-Rugenstein).

Brie, Andrè 1989: 'Reducing the Most Offensive Weapon Systems', in Borg & Smit, eds., 221-230.

Brigot, Andrè 1989: 'A Neighbour's Fears: Enduring Issues in Franco-German Relations', in Prestre, Philippe G. Le, eds.: *French Security Policy in a Disarming World. Domestic Challenges and International Constraints* (Boulder: Lynne Rienner), 85-104.

Brill, Heinz 1987: *Bogislaw von Bonin im Spannungsfeld zwischen Wiederbewaffnung, Westintegration, Wiedervereinigung. Ein Beitrag zur Entstehungsgeschichte der Bundeswehr 1952-1955* (Baden-Baden: Nomos).

—, ed. 1989: *Bogislaw von Bonin im Spannungsfeld zwischen Wiederbewaffnung, Westintegration, Wiedervereinigung. Band 2, Dokumente und Materialien* (Baden-Baden, Nomos).

Brinckley, Douglas 1987: 'Kennan-Acheson: The Disengagement Debate', *The Atlantic Community Quarterly*, Winter, 413-425.

Brock, Lothar, Mathias **Jopp**, Berthold **Meyer**, Norbert **Ropers** & Peter **Schlotter** 1988: 'France, Great Britain and West Germany. Dissenting Promoters of Security Cooperation in Western Europe', *PRIF-R*, 4.

Brodie, Bernard 1946: *The Absolute Weapon* (New York: Harcourt, Brace).

1959: *Strategy in the Missile Age*, (Princeton: Princeton U.P.).

Brooks, Linton F. 1986 : 'Naval Power and National Security. The Case for the Maritime Strategy' (IS, Fall), in Miller & Evera, eds. 1988, 16-46.

Brossolet, Guy 1976: 'Das Ende der Schlacht', in Weizsäcker, ed., 93-223.

Bruckmann, Wolfgang 1984: 'Bericht vom Hearing "Militärische Rüstung abbauen, Soziale Verteidigung aufbauen! Perspektiven einer neuen europäischen Friedensordnung jenseits von NATO und Warschauer Pakt"', *Mediatus*, 10, 10-12.

Bruns, Wilhelm 1989: 'Normalisierung oder Wiedervereinigung. Wie geht es weiter in den deutsch-deutschen Beziehungen?' (Bonn: Friedrich Ebert Stiftung).

1990, 'Von der Koexistenz über die Vertragsgemeinschaft zur Konföderation? Thesen', *Kurzp.*, 35.

1990a: 'Zur Diskussion über den sicherheitspolitischen Status des deutschen Bundesstaates', *Kurzp.*, 37.

1990b: 'Die äusseren Aspekte der deutschen Einigung', *Studie*, 40.

1991: 'Zur Rolle Deutschlands in der interna-tionalen Politik', *Studie*, 45.

— & Wulf **Lapins,** eds. 1991: 'Die Bundeswehr vor neuen Aufgaben und Herausforderungen', *Studie*, 44.

Brückner, Herbert 1990: 'Neuer deutscher Nationalismus und die Metaphysisk des Wirtschaftswunders', *NG*, 37:4, 314-326.

Buchan, Alastair 1964: 'The Multilateral Force, An Historical Perspective', in Kissinger, ed. 1965, 264-287.

Bull, Hedley 1973: 'Strategic Arms Limitation. The Precedent of the Washington and London Naval Treaties', in Kaplan, Morton A., ed.: *SALT, Problems and Prospects* (Morristown: General Learning), 26-52.

Bundeskanzleramt 1985: *Landesverteidigungsplan* (Wien: Österreichische Staatsdruckerei).

Bundesministerium der Verteidigung 1985: *Weissbuch 1985: Zur Lage und Entwicklung der Bundeswehr* (Bonn: Ministry of Defence).

Bundesregierung 1977: *Dokumentation zur Entspannungspolitik der Bundesregierung* (Bonn: Presse—und Informationsamt der Bundesregierung).

1981, *Dokumentation zur Entspannungspolitik der Bundesregierung. Deutschlandpolitik* (Bonn: Presse—und Informationsamt der Bundesregierung).

Bundy, McGeorge 1986: 'Existential Deterrence and its Consequences', in Maclean, Douglas, ed.: *The Security Gamble* (Totowa: Rowman & Allanhead), 3-13.

—, George F. **Kennan,** Robert S. **McNamara** & Gerard **Smith** 1982, 'Nuclear Weapons and the Atlantic Alliance' (Foreign Affairs, Spring 1982), in Bundy, W., ed. 1985, 23-40.

Bundy, William P. ed. 1985: *The Nuclear Controversy. A Foreign Affairs Reader* (New York: New American Library).

Burley, Anne-Marie 1989: 'The Once and Future German Question', *Foreign Affairs*, 68:5, 65-83.

Buro, Andreas 1982a: *Zwischen sozial-liberalem Zerfall und konservativer Herrschaft. Zur Situation der Friedens—und Protestbewegung in dieser Zeit* (Offenbach: 2000).

1983a, 'Principles and Problems of Alternative Peace Strategies', in Steinke & Vale, eds., 173-186.

1983b: 'Striktes Defensivkonzept als Alternative', *Antimilitarismus*, 3.

1987: 'Strukturelle Nichtangriffsfähigkeit unter friedenspolitischer Perspektive', *S + F*, 1, 16-21.

1988: 'Bemerkungen zur Diskussion über konventionelle Stabilität', in Bahr & Lutz, eds., 429-432.

1990: 'Die Zivilisierung Europas steht noch voran. Zur Begründung der Kampagne "Bundesrepublik ohne Armee" (BoA)', *Blätter*, 9, 1106-1115.

Bussmann, Walter 1983: 'Das deutsche Nationalbewusstsein im 19. Jahrhundert', in Weidenfeld, ed., 64-82.

Butterwege, Christoph 1989: 'Die Opposition auf der Suche nach einer friedenspolitischen Konzeption. Sozialdemokratische und Grüne Alternativen zur Sicherheitspolitik der Bundesregierung', in IMSF, eds., 278-291.

Buzan, Barry 1983: *People, States and Fear. The National Security Problem in International Relations* (Brighton: Wheatsheaf).

1986: 'A Framework for Regional Security Analysis', in idem, Rother Rizwi & al.: *South Asian Insecurity and the Great Powers* (London: Macmillan), 3-33.

—, Morten **Kelstrup,** Pierre **Lemaitre,** Elzbieta **Tromer** & Ole **Wæver** 1990: *The European Security Order Recast. Scenarios for the Post-Cold War Era* (London: Pinter).

Büchler, Hans 1988: 'Die zweite Phase der Deutschlandpolitik. Gedanken zur Fortentwicklung der deutsch-deutschen Beziehungen', *DA*, 21:10, 1042-1048.

Bülow, Andreas von 1984a: *Alpträume West gegen Alpträume Ost. Ein Beitrag zur Bedrohungsanalyse* (Bonn: SPD).

1984b: 'Gedanken zur Weiterentwicklung der Verteidigungsstrategie in West und Ost', in Brauch, ed., 223-244.

1985a, 'Die eingebildete Ohnmacht', *EW*, 2, 83-85.

1985b: 'Strategie vertrauensschaffender Sicherheitsstrukturen in Europa. Wege zur Sicherheitspartnerschaft', *Blätter*, 10, 1267-1274.

1986: 'Vorschlag für eine neue Bundeswehrstruktur der 90er Jahre. Einstieg in die strukturelle Nichtangriffsfähigkeit', *EW*, 11, 636-638.

1986a: 'Defensive Entanglement, An Alternative Strategy for NATO', in Pierre, ed., 112-151.

1987: 'Stellungnahme zu Christian Krauses Kritik', *S + F*, 3, 195-197.

1988a: 'Friedensordnung und Verteidigung in Europe. Technik, Taktik, Strategie und Politik, Gestaltungsraum und Sachzwänge, in —, Funk & Müller, 9-46.

1988b: 'Vorschlag für eine Bundeswehrstruktur der 90er Jahre. Auf dem Weg zur konventionellen Stabilität', in —, Funk & Müller, 95-110.

1988c: 'Neues Denken auch in den Militärdoktrinen', in —, Funk & Müller, 195-207.

1988d: 'Thesen zur strukturellen Nichtangriffsfähigkeit', *Blätter*, 11, 1376-1379.

1989: 'Conventional Stability. An Overall Concept', in Borg & Smit, eds., 45-48.

1989a: 'Restructuring the Ground Forces', in Borg & Smit, eds., 161-174.

— & Helmut **Funk** 1987: 'Zum Problem der Strukturellen Nichtangriffsfähigkeit', *S + F*, 1, 14-16.

— 1988: 'The Achievement of Mutual Conventional Forces Defender Superiority in Central Europe from the Urals to the Atlantic', *Pugwash Newsletter*, 25:3, 108-110.

— 1988a: 'Statements zur Konventionellen Stabilität', in Bahr & Lutz, eds., 422-428.

—,— & Albrecht A.C. von **Müller** 1988: *Sicherheit für Europa* (Koblenz: Bernard & Graefe).

Calleo, David P. 1986: 'Deutschland und Amerika. Eine amerikanische Sicht', in & al., 45-96.

— & al. 1986: *Geteiltes Land—halbes Land? Essays über Deutschland, eingeleitet von Richard Löwenthal* (Frankfurt: Ullstein).

Campbell, Edwina 1989: 'Nuremberg and Beyond, Defining a New SPD Security Policy', in Griffith & al., 40-65.

1990, *Germany's Past and Europe's Future* (London: Brassey's).

Canby, Steven 1983: 'Military Reform and the Art of War', *Survival*, 25: 3, 120-127.

Carton, Allan 1984: 'Dissuasion Infra-nucleaire. L'Ecole allemande de techno-guerila', *Cahiers d'etudes strategiques*, 3 (Paris: CIRPES).

Cerutti, Furio & Rodolfo **Ragionieri**, eds. 1990: *Rethinking European Security* (New York: Crane Russak).

Chalmers, Malcolm 1990: 'Beyond the Alliance System', *WPJ*, 7:2, 215-250.

— & Lutz **Unterseher** 1987: 'Is There a Tank Gap? A Comparative Assessment of the Tank Fleets of NATO and the Warsaw Pact', *Peace Research Report*, 19 (Bradford: School of Peace Studies).

— & 1988, 'Is There a Tank Gap? Comparing NATO and Warsaw Pact Tank Fleets', *IS*, 13:1, 5-49.

— & 1989: 'Correspondence: The Tank Gap Data Flap. The Authors Reply', *IS*, 13:4, 187-194.

Charlier, Michael 1990: 'Deutschland: schwierig Vaterland', *Blätter*, 2, 179-187.

Clausewitz, Carl Von 1832: *Vom Kriege, Ungekürzter Text nach der Erstauflage* (1832-1834) (Frankfurt 1980: Ullstein).

Clemens, Clay 1988: 'Beyond INF, West Germany's Centre-Right Party and Arms Control in the 1990s', *International Affairs*, 65:1, 55-74.

Clesse, Armand & Thomas C. **Schelling**, eds. 1989: *The Western Community and the Gorbachev Challenge*. (Baden-Baden: Nomos)

Committee (1983) for Basic Rights and Democracy: 'Five Proposals for a New Security Policy', in Steinke & Vale, eds., 179-186.

Conetta, Carl & Charles **Knight** 1989: 'After Conventional Cuts, New Options for NATO Ground Defence' (Brookline, Mass.: Institute for Defense and Disarmament Studies).

1990: 'How Low Can NATO Go?', *DDA*, 3:2, 1-3.

—,— & Lutz **Unterseher** 1991: 'Toward Defensive Restructuring in the Middle East', *Project on Defense Alternatives Research Monograph*, (Cambridge, MA: Commonwealth Institute).

Cooney, James A. & al., eds. 1984: *The Federal Republic of Germany and the United States. Changing Political, Social, and Economic Relations* (Boulder: Westview).

Cotter, Donald R. 1983: 'Potential Future Roles for Conventional and Nuclear Forces in Defence of Western Europe', in ESECS, 209-253.

Czempiel, Ernst-Otto 1990: 'Die Modernisierung der Atlantischen Gemeinschaft', *EA*, 8, 275-286.

Danspeckgruber, Wolfgang 1986: 'Armed Neutrality: Its Application and Future', in Flanagan, Stephen J. & Fen Osler Hampson, eds.: *Securing Europe's Future* (London: Croom Helm), 242-279.

Davis, Jacquelyn K. and Robert L. **Pfaltzgraff**, Jr. 1989: 'The West German Left: Implications for U.S. Policy', in Griffith & al., 111-126.

Davy, Richard 1990: 'Grossbritannien und die deutsche Frage', *EA*, 4, 139-144.

Dawydow, Jurij P. & Dmitrij W. **Trenin** 1990: 'Die Haltung der Sowjetunion gegenüber der Deutschen Frage', *EA*, 8, 251-263.

Däniker, Gustav 1987: *Dissuasion. Schweizerische Abhaltestrategie Heute und Morgen* (Frauenfeld: Huber).

Dean, Jonathan 1985: 'MBFR: Past and Future', in Paul, ed., 82-91.

1985a: 'Directions in Inner-German Relations', *Orbis*, Fall, 609-632.

1987a: *Watershed in Europe. Dismantling the East-West Military Confrontation* (Lexington: Lexington Books).

1987b: 'The Future of Berlin', in Moreton, ed., 157-179.

1988a: 'Berlin in a Divided Germany: An Evolving International Regime', in George & al., eds., 83-105.

—1990: 'Alternative Defence—Answer to the Bundeswehr's Post-INF Problems?', in Szabo, ed., 188-216.

Deittert, Albert 1986: 'Von der Gefahrengemeinschaft zur Gemeinsamen Sicherheit', in Gohl & Niesporek, eds., 113-126.

De Lupis, Ingrid Detter 1987: *The Law of War* (Cambridge: Cambridge U.P.).

Dettke, Dieter 1984: 'No First Use: Ein Beitrag zur Konventionalisierung der Verteidigung Europas', in SAS, eds., 103-107.

Deutsch, Karl W. & al. 1957: *Political Community and the North Atlantic Area. International Organization in the Light of Historical Experience* (Princeton: Princeton U.P.).

Dibb, Paul 1988: *The Soviet Union: The Incomplete Superpower*, (London: Macmillan/IISS).

Dick, Charles J. & Lutz **Unterseher** 1986: 'Dialogue on the Military Effectiveness of Non-provocative Defence', in Barnaby & Borg, eds., 239-250.

Digby, James 1975: 'Precision-guided Munitions', *AdP*, 118.

Dobrosielski, Marian 1990: 'Vom Rapacki—zum Jaruzelski-Plan. Ein polnischer Weg', in Lutz & Schmähling, eds., 113-142.

Doehler, Edgar & Horst **Haufe** 1989: *Militärhistorische Traditionen der DDR und der NVA* (Berlin: Militärverlag der DDR).

Dowe, Dieter & Kurt **Klotzbach**, eds. 1984: *Programmatische Dokumente der deutschen Sozialdemokratie* (Bonn: Dietz).

Dregger, Alfred 1988: 'Disarmament With Security: A German View of Current Alliance Developments', *Atlantic Community Quarterly*, Winter, 404-412.

1989: 'Sicherheit für Europa und das Atlantische Bündnis', in Wagemann, ed., 97-106.

Duke, Simon 1989: *United States Military Forces and Installations in Europe*. (Oxford: Oxford U.P.).

Dunn, Keith A. & William O. **Staudenmaier** 1985: 'The Retaliatory Offensive and Operational Realities in NATO', *Survival*, 27:3, 108-118.

Dunnigan, James F. 1983: *How to Make War. A Comprehensive Guide to Modern Warfare*, Updated Edition (New York: Quill).

Dupuy, William E. 1985: 'The Light Infantry: Indispensable Element of a Balanced Force', *Army*, June, 26-41.

Dünne, Ludger 1988: '"Strukturelle Nichtangriffsfähigkeit" und konventionelle Landstreitkräfte', in Bahr & Lutz, eds., 100-107.

1988a: 'Zur Frage der Realisierung "Struktureller Nichtangriffsfähigkeit" im Rahmen konventionell bewaffneter Landstreitkräfte', *HB*, 34.

Dürr, Hans-Peter 1987: 'Stabilitätsorientierte Sicherheitspolitik', *S + F*, 1, 22-23.

1988: 'Kooperation statt Konfrontation. Wie wir die globalen Herausforderungen gemeinsam anpacken konnen', *Wissenschaftliche Welt*, 1, 13-19.

—, Horst **Afheldt** & Albrecht A.C. von **Müller** 1984: *Exposé zu dem Forschungsprojekt* '*Stabilitätsorientierte Sicherheitspolitik*' (München: Max Planck Institute).

Earle, Edward Mead, ed. 1941: *Makers of Modern Strategy. Military Thought from Machiavelli to Hitler* (New York 1970: Atheneum).

Ebert, Theodor 1967a: 'Organization in Civilian Defence', in Roberts, ed., 255-273.

1968: *Gewaltfreier Aufstand: Alternative zum Bürgerkrieg* (Waldkirch: Waldkircher Verlag).

1981a: *Soziale Verteidigung. Vol. 1: Historische Erfahrungen und Grundzüge der Strategie* (Waldkirch: Waldkircher Verlag).

1981b: *Soziale Verteidigung. Vol. 2: Formen und Bedingungen des zivilen Widerstandes* (Waldkirch: Waldkircher Verlag).

1983: 'Techno-Commando Units or Social Defence? A Comparison', in Steinke & Vale, eds., 197-203.

1984: 'Ziviler Wiederstand im besetzten Gebiet', in Weizsäcker, ed., 231-264.

—, ed. 1970: *Ziviler Widerstand: Fallstudien aus der Innenpolitischen Friedens—und Konflik-tforschung* (Düsseldorf: Bertelsmann).

—, ed. 1971: *Soziale Verteidigung. Friedens—und Sicherheitspolitik in den 80er Jahren* (Berlin: Burchhardthaus).

Eekelen, Willem van 1990: 'WEU and the Gulf Crisis', *Survival*, 32:6, 519-532.

Ehmke, Horst 1986: 'Wege zur Sicherheitspartnerschaft. Aus der Tätigkeit der gemeinsamen Arbeitsgruppe von SPD-Bundestagsfraktion und PVAP', *Blätter*, 6, 669-674.

—, Karlheinz **Koppe** & Herbert **Wehner**, eds. 1986: *Zwanzig Jahre Ostpolitik. Bilanz und Perspektiven* (Bonn: Neue Gesellschaft).

Ehrhart, Hans-Georg 1987: *Französische Verteidigungspolitik im Wandel? Zur Problematik konventioneller Verteidigungskooperation zwischen Paris und Bonn* (Bonn: Friedrich-Ebert-Stiftung).

1989: 'Konventionelle Abrüstung als Gegenstand deutsch-französischer Sicherheitskooperation: Entwicklungen, Interesen, Perspektiven', *Studie*, 34.

1990: 'Ökonomische Aspekte des deutschen Wiedervereinigungsprozesses', *S + F*, 1, 9-12.

Eiselt, Gerhard 1988: 'Die Neutralisierung Europas als Weg zur Einheit Deutschlands', *DA*, 21, 11, 1163-1166.

Enders, Thomas 1986: 'ATM: Europas Verteidigung auch gegen Flugkörper', *EW*, 10, 560-568.

1988: 'START und europäische Sicherheitsinteressen', *EA*, 24, 722-730.

1988a: 'Nukleare Abschreckung in und für Europa. Einige grundsätzliche Überlegungen nach Unterzeichnung des INF-Vertrags', *Interne Studien*, 9 (Sankt Augustin: Konrad-Adenauer-Stiftung).

1990: 'Militärische Herausforderungen Europas in den neunziger Jahren', *EA*, 10, 321-329.

1990a: 'The Role of Nuclear Deterrence in Non-Provocative Defence', *Disarmament*, 13:2, 24-38.

— & Peter **Siebenmorgen** 1988: 'Überlegungen zu einem sicherheitspolitischen Gesamtkonzept der Bundesrepublik Deutschland', *EA*, 14, 385-392.

Engels, Dieter & Jürgen **Scheffran** 1987: Bundesdeutsche Weltraumpolitik. Grossmacht-streben im All', *Blätter*, 6, 764-779.

Eppler, Erhard 1981: *Wege aus der Gefahr* (Reinbek: Rowolt).

1988: *Wie Feuer und Wasser. Sind Ost und West Friedensfähig?* (Reinbek: Rowohlt).

Epstein, Joshua M. 1985: *The Calculus of Conventional War: Dynamic Analysis Without Lanchester Theory* (Washington: Brookings).

1988: 'Dynamic Analysis and the Conventional Balance in Europe', *IS*, 12:4, 154-165.

1990: *Conventional Force Reductions: A Dynamic Assesment*, (Washington: Brookings).

Erb, Gottfried 1989: 'Änderungsbedarf in der Polenspolitik', *NG*, 36, 11, 803-807.

Etzioni, Amitai 1962: *The Hard Way to Peace. A New Strategy* (New York: Collier).

Etzold, Thomas H. & John Lewis **Gaddis**, eds. 1978: *Containment. Documents on American Policy and Strategy, 1945-1950* (New York: Columbia U.P.).

ESECS (European Security Study Group) 1983: *Strengthening Conventional Deterrence in Europe. Proposal for the 1980s. Report of the European Security Study* (London: Macmillan).

Evera, Stephen W. Van 1984: *Causes of War*, Ph. D. Thesis (Berkeley: University of California).

1985: 'The Cult of the Offensive and the Origins of the First World War', in Miller, ed., 58-107.

Farndale, Martin 1988: 'Follow on Forces Attack', *NSN*, 3:2, 42-50.

Farwick, Dieter 1985: 'Eine nationale Option Moskaus? Überraschender Angriff mit begrenztem Ziel', *EW*, 12, 642-646.

1987: 'Modelle zur konventionellen Sicherheit', in Heisenberg & Lutz, eds., 751-762.

Fechner, Wolfgang 1990: 'Abzug, aber kein Abschied', *EW*, 11, 640-645.

Fels, Gerhard, Reiner K. **Huber**, Werner **Kaltefleiter**, Rolf F. **Pauls** & Franz-Joseph **Schulze**, eds. 1990: *Strategie-Handbuch*, Vols 1-2 (Herford: Mittler).

Finer, Samuel E. 1976: *The Men on Horseback. The Role of the Military in Politics*, Revised Edition (Harmondsworth: Penguin).

Fink, Hans Jürgen 1990: 'Die SPD in der DDR', *DA*, 23, 2, 180-185.

Fischer, **Benno** 1990: 'DDR-Rechtsextremismus als Vorbote der Systemkrise', *NG*, 37, 4, 332-338.

Fischer, **Horst** 1987: 'Koexistenz und Kooperation im modernen Völkerrecht. Gemeinsame Sicherheit und die Struktur des Rechts der Friedenssicherung', in Bahr & Lutz, eds., 55-84

Fischer, Johannes, ed. 1975 (Militärgeschichtliches Forschungsamt): *Verteidigung im Bündnis. Planung, Aufbau und Bewährung der Bundeswehr 1950-1972* (München: Bernard & Graefe).

Fischer, **Siegfried** 1990: 'Militärdoktrinen und internationale Sicherheit. Gedanken über die Zukunft der NVA', *S + F*, 1, 13-17.

FM 100-5 1982: Headquarters, Department of the Army: *Field Manual 100-5: Operations* (Washington: Government Printing Office).

Foschepoth, Josef 1988: 'Einleitung: Adenauer und die deutsche Frage', in —, ed., 7-28.

1988a: 'Westintegration statt Wiedervereinigung: Adenauers Deutschlandpolitik 1949-1955', in —, ed., 29-60.

—, ed. 1988: *Adenauer und die deutsche Frage* (Göttingen: Vandenhoech & Ruprecht).

FRAG (Forsvarsministerens Rådgivnings—og Analysegruppe) 1986: 'Mulig anvendelse af landbaserede sømålsmissiler i Danmark', *Report*, RAG 0-4/1986 (Copenhagen: Ministry of Defence).

Freedman, Lawrence 1983: *Evolution of Nuclear Strategy* (London: Macmillan).

1988: 'Britain's Nuclear Commitment to Germany', in Kaiser & Roper, eds., 184-200.

Frei, Daniel 1983: *Risks of Unintentional Nuclear War*, (Totowa, N.J.: Allanheld, Osmun/ UNIDIR).

Freundl, Siegfried 1984: 'Überlegungen zu einem Informations—und Führungsnetz für eine rein defensive Verteidigung', in Weizsäcker, ed., 167-178.

Frey, Eric G. 1987: *Division and Détente. The Germanies and Their Alliances* (New York: Praeger).

Fritsch-Bournazel, Renata 1987: 'The French View', in Moreton, ed., 64-82.

1988: *Confronting the German Question. Germans on the East-West Divide* (Oxford: Berg).

1989: 'The German Factor in Future East-West Relations', in Clesse & Schelling, eds., 225-235.

1990: *Europa und die deutsche Einheit*, (Bonn: Aktuell).

Fritzsche, Helmut 1989: 'The Security Debate in the Evangelical Church of the GDR', in Wæver & al., eds., 46-60.

Frowein, Jochen Abr. 1990: 'Rechtliche Probleme der Einigung Deutschlands', *EA*, 7, 233-238.

Fuhrer, H. R. 1987: 'Austria and Switzerland: the Defence Systems of Two Minor Powers', in Gann, L.H., ed.: *The Defence of Western Europe* (London: Croom Helm), 95-125

Funk, Helmut 1988: 'Die Integrierte Vorneverteidigung Mitteleuropas', in Bülow, — & Müller, 111-193.

1988a: 'Von der Doktrin zur Struktur', in Bülow, — & Müller, 208-219.

Gaddis, John Lewis 1982: *Strategies of Containment. A Critical Appraisal of Postwar American National Security Policy.* (New York: Oxford U.P.).

Galtung, Johan 1959: *Forsvar uten Militærvesen* (Oslo).

1964: 'Two Concepts of Defence', in 1976, 280-340.

1965: 'On the Meaning of Nonviolence', in 1976, 341-377.

1968: 'On the Strategy of Nonmilitary Defence. Some Proposals and Problems', in 1976, 378-426.

1969: 'Violence, Peace and Peace Research', *JPR*, 6, 3, 167-192.
1971: 'Nichtmilitärische Verteidigungsmassnahmen', in Ebert, ed., 84-93.
1976: *Peace, War and Defence. Essays in Peace Research. Volume Two* (Copenhagen: Ejlers).
1984: *There Are Alternatives. Four Roads to Peace and Security* (Nottingham: Spokesman).
1986: 'The Green Movement: A Socio-Historical Exploration', in 1988a, 343-356.
1988: 'The Peace Movement: A Structural-Functional Exploration', in 1988a, 322-342.
1988a: *Transarmaments and the Cold War. Essays in Peace Research. Volume VI* (Copenhagen: Ejlers).
— & Arne Næss 1955: *Ghandi's politiske etikk* (Oslo: Fanum).
Ganser, Helmut 1988: 'Konventionelle Stabilität', in Bahr & Lutz, eds., 433-437.
Garett, James M. 1989: *The Tenuous Balance. Conventional Forces in Central Europe* (Boulder: Westview).
1990: *Central Europe's Fragile Deterrent Structure*, (London: Harvester Wheatsheaf).
Garthoff, Raymond L. 1985: *Détente and Confrontation. American-Soviet Relations From Nixon to Reagan* (Washington: Brookings).
Gat, Azar 1988: 'Clausewitz on Defence and Attack', *JSS*, 11, 1, 20-26.
1989: *The Origins of Military Thought From the Enlightenment to Clausewitz* (Oxford: Clarendon).
Gates, David 1987: *Non-Offensive Defence. A Strategic Contradiction?* (London: Alliance).
Gaus, Günter 1986: *Die Welt der Westdeutschen. Kritische Betrachtungen* (Köln: Kiepenheuer & Witsch).
1990: 'Rede an die Deutschen in der DDR', *Blätter*, 3, 310-318.
1990a (interviewed by Karl D. Bredthauer): 'Not und Tugend. Von deutschem Jubel über die eigene Unzulänglichkeit', *Blätter*, 5, 531-540.
Geiss, Imanuel 1985: *Das Deutsche Reich und die Vorgeschichte des Ersten Weltkriegs* (München: Piper).
1985a: *Das Deutsche Reich und der Erste Weltkrieg* (München: Piper).
1990: *Der lange Weg in die Katastrophe. Die Vorgeschichte des Ersten Weltkriegs 1815-1914* (München: Piper).
Genscher, Hans Dietrich 1987: 'Chancen einer zukunftsfähigen Gestaltung der West-Ost-Beziehungen' (Speech in Davos, 1 February 1987), *Blätter*, 3, 439-446.
1989: 'Kooperative Strukturen der Sicherheit: eine Perspektive für die Friedensordnung in Europa', *S + F*, 7, 2, 132-136.
George, Alexander L. 1988: 'Strategies for Facilitating Cooperation', in George & al., eds., 692-711.
—, Philip J. **Farley** & Alexander **Dallin**, eds. 1988: *U.S.-Soviet Security Cooperation. Achievements, Failures, Lessons* (New York: Oxford U.P.).
Gerber, Johannes 1984: 'Fordert die Wirtschaftlichkeit eine neue Struktur des Heeres?', in Jacobsen, Hans-Adolf & Heinz-Georg Lemm, eds.: *Heere International, Vol. 3* (Herford: Mittler), 9-52.
1985: *Die Bundeswehr im Nordatlantischen Bündnis* (Regensburg: Walhalla & Praetoria).
1987: 'Die konventionelle Nichtangriffsfähigkeit als militärische Dimension der Sicherheit in Mittel—und Nordeuropa', *S + F*, 1, 23-30.
1988: 'Militärökonomische Aspekte zur militärischen Stabilität in Mitteleuropa', in Bahr & Lutz, eds., 438-444.
Gerhard, Wilfried 1989: 'Angst vor Gorbatschow? Neues Denken in der Sowjetunion und politische Bewusstseinsstrukturen in der Bundesrepublik Deutschland', in Vogt, ed., 47-66.
Gerster, Florian 1990: 'Zwei-Zonen-Staat unter alliierter Kontrolle? Der Sicherheitspolitische Rahmen der deutschen Einheit', *S + F*, 8:2, 69-73.
Geyer, Micheal 1986: 'German Strategy in the Age of Machine Warfare, 1914-1945', in Paret, ed., 527-597.
Gibson, Irving M. 1941: 'Maginot and Liddell Hart: The Doctrine of Defense', in Earle, ed., 365-387.
Gilges, Konrad 1985: *Frieden ohne NATO. Perspektiven einer linken Friedenspolitik*, (Hamburg: VSA).
Glaessner, Gert-Joachim 1989: 'Don't trust the Germans? Anmerkungen zum Deutschland-Bild in der britischen Presse', *DA*, 22, 9, 1027-1034.

Gleditsch, Nils Petter & Olav Njølstad, eds. 1989: *Arms Races. Technological and Political Dynamics.* (London: Sage).

Gloannec, Anne-Marie Le 1986: 'Die Deutschen und die französische Abschreckungsstreitmacht: deutsch-französische Zweideutigkeiten', in Kaiser & Lellouche, eds., 90-100.

Gloeckner, Eduard 1990: 'Der Minister, die Armee und die deutsche Einheit', *EW*, 7, 384-387.

Glotz, Peter 1985: ' "Common Security" und "Strukturelle Nichtangriffsfähigkeit". Plädoyer für eine Politisierung des historischen Begriffs Kollektiver Sicherheit, in Lutz, ed., 107-114.

1987: 'Mehr Sicherheit durch FOFA?', *EW*, 4, 195-199.

1990: 'Gesamteuropa—Skizze für einen schwierigen Weg', *EA*, 2, 41-50.

1990a: 'Sicherheitspartnerschaft zwischen ideologischen Blöcken in Europa', in Weizsäcker, ed., 347-358.

Glucksman, Andrè 1967: *Le Discours de la Guerre* (Paris: l'Herne).

Gnesotto, Nicole 1986: 'Der Sicherheitspolitische Dialog 1954 bis 1986', in Kaiser & Lellouche, eds., 5-26.

Goblirsch, Josef 1984: 'Neue Leitidee für die Verteidigung: Technotaktik', in Weizsäcker, ed., 121-166.

Gohl, Diethelm 1986: 'Schritte zur Abrüstung. Plädoyer für das Gradualismus-Konzept', in Gohl & Niesporek, eds., 148-164.

— & Heinrich **Niesporek**, eds. 1986: *Sicher auf neuen Wegen. Mit Beiträgen von Franz Alt, Kurt Biedenkopf, Gustav Fehrenbach und anderen* (Warendorf: Gohl).

Gorlov, Sergei, ed. 1990: 'Soviet-German Military Cooperation, 1920-1933 (Documents Published for the First Time)', *International Affairs* (Moscow), 7, 95-113.

Görner, Rüdiger 1990: 'Von deutscher Souveränität', *NG*, 37, 4, 306-310.

Grass, Bernd 1984: 'Das Wehrpotential der 90er Jahren. Eine demographisch-statistische Analyse', in SAS, eds., 35-46.

1990: 'The Personnel Shortage of the Bundeswehr Until the Year 2000', in Brauch & Kennedy, eds., 97-112.

Grebing, Helga 1970: *Geschichte der deutschen Arbeiterbewegung* (München: dtv).

Greiner, Bernd 1990: 'Angst vor Rapallo. Amerikanische Reaktionen auf den Fall der Mauer', *Blätter*, 2, 159-167.

Griffith, William E. 1978: *The Ostpolitik of the Federal Republic of Germany* (Cambridge, Mass.: MIT).

1987: 'The American View', in Moreton, ed., 49-63.

1989: 'The Security Policies of the Social Democrats and the Greens in the Federal Republic of Germany', in — & al., 1—20.

— & al. 1989: *Security Perspectives of the West German Left. The SPD and the Greens in Opposition* (Washington: Pergamon).

Grin, John 1990: 'Options for the Communication System of NATO's Land Forces', *APR*, 31.

— & Lutz **Unterseher** 1988: 'The Spiderweb Defense', *BAS*, 44, 7, 28-31.

1989: 'Spezialisierung auf die Defensive: Einige Zusammenhänge', in SAS, eds., 139-148.

1990: 'Military Restructuring for Conventional Disarmament', in Auffermann, Burkhard, ed.: 'NOD or Disarmament in the Changing Europe?', *Research Reports*, 40 (Tampere: Tampere Peace Research Institute), 103-114.

1990a: '. . .den Bedrohungszirkel unterbrechen: Spinnennetz. Ein militärtheoretischer Beitrag zur Um—und Abrüstung', in Vogt, ed., 243-262.

Grosser, Alfred 1988: *Das Deutschland im Westen. Eine Bilanz nach 40 Jahren* (München: dtv).

Grunenberg, Antonia 1983: 'Die gespaltene Identität. Gesellschaftliches Dobbeltleben in der DDR', in Weidenfeld, ed., 210-228.

Grünen, die 1981:*Das Friedensmanifest der Grünen* (Bonn: Grünen).

1985: *Frieden und Freiheit durch einseitige Abrüstung. Bei uns anfangen. Diskussionsbeiträge zum Ratschlag der Friedensbewegung 1985* (Bonn: Grünen).

—, eds. 1985: *Euromilitarismus. Zur Bedeutung der "Europäisierung der Sicherheitspolitik"* (Bonn: Grünen).

Grünen im Bundestag, die 1984: *Angriff als Verteidigung. AirLand Battle, AirLand Battle 2000, Rogersplan. Eine Dokumentation* (Bonn: Grünen im Bundestag).

1987: *Ohne Waffen, aber nicht Wehrlos. Das Konzept der Sozialen Verteidigung* (Bonn: Grünen im Bundestag).
1988: *Militärblock West. Die NATO-Broschüre der Grünen* (Bonn: Grünen im Bundestag).
Gupta, Ronjon Das 1988: 'Anregungen zur Panzerrüstung' (Bonn: SAS).
Gutjahr, Lothar 1990: 'Wachsen oder wuchern? Die Aussenpolitik der CDU zwischen deutscher Wiedervereinigung und westeuropäischer Integration', *S + F,* 1, 30-34.
Haberl, Othmar Nikola 1989: 'Die deutsch-sowjetischen Beziehungen zwischen aussenwirtschaftlicher Normalität und der aussenpolitischen Suche nach einem modus vivendi', in & Hecker, eds., 229-248.
— & Hans **Hecker,** eds. 1989: *Unfertige Nachbarschaften. Die Staaten Osteuropas und die Bundesrepublik Deutschland* (Essen: Reimar Hobbing).
Hacke, Christian 1988: *Weltmacht wider Willen. Die Aussenpolitik der Bundesrepublik Deutschland* (Stuttgart: Klett).
Hacker, Jens 1989: 'Die deutsche Frage aus der Sicht der SPD', in Blumenwitz & Zieger, eds., 39-66.
Hackett, General Sir John & al. 1979: *The Third World War* (London: Sphere).
Haeberlin, Friedrich, Hans-Joachim **Hoffmann,** Volker **Kröning,** Peter von **Oertzen,** Hermann **Scheer** & Lutz **Unterseher** 1985: 'Konservative Verteidigungsplanung erhöht die Kriegsgefahr in Europa', *Vorwärts Dokumentation,* 21 September.
Haffner, Friedrich 1990: 'Wünschenswerte Entwicklungen für die beide deutsche Staaten und die damit verbundenen Risiken und Chancen', *DA,* 23, 1, 36-48.
Haftendorn, Helga 1986: *Sicherheit und Stabilität. Aussenbeziehungen der Bundesrepublik zwischen Ölkrise und NATO-Dobbelbeschluss* (München: dtv).
1986a: 'Wurzeln der Ost—und Entspannungspolitik der sozial-liberalen Koalition', in Ehmke & al., eds., 17-28.
Hagena, Hermann 1990: 'Reform für die NVA. Vom Parteisoldaten zum Staatsbürger in Uniform', *EW,* 3, 172-175.
1990a: 'Vorschlag für die Volkskammer. Die Radikale Wende der Nationalen Volksarmee', *EW,* 4, 206-210.
1990b: *Tiefflug in Mitteleuropa. Chancen und Risiken offensiver Luftkriegsoperationen* (Baden-Baden: Nomos).
1990c: 'NVA-Soldaten in der Bundeswehr. Integration, nicht Restewertung', *EW,* 10, 568-571.
Hahlweg, Werner 1986: 'Clausewitz and Guerilla Warfare', *JSS,* 9, 2-3, 127-133.
Hahn, Erich 1987: 'Überlegungen zum Dokument "Der Streit der Ideologien und die gemeinsame Sicherheit"', *Blätter,* 11, 1486-1493.
1988: *Friedenskampf ohne Ideologie* (Berlin, GDR: Dietz).
Hakovirta, Harto 1988: *East-West Conflict and European Neutrality* (Oxford: Clarendon).
Haltzel, Michael H. 1990: 'Amerikanische Einstellungen zur deutschen Wiedervereinigung', *EA,* 4, 127-132.
Hamerow, Theodore S., ed. 1973: *The Age of Bismarck. Documents and Interpretations* (New York: Harper & Row).
Hamm, Manfred R. & Hartmut **Pohlman** 1990: 'Military Doctrines and Strategies. The Missing Keys to Success in Conventional Arms Control?', *AuP,* 1, 52-72.
1990a: 'Military Strategy and Doctrine: Why They Matter to Conventional Arms Control', *WQ,* 13:1, 185-198.
Hannig, Norbert 1979: 'Lässt sich Westeuropa konventionell verteidigen?', *IW,* 1, 1237-1241.
1981: 'Die Verteidigung Westeuropas mit konventionellen Feuersperren', *IW,* 11, 1439-1443.
1981a: 'NATO-Nachrüstungsbeschluss: Militärisch notwendig?', *Armada International,* 4, 34-46.
1984: *Abschreckung durch konventionelle Waffen: Das David-und-Goliath Prinzip* (Berlin: Spitz).
1985: 'Fiasko der NATO-Verteidigung und Wege zu einer Neuorientierung', *Armada International,* 1, 51-66.
1986: 'Das DEWA-Konzept: Eine Alternative zu FOFA', *IW,* 7, 897-898.
1986a: 'Deterrence by Means of Conventional Weapons: the David-Goliath Principle', in Tromp, Hylke, ed. 1986: *Non-Nuclear War in Europe. Alternatives for Nuclear Defence* (Groningen: Polemological Institute), 179-194.

1986b: 'NATO's Defense: Conventional Options Beyond FOFA', *IDR*, 7.

1986c: 'Verteidigen ohne zu bedrohen. Die DEWA-Konzeption als Ersatz der NATO-FOFA', *AFP*, 5.

1987: 'Die "Strukturelle Nichtangriffsfähigkeit" im weiteren und engerem Sinne', *S + F*, 1, 30-32.

1988: 'Antworten auf Fragen zur Konventionellen Stabilität', in Bahr & Lutz, eds., 445-451.

1990: 'Die DEWA-Konzeption: Verteidigen ohne zu bedrohen', in Weizsäcker, ed., 1550-157.

Hanolka, Harro 1984: 'Soziale Voraussetzungen und Konsequenzen einer Netzverteidigung der Bundesrepublik', in Weizsäcker, ed., 199-230.

Hanrieder, Wolfram 1990: 'The Federal Republic, the United States, and the New Europe: A Historical Perspective', in Jordan, ed., 67-86.

Harle, Vilho & Pekka **Sivonen**, eds. 1989: *Europe in Transition. Politics and Nuclear Security* (London: Pinter).

Hart, Basil Liddell 1937: *Europe in Arms* (London: Faber and Faber).

1939: *The Defence of Britain* (London: Faber and Faber).

1951: *The Other Side of the Hill. Germany's Generals, Their Rise and Fall, With Their Own Account of Military Events* 1939-1945, revised and enlarged edition (London: Cassell).

1967: *Strategy. The Indirect Approach*, second, revised edition (New York 1974: Signet).

1967a: 'Lessons from Resistance Movements: Guerilla and Non-violent', in Roberts, ed., 195-214.

Hartmann, Karl, ed. 1990: 'Gibt es eine deutsche Minderheit in Polen?', *Osteuropa-Archiv*, 40, 1, A25-A33.

Hartwig, Jürgen 1989: 'Bundeswehr im Personaldilemma', in SAS, eds., 108-117.

Hassner, Pierre 1983: 'Zwei deutsche Staaten in Europa. Gibt es gemeinsame Interessen in der internationalen Politik?', in Weidenfeld, ed., 294-324.

1990: 'Europe Beyond Partition and Unity: Disintegration or Reconstitution', *International Affairs*, 66:3, 461-475.

Hatschikjan, Magarditsch A. & Wolfgang **Pfeiler** 1989: 'Deutsch-sowjetische Beziehungen in einer Periode der Ost-West-Annäherung', *DA*, 22, 8, 883-889.

Hättich, Manfred 1983: 'Nationalbewusstsein im geteilten Deutschland', in Weidenfeld, ed., 274-293.

Haungs, Peter 1989: 'Parteien in westlichen Verfassungsstaaten: Übermächtig oder ohnmächtig?', in Blumenwitz & Zieger, eds., 29-38.

Hecker, Hans 1989: 'Deutschland und Osteuropa. Historische Chancen und überkommene Probleme. Die Beziehungen zwischen Osteuropa und dem Deutschen Reich von Bismarck zu Hitler', in Haberl & —, eds. pp. 9-36.

Heimann, Gerhard 1990: 'Die Auflösung der Blöcke und die Europäisierung Deutschlands', *EA*, 5, 167-172.

Heininger, Horst 1989: 'Aggresivität und Friedensfähigkeit des heutigen Kapitalismus. Methodologische Aspekte', *IPW-B*, 4, 1-7.

Heisenberg, Werner & Dieter S. **Lutz**, eds. 1987: *Sicherheitspolitik Kontrovers. Auf dem Weg in die neunziger Jahre* (Baden-Baden: Nomos).

Hennes, Michael 1985: 'Vor einer neuen Aufrüstungswelle. Die Bundeswehr-Planung für die 80er und 90er Jahre', *Blätter*, 4, 449-463.

Herbst, Ludolf 1989: *Option für den Westen. Vom Marshallplan bis zum deutsch-französischen Vertrag* (München: dtv).

Herf, Jeffrey 1990: *War by Other Means. Soviet Power, West German Resistance, and the Euromissiles*, (New York: Free Press).

Herspring, Dale R. & Ivan **Volgyes** 1980: 'How Reliable are Eastern European Armies?', *Survival*, 22:5, 208-218.

Herz, John M. 1950: 'Idealist Internationalism and the Security Dilemma', *World Politics*, 2, 157-180.

Hesslein, Bernd C. 1990: 'Abschied von Himmerod oder: Die Bundeswehr am Ende des Kalten Krieges-ratlos', *S + F*, 8:2, 107-109.

Hill, J.R. 1989: *Arms Control at Sea* (London: Routledge).

Hinrichs, Hans 1977: 'Vorneverteidigung oder Abwehr in der Tiefe?', *EW*, 3, 131-138.

Hoffmann, Lutz 1990: '"Ein Volk" statt "Das Volk". Hintergründe einer semantischen Korrektur', *Blätter*, 4, 486-494.

Hoffmann, Stanley 1990: 'Reflections on the "German Question"', *Survival*, 32:4, 291-298.

Hofmann, Hans W. & Reinar K. **Huber** 1990: 'On the Role of New Technologies for Conventional Stability in Europe', in Schmähling, ed. 1990, 137-158.

Hofmann, Hans W. & Reinar K. **Huber** & Karl **Steiger** 1986a: 'On Reactive Defense Options. A Comparative Systems Analysis of Alternatives for the Initial Defense against the First Strategic Echelon of the Warsaw Pact in Central Europe', in Huber, Reinar, ed.: *Modeling and Analysis of Conventional Defense in Europe. Assessment of Improvement Options* (New York: Plenum), 97-140.

1986b: 'Some Remarks on the Costs of Reactive Defence Options', in Barnaby & Borg, eds., 303-314.

Hogrefe, Bernd 1989: 'Wider die sichere Niederlage: Zur Forderung nach struktureller Nichtangriffsfähigkeit', *Truppenpraxis*, 4, 387-388.

Holborn, Hajo 1941: 'Moltke and Schlieffen: The Prussian-German School', in Earle, ed., 172-205.

1986: 'The Prusso-German School: Moltke and the Rise of the General Staff', in Paret, ed., 281-295.

Holden, Gerald 1989: *The WTO and Soviet Security Policy* (Oxford: Basil Blackwell).

1991: *Soviet Military Reform. Conventional Disarmament and the Crisis of Militarized Socialism*, (London: Pluto).

Holloway, David 1989: 'Gorbachev's New Thinking', *Foreign Affairs*, 68:1, 66-81.

Holmes, Kim R. 1984: *The West German Peace Movement and the National Question* (Cambridge, Mass.: Institute for Foreign Policy Analysis).

Holtzendorff, Friedrich 1990: 'Das Risiko und die Chance der einstigen NVA-Soldaten', *EW*, 10, 562-564.

Holzweissig, Gunter 1990: 'The National People's Army After the Upheaval in the GDR', *AuP*, 4, 399-404.

Hopmann, P. Terrence & Frank **Barnaby**, eds. 1988: *Rethinking the Nuclear Weapons Dilemma in Europe* (New York: St. Martin's).

Hoppe, Thomas & Hans Joachim **Schmidt** 1990: 'Konventionalle Stabilisierung. Militärstrategische und rüstungspolitische Fragen eines Kriegsverhütungskonzepts mit weniger Kernwaffen aus ethischer und politikwissenschaftlicher Sicht', *HSFK-B*, 1.

Horn, Erwin & Heinrich **Buch** 1984: 'Eine Auswertung der Anhörung "Alternative Strategien"', *S + F*, 3, 22-26.

Howard, Michael 1958: *Disengagement in Europe* (Harmondsworth: Penguin).

1976: *War in European History* (Oxford: Oxford U.P.).

1985: 'Men Against Fire: Expectations of War in 1914' (IS, 9, 1), in Miller, ed. 1985, 41-57.

Huber, Reinar K. 1986: *Some Remarks on Structural Implications of Strategic Stability in Central Europe*, Working Paper 1 for the Fifth Workshop of the Pugwash Study Group on Conventional Forces in Europe, Castilionciello, Italy, 9-12 October 1986.

1986a: 'On Strategic Stability in Europe Without Nuclear Weapons', in Avenhaus, Rudolf, & John D. Kettelle, eds.: *Modelling and Analysis in Arms Control* (Berlin: Springer), 215-238.

1987: 'Bemerkungen zur "Strukturellen Nichtangriffsfähigkeit"', *S + F*, 1, 32-38.

1988a: 'The Defence Efficiency Hypothesis and Conventional Stability in Europe: Implications for Arms Control', *Fakultät für Informatik: Bericht*, SS-8801 (München: Universität der Bundeswehr).

1988b: 'Crisis Stability in Europe Without Nuclear Weapons: Prerequisites and Implications for Security and Arms Control', *Fakultät für Informatik: Bericht*, S-8704 (München: Universität der Bundeswehr).

1990: 'Multipolare Sicherheitssysteme für Europa. Systemanalytische Überlegungen zu einer militärischen Ausgestaltung', *ÖMZ*, 5, 412-418.

1990a: 'An Analytical Approach to Cooperative Security: First Order Assessment of Force Posture Requirements in a Changing Security Environment', in —, ed. 1990, 165-184.

1991a: 'Parity and Stability: Some Conclusions from Geometrical Models of Military Operations in Central Europe', *International Interactions*, 16:4, 225-238.

1991b: 'Militärische Modelle für die künftige Stabilität', *EW*, 2, 94-99.

—, ed. 1990: *Military Stability. Prerequisites and Analysis of Requirements for Conventional Stability in Europe* (Baden-Baden: Nomos).

312 BIBLIOGRAPHY

— & **Hoffmann** 1984: 'Gradual Defensivity: An Approach to a Stable Conventional Force Equlibrium in Europe', in Brans, J.P., ed.: *Operational Research* '84 (Amsterdam: Elsevier), 197-211.

1984a: 'Some Thoughts on Unilaterally Reducing the Conventional Imbalance in Central Europe: Gradual Defensivity as a Force Design Principle', *Fakultät für Informatik: Bericht*, 8402 (München: Universität der Bundeswehr).

Huber, Reiner K. & O. **Schindler**: 'Stability Implications of Different Views on the Effects of Air Support on the Force Ratio in Main-Thrust Sectors', *Bericht*, S-9101, (München: Universität der Bundeswehr).

Huffschmid, Jörg, Werner **Voss** & Norbert **Zdrowomyslaw** 1986: *Neue Rüstung—Neue Armut. Aufrüstungspläne und Rüstungsindustrie in der Bundesrepublik Deutschland bis zum Jahr 2000* (Köln: Pahl-Rugenstein).

Huntington, Samuel 1983: 'Conventional Deterrence and Conventional Retaliation in Europe' (IS, 8:3), in Miller, ed. 1986, 251-275.

Huntzinger, Jacques 1985: 'Das Bündnis und die Entwicklung einer europäischen Position', *NG*, 5.

IFSH 1985 (Institut für Friedens—und Sicherheitspolitik an der Universität Hamburg): 'Angriff in die Tiefe. Ein Diskussionsbeitrag zum Rogers-Plan', *S + F Sonderdruck*, 1.

1990: 'Ein geeintes Deutschland in einem neuen Europa. Vom Blocksystem zur Sicherheitsgemeinschaft', *S + F*, 8:2, 74-85.

IISS 1988 (International Institute for Strategic Studies): *The Military Balance* 1988-1989 (London: IISS).

Inacker, Michael J. 1991: 'A Real People's Army After Six Months? Legends and Truths about the National People's Army After the Upheaval in the GDR', *AP*, 42:1, 31-36.

Independent Commission on Disarmament and Security Issues 1982: *Common Security. A Blueprint for Survival. With a Prologue by Cyrus Vance* (New York: Simon & Schuster).

Informationsdienst Sicherheitspolitik 1984: ' "Alternative Strategien": Machen sie den Frieden sicherer?', *ISP*, 1.

Ischinger, Wolfgang 1988: 'Jenseits der Abschreckung. Nuklearwaffen, Rüstungskontrolle und die Zukunft Europas', *EA*, 12, 339-348.

Jacobsen, Hanns-D. 1986: 'Die Technologiekontrollpolitik der Vereinigten Staaten und ihre Auswirkungen auf die West-West-Beziehungen', *EA*, 15, 443-450.

Jaeschke, Paul 1986: 'Politische Rahmenbedingungen einer neuen Sicherheitspolitik', in Gohl & Niesporek, eds., 45-61.

Jahn, Egbert 1971: 'Soziohistorische Voraussetzungen der sozialen Verteidigung', in Ebert, ed., 28-35.

1973: 'Civilian Defence and Civilian Offence', *JPR*, 10, 3, 285-294.

1977: 'Social and Political Conditions for the Expansion of the Non-Violent Movement: Historical Evolution and Future Prospects', *BPP*, 9, 4, 335-338.

1984: 'Frieden durch Pazifismus: Das Konzept waffen—und gewaltfreier Sicherheitspolitik', in Vogt, ed., 79-91.

1984a: 'Prospects and Impasses of the New Peace Movement: Alternative Horizons', *BPP*, 15. 1, 47-56.

Jankowitsch, Peter 1990: 'Die neue politische Landkarte Europas', *NG*, 37, 2, 110-116.

Jansen, Silke 1989: 'Zwei deutsche Staaten—zwei deutsche Nationen? Meinungsbilder zur deutschen Frage im Zeitablauf', *DA*, 22:10, 1132-1143.

Jervis, Robert 1976: *Perception and Misperception in International Politics* (Princeton: Princeton U.P.).

1978: 'Cooperation Under the Security Dilemma', *World Politics*, 2, 167-214.

1982: 'Security Regimes', *International Organization*, 36:2, 357-378.

Jesse, Eckhard 1989: 'Der "dritte Weg" in der deutschen Frage. Über die Aktualität, Problematik und Randständigkeit einer deutschlandpolitischen Position', *DA*, 22:5, 543-559.

Jessen. Hans, ed. 1973: *Die Deutsche Revolution 1848/49 in Augenzeugenberichte* (München: dtv).

Joffe, Josef 1984: 'Squaring Many Circles: West German Security Policy Between Deterrence, *Détente* and Alliance', in Cooney & al., eds., 174-203.

1988: *The Limited Partnership. Europe, the United States, and the Burdens of Alliance* (Cambridge MA: Ballinger).
1990: 'Once More: The German Question', *Survival*, 32:2, 129-140.
1991: 'The Security Implications of a United Germany: Paper I', *AdP*, 257, 84-91.
Johnson, Alfred Ross, Robert W. **Dean** & Alexander **Alexiev** 1980: *East European Military Establishments: The Warsaw Pact Northern Tier* (Santa Monica: RAND).
Jomini, Antoine-Henri de 1811: *Traité des grandes operations militaires*, second edition (Paris: Magimel).
Jones, Archer 1988: *The Art of War in the Western World* (London: Harrap).
Jones, Christopher D. 1981: *Soviet Influence in Eastern Europe. Political Autonomy and the Warsaw Pact* (New York: Praeger).
1981a: 'Soviet Military Doctrine and Warsaw Pact Exercises', in Leebaert, Derek, ed.: *Soviet Military Thinking* (London: Allen & Unwin), 225-258.
1984: 'National Armies and National Sovereignity', in Holloway, David & Jane M.O. Sharp, eds.: *The Warsaw Pact. Alliance in Transition* (London: Macmillan), 87-110.
Jordan, Robert 1990: Introduction: The Changing Political Environment of Europe', in —, ed., 1-25.
—, ed. 1990: *Europe and the Superpowers. Essays on European International Politics* (London: Pinter).
Jung, Lothar 1989: 'Die "deutsche Frage" und die Abschreckungspolitik', *DA*, 22:9, 1011-1015.
Kade, Gerhard 1981: *Generale für den Frieden. Interviews von Gerhard Kade* (Köln: Pahl-Rugenstein).
Kaestner, Roland 1990: 'Zur künftigen Wehrstruktur deutscher Streitkräfte in einem Europa kooperativer Sicherheit', *S + F*, 8:2, 86-93.
Kaiser, Karl 1989: 'Wozu Atomwaffen in Zeiten der Abrüstung', in Wagemann, ed., 189-202.
—, Georg **Leber**, Alois **Mertes** & Franz-Josef **Schulze** 1982: 'Nuclear Weapons and the Preservation of Peace' (Foreign Affairs, Summer 1982), in Bundy, W., ed. 1985, 77-100.
— & Pierre **Lellouche**, eds. 1986: *Deutsch-Französiche Sicherheitspolitik. Auf dem Wege zur Gemeinsamkeit?* (Bonn: Europa Union).
— & John **Roper**, eds. 1988: *British-German Defence Co-operation. Partners Within the Alliance* (London: Jane's).
Kaiser, Reinhard 1988: 'Vor Beginn der Verhandlungen über konventionelle Rüstungskontrolle in Europa', *Blätter*, 9, 1098-1110.
Kaldor, Mary 1981: *The Baroque Arsenal*, (New York: Hill & Wang).
Kaltefleiter, Werner 1989: 'German Foreign Policy: The Domestic Political Framework', in Griffith & al., 21-39.
Kamp, Karl-Heinz 1988: 'Die Modernisierung der nuklearen Kurzstreckenwaffen in Europa', *EA*, 10, 269-276.
1989: 'Konventionelle Rüstungskontrolle vom Atlantik bis zum Ural: Sachstand und Probleme', *AZ*, B 8/89 (17 February).
Kant, Immanuel 1788: *Kritik der praktischen Vernunft* (Stuttgart 1963: Reclam).
1795: *Zum ewigen Frieden. Ein philosophischer Entwurf* (Stuttgart 1963: Reclam).
Kaplan, Fred 1983: *The Wizards of Armageddon*, (New York: Simon & Schuster),
Kaser, Michael 1987: 'The Economic Dimension', in Moreton, ed., 123-140.
Kelstrup, Morten 1987: *Fælles Sikkerhed. Det tyske socialdemokratis opfattelse af sikkerhedspartnerskab.* (Copenhagen: SNU).
Kelleher, Catherine McArle 1987: 'NATO Nuclear Operations', in Carter, Ashton B., John D. Steinbruner & Charles Zraket, eds.: *Managing Nuclear Operations* (Washington: Brookings), 445-469.
1990: 'Fundamentals of German Security: The Creation of the Bundeswehr—Continuity and Change', in Szabo, ed., 13-30.
Kennan, George F. 1958: *Russia, the Atom and the West. The BBC Reith Lectures 1957* (London: Oxford U.P.).
1972: *Memoirs 1950-1963* (London: Hutchinson).
1987: 'Reflexions on Containment', in Deibel, Terry L. & John Lewis Gaddis, eds.: *Containing the Soviet Union. A Critique of US Policy* (London: Brassey's), 15-19.

314 BIBLIOGRAPHY

Kennedy, Paul M. 1988: *The Rise and Fall of the Great Powers. Economic Change and Conflict from 1500 to 2000* (London: Unwin Hyman).

Kerby, William & Götz **Neuneck** 1990: 'Überlegungen zur Modellierung von Abrüstung und Stabilität', in Weizsäcker, ed., 84-103.

Kiessling, Günter 1989: 'Zum Begriff der Neutralität in der deutschlandpolitischen Diskussion', *DA*, 22:4, 384-390.

1989a: *Neutralität ist kein Verrat. Entwurf einer europäischen Friedensordnung* (Erlangen: Straube).

1990: 'Das Ende von Jalta', in Venohr, ed., 136-159.

1990a: *NATO oder Elbe. Modell für ein europäisches Sicherheitssystem*, (Erlangen: Straube).

King-Hall, Stephen 1959: *Defense in the Nuclear Age* (New York: Fellowship).

Kipp, Jacob W. 1987: 'Conventional Force Modernization and the Assymmetries of Military Doctrine: Historical Reflections on Air/Land Battle and the Operational Manoeuvre Group', in Jacobsen, Carl G., ed.: *The Uncertain Course. New Weapons, Strategies, and Mindsets* (Oxford: Oxford U.P.), 137-166.

Kissinger, Henry A., ed. 1965: *Problems of National Strategy* (New York: Praeger).

Klein, Dieter, 1988: *Chancen für einen friedensfähigen Kapitalismus* (Berlin: Dietz).

Klein, Paul & Ekkehard **Lippert** 1987: 'Funktionswandel des Militärs und Streitkräftestruktur. Oder: Wie viele Soldaten sind genug?', in Bald, ed., 101-123.

Klessmann, Christoph 1988: 'Adenauers Deutschland—und Ostpolitik 1945-1963', in Foschepoth, ed., 61-79.

Kluge, Manfred, ed. 1990: *Schwarz-rot-gold. Ein politisches Lesebuch* (München: Heine).

Knabe, Hubertus, ed. 1989: *Aufbruch in eine andere DDR. Reformer und Oppositionelle zur Zukunft ihres Landes* (Reinbek: Rowohlt).

Knight, Charles 1988: 'New Realities. New Opportunities. A Proposal for Restructuring the U.S. Army in NATO', Preliminary version (Cambridge, Mass.: Commonwealth Institute).

Koch, Jutta 1989: 'Die Zukunft militärischer Sicherung. Strukturwandel, Defensivorientierung, Zivilisierung?', *Das Parlament*, 7 (9 February), 12-13.

Kohl, Helmut 1990: 'Europe—Every German's Future', *European Affairs*, 4:1, 16-21.

Kolboom, Ingo 1989: 'Ostpolitik als deutsch-französische Herausforderung', *EA*, 4, 115-124.

Komitee für Grundrechte und Demokratie 1981: *Frieden mit anderen Waffen. Fünf Vorschläge zu einer alternativen Sicherheitspolitik* (Reinbek: Rowohlt).

Kosthorst, Erich 1988: 'Die Frage der deutschen Einheit im Spannungsfeld politischer Optionen und historischer Traditionen', in Jeismann, Karl-Ernst, ed.: *Einheit Freiheit Selbstbestimmung. Die Deutsche Frage im historisch-politischen Bewusstsein* (Frankfurt: Campus), 19-42.

Köllner, Lutz & Burkhardt J. **Huck**, eds. 1990: *Abrüstung und Konversion. Politische Voraussetzungen und wirtschaftliche Folgen in der Bundesrepublik*, (Frankfurt: Campus).

Krause, Christian 1984: 'Kriterien für eine alternative Militärstrategie', in Bruns, Wilhelm, & Eckhard Lübkemeier: *Sicherheit durch Abrüstung. Orientierende Beiträge zum Imperativ unserer Zeit* (Bonn: Neue Gesellschaft), 125-159.

1986: 'Can NATO Renounce the First Use of Nuclear Weapons? Comments on the Current Debate Over Security Policy in the United States and in the Federal Republic' (Bonn: Friedrich Ebert Stiftung).

1987a: 'Muss Nichtangriffsfähigkeit strukturell sein? Kritische Gedanken zu einem unklaren Begriff', *S + F*, 1, 47-51.

1987b: 'Strukturelle Nichtangriffsfähigkeit im Rahmen europäischer Entspannungspolitik', *S + F*, 3, 183-194.

1987c: 'Strukturelle Nichtangriffsfähigkeit. Eine Nachlese', *S + F*, 4, 272-274.

1988: '"Strukturelle Nichtangriffsfähigkeit"—A Yardstick for Conventional Stability?', *CRPV*, 11:3, 121-129.

1990: 'Defensive Verteidigung in Europa—gestern und heute', *Studie*, 36.

1990a: 'Europe's Security 1990' (Bonn: Friedrich-Ebert-Stiftung).

1990b: 'Die Zukunft der konventionellen Abrüstung in Europa', *Studie*, 41.

Krause, Joachim 1988: 'Prospects for Conventional Arms Control in Europe', *Occasional Paper Series*, 8 (New York: Institute for East-West Security Studies).

Kreck, Walter 1990: 'Warnung vor Kurzschlüssen', *Blätter*, 2, 168-178.

Krell, Gert 1988: 'Ostpolitik Dimensions of West German Security Policy', *PRIF-R*, 1.

1989: 'Die Ostpolitik der Bundesrepublik Deutschland und die deutsche Frage: Historische Entwicklungen und politische Optionen', *HSFK-R*, 7.

1990: 'The Federal Republic of Germany and Arms Control', *PRIF-R*, 10.

—, Thomas Risse-Kappen & Hans-Joachim Schmidt 1983: 'The No-First-Use Question in Germany', in Steinbruner & Sigal, eds., 147-172.

Kremp, Herbert 1989: 'Deutschlandfrage und Sicherheit', in Wagemann, ed., 155-164.

Krippendorff, Ekkehardt 1983: 'Einseitige Abrüstung', in & R. Stuckenbrock, eds.: *Zur Kritik des Palme Berichts. Atomwaffenfrie Zonen in Europa* (Berlin: Europäische Perspektiven), 211-222.

1984: *Staat und Krieg. Die historische Logik politischer Unvernunft* (Frankfurt: Suhrkamp).

1987: 'Die NATO-Strategie der Abschreckung: auf dem Weg zur erhöhten Kriegsrisiko', in Heisenberg & Lutz, eds., 674-681.

Krockow, Christian Graf von 1983: 'Die fehlende Selbstverständlichkeit', in Weidenfeld, ed., 154-169.

Krönig, Volker 1989: 'Vertrauensbildung, konventionelle Rüstungskontrolle und Strukturwandel der Verteidigung in Europa', *Bremer Beiträge*, 1, 9-14.

1989: 'Auf dem Wege zur gemeinsamen Sicherheit', in SAS, eds., 25-33.

Krüger, Klaus 1986: 'Wege zu einer gesamteuropäischen Friedensordnung', in Gohl & Niesporek, eds., 101-112.

Kuppe, Johannes L. 1990: 'Der ausserordentliche Parteitag der SED', *DA*, 23:1, 52-58.

Küntzel, Matthias & al., eds. 1986: *Atombomben—Made in Germany?. Atomenergie—Schleichwege zum Atomwaffenstaat* (Köln: Kölner Volksblatt).

Lafontaine, Oskar 1983: *Angst vor den Freunden* (Hamburg: Spiegel).

1988: *Die Gesellschaft der Zukunft. Reformpolitik in einer veränderten Welt* (Hamburg: Hoffmann und Campe).

Lamers, Karl 1988: 'Konventionelle Abrüstung in Europa', *AZ*, B 18/88, 12-20.

Lanchester, F.W. 1916: *Aircraft in Warfare: The Dawn of the Fourth Arm* (London: Constable).

Lange, Peer H. 1989: 'NATO and WTO "Military Doctrines" in East-West Consultations', in Blackwill & Larrabee, eds., 186-211.

Lapp, Peter Joachim 1990: 'Ehemalige DDR-Blockparteien auf der Suche nach Profil und Glaubwürdigkeit', *DA*, 23:1, 62-68.

Lasalle, Ferdinand 1862: 'The Working Class Program', in Fried, Albert & Ronald Sanders, eds. 1964: *Socialist Thought. A Documentary History* (New York: Anchor), 378-389.

Lather, Karl-Heinz 1982: 'Alternative Konzeptionen der Verteidigung, Part 3: "Raumverteidigung" und "Vorneverteidigung" als operative Konzeptionen', *Truppenpraksis*, 11, 787-794.

Lemke, Hans-Dieter 1989: 'Militärische Stabilität durch Überlegenheit der Verteidigung' (Ebenhausen: Stiftung Wissenschaft und Politik, SWP-AZ 2599 Fo.Pl. II 3c/89).

1990: 'Prospects for Conventional Arms Control in Europe', *Disarmament*, 13:1, 39-57.

1990a: 'Conventional Arms Control and Defence Planning', in Huber, ed., 107-114.

Lenk, Kurt 1990: 'Grossdeutschland im Programm—Die "Republikaner" nach Rosenheim', *NG*, 37:4, 327-331.

Leonhard, Elke 1990: 'Eine junge Partei mit alter Tradition. Erster Parteitag der neuen SPD in der DDR', *DA*, 4, 506-511.

Lepingwell, John W.R. 1987: 'The Laws of Combat? Lanchester Reexamined', *IS*, 12:1 89-139.

Leski, Christian 1988: 'Strukturelle Angriffsunfähigkeit. Zur wissenschaftlichen Diskussion eines politischen Begriffes', *S + F*, 4, 253-259.

Lippert, Ekkehard, Mathias Schönborn & Günther Wachtler 1984: 'Gesellschaftliche und politische Konsequenzen alternativer Verteidigungskonzepte', in Weizsäcker, ed., 179-198.

Lippert, Günter 1987: 'GSFG. Spearhead of the Red Army', *IDR*, 5, 553-562.

Lodgaard, Sverre 1982: 'Long-range Theatre Nuclear Forces in Europe', in SIPRI: *World Armaments and Disarmament. SIPRI Yearbook* 1982 (London: Taylor & Francis), 3-50.

1983: 'Long-range Theatre Nuclear Forces', in SIPRI: *World Armaments and Disarmament. SIPRI Yearbook* 1983 (London: Taylor & Francis), 3-26.

1987: 'Threats to European Security: The Main Elements', in idem & Karl Birnbaum, eds.:

Overcoming Threats to Europe: A New Deal for Confidence and Security (Oxford: Oxford U.P.), 3-36.

Longerich, Peter, ed. 1990: *"Was ist des Deutschen Vaterland?" Dokumente zur Frage der deutschen Einheit* 1800-1990 (München: Piper).

Loquai, Heinz 1982: 'Alternative Konzeptionen der Verteidigung. II Teil: Beurteilung aus sicherheitspolitischer und strategischer Sicht', *Truppenpraxis*, 10, 703-712.

Loth, Wilfried 1989: *Ost-West-Konflikt und deutsche Frage* (München: dtv).

1989a: 'Die Bundesrepublik Deutschland und Osteuropa. Rückblick auf einen Lernprozess', in Haberl & Hecker, eds., 37-52.

1990: 'Welche Einheit soll es sein? Beobachtungen zur Lage der Nation', *Blätter*, 3, 301-309.

Lowe, Karl & Thomas-Durell **Young** 1991: 'Multinational Corps in NATO', *Survival*, 33:1, 66-77.

Löser, Jochen 1982: *Weder rot noch tot. Überleben ohne Atomkrieg: Eine Sicherheitspolitische Alternative* (München: Olzog).

1982a: *Gegen den dritten Weltkrieg. Strategie der Freien* (Herford: Mittler).

1985a: 'Defensive Optionen der NATO in den neunziger Jahren', *ÖMZ*, 6, 525-532.

1985b: 'Defensive Optionen Mitteleuropas: Ein kollektives Sicherheitssystem der kleinen Schritte', in Lutz, ed., 294-309.

1986a: 'Gedanken zur Weiterentwicklung von Strategie, Operation und Taktik', *Allgemeine Schweizerische Militärzeitschrift*, 9, 529-532.

1986b: 'Modern Defence Technologies for Non-Nuclear Border Defence' in Tromp, Hylke, ed.: *Non-Nuclear War in Europe. Alternatives for Nuclear Defence* (Groningen: Groningen U.P.), 195-200.

1987a: 'Strukturelle Nichtangriffsfähigkeit', *S + F*, 1, 51-60.

1987b: 'Europäische Friedenszone, Gemeinsame Sicherheit und Defensive Optionen,' *Dialog* 10, 111-114.

1988: 'Diskussionsbeiträge zur konventionellen Stabilität', in Bahr & Lutz, eds., 457-460.

1990: 'Gegenseitige Sicherheit durch defensive Stabilität in Mitteleuropa', in Weizsäcker, ed., 133-142.

— & Harald **Anderson** 1984: *Antwort auf Genf. Sicherheit für West und Ost* (München: Olzog).

— & Lothar **Penz** 1988: 'Verstärkung der nicht-atomaren Verteidigung, aber wie?', *Allgemeine Schweizerische Militärzeitschrift*, 1, 10-14.

— & Ulrike **Schilling** 1984: *Neutralität für Mitteleuropa. Das Ende der Blöcke* (München: Bertelsmann).

Löwe, Bernd P. 1990: 'Deutschland in Europa-zwischen Utopie und Pragmatismus', *S + F*, 8:2, 65-69.

Löwenthal, Richard 1986: 'Vom Weg der Deutschen—vorgestern, gestern und heute', in Calleo & al., 7-43.

Lucas, Michael 1986: 'SDI and Europe', *WPJ*, 3:2, 219-250.

1988: 'The United States and Post-INF Europe. The Need for a Pan-European Policy', *WPJ*, 5:2, 183-234.

1990: *The Western Alliance After INF. Redefining U.S. Policy Toward Europe and the Soviet Union* (Boulder: Lynne Rienner).

Lukic, Reneo 1984: 'La dissuassion populaire yougoslave', *Cahiers d'Etudes stratégiques* 5 (Paris: CIRPES).

Lummer, Heinrich 1988: 'Zwei Friedensverträge mit Deutschland? Zu einem Vorschlag von Egon Bahr', *DA*, 21:4, 370-374.

Luttwak, Edward N. 1987: *Strategy. The Logic of War and Peace.* (Cambridge, Mass.: Harvard U.P.).

Lutz, Dieter S. 1981: *Weltkrieg wider Willen. Eine Kräftevergleichsanalyse der Nuklearwaffen in und für Europa* (Reinbek: Rowohlt).

1982a: 'Stabilität durch Vorhersehbarkeit und Vertrauensbildung. Kriegsbilder, unkalkulierbare Realität und Worst-Case Orientierung', in Lutz & Müller, eds., 23-52.

1982b: 'Neutralität: (K)eine sicherheitspolitische Alternative für die Bundesrepublik Deutschland?', in— & Grosse-Jütte, eds., 7-42.

1983: 'Auf dem Weg zu einer Neuen Europäischen Friedensordnung. Programmatische Überlegungen zur Utopie und Machbarkeit eines Systems Kollektiver Sicherheit in und für

BIBLIOGRAPHY 317

Europa', in Deutsche Gesellschaft für Friedens-und Konfliktforschung, eds.: *DGFK Jahrbuch* 1982/83: *Zur Lage Europas im globalen Spannungsfeld* (Baden-Baden: Nomos), 505-532.
1984: 'Eröffnungsreferat zur Anhörung "Alternative Strategien"', *S + F*, 3, 65-68.
1985a: 'Für eine neue Friedens—und Sicherheitspolitik der SPD', *NG*, 9, 836-842.
1985b: 'Auf dem Weg zu einem System Kollektiver Sicherheit in und für Europa', in —, ed., 22-44.
1986a: 'Die SPD auf der Suche nach einer neuen friedens—und sicherheitspolitischen Konzeption, oder: Was ist Gemeinsame Sicherheit?', *S + F* 2, 109-114.
1986b: 'Ist eine rot-grüne Sicherheitspolitik möglich?', *S + F*, 4, 228-231.
1986c: 'Seemacht und Marinedoktrin. Eine Einführung in die theoretische Grundlagen der Rüstung zur See', in —, Müller & Pott, 7-54.
1986d: 'Sicherheitspartnerschaft und/oder Gemeinsame Sicherheit? Zur Entstehung und Entwicklung der Begriffe und ihrer Inhalte', in Bahr & —, eds., 29-42.
1986e: 'Security Partnership and/or Common Security', *HB*, 8.
1986f: 'Gemeinsame Sicherheit: das neue Konzept', in Bahr & —, eds., 45-81.
1986g: 'Common Security: The New Concept. Distinctive Features and Structural Elements of Common Security Compared With Other Security Policy Methods and Strategies', *HB*, 8.
1987a: 'Zu den verfassungsrechtlichen Rahmenbedingungen Gemeinsamer Sicherheit nach dem Grundgesetz der Bundesrepublik Deutschland', in Bahr & —, eds., 85-104.
1987b: 'Was heisst "Strukturelle Nichtangriffsfähigkeit" (i. e. S.)? Versuch einer Annäherung', *S + F*, 1, 2-3.
1987c: 'Stabilität und Abrüstung durch Umrüstung. Zur Abrüstungs—und Stabilitätsorientierung Struktureller Nichtangriffsfähigkeit im Rahmen Gemeinsamer Sicherheit', *S + F*, 3, 167-169.
1987d: 'Zur Theorie Struktureller Angriffsunfähigkeit. Genesis, Definitionen und Kriterien Struktureller Angriffsunfähigkeit im Rahmen Defensiver Abhaltung und Gemeinsamer Sicherheit', *HB*, 22.
1987e: 'Der Status Quo in Westeuropa: Die NATO', in Heisenberg & —, eds., 251-259.
1987f: 'Politische und militärische Modelle der Sicherheit', in Heisenberg & —, eds., 561-591.
1988: 'On the Theory of Structural Inability to Launch an Attack', *HB*, 25.
1988a: *Strukturelle Angriffsunfähigkeit im Rahmen Defensiver Abhaltung und einer Konzeption Gemeinsamen Friedens. Disussionsvorschläge, verabschiedet vom August-Bebel-Kreis* (Bonn: SPD).
1988b: 'Teilelement einer politischen Konzeption. Funktionen, Zielkriterien, konzeptioneller Rahmen der strukturellen Nichtangriffsfähigkeit', *NG*, 6, 547-553.
1988c: 'Vom atomwaffenfreien Korridor zur panzerfreien Zone', in Bahr & —, eds., 493-500.
1989: 'SIA and Defensive Zones', *BPP*, 20:1, 71-80.
1989a: '"Alles was fliegt, muss weg"? Luftstreitkräfte, Strukturelle Angriffsunfähigkeit und Abrüstung', *S + F*, 7:2, 145-149.
1989b: 'Luftstreikräfte, Strukturelle Angriffsunfähigkeit und Abrüstung', *HB*, 41.
1989c: 'Basic Law. Security and Peace. Armament and Disarmament', *HB*, 38.
1989d: 'Gemeinsamer Frieden und Europäische Sicherheit', in Krohn, Axel & : 'Europäische Sicherheit II', *HB*, 40, 1-39.
1989e: *Gemeinsame Sicherheit, Defensive Abhaltung und Strukturelle Angriffsunfähigkeit. Bd. IV: Zur Genesis und Theorie Struktureller Angriffsunfähigkeit im Rahmen einer Strategie Defensiver Abhaltung und ihrer konzeptionellen Einbettung in die Gemeinsame Sicherheit*, (Baden-Baden: Nomos).
1990: 'Deutsche Einheit Europäische Sicherheit oder Brauchen wir noch (deutsche) Streitkräfte?', *HB*, 43.
1990a: 'Towards a European Peace Order and a System of Collective Security', *BPP*, 21:1, 71-76.
1990b: 'Wieviel (deutsche) Soldaten braucht Europa?', *S + F*, 1, 18-22.
1990c: *Brauchen wir nich deutsche Streitkräfte. Plädoyer des August-Bebel-Kreises für ein System Kollektiver Sicherheit in und für Europa* (Bonn: August-Bebel-Kreis).
1990d: 'Ein Europa des Gemeinsamen Friedens mit der Sowjetunion?', in — & Schmähling, eds., 13-22.

1990e: 'Strukturelle Angriffsunfähigkeit und Abrüstung. Das Beispiel "Luftstreitkräfte"', in— & Schmähling, eds., 253-268.

1990f: 'Die Golfkriese, das Grundgesetz, die Gemeinsame Sicherheit', *S + F*, 8:4, 233-237.

1990g: 'Gemeinsamer Frieden. Zur Bewältigung grenzüberschreitender Gefahren durch ein System Kollektiver Sicherheit in und für Europa', in Vogt, ed., 41-51.

—, ed. 1985: *Kollektive Sicherheit in und für Europa: Eine Alternative? Beiträge zur Utopie und Umsetzung einer neuen Friedens—und Sicherheitsprogrammatik. Pro und Contra* (Baden-Baden: Nomos).

—, ed. 1987: *Lexikon Rüstung, Frieden, Sicherheit* (München: Beck).

—, Erwin **Müller** & Andreas **Pott** 1986: *Seemacht und Sicherheit. Beiträge zur Diskussion maritimer Rüstung und Rüstungskontrolle* (Baden-Baden: Nomos).

— & Alexander **Theilmann** 1986: 'Gemeinsame Sicherheit: Auf der Suche nach Inhalten. Auf dem Weg zur Akzeptanz? Zu den Kritiken und Reaktionen in der Bundesrepublik und in der DDR', in Bahr & —, eds., 223-251.

— & Annemarie **Grosse-Jütte**, eds. 1982: *Neutralität: Eine Alternative?* (Baden-Baden: Nomos).

— & Erwin **Müller**, eds. 1982: *Vertrauensbildende Massnahmen. Zur Theorie und Praxis einer sicherheitspolitischen Strategie* (Baden-Baden: Nomos).

— & Elmar **Schmähling**, eds. 1990: *Gemeinsame Sicherheit. Internationale Diskussion. Bd. V: Beiträge und Dokumente aus Ost und West* (Baden-Baden: Nomos).

Lübckemeier, Eckhard 1988: 'Abschreckung und Gemeinsame Sicherheit', *NG*, 1, 82-85.

1988a: 'Current NATO Strategy and No First Use: What Can They Accomplish?', in Hopmann & Barnaby, eds., 115-131.

1990: 'Sicherheit jenseits der Blockkonfrontation. Die strategischen Inplikationen der Revolutionen in Osteuropa', *Kurzp.*, 40.

1990a: 'Europas Sicherheit nach dem Kalten Krieg', *Reihe Eurokolleg*, 5 (Bonn: Friedrich-Ebert-Stiftung).

MacGregor, Douglas 1986: 'Uncertain Allies? East European Forces in the Warsaw Pact', *Soviet Studies*, 38:2, 227-247.

1989: *The Soviet-East German Military Alliance* (Cambridge: Cambridge U.P.).

Mager, Olaf 1990: 'Londons Vorschuss für die Abrüstung: Rheinarmee minus 50 Prozent', *EW*, 10, 592-595.

Manfrass-Sirjacques, Francoise 1990: 'Die französische Europapolitik und die deutsche Frage', *NG*, 37:2, 116-121.

Mann, Golo 1968: *Deutsche Geschichte* 1919-1945 (Frankfurt: Fischer).

Mantzke, Martin 1990: 'Eine Republik auf Abruf. Die DDR nach den Wahlen von 18. März 1990', *EA*, 8, 287-292.

Mao Tse-tung 1936: 'Problems of Strategy in China's Revolutionary War', in *Selected Works of Mao Tse-tung*, vols. 1-4 (Peking: Foreign Languages Press, 1975), 1, 179-254.

Marsh, David 1989: *The Germans. Rich, Bothered and Divided* (London: Century).

Marx, Karl & Friedrich **Engels** 1848: 'Manifest der kommunistischen Partei', in— & -: *Werke*, 4 (Berlin 1977: Dietz), 459-493.

Mattes, Brigitte 1985: 'Moskaus "Revanchismus-Kampagne" gegen Bonn', *Osteuropa-Archiv*, November, A 581-A 597.

May, Ernest 1984: 'American Forces in the Federal Republic: Past, Current and Future', in Cooney & al., eds., 153-173.

Mayne, Richard 1970: *The Recovery of Europe. From Devastation to Unity* (London: Weidenfeld and Nicholson).

McAdams, A. James 1986: 'Inter-German *Détente*: A New Balance', *Foreign Affairs*, Fall, 136-153.

1990: 'An Obituary for the Berlin Wall', *WPJ*, 7:2, 357-375.

McCausland, Jeff 1986: 'The East German Army—Spearpoint or Weakness?, *Defense Analysis*, 2, 137-153.

MccGwire, Michael 1986: *Military Objectives in Soviet Foreign Policy*, (Washington: Brookings).

1987: 'Update: Soviet Military Objectives', *WPJ*, Fall, 723-731.

1987a: 'Why the Soviets Want Arms Control', *Technology Review*, 90:2, 37-45.

1988: 'New Directions in Soviet Arms-Control Policy', *WQ*, 11:3, 185-200.

1988a: 'Rethinking War: The Soviets and European Security', *The Brookings Review*, Spring, 3-12.

1988b: 'A Mutual Security Regime for Europe', *IS*, 12:3, 361-379.

McFarland, Stephen L. 1986: 'Preparing for What Never Came: Chemical and Biological Warfare in World War II', *Defense Analysis*, 2:2, 107-121.

McNamara, Robert S. 1968: *Essence of Security. Reflections in Office* (New York: Harper & Row).

McNeil, William H. 1983: *The Pursuit of Power. Technology, Armed Force, and Society Since A.D. 1000* (Oxford: Basil Blackwell).

Mead, Walter Russell 1990: 'The One and Future *Reich*', *WPJ*, 7:4, 593-638.

Mearsheimer, John J. 1982: 'Why the Soviets Can't Win Quickly in Central Europe' (IS, 7:1), in Miller, ed. 1986, 121-157.

1983: *Conventional Deterrence* (Ithaca: Cornell U.P.).

1986: 'A Strategic Misstep: The Maritime Strategy and Deterrence in Europe' (IS, Fall 1986), in Miller & Evera, eds. 1988, 47-101.

1988: 'Numbers, Strategy, and the European Balance', *IS*, 12:4, 174-185.

1988a: *Liddell Hart and the Weight of History* (London: Brassey's).

1989: 'Assessing the Conventional Balance: The 3:1 Rule and Its Critics', *IS*, 13:4, 54-89.

1990: Back to the Future: Instability in Europe After the Cold War, *IS*, 15:1, 5-52.

Mechtersheimer, Alfred 1984: *Rüstung und Frieden. Argumente für eine neue Sicherheitspolitik*, second edition (Reinbek: Rowohlt).

1987: 'Der Stellenwert alternativer Verteidigungsstrategien fur das Ost-West-Verhaltnis', in Bühl, ed. 1987, 149-154.

—, ed. 1982: *Nachrüsten? Dokumente und Positionen zum NATO Dobbelbeschluss* (Reinbek: Rowohlt).

— & Peter **Barth** 1986: *Militarisierungsatas der Bundesrepublik. Streitkräfte, Waffen und Standorte. Kosten und Risiken* (Darmstadt: Luchterhand).

— & —, eds. 1983: *Den Atomkrieg führbar und gewinnbar machen?* (Reinbek: Rowohlt).

— & —, eds. 1985: *Militärmacht Sowjetunion. Politik, Waffen und Strategien* (Darmstadt: Luchterhand).

Mellon, Christian & Jean-Marie **Muller** & Jaques **Semelin** 1985: *La Dissuasion Civile* (Paris: Fondation pour les Etudes de Défense Nationale).

Mey, Holger H. & Michael **Rühle** 1991: 'German Security Interests and NATO's Nuclear Strategy', *AP*, 42:1, 20-30.

Meyer, Bertold 1987: 'Die Parteien in der Bundesrepublik Deutschland und die sicherheitspolitische Zusammenarbeit in Westeuropa', *HSFK-R* 2.

1989: 'Common Security Versus Western Security Cooperation? The Debate on European Security in the Federal Republic of Germany', in Wæver & al., eds., 168-185.

Meyer, Thomas 1987: 'Ein neuer Rahmen für den Ost-West Dialog. Das gemeinsame Papier von SED und SPD. Kein nationales Memorandum', *NG*, 34:10, 870-877.

Michalka, Wolfgang & Gottfied **Niedhart**, eds. 1980: *Die ungeliebte Republik. Dokumente zur Innen—und Aussenpolitik Weimars 1918-1933* (München: dtv).

Miksche, Ferdinand Otto 1955: *Atomic Weapons and Armies* (London: Faber and Faber).

1959: *The Failure of Atomic Strategy* (London: Faber and Faber)

1990: *Das Ende der Gegenwart. Europa ohne Blöcke* (Munich: Herbig).

Miller, Steven E., ed. 1984: *Strategy and Nuclear Deterrence. An International Security Reader* (Princeton: Princeton U.P.).

—, ed. 1985: *Military Strategy and the Origins of the First World War. An International Security Reader* (Princeton: Princeton U.P.).

—, ed. 1986: *Conventional Forces and American Defense Policy. An International Security Reader* (Princeton: Princeton U.P.).

— & Stephen van **Evera**, eds. 1988: *Naval Strategy and National Security. An International Security Reader* (Princeton: Princeton U.P.).

Moisi, Dominique 1990: 'The French Answer to the German Question', *European Affairs*, 4:1, 30-35.

Mommsen, Wolfgang J. 1983: 'Wandlungen der nationalen Identität', in Weidenfeld, ed., 170-192.

Moon, John Ellis van Courtland 1984: 'Chemical Weapons and Deterrence. The World War II Experience', *IS*, 8:4, 3-35.

Moreton, Edwina 1987: 'The German Question in the 1980s', in —, ed., 3-20.

—, ed. 1987: *Germany Between East and West* (Cambridge U.P.).

Morgan, Roger 1986: 'Deutschland und Europa. Die deutsche Frage aus britischer Sicht', in Calleo & al., 97-126.

Mueller, John 1990: 'A New Concert of Europe', *Foreign Policy*, 77 (Winter 1989-90), 3-16.

Muller, Jean-Marie 1984: *Vous avez dit 'pacifisme'?. De la menace nucleaire a la défense civile non-violente* (Paris: Cerf).

Mushaben, Joyce Marie 1986: 'Grassroots and Gewaltfreie Aktionen: A Study of Mass Mobilization Strategies in the West German Peace Movement', *JPR*, 23:2, 141-154.

Mutz, Reinhard 1986: 'Gemeinsame Sicherheit: Grundzüge einer Alternative zum Abschreckungsfrieden', in Bahr & Lutz, eds., 83-157.

1988: 'Konventionelle Stabilität: Eine Einführung', in Bahr & Lutz, eds., 36-43.

1988a: 'Die Kontrolle konventioneller Rüstung in Europa', in Moltmann, ed., 121-130.

1990: 'Europäische Sicherheit und deutsche Einheit. Zur Kritik Martin Müllers an der Stellungnahme des IFSH', *S + F*, 8:3, 171-176.

— & Götz **Neuneck** 1990: 'Konventionelle Stabilität und qualitative Rüstungsdynamik', in Müller & Neuneck, eds., 119-134.

Müller, Albrecht A.C. von 1984a: *Die Kunst des Friedens. Grundzüge einer europäischen Sicherheitspolitik für die 80er und 90er Jahre* (München: Hanser).

1985a: 'Confidence-Building by Hardware Measures', in Rotblat, Joseph & Sven Hellman, eds.: *Nuclear Strategy and World Security. The Annals of Pugwash 1984* (London: Macmillan), 275-286.

1986a: 'Structural Stability at the Central Front', in Boserup, Anders, L. Christensen & O. Nathan, eds.: *The Challenge of Nuclear Armaments, Essays Dedicated to Niels Bohr and His Appeal for an Open World* (Copenhagen: Rhodos), 239-256.

1986b: 'Integrated Forward Defence. Outline of a Modified Conventional Defence for Central Europe', in Tromp, Hylke, ed.: *Non-Nuclear War in Europe. Alternatives for Nuclear Defence* (Groningen: Groningen U.P.), 201-224.

1986c: 'Neue Chancen für den Rüstungskontrollprozess', *EW*, 35:7, 380-382.

1987a: 'Stellungnahme zum Thema "Strukturelle Nichtangriffsfähigkeit" ', *S + F*, 1, 60-62.

1987b: 'Conventional Stability in Europa. Outlines of the Military Hardware for a Second *Détente*' (Starnberg: Max Planck Society).

1987c: 'Technischer Fortschritt und Rüstungskontrolle. Überlegungen zur Integration von Sicherheits—und Verteidigungspolitik am Beispiel der Landstreitkräfte der Bundeswehr', in Heisenberg & Lutz, eds., 498-522.

1988: 'Die Schaffung konventioneller Stabilität. Ein modifiziertes Rahmenkonzept für die Rüstungskontrollpolitik und die Streikräfte-Modernisierung der NATO', in Bahr & Lutz, eds., 81-92.

1988a: 'Beantwortung des Fragebogens für die Anhörung zur "Konventionellen Stabilität" ', in Bahr & Lutz, eds., 461-463.

1988b: 'Die Transformation des Ost-West-Konflikts. Ein Rahmenkonzept für eine zweite Entspannungspolitik', in Bülow, Funk & —, 47-68.

1988c: 'Konventionelle Stabilität. Plädoyer für eine verstärkte Integration von Sicherheits—und Verteidigungspolitik', in Bülow, Funk & —, 69-94.

1989: 'Towards Conventional Stability in Europe', in Rotblat, Joseph & V.I. Goldanski, eds.: *Global Problems of Common Security. Annals of Pugwash 1988* (Berlin: Springer), 118-135.

1989a: 'Conventional Stability 2000. How Could NATO Regain the Initiative', in Clesse & Schelling, eds., 332-341.

1990: 'Conventional Stability and Arms Control', in Boserup & Neild, eds., 47-54.

1990a: 'Conventional Stability and Defense Dominance', in UNIDIR, eds.: *Nonoffensive Defense. A Global Perspective*, (New York: Taylor & Francis), 3-22.

1990b: 'Conventional Stability in Europe: Outlines of the Military Hardware for a Second *Détente*', in Schmähling, ed. 1990, 159-178.

— & Andrei **Karkoszka** 1988: *A Modified Approach to Conventional Arms Control*, in Bülow, Funk & —, 220-224.

Müller, Barbara, ed. 1990: 'Keine Bundeswehr in Krisengebie

Müller, Erwin 1982: 'Vertrauensbildende Massnahmen. Chancen und Probleme eines sicherheitspolitischen Konzepts', in Lutz & —, eds., 67-128.

1984: 'Dilemma Sicherheitspolitik. Tradierte Muster westdeutscher Sicherheitspolitik und Alternativoptionen:; Ein Problem—und Leistungsvergleich,' in —, ed.: *Dilemma Sicherheit. Beiträge zur Diskussion über militärische Alternativkonzepte* (Baden-Baden: Nomos), 53-170.

1985a: 'Die Supermächte und ein System Kollektiver Sicherheit in Europa', in Lutz, ed., 151-171.

1985b: 'Flexible Response oder konventionelles Alternativkonzept. Ein sicherheitspolitischer Problem—und Leistungsvergleich', in Lutz, Dieter, ed.: *Im Dienst fur Frieden und Sicherheit. Festschrift für Wolf Graf von Baudissin* (Baden-Baden: Nomos), 359-374.

1986a: 'Gemeinsame Sicherheit: Profil eines Konzepts alternativer Sicherheitspolitik', in Bahr & Lutz, eds., 159-198.

1986b: 'Rüstungsdynamik und Rüstungssteuerung im historischen Vergleich: Erfolgsbedingungen und Misserfolgsursachen von Rüstungskontrollpolitik', in Lutz,— & Pott, 165-197.

1987: 'Zur Logik politischer Bedrohungsanalysen', in Heisenberg & Lutz, eds., 79-97.

1988: 'Überlegungen zum Problemfeld "Konventionelle Stabilität"', in Bahr & Lutz, eds., 44-61.

1988a: 'Vertrauensbildung in Europa: Die KVAE und ihre Folgen', in Moltmann, ed., 131-135.

1989: 'Konventionelle Stabilität durch Strukturelle Angriffsunfähigkeit', *S + F*, 7:2, 139-145.

— & Götz **Neuneck**, eds. 1990: *Abrüstung und Konventionelle Stabilität in Europa* (Baden-Baden: Nomos).

Müller, Harald 1989: 'Transforming the East-West Conflict: The Crucial Role in Verification', in Altmann & Rotblat, eds., 2-15.

Müller, Manfred 1988: 'European Security and Non-Offensive Defence', *Scientific World*, 32:1, 11-13.

1989: 'Constraints', in Blackwill & Larrabee, eds., 405-421.

1990: 'Deutschlands Rolle in einem neugestalteten europäischen Sicherheitssystem', *EA*, 6, 221-224.

Müller, Martin 1988: 'Thesen zur Kritik der "Theorie struktureller Angriffsunfähigkeit"', *S + F*, 6:1, 41-45.

1988a: *Politik und Bürokratie: Die MBFR-Politik der Bundesrepublik Deutschland zwischen 1967 und 1971* (Baden-Baden: Nomos).

1990: 'Deutsche Einheit und europäische Sicherheit. Eine Kritik der Studie der IFSH', *S + F*, 8:3, 166-170.

Müller, Rolf-Dieter 1990: 'Ostwall und Wehrbauern. Zur historischen Hypothek der deutschen Ostgrenze', *NG*, 37:2, 126-133.

Møller, Bjørn 1987: 'A Non-offensive Maritime Strategy for the Nordic Area. Some Preliminary Ideas', *WP-CPCR*, 3.

1987a: 'The Need for an Alternative NATO Strategy', *JPR*, 24:1, 61-74.

1988: 'No-First-Use of Nuclear Weapons and Non-Offensive Defence', in Alger, Chadwick & Michael Stohl, eds.: *A Just Peace Through Transformation. Cultural, Economic, and Political Foundations for Change* (Boulder: Westview), 436-454.

1988a: 'Common Security and Military Posture', in Baudisch, ed., 41-54.

1989: 'Restructuring the Naval Forces. Maritime Aspects of a Non-Offensive Defence', in Borg & Smit, eds., 189-206.

1989a: 'Air Power and Non-Offensive Defence. A Preliminary Analysis', *WP-CPCR*, 2.

1989b: 'Common Security: Some Military and Non-Military Aspects', *WP-CPCR*, 8.

1989c: 'The Nordic Regional Security Complex. A Preliminary Analysis', in Ohlson, Leif, ed.: *Case Studies on Regional Conflicts and Regional Conflict Resolution* (Gotenburg: Padrigu Peace Studies), 45-82.

1989d: 'Crisis Stability and Non-Offensive Defence. A Nordic Perspective', in Chalmers, Malcolm, — & David Stevenson: 'Alternative Conventional Defence Structures for Europe. British and Danish Perspectives', *APR*, 22, 1-65.

1989e: 'Is War Impossible in Europe. A Critique of the Hypothesis of the Totally Destructive Conventional War (TDCW)' *WP-CPCR*, 11.

1989f: 'Ist Krieg in Europa unmöglich geworden? Eine kritik der Hypothese vom totalver-heerenden konventionellen Krieg', *S + F*, 4, 232-237.

1990: 'A Common Security System for Europe?', *WP-CPCR*, 6.

1990a: 'Gemeinsame Sicherheit und strukturelle Angriffsunfähigkeit aus dänischer Sicht', in Lutz & Schmähling, eds., 217-243.

1990b: 'Current and Alternative Trends in the Military Confrontation in the Baltic Area—With a Special Emphasis on Naval Forces', *Acta Politica*, 2 (Szczecin: Uniwersytet Szczecinski), 89-118.

1990c: 'Teknologi og Forsvar', in Sørensen, Henning, ed.: *Forsvar i Forandring* (Copenhagen: Samfundslitteratur), 63-96.

1990d: 'Non-Offensive Defence, the Armaments Dynamics, Arms Control and Disarma-ment', in Auffermann, Burkhard, ed.: 'NOD or Disarmament in the Changing Europe?', *Research Reports*, 40 (Tampere: TAPRI), 43-102.

1990e: 'Nicht-offensive Verteidigung (NOV) und die deutsche Frage', in Benjowski, Klaus, Bertel Heurlin, Gregor Putensen & Håkan Wiberg, eds.: *Endzeit für Deutschlands Zweis-taatlichkeit. Konsequenzen für Europa. Deutsch-dänische Refelxionen europäischer Sicherheit-sprobleme* (Protokolle eines Symposiums über die deutsch-nordischen Beziehungen und die europäische Sicherheit in Kopenhagen 3.-4. Mai 1990), 54-71.

1990f: 'Conversion: A Comprehensive Agenda', *WP-CPCR*, 19.

1991a: 'Civilian-Based and Non-Offensive Defence', *WP-CPCR*, 3.

1991b: 'Guerilla Strategies and Non-Offensive Defence', *WP-CPCR*, 4.

1991c: 'European Security Structures for the Nineties and Beyond: A Nordic Perspective', *APR*, 40.

1992: *Common Security and Non-Offensive Defense. A Neorealist Perspective* (Boulder, Col: Lynne Reinner, forthcoming).

— & Håkan **Wiberg** 1989: 'Non-Offensive Defence and Armaments Dynamics: A Theoretical and Empirical Assessment', *WP-CPCR*, 3.

— & 1990: 'Nicht-offensive Verteidigung als Vertrauensbildende Massnahme? Probleme und Konzepte', in Schweizerische Friedensstiftung, eds.: *Blocküberwindende Vertrauensbildung nach dem europäischen Herbst '89* (Bern 1990: Schweizerische Friedensstiftung), 39-79.

Naumann, Klaus 1989: 'Defensive Doktrinen und Streitkräftestrukturen', *EA*, 22, 667-676.

1989a: 'The Restructured Bundeswehr', *NSN*, October, 31-35.

1990: 'The Forces and the Future', in Szabo, ed., 173-187.

Nehrlich, Uwe 1986: 'Der Bedeutungswandel der französischen Nuklearstreitmacht', in Kaiser & Lellouche, eds., 165-179.

1986a: 'Folgerungen aus SDI für Strategie, Rüstungskontrolle und Politik. Zum Entscheidungsbedarf der Bundesrepublik Deutschland', *EA*, 4, 89-98.

Neild, Robert 1986: 'The Implications of the Increasing Accuracy of Non-Nuclear Weapons', in Rotblat, Joseph & Ubiratan d'Ambrosio, eds.: *World Peace and the Developing Countries. Annals of Pugwash* 1985 (London: Macmillan), 93-106. (Abridged version in Boserup & —, eds. 1990, 55-62).

1989: 'The Case Against Arms Negotitions and for a Reconsideration of Strategy', in Tromp, ed., 119-140.

1990: *An Essay on Strategy as it Affects the Achievement of Peace in a Nuclear Setting* (London: Macmillan).

Neumann, Hans Dieter 1988: 'The Special Case of Germany', in *The New Force Reduction Negotiations in Europe: Problems and Prospects, Proceedings from a AAAS Annual Meeting Symposium, February 13 1988* (Washington: AAAS), 13-16.

Newhouse, John 1973: *Cold Dawn. The Story of SALT*, (New York: Reinhard & Winston).

Niclauss, Karlheinz 1988: *Kanzlerdemokratie. Bonner Regierungspraxis von Konrad Adenauer bis Helmut Kohl* (Stuttgart: Kohlhammer).

Niesporek, Heinrich 1986: 'Verteidigung statt Selbstvernichtung', in Gohl & Niesporek, eds., 165-173.

Noelle-Neumann 1985: 'Im Wartesaal der Geschichte. Bleibt das Bewusstsein der deutschen Einheit lebendig?', in Weidenfeld, ed., 133-146.

Nolte, Hans-Heinrich & **Wilhelm Nolte** 1984: *Ziviler Widerstand und Autonome Abwehr* (Baden-Baden: Nomos).

Nolte, Wilhelm 1984: 'Die Militärstrategien von NATO und Warschauer Pakt und die Veränderungen in den Nukleardoktrinen der USA und der UdSSR', in Brauch, ed., 113-127.
1985: 'Soziale Verteidigung im System Kollektiver Sicherheit?', in Lutz, ed., 310-320.
1986a: 'Verteidigung in Deutschland. Wiedervereinigung mit militärischen Mitteln?', S + F, 3, 154-158.
1986b: 'Deutschlandargumente für Autonome Abwehr', in Gohl & Niesporek, eds., 174-186.
1987a: 'Zum Thema "Strukturelle Nichtangriffsfähigkeit"', S + F, 1, 63-72.
1987b: 'Militärische Aspekte Gemeinsamer Sicherheit. Können Soldaten Beiträge zu Gemeinsamer Sicherheit erbringen?', in Bahr & Lutz, eds., 301-307.
1987c: 'Autonome Abwehr: Alternative zu den Alternativen!', in Bühl, ed., 219-233.
1988: 'Dominanz der Defensive. Streitbare Anmerkungen zur Krause-Studie', S + F, 1, 37-40.
1988a: 'Anmerkungen und Kritik zur Konventionellen Stabilität', in Bahr & Lutz, eds., 464-471.
1989: 'Civilian-Military Security Co-Function: Autonomous Protection, Alternative Defence From a West German Perspective', in Tromp, ed., 259-280.
1990: 'Zur Transpositionsfähigkeit zu mehr nichtmilitärischen Mitteln', in Weizsäcker, ed., 158-170.
1990a: '"Wer wagt..."'. Plädoyer für das Zusammenwirken Gewaltfreien Widerstandes mit Konventioneller Verteidigung', in Vogt, ed., 263-276.
Nötzold, Jürgen 1990: 'Die deutsche Einheit und Osteuropa', Liberal. Vierteljahreshefte für Politik und Kultur, 32:3, 49-57.
O'Ballance, Edgar 1972: The Third Arab-Israeli War, (London: Faber).
Oeser, Edith 1990: 'Vier plus Zwei gelich Fünf? Vier Mächte und zwei deutsche Staaten', Blätter, 4, 426-433.
Oldenburg, Fred 1990: 'Sowjetische Deutschland-Politik nach der Oktober-Revolution in der DDR', DA, 23:1, 68-76.
Olson, William J. 1985: 'The Light Force Initiative', Military Review, 65:6, 2-17.
Ondarza, Henning von 1990: 'The German Army on its Way to the Year 2000', NSN, February-March, 31-37.
1990a: 'Das Heer in einer Phase des Übergangs. Historische Chancen der Neugestaltung', EW, 7, 406-413.
Orbons, Sjef 1986: 'Verteidigungsoptionen für Mitteleuropa: Defensivität, Technologie, Konsequenzen' (Delft/Bonn: SAS).
1989: 'A Classification and Evaluation of Concepts for the Defense of NATO's Central Sector', APR, 33.
Osgood, Charles E. 1962: An Alternative to War or Surrender (Urbana: Illinois U.P.).
OTA (Office of Technology Assessment) 1987: New Technology for NATO. Implementing Follow-On Forces Attack (Washington: Congress).
Papcke, Sven 1988: 'Mitteleuropa: Kopfgeburt oder politische Chance?', in idem & Weidenfeld, eds., 120-135.
— & Werner **Weidenfeld**, eds. 1988: Traumland Mitteleuropa? Beiträge zu einer aktuellen Kontroverse (Darmstadt: Wissenschaftliche Buchgeselllschaft).
Paret, Peter, ed. 1986: Makers of Modern Strategy From Machiavelli to the Nuclear Age (Princeton: Princeton U.P.).
Paul, Derek ed. 1985: Defending Europe. Options for Security. (London: Taylor & Francis).
Perret, Bryan 1985: Lightning War. A History of Blitzkrieg (London: Panther).
Peter, Hans 1989: 'Offensivkonzepte der NATO gefährden die Sicherheit Europas', IPW-B, 2, 16-22.
Petersen, Nikolai 1984: 'Das Scandilux-Experiment. Auf dem Wege zu einer transnationalen sozialdemokratischen Sicherheitsperspektive', EA, 16, 493-500.
Petraeus, David H. 1984: 'Light Infantry in Europe: Strategic Flexibility and Conventional Deterrence', Military Review, 64:12, 35-55.
Peuthert, Joachim 1989: 'Konventionelle Stabilität, Strukturelle Angriffsunfähigkeit: Militärische Konsequenzen sicherheitspolitischer Absichten', S + F, 7:2, 110-113.
Pfaltzgraff, Robert L., Jr., Kim R. **Holmes,** Claus **Clemens** & Werner **Kaltefleiter** 1983: The Greens of West Germany. Origins, Strategies, and Transatlantic Implications (Cambridge, Mass.: Institute for Foreign Policy Analysis).

Pfeiler, Wolfgang 1986: 'Zum Verhältnis von Abschreckung und Entspannung in der Sicherheitspolitik', in Gohl & Niesporek, eds., 127-148.

1987: 'Hat das sowjetische "neue politische Denken" auch zu einem neuen militärischen Denken geführt?', *AZ*, B 44/87 (31 October), 28-38.

Phillips, Ann L. 1990: 'The German Democratic Republic and the New European Political Order', in Jordan, ed., 87-114.

Piepmeier, Rainer 1987: 'Immanuel Kant (1724-1804). Friede als Ziel der Geschichte', in Rajewsky & Riesenberger, eds., 17-25.

Pierre, Andrew ed. 1986: *The Conventional Defense of Europe: New Technologies and New Strategies* (New York: Council on Foreign Relations).

Planer-Friedrich, Götz 1990: 'The DDR Churches in the Eastern European Revoluion', *BPP*, 21:4, 431-440.

Pleiner, Horst 1987: ' "Kecker Spatz-Moineau hardi". Deutsch-französische Heeresübung 1987', *ÖMZ*, 6, 512-527.

1990: 'Aktuelle militärstrategische Entwicklungen und mögliche Auswirkungen auf das Bundesheer der neunziger Jahre', *ÖMZ*, 5, 369-379.

Plügge, Matthias 1990: 'The East German Army. High-speed Perestroika', *IDR*, 4, 361-362.

Poch, Ulrich 1970: 'Anpassungspolitik ohne Kollaboration: Der dänische Widerstand von 1940-45', in Ebert, ed., 237-293.

Poeppel, Hans 1990: 'Wenn die direkte Drohung schwindet... Operative Planung für die Zukunft', *EW*, 9, 532-535.

Poidevin, Raymond 1986: 'Der unheimliche Nachbar. Die deutsche Frage aus französischer Sicht', in Calleo & al., 127-196.

Pontara, Giuliano 1965: 'The Rejection of Violence in Ghandhian Ethics of Conflict Resolution', *JPR*, 2:3, 197-215.

Posen, Barry R. 1984: *The Sources of Military Doctrine. France, Britain, and Germany Between the World Wars* (New York: Cornell U.P.).

1984a: 'Measuring the European Conventional Balance. Coping With Complexity in Threat Assessment' (IS, 9:3), in Miller, ed. 1986, 79-120.

1988: 'Is NATO Decisively Outnumbered?', *IS*, 12:4, 186-202.

Posser, Diether 1990: 'Die deutsche Frage. "Wiedervereinigung" oder "Oder-Neisse-Grenze" ', *S + F*, 1, 2-8.

Pott, Andreas 1985: 'Die See und ein System Kollektiver Sicherheit in Europa', in Lutz, ed., 344-357.

1986a: 'Die US-Navy zwischen Anspruch und Möglichkeit, in Lutz, Müller & —, 55-94.

1986b: 'Maritime Rüstungssteuerung als Sonderfall der kooperativen Rüstungssteuerung', in Lutz, Müller & —, 137-163.

1987: 'Die Strategie der Abschreckung: Mythenbild der Sicherheitspolitik', in Heisenberg & Lutz, eds., 153-165.

1988: 'Deutsch-französische Zusammenarbeit in der Sicherheitspolitik', in Moltmann, ed., 203-212.

1988a: 'Europäische Sicherheit. Part I: Gemeinsame Sicherheit als Strategiemodell für Europa', *HB*, 32.

— & Dieter S. **Lutz** 1986: 'Die sowjetische Marine: Ein Instrument globaler Machtpolitik?' in Lutz, Müller & —, 95-136.

Prawitz, Jan 1990: 'Naval Arms Control: History and Observations', in Fieldhouse, Richard, ed.: *Security at Sea. Naval Forces and Arms Control* (Oxford: Oxford U.P.), 43-63.

Quester, George 1977: *Offense and Defense in the International System.* (New York: Wiley).

1986: 'Avoiding Offensive Weapons and Strengthening the Defense', in idem: *The Future of Nuclear Deterrence* (Lexington, Mass.: Lexington Books), 229-250.

Rajewsky, Christiane 1987: 'Zur Geschichte des Pazifismus seit 1933', in & Riesenberger, eds., 412-446.

— & Dieter **Riesenberger**, eds. 1987: *Wider den Krieg. Grosse Pazifisten von Immanuel Kant bis Heinrich Böll* (München: Beck).

Ramsbotham, Oliver 1989: *Modernizing NATO's Nuclear Weapons. 'No Decisions Have Been Made'* (London: Macmillan).

Rathjens, George 1973: 'The Dynamics of the Arms Race', in York, Herbert, ed.: *Arms Control. Readings from the Scientific American* (San Fransisco: Freeman), 177-187.

Rattinger, Hans 1985: 'The Federal Republic of Germany: Much Ado About (Almost) Nothing', in Flynn, Gregory & Hans Rattinger, eds.: *The Public and Atlantic Defence* (London: Rowman & Allanhead), 101-174.

Rauchensteiner, Manfred 1989: 'Kriterien einer defensiven Verteidigung', in Wagemann, ed., 65-76.

Rausch, Heinz, 1983: 'Politisches Bewusstsein und politische Einstellungen im Wandel', in Weidenfeld, ed., 119-153.

Rautenberg, Hans-Jürgen & Norbert **Wiggershaus** 1977: *Die Himmeroder Denkschrift v. Oktober 1950. Politische und militärische Überlegungen für einen Beitrag der Bundesrepublik Deutschland zur westeuropäischen Verteidigung* (Karlsruhe: Militärgeschichtliches Forschungsamt).

Reeb, Hans Joachim 1990: 'Eine Botschaft der Bundeswehr: Innere Führung auch für die NVA', *EW*, 7, 388-392.

Reich, Utz-Peter 1990: 'Die Kunst der Dialektik als Methode der Friedensforschung', in Weizsäcker, ed., 104-109.

Reinhold, Otto 1988: 'Wichtiger Beitrag und viele Diskussionsfragen. Zu Egon Bahrs Buch "Zum europäischen Frieden"', *NG*, 35:10, 915-919.

Renouard, Isabelle 1986: 'Deutsch-französische Zusammenarbeit heute', in Kaiser & Lellouche, eds., 48-56.

Reusch, Jürgen 1988: *Neue Sicherheitspolitik im Nuklearzeitalter* (Köln: Pahl-Rugenstein). 1989: 'Neues Denken und die marxistische Wissenschaft vom Frieden', in IMSF, eds., 11-54.

Richtenwald, Marion 1988: 'Perestrojka in den sowjetische Streitkräften', *Berichte*, 10.

Richter, Michael 1989: 'Parteien für ganz Deutschland', *DA*, 22:10, 1144-1153.

Ries, Tomas 1989: *Cold Will. The Defence of Finland* (London: Brassey's).

Riese, Hans-Peter 1990: 'Die Geschichte hat sich an das Werk gemacht. Der Wandel der sowjetischen Position zur deutschen Frage', *EA*, 4, 117-126.

Riesenberger, Dieter 1987: 'Zur Geschichte des Pazifismus von 1800 bis 1933', in Rajewsky & Riesenberger, eds., 212-228.

Risse-Kappen, Thomas 1988: *Die Krise der Sicherheitspolitik. Neuorientierungen und Entscheidungsprozesse im politischen System der Bundesrepublik Deutschland* 1977-1984 (München: Kaiser). 1990: 'Predicting the New Europe', *BAS*, 46:8, 25-29.

Rittberger, Volker, Manfred **Efinger** & Martin **Mendler** 1990: 'Toward and East-West Security Regime: The Case of Confidence—and Security-Building Measures', *JPR*, 27:1, 55-74.

Ritter, Klaus 1985: 'The Critical Issue of the Transfer of Technology', *NSN*, March, 39-45.

Rix, Christiane 1987: 'Plädoyer für ein europäisches System Kollektiver Sicherheit', in Heisenberg & Lutz, eds., 697-709. — & Peter **Wilke** 1986: 'Gemeinsame Sicherheit zwischen Entspannungspolitik, Rüstungskontrolle und einseitiger Abrüstung', in Bahr & Lutz, eds., 197-219.

Roberts, Adam, ed. 1967: *The Strategy of Civilian Defence. Non-violent Resistance to Aggression* (London: Faber and Faber). 1976: *Nations in Arms. The Theory and Practice of Territorial Defence* (New York: Praeger). 1978: 'Civilian Defence Twenty Years On', *BPP*, 9:4, 293-300.

Robinson, Julian Perry 1986: 'NATO Chemical Weapons Policy and Posture', *ADIU Occasional Papers*, 4.

Rochon, Thomas 1989: *Mobilizing for Peace. The Antinuclear Movements in Western Europe* (London: Adamantine).

Rogers, Bernard 1983: 'Sword and Shield: ACE Attack of Warsaw Pact Follow-On Forces', *NSN*, 28:1, 16-26. 1985: 'Follow-On Forces Attack', *NATO Review*, 1, 1-9.

Romberg, Walter 1986: *Krisenstabile militärische Sicherheit in Mitteleuropa: Kriterien, Modelle und ethische Aspekte* (Berlin: Bund der Evangelischen Kirchen in der DDR). 1988: 'Towards Non-Offensive Defence Through Unilateral, Limited and Reciprocated Reductions. On a Gradualistic Approach to Military Crisis Stability in Central Europe', in Baudisch, ed., 62-67. 1989: 'Ein gradualistischer Zugang zu militärischer Krisenstabilität', in SAS, eds., 215-222. 1989a: 'The Relation Between Unilateral and Bilateral Steps', in Borg & Smit, eds., 239-244. 1990: 'Thesen zu sicherheitspolitischen Alternativen für Osteuropa', *Bremer Beiträge*, 3, 6-8.

326   BIBLIOGRAPHY

Ropp, Theodore 1941: 'Continental Doctrines of Sea Power', in Earle, ed., 446-456.

1962: *War in the Modern World* (New York: Collier).

Rose, Francois de 1986: 'Die nukleare Hürde zwischen Paris und Bonn', in Kaiser & Lellouche, eds., 180-186.

Rosolowsky, Diane 1987: *West Germany's Foreign Policy. The Impact of the Social Democrats and the Greens* (New York: Greenwood).

Rotfeld, Adam & Walther **Stützle** 1991: *Germany and Europe in Transition*, (Oxford: Oxford U.P./SIPRI).

Roth, Günter 1987: 'Die Trias strategischer Herausforderungen der Zukunft', in Bald, ed., 83-100.

1989: 'Deutsche Rüstungspolitik im Zeitalter der Weltkriege', in Wagemann, ed., 47-56.

Rothenberg, Günther E. 1986: 'Moltke, Schlieffen, and the Doctrine of Strategic Envelopment', in Paret, ed., 296-325.

Rotter, Manfred 1984: 'Bewaffnete Neutralität. Das Beispiel Österreich', *Militärpolitik Dokumentation*, 8, 38.

Rovan, Joseph 1983: 'Staat und Nation in der deutschen Geschichte', in Weidenfeld, ed., 229-247.

Rudolph, Hermann 1983: 'Wie sieht das Selbstverständnis der DDR-Gesellschaft aus?', in Weidenfeld, ed., 193-209.

1987: 'The Human Dimension', in Moreton, ed., 141-156.

Rühl, Lothar 1982: 'MBFR: Lessons and Problems', *AdP*, 176.

1986a: 'Der Aufschwung der sicherheitspolitiscen Zusammenarbeit', in Kaiser & Lellouche, eds., 27-47.

1990: 'Konventionelle Abrüstung im Sturmwind der Ereignisse', *EA*, 8, 264-274.

1991: 'Der Vertrag über Konventionelle Streitkräfte inm Europa und die neue Konstellation der europäischen Sicherheit', *EA*, 46:3, 81-90.

Rühle, Hans 1984: 'Wunschträume statt Alpträume', *EW*, 11.

Sailer, Michael 1989: 'Die Bedeutung des kerntechnischen Risikopotentials für die Kriegsfähigkeit einer Industriegesellschaft', *S + F*, 7:4, 211-219.

SALSS (Sozialwissenschaftliche Analysen zur Leistungssteigerung Sozialer Systeme) 1984a: 'Konventionelle Landstreitkräfte für Mitteleuropa: Eine Militärische Bedrohungsanalyse' (Bonn: SALSS).

1984b: 'Spezialisierung auf die Defensive. Einführung und Quellensammlung. Ein Übersichtsgutachten' (Bonn: SALSS).

1985: 'Die Zukunft der Bundeswehr: Eine Durchleuchtung der amtlichen Planung. Gutachten' (Bonn: SALSS).

SAS (Studiengruppe Alternative Sicherheitspolitik), eds. 1984: *Strukturwandel der Verteidigung: Entwürfe für eine konsequente Defensive* (Opladen: Westdeutscher).

1984a: 'Über die Luftstreitkräfte einer defensiven Verteidigung', in —, eds., 181-182.

1984b: 'Landstreitkräfte zur Verteidigung der Bundesrepublik Deutschland. Ein Modell für die 90er Jahre', in —, eds., 156-173.

1984c: 'Das Personal alternativer Landstreitkräfte', in —, eds., 176-180.

1987: 'Das SAS-Konzept: Strukturwandel für die 90er Jahre (Stand Herbst 1987)' (Bonn: SAS).

1989: 'Prüfsteine für die Entwicklung einer stabilitätsgerechten konventionellen Verteidigung in Mitteleuropa', in —, eds., 235-239.

1989a: '"Verteidigerüberlegenheit" (SWP) und "Vertrauensbildende Verteidigung" (SAS)' (Bonn: SAS).

—, eds. 1989: *Vertrauensbildende Verteidigung. Reform deutscher Sicherheitspolitik.* (Gerlingen: Bleicher).

Scheer, Hermann 1984: 'Der Ost-West Konflikt und die Antwort der NATO. Eine kritische Auseinandersetzung mit dem AirLand Battle-Konzept', in Brauch, ed., 204-13.

1985a: 'Chancen und Klippen einer deutsch-französischen Sicherheitskooperation', *NG*, 8, 732-736.

1985b: 'Eureka: Eine Alternative zu SDI und EVI? Kriterien zur Beantwortung', *Blätter*, 11, 1339-1343.

1986a: *Die Befreiung von der Bombe. Weltfrieden, europäischer Weg und die Zukunft der Deutschen* (Köln: Bund).

1986b: 'Mit Schlagworten gegen eine Denkschule', *EW*, 1, 5-6.
1987: 'Miliz—nüchtern betrachtet', in Bald, ed., 125-133.
1989: 'Sind Atomwaffen zur Kriegsverhütung erforderlich?', in SAS, eds., 48-54.
Scheffran, Jürgen 1987: 'Ein Einstieg in die westeuropäische SDI-Diskussion', in Engels, Dieter, & Ekkehard Sieker, eds.: *SDI—Falle für Westeuropa. Politik, Wirtschaft und Wissenschaft im Schatten der Weltraumrüstung* (Köln: Pahl-Rugenstein), 11-58.
Scheler, Wolfgang, ed. 1989: *Frieden, Krieg, Streitkräfte. Historisch-materialistischer Abriss* (Berlin: Militärverlag der DDR).
Schelling, Thomas 1960: *The Strategy of Conflict* (Cambridge Mass.: Harvard U.P.).
1966: *Arms and Influence* (New Haven: Yale U.P.).
— & Morton **Halperin** 1961: *Strategy and Arms Control* (New York 1985: Brassey's).
Schierholz, H. 1986: 'Scheitert ein rot-grünes Bündnis an der NATO-Frage? Anmerkungen zur Friedenspolitik der Grünen', *Blätter*, 7, 1214-1225.
Schilling, Hans-Jürgen 1989: 'Die Mitteleuropäische Union. Ein vergessener französischer Versuchsballon', *DA*, 22:10, 1126-1131.
Schirmeister, Helga, 1989: *Sicherheit durch Vertrauen* (Berlin, GDR: Staatsverlag).
Schlaga, Rüdiger 1990: 'Peace Movement as a Party's Tool? The Peace Council of the German Democratic Republic', in Kodama, Kaysuya & Unto Vesa, eds.: *Towards a Comparative Analysis of Peace Movements* (Aldershot: Dartmouth), 129-146.
Schlotter, Peter 1982: 'Die Ost-West Beziehungen als pluralistisches Sicherheitssystem', in Hessische Stiftung für Friedens—und Konfliktforschung, eds.: *Europa zwischen Konfrontation und Kooperation. Entspannungspolitik für die achtziger Jahren* (Frankfurt: Campus), 42-61.
Schlögel, Karl 1989: 'Mitteleuropa hört auf, eine Ideologie zu sein', *NG*, 36:11, 986-990.
Schmähling, Elmar 1986a: 'The Survivability of Static and Large Weapons Systems Against Modern Stand-Off Weapons' (Working Paper 3 for the Fifth Workshop of the Pugwash Study Group on Conventional Forces in Europe, Castilionciello, Italy, 9-12 October).
1986b: 'Thoughts on the Future of Surface Forces' (Working Paper 2 for the Fifth Workshop of the Pugwash Study Group on Conventional Forces in Europe, Castilionciello, Italy, 9-12 October).
1987: 'Bemerkungen zum Problemfeld "Strukturelle Nichtangriffsfahigkeit"', *S + F*, 1, 72-77.
1988: 'Das Ende unserer Sicherheit oder Abschied von einer Illusion? Warum die Falken gegen das INF-Abkommen sind', *S + F*, 1, 34-37.
1988b: 'Von der "Strukturellen Nichtangriffsfähigkeit" zur "Verteidigerüberlegenheit"', in Bahr & Lutz, eds., 62-80.
1988b: 'Gedanken zu den gestellten Fragen über konventionale Stabilität', in Bahr & Lutz, eds., 472-476.
1988c: 'Auch wir brauchen ein "Neues Denken". Abschied von der Militarisierung der äusseren Sicherheit', *NG*, 6, 542-547.
1989: 'German Security Policy Beyond American Hegemony', *WPJ*, 6:2, 371-384.
1989a: 'Seestreitkräfte und Rüstungsbeschränkung. Möglichkeiten und Probleme der Einbeziehung von Seestreitkräften in den Prozess von Abrüstung, Rüstungskontrolle und Vertrauensbildung', *AZ*, B 8/89, 17 February.
1989b: 'Rüstungskontrolle und Abrüstung bei Seestreitkräften', *S + F*, 7:2, 150-152.
1989c: 'Armee als Wagenburg? Über Tendenzen der Abschrottung in der Bundeswehr und falsche Reaktionen auf den gesellschaftlichen Wandel-ein Plädoyer für demokratisierte Streitkräfte', in Vogt, ed., 252-264.
1990: *Der unmögliche Krieg. Sicherheit und Verteidigung vor der Jahrtausendwende* (Düsseldorf: ECON).
1990a: 'Geht die Nachkriegszeit für die Bundesrepublik Deutschland zu Ende?', Lutz & —, eds., 23-34.
1990b: 'The Vulnerability of Surface Forces to Modern Stand-Off Weapons', in Boserup & Neild, eds., 173-178.
1990c: 'Conclusion: A New Way of Thinking for a Future Security Regime', in —, ed., 189-199.
1990d: 'NATO's Nuclear Strategy in a Dilemma', in —, ed., 3-10.
1990e: 'Vom nationalen Kriegsdienst zum europäischen Friedensdienst—die Zukunft der Bundeswehr', in Bahr, H-E., ed., 119-126.

—, ed. 1990: *Life Beyond the Bomb. Global Stability Without Nuclear Deterrence* (München: Berg).

— & Dieter **Mahncke** 1990: 'Hoffnung ohne Garantie', *NG*, 37:2, 150-156.

Schmid, Günther 1983: 'Positionen in der sicherheitspolitischen Diskussion und ihre Vertreter in der Bundesrepublik Deutschland', *ÖMZ*, 6, 504-512.

Schmidt, Hans-Joachim 1988: 'Conventional Arms Control in Europe', *PRIF-R*, 6.

Schmidt, Helmut 1984: 'Zur Lage der Sicherheitspolitik. Zweiter Verhandlungstag des ausserordentlichen Parteitages der SPD in Köln vom 18. bis 19.11 1983', in Maruh, Jürgen & Manfred Wilke, eds.: *Wohin treibt die SPD? Wende oder Kontinuität sozialdemokratischer Sicherheitspolitik* (München: Olzog), 129-164.

1986: *Eine Strategie für den Westen* (Berlin: Siedler).

1987: 'Deutsch-französische Zusammenarbeit in der Sicherheitspolitik', *EA*, 11, 303-307.

Schmidt, Helmut F. 1988: 'Rahmenbedingungen und Planungen für die Personalstruktur in den 90er Jahren', in Bald & Klein, eds., 23-40.

Schmidt, Max & al. 1989: *Sicherheit und Friedliche Koexistenz. Umfassende internationale Sicherheit Umsetzung freidlicher Koexistenzbeziehungen heute* (Berlin: Staatsverlag der DDR).

— & Wolfgang **Schwarz** 1988: 'Das Gemeinsame Haus Europa: Realitäten, Herausforderungen, Perspektiven', Parts 1 and 2, *IPW-B*, 9 and 10, 1-10 and 1-11.

1989: 'Strukturelle Angriffsunfähigkeit in Europa. Vernünftige Alternative zur Abschreckung', *Horizont*, 3, 3-4.

1989a: 'Herausforderungen und Perspektiven für Gemeinsame Sicherheit und das gemeinsame Haus Europa', in IMSF, eds., 248-267.

1989b: 'From East Germany: It's NATO's Move Now', *BAS*, 45:7, 5-7.

1989c: 'DDR und BRD: Sicherheitspartner im gemeinsamen Haus Europa', *IPW-B*, 8, 1-10.

1989d: 'Umfassende internationale Sicherheit Erfordernis unserer Zeit', in Schmidt & al., 10-61.

1989e: 'Frieden als Überlebungsbedingung', *S + F*, 7:4, 206-211.

1990: 'Mutual Inability to Launch Attacks, and Arms Reductions in Europe', *Disarmament*, 13:1, 69-82.

1990a: 'Von der nuklearen Abschreckung zur Gemeinsamen Sicherheit', in Lutz & Schmähling, eds., 85-112.

1990b: 'German Unity and European Security', *Peace and the Sciences* (Vienna: International Institute for Peace), 1-9.

Schmidt, Peter 1986: 'Die deutsche Debatte über die nuklearen und konventionellen Streikräfte Frankreichs', in Kaiser & Lellouche, eds., 101-110.

Schmidt-Eenboom, Erich 1989: 'Strukturelle Verteidigungsuntauglichkeit urbaner Zentren und Regionen', *S + F*, 7:4, 226-231.

Schmige, Georg 1988: 'Staatenvertrag statt Friedensvertrag', *DA*, 21:11, 1167-1170.

Schmitt, Matthias 1988: *Das Ostgeschäft von Morgen. Neue Perspektiven und Chancen* (Baden-Baden: Nomos).

Schmückle, Gerd & Albrecht A.C. von **Müller** 1988: 'Das Konzept der "Stabilen Abhaltung". Umrisse eines Gesamtkonzepts zur Um—und Afrüstung in Europa' (Starnberg: Max Planck Society).

Schoenbaum, David 1988: 'The World War II Allied Agreement on Occupation and Administration of Postwar Germany', in George & al., eds., 21-45.

Scholz, Rupert 1989: 'Alternative Verteidigung? Die Strategie der "Spinne im Netz"', *EW*, 11, 643-646.

1989a: 'Sicherheit trotz Abrüstung?', in Wagemann, ed., 107-114.

1990: 'Deutsche Frage und europäische Sicherheit. Sicherheitspolitik in einem sich einigenden Deutschland und Europa', *EA*, 7, 239-246.

Schölch, Ingrid 1990: *Abschreckung, Sicherheit und Stabilität. Grundsatzprobleme der sicherheitspolitischen Situation in Europa* (Baden-Baden: Nomos).

Schramm, Friedrich-Karl, Wolfram-Georg **Riggert** & Alois **Friedel**, eds. 1972: *Sicherheitskonferenz in Europa. Dokumentation 1954-1972. Die Bemühungen um Entspannung und Annäherung im politischen, militärischen, wirtschaftlichen, wissencahftlich-technologischen und kulturellen Bereich* (Frankfurt: Metzner).

Schreiner, Karl H. 1987: '"Strukturelle Nichtangriffsfähigkeit": Eine Auseinandersetzung mit den Thesen von Albrecht A.C. von Müller', in Bühl, ed., 173-183.

Schröder, Diethelm, ed. 1984: *Krieg oder was sonst? NATO: Strategie des Unsicherheit* (Reinbek: Rowohlt).

Schröder, Hans-Henning 1989: 'Die Verteidigungspolitik der UdSSR 1987-1989', *Berichte*, 14.

Schröder, Hans-Jürgen 1988: 'Kanzler der Alliierten? Die Bedeutung der USA für die Aussenpolitik Adenauers', in: Foschepoth, ed., 118-145.

Schubert, Klaus von 1970: *Wiederbewaffnung und Westintegration. Die innere Auseinandersetzung um die militärische und aussenpolitische Orientierung der Bundesrepublik* 1950-1952 (Stuttgart: Deutsche Verlags-Anstalt).

1988: 'Strategische Voraussetzungen einer zukünftigen Wehrstruktur', in Bald & Klein, eds., 11-22.

1989: 'Gemeinsame Sicherheit—das neue Paradigma. Ein Beitrag aus der Sicht der Bundesrepublik Deutschland', *NG*, 36:11, 978-982.

1990: 'Mutual Responsibility: A Strategy for West and East', in Schmähling, ed., 73-86.

—, Egon **Bahr** & Gert **Krell** 1988: 'Stellungnahme. Zur Entwicklung der Ost-West-Beziehungen nach dem INF-Vertrag', in Moltmann, ed., 9-14.

Schulte, Ludwig 1985: 'Das Schlagwort von der "defensiven Umrüstung"', *EW*, 9, 474-479.

1990: *Trumpf der Verteidigung. Mehr Stabilität durch moderne Technologien* (Baden-Baden: Nomos).

Schultz, Eberhard 1988: 'Militärische und politische Sicherheit', *NG*, 6, 525-531.

1989a: 'Europäische Sicherheit als ein Aspekt der deutschen Frage', *DA*, 22:5, 524-532.

1989b: 'Berlin-Politik: Über das Provisorium hinausgedacht. Ein Ansatz zu einer Antwort auf die deutsche Frage in Selbstbestimmung', *DA*, 22:10, 1094-1106.

Schulze, Franz-Joseph 1986: 'Die Notwendigkeit unverzüglicher gemeinsamer Abwehrreaktionen', in Kaiser & Lellouche, eds., 150-159.

Schulze, Hagen 1987: 'The Revolution of the European Order and the Rise of German Nationalism', in —, ed., 5-18.

—, ed. 1987: *Nation-Building in Central Europe* (Leamington Spa, U.K.: Berg).

Schulze-Marmeling, Dieter 1987: *Die NATO. Anatomie eines Militarpaktes* (Göttingen: Werkstatt).

Schuster, Dieter & Ulrike C. **Washmuth** 1984: '"Alternative Strategien". Eine Auswertung der öffentlichen Anhörung im Verteidigungsausschuss des Deutschen Bundestages', *S + F*, 3, 2-16.

Schütze, Walter 1990: 'Frankreich angesichts der deutschen Einheit', *EA*, 4, 133-138.

1990a: 'Bauplan für eine gesamteuropäische Architektur', *Blätter*, 5, 585-591.

Schwarz, Wolfgang 1988: 'Non-offensive Defence: Goals and Issues of Disarmament Between NATO and WTO in Europe', *IPW-P*, November.

1989: 'Strukturelle Angriffsfähigkeit in Europa. Erfordernisse, Konzepte, Hemnisse', *IPW-F*, 2.

1989a: 'Strukturelle Angriffsunfähigkeit in Europa. NATO und Warschauer Vertragsorganisation', *Beiträge zur Konfliktforschung*, 2.

Schweisfurt, Theodor 1989: 'Die deutsche Frage aus der Sicht der Grünen', in Blumenwitz & Zieger, eds., 109-120.

Seidelmann, Reimund 1987: 'SPD und SED zur Schaffung eines atomwaffenfreien Korridors', *DA*, 2, 134-148.

1989: 'Zu den europapolitischen Aussagen des neuen SPD-Programms', *NG*, 36:9, 1035-1037.

Seiffert, Wolfgang 1986: *Das ganze Deutschland. Perspektiven der Wiedervereinigung* (München: Piper).

1989: *Die Deutschen und Gorbatschow. Chancen für einen Interessenausgleich* (Erlangen: Straube).

1990: 'Das Selbstbestimmungsrecht der Deutschen', in Venohr, ed., 91-102.

Senghaas, Dieter 1972: *Rüstung und Militarismus* (Frankfurt: Suhrkamp).

1985: 'Die Ostproblematik eines europäischen Systems Kollektiver Sicherheit', in Lutz, ed., 294-309.

1986: *Die Zukunft Europas. Probleme der Friedensgestaltung* (Frankfurt: Suhrkamp).

1987: 'Conventional Forces in Europe: Dismantle Offense, Strengthen Defense', *BAS*, 10, 9-11.

1988: *Konfliktformationen im internationalen System* (Frankfurt: Suhrkamp).

1989: 'Die Entmilitarisierung des Systemkonflikts: Europas Chance. Ein Vorschlag für die nächste Etappe', *Dialog*, 14:1, 7-17.

1989a: 'Arms Race Dynamics and Arms Control', in Gleditsch & Njølstad, eds., 15-30.

1989b: 'Systemic Confrontation, Armament Competition, and Armaments Dynamics', in Gleditsch & Njølstad, eds., 346-351.

1990: *Europa 2000. Ein Friedensplan* (Frankfurt: Suhrkamp).

1990a: 'Die Zivilisierung des Ost-West-Konfliktes', in Weizsäcker, ed., 171-188.

1990b: 'Was friedenspolitisch jetzt zu tun wäre', in Bahr, H-E., ed., 169-188.

1990c: 'Requirements for a Timely Peace Policy', *BPP*, 21:4, 441-447.

1990d: 'Europa an der Schwelle der neunziger Jahre', *Friedensforum*, 5, 3-7.

1990e: 'Europe 2000: A Peace Plan', *Alternatives*, 15:4, 467-478.

1990f: 'Friedensforschung an der Schwelle der neunziger Jahre', *EA*, 20, 607-614.

Sharp, Gene 1973: *The Politics of Non-violent Action*, vol. 1-3 (Boston: Porter & Sargent).

1985: *Making Europe Unconquerable. The Potential of Civilian-Based Deterrence and Defence* (London: Taylor & Francis).

Sharp, Jane M.O. 1987: 'After Reykjavik: Arms Control and the Allies', *International Affairs*, 2, 239-257.

—, ed. 1990: *Europe After an American Withdrawal. Economic and Military Issues* (Oxford: Oxford U.P.).

Siegmann, Heinrich 1989: 'Enhancing Conventional Stability in Europe', in Altmann & Rotblat, eds., 131-139.

Sigal, Leon V. 1983: *Nuclear Forces in Europe. Enduring Dilemmas, Present Prospects* (Washington: Brookings).

Simpkin, Richard 1983: *Red Armour. An Examination of the Soviet Mobile Force Concept* (London: Brassey's).

1986: *Race to the Swift. Thoughts on 21st Century Warfare* (London: Brassey's).

Skubiszewski, Krzystof 1990: 'Die völkerrechtliche und staatliche Einheit des deutschen Volkes und die Entwicklung in Europa', *EA*, 6, 15-202.

Smit, Wim A. 1989: 'Conventional Attack on Nuclear Facilities', in Tromp, ed., 293-318.

Smith, Roland 1985: 'Soviet Policy Towards West Germany', *AdP*, 203.

Smyser, William P. 1989: 'Partner im Widerstreit. Die Bundesrepublik und die Vereinigten Staaten vor dem Beginn einer neuen Ära', *EA*, 21, 645-654.

Snyder, Glenn H. 1984: 'The Security Dilemma in Alliance Politics', *World Politics*, 36:4, 461-495.

Snyder, Jack 1984: *The Ideology of the Offensive. Military Decision Making and the Disasters of 1914* (New York: Cornell U.P.).

1985: 'Civil-Military Relations and the Cult of the Offensive 1914 and 1984', in Miller, ed., 108-146.

1987: 'The Gorbachev Revolution: A Waning of Soviet Expansionism?', *IS*, 12;3, 93-131.

1988: 'Limiting Offensive Conventional Forces: Soviet Proposals and Western Options', *IS*, 12:4, 48-77.

1990: 'Averting Anarchy in the New Europe', *IS*, 14:4, 5-41.

Sommer, Karl-Ludwig 1988: 'Wiederbewaffnung oder Wiedervereinigung? Adenauer und die Diskussion um die EVG im Bundesrat', in Foschepoth, ed., 146-168.

Sonntag, Philip 1990: 'Quantität und Qualität in der Rüstungssteuerung', in Weizsäcker, ed., 77-83.

Sontheimer, Kurt 1983: 'Ein deutscher Sonderweg?', in Weidenfeld, ed., 324-336.

Souchon, Lennart 1990: *Neue deutsche Sicherheitspolitik*, (Herford: Mittler).

Spanger, Hans-Joachim 1989: 'The GDR in East-West Relations', *AdP*, 240.

Spannocchi, Emilio 1976: 'Verteidigung ohne Selbstzerstörung', in Weizsäcker, ed., 15-91.

SPD 1986: 'Leitantrag "Friedens—und Sicherheitspolitik" in der vom Bundesparteitag der SPD in Nürnberg am 27. August 1986 beschlossenen Fassung', *Blätter*, 10, 1268-1278.

1988: 'Frieden und Abrüstung in Europa. Beschluss zur Friedens—und Abrüstungspolitik des SPD-Bundesparteitages in Münster 30.8-2.9.1988', *Politik. Informationsdienst der SPD*, 10 September.

— & **PVAP** 1985: 'Gemeinsame Erklärung von SPD und PVAP zur Sicherheit und Zusammenarbeit in Europa durch Massnahmen der gegenseitigen Vertrauensbildung', *Blätter*, 12, 1515-1519.

1988: 'Kriterien und Schritte zu vertrauensschaffende Sicherheitsstrukturen in Europa', *Blätter*, 4, 508-510.

SPD & SED 1985: *Für eine chemiewaffenfreie Zone in Europe. Gemeinsame politische Initiative der Sozialistischen Einheitspartei Deutschlands und der Sozialdemokratischen Partei Deutschlands* (Dresden: Zeit im Bild).

1987a: 'Initiative von SPD und SED für eine atomwaffenfreie Zone in Mitteleuropa', *DA*, 2, 211-215.

1987b: '"Der Streit der Ideologien und die gemeinsame Sicherheit". Gemeinsame Erklärung der Grundwertekommission der SPD und der Akademie für Gesellschaftswissenschaften beim ZK der SED vom 27. August 1987', *Blätter*, 10, 1365-1371.

SPD-Fraktion im Deutschen Bundestag 1988: 'Positionspapir zur Streitkräfte—, Personal, Rüstungs—und Finanzplanung der Bundeswehr (1 April)', in Horn, Erwin: 'Brief an die Fraktion, 28. April'.

Spittmann, Ilse 1990: 'Deutschland einig Vaterland', *DA*, 23:2, 187-190.

Stadelmann, Rudolph 1975: *Social and Political History of the German 1848 Revolution* (Athens, Ohio: Ohio U.P.).

Staritz, Dietrich 1990: 'Ursachen und Konsequenzen einer deutschen Revolution', in Baumann et al., 13-44.

Statz, Albert 1988: 'Unilateral Steps to Disarmament and Deliberate Self-Containment. Elements of a Green Foreign Policy Strategy for West Germany', *Green Peace Policy*, 13, 2-4.

1988a: *Militärzwillinge. Bundesrepuplik/Frankreich: Eine Achse der Aufrüstung* (Bonn: Grünen im Bundestag).

Stechow, Christian von 1987: 'Sicherheitspolitische Perspektiven der neunziger Jahre', in Heisenberg & Lutz, eds., 834-843.

Stefanic, David 1988: 'The Rapacki Plan: A Case Study of East European Diplomacy', *East European Quarterly*, 21:4, 401-412.

Stehle, Hans-Jakob 1989: 'Adenauer, Polen und die deutsche Frage', in Foschepoth, ed., 80-98.

Steinbach, Peter 1990: 'Traditionsbruch? Von der Neurose zur versuchten Traditionsbildung', *NG*, 37:2, 139-146.

Steinbruner, John D. & Leon V. Sigal, eds. 1983: *Alliance Security: NATO and the No-First-Use Question* (Washington: Brookings).

Steiner, Kurt 1988: 'Negotiations for an Austrian State Treaty', in George & al. eds., 46-82.

Steininger, Rolf 1989: *Wiederbewaffnung. Die Entscheidung für einen westdeutschen Verteidigungsbeitrag: Adenauer und die Westmächte 1950* (Erlangen: Straube).

1990: 'Deutsche Frage und Berliner Konferenz 1954', in Venohr, ed., 37-90.

Steinke, Rudolph & Michel Vale, eds. 1983: *Germany Debates Defence. The NATO Alliance at the Crossroad* (New York: Sharpe).

Steinsecker, Heinz-Eberhard Freiherr von 1982: 'Zur "Raumverteidigung"', *Wehrwissenschaftliche Rundschau*, 1, 1-11.

Stoltenberg, Gerhard 1990: 'Die transatlantische Allianz: Lebenswichtiger Faktor der Zukunft', *EW*, 3, 136-144.

Stratmann, K.-Peter 1989: 'The Military Objectives of Conventional Arms Control', in Blackwill & Larrabee, eds., 140-164.

Stromseth, Jane E. 1988: *The Origins of Flexible Response. NATO's Debate Over Strategy in the 1960's* (New York: St. Martin's).

Studiengruppe Alternative Sicherheitspolitik: see under: SAS.

Stürmer, Michael 1983: 'Kein Eigentum der Deutschen: die deutsche Frage', in Weidenfeld, ed., 83-101.

1987: 'The Evolution of the Contemporary German Question', in Moreton, ed., 21-32.

1989: 'Die Deutschen in Europa. Auf dem Weg zu einer zwischenstaatlichen Innenpolitik', *EA*, 24, 721-732.

1990: 'Making the GDR "Clubable"', *European Affairs*, 4:1, 22-29.

Surotchak, Jan Erik 1989: 'One Step Forward, Two Steps Back? Assessing the Status and Influence of the West German Greens', in Griffith & al., 66-82.

Szabo, Stephen F. 1990: *The Changing Politics of German Security* (London: Pinter).

—, ed. 1990: *The Bundeswehr and Western Security*, (London: Macmillan).

Szilard, Leo 1964: '"Minimal Deterrent" vs. Saturation Parity' (BAS, March), in Kissinger, ed. 1965, 376-391.

Sørensen, Henning & Lutz **Unterseher** 1989: 'NOD Principles Implemented in Danish Defence', *WP-CPCR*, 14.

Teltschik, Horst 1990: 'The Federal Republic and Poland—A Difficult Partnership in the Heart of Europe', *AuP*, 1, 3-14.

Tetzlaff, Martin 1988: 'Überlegungen zur Konventionellen Stabilität', in Bahr & Lutz, eds., 477-480.

Thadden, Rudolf von 1983: 'Das Schwierige Vaterland', in Weidenfeld, ed., 51-63.

Theilmann, Alexander 1986: 'Die Diskussion über militärische Defensivkonzepte. Entwicklungen, Inhalte, Perspektiven', *HB*, 9.

Thimann, Christian 1989: 'Das Personalmodell einer alternativen Verteidigung', in SAS, eds., 204-211.

1989a: 'Drei militärische Modelle auf einen Blick', in SAS, eds., 17-22.

— & al. 1988: 'Zum Personalmodell von H. Funk: "Die Integrierte Vorneverteidigung Mitteleuropa"' (Bonn: SAS).

Trähnert, Oliver, ed. 1991: 'Nach Wien I: die Zukunft der nuklearen und konventionellen Abrüstung auf dem Weg zu einer neuen europäischen Friedensordnung', *Studie*, 42.

Tiedtke, Stephan 1986: 'Abschreckung und ihre Alternativen. Die sowjetische Sicht einer westlichen Debatte', *Texte und Materialien der Forschungsstätte der Evangelischen Studiengemeinschaft*, Reihe A, 20 (Heidelberg: F.E. St.).

Till, Geoffrey 1982: *Maritime Strategy and the Nuclear Age* (London: Macmillan).

Todenhöfer, Jürgen 1989: *Ich denke Deutsch. Abrechnung mit dem Zeitgeist* (Erlangen: Straube).

Trempnau, Thomas 1983: 'Horst Afheldt's Defensive Response Model', in Steinke & Vale, eds., 187-196.

Tromp, Hylke W., ed. 1989: *War in Europe. Nuclear and Conventional Perpectives* (Aldershot: Gower).

Tuchman, Barbara 1962: *The Guns of August* (New York: Macmillan).

Türpe, Andrè 1989: 'Von der Philosophie der Abschreckung zu einem gesichertem Frieden für Europa', in Wagemann, ed., 133-142.

Uhle-Wettler, Franz 1966: *Leichte Infanterie im Atomzeitalter* (Darmstadt: Wehr und Wissen).

1980: *Gefechtsfeld Mitteleuropa. Gefahr der Übertechnisierung von Streitkräften* (Gütersloh: Bernard & Graefe).

1989: *Die Gesichter des Mars. Krieg im Wandel der Zeiten* (Erlangen: Straube).

1990: 'Geographische Faktoren in der Verteidigung', in Weizsäcker, ed., 123-132.

Ungerer, Werner 1990: 'Die Europäische Gemeinschaft und die Einigung Deutschlands', *Blätter*, 4, 434-444.

Union of Concerned Scientists 1983: *No-First-Use.* (Washington: UCS).

Unterseher, Lutz 1984a: 'Friedenssicherung durch Vermeidung von Provokation? Ein pragmatischer Vorschlag für eine alternative Landesverteidigung', in Vogt, ed., 95-103

1984b: 'Für eine tragfähige Verteidigung der Bundesrepublik: Grundgedanken und Orientierungen', in SAS, eds., 108-130.

1984c: 'Konventionelle Verteidigung Mitteleuropas: Etablierte Struktur und Alternativen im Test', in Brauch, ed., 214-222.

1987: 'Fünf Thesen zur Vermeidung von Missverständnissen um eine alternative Verteidigung', in Bahr & Lutz, eds., 283-300.

1987a: 'Stellungnahme der Studiengruppe Alternative Sicherheitspolitik (SAS) zum Thema "Vertrauensbildende Strukturen"', *S + F*, 1, 77-83.

1987b: 'Bewegung, Bewegung! Zur Kritik eingefahrener Vorstellungen vom Krieg', *S + F*, 2, 90-97.

1987c: 'The Standard Battalion of Line Infantry: An Exercise in Force Design With Robust Technologies' (Bonn: SAS).

1988: 'Spider and Web: The Case for a Pragmatic Defence Alternative' (Bonn: SAS).

1988a: 'Some Naughty Thoughts on Italy's Defence' (Paper Prepared for the International Conference "Rethinking European Security", at the Istituto Universitario Europeo, University of Florence, 23-24 September).

1988b: 'Tactical Air Forces. For a Disarmament Initiative of the West' (Bonn: SAS).
1988c: '7 Theses on Defusing Europe as a Potential Source and Theatre of Military Conflict', in Baudisch, ed., 76-82
1988d: 'Defusing the Military Confrontation in Europe. Some Guidelines for Bilateral Talks', in Baudisch, ed., 83-85.
1989: 'Ein anderes Heer: Wesentliche Einzelheiten', in SAS, eds., 240-270.
1989a: 'Bauprinzipien alternativer Landstreitkräfte', in SAS, eds., 149-164.
1989b: 'Umrisse einer stabilen Lutfverteidigung', in SAS, eds., 188-203.
1989c: 'Spinne im Netz. Ein tragfähiger Weg zur Vertrauensbildenden Verteidigung', *Bremer Beiträge*, 1, 15-26.
1989d: 'MP(S)G. The Mobile Protected (Shot) Gun. An Exercise in Alternative Weapons Design' (Bonn: SAS).
1989e: 'Urban Warfare', for Dupuy, Trevor, ed.: *Military Encyclopedia* (Manuscript).
1989f: '"Sicher ist Sicher". Militärisches Rückversicherungsdenken gegen strikte Defensivorientierung', in Vogt, ed., 82-98.
1989g: '...Der Ost macht ernst. Über die militärische und politische Bedeutung einseitiger Truppenreduzierungen der UdSSR und ihrer Verbündeten', *S + F*, 7:4, 248-251.
1989h: 'Defending Europe: Toward a Stable Conventional Deterrent', in Shue, Henry, ed.: *Nuclear Deterrence and Moral Restraint, Critical Choices for American Strategy*(Cambridge: Cambridge U.P.), 293-342.
1990: 'Vertrauensbildende Verteidigung', in Weizsäcker, ed., 143-149.
1990a: 'A Note on the Intricacies of Military Force Assessment', in Brauch & Kennedy, eds., 69-78.
1990b: 'The Case for Alternative Defence: A Detailed Proposal and Its Implications', in Cerutti & Ragionieri, eds., 105-117.
1990c: 'The Case for a Confidence-Building Defence: the SAS Proposal and its Implications', in Brauch, Hans Günter & Robert Kennedy, eds. 1990: *Alternative Conventional Defense Postures in the European Theatre. Vol. 2* (New York: Taylor & Francis, forthcoming).
1990d: 'Der Abrüstungsprozess ist kein Selbstläufer', *BB*, 3, 40-44.
1990e: 'Conventional Land Defence in Central Europe', *APR*, 30.
Valentin, Francois 1986: 'Deutsch-französische Zusammenarbeit in Europa-Mitte', in Kaiser & Lellouche, eds., 142-149.
Väyrynen, Raimo, ed. 1985: *Policies for Common Security*. (London: Taylor & Francis).
Venohr, Wolfgang 1990a: 'Das Vermächtnis des deutschen Widerstandes', in —, ed., 19-36.
1990b: 'Der erste Aufstand in der DDR', in —, ed., 161-178.
—, ed. 1990: *Deutschland wird es sein* (Erlangen: Straube).
'Vertrag zwischen der Bundesrepublik Deutschland und der Deutschen Demokratischen Republik über die Herstellung der Einheit Deutschlands. Einigungsvertrag', *Bulletin*, 104 (6.9.1990), 877-1120.
Vetschera, Heinz 1985: 'Der Weg zu Staatsvertrag und Neutralität', *ÖMZ*, 3, 223-228.
1985a: 'Die Rüstungsbeschränkungen des Österreichischen Staatsvertrags aus rechtlicher und politischer Sicht', *ÖMZ*, 6, 500-505.
— & James V. **Rocca** 1985: 'Österreich in den Ost-West-Beziehungen', *ÖMZ*, 3, 229-305.
Vigor, Peter 1983: *Soviet Blitzkrieg Theory*, (New York: St. Martin's).
Visuri, Pekka 1989: 'Alternative Defence in Central European Debate', in Harle & Sivonen, eds., 93-109.
Vogt, Wolfgang R. 1989: 'Legitimitätsverfall der Sicherheitspolitik', in SAS, eds., 67-101.
1989: 'Militär und Risikogesellschaft', *S + F*, 7:4, 198-205.
1990: 'The Crisis of Acceptance of the Security Policy With Military Means in the Federal Republic of Germany', in Brauch & Kennedy, eds., 165-188.
—, ed. 1984: *Streitfall Frieden. Positionen und Analysen zur Sicherheitspolitik und Friedensbewegung* (Heidelberg: Müller).
—, ed. 1989: *Angst vorm Frieden. Über die Schwierigkeiten der Friedensentwicklung für das Jahr 2000* (Darmstadt: Wissenschaftliche Buchgesellschaft).
—, ed. 1990: *Mut zum Frieden. Über die Möglichkeiten einer Friedensentwicklung für das Jahr 2000*, (Darmstadt: Wissenschaftliche Buchgesellschaft).
Voigt, Karsten 1985: 'Gemeinsame Wege zur chemischen Abrüstung', *NG*, 8, 736-741.

1986: 'Die Grünen nach Hannover, oder Warum es zwischen ihnen und der SPD keine Koalition geben kann', S + F, 4, 220-222.

1987a: 'Der Vorschlag für einen nuklearwaffenfreien Korridor. Ein deutsch-deutsches Pilotprojekt für eine Sicherheitspartnerschaft im Ost-West Konflikt', DA, 2.

1987b: 'New Strategies and Operational Concepts'. Sub-Committee on Conventional Defence: Report, (Brussel: NAA. Military Committee).

1987c: 'Von der nuklearen zur konventionellen Abrüstung in Europa. Kriterien konventioneller Stabilität und Möglichkeiten der Rüstungskontrolle', EA, 14, 409-418.

1988: 'Konventionelle Stabilisierung und Strukturelle Nichtangriffsfähigkeit. Ein systematischer Vergleich verschiedener Konzepte', AZ, B 18/88 (29 April), 21-34. (English version: 'The Prospects of Conventional Stabilization in Europe, in Kaldor, Mary, Gerard Holden & Richard Falk, eds. 1990: The New Détente. Rethinking East-West Relations (London: Verso), 207-234).

1988a: 'Mitteleuropa—ein Konzept mit unklarer politischer Substanz, ein Raum mit wechselnden Grenzen', in Papcke & Weidenfeld, eds., 96-102.

1989: 'Durch "Neues Denken" zur Neuen Friedenspolitik', NG, 4, 305-311.

1989a: 'Defense Alliances in the Future: West European Integration and All-European Co-operation', BPP, 20:4, 355-361.

1989b: 'Durchbruch bei der konventionellen Abrüstung möglich: Analyse und Bewertung des bisherigen Verlaufs der Wiener Verhandlungen zur konventionellen Abrüstung', S + F, 7:2, 136-139.

1989c: 'Eine Sicherheitspolitik für Europa', in Wagemann, ed., 115-122.

1990: 'Overcoming the Division of Europe', BPP, 21:1, 3-14.

1990a: 'Eine europäische Friedensordnung ohne den Ungeist des Nationalismus', EW, 3, 146-154.

1990b: 'Schritte zur Demilitarisierung Europas', in Weizsäcker, ed., 317-331.

1990c: 'Deutsche Einheit und gesamteuropäische Ordnung des Friedens und der Freiheit', DA, 4, 562-568.

1990d: 'KSZE und europäische Gemeinschaft als wichtigste Grundlagen einer europäischen Friedensordnung', in Bahr, H-E., ed., 207-211.

Volgyes, Ivan 1982: 'Regional Differences Within the Warsaw Pact', Orbis, Fall, 665-678.

Voslensky, Michael 1986: 'Die sowjetische Deutschlandpolitik. Sinn, Strategie und Taktik', in Calleo & al., 17-234.

Vossler, Otto 1974: Die Revolution von 1848 in Deutschland (Frankfurt: Suhrkamp).

Wagemann, Eberhard, 1989, ed.: Frieden ohne Rüstung? (Herford: Mittler).

Wagenlehner, Günther 1989: 'Gorbatschow und die deutsche Frage', DA, 22:9, 1005-1011.

Wagner, Jay 1988: 'West German Naval Policy on the Northern Flank: Determinants and Perspectives 1955-1988', NUPI Rapport, 117 (Oslo: NUPI).

1990: 'The West German Response to Soviet Naval Activity in the North', in Skogan, John & Arne Olav Brundtland, eds.: Sovjet Sea Power in Northern Waters. Facts, Motivation, Impact and Reponses (London: Pinter), 131-150.

Wagner, Richard L. 1990: 'A Path to Enduring Improvements, Over the Long Term, in the East/West Security Relationship', in Huber, ed., 29-50.

Wagner, Wolfgang 1989: 'Auf der Suche nach einer neuen Ordnung in Europa', EA, 23, 693-702.

1990: 'Die Dynamik der deutschen Wiedervereinigung. Suche nach einer Verträglichkeit für Europa', EA, 3, 79-88.

Wallach, Jehuda L. 1967: Das Dogma der Vernichtungsschlacht. Die Lehren von Clausewitz und Schlieffen und ihre Wirkungen in zwei Weltkriegen (Frankfurt: Bernard & Graefe).

1972: Kriegstheorien. Ihre Entwicklung im 19. und 20. Jahrhundert (Frankfurt: Bernard & Graefe).

1986: 'Misperceptions of Clausewitz's "On War" by the German Military', JSS, 9:2-3, 213-239.

Walter, Gert 1990: 'Die DDR und die nationale Frage', in Venohr, ed., 103-136.

Walzer, Michael 1977: Just and Unjust Wars. A Moral Argument with Historical Illustrations (New York: Harper).

Wasmuht, Ulrike 1987: Friedensbewegungen der 80er Jahre. Zur Analyse ihrer strukturellen und aktuellen Entstehungsbedingungen in der Bundesrepublik Deutschland und den Vereinigten Staaten von Amerika nach 1945: Ein Vergleich (Giessen: Focus).

Weber, Wolfgang & al. 1985: *Die Streitkräfte der NATO auf dem Territorium der BRD* (Berlin: Militärverlag).

Wegener, Bernd, ed.: *Zwei Wege nach Moskau. Vom Hitler-Stalin-Pakt bis zum 'Unternehmen Barbarossa*, (München: Piper).

Weidenfeld, Werner 1983: 'Die Identität der Deutschen-Fragen, Positionen, Perspektiven', in —, ed., 13-50.

— 1985: 'Land im Brennpunkt Europas. Die europäische Qualität der Deutschen Frage', in —, ed., 69-79.

— 1988: 'Mitteleuropa: Traum oder Trauma von der Zukunft Europas?', in Papcke & —, eds., 87-95.

—, ed., 1983: *Die Identität der Deutschen* (Bonn: Bundeszentrale für politische Bildung).

—, ed. 1985: *Nachdenken über Deutschland. Materialien zur politischen Kultur der Deutschen Frage* (Köln: Wissenschaft und Politik).

Weiner, Klaus-Peter 1989: 'Die "Europäisierung der Sicherheitspolitik": Tendenzen, Probleme, in IMSF, eds., 212-223.

Weisenfeld, Ernst 1984: 'Ostpolitik und die deutsche Frage. Französische Initiativen und deutsche Ostpolitik', in Manfrass., Klaus, ed.: *Paris-Bonn. Eine dauerhafte Bindung schwreriger Partner* (Sigmaringen: Thorbecke), 247-259.

— 1989: *Quelle Allemagne pour la France?* (Paris: Armand Colin).

Weizsäcker, Carl Friedrich von 1979: *Wege in der Gefahr. Eine Studie über Wirtschaft, Gesellschaft und Kriegsverhütung* (München: dtv).

— 1983: *Der bedrohte Friede. Politische Aufsätze 1945-1981* (München: dtv).

— 1990: 'Bedingungen des Friedens in Europa, in —, ed., 17-22.

—, ed. 1971 : *Kriegsfolgen und Kriegsverhütung*, 2nd edition (München: Hanser).

—, ed. 1976: *Verteidigung ohne Schlacht* (München: dtv).

—, ed. 1984: *Die Praxis der defensiven Verteidigung* (Hameln: Sponholz).

—, ed. 1990: *Die Zukunft des Friedens in Europa. Politische und militärische Voraussetzungen* (München: Hanser).

Weizsäcker, Richard von 1985: *Die deutsche Geschichte geht weiter* (München: dtv).

— 1987: 'Speech in Moscow, 6 July 1987', *Bulletin*, 73 (15 July).

Well, Günther van 1990: 'Zur Europa-Politik eines vereinigten Deutschland', *EA*, 9, 293-300.

Wellershoff, Dieter 1989: 'Menschen und Waffen im Dienst der Sicherheitspolitik', in Wagemann, ed., 203-210.

—, ed. 1991: *Frieden ohne Macht? Sicherheitspolitik und Streitkräfte im Wandel*, (Bonn: Bouvier).

Wernicke, Joachim & Ingrid **Schöll** 1985: *Verteidigen statt vernichten. Wege aus der atomaren Falle* (München: Kösel).

Wette, Wolfram 1989: 'Die Deutschen zwischen Militarismus und Pazifismus', *Blätter*, August, 974-980.

Wettig, Gerhard 1967: *Entmilitarisierung und Wiederbewaffnung in Deutschland 1943-1955. Internationale Auseinandersetzungen um die Rolle der Deutschen in Europa* (München: Oldenburg).

— 1989a: 'Krise der Deutschland-Politik?', *DA*, 22:11, 1212-1216.

— 1990: 'The German Problem in Soviet Policy', *AuP*, 1, 38-51.

Wheeler, Nicholas J. & Ken **Booth** 1987: 'Beyond the Security Dilemma: Technology, Strategy and International Security', in Jacobsen, Carl G., ed.: *The Uncertain Course. New Weapons, Strategies and Mindsets* (Oxford: Oxford U.P.), 313-337.

Wickert, Ulrich, ed. 1990: *Angst vor Deutschland* (Hamburg: Hoffmann & Campe).

Wieczorek-Zeul, Heidemarie & Hermann **Scheer** 1990: 'Politischer Strukturwandel in Europa und das Ende der Abschreckung', *F&A*, 1, 5-10.

— 1990a: 'Deutschland und die NATO. Denkschrift zur Frage der Mitgliedschaft des vereinigten Deutschland in der NATO', *F&A*, 1, 11-16.

Wieland, Lothar 1990: 'Sozialdemokratie und Abrüstung in der Weimarer Republik', in Steinweg, Reinar, ed.: *Lehren aus der Geschichte? Historische Friedensforschung* (Frankfurt: Suhrkamp), 160-185.

Wiesendahl, Elmar 1989: 'Militärische Funktionskriese durch Frieden? Zum Verschwinden von Verteidigungswillen und Kampfbereitschaft in der Bundesrepublik Deutschland', in Vogt, ed., 229-238.

Wittgenstein, Ludwig 1953: *Philisophische Untersuchungen* (Oxford: Basil Blackwell).

Wittmann, Klaus 1989: 'Challenges of Conventional Arms Control', *AdP*, 239.

Wohlstetter, Albert 1958: 'The Delicate Balance of Terror', in Kissinger, ed. 1965, 34-58.

Wolter, Gustav-Adolf & Alexander **Meurer** 1970: *Die See. Schicksal der Völker. Eine Geschichte der Seefahrt und der Seemacht als Einführung in die Weltgeschichte* (Herford: Mittler).

Wörmann, C. 1986: 'Osthandel als Problem der Atlantischen Allianz. Erfahrungen aus dem Erdgas-Röhren-Geschäft mit der UdSSR', *Arbeitspapiere zur Internationalen Politik*, 38 (Bonn: Deutsche Gesellschaft für Auswärtige Politik e.V.).

Wörner, Manfred 1985: 'Kritik an den Entwürfen zur Alternativen Verteidigung', in Lutz, ed., 366-378.

1986: 'A Missile Defence for NATO Europe', *Strategic Review*, Winter, 13-20.

1989: 'Managing European Security', *Survival*, 31:1, 3-12.

1990: 'NATO's New Decade', *European Affairs*, 4:1, 8-15.

Wæver, Ole 1989: 'Ideologies of Stabilization, Stabilization of Ideologies: Reading German Social Democrats', in Harle & Sivonen, eds., 110-139.

1989a: 'Conceptions of *Détente* and Change: Some Non-Military Aspects of Security Thinking in the FRG', in & al., eds., 186-224.

1990: 'Three Competing Europes: German, French, Russian', *International Affairs*, 66:3, 477-493.

—, Pierre **Lemaitre** & Elzbieta **Tromer**, eds. 1989: *European Polyphony: Perspectives Beyond East-West Confrontation*. (London: Macmillan).

Yost, David 1984: 'European Anxieties About Ballistic Missile Defences', *WQ*, 7:4, 112-129.

1984a: 'France's Deterrent Posture and Security in Europe. I-2' (Part I: 'Capabilities and Doctrine', and Part II: 'Strategic and Arms Control Implications'), *AdP*, 194-195.

1990: 'Franco-German Defence Cooperation', in Szabo, ed., 217-258.

Zellner, Wolfgang 1989: 'Abrüstung: das Mandat von Wien', *Blätter*, 3, 323-338.

Zieger, Gottfried 1988: *Die Haltung von SED und DDR zur Einheit Deutschlands* 1949-1987 (Köln: Wissenschaft und Politik).

Zinner, Paul E.: 'German and U.S. Perceptions of Arms Control', in Hanrieder, Wolfram E., ed.: *Arms Control, the FRG, and the Future of East-West Relations* (Boulder: Westview), 11-28.

Ørvik, Niels 1986: 'Introduction', in —, ed.: *Semi-alignment and Western Security* (London: Croom Helm), 1-14.

Name Index